T0181940

Lecture Notes in Computer Science

Lecture Notes in Artificial Intelligence   13495

Founding Editor

Jörg Siekmann

Series Editors

Randy Goebel, *University of Alberta, Edmonton, Canada*
Wolfgang Wahlster, *DFKI, Berlin, Germany*
Zhi-Hua Zhou, *Nanjing University, Nanjing, China*

The series Lecture Notes in Artificial Intelligence (LNAI) was established in 1988 as a topical subseries of LNCS devoted to artificial intelligence.

The series publishes state-of-the-art research results at a high level. As with the LNCS mother series, the mission of the series is to serve the international R & D community by providing an invaluable service, mainly focused on the publication of conference and workshop proceedings and postproceedings.

Qi Su · Ge Xu · Xiaoyan Yang
Editors

Chinese Lexical Semantics

23rd Workshop, CLSW 2022
Virtual Event, May 14–15, 2022
Revised Selected Papers, Part I

 Springer

Editors
Qi Su (ID)
Peking University
Beijing, China

Ge Xu
Minjiang University
Fuzhou, China

Xiaoyan Yang
Minjiang University
Fuzhou, China

ISSN 0302-9743   ISSN 1611-3349 (electronic)
Lecture Notes in Artificial Intelligence
ISBN 978-3-031-28952-1   ISBN 978-3-031-28953-8 (eBook)
https://doi.org/10.1007/978-3-031-28953-8

LNCS Sublibrary: SL7 – Artificial Intelligence

© The Editor(s) (if applicable) and The Author(s), under exclusive license
to Springer Nature Switzerland AG 2023
This work is subject to copyright. All rights are reserved by the Publisher, whether the whole or part of the material is concerned, specifically the rights of translation, reprinting, reuse of illustrations, recitation, broadcasting, reproduction on microfilms or in any other physical way, and transmission or information storage and retrieval, electronic adaptation, computer software, or by similar or dissimilar methodology now known or hereafter developed.
The use of general descriptive names, registered names, trademarks, service marks, etc. in this publication does not imply, even in the absence of a specific statement, that such names are exempt from the relevant protective laws and regulations and therefore free for general use.
The publisher, the authors, and the editors are safe to assume that the advice and information in this book are believed to be true and accurate at the date of publication. Neither the publisher nor the authors or the editors give a warranty, expressed or implied, with respect to the material contained herein or for any errors or omissions that may have been made. The publisher remains neutral with regard to jurisdictional claims in published maps and institutional affiliations.

This Springer imprint is published by the registered company Springer Nature Switzerland AG
The registered company address is: Gewerbestrasse 11, 6330 Cham, Switzerland

CLSW 2022 Preface

The 2022 Chinese Lexical Semantics Workshop (CLSW 2022) was the 23th annual meeting in a series that began in 2000, and the series has been hosted in Beijing, Hong Kong, Taipei, Singapore, Xiamen, Hsin Chu, Yantai, Suzhou, Wuhan, Zhengzhou, Macao, Leshan, and Chia-Yi, etc. The Chinese Lexical Semantics Workshop (CLSW) is well known for both linguists and computer science academics reporting and discussing their thoughts. Theoretical and applied linguistics, computational linguistics, information processing, and computational lexicography are some of its topics. CLSW serves as one of the most prominent gatherings in Asia for Chinese Lexical Semantics, having a great impact on as well as promoting academic research and application development in those topics.

CLSW 2022 was hosted by Minjiang University (MJU for short), Fuzhou, China, on May 14–15, 2022. 214 papers were submitted to the conference; at least two independent reviewers conducted a double-blind review of each submission. Of all submissions, we were only able to accommodate 42.99% (92 papers) as oral presentations and 24.77% (53 papers) as poster presentations. Among accepted papers, selected English papers are included in Springer's LNAI series. They are organized in topical sections covering all major topics of lexical semantics, semantic resources, corpus linguistics, and natural language processing, etc.

We heartily thank the invited speakers for their excellent keynote addresses. Furthermore, we are very appreciative to the conference chairs on behalf of the Program Committee: Zonghua Wang (President of MJU) and Houfeng Wang (Peking University), honorary members of the Advisory Committee: Shiwen Yu (Peking University), Chin-Chuan Cheng (National Taiwan Normal University), Benjamin Ka Yin T'sou (The Education University of Hong Kong), and other members of the Advisory Committee for their guidance in supporting the conference. Also, we would like to acknowledge the chairs of the Organization Committee: Ge Xu (MJU), Guomei Cai (MJU), Xiaoyan Yang (MJU), Hua Zhong (Fujian Normal University) and Xiangwen Liao (Fuzhou University).

Thanks should also be given to the student volunteers of Minjiang University for their tremendous contribution in this event. We appreciate the time and effort put forth by the Program Chairs: Jia-fei Hong (National Taiwan Normal University), Peng Jin (Leshan Normal University), and Jingxia Lin (Nanyang Technological University), as well as the entire Program Committee, and all the reviewers in order to have the submitted papers properly evaluated. We are pleased that the accepted English papers are published by Springer as part of their Lecture Notes in Artificial Intelligence (LNAI) series and are indexed by EI and SCOPUS.

Last but not least, we would like to express our gratitude to all authors and attendees for their scholarly work and cooperation in making CLSW 2022 a success.

January 2023   Zonghua Wang

Organization

General Chairs

Wang, Zonghua — Minjiang University
Wang, Houfeng — Peking University

Wang, Zonghua	Minjiang University
Wang, Houfeng	Peking University

Steering Committee Honorary Members

Cheng, Chin-Chuan	Taiwan Normal University
T'sou, Ka Yin Benjamin	The Education University of Hong Kong
Yu, Shiwen	Peking University

Steering Committee Members

Diao, Yanbin	Beijing Normal University
Hong, Jia-Fei	Taiwan Normal University
Hsieh, Shu-Kai	Taiwan University
Huang, Chu-Ren	Hong Kong Polytechnic University
Ji, Donghong	Wuhan University
Jin, Peng	Leshan Normal University
Jing-Schmidt, Zhuo	University of Oregon
Liu, Meichun	City University of Hong Kong
Lu, Qin	The Hong Kong Polytechnic University
Lua, Kim-Teng	National University of Singapore
Qu, Weiguang	Nanjing Normal University
Su, Xinchun	Xiamen University
Sui, Zhifang	Peking University
Wu, Jiun-Shiung	Taiwan Chung Cheng University
Xu, Jie	University of Macau
Zan, Hongying	Zhengzhou University
Zhang, Yangseng	Beijing Information Science & Technology University

Program Committee Chairs

Hong, Jia-Fei   Taiwan Normal University
Jin, Peng   Leshan Normal University
Lin, Jingxia   Nanyang Technological University

Organization Chairs

Cai, Guomei   Minjiang University
Liao, Xiangwen   Fuzhou University
Xu, Ge   Minjiang University
Yang, Xiaoyan   Minjiang University
Zhong, Hua   Fujian Normal University

Publication Chairs

Su, Qi   Peking University
Tang, Xuri   Huazhong University of Science and Technology

Contents – Part I

Contents – Part II

General Linguistics, Lexical Resources

Lexical Semantics

Divergence and Convergence in Tense and Aspect Meanings of "guo" and "le"

Zhao Xu[1] and Zheng Wu[2(⊠)]

[1] School of Humanities, Zhejiang University, Hangzhou 310058, China
[2] Faculty of Arts, Hong Kong Baptist University, Hongkong 999077, China
21482993@life.hkbu.edu.hk

Abstract. The paper discusses the divergence and convergence in aspect and tense meanings via semantic feature analysis. Arguably, the divergence of the experiential marker *guo*过 and the actualize marker *le*了 are embodied in aspect and tense meanings. In particular, the tense and aspect meanings of *guo*过 indicates factual connection between the past event and current one. As such, the reality of event is accentuated by backtracking the past experience. The tense and aspect meanings of *le*了 is involved with eventual connection between the past event and current one, which express the actualization of event via highlighting the action perfective. The convergence of the tense of *guo*过 and *le*了 can be rendered by a couple of conditions, including (1) the suppression of *le*了 on *guo*过 in the syntactic structure of "V-*guo-le*-O", which leads to the semantic meaning of the close-temporal past event; (2) the force of temporal adverbials on the distance between the event time and speech time (reference time); (3) the compliment of frequency induce the number of times that the past event happened, which emphasized the same "Perfective" meaning of *guo*过 and *le*了.

Keywords: *le* · *guo* · Tense · Aspect · Semantic features

1 Introduction

Tense aspect function is believed as the grammatical tool to systematically express the meaning of Tense and Aspect in Modern Chinese. The meaning of tense aspect function differs from one to another, with *guo*过 presenting "past tense- experiential aspect" and the verbal suffix *le*了 expressing "actualized aspect" [2]. The grammatical meaning of *guo*过 and *le*了 is not the same, but they are impacted other components in the sentence, which lead to convergence of tense and aspect meanings *guo* and *le*了. For example:

(1) a. "你和他聊了吗？"   "我和他聊了。"[1]
     "nǐ hé tā liáo le ma?"   "wǒ hé tā liáo le."
     "Have you talked to him yet?"   "I have."

The data of examples in current paper are sourced from both the annotated Modern Chinese Corpus by Beijing Language and Culture University (BCC) and the self-prepared corpus.

© The Author(s), under exclusive license to Springer Nature Switzerland AG 2023
Q. Su et al. (Eds.): CLSW 2022, LNAI 13495, pp. 3–13, 2023.
https://doi.org/10.1007/978-3-031-28953-8_1

   b. "你和他<u>聊过了</u>吗？"   "我和他<u>聊过了</u>。"

   nǐ hé tā liáo guò le ma?"   "wǒ hé tā liáo guò le."

   "Have you talked to him yet?"   "I have."

(2) a. 我<u>去了</u>两次中国，感觉好极了。

     wǒ qù le liǎng cì zhōng guó, gǎn jué hǎo jí le.

     I went China twice and it feels so good.

   b. 我<u>去过</u>两次中国，感觉好极了。

     wǒ qù guò liǎng cì zhōng guó. gǎn jué hǎo jí le.

     I went to China twice and it feels so good.

As for the examples (1a-b), *le* 了 and *guo* 过 both have the meaning of "Perfective", for denoting the perfective of *liáo* 聊 (talk). With regard to (2a-b) examples, both *le* 了 and *guo* 过 have the sense of "experience" for accentuating the fact that the event had actually happened in the past, rather than the perfective of the event.

We therefore explore the induced factors causing the convergence in aspect and tense meanings of *le* 了 and *guo* 过, which seldomly is touched upon by the previous literature. This paper first provides the overview of aspect and tense meanings of *le* 了 and *guo* 过 respectively via the semantic feature. Second, the analysis of reasons inducing convergence in aspect and tense meanings of *le* 了 and *guo* 过, i.e., the semantic suppression of *le* 了 on *guo* 过, temporal words, and Perfective, followed by the conclusion part.

2   Divergence in Aspect and Tense Meanings of guo and le

As the aspectual markers used to observe a situation from an external perspective, the common semantic feature of *le* 了 and *guo* 过 is "Perfective", i.e., the speaker focuses on the whole process of the event from the starting point to the perfective point [1]. Through this process, "V + *le* 了" and "V + *guo* 过" present the complete aspectual meaning of the event, in contrast to the imperfective aspectual marker *zhe* 着. However, *le* 了 and *guo* 过 are aspect markers at different levels. In other words, *le* 了 is the aspectual marker at the "concept-reality" level, which is concerned with the actualization of the event. While *guo* 过 is the "event-fact" aspectual marker concerning the event has once happened in the past. The most prominent divergence between these two is the connection between the event and the speaking time (reference time). That is, "V + *le* 了" represents the result of the event or the state of the event expanding to the speaking time, while "V + *guo* 过" denotes the event is real at the speaking time. The next content further clarifies the differences in association with the speaking time between *le* 了 and *guo* 过.

2.1   Aspect and Tense Meanings of *le* 了 Sample

Dai [2] refers to *le* 了 as the "reality aspect" marker, which marks the real occurrence of an event. For example, "tā chī píng guǒ (he eats the apple)" can only be regarded as a concept or habitual behavior that does not have the eventual meaning. Another example "tā chī le píng guǒ (he ate the apple) means that the concept is transformed into a real event. That "concept-to-reality" transformation requires the mandatory presence of the grammatical marker *le* 了.

Langacker [3] argues that this transformation is a linguistic expression based on epistemic immediacy, indicating the impact of the event occurrence on speech time. The impact is epitomized in two aspects: the result state of the event affects the behaviors at the speech time, as seen in the (4a) example "kǎo le mǎn fēn (got a full mark)" affecting the behavior at the speech time. In the (4b) example, the result state of "bēi zi suì le (broke cup)" causes the claiming behavior. Neither example sentence can be replaced by *guò* 过. The other aspect identifies the behavior of the event possibly continuing after the speech time, which can be seen that the behaviors "kàn shū (read book)" in (5a) and the "zài běi jīng zhù (live in Beijing)" in (5b) perhaps continue in the coming future. The two above elaborations between the event time and the speech time are named as "Current Relevance" [3, 5–7].

（4）a. 这次考试他考了满分，所以现在洋洋得意。

     zhè cì kǎo shì tā kǎo le mǎn fēn, suǒ yǐ xiàn zài yáng yáng dé yì.

     He got full mark on this test, so now he is smug.

  b. 我打碎了杯子，所以需要赔钱。

     wǒ dǎ suì le bēi zi, suǒ yǐ xū yào péi qián.

     I broke the cup, so I need to pay for it.

（5）a. 这本书我看了三天，还没看完。

     zhè běn shū wǒ kàn le sān tiān, hái méi kàn wán.

     I've been reading this book for three days, and I haven't finished it yet.

  b. 我已经在北京住了五年了。

     wǒ yǐ jīng zài běi jīng zhù le wǔ nián le.

     I've been living in Beijing for five years

Since *le* 了 can mark the relevance of the event toward the present, "V + *le* 了" can indicate the tense meaning of "perfect". For example:

（6）a. I have read a book.

  b. I have written some poems, but I have not finished writing them.

The perfect tense in English can be seen in the (6a-b) examples, which is reflected by the "have/has" past participle form. In Chinese, it can be reflected by the reality marker *le* 了. For instance, (6a) can be expressed by "wǒ kàn le yī běn shū", and (6b) expressed as "I have written some poems, but I haven't finished them yet" to illustrate the effect of the event on the speech time.

It should be noted that the current relevance of the reality marker *le* 了 is a pragmatic meaning, not grammatical semantics [8]. For example:

（7）问："你昨天去了哪里？"
Wèn: "nǐ zuó tiān qù le nǎ lǐ?"
Q: "Where did you go yesterday?"
答："我昨天去了超市。"
Dá: "wǒ zuó tiān qù le chāo shì."
A: "I went to the supermarket yesterday."

In contrast to (4–5) examples, the question in (7) example is driven by curiosity, and the answer is based on the objective statement of the existing event. Since the event is not inclined to be linked with the present time, the perfect tense meaning of "V + *le* 了" is rendered by the temporality of the verb along with the result state of the argument, instead of by *le* 了. In short, the current relevance of *le* 了 in the aspect category pertains to pragmatic semantics.

Current correlation is a pragmatic meaning rather than a grammatical one with reason that *le* 了 being the aspect marker but not a tense marker. *le* 了 firstly marks the Perfective of the event itself, which is through the course of time, thus it helps to associate with the speech time (reference time) and eventually induces the tense meaning. In short, *le* 了 is a grammatical marker at the "concept-reality" level, with the grammatical function of turning concepts into events. In addition, it contributes the extension of "aspect" to "tense" via current relevance, for indicating the relevance relationship between existing events and current behavior reflected by result relevance, state relevance or behavior continuation.

2.2 Aspect and Tense Meanings of guo过

Chao [9] and Smith [10] refer to *guo*过 as the "experiential marker", indicating that the event occurred at least once in the past [3,11], which covers the semantic features "ephemerality, perfectiveness, and termination" [2]. The semantic meaning of "perfectiveness and termination" originates from the meaning of Aspect while that of ephemerality from the meaning of Tense

"Ephemerality" is differentiated from "distant-temporality" since "distant-temporality" entails that the event time is far from the speech time (reference time), while "ephemerality" asserts that the event occurred completely in the past, which conceptualizes the process from the event expression to the fact expression. Thus, "ephemerality" is not necessarily to temporal distance. The "V + *guò*过" can be paired with yǐ qián (before) and céng jīng (once) for constructing "distant-temporality" and also be co-occurred with gāng gāng (just now) and cái (only then) to express a close-past event. "V + *guò*过" therefore is called as "indefinite past tense" marker by [12].

The noteworthy difference from *le* 了 is that *guo*过does not denote an event-based transformation from concept to reality, but rather a conceptualized process from event to fact. It can be reflected that "V + *guò*过" event is identified as a real occurrence of the experience, stressing the fact to provide contextual information for the current event. The association of the experiential aspect with the current event is referred as "Experiential Perfect" coined by [3] and argues that the experienced event can be associated with the current event. [3]:59 regards the (8b) example as the result association, which implicitly reflects that "Bill is still in the United States", and he regards the (8a) example as the experience association, which implicitly reflects that "Bill is no longer in the United States". However, Comrie fails to explain the difference between these two associations. On the other hand, the experiential aspect in English is significantly different from the experiential meaning in English[1]. We are in line with Comrie's statement that the experiential aspect is associated with current events, and any past event actually can be associated with the present or the future. However, the relevancy of the current event of "V + *guò*过" and that of "V + *le*了" is distinctive. Particularly, "V + *guò*过" mainly presents past facts while "V + *le*了" mainly expresses event relevance.

As Vendler [13]: 244 states, "'facts' are not in space and time at all. They are not located, cannot move, split, or spread, and they do not occur, take place, or last in any sense", and this paper argues that "event" emphasizes the truth-value meaning of events, axioms, theorems, etc., and does not help to elaborate events on the present[2]. The (7) example demonstrates that "fact" focus on both the truth-value meaning while the (4–5) examples show the direct impact on the present event. The distinction between "fact" and "event" relies on whether the event has a direct impact on the present[3]. As such, the result state of "fact" cannot extend to the speech time, but the state of the "event" causes the effect on the speech time. Based on that, [14] proposes a temporal schema, as shown in Fig. 1, where source represents the event itself, the target represents the result state, and "fact" (here in Klein, that is "V + *guò*过") is not associated with the speech time while the result state of the "event" ("V + *le*了") can continue to the speech time. Taking (8c-d) as examples, the active situation "qù lún dūn (went to London)" is marked by "*le*了", which has the complete aspectual meaning. It becomes an event indicating the whole process through "departed from the domestic" to "arrived in London". In that case, the speaker is in the continuum state of being in London, thus bringing up the situation of not being in the domestic at the current time. Conversely, the perfective event marked by guò过 goes through "departure from the domestic" to "return to the domestic". Since the perfective event is disconnected with the current time [9]:439, the state of being in London no longer exists, thus deriving the pragmatic meaning that "the speaker is not currently in London."

---

[1] The detailed description can be seen in [6]: 166–168.

[2] The "fact" is the indirect forces for the elaboration see details in Sect. 3 "V + *guò*过 + *le*了 + O".

[3] Ass the claim by Michaelis [15], "direct impact" means that the result of the event is irrevocable in current time. For example, the direct impact in "tā dǎ suì le bēi zi (he has broken the cup)" is "the broken cup". The "indirect effect" means that the result of the event is revocable in current time. For instance, the cup is not necessary for being broke in the sentence "tā dǎ suì guò bēi zi (he broke the cup)".

（8）a. Bill has been to America.

b. Bill has gone to America.

c. * 我去过伦敦，所以现在不在国内。

* wǒ qù guò lún dūn, suǒ yǐ xiàn zài bù zài guó nèi.

* I went to London, so I'm not in the country now.

d. 我去了伦敦，所以现在不在国内。

wǒ qù le lún dūn, suǒ yǐ xiàn zài bù zài guó nèi.

I've been to London, so I'm not in the country now.

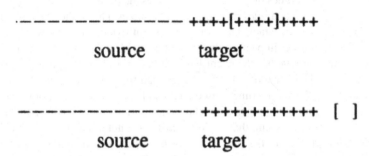

Fig. 1. Temporal schema of *guò*过 (cited in Klein, 2000: 76)

The current paper deems that the result state of "event" is able to extend to the speech time, but it does not necessity extend to speech time. The above (7) example is the case in that since it the state of "qù le chāo shì (went to the supermarket)" does not expand to speech time. The "V + *le*了" event, therefore shows the possibility of extending the result state to the speech time. On the other hand, the result state of "fact" fails to extend to the speech time, but it serves as the indirect driving force of speech time. The upcoming section is developed how the force can be achieved through the co-occurrence of *le*了 and *guo*过.

3   Convergence in Aspect and Tense Meanings of guo and le

Despite the divergences exiting in the aspect and tense meanings of guo "过" and le "了", the convergence also occurs in in the aspect and tense meanings. The coverage can be epitomized as follows: (1) the suppression of le 了 on guo过 in the syntactic structure of "V-guo-le-O", which leads to blur the ephemeral meaning of guo过 while spotlighting the "perfective" meaning; (2) the temporal words in the sentence close the temporal distance between "V + guò过" and the speech time, foregrounding the "perfective" meaning of the event; (3) the temporal words in the sentence distant the temporal distance between "V + guò过" and the speech time, highlighting the ephemeral meaning of the event; (4) the verbal complement in the sentence indicates the frequency of "V + le 了" and "V + guò过", prioritizing the frequency of the event rather than the process with the event shows as "dot-like" in the temporal schema.

3.1 Semantic Convergence Caused by Co-occurrence of Aspect Markers

In this paper, the co-occurrence of "aspect markers" is restricted to the structure of "V-*guo-le-O*", and "V-*guo-O-le*" is not involved here. Please see the following (9) example:

（9）a. 打过针的人请举手！
dǎ guò zhēn de rén qǐng jǔ shǒu!
Raise your hand if you had the shot!
b. 打过了针的人请举手！⁵
dǎ guò le zhēn de rén qǐng jǔ shǒu
Raise your hand if you've had the shot!

Kong [15] and other scholars argue that the *guò*过 in (9a) is the experiential auxiliary "*guò*过2", which indicates the past event and not being co-occurred with *le* 了. While the word *guò*过 in (9b) is the completive auxiliary "*guò*过1", which means "finished" or "completed" and needs to be co-occurred with *le* 了. Despite that the above argument is the mainstream, other scholars hold different views, i.e., [17] [18]. They maintain that *guò*过 in the two sentences belong to the same auxiliary *guò*过. These two are caused by the meaning of past in different contexts, with the "perfective" meaning is impacted by *le* 了. The behind rationale exists that *le* 了 can make concepts into reality and facts into events. Given that X in "X *le* 了" is used as a factual "V + *guò*过", the *le* 了 marks it as an event associated with the present.

Both strands gain rapports from relevant studies, and the former mainstream view is more identical with language intuition. It also makes semantic distinctives between "*guò*过1" and "*guò*过2" stand out, in order reduce the difficulty in teaching Chinese as a foreign language and ease the burden of comprehension for the corresponding learners. The latter view is inclined to the homogeneity of linguistic units and explore the interaction between form and meaning, for attributing the semantic diversity to the suppressive effect from collocations.

This paper boasts the homogeneity of the auxiliary *guò*过 while incorporating "*guò*过1" and "*guò*过2" into the same experiential aspect *guò*过.

We hold the view that both "*guò*过1" and "*guò*过2" can express the "tense" meaning, and "*guò*过1" expresses the tense meaning of "past-close temporal" while "*guò*过2" refers as "past-far". Concerning that "V + *guò*过" is treated as time period including "start - continue – finish" in the time coordinates, the inconsistence in distance between that time and speech time causes the speakers stress different "time period" at various stages. In particular, the speaker does not observe the internal stages of the time period, but only treats it as a "timepoints" in the temporal coordinates under the condition that time period is far from the speech time. Conversely, when the time period is close to the speech time, the speaker observes the internal stages of the time period clearly. Under this circumstance, the "perfective" time phase is more likely to be observed and focused since it is the closest phase to the speech time, and thus induce the meaning of "perfective". The above example can demonstrate that the meaning of "perfective" can be achieved by grammar usage of the *le* 了's suppression on *guo*过, which is reflected by "V-*guo-le-O*". In the syntactic structure of "V-*guo-le-O*", "V + *guò*过" is regarded as a "concept" that has not been transformed into an event yet, which is in line with the factual nature of "V + guò过". During the process of being marked by le 了, the experiential event is mentioned once more for the indirect effect on the present along with the temporal distance between the event and the speech time becoming close, thus producing the "perfective" meaning. Therefore, it can be seen that the different time distance does not affect the common tense meaning of "guò过1" and "guò过2". The "far-temporal distance" and "close-temporal distance" are relative and flexible. The guo 过 can be allied with temporal words and céng jīng (once) and yǐ qián (before) for constructing "distant-temporality", and it can also be allied with gāng gāng (just now) and cái (only then) for the near-temporal event. It should be reported that "far-temporal" and "close-temporal" have no absolute semantic divergence. More specially, both two display the past in "tense", and exist "discontinuity" (that is interval from the speech time (reference time) in time coordinates). Regardless of the longitude of time interval, the event is an objective experience all the time. From the meaning of "aspect", the distance between the time period and the speech time gives rise to different aspectual meaning, "perfective" for guo过1 and "perfectiveness" for guo过2 in specific.

In the nutshell, "guò过1" and "guò过2" can be treated as same guo过. "V + guò 过" stands alone for indicates that the event has happened. When "V-guo-le-O" comes, it is suppressed by the current relevance of le 了. Under this condition, the event that has happened is brought closer to the speech time, and the perfective point is the closest to the speech time along with the most easily perceived semantics, thus triggering the aspect meaning of "perfective".

3.2 Aspect and Tense Meanings Caused by Other Sentence Components

The aspect and tense meanings are not only afflicted to the verb [19], and it is also linked to the temporal words/phrases and verbs in the sentence.

Foremost, the aspect and tense meanings can render the "V + le 了" event as "past-far distant tense" and converge with the meaning of guo过.

（11）a. 小时候，我在上海住了三年。
　　　 xiǎo shí hòu, wǒ zài shàng hǎi zhù le sān nián.
　　　 When I was a child, I've lived in Shanghai for three years.

　　 b. 小时候，我在上海住过三年。
　　　 xiǎo shí hòu, wǒ zài shàng hǎi zhù guò sān nián.
　　　 When I was a child, I lived in Shanghai for three years.

When I was a child, I lived in Shanghai for three years.

Comparing (11a) and (11b), "far temporal" and "close temporal" share the same meaning of the two sentences. Both two suggest that the event is far from the speech time, since the temporal phrase "as a child" hints at the background time for the sentence, and this temporal phrase forwards the event in (11a) in time coordinates. Consequently, the sentence's semantic meaning perceivably is related to past distant temporal. In this case, the aspect and tense meanings of le 了 converge with guo过. To be more specific, the *le* 了 not only marks the "lived for three years" events' transition from the concept to reality, but also is framed in the "past distant temporal" time domain by the reference time "when I was a child", indicating the convergence of the events' meaning between "V + *le* 了" (the event that had achieved long time ago) and "V + *guò* 过" (the event that happened in the past).

Second, the temporal words can render "V + *guò* 过" as the "perfective" meaning, which converges with the meaning of *le* 了.

（12）a. 我刚说了这句话，你转头就忘了。
　　　　wǒ gāng shuō le zhè jù huà, nǐ zhuǎn tóu jiù wàng le.
　　　　I've just said that, and you forgot it.
　　　b. 我刚说过这句话，你转头就忘了。
　　　　wǒ gāng shuō guò zhè jù huà, nǐ zhuǎn tóu jiù wàng le.
　　　　I just said this, and you turned your head and forgot it.

（13）a. 今天打了针的明天来复查
　　　　jīn tiān dǎ le zhēn de míng tiān lái fù chá.
　　　　Those who had the injection today will be reviewed tomorrow.
　　　b. 今天打过针的明天来复查。
　　　　jīn tiān dǎ guò zhēn de míng tiān lái fù chá.

Those who have had their shots today will come back tomorrow for a review.

As discussed above, the "V + *guò* 过" event carries the indefinite character in past tense mechanism, and it is given the "close temporal" meaning driven by the temporal adverbs like "gang(just), cái (just now), yǐ jīng (already), and bù jiǔ qián (shortly)". The "V + *guò* 过" event is close to the reference time, with the easily-perceived termination point of the event, highlighting the perfective meaning of the event. In example (12b), the temporal adverb "gāng (just)" indicates that the event occurred shortly before the reference time and similarly, the time domain (background time) of example (13) is "jīn tiān (today)" as the past temporal time, while the event is framed near the reference time, so the ephemerality of *guò* 过 is greatly weakened, causing the convergence with *le* 了 in semantic meaning.

Furthermore, the verbal phrases render *guo* 过 as being in convergence with *le* 了 in meanings.

（14）a. 北京我去了两次，以后还想再去。
　　　　běi jīng wǒ qù le liǎng cì, yǐ hòu hái xiǎng zài qù.
　　　　I went to Beijing twice and would like to go there again in the future.

　　　b. 北京我去过两次，以后还想再去。
　　　　běi jīng wǒ qù guò liǎng cì, yǐ hòu hái xiǎng zài qù.
　　　　I have been to Beijing twice and would like to go there again in the future.

The *le* 了 and *guo*过 in (14) example is not obvious in the distant and close temporal, due to the fact that the verbal phrase "liǎng cì (twice)" shows that the event occurred twice before the speech time. The focus exits in momentum rather than temporal quantity, and the completeness of the event is presented in the "dotted" form. The "dotted" form means that the event in the temporal schema does not underline "beginning-continuity-end" of the time period, but only illustrates that that event occupies a position in the time coordinate. The distinction among the nodes of the time period is weaken as the "start node" and "perfective node" overlap with each other. In that way, any point of the event can represent the whole event. As for the (14) example, the semantic meanings of "qù le" and "qù guò" are metaphorized, with the beginning of the action representing the whole action. In other words, "qù" replaces the process of "going - living -returning". The information importance of two sentences in the (14) example are shown as below: [+past] > [+momentum] > [+point] > [+perfective].

In the nutshell, temporal words/phrases and verbal complements produce the convergent effect on the "aspect" meaning, as reflected in the fact that temporal words/phrases for "close temporal" weaken the ephemerality of *guo*过, and temporal words/phrases for "far temporal" weaken the current relevance of *le* 了, with the integrity of "aspect" emphasized by the verbal phrases.

4   Summary

The convergence of tense and aspect markers in Chinese is a systematic phenomenon. For example, [19] analyzes the semantic convergence of *le* 了 and *zhe*着in the sentence "qiáng shàng guà zhe zhōng (the clock is hanging on the wall)" and "qiáng shàng guà le zhōng (the clock hung on the wall) respectively. Moreover, Smith [8,10]and Ouyang [20] identify the semantic convergence of zài 在 and *zhe*着. The current paper investigates the semantic convergence of *le* 了 and *guo*过. The term "convergence" can be explained that each tense-aspect marker performs its own function originally but is interpreted as the same tense meaning due to specific syntactic structure and sentence components. Additionally, this paper explores the co-occurrence of *le* 了 and *guo*过 in "V-*guo-le*-O" structure for providing the insights into the semantic suppression of *le* 了 on *guo*过. When the past experience is employed to elaborate the effect on the current event, the past distant tense meaning also changes to the close tense one. As such, the time interval between the event and the speech time is subjectively shortened while accentuating the node of perfective nearest to the speech time, followed by producing the "perfective" meaning for the experiential *guo*过 (also called as "*guò*过1"). Regarding that the event marked *le* 了 is influenced by temporal words for "past distant temporal" meaning, the "perfective" meaning of the event is weakened while enhancing the factuality of the event for its truth, which inclines to ephemeral meaning of *guo*过. Finally, the momentum complements lead to the convergence in the aspect and tense meanings of *le* 了 and *guo*过 as well. This view can be reflected that the "V *guo-le* + momentum complement" structure stress the frequency of events rather than the process. In that way, the "perfective" of the whole through "start node - process - perfective node" is blurred as the occurrence of events, which can be interpreted as a shift from a line-segment form to a point form in the temporal schema, without concerning any stages of the perfective.

Acknowledgments. This study was funded by the National Social Science Foundation of China under the project "Development of a grammar syllabus for teaching Chinese as a foreign language and a reference grammar book series (multi-volume version)" (17ZDA307).

References

1. Smith, C.: The Parameter of Aspect. Kluwer Academic Publishers, Dordrecht (1991)
2. Dai, Y.J.: Research on the Modern Chinese Tense System. Zhejiang Education Publishing House, Zhejiang (1997). (in Chinese)
3. Langacker, R.W.: The English present: temporal coincidence vs. epistemic immediacy. In: Patard, A., Brisard. F. (eds.) Cognitive Approaches to Tense, Aspect, and Epistemic Modality, pp. 45–86. John Benjamins Pub. Co. (2011)
4. Comrie, B.: Aspect. Cambridge University Press, Cambridge (1976)
5. Li, C.N., Thompson, S.A.: Mandarin Chinese: A Functional Reference Grammar. University of California Press, Berkeley (1981)
6. Yeh, M.: Stative situations and the imperfective -zhe in Mandarin. J. Chin. Lang. Teach. Assoc. **28**, 69–98 (1993)
7. Givón, T.: Syntax. John Benjamins, Amsterdam/Philadelphia (2001)
8. Smith, A.: Theory of Aspectual Choice. Linguistic Society of America, Language (1983)
9. Chao, Y.R.: A Grammar of Spoken Chinese. University of California Press, Berkeley (1968)
10. Smith, C.S.: The syntax and interpretation of temporal expressions in English. In: Meier, R., Aristar-Dry, H., Destruel, E. (eds.) Text, Time, and Context, pp. 95–146. Studies in Linguistics and Philosophy, vol. 87. Springer, Dordrecht (2009). https://doi.org/10.1007/978-90-481-261 7-0_4
11. Dahl, Ö.: Tense and Aspect System. The Bath Press, Bath (1985)
12. Lu, S.X: Xiandao Hanyu Babai Ci [800 Words of Contemporary Chinese], Beijing: Shangwu Publishers (1980). (in Chinese)
13. Vendler, Z.: Linguistics in Philosophy. Cornell University Press, Itchaca (1967)
14. Klein, W., Li, P., Hendriks, H.: Aspect and assertion in Mandarin Chinese. Nat. Lang. Linguist. Theory **18**(4), 723–770 (2000)
15. Michaelis, L.: Toward a grammar of aspect: the case of the English perfect construction. Dissertations. UC Berkeley (1993)
16. Kong, L.D.: About the dynamic auxiliaries *guò*过1" and "*guò*过2". J. Anhui Normal Univ. (Natural Science) **4**, 104–110 (1986). (in Chinese)
17. Wang, Y.G.Z.: The "perfective aspect" in Chinese. Chinese Lang. Learn. **1**, 12–16 (2000). (in Chinese)
18. Liu, M.C., Xu, Z.: The Grammatical Evolution and Constructive Function of *guo*过-An Application to Teaching Chinese as a Foreign Language: Essays in Honor of Mr. Dong Pengcheng (2021). (in Chinese)
19. Dai, Y.J.: Semantic analysis of the modern Chinese "*zhe*着" word for continuum. Lang. Teach. Linguist, Stud. **2**, 92–106 (1991). (in Chinese)
20. Ouyang, X.F.: Reanalysis of the function of "zheng" "zai" and "zhe." Stud. Lang. Linguist. **40**(3), 59–68 (2020). (in Chinese)

A Corpus-Based Study on the Syllablic Form Selection of Ancient Chinese High-Frequency Nouns in the Middle Ages

Bing Qiu$^{(\boxtimes)}$ and Jia Yi

Department of Chinese Language and Literature, School of Humanities and Social Sciences, Tsinghua University, Beijing100084, China
qiubing@mail.tsinghua.edu.cn

Abstract. Polysyllablization was one of the trends governing the development of Chinese lexis, and the Middle Ages, linking the preceding era and the next, was the key stage. Under the macro trend of lexical polysyllablization, different words could select different syllabic forms. Due to lack of basic data on syllabic form selection from Ancient Chinese to Middle Chinese, there remain considerable ambiguities and even blanks in research. Nouns are the bulk of the lexical system. Focusing on high-frequency nouns in Ancient Chinese, this paper constructs lexical data on syllabic form selection from Ancient Chinese to Middle Chinese based on the corpus linguistics method. After a quantitative survey and statistical analysis, it preliminarily reveals the rules of syllabic form selection in the evolution of Chinese lexis from various aspects, such as overlapping morphemes, nature of the source text, word formation, etc.

Keywords: Syllablic form selection · Polysyllablization · High-frequency nouns · Middle Chinese

1 Introduction

Polysyllablization, a governing trend in the development of the Chinese language which profoundly changed the features of the Chinese lexical system, has become a research focus and hotspot in the study of the history of Chinese lexis. The Middle Ages, linking the preceding era and the next, was the key stage. Zhu Qingzhi pointed out that in light of the internal laws of the development of Chinese, its lexis would eventually achieve disyllablization; this progression was, however, extremely slow before the Wei and Jin Dynasties, but suddenly accelerated after entering the Middle Ages, and in just two or three hundred years, the monosyllable-dominated Chinese lexical system (mainly referring to that of literature language) was fundamentally changed [1]. The academia has conducted much research on polysyllabic words and polysyllablization in Middle Chinese. For example, Zhou Shengya [2], Dong Yuzhi [3], and Zhou Rijian [4], studied polysyllabic words in individual books 世说新语 (*Shishuo Xinyu*), 抱朴子 (*Baopuzi*), and 颜氏家训 (*Yanshi Jiaxun*), respectively. Qiu Bing systematically discussed the polysyllablization of Middle Chinese lexis, pointing out that in Middle Ages

© The Author(s), under exclusive license to Springer Nature Switzerland AG 2023
Q. Su et al. (Eds.): CLSW 2022, LNAI 13495, pp. 14–24, 2023.
https://doi.org/10.1007/978-3-031-28953-8_2

polysyllablization demonstrated a complex state of "leaping growth at the macro level and varying growth at the micro level" [5], that is, the number of polysyllabic words showed a leaping growth, and the frequency of use of polysyllabic words experienced a continual increase, while the growth trends were different in native Chinese texts and Chinese translated Buddhist texts.

It is worth noting that the Middle Ages was the first period to witness large-scale contact between Chinese and foreign languages. In the Eastern Han Dynasty, Buddhist scriptures were introduced from the Western Regions, and then translated into Chinese in large quantities. Liang Xiaohong noted that in the development of the Chinese language, it was an inevitable trend for its lexical system to transit from monosyllabic word-dominated to disyllabic word-dominated. With the introduction, rapid spread, and flourishing of Buddhism in China, translated Buddhist scriptures abounded; as a result, new words and expressions were created in batches, which was bound to exert a significant impact on the aforementioned trend [6]. The degree of polysyllablization in Chinese translated Buddhist scriptures, in terms of both the number of polysyllabic words and their frequency of use, was higher than that in native literature of the same period [7], and research showed that both external language contact and internal literary style accounted for the stronger tendency of polysyllablization in translated Buddhist scriptures.

Polysyllablization was a macro trend in the development of the lexical system. At the micro level, with regard to specific words, different words could still select different syllabic forms, illustrated as follows: Some monosyllabic words have been kept in use till today, such as "人" (ren in pinyin, literally, person), "手" (shou in pinyin, literally, hand), "水" (shui in pinyin, literally, water), etc. Some monosyllabic words have developed polysyllabic forms, which might have common morphemes with the original monosyllabic word, such as "月" (yue in pinyin, literally, moon) and its disyllabic form "月亮" (yueliang in pinyin), or no common morphemes, such as "日" (ri in pinyin, literally, sun) and its disyllabic form "太阳" (taiyang in pinyin). In addition, reduplication such as "星" (xing in pinyin, literally, star) and its disyllabic form "星星" (xingxing in pinyin), and derivation such as "杯" (bei in pinyin, literally, cup) and its disyllabic form "杯子" (beizi in pinyin) could also be found. There have been some achievements in the study of syllabic form selection [8–11], from the perspectives of presentation of sememe, transition of latent morpheme to dominant morpheme, core meaning, etc., but mainly aimed at specific cases. Since different words selected different syllabic forms, which was the most prevailing? When a compound form was selected, which type of structure was preferred? What about their appearances in native literature and translated Buddhist scriptures, respectively? Were they affected by external language contact? Due to lack of statistical analysis and systematic depiction of the selection of specific syllabic forms in the diachronic evolution of the Chinese lexical system, especially lack of basic data on such selection from Ancient Chinese to Middle Chinese, these questions have not yet been well discussed or answered.

Therefore, with the syllabic form selection of specific words in the key stage of polysyllablization of Chinese lexis as the research object, we will construct lexical data on the syllabic form selection from Ancient Chinese to Middle Chinese, and conduct a statistical survey and systematic depiction of the paths of selection, morphemic connections between new and old words, their appearances in native literature and Buddhist scriptures, etc. This is not only fundamental in the study of the polysyllablization of Chinese lexis, but also conducive to a clearer understanding of the impact of language contact on the development of Chinese. Nouns are the bulk of the lexical system. This paper will focus on high-frequency nouns in Ancient Chinese, construct lexical data on the syllabic form selection from Ancient Chinese to Middle Chinese based on the corpus linguistics method, and then conduct multi-perspective quantitative analysis and discussion.

2   Workflow and Results

In this paper, based on the corpus linguistics method, lexical data on the syllabic form selection from Ancient Chinese to Middle Chinese would be established. The specific process is shown in Fig. 1.

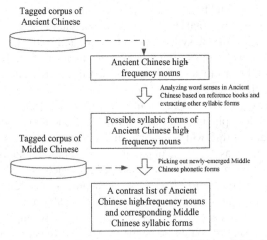

Fig. 1. Flowchart of constructing lexical data on Ancient Chinese high-frequency nouns and corresponding Middle Chinese syllabic forms.

First, based on the tagged corpus of Ancient Chinese [12], we took 16 texts, including 论语 (*Lunyu* in pinyin), 左传 (*Zuozhuan* in pinyin), 史记 (*Shiji* in pinyin) and so on, with a total of 1.64 million characters, and identified Ancient Chinese high-frequency nouns according to the word segmentation and part-of-speech tagging information of the corpus. Then, those nouns were ranked according to their number of instances in the corpus. "人" (*ren* in pinyin, literally, person) ranked first, followed by "王" (*wang* in pinyin, literally, king), "民" (*min* in pinyin, literally, people), "秦" (*qin* in pinyin, literally, Qin state), "国" (*guo* in pinyin, literally, state), "天下" (*tianxia* in pinyin, literally, world), etc.

Second, we analyzed the sememes of the Ancient Chinese high-frequency nouns one by one based on reference books and extracted other syllabic expressions. Here only common nominal sememes produced in the Ancient Chinese period were considered.

Take the Ancient Chinese high-frequency noun "人" (*ren* in pinyin, literally, person) as an example. Among its many sememes, three common ones were selected, based on reference books including 汉语大字典 (*Hanyu Da Zidian* in pinyin, literally, Comprehensive Chinese Character Dictionary, abbr. HDZ), 汉语大词典(*Hanyu Da Cidian* in pinyin, literally, Comprehensive Chinese Word Dictionary, abbr. HDC), etc.: Sememe 1: an advanced animal that can make and employ tools to work and use language to think; Sememe 2: every person, each person; Sememe 3: a talent or outstanding person. In Modern Chinese, Sememe 1 retains its monosyllabic form "人", while Sememe 2 and 3 take corresponding disyllabic forms "人人" (*renren* in pinyin, literally, every person) and "人才" (*rencai* in pinyin, literally, talent), respectively. "人" in Ancient Chinese also had the sense of "sexual intercourse" such as in "荒侯市人病不能为人" (《史记·樊郦滕灌列传》), which, however, had a very low frequency of use. In addition, "人" could also refer to "reputation, honor", which did not emerge until Early Modern Chinese. Senses as such were not within the scope of this paper.

Third, based on the tagged corpus of Middle Chinese, newly emerged Middle Chinese syllabic forms were picked out. Middle Chinese texts could be classified into two categories, say, native literature and Buddhist scriptures. The former was represented by 5 texts, namely, 抱朴子内篇 (*Baopuzi Neipian* in pinyin), 世说新语 (*Shishuo Xinyu* in pinyin), 齐民要术 (*Qimin Yaoshu* in pinyin), 洛阳伽蓝记 (*Luoyang Qielan Ji* in pinyin), and 颜氏家训 (*Yanshi Jiaxun* in pinyin), and the latter by 23 texts, including 阴持入经 (*Yin Chi Ru Jing* in pinyin) and 道地经 (*Dao Di Jing* in pinyin) translated by 安世高, 道行般若经 (*Dao Xing Bo Re Jing* in pinyin) translated by 支娄迦谶, 佛说义足经 (*Fo Shuo Yi Zu Jing* in pinyin), 佛说菩萨本业经 (*Fo Shuo Pu Sa Ben Ye Jing* in pinyin), and 了本生死经 (*Liao Ben Sheng Si Jing* in pinyin) translated by 支谦, 佛本行集经 (*Fo Ben Xing Ji Jing* in pinyin) translated by 阇那崛多, etc. Altogether, the 28 selected Middle Chinese texts, including both native texts and Buddhist scriptures, totaled 1.62 million characters. Still take "人" (*ren* in pinyin, literally, person) as an example. Its corresponding disyllabic form "人人" (*renren* in pinyin, literally, every person) had already existed in Ancient Chinese, such as in "子曰：'仁之难成久矣。人人失其所好, 故仁者之过易辞也。'" (《礼记·表记》), while its corresponding disyllabic form "人才" (*rencai* in pinyin, literally, talent) was not produced until in Middle Chinese, such as in "褒贤贵德, 乐育人才" (《抱朴子·逸民》).

Following the above procedure, newly emerged lexical forms of Ancient Chinese words in the Middle Ages could be obtained in an exhaustive manner, marked in "A—M" format below, where A is an Ancient Chinese high-frequency noun (or a group of synonyms), and M is the newly emerged Middle Chinese word corresponding to a specific sememe of A, which is still in use in Modern Chinese. After a survey of the top 500 high-frequency nouns, we obtained 100 sets of items. Due to space limitations, we will only present some of the typical cases as follows.

1. 'A: 人 (*ren* in pinyin)—M: 人才 (*rencai* in pinyin)

"人" in Ancient Chinese had the sense of "talent", such as in "子无谓秦无人, 吾谋适不用也。" (《左传·文公十三年》). Its corresponding disyllabic form "人才" emerged in Middle Chinese, only found in native literature:

尔朱荣马邑小胡, 人才凡鄙, 不度德量力, 长戟指阙, 所谓穷辙拒轮, 积薪候燎。(《洛阳伽蓝记》卷一).

2. A: 王 (*wang* in pinyin)—M: 国王 (*guowang* in pinyin)

The newly emerged disyllabic form "国王" meant "a ruler of a state," found in both translated Buddhist scriptures and native literature in the Middle Ages. Examples are:

即时佛到, 国王臣民、长者居士、眷属围绕, 数千百重, 菩萨欲前散花, 不能得前。(《修行本起经》卷上).

以其疾故, 国王大臣、长者居士、婆罗门等, 及诸王子并余官属, 无数千人, 皆往问疾。(《维摩诘所说经》上卷).

父老传云: 此像本从南方腾空而来, 于阗国王亲见礼拜, 载像归, 中路夜宿, 忽然不见, 遣人寻之, 还来本处。(《洛阳伽蓝记》卷五).

3. A: 今 (*jin* in pinyin)—M: 现在 (*xianzai* in pinyin)

The disyllabic form "现在" (literally, now), as a time indicator, abounded in Chinese translated Buddhist scriptures. Examples are:

闻如是: 一时佛游于摩竭道场, 初始得佛, 光景甚明, 自然莲华宝师子座, 古昔诸佛所坐皆尔, 道德威仪相好如一, 身意清净, 福行普具, 明彻彻照人刹法处, 去来现在无复罣碍, 成兴于世, 一切悉等。(《佛说菩萨本业经》).

法行天子又复白言: "不以是行得成至佛, 现在行道所修甚难, 当察己身等之山谷, 是则究竟菩萨大士一生补处。" (《普曜经》第四卷).

便谓过去未来现在唯是一识无有迁谢。(《百喻经》卷三).

4. A: 公 (*gong* in pinyin)—M: 公务 (*gongwu* in pinyin)

"公" could be used to refer to "公事" (*gongshi* in pinyin, literally, official business), such as in "肃肃宵征, 夙夜在公。" (《诗·召南·小星》). "公, 指公事。" (annotated by 余冠英). The newly emerged Middle Chinese disyllabic form "公务" (literally, official business) was found in both translated Buddhist scriptures and native literature. Examples are:

但自营私何虑公务。(《出曜经》卷二十三).

所以然者, 以其当公务而执私情, 处重责以怀薄义也。(《颜氏家训·兄弟》).

5. A: 地 (*di* in pinyin)—M: 大地 (*dadi* in pinyin)

The newly emerged disyllabic form "大地" meant "vast expanse of ground; the whole world under heaven", which could also refer to "related to the earth", only found in Chinese translated Buddhist scriptures:

一切大地庄严映饰未曾有。(《大庄严论经》卷十四).

此善华世界诸菩萨等皆得神通, 于诸菩萨功德自在, 今日清旦见是大光, 其光悉从诸佛世界来至于此, 大地时时六种震动, 雨种种华。(《悲华经》卷十).

尔时世尊, 与诸四众, 前后围遶, 放大光明震动大地, 至舍卫国, 所经客舍, 悉于中止, 道次度人, 无有限量, 渐渐来近舍卫城边, 一切大众, 持诸供具, 迎待世尊。(《贤愚经》卷十).

6. A: 日 (*ri* in pinyin)—M: 太阳 (*taiyang* in pinyin)

The newly emerged disyllabic form "太阳" was a general term for "日," found in native literature:
王公曰: "使太阳与万物同晖, 臣下何以瞻仰?" (《世说新语·宠礼》).

7. A: 时 (*shi* in pinyin)—M: 时间 (*shijian* in pinyin)

The newly emerged disyllabic form "时间" meant "the present, the moment". The earliest textual instance in HDC was "时间尚在白衣, 目下风云未遂。" (《西厢记诸宫调》卷一, by 董解元 in Jin Dynasty). It was quite late. In fact, instances had emerged in Middle Chinese translated Buddhist scriptures:
是诸菩萨摩诃萨, 从初踊出, 以诸菩萨种种赞法而赞于佛, 如是时间, 经五十小劫. (《妙法莲华经》卷五).
如是念念刹那时间。(《佛本行集经》卷二十一).

8. A: 时 (*shi* in pinyin)—M: 光阴 (*guangyin* in pinyin)

The newly emerged disyllabic form "光阴" meant "time; years" and was only found in native literature:
光阴可惜, 譬诸逝水。(《颜氏家训·勉学》).

9. A: 臣 (*chen* in pinyin)—M: 奴隶 (*nuli* in pinyin)

The word "臣" in Ancient Chinese had a sense of "slave." According to HDZ, "臣" meant "奴仆" (*nupu* in pinyin, literally, slave and servant). "臣, 男子贱称。" (《广韵·真韵》). "臣妾逋逃。" (《书·费誓》). "役人贱者, 男曰臣, 女曰妾。" (孔传). The newly emerged disyllabic form "奴隶" was only found in native literature:
爰及农商工贾, 厮役奴隶, 钓鱼屠肉, 饭牛牧羊, 皆有先达, 可为师表, 博学求之, 无不利于事也。(《颜氏家训·勉学》).

10. A: 后/后世 (*hou/houshi* in pinyin)—M: 后代 (*houdai* in pinyin)

Both "后" and "后世" entered the list of high-frequency nouns in Ancient Chinese, and could be used to refer to "offspring, descendants," such as in "无忝皇祖, 式救尔后。" (《诗·大雅·瞻卬》). "后, 谓子孙也。" (annotated by 郑玄). "上古穴居而野处, 后世圣人易之以宫室。" (《易·击辞下》). The newly emerged disyllabic form "后代" was only found in native literature:
余若欲以此辈事, 骋辞章于来世, 则余所著外篇及杂文二百余卷, 足以寄意于后代, 不复须此。(《抱朴子内篇》).

11. A: 外 (*wai* in pinyin)—M: 外边 (*waibian* in pinyin)

The newly emerged disyllabic form "外边" meant "a place beyond a certain boundary." The earliest textual instance in HDC was "绿树碧檐相掩映, 无人知道外边寒" (

《华清宫》by吴融 in Tang Dynasty). It was quite late. In fact, instances were found in Chinese translated Buddhist scriptures:

其园林中作种种伎乐, 其园外边有四兵宝周匝围遶。(《悲华经》卷二).

时有大臣, 从外边来, 见此一人, 而被囚执, 便问左右: "何缘乃尔?" (《贤愚经》卷一).

12. A: 周 (*zhou* in pinyin)—M: 周围 (*zhouwei* in pinyin)

The newly emerged disyllabic form "周围" meant "the part that surrounds the center" and was only found in Chinese translated Buddhist scriptures:

菩提树下地周围。(《佛本行集经》卷二十七).

13. A: 故 (*gu* in pinyin)—M: 缘故 (*yuangu* in pinyin)

The newly emerged disyllabic form "缘故" meant "reason." The earliest textual instance in HDC was "伏望圣慈, 从其所请, 若除受别有缘故, 即乞明降指挥。" (《论安焘辞免迁官恩命事札子》by苏轼 in Song Dynasty). It was quite late. In fact, the earliest use of this disyllabic form was found but in Chinese translated Buddhist scriptures:

由是缘故, 速得无上正真道成最正觉。(《正法华经》卷五).

某可愍之, 了身行恶、口言恶、心念恶, 具足恶行, 诽谤贤圣奉于邪见, 以此缘故碎身寿命, 趣于勤苦、堕于地狱。(《光赞经》卷二).

14. A: 利/益 (*li/yi* in pinyin)—M: 利益 (*liyi* in pinyin)

The disyllabic form "利益" meant "benefit" and was found in both native literature and Chinese translated Buddhist scriptures:

当觉成佛, 所在供养, 为饶利益, 诸天世间。(《正法华经》卷八).

汝今速往, 至于佛所, 头顶礼足, 作大利益。(《悲华经》卷五).

凡种榆者, 宜种刺、梜两种, 利益为多; 其余软弱, 例非佳木也。(《齐民要术》卷五).

15. A: 世 (*shi* in pinyin)—M: 一生 (*yisheng* in pinyin)

The disyllabic form "一生" meant "the whole life" and was found in both native literature and Chinese translated Buddhist scriptures:

夫人一生中不怀众想念。(《出曜经》卷六).

友闻白羊肉美, 一生未曾得吃, 故冒求前耳, 无事可咎。今已饱, 不复须驻。(《世说新语·任诞》).

何惜数年勤学, 长受一生愧辱哉! (《颜氏家训·勉学》).

Due to space limitations, other sets of items will not be presented here in this paper.

3 Analysis of Newly Emerged Lexical Syllabic Forms

The lexical data of Ancient Chinese high-frequency nouns and their corresponding syllabic forms in the Middle Ages contain quantitative statistical laws of syllabic form selection. In the contrast list in the previous section, there are mainly two categories of situation: In the first category, the Ancient Chinese high-frequency words are monosyllabic, and the newly emerged Middle Chinese words are disyllabic. In the second category, both the Ancient Chinese high-frequency words and the newly emerged Middle Chinese words are disyllabic. The first category is more common, such as "王—国王", "地—大地", etc., while the second is less common, such as "后世—后代." Theoretically, there is a third category of situation, say, the Ancient Chinese high-frequency words are disyllabic while the newly emerged Middle Chinese words are monosyllabic. However, since the high-frequency words we examined were limited in range, no case of the third category was observed. Therefore, the major path of syllabic form selection in the Middle Ages was for monosyllabic words to take a disyllabic word as their newly emerged form, which is worth more detailed investigation. In addition, since there exists a complex situation of "multiple to one", such as "A:后/后世—M:后代," we only took the "one to one" evolution path, say, one monosyllabic word to one disyllabic word, into consideration, which was found in 91 sets of items.

For cases following the "one monosyllabic word to one disyllabic word" evolution path, we conducted a statistical investigation from three aspects, and the data are shown in Table 1.

Table 1. Statistics of syllabic selection types of Ancient Chinese high-frequency nouns in the Middle Ages.

Classification criteria	Data
Whether the newly emerged disyllabic word and the old word have overlapping morphemes	The new word absorbed the old word as its morpheme: 65 items (71.4%) The new word shared no common morpheme with the old word: 26 items (28.6%)
Nature of the source text of the newly emerged disyllabic word	Seen in native literature only: 23 items (25.3%) Seen in both native literature and Buddhist scriptures: 17 items (18.7%) Seen in Buddhist scriptures only: 51 items (56.0%)
Word formation of the newly emerged disyllabic word	Coordinative structure: 53 items (58.2%) Attributive structure: 36 items (39.6%) Derivative structure: 2 items (2.2%)

In the first aspect, in terms of whether there are overlapping morphemes between the newly emerged disyllabic word and the old word, the surveyed items can be divided into two types. One is that the Middle Chinese newly emerged disyllabic word took the Ancient Chinese monosyllabic word as its morpheme, such as "王"—"国王", "地"—"大地", "时"—"时间", with a total of 65, accounting for 71.4% of all items. The other is that the Middle Chinese new word shared no common morpheme with the old, such as "日"—"太阳", "臣"—"奴隶", "今"—"现在", with a total of 26, accounting for 28.6% of all items. It can be seen that taking the original monosyllabic word as a morpheme was a major path of syllabic selection in the formation of a new polysyllabic word. Specifically, absorbing the original morpheme (especially a high-frequency one) helped to better express the semantic range of the newly produced word, while its semantic accuracy was improved through the restriction of other morphemes; therefore, this path was a more direct and economical approach in the polysyllabic form selection. In contrast, if there was a lack of common morphemes between the old and new words, the new word was usually a polysyllabic form that had evolved from another monosyllabic word, merely semantically overlapping with the old word. Only when the newly emerged polysyllabic word gained an advantage in the competition of the lexical system could an association of syllabic selection be established between the new word and the old word. This process was usually very slow and mostly could not be truly completed until in Modern Chinese. Take Ancient Chinese monosyllabic word "今" (*jin* in pinyin, literally, now) as an example. Its corresponding disyllabic form "现在" (*xianzai* in pinyin, literally, now) was newly produced in Middle Chinese, used in large quantities in Chinese translated Buddhist scriptures. Yet not until in Modern Chinese did the disyllabic form "现在" become a dominant word, where the monosyllabic form "今" generally cannot be used independently, say, it usually serves as a morpheme to form a word but is rarely used on its own.

In the second aspect, according to the nature of the source text of the newly emerged disyllabic words, they can be divided into three types: First, newly emerged words that were found only in the native literature and not in the Buddhist scriptures of the same period totaled 23 items, accounting for 25.3% of all. Second, newly emerged words that were found only in the Buddhist scriptures and not in the native literature of the same period totaled 51 items, accounting for 56.0% of all. Third, newly emerged words that were found in both the Buddhist scriptures and the native literature totaled 17 items, accounting for 18.7% of all. It can be seen that those only found in the Buddhist scriptures occupied a major part, indicating that polysyllabic forms were more abundant in Buddhist scriptures, that is, the lexical system of Chinese translated Buddhist scriptures featured a more active presence of newly emerged polysyllabic words compared with that of the native literature of the same period. Since Chinese translated Buddhist scriptures were a product of Sanskrit-Chinese language contact, the activeness of polysyllabic words is believed to have been closely related to language contact.

In the third aspect, from the perspective of word formation, the newly emerged nouns can be divided into three types, namely, coordinative structures which totaled 53 in number and accounted for 58.2% of all, attributive structures, 36 and 39.6%, and derivative structures, 2 and 2.2%. Coordinative structures, as one of the most productive compound word-formation methods, accounted for the majority, followed by attributive structures. Derivation was rarely seen, as affixes in Chinese were small in number and late in appearance. In fact, only 2 derivative structures were found. One is Ancient Chinese "木" (*mu* in pinyin) and Middle Chinese "木头" (*mutou* in pinyin), literally, a general term for wood and timber. The earliest textual instance in HDC was "木头雕作小唐鸡, 箸子拈来壁上栖。" (《五冠山》by 李齐贤 in the Liao Dynasty). It was quite late. Actually this disyllabic word had been in use in Chinese Buddhist scriptures, such as in "时妇常以三奇木头, 擎镜照面。" (《贤愚经》卷四) and "是时, 迦叶祭祀火时, 火及木

头, 东西驰走, 不能一住。" (《佛本行集经》卷四十二). The other is Ancient Chinese "种" (*zhong* in pinyin) and Middle Chinese "种子" (*zhongzi* in pinyin), literally, seed, such as in "至春, 治取别种, 以拟明年种子。" (《齐民要术·收种》) and "何有田中, 不下种子, 望有收获?无有是事。" (《大庄严论经》卷十).

4 Conclusion

After a systematic survey of the top 500 high-frequency nouns in Ancient Chinese, this paper obtained a contrast list of Ancient Chinese high-frequency nouns and their corresponding Middle Chinese words, which offers a comprehensive representation of the diachronic evolution of the phonetic forms of high-frequency nouns from Ancient Chinese to Middle Chinese, and forms basic data on the syllabic selection mechanism of Middle Chinese words. Then, based on the above word list, various paths of phonetic form development from Ancient Chinese to Middle Chinese were statistically analyzed, and the statistical rules governing the phonetic form development of Ancient Chinese high-frequency nouns in the Middle Ages were preliminarily explored. The main conclusions are:

First, inheritance was the mainstream in the lexical evolution and development. High-frequency nouns in Ancient Chinese had certain stability that most of them were retained and continued to be used in the Middle Chinese period, which reflects the stability in the process of language development. Newly emerged Middle Chinese words and inherited Ancient Chinese words coexisted in the lexical system, competing with each other in a dynamic development. Some of the Middle Chinese newly emerged words would eventually gain a competitive advantage and then replace the retained original word, but this process was usually very slow and gradual and could not be completed until the Modern Chinese period.

Second, polysyllablization was a main form of lexical development in Middle Chinese. In the vast majority of cases, disyllabic forms were used in this period as an alternative to the original monosyllabic words, because polysyllabic words (especially disyllabic words) were more productive compared with monosyllabic words. It was a significant governing trend for polysyllabic words to serve as a newly selected syllabic form of the original monosyllabic words in the development of the lexical system.

Third, taking the original monosyllabic words as morphemes to form new polysyllabic words was a main path of syllabic selection. According to the statistical survey on the word list, those that took the original monosyllabic words as morphemes accounted for more than half of all the newly emerged polysyllabic words. That was because taking the original high-frequency morphemes and restricting the word sense with a compounding structure helped to make a full and economical use of existing morphemes and achieve better semantic precision at the same time.

Fourth, language contact had a certain impact on the selection of polysyllabic forms. In the Middle Ages, Buddhist scriptures, mainly in Sanskrit, were translated into Chinese on a large scale. Due to the influence of external languages, polysyllabic words were more abundant and more active in the lexical system of Chinese translated Buddhist scriptures. For example, the time indicator "现在" (*xianzai* in pinyin, literally, now) was formed in translation by imitating the Sanskrit word prati-ut-√pad. With the spread of

Buddhism in China, such words gradually entered the mainstream of Chinese lexis and exerted a positive impact on its development ever after.

This paper, taking high-frequency nouns as the starting point, established for the first time a contrast list reflecting the syllabic form selection of Chinese words, which provides basic data for the study of the history of Chinese lexis, preliminarily proved the feasibility of the approach, and conducted a quantitative discussion from various aspects. In the future, the research object and research scope of this paper will be further expanded. The syllabic form selection of words of various parts of speech from a larger range of frequency ranking will be investigated and described, in order to obtain a more systematic and substantial word list and enrich the fundamental data for the study of the history of Chinese lexis.

Acknowledgments. This paper was sponsored by the Beijing Social Science Foundation project "A Study on New Words and New Senses in *Fo Suo Xing Zan* Based on Sanskrit-Chinese Collation" (Grant No. 17YYC019), Major Program of National Social Science Foundation of China (Grant No. 21&ZD310) and the independent scientific research project of Tsinghua University "A Study on the Formation of Chinese Polysyllabic Nouns and Their Syllabic Selection Mechanism" (Grant No. 2019THZWLJ28).

References

1. Zhu, Q.: On the various influences of translated Buddhist scriptures on the development of Middle Chinese lexis. Stud. Chinese Lang.. **4**, 297–306 (1992). (in Chinese)
2. Zhou, S.: Issues on polysyllabic words in Shishuo Xinyu. J. Jilin Univ. (Social Sciences Edition). **02**, 81–88 (1982). (in Chinese)
3. Dong, Y.: An exploration of the word formation of polysyllabic words in Baopuzi. Res, Ancient Chinese Lang. **04**, 82–85 (1994). (in Chinese)
4. Zhou, R.: Word formation of polysyllabic words in Yanshi Jiaxun. J. South China Normal Univ. (Social Sciences Edition). **02**, 80–87 (1998). (in Chinese)
5. Qiu, B.: A Multi-perspective Study on the Polysyllablization of Middle Chinese Lexis. Nanjing University Press (2012). (in Chinese)
6. Liang, X.: Influence of the Han, Wei and six dynasties on the polysyllablization of Chinese lexis. J. Nanjing Normal Univ. (Social Sciences Edition). **2**, 73–78 (1991). (in Chinese)
7. Qiu, B.: A Study on the Lexicon of Fo Suo Xing Zan. Nanjing University Press (2020). (in Chinese)
8. Che, S.: From latent morpheme to dominant morpheme—on the polysyllabic process of the compound verb zhāoshǒu. Stud. Lang. Linguist.. **33**(04), 88–91 (2013). (in Chinese)
9. Che, S., Li, X.: The presentation of the sememe: on the polysyllabic process of the compound noun tóufà. J. Shanxi Normal Univ. (Social Sciences Edition). **41**(01), 147–152 (2014). (in Chinese)
10. Che, S., Li, X.: On the polysyllabic approach and mechanism of the compound noun Shǒuzhǎng. J. Sch. Chinese Lang. Cult. Nanjing Normal Univ. **02**, 160–165 (2017). (in Chinese)
11. Wang, C., Wang, Y.: On the underlying mechanism of morpheme combination of coordinative compound words: from the perspective of core meaning. J. Zhejiang Univ. (Humanities and Social Sciences). **50**(01), 204–217 (2020). (in Chinese)
12. Huang, C.R., Chen, K.: A Chinese corpus for linguistic research. In: COLING 1992 Volume 4: The 14th International Conference on Computational Linguistics. Nantes, French, pp. 23–26 (1992)

On the Emergence of Positive Meaning of *Xiāngdāng* from the Structure of *Xiāngdāng de NP*

Mengmeng Song[(✉)]

Department of Chinese Language and Literature, School of Humanities and Law Henan Institute of Science and Technology, Xinxiang, China
1350950393@qq.com

Abstract. *Xiāngdāng (相当)* can modify nominal component more freely and express positive meanings such as 'very large/good/outstanding/excellent'. The positive meanings of *xiāngdāng* emerged under the joint action of multiple factors. The inherent quantitative feature of *xiāngdāng* has accompanied its semantic evolution throughout. Therefore, under the dual effects of the shift of cognitive focus and the semantic constraint of *yǒu(有)* sentences, the degree implication of *xiāngdāng* presents high-order prominence so that the degree of high quantity meaning is solidified and became the source power of the positive meaning. At the synchronic level, the close adjacency in syntactic order, the direct relation in semantics and the shift of communicators' focus further accelerate and solidify the semantic fusion between degree adverb *xiāngdāng* and the modified attribute concept.

Keywords: *Xiāngdāng* · Positive meaning · Quantitative feature · Semantic fusion

1 Introduction

In modern Chinese, there exists such a special kind of positive meaning structure -- *xiāngdāng (de) NP*. The construction component *xiāngdāng* often contains the high quantity meaning in the internal degree level of the specific attribute concept. For example:

(1) 他的父亲和洗桂秋的父亲有相当的交情。

> *Tā de fùqīn hé Xǐ Guìqiū de fùqīn yǒu xiāngdāng de jiāoqíng.*
> His father and Xi Guiqiu's father have very close fellowship
> 'His father had a considerable relationship with Xi Guiqiu's father.' (老舍《蜕》).

Funding. Youth Project for Humanities and Social Sciences Research of Hebei Province (Semantic Word-formation of Chinese Modifier-head VN Compounds From The Generative Lexicon Theory) (HB22YY021); International Chinese Language Education Project of Center For Language Education and Cooperation (Research on Polysemic Compounds for International Chinese Language Education) (22YH65D).

© The Author(s), under exclusive license to Springer Nature Switzerland AG 2023
Q. Su et al. (Eds.): CLSW 2022, LNAI 13495, pp. 25–41, 2023.
https://doi.org/10.1007/978-3-031-28953-8_3

(2) 各种创作也都有相当的成绩。

Gèzhǒng chuàngzuò yě dōu yǒu xiāngdāng de chéngjì.
All kinds of creation also have very big achievement
'Each kind of creation also has the quite achievement.' (周作人《地方与文艺》).

(3) 说出话来有相当分量谁都乐意听他的。

Shuōchū huà lái yǒu xiāngdāng fènliang shuí dōu lè yì tīng tā de.
Speak have great strength everyone willing to listen to him
'If he spoke authoritatively, everyone is willing to listen to him.' (张爱玲《论写作
》).

It is precisely because the special usage of *xiāngdāng* is abundant in language facts, so its attribution of the part of speech is still controversial. Most scholars regard *xiāngdāng* in such usages as an adjective based on its grammatical function of modifying substantive components [1–5], and others judge it as an adverb [6] or an attributive word [7] based on semantics. In fact, the origin of this controversy lies in different scholars' different cognition of the derivation path of the *xiāngdāng (de) NP* structure mentioned above. How does the *xiāngdāng*, which formally modifies the substantive components and semantically highlights the positive quantity feature, emerge? Some studies have discussed the semantic evolution of *xiāngdāng* in detail when research its grammaticalization process [4, 5, 8]. However, these studies mainly focus on revealing the trigger mechanism of grammaticalization of *xiāngdāng* and their observation point is mostly based on the static result dimension. Therefore, the above usages of the dynamic grammaticalization process have not received due attention.

When discussing the formation path of degree adverb *xiāngdāng*, Lei Dongping pointed out that the high quantity meaning *xiāngdāng* in examples (1)-(3) was formed in the construction of *yǒu xiāngdāng (de) NP* in order to solve the contradiction of semantic [5]. We agree with the judgment that the *yǒu* sentence is the source of the above usage of *xiāngdāng*. However, the emergence of the degree high quantity meaning of attributive position *xiāngdāng* is not so direct and the extensive use of the positive meaning of *xiāngdāng (de) NP* structure is not just grammaticalization. Because this view cannot solve the following two problems: One is the exclusive problem, that is, why the degree adverb *tèbié(特别)*, which is also caused by the grammaticalization of adjectives, does not emerge new meanings under the suppression of the *yǒu* sentences? The other is the compatibility problem, that is, why some NP that cannot act as the object component of the word *yǒu* can be compatible with this structure (for example, '*yǒu shù'é(有数额)'-'xiāngdāng de shù'é(相当的数额))*'?

In view of the above, this paper will explore the semantic characteristics of *xiāngdāng* by analyzing the internal correlation between different meanings from the perspective of the semantic evolution of *xiāngdāng*, and then analysis the influencing factors of the final solidification of the positive meaning of *xiāngdāng*.

2 The Emergence Process of the High Quantity Meaning of *Xiāngdāng (de) NP*: Attribute Prominence to Quantity Prominence

The attributive function of *xiāngdāng* was quite mature in the Qing Dynasty. However, the structure of *xiāngdāng (de) NP* in Chinese language history is not completely homogeneous, such as *xiāngdāng de zhíwèi* (相当的职位), *xiāngdāng de jiāoqíng* (相当的交情) and *xiāngdāng de nǚrén* (相当的女人).It means that not all *xiāngdāng (de) NP* structures belong to the research object of this paper. The main reason for the constructional homonymy is that the grammatical quality and semantic reference of the construction component *xiāngdāng* are quite different. So, we need to first research the semantic evolution of *xiāngdāng* in order to clarify the research object and then observe its emergence process through the specific distribution context of the structure.

2.1 The Semantic Evolution of *Xiāngdāng*

Generally speaking, the grammaticalization of *xiāngdāng* follows the development sequence from verb to adjective to adverb [4, 9, 10]. It should be noted that since the semantic evolution is a gradual process and this paper intends to observe what the meaning of *xiāngdāng* enters *xiāngdāng (de) NP* structures rather than the exact time each meaning of *xiāngdāng* appears, so the time nodes mentioned in this paper are relatively general. What's more, this paper mainly focuses on the internal correlation between different meanings and the trigger mechanism for the high quantity meaning of *xiāngdāng*.

According to the Ancient Chinese Corpus of Peking University Center for Chinese Linguistics (CCL), the usage of *xiāngdāng* in different historical periods can be summarized as follows: ① It means that different entities are sufficient to 'match each other' on the specific attributes; ② It means that the 'relative' relationship in spatial distribution; ③ It means that one entity can 'matching' another entity on the specific attribute; ④ It means that the quantity value presented by a certain entity on the specific attribute is 'corresponding/reasonable/appropriate'; ⑤ It means that the entity presents 'high quantity meaning' on the specific attribute; ⑥ It means that the entity presents 'high quantity meaning' on the dimension of degree. The specific usages are shown in the following table:

It can be seen from the table that the usage of *xiāngdāng* in diachronic evolution shows certain regularity: (1) The predicate feature of *xiāngdāng* is particularly prominent. The phrase *xiāngdāng* in the Warring States Period is a free combination of the morpheme *xiāng* (相) and *dāng* (当) at the syntactic level and it is an attributive structure. The verb *dāng* acts as the structure and semantic center of the phrase, so after the lexicalization of *xiāngdāng*, its usage of verbal parts takes a dominant position, which runs through the whole semantic evolution. The usage of adjective derived from it is relatively early and has been used to the greatest extent in the Republic of China. (2) The semantic function of *xiāngdāng* is positive correlation with its frequency of use. Before the Qing Dynasty, the use frequency of *xiāngdāng* was relatively limited and the applicable register was concentrated. The phrase *xiāngdāng* is mainly used to describe the mutual

Table 1. The usage statistics of *xiāngdāng* in diachronic evolution.

Period \ Quantity / Meaning	Meaning ①	Meaning ②	Meaning ③	Meaning ④	Meaning ⑤	Meaning ⑥
Warring States	8	/	/	/	/	/
Han Dynasty	12	2	1	/	/	/
Six Dynasties	8	7	3	/	/	/
Tang & the Five Dynasties	1	/	18	3	/	/
The Northern Song Dynasty	7	5	42	4	/	/
The Southern Song Dynasty	/	/	4	10	/	/
Yuan Dynasty	1	/	2	/	/	/
Ming Dynasty	5	/	44	1	/	/
Qing Dynasty	8	/	85	11	/	/
The Republic of China	15	/	110	70	21	2

checks and balances of the army in terms of strength, quantity, military strength and damage, the vertical and horizontal relationship in spatial orientation and the matching relationship between the main entities in terms of qualifications, talent and appearance, age, morality and other attributes. After the Republic of China, with the proliferation of *xiāngdāng* use cases, their semantic functions becoming increasingly rich, the communicators gradually paid less attention to the reference subject and instead focused on the comparison results. The meaning ⑤ and the meaning ⑥ gradually emerged. It can be said that the different meanings of *xiāngdāng* are not formed along a specific single path, which can be expressed as follows:

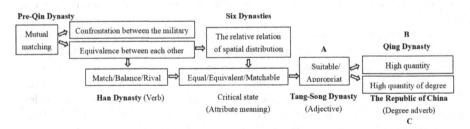

Fig. 1. Semantic evolution of *xiāngdāng*.

2.2 The Emergence Process and Restrictive Factors of High Quantity Meaning of *Xiāngdāng*

As far as our current corpus is concerned, the structure of *xiāngdāng (zhī/de (之/的))* NP first appeared in the Tang Dynasty (Example (4)), which means 'appropriate'. Obviously, this kind of structure is not the positive meaning this paper called *xiāngdāng (de)* NP structure. In fact, in addition to the *xiāngdāng (zhī/de)* NP structure which means 'appropriate', there is another heterogeneous structure that highlights the degree meaning in Modern and Contemporary Chinese (Example (6)). The *xiāngdāng* in example (4)–(6) respectively corresponds to the meanings generated on the time nodes A, B and C in Fig. 1. It can be seen that the origin of these heterogeneous structures mainly lies in the distinct semantic and syntactic functions of *xiāngdāng*. Therefore, to explore the derivation path of positive meaning *xiāngdāng (zhī/de)* NP structure, to some extent, is actually to explore the emergence process of the positive meaning of *xiāngdāng*, while high quantity meaning itself is the initial manifestation of the emerging positive meaning. So how does *xiāngdāng* derive the meaning 'high quantity' from the meaning 'appropriate'?

(4) 任人如本道有相当职员, 任奏请改转。

Rèn rén rú běn dào yǒu xiāng dāng zhí yuán, rèn zòu qǐng gǎi zhuǎn.
Selecting officials if this area has appropriate clerk reported please transferring
'If there are officials with similar positions in this area while choosing officials, please inform the emperor so they can be transferred to another post.' (《唐会要·卷七十九》)

(5) 高凌霨呢, 内阁还在他的手中, 也还有相当的能力。

Gāo Língwèi ne, nèigé háizài tā de shǒuzhōng, yě háiyǒu xiāngdāng de nénglì.
Gao Lingwei cabinet is still in his hand and have considerable ability
'Gao Lingwei is still take charge of cabinet and has considerable ability.' (《民国演义》).

(6) 选景相当的中国, 相当的城乡结合部。

Xuǎn jǐng xiāng dāng de zhōng guó, xiāng dāng de chéng xiāng jié hé bù.
Scenery selection very China very urban periphery
'The scenery selection is particularly Chinese style and rural-urban fringe style.'

(7) 大军相当之际, 将士用命之时, 丞相何故出此不吉之言?

Dàjūn xiāngdāng zhī jì, jiàngshì yòngmìng zhī shí, chéngxiàng hégù chū cǐ
The military confrontation time soldiers use their life time 2PL why say such *bùjí*
zhī yán?
unlucky words

'Why did the Prime minister make such unfortunate remarks at the time when the military confrontation and the soldiers were fighting?' (《三国演义》)

Based on the initial distribution context of the high quantity of *xiāngdāng (zhī/de)* NP, which often acts as an object component of [+possessive] verbs. Among them, the most common structure is in the *yǒu* structures. From a textual perspective, this structure often resides in subsequent turn-talking, following the reference information mentioned in the originating turn-talking. For example:

(8) 咱们大家回到镖局之内，自有相当的待遇。

    Zánmen dàjiā huídào biāojú zhī nèi, zì yǒu xiāngdāng de dàiyù.
We go back to Escort agency naturally have appropriate remuneration
'When we return to the Escort agency, we will be treated fairly.' (《三侠剑》).

(9) 这完全是我十年前所经受相当惨劫所造成的一种结局罢了。

    Zhè wánquán shì wǒ shínián qián suǒ jīngshòu xiāngdāng cǎnjié suǒ zàochéng de
This completely 1SG ten years ago experience quite a disaster cause *yìzhǒng jiéjú bà le.*
an ending
'This is entirely the result of a rather miserable misery I suffered ten years ago.' (《八仙得道·第七十三回》)

The *xiāngdāng* in example (8) is an echo of the '*sānwèi shàonián biāotóu de sǐ*(三位少年镖头的死)' mentioned in the previous part of article in order to cue to give their families adequate compensation to match their early death. The *xiāngdāng* in example (9) refers to the '*cǎnjié*(惨劫)' matched with the '*kěyǐ hōngdòng shìjiè rénmín de mólì*(可以轰动世界人民的魔力)' in the preceding sentence. Most of the *xiāngdāng* in these initial states have multiple interpretations, which can be understood not only as the action meaning of 'commensurate' with the specific standard provided by the background context information, but also as the attribute meaning of 'almost' with the communicator's subjective standard. At the same time, since these reference quantities are higher than social averages so they can naturally be construed as high quantity. It can be said that the frequent use of the object component of a [+possessive] verb provides sufficient syntactic preparation for the emergence of high quantity of *xiāngdāng*.

Since the Republic of China, with the increasing frequency of *xiāngdāng (zhī/de)* NP, *xiāngdāng* gradually reduced its dependence on contextual information, lost its information of indication, and loosened its restriction on possessive verbs. Thus, its high quantity meaning was solidified, which can increase the connotation and reduce the extension by clearing intrinsic quantitative information of modified NP. From example (10) to example (14), *xiāngdāng* gradually weakens its dependence on the reference information in the text structure until it is completely hidden.

(10) 现在贼人拥百万之众，俺如没有相当的实力，只怕未必能够成功。

    Xiànzài zéirén yōng bǎiwàn zhī zhòng, ǎn rú méiyǒu xiāngdāng de shílì,

Now enemy have millions of people 1SG if NEG considerable strength *zhǐpà wèibì*
nénggòu chénggōng.
just afraid won't succeed
'Now there are millions of enemies. If I have no considerable strength, I am afraid I
may not be able to succeed.' (《明代宫闱史》)

(11) 四面的冷水汇集拢来, 和沸水相混, 到了<u>相当的水量和热度</u>, 然后渐渐腾起,
      愈腾愈高, 就向穴中喷出。

Sìmiàn de lěngshuǐ huìjí lǒng lái, hé fèishuǐ xiānghùn, dàole xiāngdāng de
All sides cold water collect and boiling water mix reach a considerable amount of
shuǐliàng hé rèdù, rán hòu jiànjiàn téngqǐ, yù téng yù gāo, jiù xiàng xuézhōng pēnchū.
water and heat then gradually ebbed higher and higher rushed into the cave
'The cold water on all sides gathered together, mixed with boiling water, reached
a considerable amount of water and heat, and then gradually ebbed, and the higher the
ebbed was, the more it was sprayed into the cave.' (《上古秘史》)

(12) 戴天仇本也不算什么人物。但是同孙先生来, 你也应得表<u>相当的敬意</u>。

Dài Tiānchóu běn yě búsuàn shénme rénwù. Dànshì tóng Sūn xiānshēng lái,
Dai Tianchou originally NEG counting what figure Q with Mr. Sun
nǐ yě yīng dé biǎo xiāngdāng de jìng yì.
2SG also should show considerable respect
'Dai Tianhou is not a big deal. But he's coming with Mr. Sun, you should also show
considerable respect.' (《留东外史》)

(13) 这些亡命先生, 我起初对于他们还表<u>相当的敬意</u>。

Zhèxiē wángmìng xiānshēng, wǒ qǐchū duìyú tāmen hái biǎo xiāngdāng de jìngyì.
These dead gentlemen 1SG initially for them expressed considerable respect
'At first, I showed considerable respect to these fugitives.' (《留东外史》)

(14) 须得见面的日子多了, 有了<u>相当的感情</u>, 才能渐渐用手段, 使她的感情变成爱
      情。

Xū dé jiànmiàn de rìzǐ duō le, yǒu le xiāngdāng de gǎnqíng, cáinéng jiànjiàn yòng
Should meet days more have considerable feelings can gradually use
shǒuduàn, shǐ tā de gǎnqíng biànchéng àiqíng.
means make her feelings into love
'There must be more days to meet, with considerable feelings, in order to gradually
use means to make her falling in love.' (《留东外史续集》)
   Indeed, *yǒu* sentences is the initial context and common context of the high quantity meaning of *xiāngdāng*, but this does not mean that the high quantity meaning of
xiāngdāng is given by the *yǒu* sentences. The reasons are as follows: First, *yǒu* sentences
shows high quantity meaning is the consensus of academic, but the lexical semantic information of such verbs as '*jīngshòu*(经受)', '*méiyǒu*(没有)', '*dào* (到)', '*biǎo*'(表) in the

above examples obviously does not reflect high quantity meaning, the construction itself does not naturally highlight high quantity meaning. However, *xiāngdāng* still shows the obvious quantitative characteristics. Second, *yǒu* + *[]* + *(zhī/de +) NP* are not only compatible with the modifier *xiāngdāng*. For example, the degree adverb '*tèbié(特别)*', which has also experienced the grammaticalization of adjectives into adverbs with high degree of quantity, can also be freely accessible to the structure('国人必有特别之报酬'), but it didn't show high quantity meaning.

In fact, like other constructions in the above examples, *yǒu* sentences is only an occasional context where the usages of high quantity of *xiāngdāng*. However, high quantity meaning of *yǒu* sentences itself is more prominent, so when a large number of *xiāngdāng* appear in the structure, high quantity naturally becomes the primary semantic connotation that *xiāngdāng* can activate under the suppression of the construction meaning. That is to say, the construction suppression of the *yǒu* sentences is only a catalyst for the emergence of high quantity meaning of *xiāngdāng*, which value lies in accelerating the derivation and solidification of high quantity meaning of *xiāngdāng*, rather than a decisive factor in absolute meaning. For example:

(15) 她能翻译英国书, 英文总有个<u>相当程度</u>。

Tā néng fānyì yīngguó shū, yīngwén zǒngyǒu gè <u>xiāngdāng chéngdù</u>.
3SG can translate English books English always has a considerable extent.
'She can translate English books. She always has a good command of English.' (《留东外史续集》)

(16) 舆论之对于执事, 已从沸点而渐降下矣, 今犹保持<u>相当之温度</u>, 以观执事对于今兹之役。

Yúlùn zhī duìyú zhíshì, yǐ cóng fèidiǎn ér jiàn jiàng xià yǐ,
Public opinion for the executive already from boiling point gradually dropped
jīn yóu bǎochí <u>xiāngdāng zhī wēndù</u> yǐ guān zhíshì duìyú jīn zī zhī yì.
now still maintain a considerable temperature to watch the executive for today's duties
'Public opinion for the executive has gradually dropped from the boiling point, now a considerable temperature should be maintained, to watch the executive for today's service.' (《民国演义》)

The phrase '*Xiāngdāng chéngdù*' in Example (15) seems to be placed in the *yǒu* sentences as in Example (4) (5) (8) (10) (14), but the two types are not exactly the same. There is a quantifier *gè(个)* in the *yǒu* sentence in Example (15), which has a relatively stronger objective factuality. Like the phrase '*yǒuběnshū(有本书)*', the omitted numeral is '*yī(一)*' and the whole structure itself is not intend to highlight 'a large number of meanings' but rather to describe certain facts. However, *xiāngdāng* still shows high quantity meaning in this structure. The evidence is in this article: the high quantity of '*hěnhǎo (很好)*' in the preceding text '*tīngshuō èr gūniang de yīngwén hěnhǎo (听说二姑娘的英文很好)*', corresponds to the high quantity of *xiāngdāng*. The '*xiāngdāng zhī wēndù(相当之温度)*' in Example (16) does not appear in the *yǒu* sentence, but it still represents the significant high quantity meaning. In fact, since high quantity itself is one of the benchmarks corresponding to *xiāngdāng* in the conventional context, it is an inevitable trend for *xiāngdāng* itself to develop high quantity. The construction of *yǒu* only accelerates the process of semantic evolution. So what are the deep constraints that really restrict the emergence of high quantity meaning of *xiāngdāng* ?

From the perspective of semantic evolution, although the semantic evolution of *xiāngdāng* radiates along several different development directions, these meanings are not unrelated. They follow a common development path in the underlying logical sense, that is, the attentive focus of the speaker and listeners on the comparative event where *xiāngdāng* is located. As follows:

During the Warring States Period, *xiāngdāng* was a free combination at the syntactic level. The word *xiāng* means 'interaction' and the sememe constituting the semantic could be summarized as [+two entities]. The use of the phrase must be accompanied by two entities. The word *dāng* acts as the structural center and semantic center of the phrase so *xiāngdāng* often acts as a predicate component in the syntactic combination, expressing the mutual matching of two specific subjects on a certain attribute side such as quantity, value, status, degree, condition and reason. That is to say, from the logical point of view, *xiāngdāng* sentences often implies a comparative event at the bottom of the mind, that is, 'after comparing the subject A and the subject B, it is found that the two are similar on X'. The semantic status of the reference subjects A and B is equal, so the conclusion of the 'equivalent' is based on comparison. Therefore, lexical semantics of *xiāngdāng* implies certain time characteristics. For example:

(17) 以百与六十为无穷者之虑, 其情必不相当矣。

Yǐ bǎi yǔ liùshí wéi wúqióng zhě zhī lǜ,
According to the person of 100-year-old and 60-year-old the infinitely consider
qí qíng bì bù xiāngdāng yǐ.
situation must NEG suitable
'According to the needs of the person of 100-year-old or 60-year-old, considering the infinitely long dead, their actual situation must not be suitable.' (《吕氏春秋·卷十》)

After the Han Dynasty, as the frequency of adjacent co-occurrence of *xiāng* and *dāng* on syntactic combination increases, their dependence on entities gradually weakened. At this time, the focus of the communicator changes from the whole process event in the underlying logic to the static result judgment. Therefore, the lexical meaning of *xiāng* is gradually weakened, and the 'equivalent' of *dāng* is increasingly prominent. As a result, in addition to expressing the confrontation between the two forces in strength, quantity the applicable scope of *xiāngdāng* is more extensive and the subject involved is more and more abundant. The semantic status of subject A and B is no longer balanced in comparative events. The focus of the conversation is mainly to highlight the quantity of a certain attribute of subject A, and subject B plays a more benchmark role. It is worth mentioning that although the lexical meaning of *xiāng* is gradually implicit and the meaning of *xiāngdāng* is gradually closeted, the *xiāngdāng* in the early lexicalization still retains a strong objective reality. Even if B as a reference does not appear mandatory in the surface of the sentence, it will not affect the communicators' perception of its existence. That is to say, the contest between the subject A and the subject B involved in the verb *xiāngdāng* is true in the speaker's subjective mental field, so the static result of *xiāngdāng* still more or less implies a certain time meaning. For example:

(18) 卒取小民, 不相当。

> *Zú qǔ xiǎo mín, bù xiāng dāng.*
> Finally marry common people NEG equivalent
> 'Immortal finally marry common people, which is not match.' (《风俗通义》).

During the Six Dynasties, the use cases of *xiāngdāng* expressing spatial relative relations surged and the narrative in the lexical semantics of *xiāngdāng* was also greatly weaken, as shown in Example (19). The semantic function of expressing spatial relative relations brings great convenience to the further abstraction of the meaning of *xiāngdāng*. The declarative results of *xiāngdāng* are no longer an explicit or implicit contest attached to the entities, but a description of the equilibrium distribution state in the abstract material space. Its time attributes are completely eliminated, which provides the possibility for its transformation from temporary attribute to constant attribute.

(19) 必须稀概均调, 行伍条直相当。

> *Bì xū xī jì jūn diào, háng wǔ tiáo zhí xiāng dāng.*
> Must sparse and dense balanced vertical and horizontal equal
> 'The density should be proper, the distance between horizontal and vertical should be equal.' (《齐民要术》)

In the Tang Dynasty, the attributive function of the adjective *xiāngdāng* appeared initially. Because the verbs and adjectives are located in the adjacent nodes of the word class continuum, and the verbs and adjectives are the description of the attribute characteristics of the specific subject, so in some *xiāngdāng (zhī/de) NP* structures, *xiāngdāng* still clearly retains the verb meaning of 'matching', such as example (4). However, since the verb usage of *xiāngdāng* is still the mainstream at this time, it is not common to occupy the attributive position of the typical syntactic function of adjectives, and there is almost no examples in the Song, Yuan and Ming Dynasties. Until the Qing Dynasty, the attributive function of *xiāngdāng* gradually matured and a large number of *xiāngdāng(de) NP* structures emerged in language facts. Driven by the usage of 'relative relation in spatial distribution', the communicators' attention to comparative events involved in the underlying logic of *xiāngdāng* is further reduced, while more attention is paid to the subsequent state of comparative results. In other words, the reference items and comparative focus involved in the process of comparison have become the background semantic information in the context, which is hidden in the mental field of the communicator. While the result of 'equivalent' is further abstract after subjective action, thus completing the transformation from the temporary attribute feature of subject A to the constant attribute feature. Corresponding to the structural relation, the comparison result and subject A change from subject-predicate relation to definite-center relation. At the same time, since the attention of subject B in the communicators' mind is more weakened, its acting form has gradually changed from the entity to the standard of conventional experience or subjective judgment in a certain social life.

In fact, the communicators' attention is not only reflected in comparison results' subsequent state, but also reflected in the specific content covered by the results. Since 'seeking greatness and goodness' is a common cognitive psychology of human beings, the benchmarks used for comparison in comparative events are often higher than social averages. When the focus of communicators shifts to the coverage of the comparison results, this kind of high quantitative meaning is naturally easy to be understood. In other word, whether the high quantity of some characteristic implication on the character side or the high quantity of degree implication on the degree side, it is actually the semantics derived from the focus shift to the specific content of the comparison results.

It can be seen from the above that each meaning of *xiāngdāng* is more or less related to the comparative events in the underlying logic. The comparison is bound to involve the established quantification. Therefore, the quantitative characteristics of *xiāngdāng* run through its entire semantic evolution. The high quantity of *xiāngdāng* is actually the mapping of the high quantity stage of its inherent quantitative characteristics. Its emergence is the inevitable result of the focus shift of communicators on comparative events in the underlying logic. The construction suppression of the *yǒu* sentence is the catalyst that triggers the derivation of the meaning and this semantic function is solidified through context expansion. The changes in communicators' focus at cognitive level can be illustrated as follows (Fig. 2):

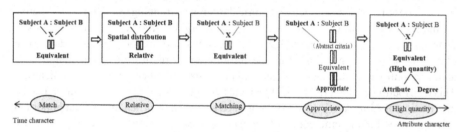

Fig. 2. Communicators' focus on comparative events of *xiāngdāng*.

3   The Emergence Process of Positive Meaning of *Xiāngdāng (de) NP*: Form Quantity Prominence to Attribute Prominence

According to Table 1, the usage of *xiāngdāng* to represent the positive meanings of 'very large/good/prominent/excellent' has not appeared in the history of ancient Chinese, but this usage has many examples in Mandarin Chinese. In CCL Mandarin Chinese Corpus, this paper respectively study 1000 examples of spoken language, historical biography, practical writing, newspapers and literature. The meaning of *xiāngdāng* in these examples is not fully covered in Table 1. This means that *xiāngdāng* has emerged new meanings in Mandarin Chinese, which are positive meanings. There are 635 examples of *xiāngdāng* that express positive meaning with the proportion of 13%, which is very close to the average probability value (14%) of the seven meanings of *xiāngdāng* in specific use. This is enough to show that positive meaning is not a temporary contextual meaning of *xiāngdāng* in a specific discourse. However, neither the constructional repression of the *yǒu* sentences nor the phased prominence of the quantitative feature of *xiāngdāng* can reasonably explain the emergence of the positive meaning of *xiāngdāng*. So what is the mechanism that triggers the further extension of *xiāngdāng*?

3.1 The Relationship Between Positive Meaning and High Quantity of Degree Meaning of *Xiāngdāng*

Based on the real language practice, the positive meaning of *xiāngdāng* actually emerges to a considerable extent under the influence of its high quantity meaning of degree. This assertion can be supported by three aspects:

First, from the perspective of the history of semantic evolution, high quantity meaning of the degree adverb *xiāngdāng* (hereinafter referred to as '*xiāngdāng*$_{high-quantity}$') appeared at the latest in the early Republic of China [8], while the positive meaning of *xiāngdāng* (hereinafter referred to as '*xiāngdāng*$_{positive}$') mainly used in mandarin Chinese. The temporal succession provides the possibility for the semantic reference of *xiāngdāng* to expand from the quantitative category to the attribute category.

Secondly, from the perspective of context distribution, because the lexical meaning of *xiāngdāng*$_{high-quantity}$ itself is an attribute concept that contains process characteristics, its syntactic combination inevitably also infects certain process characteristics, which implies cognitive processes such as empirical inference, thinking operation or subjective estimation. Specifically, the *xiāngdāng*$_{high-quantity}$ *of VP (de) NP* structure is mostly distributed in the object position that bears the focus information. When it wants to be placed in the subject position as an old information, it often needs to be bounded by adding quantity qualifiers or demonstrative pronouns and other compensation methods. This distribution characteristics of object and subject is exactly the same as the syntactic distribution of *xiāngdāng*$_{positive}$. As mentioned above, the *yǒu* sentences is an important driving factor for the emergence of *xiāngdāng*$_{positive}$. Therefore, under the influence of grammaticalization retention, the structural formula of *xiāngdāng*$_{positive}$ in mandarin Chinese is still often in the object position. The structure of the subject position is mostly used as the definite component of the expression subject, and the phrase '*xiāngdāng* (yí) bùfen (相当(一)部分)' is widely used. The similarity in distribution provides the preparation for *xiāngdāng* to achieve semantic extension across categories in similar contexts.

Thirdly, from the perspective of combinational form, '程度并不是由某个词来表现的'[11:3]. The high quantity contained in *xiāngdāng* as a standby language unit at the static lexical level is potential. Only when it co-occurrence with the concept of specific attributive conception at the dynamic syntactic level, can it jointly express a complete concept of degree. That is to say, a large number of this positive usage in the quantitative category is often reflected by the combining forms of *xiāngdāng*$_{high-quantity}$ *of VP*, and modifying NP is the usual usage of this form of degree combination. Thus, the expression of *xiāngdāng*$_{high-quantity}$ *VP (de) NP* naturally becomes a typical form of *xiāngdāng* in highlighting the specific characteristics on the side of NP's intrinsic degree. Similarly, when *xiāngdāng* highlights the specific characteristics of NP's other attributes, it also needs to use the attribute-center structure to express and form the expression form of *xiāngdāng*$_{positive}$ *VP (de) NP*. The identity of syntactic combination form brings convenience for *xiāngdāng* to integrate adjacent concept of property. Therefore, since the positive meaning and high quantity of degree meaning of *xiāngdāng* respectively belongs to trait category and degree category, which all belong to the attribute category. The similarity and relevance of connotation naturally provide the possibility for *xiāngdāng* to generate new meanings through the effect of metonymy mechanism. It can be said that high quantity of degree meaning is a category mapping of positive meaning.

3.2 The Solidification of Positive Meaning of *Xiāngdāng*

The semantic evolution history of *xiāngdāng* only reveals the semantic bedding for the emergence of its positive meaning. It does not mean that after the complete grammaticalization of *xiāngdāng*, it is led by the word *yǒu* to express the positive meaning usage in the category of quantity (Node B in Fig. 1) completely becomes the grammaticalization retention phenomenon. On the contrary, the typical syntactic function of the degree adverb *xiāngdāng* at the synchronic level further consolidates and extends the meaning. The main semantic contribution of the degree adverb *xiāngdāng* is realized by modifying the predicate components. Manifested in the combination relationship, its limitation on the degree of hierarchy can be roughly expressed as:

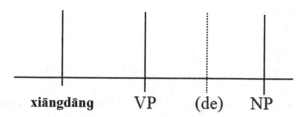

Fig. 3. Sequence of insertion combination of degree adverb *xiāngdāng*.

As shown in the figure, the specific meaning of NP is limited by the conceptual integration of *xiāngdāng* VP, which contains the [+hierarchy] feature. The close proximity in sentence position and semantic direct association of degree adverb *xiāngdāng* and VP create congenital advantages for the semantic integration of the two entities. Just like the series of electronic components in physics, there is a certain order between the horizontal combinations of the components in *xiāngdāng* VP (de) NP. The word *xiāngdāng* and VP are first combined into a semantic unit and then modify the limited central component NP. The different semantic relations between language units determine the hierarchy of the internal structure of the combining forms, which further consolidates the close relationship between *xiāngdāng* and VP, thus promoting the semantic integration between the two entities. At the same time, from the perspective of semantic evolution history, *xiāngdāng* could be used as an adjective and when its adjective usage is active in the *yǒu* sentences, it can also express the high quantity meaning in the quantitative category (Node B in Fig. 1). Therefore, under the dual constraints of the above syntactic order and semantic features, *xiāngdāng* gradually integrates the inherent quantitative characteristics of VP, and the meaning is generalized from high quantity meaning in the quantitative category to other attribute categories. The functional usage also changes under the influence of the attributive function of the structure *xiāngdāng VP*, showing an adjective tendency. This also partly confirms Cui Yingxian's view: *xiāngdāng* '在一定程度上获得了形容词的功能及意义'[12]. Because of this, there are a considerable number of cases of *xiāngdāng* and other adjective structures that correspond remotely at the synchronic level. For example:

(20)　上海的大部分寻呼台经营比较规范, 保持了<u>相当的规模和一定的服务水准</u>。

Shànghǎi de dàbùfēn xúnhūtái jīngyíng bǐjiào guīfàn, bǎochí le xiāngdāng de
Shanghai most paging center operate relatively standard maintain considerable
guīmó hé yídìng de fúwù shuǐzhǔn.
scale and a certain service level
'Most paging center in Shanghai are relatively standardized in operation, maintaining a considerable scale and a certain level of service.' (《文汇报》2002年12月13日)

(21)　我国的公共艺术教育已形成了<u>相当的规模和不小的影响</u>。

Wǒguó de gōnggòng yìshù jiàoyù yǐ xíngchéng le xiāngdāng de guīmó hé
China public art education already form considerable scale and
bùxiǎo de yǐngxiǎng.
NEG small impact
'China's public art education already has formed a considerable scale and great impact.' (《人民日报》2016年4月26日)

In fact, the emergence of *xiāngdāng*$_{positive}$ is also more or less affected by constructional repression, just as the causative factors of the generation of the high quantity meaning at the diachronic level. In the attribute combination forms composed of degree adverb *xiāngdāng*, the semantic limit of NP is [+quantity scalability]. The overall structure contains a significant high quantity meaning, which determines that when there is a component vacancy in the VP sequence in Fig. 3, the communicators can still complete the overall understanding of the meaning of the structure without consuming too much cognitive resources by the top-down permission of the independent coding structure itself. That is to say, in the conventional combination combination of *Degree Adverb VP (de) NP*, the intrinsic lexical semantics of *xiāngdāng* and NP play a diffusion activation function. The force transmission within the language structure makes the VP even default will not affect the communicator in the original semantic potential to choose a suitable meaning to understanding the semantic. In fact, this semantic fusion is not a special case and there is a similar phenomenon at the lexical level. For example, '*béng(甭)*', '*nāo(孬)*', '*ēn(奀)*', '*biáo(嫑)*', '*gū(兲)*' are integrated concepts formed by fusion of different word forms, which is a way of creating new words through semantic fusion. However, since Chinese is not a typical morphological language, this word-formation is rare. If the '*béng(甭)*' category is the formal representation of the fusion of different word meanings, then *xiāngdāng*$_{positive}$ should belong to the product of the fall of the word VP in the structure of *xiāngdāng VP*. Just as the production of homophones needs to rely on specific phonetic conditions, the fusion of different lexical meanings also needs to be dependent on certain semantic conditions. Specifically, subject to the high quantity feature of *xiāngdāng* on node C, the semantic fusion of *xiāngdāng* and VP is possible only when the component VP express the corresponding positive meaning. Therefore, although in the structure of *yǒu xiāngdāng xiǎo de bǐlì*(有相当小的比例), the component of *xiāngdāng* and *xiǎo* is also shown in Fig. 3, *xiāngdāng* is not compatible with the negative concept of *xiǎo*. This matching requirement in turn solidifies of *xiāngdāng*$_{positive}$. When this usage is mature, even if the default content of VP sequence cannot be supplemented, *xiāngdāng* can also form a linguistic unit together with the positive meaning of adjectives, freely modifying NP with [+quantity scalability]. For example:

(22) 由于保守党政府推行的私有化已经有了相当的规模和深度，工党在这次大选中也没有提出要把已经私有化的企业再全部收归国有。

Yóuyú bǎoshǒudǎng zhèngfǔ tuīxíng de sīyǒuhuà yǐjīng yǒu le xiāngdāng de
Because Conservative government implement privatization already have considerable
guīmó hé shēndù, gōngdǎng zài zhècì dàxuǎn zhōng yě méiyǒu tíchū yào bǎ yǐjīng
scale and depth the Labor Party in this election NEG propose already
sīyǒuhuà de qǐyè zài quánbù shōuguī guóyǒu.
privatized enterprise wholly reclaim national ownership
'Due to the privatization of the Conservative government already has a considerable scale and depth, the Labor Party in this election did not propose to have all the privatization of enterprises to national ownership.' (《人民日报》1987年6月25日)

(23) 上层建筑中的伦理道德价值观念，是一个民族区别于其他民族的特质，具有相当的稳定性。

Shàngcéngjiànzhù zhōng de lúnlǐ dàodé jiàzhí guānniàn, shì yígè mínzú qūbié yú
Superstructure ethical moral values is a nation different from
qítā mínzú de tèzhì, jùyǒu xiāngdāng de wěndìngxìng.
other nations characteristics have considerable stability
'Ethical and moral values in superstructure are the characteristics of a nation different from other nations and have considerable stability.' (《人民日报·海外版》2017年10月12日)

(24) 这类图书仍以相当的数量和品种，构成一种规模，在图书市场占据一席之地。

Zhèlèi túshū réng yǐ xiāngdāng de shùliàng hé pǐnzhǒng, gòuchéng yìzhǒng guīmó, zài
Such books still considerable number and varieties constitute one kind scale in
túshū shìchǎng zhànjù yìxízhīdì.
the book market occupy a place
Such books still constitute a scale with a considerable number and varieties, occupying a place in the book market. (《人民日报》1993年10月12日)

Of course, the further semantic extension of *xiāngdāng* at the synchronic level is still closely related to the attentive focus of communicators at the cognitive level. Since the high quantity usage of *xiāngdāng* in the degree category has become its prominent feature, when it is used to modify a specific NP, the structure itself naturally shows a certain high quantity meaning. This is true of real language practice. Whether *xiāngdāng* NP emphasizes 'big' in volume dimension or 'good' in quality dimension, it is self-evident that the whole structure contains high quantity. As high quantity has become the natural semantic potential of the structure, then of course communicators will no longer focus on the intrinsic quantitative characteristics when they use *xiāngdāng*, but pay more attention to the attribute dimension of the high quantity. Therefore, the semantic connotation of the *xiāngdāng* structure is transformed from quantitative prominence to attribute prominence again, and the meaning of *xiāngdāng* is extended to positive meaning, which is reasonable.

4 Conclusion

From the perspective of positive meaning of *xiāngdāng (de) VP* structure, the emergence process of the phrase *xiāngdāng$_{positive}$* is not single. From the perspective of genesis, the inherent quantitative characteristics accompanied by semantic evolution have created semantic bedding for the emergence of the *xiāngdāng$_{positive}$*. Under the construction suppression of *yǒu* sentences with high quantity meaning, the semantics of *xiāngdāng* show high-order prominence. The generation of the high quantity of degree meaning is the inevitable result of the communicator's focus shift on the comparative events in the underlying logic. From the perspective of pragmatics, the solidification of the *xiāngdāng$_{positive}$* implies a very complex strategic mental process. The adjacent sentence positions, semantic direct connection between *xiāngdāng* and the modified attribute components create a congenital advantage for the fusion of the two semantics. And the shift of communicators' focus creates future preparation. It can be seen that the semantic evolution of *xiāngdāng* has undergone a category rotation from attribute prominence ('appropriate') to quantity prominence ('high quantity of degree'), and then from quantity prominence ('High quantity of degree') to attribute prominence ('Relatively large/good/prominent/excellent').

References

1. Liu, Z.P.: These '*Xiāngdāng*' are adjectives or adverbs. Chinese Lang. Learn. **5**, 27–29 (1984). (In Chinese)
2. Si, P.: The meanings and word class's separation of '*Xiāngdāng*.' Chinese Lang. Learn. **6**, 23–24 (1985). (In Chinese)
3. Dai, J.T.: The identification of the word class of '*Xiāngdāng*.' J. Liaoning Educ. Inst. (Social Science Edition). **1**, 64–66 (1988). (In Chinese)
4. Cao, X.L.: The virtualization of '*Xiāngdāng*' and related issues. Stud. Chinese Lang. **4**, 317–321 (2008). (In Chinese)
5. Lei, D.P.: On the special path of formation of degree adverb '*Xiāngdāng*.' Chinese Lang. Learn. **3**, 66–73 (2018). (In Chinese)

6. Guo, C.: Adverb characteristics of 'Xiāngdāng.' Chinese Lang. Learn. **5**, 24–26 (1984). (In Chinese)
7. Sha, P.: Analysis on the Word Class of 'Xiāngdāng' –Discussion with Guo Chao and other comrades. J. Fujian Normal Univ. (Philosophy and Social Sciences Edition). **2**, 74–77 (1987). (In Chinese)
8. Hu, X.L.: Doubts on the virtualization of 'Xiāngdāng' and related issues. Stud. Lang. **4**, 371–373 (2013). (In Chinese)
9. Shan, B.S.: On 'Xiāngdāng.' Lang. Plann. **2**, 59–62 (2009). (In Chinese)
10. Li, J.L.: From Comparison to Degree: Analysis on the Grammaticalization of Adverbs of Degree 'Xiāngdāng' and 'Bǐjiào.' Beijing Language and Culture University, Beijing (2009). (In Chinese)
11. Wu, L.H.: A Study on the Combination of Degree Adverb in Mandar in Chinese. Jinan University, Guangzhou (2006). (In Chinese)
12. Cui, Y.X.: Part-of-speech tagging of 'Xiāngdāng', 'Yǒngyuǎn' and 'yě.' Lang. Plan. **9**, 26–29 (1997). (In Chinese)

Active and Passive Expressions of Tolerance: A Semantic Analysis of the Near-Synonyms *ren3* and *shou4* Based on MARVS Theory

Chunhong Huang[1], Panyu Qin[2], and Xiaowen Wang[1(✉)] ⓘ

[1] School of English Education, Guangdong University of Foreign Studies, Guangzhou, China
chunhong_huang@yeah.net, xiaowen-annie.wang@connect.polyu.hk
[2] School of Foreign Languages, Zhaoqing University, Zhaoqing, China

Abstract. This paper examines the representation of verbal semantics for a pair of near-synonyms expressing tolerance in Chinese: *ren3* and *shou4*. Following Churen Huang's MARVS theory, we explore the differences in the eventive information of the two words with results from the Chinese Gigaword corpus as evidence. Although they both belong to the state event type, our corpus analyses reveal their distinctive attributes in the event and role modules. First, they vary in the range of the subjects and objects, showing that *ren3* underlines active endurance and *shou4* predominately indicates passive suffering or acceptance. Second, *ren3* and *shou4* differ greatly in the connotation they carry: *ren3* can exhibit a positive spirit that highlights one's strong will to overcome obstacles, while *shou4* carries both negative and positive meanings. This study demonstrates that the combination of corpus-based methodology and the lexical semantics approach is highly useful in distinguishing subtle differences between near-synonym pairs.

Keywords: Near-synonyms · MARVS · Verbal semantics

1 Introduction

Linguistic behaviours of verbs expressing tolerance have caught scholarly attention in China and abroad [1–3], yet the differences between verbs of active and passive tolerance in Chinese have not been systematically investigated. In this study, we present a corpus-based study of Chinese verb synonyms: *ren3* 忍 'endure' and *shou4* 受 'suffer'. Generally, the two verbs can be viewed as indicating the behaviour of tolerating certain conditions. To comprehensively represent and distinguish the subtle semantic behaviours of the two verbs, this study adopts the MARVS theory – a new, creative approach to examine lexical semantics of near-synonyms [4]. We expect to capture the semantic properties on the basis of the event structure of verbs. The following research questions are explored in this paper:

(1) What are the event representations for *ren3* and *shou4* used in the corpus of Mainland Chinese usage?
(2) What are the similarities and differences in the event representations of *ren3* and *shou4*?

© The Author(s), under exclusive license to Springer Nature Switzerland AG 2023
Q. Su et al. (Eds.): CLSW 2022, LNAI 13495, pp. 42–51, 2023.
https://doi.org/10.1007/978-3-031-28953-8_4

2   Previous Studies on *ren3* and *shou4*

In The Contemporary Chinese Dictionary [5], *ren3* has two meanings: (1) endure; (2) bring oneself to (do sth.). Previous studies have provided insight into the lexical meaning of *ren3*, focusing on specific structures containing *ren3*, including *ren3wu2ke3ren2* 忍无可忍 'be driven beyond endurance' [6], *ren3jun4bu4jin1* 忍俊不禁 'simmer with laughter' [7] and *ren3(bu4)zhu4bu4* 忍(不)住不VP 'cannot help but VP'/*ren3zhu4bu4* 忍住不VP 'refrain from VP' [8]. However, relatively little attention has been paid to the subtle differences between *ren3* and its near-synonym.

As shown in The Contemporary Chinese Dictionary [5], there are four meanings for *shou4*: receive, suffer, endure and be pleasant. Prior studies on *shou4* mainly focused on its role as a passive marker. For instance, Lü [9] pointed out the syntactic similarity between *shou4* and *bei4*. Xiao et al. [2] compared *shou4* with other passive markers. The results revealed that *shou4* frequently occurs without an agent and is of negative semantic prosody. Li [10] probed into two syntactic frames, "S + *shou4* 受 'suffer' + N + V" and "S + *shou4* 受 'suffer' + V" and found that *shou4*, an atypical passive marker, can be used to introduce agents. In addition, Li [11] examined the differences between *bei4* 被 'be', *shou4* 受 'suffer', and *ai1* 挨 'endure'. Nonetheless, its semantic properties deserve further investigation.

Therefore, taking into account eventive information, the present study aims to provide a more systematic and detailed comparison of *shou4* and *ren3*.

3   MARVS Theory

MARVS theory has been proven effective in identifying syntactic and semantic differences of near-synonyms pairs [12–15]. It hinges on the assumption that eventive information is closely related to verb senses. The eventive information contains two aspects: (1) event types and their semantic attributes (event-internal attributes); (2) role modules and their semantic attributes (role-internal attributes) [15]. Notably, event types are characterized by five "atomic event structures" [15], including boundary, punctuality, process, state, and stage. They are shown as follow [15, p.26]:

(1)   · Boundary (includes a Complete Event)

Boundary is an event module that can be identified by means of a temporal point and must be regarded as a whole.

(2)   / Punctuality

Punctuality is an event module that represents a single occurrence of an activity that cannot be measured by duration.

(2)   ///// Process

Process is an event module that represents an activity that has a time course, i.e., that can be measured in terms of its temporal duration.

(4) _____ State

State is a homogeneous event module in which the concept of temporal duration is irrelevant; i.e., it is neither punctual nor does it have a time course.

(5) ^^^^^ Stage

Stage is an event module consisting of iterative subevents [15, p. 26].

Event-internal attributes refer to the properties of the event, such as [control], [realized] and [disposal] [16, p. 8]. Role-internal attributes are the properties of the role, including [sentience], [volition], [affectedness], [design] and so forth [15, p. 32].

Based on the MARVS theory, this study first discuss the event modules and event-internal attributes, then the role modules and role-internal attributes.

4 Methodology

This study takes a corpus-based method. The corpus used is the Chinese Gigaword 2 corpus: Mainland, simplified (Giga2) loaded in the Sketch Engine platform (https://www.sketchengine.eu/), which contains 250, 124, 230 tokens in simplified Chinese. It is a comprehensive archive of newswire data from the Xinhua News Agency, Beijing from 1991 and 2002. We will adopt the steps recommended by Huang et al. [15]: (1) characterizing grammatical relations between *ren3* and *shou4* based on their distributional differences; (2) examining and deducing event structure elements based on corpus results.

5 Results and Analysis

5.1 Overall Distribution

A great difference can be spotted in the frequency distribution of this near-synonym pair, with *shou4* (frequency = 60927 in Giga2) being overused than *ren3* (frequency = 1576 in Giga2).

5.2 Event Module: Structure and Attributes

When looking into the concordances of *ren3*, we found that *yi1zhi2* 一直 'constantly' can precede *ren3* in the Giga2, as shown in (1). Moreover, it can be followed by tense marker *le* 了, such as *ren3le yi1ye4* 忍了一夜 'endured all night'. A deeper look into the context, as shown in (2), revealed that *ren3le* 忍了 'endured' is a continuous state that initiates an afflicting state without knowing when it is going to end. Therefore, *ren3* can normally be viewed as an inchoative state event.

(1) 刘小强 一直 忍 着 常人 难以 忍受 的 剧烈 疼痛

Liu2Xiao3qiang2 yi1zhi2 ren3 zhe chang2ren2 nan2yi3ren3shuo4 de ju4lie4 teng2tong4.

Liu Xiaoqiang has been enduring severe pain that is unbearable for ordinary people.

(2) 可是 他们 都 咬咬牙 忍 了。

Ke3shi4, ta1men dou1 yao3yao3ya2 ren3le.

However, they all gritted their teeth and endured it.

Similarly, *shou4* can collocate with *yi1zhi2* 一直 'constantly' and/or *bu4duan4* 不断 'continuously'. Besides, we observed collocations like *shou4le shang1* 受了伤 'get injured', indicating a clear beginning point of the state of being injured. See examples below:

(3) 奥运会 后, 他 一直 受 伤痛 的 困扰。

Ao4yun4hui4 hou4, ta1 yi1zhi2 shou4 shang1tong4 de kun4rao3.

Since the Olympics, he has been plagued by injuries and pain.

(4) 你 老父亲 也 受了 伤, 快 回家 看看 吧。

Ni3 lao3 fu4qin1 ye3 shou4le Shang1, kuai4 hui2 jia1 kan4 kan4 ba.

Your father also got injured, go home quickly and have a look.

Therefore, *shou4* can also be represented as an inchoative state. For the event-internal attributes, however, there is a great difference between the two verbs. The subjects of *shou4* are all patients, having no control over the whole event. As opposed to *shou4*, the subjects of *ren3* are the agents, who initiate the state. Therefore, only *ren3* can be controlled. The event structure and event-internal attributes can be presented as follow:

ren3 · _____ [+control].

shou4 · _____ [-control].

5.3   Role Module: Roles and Attributes

To figure out the role module of *ren3* and *shou4*, the typical subjects and objects in context were carefully observed based on the sketch difference results in Sketch Engine (Fig. 1). The subjects preceding *ren3* are the agents, and the objects following it are often nouns serving as the goals. In contrast, the subjects preceding *shou4* normally play the role of a patient rather than an agent. For objects in their transitive usages, both verbs can take a noun as an object, such as *ren3lei4* 忍泪 'hold back the tear' and *shou4li4* 受力 'be under stress'; however, *shou4* is eventive and can take a verbal *shou4yao1* 受邀 'get invited' or adjective *shou4liang2* 受凉 'get cold' object. To be specific, most objects of *shou4* are abstract and negative (see (5)), such as *zai1* 灾 'disaster', *tai2feng1 ying3xiang3* 台风影响 'the influence of Typhoon', *sun3shi1* 损失 'loss', *shang1hai4* 伤害 'damage' and *kun4rao3* 困扰 'trouble'. Other objects such as *huan1ying2* 欢迎 'welcome', *xi3'ai4* 喜爱 'like' and *hao3ping2* 好评 'acclaim' have a positive meaning (see (6)). On the contrary, objects of *ren3* are more concrete and closely related to mental or physical negative aspects, such as *ju4tong4* 巨痛 'great pain', *shang1tong4*

伤痛 'injury', *teng2tong4* 疼痛 'ache', *zhe2mo2* 折磨 'torture', *wen2chong2ding1yao3* 蚊虫叮咬 'mosquito sting' and *ji1* 饥 'hunger'.

(5) 受 台风 影响, 汕头市 大 部分 地区 降 了 暴雨。

  Shou4 tai2feng1 ying3xiang3, shan4tou2shi4 da1 bu4fen4 di4qu1 jiang4 le bao4yu3.
  Typhoon has brought heavy rain to most parts in Shantou City..

(6) 电视剧《围城》也 颇 受 好评。

  Dian4shi4ju4 "wei2cheng2" ye3 po1 shou4 hao3ping2.
  The TV series "Besieged City" was also highly acclaimed .

WORD SKETCH DIFFERENCE   Chinese GigaWord 2 Corpus: Mainland. simplified

忍 1,576+ | 8.0 | 4.0 | 2.0 | 0 | -2.0 | -4.0 | -6.0 | 受 60,927+

SentObject_of   Subject_of   Modifies   Modifier   PP_

Object

目痛	16	0	10.6	— ...
钻心	10	0	10.1	— ...
沙砾	2	0	7.7	— ...
疼痛	5	0	7.5	— ...
膝关节	2	0	6.9	— ...
多久	3	0	6.6	— ...
胃	3	0	6.6	— ...
臀部	2	0	6.4	— ...
肝病	2	0	6.0	— ...
伤口	3	0	6.0	— ...
眼泪	4	0	5.9	— ...
手臂	2	0	5.7	— ...
腹部	2	0	5.5	— ...
内心	3	0	5.5	— ...
2 5 年	2	0	5.4	— ...
伤痛	39	5	10.4	2.5 ...
病痛	27	4	9.7	2.2 ...
蚊虫	4	3	7.7	1.8 ...
常人	7	5	7.5	2.5 ...
膜	9	9	6.6	3.2 ...
折磨	5	30	6.7	5.0 ...
威胁	0	156	—	6.5 ...
程度	0	158	—	6.5 ...
因素	0	179	—	6.6 ...
消费者	0	192	—	6.6 ...
教育	0	832	—	6.7 ...
损害	0	153	—	6.9 ...
困扰	0	140	—	7.0 ...
贿案	0	114	—	7.0 ...
损失	0	307	—	7.0 ...
空气	0	178	—	7.1 ...
国务院	0	400	—	7.2 ...
股市	0	274	—	7.2 ...
台风	0	155	—	7.2 ...
冲击	0	210	—	7.3 ...
青睐	0	231	—	7.8 ...

Subject

急用	187	0	12.5	— ...
疼痛	24	0	9.4	— ...
孰	11	0	9.0	— ...
李书深	4	0	7.7	— ...
李离令	3	0	7.2	— ...
病痛	5	0	6.9	— ...
尹敬芝	2	0	6.9	— ...
凤飞	2	0	6.8	— ...
伤痛	4	0	6.7	— ...
王立军	2	0	6.4	— ...
常人	4	0	6.4	— ...
吴文凯	3	0	6.4	— ...
赵震芳	2	0	6.2	— ...
徐洪刚	2	0	5.3	— ...
王义夫	2	0	5.0	— ...
床	2	0	3.7	— ...
军区队	2	0	3.5	— ...
高敏	7	11	7.2	5.4 ...
他	98	89	2.4	2.2 ...
她	24	24	2.8	2.7 ...
战士	2	10	1.4	3.4 ...
大家	2	11	1.1	3.3 ...
菜田	0	7	—	4.6 ...
臀部	0	6	—	4.7 ...
驾驶员	0	9	—	4.7 ...
罪	0	9	—	4.7 ...
书籍	0	12	—	4.9 ...
平民	0	15	—	4.9 ...
本人	0	15	—	4.9 ...
们经	0	7	—	4.9 ...
买气	0	7	—	4.9 ...
人身	0	12	—	5.0 ...
乘客	0	17	—	5.0 ...
人	0	597	—	5.2 ...
膝盖	0	10	—	5.3 ...
财产	0	43	—	5.5 ...

Fig. 1. A comparison of the objects and subjects between *ren3* and *shou4*.

As for subjects, the subjects of *ren3* predominantly include specific individuals like *xu2yong3fa3* 徐永法 'the name of a brave policeman' (see (7)) and singular third person pronouns like *ta1* 他 'he' and *ta1* 她 'she'. It is important to note that the pronouns 'he' (frequency = 98, LogDice = 2.4) and 'she' (frequency = 24, LogDice = 2.8) collocate far more closely with *ren3* than *ta1men* 他们 'they' (frequency = 12, LogDice = 0.6) and *wo3* 'I' (frequency = 8, LogDice = 1.0).

(7) 徐永法 忍 着 巨 痛 追赶 歹徒。

    Xu2yong3fa3 ren3 zhe ju4 tong4 zhui1gan3 dai3tu2.
    Xu Yongfa endured the pain to chase the gangster.

    In contrast, the patients of *shou4* are often people in a collective sense. The most commonly seen subjects of *shou4* are *er2tong2* 儿童 'children', *ping2min2* 平民 'the public', *shi4bing1* 士兵 'soldiers' and *chuan2yuan2* 船员 'boatmen' – groups vulnerable to damages or hurts. As for pronoun subjects, *shou4* collocates closely with not only 'he' (frequency = 89, LogDice = 2.2) and 'she' (frequency = 24, LogDice = 2.7) but also *ta1men* 他们 'they' (frequency = 88, LogDice = 3.4) and *wo3* 我 'I' (frequency = 87, LogDice = 4.3). A deeper look into the context reveals that most objects following *wo3* + *shou4* 我 + 受 have a positive meaning, such as *gu3wu3* 鼓舞 'encouragement', *qi3fa1* 启发 'inspiration', *jiao4yu4* 教育 'education' and *gan3dong4* 感动 'gratitude'. See examples below:

(8) 国家 可以 保证 他们 不 受 损失。

    Guo2jia1 ke3yi3 bao3zheng4 ta1men bu4 shou4 sun3shi1.
    The country can guarantee that they do not suffer from losses.

(9) 这 封 信 令 我 感到 很 受 鼓舞。

    Zhe4 feng1 xin4 ling4 wo3 gan3dao4 hen3 shou4 gu3wu3.
    I am very encouraged by this letter.

    Regarding role-internal attributes, there are sharp differences between *ren3* and *shou4*. For the modifiers (Fig. 2), *ren3* collocates saliently with *ying4shi4* 硬是 'tenaciously' (LogDice = 8.5) and *reng2ran2* 仍然 'still' (LogDice = 3.4), indicating that the agent is volitional. Besides, many of the consequences of endurance *ren3* in the corpus are promising. In other words, individuals allow themselves to be in an undesirable state for the time being only because they are looking forward to a better future. In this sense, *ren3* can be regarded as a positive state embodying one's active efforts and strong will to overcome difficulties, and the individual agents of *ren3* are often praised as heroes or role models to be appreciated (see (7), (10)).

(10) 她 硬是 忍着 自己 的 病痛 每天 陪床。

    Ta1 ying4shi4 ren3zhe zi4ji3 de bing4tong4 mei3tian1 pei2chuang2.
    She endures the pain and takes care of the patient every day.

    Shou4 often occurs with adverbs of degree *zui4* 最 'most', *hen3* 很 'very', *po1* 颇 'quite', and *shao3* 少 'less' when taking objects of feelings or emotion (see (6)). In addition, *shou4* often contributes to the construction of passive sentences. No matter collocating with positive (see (6)) or negative events (see (5)), *shou4* is linked to passive results of a certain extent, and patients of this event cannot be counted as volitional.

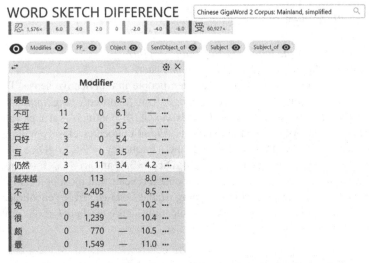

Fig. 2. A comparison of the modifiers between *ren3* and *shou4*.

In addition, *ren3* 忍 'endure' and *shou4* 受 'suffer' can be combined as a compound verb *ren3shou4* 忍受 'withstand', with eventive information bearing features from *ren3* 忍 'endure' and *shou4* 受 'suffer'. The subjects of *ren3shou4* 忍受 'withstand' include specific individuals like *ta1* 她 'she' (frequency = 17, LogDice = 2.3), *ta1* 他 'he' (frequency = 37, LogDice = 1.0), and *wo3* 我 'I' (frequency = 14, LogDice = 1.8) and people in a collective sense like *ren2* 人 'the public' (frequency = 72, LogDice = 2.2), *ta1men* 他们 'they' (frequency = 19, LogDice = 1.3), and *lao2gong1* 劳工 'workers' (frequency = 9, LogDice = 5.1). The objects following *ren3shou4* 忍受 'withstand' are concrete and closely related to negative physical and mental conditions, such as *e4chou4* 恶臭 'stink', *wen2chong2ding1yao3* 蚊虫叮咬 'mosquito sting', *bing4tong4* 病痛 'diseases', *gao1wen1* 高温 'heat', *ya1li4* 压力 'pressure', *kun4rao3* 困扰 'trouble', and *jian1ao2* 煎熬 'torment'. Modifiers of *ren3shou4* 忍受 'withstand' indicate people's passive sufferings in irresistible situations. Specifically, *ren3shou4* is often modified by *wu2fa3* 无法 'incapable', *bu4neng2* 不能 'unable', *nan2yi3* 难以 'hard', *bei4po4* 被迫 'be forced to' (see (11)), and *bu4de2bu4* 不得不 'have to', and the sense that the agent can not control this situation is emphasized (see (11)).

(11) 人们 最为 担忧 的 是 部分 发展 中 国家 经济 出现 负增长, 这些 国

家 的 人民 被迫 忍受 饥饿 和 贫困 。

Ren2men zui4wei2 dan1you1 de shi4 bu4fen4 fa1zhan3 zhong1 guo2jia1 jing1ji4 chu1xian4 fu4zeng1zhang3, zhe4xie1 guo2jia1 de ren2min2 bei4po4 ren3shou4 ji1e4 he2 pin2kun4.

The biggest worry is the negative economic growth in some developing countries, where people are forced to endure hunger and poverty.

However, we can also find cases where the agents suffer on their own will because of their sense of responsibility or hope for future development (see (12), (13)).

(12) 耳鼻喉科 张传仁 教授, 胃癌 到了 晚期, 仍 忍受着 病痛, 拖着 干

瘦 的 身躯, 坚持 每天 到 病房 查房、 治病......

er3bi2hou3ke1 zhang1chuan2ren2 jiao4shou4, wei4ai2 dao4le wan3qi2, reng2 ren3shou4zhe bing4tong4, tuo1zhe gan1shou4 de shen1qu1, jian1chi2 mei3tian1 dao4 bing4fang2 cha2fang2, zhi4bing4......

Despite the overwhelming pain caused by advanced gastric cancer, Zhang Chuanren, Professor of the Department of Otolaryngology, insists on visiting the patients on a daily basis to provide treatment with his skinny body.

(13) 为了 获得 这些 大 公司 的 信任, 有时 不得不 做 亏本 生意, 但 为

了 更 好 地 发展, 只 能 默默 忍受。

wei4le huo4de2 zhe4xie1 da4 gong1si1 de xin4ren4, you3shi2 bu4de2bu4 zuo4 kui1ben3 sheng1yi4, dan4 wei4le geng4hao3 de fa1zhan3, zhi3neng2 mo4mo4 ren3shou4.

To gain the trust of these big companies, sometimes you have to do business at a loss and suffer in silence for better development.

6 Discussion

Following the MARVS theory in Sect. 5, *ren3* and *shou4* can be represented based on corpus results as below:

ren3 ·_____ [+control] [active] <agent, goal>
                                  | |
                         [+volition] [negative]
shou4 ·_____ [-control] [passive] <patient, (agent,) event>[eventive]
                                  | |
                         [-volition]   [negative/positive]

The major similarity between the two verbs is that both can initiate state events of tolerating certain conditions. The main differences lie in voice and polarity: *ren3* typically describes an active mental or physical state and it can be regarded as a positive event to overcome obstacles; however, *shou4* tends to be attached to a passive event involving negative or positive results, mostly negative, which echoes the statistical results presented by Xiao et al. [2]. The agents of *ren3* are usually individuals while the patients of *shou4* are more of vulnerable groups. Since *ren3* is active, its agent is supposed to take volitional action over the goal. In contrast, *shou4* requires no volition from the patient.

In addition, the compound verb *ren3shou4* 忍受 'withstand' predominantly indicates negative sufferings, but it sometimes embodies people's volition. Therefore, it is a special case that mitigates the disparate eventive information of *ren3* and *shou4*. This interesting phenomenon deserves more careful analyses in future studies.

In conclusion, the syntactic differences between near-synonym verbs signal the existence of subtle semantic differences. This work demonstrates that our usage of *ren3* and *shou4* is essentially based on our underlying perception of events and their attributes. Pedagogically, with comprehensive analyses based on corpus results, this study can help Chinese learners to better differentiate this near-synonym set. In addition, the study may improve our understanding of the relations between verbal semantics and associated syntactic patterns.

Acknowledgments. Panyu Qin and Chunhong Huang contributed equally to this paper.

References

1. Park, T.-S.: A Corpus-based analysis of bear, stand, endure, and tolerate. Stud. Linguist. **2**, 61–74 (2011). https://doi.org/10.17002/sil..20.201108.73
2. Xiao, R., McEnery, T., Qian, Y.: Passive constructions in English and Chinese: a corpus-based contrastive study. Lang. contrast. **6**, 109–149 (2006)
3. Chang, L., et al.: Alternation across semantic fields: a study on mandarin verbs of emotion. Comput. Linguist. Chinese Lang. Process. **5**, 61–80 (2000)
4. Huang, C.-R., Ahrens, K.: The module-attribute representation of verbal semantic. In: Proceedings of the 14th Pacific Asia Conference on Language, Information and Computation (PACLIC 14), pp. 109–120 (2000)
5. Dictionary Compiling Office of the Institute of Language Studies of the Chinese Academy of Social Sciences: The Contemporary Chinese Dictionary. Foreign Language Teaching and Research Press, Beijing (2002)
6. Gao, L.: A probe into the source of "Ren Wu Ke Ren." J. Zhejiang Int. Stud. Univ. **3**, 6–8 (2012). (in Chinese)
7. Lei, H., Li, J.: Analysis on "Ren Jun Bu Jin." Res. Anc. Chinese Lang. **3**, 91–102 (2019). (in Chinese)
8. Dai, Y.: Analysis on "Ren Bu Zhu Bu VP" and "Ren Zhu Bu VP." Overseas Dig. **6**, 1–3 (2021). (in Chinese)
9. Lü, S.: Collection of the Works by Lü Shuxiang (First volume). The Commercial Press, Beijing (2010). (in Chinese)
10. Li, S.: Study on Shou. Res. Anc. Chinese Lang. **1**, 88–96 (2014). (in Chinese)
11. Li, M.: Differences in the Words "Bei" "Shou" "Ai." J. Tianjin Adult High. Learn. **3**, 44–46 (2001)
12. Tsai, M.-C., Huang, C.-R., Chen, K.-J., Ahrens, K.: Towards a representation of verbal semantics-an approach based on near-synonyms. Comput. Linguist. Chinese Lang. Process. **3**, 61–74 (1998)
13. Wang, X., Huang, C.R.: From contact prevention to social distancing: the co-evolution of bilingual neologisms and public health campaigns in two cities in the time of COVID-19. SAGE Open **11**, 1–17 (2021). https://doi.org/10.1177/21582440211031556

14. Wang, X., Huang, C.-R.: From near synonyms to power relation variations in communication: a cross-strait comparison of "Guli" and "Mianli." In: Hong, J.-F., Su, Q., Wu, J.-S. (eds.) CLSW 2018. LNCS (LNAI), vol. 11173, pp. 155–166. Springer, Cham (2018). https://doi.org/10.1007/978-3-030-04015-4_13

15. Huang, C.-R., Ahrens, K., Chang, L.-L., Chen, K.-J., Liu, M.-C., Tsai, M.-C.: The module-attribute representation of verbal semantics: from semantic to argument structure. Int. J. Comput. Linguist. Chinese Lang. Process. **5**, 19–46 (2000)

16. Chang, L., Chen, K., Huang, C.: A lexical-semantic analysis of Mandarin Chinese Verbs : representation and methodology. Comput. Linguist. **5**, 1–18 (2000). (in Chinese)

A Study of Nominal Verbs in Modern Chinese Based on Shannon-Wiener Index——Case Studies on *"Bianhua"* Words

Siyu Chen, Lijiao Yang[(✉)], and Jiaomei Zhou

Institute of Chinese Information Processing, Beijing Normal University, Beijing, China
{chensiyu313,zhoujiaomei}@mail.bnu.edu.cn, yanglijiao@bnu.edu.cn

Abstract. Part of speech (POS) has always been a significant problem in Chinese grammar research, and the research on nominal verbs is especially hot and complicated. It not only relates to the establishment of dictionary sense, but also involves the specification of POS tagging in language knowledge engineering, which is of great significance. Based on the concept of "entropy" in information theory, this paper applies Shannon-Weiner index, a measurement tool of information diversity, to linguistic research, which is called "word pluripotency index". At the same time, based on the BCC corpus of Beijing Language and Culture University, this paper studies the lexical pluripotency of five words under the "变化(*Bianhua*, change)" sense category. The experimental results demonstrate that the word pluripotency indexes of these words are all bigger than 0.6, and reveal the uniformity of word distribution under different word classes and the degree of verb-to-noun shifting. This paper also explores the significance of the word pluripotency index to the establishment of dictionary sense and the tagging of word class.

Keywords: Nominal verb · Shannon-Wiener index · Word class · Part of speech · Dictionary sense · POS tagging

1 Introduction

The ambiguity of the word class boundary makes an obvious continuum between word classes. There is a class of verbs in modern Chinese that have the grammatical properties of nouns, and it is difficult to determine whether they are nouns or verbs in some specific context, such as "学习(*Xuexi*, study) ", "研究(*Yanjiu*, research) " and other words.

In response to this problem, Zhu [1] put forward the concept of "nominal verb", pointing out that nominal verbs refer to words that have lost the grammatical characteristics of verbs in certain context, and behave the same as nouns in some key oppositions. For the issue of Chinese nominal verbs, there are constant disputes in theory, and it is difficult to reach a unified conclusion in practice. The establishment of semantic items in dictionaries and the POS tag set in language knowledge engineering of nominal verbs have always been controversial, and it is hard to reach a consensus. Therefore, as a special linguistic phenomenon in modern Chinese, nominal verbs urgently need new research perspectives and research methods.

© The Author(s), under exclusive license to Springer Nature Switzerland AG 2023
Q. Su et al. (Eds.): CLSW 2022, LNAI 13495, pp. 52–64, 2023.
https://doi.org/10.1007/978-3-031-28953-8_5

The Shannon-Wiener index [2,3] is used to describe the disorder of system in information theory and is widely used to measure the species diversity and richness of ecosystems in biology. At present, many studies have applied this theory to other disciplines. This paper attempts to apply the Shannon-Wiener index, a measurement tool of information diversity, to the problem of nominal verbs in linguistic research, which is called "word pluripotency index". Through quantitative indicators, the actual distribution of nominal verbs as verbs and nouns in large-scale corpus is investigated, so as to measure the uniformity of word distribution in different word classes and the degree of verb-to-noun shifting.

The word pluripotency index relies on the actual usage of the language in large corpus, not just the usage in dictionaries. Compared with dictionaries that reflect static and limited linguistic knowledge, the knowledge in corpus is dynamic and diverse, and can provide frequency information, co-occurrence information and distribution information for linguistic research. The calculation of the word pluripotency index based on corpus can not only play an important reference role in the establishment of dictionary sense, but also provide scientific and objective data support for the rationality, scientificity and interpretability of POS tag specifications for nominal verbs, which is of great significance.

Our research is based on the BCC corpus of Beijing Language and Culture University. BCC corpus covers newspapers, literature, microblogs, science and technology, ancient Chinese and other fields of corpora, with a total scale of about 15 billion words [4]. It is currently the largest and most powerful Chinese corpus at home and abroad. Therefore, based on the BCC corpus, this paper applies the Shannon-Wiener index, a measurement tool for information diversity, to study the problem of nominal verbs in modern Chinese with a new research perspective, and to investigate its significance for the establishment of dictionary meaning items and the specification of POS tagging.

2 Related Work

As the boundaries of Chinese word classes are ambiguous, the problem of word classes has always been a complicated issue in the research of Chinese grammar. Moreover, the relationship between Chinese nouns and verbs is especially a hot and major problem.

Most scholars believe that Chinese nouns and verbs are in a "discrete mode" with a small overlap in between. Taking the overlapping words into consideration, Zhu [1] put forward the concept of "nominal verb", acknowledging that some verbs have the grammatical properties of nouns, and pointed out that the difference between these words and general verbs was the similarity with nouns. After that, Zhu [5] put forward the theory of Chinese nominal verb, which considered that some predicate components have semantic function changes in the position of subject and object, and characterized them as the referentialization of verbs, which are functionally close to nouns. Subsequently, Zhu [6] further explored this complicated issue of nominal verbs, pointing out that nominal verbs have the dual nature of verbs and nouns at the same time. When these words are in the object position of a defunct verb (that is, a formal verb), they reflect their nominal aspect. Lu [7] agreed with the statement of nominal verbs in Chinese, and believed that such words had a certain scale in modern Chinese and needed to be studied and dealt with separately. In response to this problem, Hu [8] pointed out that some verbs were transferred to nouns, and put forward the theory of "noun-to-verb drifting" in view of this phenomenon, and believed that many Chinese verbs were in the process of drifting to nouns. After that, Yu [9] investigated the dynamic process of some disyllabic verbs drifting to nouns in Chinese through quantitative analysis based on the theory of "noun-to-verb drifting", and respectively distinguished three different degrees. Moreover, Wang [10] explored the inter-conversion of verbs and nouns in modern Chinese from the perspective of cognitive linguistics, and found that it had asymmetry, in which the frequency of occurrence of verb-to-noun shifting was much higher than that of noun-to-verb shifting.

Different from the above studies claiming that Chinese nouns and verbs are in the "discrete mode", Shen [11] proposed the noun-verb inclusion theory of "Mutual Inclusion of Chinese Verb and Noun", arguing that Chinese verbs and nouns are not discrete categories, and Chinese verbs are a subtype of noun category. Figure 1 shows the two different modes of Chinese word classes. In fact, the noun-verb inclusion theory is a theoretical attempt to find the characteristics of Chinese language made by grammar research eager to get rid of the Indo-European perspective. However, due to the lack of operability in specific practice, it is still in the stage of theoretical theory.

Fig. 1. The discrete mode (left) and the inclusive mode (right) of Chinese verb and noun

Regarding the problem of Chinese word classes, there are endless debates in theory, and it is even more difficult to come up with a unified solution in practice.

Since the 1990s, the construction of Chinese corpus has been carried out vigorously, and a series of remarkable achievements have been made today. However, due to the difference of corpus POS tag specification, language application research and language information processing both face challenges. Language information processing needs to divide the words into different classes, and classify each word according to a certain specification. Therefore, the tagging set of nominal verbs in Chinese language information processing and corpus construction has also become a tough problem in related researches. CCL corpus of Peking University constructively incorporates gerunds and generics into the POS tagging specification, and uses combined tagging codes to mark nominal verbs, which are regarded as the marking of the special usage of verbs [12]. The problem of the concurrence of verbs in special grammatical positions, that is, they have the properties of nouns and verbs at the same time. In view of the special function and frequent use of nominal verbs, Beijing Normal University revised the "Standard of POS Tag of Contemporary Chinese for CIP" [13–14], which also put forward the principle of combined application of POS markers to process the POS tagging problem of nominal verbs, indicating the word class to which the current and the original grammatical position of the word belongs, which greatly improves the accuracy and consistency of POS tagging, serving for language information processing and language application research. However, there is still ambiguity and uncertainty in how to choose between single POS tags and combined POS tags for a certain verb, lacking of scientific and objective quantitative indicators.

The Shannon-Wiener index is a commonly used index to measure diversity and has been widely used in biology and other fields. Wang et al. [15] applied Shannon-Wiener index to the education field. Based on this index, they explored the academic relationship structure of college teachers and provided an effective measurement tool for higher education development research. Yin et al. [16] used Shannon-Wiener index to analyze the community structure of benthic animals, and analyzed the characteristics of benthic animal communities and water environment factors to characterize the species diversity and richness of the ecosystem. Furthermore, Hieber [17–19] applied Shannon-Wiener index to examine the lexical polyfunctionality of English Words. Lexical polyfunctionality refers to the fact that a lexical item has more than one discursive or syntactic function, such as predication, reference, or modification, as opposed to verb, noun and adjective. Yang et al. [20] took the central urban area of Chengdu as the research area, using Shannon-Wiener index to measure the richness and evenness of training institutions, and made use of the method of systematic clustering to analyze the spatial form of training institutions of Chengdu. However, there is still a lack of relevant researches on applying Shannon-Wiener index to characterize the diversity of word classes in modern Chinese, which is the focus of our research.

It can be seen that the current academic research on the issue of Chinese nominal verbs mostly stays at the level of theoretical analysis, lacking scientific and reliable data indicators. Shannon-Wiener index applies the concept of "entropy" in information theory, which can be used to measure the degree of disorder and uncertainty of information, and can also be used to describe the uncertainty of individuals. When the amount of information is greater, the uncertainty is larger, and the diversity is higher as well. Therefore, this paper applies the Shannon-Wiener index to the diversity of word classes in modern Chinese, and proposes the word pluripotency index as a basis for measuring the pluripotency of nominal verbs. The distribution of the lexical category of "变化(Bianhua, change)" words in a large-scale corpus is taken as an example to carry out research, in order to provide scientific and objective data support for the establishment of dictionary sense and the setting strategy of POS tag. In addition, this research contributes to the study of modern Chinese word classes.

3   Words Under the "变化(*Bianhua*, Change)" Sense Category

Wang and Huang [21] pointed out that the POS tagging of five words ("*Bianhua*变化", "*Liangbian*量变", "*Zhibian*质变", "*Jianbian*渐变", "*Tubian*突变") under the "变化(*Bianhua*, change)" sense category in the Modern Chinese Dictionary (6th edition) did not grasp the principle of symmetry. This problem still exists in the Modern Chinese Dictionary (7th edition). The Modern Chinese Dictionary (7th Edition) sets up two meanings for the word "*Bianhua*(变化)", which is considered to have the dual nature of a verb and a noun. However, "*Zhibian*质变" and "*Liangbian*量变" are treated as verbs, corresponding to the verb meaning of "*Bianhua*变化", and the noun meaning of these two words is not marked. In the Modern Chinese Standard Dictionary (3rd Edition), the five words under the "变化(*Bianhua*, change)" sense category are only marked with verb meaning items, but no noun meaning items. Therefore, the tagging strategy of the Modern Chinese Standard Dictionary is not consistent with the Modern Chinese Dictionary. The specific definitions of five words in the two dictionaries are shown in Table 1.

By comparison, it can be seen that there are differences in the meanings of those "变化(*Bianhua*, change)" words in Modern Chinese Dictionary and Modern Chinese Standard Dictionary. In addition, we find that the tagging strategy of these words in the modern Chinese corpus of the State Language Commission is basically the same as that of the Modern Chinese Dictionary. It can be clearly seen that there are differences in the establishment of dictionary meanings and POS tagging strategies for the five words under the "变化(*Bianhua*, change)" sense category in current language knowledge engineering, and it is difficult to reach a unity.

In response to this problem, this paper will examine the distribution of the five words (including "*Bianhua*变化", "*Liangbian*量变", "*Zhibian*质变", "*Jianbian*渐变", "*Tubian*突变") in large scale real corpus based on the facts of Chinese language, and utilize the information diversity measurement tool Shannon-Wiener index (i.e., word pluripotency index in this paper) to calculate the POS pluripotency of these five words in actual context, which provides a scientific and objective method for the establishment of dictionary sense and POS tagging strategies from a new research perspective.

Table 1. Comparison of definition of the five "变化(*Bianhua*, change)" words in two dictionaries

Words	The Modern Chinese Dictionary (7th Edition)	The Modern Chinese Standard Dictionary (3rd Edition)
Bianhua (变化)	[v] Things produce a new situation in form or essence: The situation ~ quickly [n] A new situation in form or essence: In recent years, the ~ in my hometown is very large	[v] *Bian*(变)①[1]: 'impermanently; thought ~
Zhibian (质变)	[n] A change in the fundamental nature of things	[v] Philosophically refers to the fundamental change in the nature of things, and things leap from an old state to a new state. (distinct from "*Liangbian*量变")

(continued)

---

[1] *Bian*(变)① refers to the same dictionary sense as *Bian*(变).

Table 1. (*continued*)

Words	The Modern Chinese Dictionary (7th Edition)	The Modern Chinese Standard Dictionary (3rd Edition)
Liangbian (量变)	[n] A change in the quantity or degree of things	[v] Philosophically refers to the gradual and insignificant change of things, including increase or decrease in quantity, place replacement, composition changes in the arrangement of ingredients, etc. (distinct from "*Zhibian*质变")
Tubian (突变)	[v]Suddenly and drastically change: the current situation ~ [v] Qualitatively change	[v] Suddenly change (distinct from "*Jianbian*渐变"): situation ~
Jianbian (渐变)	[v] Gradually change	[v] Slowly change (distinct from "*Tubian*突变"): the process of language ~

4 Word Pluripotency Index

From the concept of nominal verbs, it can be seen that its essence reflects the degree of diversity of classes to which words belong, and its quantitative indicators can be inspired by relevant theoretical concepts of information theory. Information theory uses the concept of "entropy" to describe the degree of internal chaos of the system. When the "entropy" of the system is larger, it indicates that the degree of internal chaos is higher, and the homogeneity of the elements in the system is lower. Then, the degree of diversity of the system is higher. The theoretical concept of "entropy" is known in practice as Shannon-Wiener index.

Shannon-Wiener index is also known as Shannon species diversity, Shannon entropy or Shannon information. It is widely used as a tool of information diversity to measure the species diversity and richness of ecosystems in biology. This paper attempts to apply the Shannon-Wiener index to the study of Chinese nominal verbs in linguistics. For Shannon-Wiener index, its initial definition is:

Suppose a system is divided into I categories($A_1, A_2, A_3 \ldots \ldots A_I$), and each individual in the system belongs to one and only one of the categories. At this time, the probability that an individual is randomly selected to belong to the A_i category is P_i ($\sum P_i = 1$). Then, the function H' of P_i is the metric function of system diversity:

$$H' = -C \sum_{i=1}^{I} (p_i * \ln p_i) \tag{1}$$

where C is a constant, and the value of C is generally set to 1.

Based on the above theoretical basis, this paper uses Shannon-Wiener index to research the diversity of modern Chinese word classes, which is called "word pluripotency index" in this paper. The description is as follows:

The frequency of words marked as a certain word class i in the corpus is:

$$p_i = \frac{n_i}{N} \qquad (2)$$

where N is the total number of selected corpora, and n_i is the number of word instances marked as a certain word class i in selected corpora.

Referring to the measurement function of system diversity, the Shannon-Wiener index of words in the corpus is:

$$H' = -\sum_{i=1}^{I} (p_i * \ln p_i) \qquad (3)$$

where I is the number of word classes that the word is marked in the corpus.

In order to avoid different words being marked with different word classes in the corpus, we need to standardize formula (3). According to the judging conditions of Shannon-Wiener index, the maximum value H'_{max} of the Shannon-Wiener index under the ideal condition is:

$$H'_{max} = -\sum \frac{1}{I} * \ln \frac{1}{I} = -(\ln 1 - \ln I) = \ln I \qquad (4)$$

Dividing formula (3) by (4) yields the word pluripotency index required for this paper:

$$H = \frac{H'}{H'_{max}} \qquad (5)$$

The word pluripotency index (H) obtained after normalization is a value between 0 and 1.

This paper applies the Shannon-Wiener index to the problem of Chinese POS diversity and obtains a new quantitative index, the word pluripotency index. The word pluripotency index includes two key factors: one is the number of word categories, and the other is the uniformity or balance of word distribution under different word categories. For a word, the more evenly distributed the word under each category, the higher the word pluripotency index of the word, the closer it is to 1. At this time, it means that the more flexible the use of this word, the more balanced it is to serve as different grammatical functions in different context. On the contrary, if the difference in the distribution of the word under each category is greater, then the word pluripotency index of this word will be lower and closer to 0. At this time, it means that the word is less flexible in the actual use of language, and mainly reflects a single grammatical function in the context.

Therefore, based on the BCC corpus, this paper will calculate the word pluripotency index of five words under the "变化(Bianhua, change)" sense category (including "Bianhua变化", "Liangbian量变", "Zhibian质变", "Jianbian渐变", "Tubian突变") based on the above formula, and conduct researches on the pluripotency of these words.

5   Experimental Results and Analysis

BCC Corpus of Beijing Language and Culture University covers newspapers, literature, microblogs, science and technology, ancient Chinese and other fields of corpus, with a total scale of about 15 billion words. It is currently the largest and most powerful Chinese corpus at home and abroad. It reflects the language usage of today's society in an all-round way, and provides a powerful boost to the fields of applied linguistics research and language information processing in the era of big data [22–25]. Nowadays, the BCC corpus is still being dynamically updated, which can more comprehensively reflect the actual language phenomena in today's social life.

By comparing the corpus size of research object in BCC corpus and other corpus (such as CCL corpus, Taiwan Academia Sinica Balanced Corpus, etc.), this paper selects the large-scale and multi-domain BCC corpus and randomly selects 500 corpora for each word (including *"Bianhua*变化*"*, *"Liangbian*量变*"*, *"Zhibian*质变*"*, *"Jianbian*渐变*"*, *"Tubian*突变*"*). Their word pluripotency index (*H*) was calculated respectively. The specific results are summarized in Table 2.

Table 2. POS frequency and word pluripotency index of "变化(*Bianhua*, change)" words in BCC corpus

Words	Times marked as verb(Frequency)	Times marked as noun(Frequency)	Total number	*H*
Bianhua (变化)	88 (17.6%)	412 (82.4%)	500	0.67
Liangbian (量变)	74 (14.8%)	426 (85.2%)	500	0.61
Zhibian (质变)	80 (16%)	420 (84%)	500	0.63
Jianbian (渐变)	180 (36%)	320 (64%)	500	0.94
Tubian (突变)	150 (30%)	350 (70%)	500	0.88

Figures 2 and 3 intuitively show the distribution of the occurrences of "变化(*Bianhua*, change)" words in different word classes and the word pluripotency index (*H*) of each word. As an index to measure the flexibility of words, the word pluripotency index can reflect the uniformity and balance of the distribution of words in different categories, and provide an objective data support to measure the nominalization degree of words.

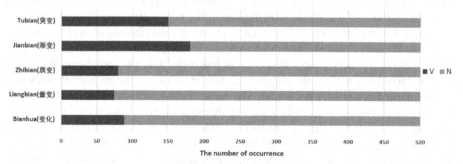

Fig. 2. The distribution of "变化(*Bianhua*, change)" words in different word classes

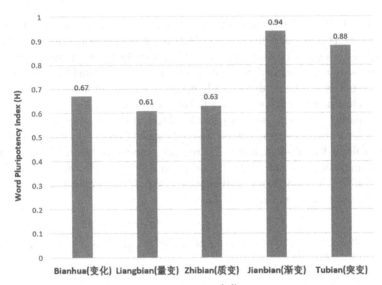

Fig. 3. The word pluripotency index of "变化(*Bianhua*, change) " words

Analyzing the experimental results above, it is found that the word pluripotency index of five words (including "*Bianhua*变化", "*Liangbian*量变", "*Zhibian*质变", "*Jianbian*渐变", "*Tubian*突变") have all reached 0.6, and the average pluripotency index of these five words is 0.746. Among them, the word "*Jianbian*(渐变)" is marked 320 times as a verb and 180 times as a noun, and the word pluripotency index of it is 0.94, indicating that "*Jianbian* (渐变)" has the strongest versatility among the five words. What's more, the word "*Liangbian* (量变)" is marked 74 times as a verb and 426 times as a noun, the word pluripotency index of it is 0.61, indicating that "*Liangbian* (量变)" in versatility among the five words is relatively weak. Based on the results, it can be seen that the five words are more flexible in the actual use of language and have a certain degree of versatility. The distribution of these five words under the noun and verb category reflects a certain degree of balance. As a verb with noun properties, the smaller the *H* value of the word, the smaller its lexical polyfunctionality, and the greater the *H* value of the word, the greater its lexical polyfunctionality. Generally speaking, the higher the word pluripotency index of a nominal verb, the deeper the nominalization of the word.

Figure 4 shows the word pluripotency index (*H*) distribution of five words (in which, the *H* value distribution of three words "*Bianhua*(变化)", "*Zhibian* (质变)" and "*Liangbian* (量变)" is partially enlarged). The horizontal axis is the number of times the word is marked as a noun in the corpus, and the vertical axis is the number of times the word is marked as a verb in the corpus. The curve *H*=1 is the maximum value curve of the word pluripotency index, indicating that the probability of a word being used as a noun and a verb in actual context is equivalent. When the word is above the curve *H*=1, it indicates that the probability of the word being used as a verb in actual context is greater than that of being a noun, and the degree of nominalization is low. When the word is below the curve *H*=1, it indicates that the probability of the word being used as a noun in actual context is greater than that of being a verb, and the degree of nominalization is higher. Also, the figure shows that the farther from the curve $H=1$, the higher the degree of nominalization of the word.

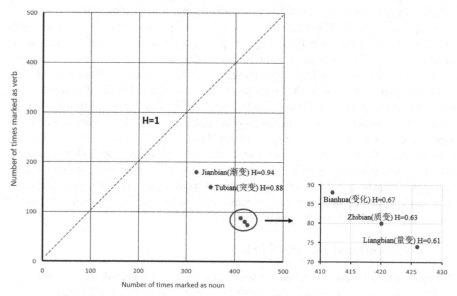

Fig. 4. The distribution of H value of the five words

Specifically, the five words "*Bianhua*(变化)", "*Liangbian* (量变)", "*Zhibian* (质变)", "*Jianbian* (渐变)" and "*Tubian* (突变)" are all located below the curve $H = 1$, and the probability of these words being marked as nouns is much greater than that of being marked as verbs, indicating that these words have a deeper degree of drift to nouns and a higher degree of nominalization. Therefore, by comparing the relative positions of words to the curve $H=1$, it helps to clearly and intuitively judge the degree of the nominalization of the word.

6 Discussion

Through the research in this paper, it can be seen that the word pluripotency index can better reflect the uniformity of the distribution of words in different word classes and the degree of drift to nouns. The problem of Chinese word classes is complex and complicated, and the phenomenon of multiple classes of words greatly increases the difficulty of establishing dictionary sense and the inconsistency of POS tagging. For language information processing, it is difficult to scientifically and reasonably deal with multiple types of words in real corpus by using a single POS tag set. In this situation, the combined application mode of POS tags is an effective strategy.

The "Standard of POS Tag of Contemporary Chinese for CIP " revised by Beijing Normal University stipulates the combined code n_v of nominal verbs in context [13, 14], which covers the word category at the current and the original grammatical position, such as marking "*Xuexi*学习" in "*Chuantong*传统/f *Wenhua*文化/n *De*的/u *Xuexi*学习/n_v *Tebie*特别/d *Zhongyao*重要/a " as n_v, putting forward the modern Chinese nominal verbs in a practical and self-consistent way. The tagging strategy greatly improves the scientificity, rationality and operability of POS tagging. Based on the principle of combined application of POS markers, the proposed word pluripotency index can be used as a reference indicator for POS tagging. By quantifying the degree of polyfunctionality of words, we can flexibly choose a reasonable tagging set.

Based on the calculated word pluripotency index, this paper believes that: on one hand, nominal verbs with high pluripotency indicate a high degree of uniformity in the distribution of the word among different word classes, it is possible to consider establishing both noun and verb meaning items in the dictionary and adopting a combined application pattern of POS tagging codes for them in the POS tagging specification, which reflects the fact that they have the properties of both verbs and nouns in actual use of language. On the other hand, the less pluripotent nominal verbs indicate a less uniform distribution of the word across different word classes, the dictionary meaning items and the choice of POS tagging codes can be set up flexibly according to actual needs, thus serving specific language studies.

7 Conclusion and Future Work

The problem of Chinese word classes is very complex and complicated, which has always been the focus of research and debate in the field of Chinese grammar. Nowadays, with the development of natural language processing technology, the research on Chinese word classes also needs to keep pace with the times.

This paper proposes a research method of nominal verbs based on the word pluripotency index, taking five words under the "变化(*Bianhua*, change)" sense category as the research object (including "*Bianhua*变化", "*Liangbian*量变", "*Zhibian*质变", "*Jianbian*渐变", "*Tubian*突变"), and innovatively applies the Shannon-Wiener index to the research on the pluripotency of modern Chinese nominal verbs. The experimental results show that the word pluripotency index of "变化(*Bianhua*, change)" words is all higher than 0.6, indicating that these words are more flexible in the actual use of language, and their distribution under both nouns and verbs reflects a certain degree of balance. Moreover, these words have a deeper degree of drift towards nouns. Further, this paper discusses that the quantitative index of word plurality can help provide scientific and reasonable data support for the establishment of dictionary sense and the setting of POS tagging specifications, which reflects important research significance and application value.

Due to the relatively small scale of "变化(*Bianhua*, change)" words in CCL Corpus and Taiwan Academia Sinica Balanced Corpus, this paper does not conduct a comparative study on different corpus. In the next step, in order to promote a more comprehensive and in-depth exploration of Chinese word classes, we will expand the scale of the experiment and carry out word pluripotency experiments on more words. Also, we will further consider the relationship of other parthenogenic words. It is noted that when conducting large-scale experiments, there may be data sparse problems due to the difference in word frequency of different terms, so the expansion and development of the corpus is also of great significance to the study of word pluripotency research.

Acknowledgments. I am grateful to the anonymous reviewers of CLSW 2022 for helpful suggestions and comments. This work is supported by the Fundamental Research Funds for National Language Committee Research Program of China (No. ZDI135-141).

References

1. Zhu, D., Lu, J., Ma, Z.: On the problem of verb adjective "nominalization." J. Peking Univ. (Humanities and Social Sciences) **4**, 53–66 (1961). (in Chinese)
2. Shannon, C.E.: A mathematical theory of communication. Bell Syst. Tech. J. **27**(3), 379–423 (1948)
3. Shannon, C.E., Weaver, W.: The Mathematical Theory of Communication. Philos. Rev. **60**. 3 (1949)
4. Xun, E., Rao, G., Xiao, X., Zang, J.: The construction of the bcc corpus in the age of big data. Corpus Linguist. **1**, 93–109 (2016). (in Chinese)
5. Zhu, D.: Self-referring and turning-referring—the grammatical and semantic functions of the Chinese nominalization marks "*De*(的)、*Zhe*(者)、*Suo*(所)、*Zhi*(之)". Dialects. **1**, 16–31 (1983). (in Chinese)
6. Zhu, D.: Definitive verbs and nominal verbs in modern written Chinese. In: World Chinese Teaching Society. Selected Papers of the First International Chinese Teaching Symposium. World Chinese Teaching Society (1985). (in Chinese)
7. Lu, J.: On the problem of concurrent categories of words. Stud. Chinese Lang. **1**, 28–34 (1994). (in Chinese) CNKI:SUN:YWZG.0.1994.01.010
8. Hu, M.: A Quantitative study on nominal verbs. Stud. Lang. Linguist. **2**, 91–99 (1995). (in Chinese). CNKI:SUN:YYYJ.0.1995.02.005
9. Yu, S., Duan, H., Zhu, X.: A Quantitative analysis on multi-class words and shift from verbs to Nouns in Chinese. In: Proceedings of the Eighth National Joint Conference on Computational Linguistics (JSCL-2005) (2005). (in Chinese)
10. Wang, D.: Nominalization and Verbalization in Contemporary Chinese: A Cognitive Linguistic Inquiry. China Social Sciences Press, Beijing (2010). (in Chinese)
11. Shen, J.: My View of word Classes in Chinese. Linguist. Sci. **1**, 1–12 (2009). (in Chinese). CNKI:SUN:YYKE.0.2009.01.000
12. Yu, S, Zhu, X., Duan, H.: The guideline for segmentation and part2OF2speech tagging on very large scale corpus of contemporary Chinese. J. Chinese Inf. Proces. **6**, 58–64 (2000). (in Chinese). https://doi.org/10.3969/j.issn.1003-0077.2000.06.010
13. Yang, L., Xiao, H., Liu, Z.: On the revision of standard of POS tag of contemporary Chinese for CIP. Appl. Linguist. **3**, 87–95 (2019). (in Chinese)
14. Yang, L., Xiao, H., Liu, Z.: On the revision of standard of POS tag of contemporary Chinese for CIP. Appl. Linguist. **3**, 111–120 (2021). (in Chinese)
15. Wang, J., Yue, S., Li, Lu.: The measurement index of faculty in colleges and universities for the academic origin structure. Teach. Educ. Forum **7**, 48–54 (2015). (in Chinese)
16. Yin, X., Han, J., Wang, B., Jin, W., Yang, L., Chen, H., et al.: Macrobenthic community and relationship with environmental factors in Taizi River Basin. Chinese J. Fishers **3**, 40–44 (2017). (in Chinese). CNKI:SUN:SCXZ.0.2017.03.008
17. Hieber, D.W.: Lexical flexibility: expanding the empirical coverage. In: UCSB Linguistics Colloquium (2020)
18. https://files.danielhieber.com/publications/ucsb-doctoral-colloquium/slides.pdf, Accessed 12 2020
19. Hieber, D.W.: Lexical polyfunctionality in discourse: a quantitative corpus-based approach (2021)

20. Yang, S., Zhang, C., Wu, W., Chen, H.: Discussion on the aggregation mode of Chengdu training institutions based on big data. Shanxi Archit. **19**, 27–29 (2021). (in Chinese). https://doi.org/10.13719/j.cnki.1009-6825.2021.19.010

21. Wang, R., Huang, C.: Heterosemy of self-reference lexemes in Modern Chinese from the perspective of the two-level word class categorization theory. Foreign Lang. Lit. **1**, 87–96 (2017). (in Chinese). https://doi.org/10.3969/j.issn.1674-6414.2017.01.014

22. Zhang, Y., Liu, P.: The semantic features of "changchang", "jingchang", "wangwang" and "tongchang"—a corpus-based perspective. In: Lu, Q., Gao, H. (eds.) Chinese Lexical Semantics. CLSW 2015. LNCS (LNAI), vol. 9332, pp. 148–159. Springer, Cham (2015). https://doi.org/10.1007/978-3-319-27194-1_16

23. Wang, X., Wang, Y.: The Discrimination of the synonyms of yǐnqǐ: a corpus-based study. In: Dong, M., Gu, Y., Hong, J.F. (eds.) Chinese Lexical Semantics. CLSW 2021. LNCS (LNAI), vol. 13249, pp. 56–67. Springer, Cham (2022). https://doi.org/10.1007/978-3-031-06703-7_5

24. Bian, W.: The differences between Jiùshì and Jiùsuàn as conjunctions and their formation mechanisms. In: Dong, M., Gu, Y., Hong, J.F. (eds.) Chinese Lexical Semantics. CLSW 2021. LNCS (LNAI), vol.13249, pp.144–159. Springer, Cham (2022). https://doi.org/10.1007/978-3-031-06703-7_11

25. Wang, C., Rao, G., Xun, E., Sui, Z.: Chunk extraction and analysis based on frame-verbs. In: Dong, M., Gu, Y., Hong, JF. (eds.) Chinese Lexical Semantics. CLSW 2021. LNCS (LNAI), vol. 13249, pp. 423–431. Springer, Cham (2022). https://doi.org/10.1007/978-3-031-06703-7_32

The Causativity of Preposition "Dui (for)"

Enxu Wang[(✉)] and Xu Ding

College of Chinese Language and Literature, University of Jinan, No. 336 Nanxinzhuang West Road, Shizhong District, Jinan 250022, China
wangbush000@126.com

Abstract. In previous studies, the preposition "dui" has two usages: one is to introduce a directed object, and the other is to introduce a treated object. This paper shows the third usage of "dui(for)", that is, to introduce a causer. When affective adjectives act as the predicates of "dui(for)" sentences, the characteristics of affective adjectives determine what the preposition "dui(for)" introduced is not a directed or treated object but a causative force, which can be proved by the object movement of "dui(for)". Semantically, there are some similarities between the third "dui(for)" and the first two "dui". Both of them have an explicit target object, which is the basis of the semantic extension of the preposition "dui". On this basis, three meanings of the preposition "dui" are extended one after another: "dui"① (to introduce a directed object) → "dui"② (to introduce a treated object) → "dui"③ (to introduce a causer).

Keywords: "dui(for)" · causer · affective adjectives

1 Introduction

The previous research revealed that the preposition "dui" has two usages: one is to introduce a directed object, which is equivalent to "chao/xiang(towards/to)"; and the other is to introduce a treated object, which is equivalent to "duiyu(with regard to)" [1–3]. Actually, in addition to introducing a directed object or a treated object, "dui(for)" can also be used to introduce a causer. Please see the following examples.

(1) Usages in previous studies

   a. To introduce a directed object: xiao huang **dui** wo xiao le xiao. (Xiao Huang smiled at me.) [1:182]

   b. To introduce a treated object: dajia **dui** wo hen reqing. (Everyone was very warm to me.) [1:182]

   c. To introduce an involved object: zhe zhong qiti **dui** renti youhai. (The gas is harmful to humans.) [4:192]

   d. To introduce a patient: women **dui** zhe jian shi yijing diaocha guo le. (We have investigated this matter.) [5:74]

(2) Usages of introducing causers

© The Author(s), under exclusive license to Springer Nature Switzerland AG 2023

Q. Su et al. (Eds.): CLSW 2022, LNAI 13495, pp. 65–76, 2023.
https://doi.org/10.1007/978-3-031-28953-8_6

a. Keren **dui** wo de shouyi gandao manyi.[1] (The guest is satisfied with my craft.)
   → Wo de shouyi ling keren manyi. (My craft satisfies the guest.)
b. b. Ta **dui** jintian de canshi feichang nanguo. (He is very sad about today's tragedy.)
   → Jintian de canshi rang ta nanguo. (Today's tragedy makes him sad.)
c. Zongshuji **dui** shishi fazhan fuzhuangye shifen gaoxing. (The general secretary is very happy about Shishi's development of the clothing industry.)
   → Shishi fazhan fuzhuangye rang zongshuji gandao gaoxing. (Shishi's development of the clothing industry made the general secretary happy.)

The "dui" of examples (1) and (2) look similar, both of which indicate "what the subject does to the object of the preposition (hereinafter referred to as 'the object')". But in fact there are great differences. Syntactically, the former "dui" introduces mainly noun components, while the latter "dui"(hereinafter referred to as "dui(for)") can introduce not only noun components (2a), event components (2b), but also clause components (2c). Semantically, the former subject only affects the object, while the latter subject is often affected by the object, such as example (2a) "My craft satisfies the guest". In other words, the affective response of "satisfies" is not caused by the subject but by the object, and the object is the causative argument of the sentence. Then why can "dui(for)" introduce a causative argument? What are the syntactic-semantic conditions, and what is the relationship between this usage and other usages? In this paper, we will answer these questions.

2   The Syntactic Condition that "DUI(FOr)" Introduces a Causer

The syntactic structure of "dui" sentences is "Subject + 'Dui' + Object + Predicate". Based on this structure, we compared various usages of the preposition "dui" and found the following differences between them.

2.1   Differences in Predicates

The predicate determines the syntactic-semantic environment of "dui" sentences. Different predicates have different meanings and usages. Based on references [5–7], this paper reclassifies the predicates of "dui" sentences into three types according to the differences of replaceable prepositions.

A-type: speech verbs, such as "shuo(say)", "han(shout)", "sahuang(lie)", "jieshi (explain)", "xuanchuan(propagate)", etc.; posture verbs, such as "ku(cry)", "xiao(laugh), "baishou(wag)", "diantou(nod)", "jugong(bow)", etc.; abstract action verbs, such as "fa piqi(lose one's temper)", "bai jiazi(put on airs)", "sajiao(act in a spoilt way)", etc.. In these predicate sentences, the preposition "dui" can be replaced by "chao/xiang(towards/to)".

---

[1] The corpus in this paper is derived from the CCL corpus of Peking University unless otherwise specified.

B-type: psychological verbs, such as "huaiyi(doubt)", "ganxie(gratitude)", "zengwu(hate)", "liangjie(understand)", "haipa(fear)", "rongren (tolerate)", ect.; concrete behavior verbs, such as "chuanhuan(summon)", "diaocha (investigate)", "ganshe(intervene)", "zhuabu (arrest)", etc.; and the perceptual or affective "'you(have)' + noun" structure, such as "you xingqu(have interest in)", "you yijian(have a different opinion)", "you zeren(have a responsibility)" etc.. In these predicate sentences, the preposition "dui" cannot be replaced by "chao/xiang(towards/to)" but can be replaced by "duiyu(with regard to)".

C-type: affective adjectives, such as "nanguo(sorry)", "gaoxing(happy)", "cankui (ashamed)", etc.. The preposition "dui(for)" in these predicate sentences cannot be replaced by "chao/xiang(towards/to)" but can be replaced by "yin/wei(for)".

In addition to the differences in replaceable prepositions, the predicate sentences above also differ greatly in subject autonomy, the syntactic position of the object, and the influence of the object on the predicate. The latter two aspects will be discussed in Sects. 2.2 and 3.3. Here, we only discuss the differences in subject autonomy.

A-type predicates is often autonomous, and their actions are caused by the subject autonomously and are not affected by the causative force, noted by [+autonomy].

B-type predicates is also autonomous, but there seems to be some kind of causative force behind the autonomy. And sometimes it is the causative force that causes the subject's behavior. Take "haizi men dui donghuapian you xingqu(kids have interest in cartoons)" as an example, the predicate "you xingqu(have interest in)" can be understood in the following two ways: one is the static "huaiyou(harbor)", "chiyou (hold)", "baoyou(cherish)", e.g. "haizi men dui donghuapian huaizhe hen da de xingqu(kids harbor a great interest in cartoons)"; the other is the dynamic "biancheng you(become…have)", "chansheng(yield)", e.g. "haizi men dui donghuapian chansheng le hen da de xingqu (kids became very interested in cartoons)" [8]. In the first understanding, the subject is autonomous; in the second understanding, the subject may be autonomous (e.g. kids are naturally fond of cartoons) or partially autonomous (e.g. some external forces, such as cartoons, have influenced kids and made them become interested). In order to highlight this property of B-type predicates implying external force, this paper notes it as [+partial autonomy].

C-type predicates are non-autonomous and are noted as [+non-autonomy]. The non-autonomy of C-type predicates is related to affective adjectives. The affective responses of adjectives is caused by external forces [9], and "subjects do not have the ability to manipulate their perceptual experiences" [10]. There is an implicit causative usage in affective adjectives, and its syntactic structure is "causative verb + person + (perceive/feel+) affective adjective" [11–13]. For example (2a), if expressed by the causative structure, it will be: "Wo de shouyi ling keren manyi (My craft satisfies the guests)". In this case, the object of "dui(for)" appears at the beginning of the sentence, and acts as the causative force that triggers the affective response, namely causers. From the corpus survey, the affective adjectives are often used as the predicate of "dui(for)" sentences are as follows: "huanghuo(perplexed)", "e'ran(astounded)", "aishang (grieved)", "huangluan(flurried)", "youchou(worried)", "gaoxing(happy)", "zihao (proud)", "jiao'ao(be proud of)", "shiwang(disappointed)", "xinwei(gratified)", "jingqi(amazed)", "kun-huo(puzzled)", "qinqie(warm)", "kongju(frightened)", "xiukui (ashamed)", "nan-guo(sad)", "xingfen(excited)", "mosheng(strange)", "cankui (ashamed)", "bukuai (unhappy)", "tongxin (distressed)", "fennu (irate)", "xiuchi (ashamed)", "wennuan (warm)", "neijiu (conscience-stricken)", "bei'ai (mournful)", "jimo (lonely)", "rongxing (honoured)", "jingyi (astonished)", "jusang (depressed)", "mangran (depressed)", "nankan (embarrassed)", "shangxin (break-hearted)", "ganga (embarrassed)", "yayi (oppressed)", "fenkai (indignant)", "haoqi (inquisitive)", "fannao (annoyed)", "chen-zhong (heavy)", "jiaolv (worried)", "beishang (sorrowful)", "konghuang (frightened)", "touteng (troublesome)", "jinghuang (alarmed)", "kuijiu (guilty)", "huangkong (terri-fied)", "deyi (pleased with oneself)", "jiongpo (embarrassed)", "shengshu (unfamil-iar)", "kumen (sick at heart)", "yuyue (cheerful)", "tongchu(painful)", "qieyi (satis-fied)", "xinhan (bitterly disappointed)", "qiguai (weird)", "qingsong (relaxed)", "nan-shou(uncomfortable)", "weiqu (wronged)", "nanweiqing (embarrassed)", "haoxiao (funny)", "kexi (regrettable)", "yanshu (familiar)", etc..

2.2 Differences in Syntactic Position of Objects

There are four possible ways to move the object of "dui": moving it to the beginning of sentences together with its preposition, moving to the beginning of sentences alone, moving to the end of sentences or to the middle of "yin...er(for)".

A-type predicates are quasi-transitive verbs, which have a strict restriction on object movement. The object can only be moved to the beginning of the sentence. Moreover, when moving to the beginning of the sentence, the object must appear with the preposition "dui(to)" [14:207], such as (3a-c). Sometimes even if appearing with prepositions, the sentence is still unnatural and needs to be turned into a complex form or appear in a comparative sentence [6:2]. Such as (3c), it needs to be turned into a comparative form, e.g. "dui meimei, ta changchang fa piqi; dui wo, que hen shao fa piqi(with his sister, he often lose his temper; with me, he rarely lose their temper).

(3) The object position of A-type predicates

    a.   Liu siye **dui** Xiangzi xiao le xiao (Master Liu smiled at Xiangzi). [5:12]
         ? Dui Xiangzi, Liu siye xiao le xiao (To Xiangzi, Master Liu smiled).
    b.   Ta **dui** cangqiong dadi gao han (He shouted to heaven and earth). [6:3]
         ? Dui cangqiong dadi, ta gao han (To heaven and earth, he shouted).
    c.   Ta changchang **dui** meimei fa piqi (He often lost his temper with his sister).
         ? Dui meimei, ta changchang fa piqi (With his sister, he often loses his temper).

B-type predicates are bivalent verbs whose objects can be moved relatively freely to the end or beginning of sentences. Among B-type predicates, the "'you(have)' + noun" construction is more special. So the following discussion will concentrate on this construction. 1) The "'you(have)' + noun" structure is equivalent to a psycho-logical perceptual verb, such as "you xingqu(have interest in)" ≈ "xihuan(like)", "you yinxiang(have an impression)" ≈ "jide(remember)", "you yijian(have a different opinion)" ≈ "buman(dissatisfaction)", etc.. Therefore, the "'you(have)' + noun" structure is the same as other B-type predicates, which are all divalent transitive verbs. 2) The "'you(have)' + noun" structure, like other B-type predicates, contains a common semantic component "you(have)". And the "you(have)" can be understood in two ways. One is the static "huaiyou(harbor)", "huaizhe(hold)", "baoyou(cherish)", "fuyou(have a responsibility)", "cunyou(keep)", "daiyou(take)", etc.. The other is the dynamic "biancheng you(become...have)", "chansheng(yield)", "qingzhu(pour into)", "caiqu(adopt)", etc.(See reference 8 for further details). 3) The "'you(have)' + noun" sentence has the same syntactic moving form as other B-type predicate sentences. Take the object of "dui(for)" as an example, it can be moved to the end of the sentence as the object of the predicate, or to the beginning of the sentence with "dui(for)" as the adverbial modifier of the sentence. More importantly, the preposition "dui(for)" that move forward can be omitted. In short, there are three ways to move the object of B-type predicate sentences. Except for the middle of "yin...er(for)", all other movements are allowed. As shown in example (4).

(4) The object position of B-type predicates

    a. Haizi men **dui** donghuapian you xingqu (Kids have interest in cartoons). | Haizi men xihuan(you xingqu) donghuapian (Kids like cartoons). | **Dui** donghuapian haizi men hen gan xingqu (As for cartoons, kids are very interested). | Donghuapian haizi men hen gan xingqu (Cartoons kids are very interested). [8]

    b. Kaiyi **dui** 20 zhong yuyan zuo guo diaocha(Kay has done a survey on 20 languages). | Kaiyi diaocha guo 20 zhong yuyan (Kay has surveyed 20 languages). | **Dui** zhe 20 zhong yuyan Kayi dou zuo guo diaocha (On these 20 languages Kay has surveyed). | Zhe 20 zhong yuyan Kaiyi dou diaocha guo (All these 20 languages Kay has surveyed).

    c. Jizhe **dui** Li Xiaolong de gongfu hen huaiyi (Reporters are very suspicious of Bruce Lee's Kung Fu). | Jizhe hen huaiyi Li Xiaolong de gongfu (Reporters doubted Bruce Lee's Kung Fu). | **Dui** Li Xiaolong de gongfu jizhe chansheng le huaiyi (To Bruce Lee's Kung Fu reporters was very suspicious). | Li Xiaolong de gongfu jizhe feichang huaiyi (Bruce Lee's Kung Fu reporters was very suspicious).

That the object can appear at the beginning of the sentence alone is not only an important characteristic that distinguishes B-type predicate sentences from A-type predicate sentences, but also a necessary condition for the object to be understood as a causer. Only when the object appears at the beginning of a sentence alone, can it be understood as a causer. Otherwise, it is difficult to be understood as a causer (see Sect. 3.2.2 for further discussion).

Compared with A- and B-type predicate sentences, the objects of C-type predicate sentences move more freely and can appear in all 4 syntactic positions. This is, it can be moved to the beginning or end of sentences as the adverbial modifier, subject or object of sentences. When moving to the beginning of sentences, there is usually a causative relationship between the subject and the predicate, in which causative markers "shi(make)", "jiao(ask)", "rang(let)" can be inserted. The causative relation is one of the causal relation, so the object can appear at the beginning of sentences as a causer or in the middle of "yin…er(for)" as a reason. Details are shown in example (5).

(5) The object position of C-type predicates

    a. Ta **dui** jintian de canshi feichang nanguo (He was very sad about today's tragedy). | (**Dui**) jintian de canshi, ta gandao nanguo (Today's tragedy, he was very sad). | Ta hen nanguo jintian de canshi (He was very sad about today's tragedy). | Jintian de canshi rang ta nanguo (Today's tragedy made him sad). | Ta yin jintian de canshi er nanguo (He was sad because of today's tragedy).

    b. keren **dui** wo de shouyi gandao manyi (The guest is satisfied with my craft). | (**Dui**) wo de shouyi, keren gandao manyi (With my craft, the guest was satisfied). | Keren hen manyi wo de shouyi (The guest is satisfied with my craft). | Wo de shouyi ling keren manyi (My craft makes the guest satisfied). | Keren yin wo de shouyi er manyi (The guest is satisfied because of my craft) .

As has been mentioned above, there are many syntactic conditions need to be satisfied for the preposition "dui(for)" introducing a causer, of which the most important two are that the "dui(for)" needs appear in B- or C-type predicate sentences, and the object of "dui(for)" needs appear alone at the beginning of sentences or in the middle of "yin…er(for)".

3   The Semantic Condition that "Dui(for)" Introduces a Causer

Most of prepositions come from verbs, and the semantic features of the verb determine whether it can be evolved into a preposition [15, 16]. As for the semantic feature or source of the preposition "dui(for)", there are different opinions. Some studies insist that it is derived from the verb "duida(answer)" [16:24], some believe the core semantic features of "dui(for)" are "zhenduixing(aim)" or "guanshexing (relevance)" [17:154], while others think the preposition usage of "dui" come from the verb "dangdui/miandui(face)" [18:235]. Perhaps the opinions above may explain why "dui(for)" can be used to introduce directed objects or treated objects, but they cannot explain why "dui(for)" can also be used to introduce causers.

3.1   The Core Semantic Feature of Preposition "Dui(for)"

According to the observation of this paper, the core semantic feature of "dui(for)" is that it contains an explicit target object. Before the event occurs, there is an explicit target object; when the event occurs, which proceeds toward the definite target object.

    The preposition "dui(for)" contains an explicit target object, which can also be found in previous studies. Taking a closer examination on the dictionary definitions of "duida(answer)", "zhendui(aim at)", "huiying(respond to)", etc., we will find they all contain the semantic feature of "explicit target object". As shown in example (6).

(6) a. [duida(answer)] huida(answer). [huida(answer)] dui wenti jiyv jieshi (giving explanations to questions). [3:329, 579]

b. [zhendui(aim at)] yinjin you mingque mudi de xingwei duixiang(to introduce behavior objects with explicit purposes). [19:1671]

c. [huiying(respond to)] huida(answer); daying(answer in response to the voice). [3:582]

In these definitions, the object of "duida(answer)" is explicit, i.e. a definite "wenti (question)"; the object of "zhendui(aim at)" or "huiying(respond to)" is also explicit, i.e. a "behavior object with explicit purposes" or a known voice, word, action, etc.

3.2 The Semantic Derivation of Preposition "Dui(for)"

Based on the semantic feature of "explicit target object", the preposition "dui(for)" has derived three meanings one after another.

[dui] ① to introduce a directed object, which is equivalent to "chao/xiang(towards)";
[dui] ② to introduce a treated object, which is equivalent to "duiyu(with regard to)";
[dui] ③ to introduce a causative object, which is equivalent to "yin/wei(for)".

Among the three meanings, "dui"① appeared first, and related examples can be found as early as the Eastern Han Dynasty. For example, "gui, dui qi mu qi (when coming back, he cried to his mother)." [20] "Dui"② appeared relatively late. There were only a few examples in the Sui and Tang dynasties, such as "Ting mei dui wo you lian yi (Mei in the yard take pity on me)". [20] The formal appearance of "dui"② was around the end of the Qing Dynasty. [16].

Relatively speaking, "dui"③ appeared much later. According to the survey on the CCL ancient and modern Chinese corpora of Peking University, before the Republic of China, the number of "dui"③ was extremely limited. Searching the keywords "dui(for) $10 gaoxing(happy) / nanguo(sad) / manyi(satisfied) / shiwang(disappointed) / jimo(lonely) / (kongjv)fearful / huangluan(panicked) / youchou(worried) / zihao(proud) / jiao'ao(proud) / xinwei(gratified) / jingqi(surprised) / kunhuo(confused) / qin-qie(affectionate) / xiukui(ashamed) / xingfen(excited) / mosheng(unfamiliar) / cankui(ashamed) / xiuchi(shamed) / wennuan(warm) / neijiu(guilty) / bei'ai(mournful) / rongxing(honored) / jingyi(astonished) / jusang(depressed)", only five cases were found. Distributed in the Tang, Song, Ming, Qing, and Republic of China five dynasties, one case in one dynasty. For example:

(7) a. Du **dui** chunguang hai jimo (The poet feels lonely when facing the beautiful spring scene). (Tang Dynasty)

b. Wo **dui** tianzi yi wu kongju(Even in the face of the emperor, I did not feel scared). (Northern Song Dynasty)

c. Qita jiangling **dui** ci dou hen bu gaoxing(The other generals are all unhappy about this). (Ming Dynasty)

It was not until the modern Chinese that "dui"③ began to be widely used. Taking "dui(for) $10 gaoxing(happy) / nanguo(sad) / manyi(satisfied) / shiwang (disappointed)" as an example, for every 100 cases, there were on average 67 cases of "dui(for)...gaoxing(happy)", 65 cases of "dui(for)... shiwang(disappointed)", 51 cases of "dui(for)...manyi(satisfied)", 49 cases of "dui(for)... nanguo(sad/sorry)". For example, "Sun Zhongshan dui xuanze zheli bijiao manyi(Sun Yat-sen was satisfied with choosing here)".

3.3 The Semantic Structure of Preposition "Dui(for)"

In previous parts, we have roughly clarified the derived order of the three meanings of "dui(for)". This is, "dui"① → "dui"② → "dui"③. This part will analyze the semantic structures and their changing conditions of each meaning.

Grammaticalization involves "a structural formula rather than a specific lexical or grammatical morpheme" [21:21]. When a component changes, the corresponding component will change accordingly. In the case of "dui(for)", there are two main factors that affect the change of its semantic structure: the predicate and the relationship between the subject and the object. The former determines the context in which "dui(for)" may appear, and the latter determines what understanding of "dui(for)" is possible in this context. In the following, we will discuss in detail based on the structure of "subject + 'dui' + object + predicate".

3.3.1   "Dui"①:Subject$_{autonomy-agent}$+"dui"+Object$_{no\ influence\ on\ the\ subject-directed\ object}$ + Predicate

The characteristics of this structure: 1) The "dui"① introduced the directed object appears the earliest and can be replaced by "chao/xiang(towards)". 2) Using A-type predicates, the action expressed by the predicate occurs in the objective world, with an explicit directed object, which can be seen and felt. 3) The subject is the agent of the action, which is autonomous; the object is the target to which the action is directed, which is non-autonomous.

(8)   a.   Ta jidong di **dui** shenbian de ren shuo: "...". (He excitedly said to the people around him: "...".)

    b.   Guitai houmian di riben xiaojie **dui** wo diantou jugong.... (The Japanese lady behind the counter nodded and bowed to me....)

    c.   Yin Xiaotiao conglai bu hui **dui** ta sajiao, ye cong bu gen ta ku nao. (Yin Xiaotiao never spoiled her or cried with her.)

Combined with part 2.2, the object of "dui"① cannot appear alone at the beginning of the sentence and cannot affect the subject. In other words, the influence of the subject on the object is one-way, only the subject can affect the object, not vice versa. For example (8a), the subject "ta(he)" may affect the object "shenbian de ren(the people around him)", but the object cannot affect the subject.

3.3.2 "Dui"②: Subject partial autonomy – agent/causer + **"dui"** + Object probably influence on the subject - treated object + Predicate

The characteristics of this structure: 1) The "dui"② indicating the treated object appears earlier and can be replaced by "duiyu(with regard to)" [4:184]. 2) Using B-type predicates, they are all bivalent predicates or can be turned into bivalent predicates, whose objects can be moved to the beginning of the sentence alone, acting as agents or causers. 3) B-type predicates contain a common semantic component "you(have)", which can be understood as static "huaiyou(harbor)", "chiyou(hold)" etc. or dynamic "biancheng you(become...have)", "chansheng(yield)", "sangshi(lose),etc..[8] When doing the dynamic understanding, the action of the subject may be influenced by some external force, whereas the external force may exactly be the object of "dui"②. For example (9a), when the "you xingqu(have interest in)" is understood dynamically, the external force that makes children interested is probably "donghuapian(cartoons)". That is, "donghuapian rang haizi men dui zhi chansheng le xingqu(cartoons make kids be interested in it)". Based on the different understandings of "you(have)", the different meanings of the B-type predicate sentences can be described as follows.

(9) a. Haizi men **dui** donghuapian you xingqu. (Kids have an interest in cartoons.)

→Haizi men **dui** donghuapian bao zhe hen da de xingqu. (Kids have great interest in cartoons.)   (static "you(have)")

→...rang haizi men **dui** donghuapian chansheng le xingqu. (... makes kids interested in cartoons.)   (dynamic "you(have)")

→Donghuapian rang haizi men **dui** zhi chansheng le xingqu. (Cartoons make kids interested in them.)   (dynamic "you(have)")

   b. Ji Erhalang **dui** fuqin hen you yijian. (Zilhalang has great dissatisfied with his father.)

→Ji Erhalang **dui** fuqin huaiyou hen da de buman. (Zilhalang has great dissatisfied with his father.)   (static "you(have)")

→...rang Ji Erhalang **dui** fuqin chansheng le buman. (...made Zilhalang dissatisfied with his father.)   (dynamic "you(have)")

→Fuqin de pianxin rang Ji Erhalang gandao buman. (Father's bias made Zilkhalang dissatisfied with him.)   (dynamic "you(have)")

   c. Luosifu **dui** ta feichang xinren. (Roosevelt trusted him very much.)

→Luosifu **dui** ta huaizhe feichang xinren de taidu. (Roosevelt had a very trusting attitude towards him.)   (static "you(have)")

→...rang Luosifu **dui** ta yuyi chongfen de xinren. (...let Roosevelt give him full trust.)   (dynamic "you(have)")

→Ta ling Luosifu **dui** zhi yuyi le chongfen de xinren. (He made Roosevelt fully trust him.)   (dynamic "you(have)")

d. Jingfang **dui** Wu Lan shishi le zhuabu. (The police made an arrest of Wu Lan.)

→Jingfang **dui** Wu Lan caiqu le zhuabu cuoshi. (The police took measures to arrest
  Wu Lan.)   (static "you(have)")
→…shi Jingfang **dui** Wu Lan shishi le zhuabu. (... made the police made an arrest of
  Wu Lan.)   (dynamic "you(have)")
→Wu lan de pantao shi Jingfang **dui** zhi shishi le zhuabu. (Wu Lan's defection led the
  police to arrest him.)   (dynamic "you(have)")

3) Combined with example (9), when the predicate is understood as the static
"huaiyou (harbor)" or "chiyou(hold)", the subject is autonomous; when it is understood as the dynamic "biancheng you(become…have)", "chansheng(yield)", the subject
is partially autonomous and may be influenced by the object of "dui"②. In this case, the
object of "dui"② is a causer, and the subject becomes a causee.

As mentioned above, there are three conditions need to be satisfied for "dui"② to
introduce a causer. 1) The object can be moved to the beginning of the sentence alone,
which satisfies the syntactic condition of acting as a causer. 2) The predicate may be
affected by external forces when being understood as the dynamic "biancheng you
(become…have)", "chansheng(yield)", etc., which satisfies the semantic condition of
introducing a causer. 3) The relevance of "dui"② determines that its object is closely
related to the predicate and the subject and affects each other. When the object is no
longer only affected by the predicate, but can also affect the predicate, the causative
usage will appear.

Emphasizing that "dui"② can introduce causers has three advantages. First, it can
explain why many unrelated verbs predicates (e.g. specific action verbs, psychological verbs, emotional "'you(have)' + noun" structure, etc.) can enter "dui" sentences.
Because all of them can provide a suitable syntactic and semantic environment for
"dui"② to introduce a causer. Second, it can explain why other predicates cannot enter
"dui"② sentences. Taking the existential sentence as an example, although its predicate
contains the meaning of "biancheng you(become…have)" or "chuxian(appear/born)",
such as "Zhongguo chu le ge Mao Zedong(There is a Mao Zedong born in China)". And
its object can also be moved to the beginning of the sentence, such as "Mao Zedong
sheng zai Zhongguo(Mao Zedong was born in China)". But there is no mutual influence
relationship between the object and the predicate, so it cannot introduce a causer. Third,
it can connect "dui"① and "dui"③ to prepare conditions for the unified interpretation of
"dui"①, "dui"② and "dui"③. Based on the core semantic feature, the preposition "dui"
has derived three meanings. "Dui"① introduces an explicit target object; "dui"② implies
some kind of causative force, and some of the causative force come from the target object
introduced by "dui"②; "dui"③ implies some kind of causative force, and most of the
causative force come from the object introduced by "dui"③. (See the following section
for more details).

3.3.3 "Dui"③:Subject_non-autonomy-experiencer+"dui"+Object_influence on the subject–causer + Predicate

The characteristics of this structure: 1) Compared to "dui"① and "dui"②, "dui"③appeared relatively later and can be replaced by "yin/wei(for)". 2) Using C-type predicates or affective adjectives. Because affective responses do not appear in the external world but in one's inner world, they are not easily perceived. 3) The affective response is not caused by the subject but by some causative force, where the causative force usually come from the object. In other words, it is the object of "dui"③ that causes the affective response, therefore it can be moved to the beginning of the sentence as the causative subject. As shown in example (10).

(10) a. Diwengku'enda **dui** you jihui lai zhongguo fangwen gandao gaoxing. (Dioncuenda is happy about the opportunity to visit China.)
　　　→ You jihui lai zhongguo fangwen, rang Diwengku'enda gandao gaoxing. (The opportunity to visit China made Dioncuenda happy.)
　　b. Zhangbolun xiansheng **dui** neige de kunao ye hen nanguo. (Mr. Chamberlain was also sad about the distress of the cabinet.)
　　　→ Neige de kunao rang Zhangbolun nanguo. (The Cabinet's distress made Chamberlain sad.)
　　c. Hen duo kehu **dui** mianhua fayun qingkuang jiwei shiwang. (Many customers were extremely disappointed with the cotton shipment situation.)
　　　→ Mianhua fayun qingkuang rang kehu men shiwang. (The cotton shipment situation disappointed the customers.)

Although "dui"② also implies the causative force, it only appears when the predicate is understood as dynamic "biancheng you(become...have)", and does not appear when the predicate is understood as static "chiyou(hold)". Therefore, that introducing a causer is not the stable usage of "dui"②. Relatively speaking, the usage of "dui"③ is stable, whose object is almost the causative force of affective response. Therefore, it is necessary to establish a meaning entry separately for the preposition "dui".

4 Conclusion

The appearance of a new usage needs to satisfy certain syntactic and semantic conditions [15, 22]. From the syntactic point of view, the preposition "dui" can introduce a causer is mainly influenced by the affective adjectives. The characteristics of the affective adjectives determine what "dui" introduced is not a directed or treated object but a causative force, which can be proved by the object movement of "dui". From the semantic point of view, there is some similarity between the "dui"③ and "dui"①, "dui"②. Both of them contain an explicit target object, which is the basis of the semantic extension of "dui". On this basis, three meanings of preposition "dui" are extended one after another: "dui"① → "dui"② → "dui"③.

Acknowledgments. This paper is supported by the National Social Science Fund (19BYY030). The anonymous reviewers of CLSW2022 put forward many valuable comments. Here, we express our sincere thanks for them!

References

1. Lü, S.X. (ed.): 800 words in modern Chinese (Revised). The Commercial Press, Beijing (1999). (in Chinese)
2. Liu, Y.H., et al.: Practical modern Chinese grammar. Commercial Press, Beijing (2001). (in Chinese)
3. The Linguistics Institute of Chinese Academy of Social Sciences: Modern Chinese Dictionary, 7th edn. Commercial Press, Beijing (2016). (in Chinese)
4. Fu, Y.X., Zhou, X.B.: Research on prepositions in modern Chinese. Sun Yat-sen University Press, Guangzhou (1997). (in Chinese)
5. Li, L.Y.: Investigation on the meaning and usage of the preposition "dui." J. Tianjin Normal Univ. 4, 71–75 (1999). (in Chinese)
6. Xu, S.: Several main forms of "dui" sentence. Chin. Lang. Learn. 3, 1–7 (1984). (in Chinese)
7. Zhou, W.H.: The study of the senses of "dui" in Chinese interlanguage. TCSOL Stud. 1, 27–35 (2011). (in Chinese)
8. Yuan, Y.L.: Study on valence of nouns in modern Chinese. Chin. Soc. Sci. 3, 205–223 (1992). (in Chinese)
9. Zhang, H.Q., Liu, F.: Research on psychological adjective with object structure in modern Chinese. J. Dalian Univ. 5, 83–87 (2011). (in Chinese)
10. Mei, G.: An outline of classical Chinese grammar. Shanghai Education Press, Shanghai (2018). (in Chinese)
11. Zhao, C.: Some principle of co-occurrence of affective adjectives and nouns. Stud. Chin. Lang. 2, 125–132 (2007). (in Chinese)
12. Yu, W.Q.: Research on the structure of "one + classier + affective" in modern Chinese. East China Normal University, Shanghai (2012). (in Chinese)
13. Kong, L.R.: A study on the phenomenon of affective adjectives with objects in modern Chinese. East China Normal University, Shanghai (2014). (in Chinese)
14. Yuan, Y.L.: A study of Chinese valence grammar. The Commercial Press, Beijing (2010). (in Chinese)
15. Shi, Y., Li, N.: A history of The process of grammaticalization in Chinese: motivation and mechanism of evolution of Chinese morpho-syntax. Peking University Press, Beijing (2001). (in Chinese)
16. Zhou, Sh.: On the grammaticalization of the preposition "dui". Linguist. Res. 1, 24–30 (2006). (in Chinese)
17. Zhou, W.H., Xiao, X.Q.: Object-introducing phrases headed by "Xiang" and "dui" their collections with predicate verbs. J. Nanjing Normal Univ. (Soc. Sci.) 5, 153–157 (2012). (in Chinese)
18. Deng, F.: On the source of "dui" having the recipient object of the whole sentence based on the Oracle Inscriptions and Bronze Inscriptions. J. Mianyang Teach. Coll. 10, 14–18 (2016). (in Chinese)
19. Li, X.J. (ed.): Dictionary of Modern Standard Chinese (3rd edition). Foreign Language Teaching and Research Press & Language and Culture Press, Beijing (2014). (In Chinese)
20. Ma, B.J.: Prepositions in modern Chinese. Zhonghua Book Company, Beijing (2002). (in Chinese)
21. Wu, F.X.: Current issue in the study of grammaticalization of Chinese. Linguist. Sci. 2, 20–32 (2005). (in Chinese)
22. Wang, E.X., Zhang, Z.: The pragmatic distribution and semantic explanation of evidential prepositions. In: Liu, M.J., et al. (eds.) Chinese Lexical Semantics. LNAI, vol. 13249, pp. 219–229. Springer, Cham (2021)

Construction of Grammar Collocation Library for International Chinese Language Education and Difficulty Standard

Yu Wang, Xingyu Hu, Xuan Mou, Endong Xun, and Gaoqi Rao(⊠)

Beijing Language and Culture University, Beijing 100083, China
202021198046@stu.blcu.edu.cn

Abstract. Grammar teaching is the focus of International Chinese Language Education, and grammar collocation resources play an essential role in promoting grammar teaching. Based on the three-dimensional grammar description of the formal structure, function, and typical context of the predecessors, this paper uses the BCC corpus to search the sentences of grammar points. This study explores a novel method to accurately acquire practical collocations and sample sentences in large quantities and constructs a collocational library containing 264 grammar points.

Keywords: International Chinese Language Education · Grammar Collocation · Collocation Library

1 Introduction

Grammar teaching is the key point and difficulty of the practice of International Chinese Language Education. Since Chinese lacks the morphological changes of the external display, its grammatical significance is more reflected by matching and word order. Under the influence of Generative Lexicon Theory and Construction Grammar Theory, the views of the Lexicalization of Grammer make the boundary between grammar teaching and vocabulary teaching more blurred. Based on these two reasons, grammar teaching is more conducted through grammatical words and their matching practice in most cases. Therefore, the construction of the grammar collocation library that is oriented to teaching practice and meets the difficulty requirements of the *Chinese Proficiency Grading Standards for International Chinese Language Education* (GF0025–2021, hereinafter referred to as the *Standards*) is of great significance in meeting the requirements for front-line teaching practice.

Based on the knowledge of the importance of the language of semantic acquisition [1, 2], the use of language [3, 4], and language learning [5], scholars of International Chinese Language Education have already started research on collocation [6] and proposed the concept of "collocational knowledge" [7]. That is to say, "collocational knowledge" is the storage and representation of a word relation system in learners' mental lexicon, composed of words and words that can form a specific collocative relationship with them

© The Author(s), under exclusive license to Springer Nature Switzerland AG 2023
Q. Su et al. (Eds.): CLSW 2022, LNAI 13495, pp. 77–90, 2023.
https://doi.org/10.1007/978-3-031-28953-8_7

in the process of use. Research on how to build collocation knowledge has gradually caught much scholarly attention, especially those on the construction of the word collocation knowledge base [8–11]. Some collocation libraries for intelligent service language applications pay attention to grammatical phenomena such as preposition structure collocation [12], VN collocation [13], and the semantic change and distribution of adjoining adverbs [14]. Coincidentally, some scholars have proposed the "grammatical teaching of vocabulary" [15] and the "lexis-grammar pedagogical model" [16], both of which have broken the boundaries of vocabulary teaching and grammar teaching. [17] believes these propositions are put forward from the perspective of grammar teaching. However, they attach importance to word collocation and usage as well as the role of chunks, which is conducive to promoting vocabulary and grammar teaching.

However, most current research on collocation knowledge and resource library construction focuses on language intelligence and Chinese ontology research, which weakens its applicability in International Chinese education. This weakness can be detected from two aspects: (1) the selection of the collocation library cannot fit the teaching, and it also lacks difficult control; (2) the construction and research of the current library are still limited to the scope of vocabulary research, with less attention paid to the support for grammar teaching. From the perspective of technology and corpus scale, the current research relies on more than a limited corpus scale, which is needed to reflect the real appearance of the real Chinese language life, and the adopted technology should also be improved. Given these reasons, this paper selects the largest online BCC corpus as the database, uses the BCC search strategy, adopts the *Standards* and *Trinitarian Grammar: Structure, Function, and Context: The Guidebook of Teaching Elementary and Intermediate Chinese Grammar Items* (hereinafter referred to as the *Trinitarian Grammar*) as the vocabulary sources, and uses the *Standards* as the difficulty control standard to explore the method of building a grammar collocation library for International Chinese Language Education.

2   Basic Data and Technical Methods

The data of this article is mainly based on the BCC corpus built by the Beijing Language and Culture University, and the BCC search strategy is used for data extraction.

2.1   BCC Corpus

With a total number of words of about 15 billion words, the BLCU Corpus Center (BCC) is a large-scale corpus that can fully reflect the linguistic landscape in contemporary China. As an online corpus with massive Chinese data, it is beneficial to language ontology and language application research [18]. Its extended version includes corpus in various fields, such as newspapers, literature, technology, and microblog. Moreover, the size of the data has reached 1.1 trillion words. This corpus can support complex queries integrating characters, attributes, and structural information, and with a fast retrieval speed.

The data of this paper is a sub-corpus specially constructed by the inner BCC corpus that aims to serve International Chinese Language Education. The type of corpus can be divided into four channels: subtitles of film and television, teaching materials for International Chinese Language Education, non-native language HSK compositions, and primary and secondary schools' compositions of native Chinese speakers.

2.2 BCC Search Strategy

BCC search strategy refers to the search specifications such as language units, grammar attribute attributes, syntax function, and structural relationships in the grammatical structure. It supports complex queries of characters, words, phrases, attributes, and structural information and can meet the demand for refined and large-scale corpus retrieval.

In the process of teaching in International Chinese Language Education, the text resources that meet the requirements of the clause structure in batches are the cornerstone of teaching activities. Take the "*piàoliang de* (beautiful) ~" as an example, and transform these linguistic needs into various symbols and parameters that BCC can understand (As shown in Fig. 1, the tree structure diagram of the example sentence after chunk structure analysis in BCC), formulate the corresponding BCC search strategy—NP-SBJ [*piàoliang de* (beautiful) ~] Freq, run the retrieval in the BCC to get the result. A total of 87 results were obtained under the channel of teaching materials for International Chinese Language Education. Such as: "*húdié* (Butterfly) 6, *hóngcǎi* (Rainbow) 3, *huā* (Flower) 10, *sàichē* (Racing) 1" (the number after a word is the frequency information in its corpus).

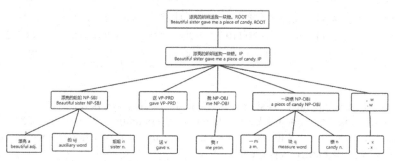

Fig. 1. The sentence "Sister's beautiful sister gave me a piece of sugar." Tree-shaped structural map.

3   The Experimental Data

This article selects the *Standards* and *Trinitarian Grammar* as the fundamental source of vocabulary and grammar formats, and the former has determined the reference standard for the difficulty.

3.1 The *Standards*

Since July 1, 2021, the *Standards* have been officially implemented as a language standard of the State Language Commission, which has caused a tremendous response. The *Standards* facilitates building resources for International Chinese Language Education in the post-epidemic era.

Based on the grammar point[1] and the difficulty level information provided by the *Standards*, this article builds a grammar collocation library. The grammatical syllabus of the *Standards* adopts a three-stage-nine-level arrangement method, focusing on coordination with syllables, Chinese characters, vocabulary, and other linguistic elements [19]. It is an introduction and analysis of the grading of grammar and vocabulary in the *Standards* (Table 1 from the *Standards*).

Table 1. General List of Language Quantitative Indicators of the *Standards*.[2]

Stage	Level	Syllable	Characters	Vocabulary	Grammar
Elementary	Level 1	269	300	500	48
	Level 2	199/468	300/600	772/1272	81/129
	Level 3	140/608	300/900	973/2245	81/210
Medium	Level 4	116/724	300/1200	1000/3245	76/286
	Level 5	98/822	300/1500	1071/4316	71/357
	Level 6	86/908	300/1800	1140/5456	67/424
High	Level 7–9	202/1110	1200/3000	5636/11092	148/572
Total		1110	3000	11092	572

In terms of vocabulary, as shown in Table 1, the increase is relatively stable. One of the reasons is that student's knowledge and understanding of vocabulary cannot be separated from teaching Chinese characters. And the size of Chinese characters has increased by 300 characters per level.

In terms of grammar points, we can also see in Table 1 that the increased amount decreases step by step. This is to match other language elements and to strictly control the number of new grammar points learned at each level so that in the future grammar testing and teaching can achieve the goal of "*shù liàng jiǎn bàn* (halving the number of grammar items)" and "*jí yòng xiān xué* (prioritizing the learning of grammar points

---

[1] Grammar point is a term redefined in this paper according to the minimum principle of modern Chinese grammar items. We assume that in teaching practice if a grammar item is not the smallest teaching unit but can be further divided, the grammar item needs to be divided into the smallest teaching unit. And this smallest teaching unit can be named a grammar unit.

[2] As for the "/" in the table, the previous numbers indicate the number of new language elements in this level, and the number of the later numbers represents the number of language elements accumulated in this level. Higher language quantification indicators are no longer subdivided by level.

needed for communication)" [20]. Classifying graded and quantitative grammar points is helpful to classroom teaching and constructing a resource library. For example, the positional nouns "*shàng* (up), *xià* (down), *lǐ* (inside), and *wài* (outside)" belong to Level 1 grammar, and the verb "*kěnéng* (may) and *kéyǐ* (can)" belong to Level 2 grammar. Teachers can choose the level of grammar points according to the stage of Chinese learners. For the grammatical collocation library, the classification of grammar points can assist in building an orderly collocation library and help teachers extract collocation knowledge quickly.

In addition to classifying grammar points, the *Standards* rank each level of grammar points at three levels (those without the three levels are treated according to the actual number of levels). The first level category has 12 items: morpheme, word class, phrase, fixed format, sentence component, and so on. The grading and classification system of grammar points is conducive to locating grammar points outside the grammar outline. For example, when some grammar points are not included in the corresponding level, the specialist can use the system to restrict the category and rank of the grammar points according to their characteristics to build a grammar library based on the category and rank information.

However, the *Standards* is only a guiding document rather than a teaching grammar manual that meets the teaching process. The grammatical points in *Standards* only give a few grammatical examples sentences without putting forward how to use specific syntactic structures and structures.

3.2 The *Trinitarian Grammar*

Trinitarian Grammar is the carrier of Trinitarian Grammar, serving grammar teaching at elementary and intermediate levels. Trinitarian Grammar is a new model of teaching and learning Chinese proposed by Feng Shengli [21].

The basic framework of this model includes three dimensions: the structure of sentences, the function of the structure, and the contexts of the structure and the function used in Mandarin Chinese. The structure of sentences is mainly based on the inductive structure, which adopts the description method of "symbol format + marker word". For example, the formal structure of the *Bei*-sentence can be summarized as "A + *bèi* (by) + B + V + R". The function of the structure is mainly to summarize the grammatical function of the grammar point. And "*bié* (do not)" functions are used to express in-person discouragement, reminder or comfort, and courtesy. The contexts of the structure and function refer to the contexts selected and refined based on learners' cognitive experience and learning stage. For example, the context of "clause + ne (auxiliary word)" includes life and weather, which mainly describes "what is it, what to do, and where to use" [21, 22].

According to the principle of practicability and systematization, 264 elementary and intermediate Chinese grammar points are selected as research objects, and the three-dimensional information is explained and interpreted one by one, including 166 lexical grammar points, 93 lexical chunks grammar points, and five sentence patterns grammar points. Each grammar point is equipped with one or more structures, each structure is associated with one or more functions, each function corresponds to one or more contexts, and each context is equipped with several example sentences. The book contains

456 structures, 275 functions, 667 classical contexts, and 1882 example sentences. For example, the three-dimensional description of the grammatical point Ba-sentence is as follows (excerpt):

Structure: A + *bǎ* (to grasp; to hold) + B + V + R/PP
Function: Used to express the movement of an object or the result of an action.
Context: Related to the shift/result.

Besides, the three-dimensional description information can be connected to the *Standards* through the grammar point, and each grammar point is endowed with corresponding level information. For example, the grammar point "*néng* (can)" is a first-level grammar point in the *Standards*, so teachers can use the three-dimensional information to teach the grammar point "*néng* (can)" in the primary stage.

4   Mining and Extraction of Collocation Knowledge

In this paper, we use the information provided by the *Standards* and *Trinitarian Grammar* to construct a grammatical collocation library system from the perspective of grammatical item levels and types. Specifically, the *Standards*, as a national normative document, provides only the content and typical examples of grammar points, but the formal and symbolic formal structure of grammar points is required to obtain an accurate corpus with the help of the BCC search strategy, and the information of this document is obviously insufficient. For example, in "passive sentences", the *Standards* gives five types of passive sentences and corresponding example sentences, such as the form "*bèi* (by) ... *suǒ* (auxiliary word) ......" with a difficulty scale of seven to nine, and the sentence "*zhè shì wǒ dìyīcì gǎndào zìjǐ bèi yī gè rén suǒ xīyǐn.* (This is the first time I've ever felt attracted by a person.)" But this kind of information is insufficient to support the batch and accurately obtain the teaching example of the "passive sentences".

This deficiency can be improved by referring to the interpretation of grammar points in *Trinitarian Grammar*. It can be seen from Sect. 3.2 that grammar points included in *Trinitarian Grammar* cover the three-dimensional description information. This information helps to translate grammar points into BCC search strategy and use function and contexts to adjust the search strategy to obtain results that meet the requirements.

Therefore, based on the level and classification information of grammar points provided by the *Standards*, this paper takes 264 grammar points supplied by the *Trinitarian Grammar* as the starting point of the work, and the three dimensions of structure, function, and context provided by the book as the reference basis for the construction of the grammar collocation library. The three-dimensional linguistic description is transformed and written into the BCC search strategy, which is used to extract grammar collocation knowledge and construct a grammar collocation library. When this part of the work is completed, the grammar points not involved in *Trinitarian Grammar* in the *Standards* are extended with the help of this achievement and experience, and the BCC search strategy is also formulated for these grammar points to expand the content of the grammar collocation library.

4.1 Mining Method

In the construction process of the grammar collocation library, this paper integrates the advantages of the grammar level outline in the *Standards* and the *Trinitarian Grammar* to carry out the construction work: With the levels and categories in the *Standards* as the construction framework, and the three-dimensional interpretation information of the grammar points in *Trinitarian Grammar* as the content elements, the vocabulary level is used to control the relative difficulty of sentences, and sentences with level information are provided to assist the International Chinese Language Education practice better.

Taking the Level and Category as the Construction Framework. The *Standards* contains a detailed classification of a three-stage-nine-level arrangement. So, this paper aligns the difficulty level of grammar points in *Trinitarian Grammar* with the *Standards*. For grammar points with missing level difficulty information, the level of grammar points with the same category information is used to determine the level difficulty. In this paper, we adopt a three-dimensional approach to build a grammar collocation database classification system based on the grammar item classification information of the *Standards* so as to build a framework for the grammar collocation library by using levels and categories to complement each other. At the same time, we also assimilated the three-dimensional description of grammar points in *Trinitarian Grammar* to supplement the content elements of grammar points in the grammar collocation library. So, the corresponding resource processing flow is constructed in this paper (as shown in Fig. 2).

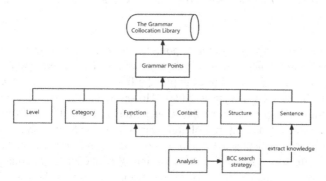

Fig. 2. The process of resource processing.

Teachers can get the corresponding level, formal structure, example sentences, and other information from grammar points based on a grammar collocation library. The corresponding BCC search strategy can be used to obtain a more dynamic corpus for teaching practice when necessary.

Use Vocabulary Levels to Control the Difficulty. The *Standards* emphasize the harmonization of grammar point levels with syllables, Chinese characters, vocabulary, and other linguistic elements, that is to say, "syllables, Chinese characters and especially words in each level of grammar points and their example sentences should be at the same level as the corresponding grammar points" [20]. Difficulty dislocation often occurs in the existing research on collocation knowledge in the academic field: the extracted corpus from low-level grammar points is composed of high-level words or a mixture of high-level and low-level words. Although certain superclass vocabulary is allowed in teaching, it is inappropriate to only provide high-difficulty sentences when teaching low-difficulty grammar points, which reduces the utilization degree of collocation knowledge and user experience.

For this reason, this paper adds one more part to the work path of "grammar point analysis → BCC search strategy writing → extraction of corresponding corpus" from the viewpoint of students' acceptability [20]: to provide word rank information for the extracted sentences, to match the extracted corpus with the grammar point rank as much as possible, and to attach word level information to the sentences for users' reference.

4.2 Collocation Extraction

In this paper, the data mining process is divided into two stages. The first stage is to build the seed grammar points collocation based on *Trinitarian Grammar*, and the second stage is to expand the grammar points in the *Standards* based on the results of the first stage.

To Build the Seed Grammar Points Collocation. In the first stage, this paper mainly collates and merges the grammar and vocabulary list in *Standards* and the grammar format in *Trinitarian Grammar* and carries out BCC search strategy writing. The steps are as follows.

Step 1: Add information about grammar point levels and grammar item categories.
The grade information of *Standards* determines the grade information of grammar points in *Trinitarian Grammar*. For example, the Ba-sentence in *Trinitarian Grammar* has a corresponding level of 3 in the *Standards*. However, the grade information should be temporarily empty if there is no corresponding grammar point in the *Standards*. In terms of categories, the detailed categories of grammar point in the *Standards* are not suitable for transformation into machine data for the time being. Therefore, category classification is carried out in the form of lexical grammar points, lexical chunks grammar points, and sentence patterns grammar points. For example, the category of the Ba-sentence is a sentence patterns grammar point.
Step 2: Write the BCC search strategy. The final determination of each retrieval mode must go through three rounds of inspection by two people, from the grammar point of three-dimensional description to the search strategy.
Step 2.1: The first person analyzes the information on lexical and syntactic blocks corresponding to the structure of grammar points and sorts out the exact POS sequence + syntactic structure.
Step 2.2: Write the BCC search strategy for the structure, and then dynamically adjust the search strategy according to the contextual results extracted from the BCC corpus so that the results can be as close as possible to the functional role and typical context of the form where the grammar points are located.

Step 2.3: The second person checks whether the result of the BCC search strategy is consistent with the three-dimensional description of grammar points: for the consistent grammar point, the grammar point example sentences are extracted in the internal corpus of BCC, and 100 sentences are extracted for each retrieval formula; after discussing the inconsistent grammar point to reach an agreement, the BCC search strategy is rewritten, and then the example sentences are extracted for the grammar point again.

To illustrate the above steps, we can take the grammar point of "Ba-sentence" in *Trinitarian Grammar* as an example: When the Ba-sentence is used to express the shift of objects and the result caused by the shift, its structure is "A + *bǎ* (to grasp; to hold) + B + V + R (general complement)/PP (place component)". After three rounds of processing, its corresponding BCC search strategy is:

NULL-MOD [*bǎ* ~] VP-PRD [] { } Context.

The overall meaning of this search strategy is to obtain the context in which the prepositional phrase is composed of the preposition "*bǎ* (to grasp; to hold)", and its introductory elements are used as modifiers to modify the predicate block. In the search strategy, "NULL-MOD" is the modifier chunk, "VP-PRD" is the predicate chunk, "[]" represents the range of a chunk, "~ " represents any word, and "Context" represents the Context corresponding to the output retrieval requirement. We can obtain the results under the current description limitation of the word "*bǎ* (to grasp; to hold)" by using this search strategy. Its results in the BCC corpus under the channel of teaching materials for International Chinese Language Education are as follows (the number before a sentence is the label of the sentence in the corpus, and the retrieval content is between two "<Q>").

436996_*Tā zhǐ le zhǐ mén, shìyì wǒ* <Q> *bǎ mén guān shàng* </Q>.
436996_She pointed to the door and motioned for me to close it.
188504_*Tā* <Q> *bǎ mén kāi le* </Q> *yì tiáo fèng, bìng qù wūlǐ bǎ yīnxiǎng de yīnliàng tiáo xiǎo le xǔduō.*
188504_He opened the door and went inside to turn down the stereo a lot.
404608_*Kěshì, tā* <Q> *bǎ tóu mái le* </Q> *xià qu.*
404608_But she buried her head.
466038_*Shuōwán, tā*<Q> *bǎ tóu mái* </Q> *zài wǒ de xīgài shàng.*
466038_Then he buried his head in my lap.
188927_*Yīqiè dōu ànzhào yìngyǒu de chéngxù* <Q> *bǎ jiǔ dǎkāi* </Q>, *zuò xià lái yìbiān tánhuà yìbiān chī dōngxi.*
188927_ Everything goes the way it's supposed to go opening the wine, sitting down and eating while we talk.
......

Grammar Point Extension. There are 572 grammar points in the *Standards* and 264 for elementary and intermediate Chinese learners in *Trinitarian Grammar*. The range of grammar points is quite different between them. The three-dimensional description of grammar points in *Trinitarian Grammar* is a scientific and referential description system. Therefore, this paper will fully use the experience and achievements in the first stage of collocation library construction based on *Trinitarian Grammar* to write the three-dimensional description for the rest of the grammar points in the *Standards*.

We can not only extract relatively correct grammatical structures from the grammatical example sentences in the *Standards* but also rely on the vast corpus data of BCC to continuously verify the correctness of grammatical and structural formulas, further supplement the function and context of grammar points, and constantly correct errors to ensure the relatively accurate three-dimensional description of grammar points. Then, the work in the first stage is repeated to build a comprehensive foundation of grammar collocation. In the future, more grammar points will be collected constantly to enrich the foundation of the grammar collocation library so that it can meet the needs of various aspects.

5   Results Analysis

5.1   The Result of the Extraction

Two hundred sixty-four grammar points are transformed from a three-dimensional description into formal and symbolic BCC search strategy, with a total of 576 search strategies by investigating the three-dimensional description of structure, function, and context of grammar points in *Trinitarian Grammar*. The transformation process has been introduced in the previous article and will not be described in detail.

For 264 grammar points, all the three-round verification work has been completed, and batch extraction has been completed under the four channels of the BCC corpus. Table 2 shows the distribution of results.

Table 2. Distribution Table of the number of extracted sentences in *Trinitarian Grammar*.

BCC corpus channel name	Number of sentences	Average number of sentences for grammar points
Subtitles of film and television	22729	85
Textbook for International Chinese Language Education	15660	59
HSK compositions for the non-native language	27698	105
Primary and secondary schools' compositions of native Chinese speakers	50021	189
Total	116108	–

5.2   Results Analysis

Here are the analyzes of the results of the collocation library constructed from the level of difficulty, the quantity of content, the quality of results, and the application scenarios in this paper.

First, as for the difficulty level of the collocation library, the work in this stage is to build the grammar collocation library based on the grammar points in *Trinitarian Grammar*. This book is aimed at Chinese learners at the level of elementary and intermediate, and its grammar points are mainly lexical forms, such as "*āi* (suffer)" "*ràng* (let)", and "*jiào* (by)", but a few grammar points are more abstract, such as passive sentences. Therefore, the results of the collocation library constructed are also oriented to the elementary and intermediate stages at present. To make the results easier to use in teaching, we add word-level information to all the results of the example sentences to associate grammar points with sentence, structure, function, context, source, type, level, and other information. Part of the results is shown below with the word Ba sentence as an example.

yǔfǎ diǎn: bǎ zì jù
Grammar point: Ba sentence
xíngshì jiégòu: A+ *bǎ* +B+V+R *(yìbān búyǔ)/PP (dìdiǎnxìng chéngfen)*
Structure: A + *bǎ* (to grasp; to hold) + B + V + R/PP
gōngnéng zuòyòng: yòng lái biǎodá wùtǐ de yíwèi huò xíngwéi yǐnfā de jiéguǒ
Function: Used to express the movement of an object or the result of an action
diǎnxíng yǔjìng: hé yíwèi/jiéguǒ yǒuguān de
Context: Related to the shift/result
jùzi wénběn: 436996_tā zhǐ le zhǐ mén, shìyì wǒ <Q> bǎ mén guān shàng </Q>.
Sentence: 436996_ She pointed to the door and motioned for me to close it.
láiyuán chūchù: chénggōngzhīlù tígāopiān dìyícè/L3 xióngmāobàba – Pān Wénshí
Source: The Road to Success Volume 1/L3 Panda Father – Pan Wenshi
cíyǔ děngjí: Tā/1 zhǐ/3 le/3 zhǐ/3 mén/1, shìyì/7 wǒ/1 bǎ/3 mén/1 guānshàng/1.
Level: She/1 points to/3 and/3 points to/3 door/1, indicating/7 I/1 close/1 to/3 door/1.
jùzi wénběn: 404608_Kěshì, tā <Q> bǎ tóu mái le </Q> xià qu.
Sentence: 404608_ But she buried her head.
láiyuán chūchù: chénggōngzhīlù chénggōngpiān dìèrcè/L10 xībù cǎifēng
Source: The Road to Success Volume 2/L10 The West
cíyǔ děngjí: Kěshì/2, tā/1 bǎ/3 tóu/3 mái/6 le/3 xià qu/3.
Level: But/2, she/1 buried/6 her/1 head/3.
......

Second, from the perspective of the content quantity of the collocation library, the grammar collocation library constructed in this work currently contains 264 grammar points and 576 BCC search strategies, with an average of 202 sentences in each search strategy and an average of 440 sentences in each grammar point. This scale can support the teaching and research use of international Chinese teachers at the elementary and intermediate levels. For example, there are 36 primary grammar points in *ERYA ZHONGWEN CHUJI HANYU ZONGHE JIAOCHENG (SHANG) 1* (37 grammar points are involved in the whole book), which can be queried in the grammar collocation library constructed in this paper.

Third, as for the perspective of the quality of the results of the collocation library, the corpus is derived from International Chinese Language Education, including subtitles of film and television, the textbook for International Chinese Language Education, HSK compositions for the non-native language, and primary and secondary schools' compositions of native Chinese speakers, etc. The corpus source is not only standardized and reliable but also actively absorbs the corpus commonly used in modern Chinese society. The corpus is analyzed by Part-of-speech tagging and chunk models in BCC, and the sentence structure is retrieved by the BCC to make the quality of results credible. Take the lexical grammar point "*zuì* (most)" as an example, when its function is "used to express the comparison with others", there are two common formal structures: *zuì* (most) + *xíngróngcí* (adjective), *zuì* (most) + *dòngcí* (verb). Taking "*zuì* (most) + *xíngróngcí* (adjective)" as an example, the retrieval results of the grammar points are as follows (excerpts).

Teaching materials for teaching Chinese as a foreign language channel extraction result:

384052_<Q>Zuì huálì </Q> de jiànzhù, yě shì xiǎngxiàng zhōng lí tiān zuì jìn de dìfang.
384052_The most gorgeous building, but also the closest to the sky in the imagination.
487874_<Q> Zuì jiǎndān </Q> de wènfǎ "shì nǐ duō dà"?
487874_The easiest way to ask is "How old are you"?
......
Non-native language HSK compositions channel extraction results:
6435278_<Q> Zuì líxiǎng </Q> de jiātíng.
6435278_The ideal family.
6446822_<Q> Zuì làngmàn </Q> de fāngshì.
6446822_The most romantic way.
......

Fourth, from the perspective of the application of the collocation library, it not only directly facilitates teachers but also benefits students. More than 400 example sentences in each grammar point can help teachers eliminate the problem of example sentences being insufficient in textbooks and complicated and challenging to obtain corpus on Internet platforms. Grammar points are associated with sentence, structure, function, context, source, type, level, and other information (as shown in Fig. 3), which significantly increases the usability of this grammar collocation library: The association of structure can facilitate teachers to practice the same sentence pattern, and facilitate students to learn and practice the same sentence pattern, and help students increase the accumulation of collocation knowledge; The relationship between function and context will enrich teachers' classroom content. The connection of provenance sources makes the result more accessible for the teacher to win the trust. The association of types and levels helps teachers to select grammar points conveniently and example sentences in line with students' learning stages.

This figure is a schematic diagram of the correlation between the attribute information of the grammar points in the grammar collocation library. The six attributes on the dotted circle can be directly related to each other, and each attribute is directly related to the grammar point.

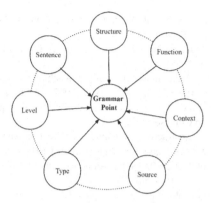

Fig. 3. Schematic diagram of grammar points associated with their attributes

6 Conclusion

Based on the idea of the three-dimensional interpretation of grammar points in the form structure, function, and context provided by *Trinitarian Grammar*, this paper took the grammar word list provided by the *Standards* as the difficulty control method. This paper, combined with the BCC search strategy, explored the method of batch and accurate acquisition of practical collocation of specified grammar points, and associated grammar points with sentence, structure, function, context, source, type, level, and other information. This paper tries to expand the idea of *Trinitarian Grammar* to more grammar points in the analysis process so that we can get more grammar points collocation knowledge suitable for teaching. As for the analysis of current practice, this method is feasible.

Further interpretation of the remaining grammatical points and the extraction of example sentences in the *Standards* is needed, as our study will address in the future. The results of this paper will be shared with the academic community later.

Acknowledgments. Project supported by The National Natural Science Foundation of China, "Study on the Characterization and Generation Method of Chinese Parataxis Graph" (No. 62076038).

References

1. Benson, M., Benson, E., Ilson, R.: The BBI combinatory dictionary of English: a guide to word combinations. John Benjamins Publishing Company, Amsterdam; Philadelphia (1986)
2. Firth, J.: A synopsis of linguistic theory 1930–1955. Studies in Linguistic Analysis. Oxford the Philological Society (1957)
3. Church, K.W., Hanks, P.: Word association norms, mutual information, and lexicography. In: Proceedings of the 27th Annual Meeting on Association for Computational Linguistics, Vancouver, British Columbia, Canada, pp. 76–83. Association for Computational Linguistics (1989). https://doi.org/10.3115/981623.981633

4. Zhang, S., Lin, X.: Dictionary of Modern Chinese Content Words Collocation. The Commercial Press, Beijing (1992). (in Chinese)
5. Lin, X.: Theory of word collocation and its research. Lang. Teach. Linguist. Stud. (04), 18–25 (1994).(in Chinese)
6. Zhou, X.: The study of collocation and the study of teaching Chinese as a second language. Doctor, Shanghai International Studies University (2007).(in Chinese)
7. Xing, H.: Collocation knowledge and second language lexical acquisition. Appl. Linguist. (04), 117–126 (2013). (in Chinese)
8. Hu, R., Xiao, H.: The construction of Chinese collocation knowledge bases and their application in second language acquisition. Appl. Linguist. (01), 135–144 (2019). (in Chinese)
9. Qian, X.: Construction of the knowledge base of notional word collocation for TCSOL. Appl. Linguist. 04, 132–142 (2020).(in Chinese)
10. Wang, S., Yang, J., Zhang, W.: Automatic acquisition of Chinese collocation. J. Int. Chin. Teach. **20**(06), 31–37 (2006). (in Chinese)
11. Wei, N.: Corpus-based and corpus-driven approaches to the study of collocation. Contemp. Linguisti. (02), 101–114+157 (2002).(in Chinese)
12. Xing, D., Rao, G., Xun, E., Wang, C.: Large-scale corpus based preposition structure collocation base. J. Chin. Inf. Process. **11**, 1–8 (2020). (in Chinese)
13. Wang, G., Rao, G., Xun, E.: Construction of verb-object knowledge base from BCC corpus. J. Chin. Inf. Process. (01), 34–42+53 (2021).(in Chinese)
14. Shao, T., Wang, C., Rao, G., Xun, E.: The semantic change and distribution of adjoining adverbs in modern Chinese. In: Su, Q., Zhan, W. (eds.) From Minimal Contrast to Meaning Construct. FCL, vol. 9, pp. 149–163. Springer, Singapore (2020). https://doi.org/10.1007/978-981-32-9240-6_11
15. Wu, Y.: The problem of "generative lexicon" in Chinese grammar teaching as a second language. TCSOL Stud. (04), 14–18 (2002).(in Chinese)
16. Li, X.: On the construction of a pedagogical model for Chinese L2 lexical-syntax teaching. Lang. Teach. Linguist. Stud. (01), 23–29 (2004).(in Chinese)
17. Li, R.: An overview of the vocabulary teaching of teaching Chinese as a second language in recent years. TCSOL Stud. (02), 32–45+51 (2017).(in Chinese)
18. Xun, E., Rao, G., Xiao, X., Zang, J.: The construction of the BCC corpus in the age of big data. Corpus Linguist. (01), 93–109+118 (2016).(in Chinese)
19. Jin, H., Ying, C.: The development principle of grammar grade outline for Chinese proficiency level standards. J. Int. Chin. Teach. (03), 12–22 (2021). (in Chinese)
20. Wang, H.: The path of the grammar grading outline and the development of the grammar grading resource database of chinese proficiency grading standards for international Chinese language education. J. Int. Chin. Teach. (03), 23–36+45 (2021).(in Chinese)
21. Feng, S., Shi, C.: Trinitarian Grammar: Structure, Function and Context: The Guidebook of Teaching Elementary and Intermediate Chinese Grammar Items. Peking University Press, Beijing (2015). (in Chinese)
22. Feng, S., Shi, C.: Trinitarian grammar in teaching and learning Chinese. Linguist. Sci. (05), 464–472 (2011). (in Chinese)

The Study of Causal Nouns in Mandarin Chinese: From the Perspective of Syntactic Realization and Pragmatic Function

Xin Kou[✉]

Shandong University, Jinan 250100, Shandong, China

Abstract. Causal nouns can express two types of information, namely, the cause and the effect. These two types of information can be realized in different syntactic positions in the sentence and discourse where causal nouns appear. This paper first explains the definition of the information of cause and effect in causal nouns and proposes syntactic standards to distinguish them. Then, by describing and summarizing the distribution and combination of cause information and effect information in the texts and sentences, it is found that there are syntactic differences between the two types of information of causal nouns. Finally, in terms of pragmatics, based on the comparison with the causal conjunction *"yinwei"* (because), the study discovered that the causal noun tends to appear in the formal style. Besides, causal nouns can achieve the coordination of foreground and background information, regulate the amount of information and arouse the expectation of listeners.

Keywords: Causal nouns · Syntactic realization · Causal relation · Pragmatic function

1 Introduction

Causal nouns are usually regarded as abstract nouns which summarize the factors that lead to effects. Typical causal nouns include 原因 (cause), 因由 (reason), 缘故 (cause), 根源 (source), 理由 (reason), 动机 (motivation) and so on. The previous studies found that the self-referential *De*-structure formed by causal nouns can be divided into two types, i.e. cause meaning and effect meaning, according to the relationship between the VP in the *De*-structure and the causal noun [1–5], such as (1).

(1) a. 生病的原因

   the cause of illness
   b. 由于生病的原因, 现在只能请假在家。(Cause meaning)
   Due to illness, I can only take time off at home now.
   c. 导致生病的原因是着凉。(Effect meaning)
   The cause of illness is the cold.
   The VP 生病 (sickness/fall ill) in (1a) can be interpreted as the content of the cause in (1b). In this interpretation, 生病的原因 (the cause of sickness) can be transformed to

© The Author(s), under exclusive license to Springer Nature Switzerland AG 2023
Q. Su et al. (Eds.): CLSW 2022, LNAI 13495, pp. 91–102, 2023.
https://doi.org/10.1007/978-3-031-28953-8_8

the cause of something is sickness. Simultaneously, 生病 in (1a) can also be interpreted as an effect of a cause such as (1c). It can be seen from (1) that although causal nouns are usually studied as abstract nouns together with *fact* and *thing* which can only form the self-referential structure with content meaning VP, their semantic structures are different from each other. Moreover, the distinction is not only reflected in the modifier structures of causal nouns, but also represents in other syntactic structures and discourse. In the aspect of discourse coherence, abstract nouns play important roles. Because of the semantic vacancy, abstract nouns are usually used to refer to specific content. So they are also called *shell nouns* or *signal nouns* in related studies. Abstract nouns can function as two kinds of reference, anaphora and cataphora, according to the textual appearance order of abstract nouns and the content they refer to. Some researches argued that abstract nouns are mainly used to package the content they refer to [6–8]. Wang Xiuli [9] proposed that the referential function of abstract nouns is *resomptif anaphore*, which means "abstractly generalize the preceding information". However, as for causal nouns, due to their complex semantic components, the discourse function of causal nouns is more various, and they can be used to correlate two events (cause and effect). For example:

(2) 这一问题不能得到圆满解决，可能有两个原因。一是把两种城镇化的地域尺度混在一起。二是把反映城镇化不同侧面的指标混在一起。

This problem cannot be solved satisfactorily for two *reasons*. One is to mix the two urbanization scales together. The second is to mix together indicators that reflect different aspects of urbanization.

In (2), 原因 (cause) is related to the effect "this problem cannot be satisfactorily solved", meanwhile it also refers to the two causes which is the content of 原因. It can be seen that causal nouns are different from general abstract nouns in that the semantic structures of the former are richer. Therefore, the syntactic and discourse distribution of the two types of information, content meaning and effect meaning, is more complex. This paper will focus on investigating the differences between the distribution of the content meaning and the effect meaning of causal nouns in discourse, exploring how the effect information and content information are syntactically realized. Moreover, the paper will also discuss the coding preference of the two kinds of information of causal nouns. Finally, the difference between the causal noun 原因 (cause) and the causal conjunction 因为 (because) will be analyzed in terms of discourse functions.

2 The Semantic Information of Causal Nouns

2.1 Content Information and Effect Information

As mentioned above, causal nouns contain content meaning and effect meaning. The former describes the content of the cause, and the latter is the effect associated with the noun. Therefore, the content meaning can be diagnosed by the transformation of *N is VP*. In general, the causal noun and its content event can form this construction. For example:

(3) a. 得刚才院长讲的非常好，我是听得挺有味道，大概因为<u>不懂技术的原因</u>。

What the dean just said is very good. And I really enjoy it, probably because I do not understand the technology.

b. 原因是不懂技术。

The reason is that I don't understand the technology.

The content of 原因 (reason) is "I don't understand the technology". Only the content meaning of nouns can constitute the *be*-structure. The effect information of causal nouns is forbidden to appear in the construction, e.g. "*The reason is that I really enjoy it." The information indicating the effect meaning is usually linked to causal nouns by other predicates rather than *be* [4], such as in (4a-b):

(4) a. 原来她的憔悴尚有许多因由。

It turned out that there were many reasons for her haggardness.

b. 导致机器无法正常工作的缘故有很多。

There are many reasons why a machine may not work properly.

In (4), the effect information can occur in the structures VP/NP *you* N and *Daozhi* VP *de* N. Therefore, the different syntactic realization of content and effect information of causal nouns can be used as criterions for distinguishing the two kinds of information. Based on the analysis above, we conclude the two syntactic features as the criterions:

A. If a VP can enter the structure N *be* VP, and the VP and N can be only connected with predicates such as *be, say, express, lie in*, then the information represented by VP is the content information of the causal noun.

B. If a VP can enter the structure of VP/NP *has* N and *Cause* VP *de* N, and the VP cannot use *be* to connect with N, then the information represented by VP is the effect information of the causal noun.

2.2 Syntactic Distribution of Effect Information

We selected 12 causal nouns, i.e. 原因(reason), 原委(reason), 根源(root), 来源(source), 来由(origin), 根由(root cause), 因由(reason), 情由(emotion), 缘由(reason), 原由(reason), 缘故(reason), 原故(reason), and search them in the CCL corpus. A total of 150 data were extracted. Through the analysis of these data, the syntactic realization and discourse distribution of content information and effect information of the causal nouns are summarized. The distribution of effect information can be classified into the following categories:

Within Sentences. The effect information and the causal noun can be connected by a predicate, in which, the effect information functions as subject. For example:

(5) 这千奇百怪的现象之所以都出现在此地, 定有缘由。

There must be a reason why all these strange phenomena appear here.

(6) 这一问题不能得到圆满解决可能有两个原因。

There may be two reasons why this issue cannot be satisfactorily resolved.

The effect information and causal nouns can also be linked by causal conjunctions. In such structures, effect information usually appears in subsequent positions, constituting the structure as *due to/for* N + VP:

(7) 出于同样的原因, urbanization也被翻译为城市化。

For the same *reason*, urbanization is also translated as *chengshihua*.

(8) 由于这个原故, 希腊人就围绕着城邦而组织其社会, 与中国社会制度形成对照
。

Due to this *reason*, the Greeks organized their society around the city-state, in contrast to the Chinese social system.

Effect information and causal nouns can also form nominal modifier constructions, in which the effect information appears as the attributive clause:

(9) 关于曹雪芹的族属与家世、曹家被抄的缘由等红学界争论多年悬而未决的
问题, 亦因发现了有关满文资料迎刃而解。

The unresolved issues that have been debated in the red academic circles for many years, such as Cao Xueqin's clan and family background, and the *reason* why Cao's family was raided, were also solved by the discovery of relevant Manchu data.

(10) 忧虑死亡的到来, 是人类不幸的主要来源。

Anxiety about death is the main *source* of human misery.

There is also a case where anaphoric pronouns of the effect information function as modifier of causal nouns. For example:

(11) 日本前首相福田赳夫说: “资源少的我国, 经历诸多考验, 得以在短期内建成
今日之日本, 其原因在于国教育水平和教育普及的提高。”

Former Japanese Prime Minister Takeo Fukuda said: "Our country, which has few resources, has gone through many challenges and has been able to build today's Japan in a short period of time. The *reason* is the improvement of national education level and education popularization."

Across Sentences. The causal noun and its effect information can appear over sentences, and there is no correlative word to mark their logical relationship. Usually, causal nouns refer back to the effect information, such as in (12–13):

(12) 有些不良的社会风气屡禁不止, 原因固然很多, 但一个重要的原因是劳动者
素质低。

There is a lot of adverse social environment, for which there are many *reasons*. Among them, an important one is the low quality of laborers.

(13) 资本主义社会的教育比奴隶社会的教育、封建社会的
教育发展得快、规模大, 根本原因是采用机器生产, 社会财富有了迅猛的增
加, 同时要求具有一定文化科学知识的人去从事生产。

Education in capitalist society develops faster and on a larger scale than education in slave society and feudal society. For this phenomenon the fundamental reason is that machine production is used, social wealth has increased rapidly, and people with certain cultural and scientific knowledge are required to engage in production.

2.3 Syntactic Distribution of Content Information

Through analyzing the data of causal nouns, the distribution of content information of causal nouns can be classified into the following categories:

Within Sentences. Causal nouns can serve as subjects or objects, and are connected with content information by predicates such as 是 (is) and 在于 (is). For example:

(14) 造成上述两方面问题的根本原由是国家科学技术力量薄弱。

The fundamental *reason* for the above two problems is the weakness of the country in science and technology.

(15) 在众说纷纭的诸多主张中, 一个重要的观点认为, 根本原因在于教育落后。

Among the many claims with different opinions, an important point is that the fundamental *reason* is that the education is backward.

Content information can also be used as attributives of causal nouns. For example:

(16) 由于历史的原因, 目前作为过渡学制将长期存在。

Due to historical *reasons*, the current transitional school system will exist for a long time.

(17) 不足的是, 因为刚刚松绑的缘故, 对意识流手法的运用还比较生硬。

The downside is that the use of stream-of-consciousness techniques is still relatively rigid because of the just loosening of the binding.

Across Sentences. When the content information and the causal noun do not appear in a sentence together, the content information usually appears in the subsequent sentences of the sentence includes a causal noun. In discourse analysis, this phenomenon is called cataphora.

(18) 如果企业真的想留住人, 要看员工离职的原因是哪一类。做得不开心、不看好前景, 在公司内部就可以解决。

Whether a company can retain talents depends on what kind of reasons employees leave. If the reason is unhappiness and no hope, these problems can be solved within the company.

(19) 我未假思索地回答: 我会选择权力。原因很简单: 获得权力, 是个人能力的表现; 掌握权力, 可以使我实现许多梦想, 完成许多我想做的事情。

I answered without hesitation: I would choose power. The reason is simple: gaining power is an expression of personal ability. And having power allows me to achieve many dreams and accomplish many things I want to do.

Without Content Information. Unlike effect information, content information can be absent in discourse. That is to say, the cause has no specific content. For example:

(20) 企业里并最终操起刀斧, 是智力优秀分子命运的沦落, 而这种沦落, 因由非在陆步轩本人。

The enterprise reformed radically, which is the fall of reduced the outstanding intellectuals. But the *reason* for this misery is not Lu Buxuan himself.

(21) 纵然"绿条"形成有种种情由, 欠账也是暂时的, 但和"白条"一样, "绿条"有损广大农民的利益。

Although there are various *reasons* for the formation of "green bars", and the debts are temporary, but just like "white bars", "green bars" are detrimental to the majority of farmers.

However, compared with the content information, the effect information must have a specific reference in discourse. And there is no case without effect information appearing in CCL corpus.

2.4 Distributional Difference of Effect and Content Information

Through the analysis of 150 causal noun data, we find that although the effect meaning and the content meaning are both important sematic features of causal nouns, their distributions in syntax and discourse are significantly different. The specific performance is shown in Table 1.

Table 1. The distribution of effect information and content information of causal nouns.

Types		Effect information	Content information
Within sentences	Subject	16 (10.67%)	13 (8.67%)
	Object	1 (0.67%)	50 (33.33%)
	Conjunction	18 (12%)	0
	Modifier	67 (44.67%)	10 (14.49%)
Across sentences	Anaphora	48 (32%)	9 (6%)
	Cataphora	0	25 (16.67%)
Absence		0	43 (28.67%)

It can be seen from Table 1 that there are two distinctions in the distribution of effect information and content information. First, the effect information tends to appear before causal nouns, as subjects of sentences or antecedents of anaphora. While the content information tends to appear after causal nouns, as the objects of sentences or the referents of cataphora. Second, the effect information must appear in the context, while the content information may not.

3   The Semantic Status of Content and Effect Information

Causal nouns contain content and effect information. This point has also been mentioned in many previous studies. The related research is mainly based on the observation of two attributives of causal nouns. And the attributives are called identity attribute and ownership attribute respectively [1]. Kou and Yuan [4] considered that both effect-defining clauses and content-defining clauses are syntactically unmarked attributive clauses from the syntactic perspective, and they are both defined by the inherent semantic structure of the head nouns. However, in terms of syntactic distribution, both of the two kinds of information cannot be realized at the attributive position at the same time. So it is debated that both types of attributive clauses can be called noun complement clauses. Moreover, it is also believed that there are differences between the two [10]. But there is no convincing evidence to prove that.

According to the above analysis, we find that there are differences in the syntactic distribution of content and effect information, which shows that these two types of information do have different status in the semantic structure of causal nouns. Relatively speaking, effect information occupies a more central and important position in the meaning of causal nouns. In addition, from the perspective of discourse function, the effect information always appears before the causal noun as a premise, which is necessary in the context. At contrast, the content information is not indispensable. And these two types of information also have different syntactic combination and transformation.

3.1   Interrogative Test

When 什么 (what) is used as an attribute to ask about a noun, the speaker asks about the definition of the noun or some aspect of the attribute. For example:

(22) a. 什么人? 我是这里的学生。
Who are you? I am a student.
   b. 什么桌子? 红木桌子.
   Which desk? Mahogany desk.
   When 什么 is used to ask a question with causal nouns, it can only answer the content information other than the effect information. For example, when a student did not do homework because of illness, the teacher may ask him (23), and the student would only answer (23a) instead of (23b).

(23) 什么原因?

For what reason?

a. 我生病了。

I am sick.

b. *我没写作业。

*I did not do the homework.

It proves that effect information is often the known information for both speaker and listener when they use a causal noun. Therefore, there is impossible to ask about this type of information.

3.2 Negative Test

Based on the data collected in the corpus, we find that the content information of causal nouns can appear in a negative form. Occasionally, the affirmative description of content information can be negated in the following. For example:

(24) 认真说来, 清政府失败的原因并不是技术的落后。

Seriously, the *reason* for the failure of the Qing government was not technolog- -ical backwardness.

(25) 这些单位不是不愿意收留我, 就是试用两天后就把我赶走了, 原因是我"笨手笨脚, 不适合干这种工作"其实我觉得自己还是挺灵敏, 并不是那么笨。

These companies either did not want to give me jobs, or they kicked me out after two days of probation. Just because I was clumsy and not suitable for this kind of work. Actually, I thought I was quite sensitive, not that stupid.

In (24–25), the content information is allowed to be denied, but the effect information is difficult to be denied in discourse:

(26) *有些不良的社会风气屡禁不止, 原因很多。但不良的社会风气并没有屡禁不止。

*Some bad social morals persist for many *reasons*. But the bad social morals have not persisted.

3.3 Meaning of Causal Nouns

Although both event information and content information can be used as attributives of causal nouns, their semantic status and syntactic properties are different. According to the above analysis, it can be found that the syntactic restrictions of content information are relatively less, and it can be questioned or negated as an attribute of nouns. But the performance of effect information is more limited. In terms of the representation of effect information in discourse, it cannot be questioned or negated, and tends to appear before causal nouns in the context. In brief, all these point to the fact that effect information is the presupposition of causal nouns. That is, a causal noun can also be regarded as a kind of presupposition trigger, which triggers a proposition that there is a specified event which is generated by another event (i.e. content information).

4 Differences Between Causal Nouns and Causal Conjunctions

Causal nouns are used to express causal relationship between events, which is similar to causal conjunctions in the logical and semantic functions. And both of them have similarities in other performances. The research found that in both written and spoken Chinese, the syntactic configuration of causality has the predominant word order of "postpositive cause clause" [11, 12]. At this point, there is the same tendency in using causal nouns to express causality. The effect information descripts the result, and the content information is the causal event. When the information is configured in the subject, attributive or be referred to by anaphoric causal nouns, it is the information preposed. While when it is configured in the object or be referred to by cataphoric causal nouns, it belongs to the information postposed. According to Table 1, the preposition of effect information is as high as 86%, while the preposition of content information is only 29%. It can be seen that when causal nouns encode causal relations, they also follow the configuration preferences of Chinese in the sequence of causal events. But at the same time, as the main components of sentences, nouns are significantly different from conjunctions in coding and function, which also makes the two different in some aspects.

4.1 Stylistic Differences

The use of causal nouns in spoken language is very limited. Taking the dialogue sub-database in the BCC corpus as an example, the research result of the causal conjunction 因为 (because) exceeded 340,621. While the causal noun 原因 (cause) occurred in 33,781 times. On the contrary, in the newspapers and periodicals database, the use of 因为 (because) was 318,376 times, and the use of 原因 (cause) increased significantly, with a total of 156,679 times. What is more noteworthy is that in special styles such as academic discourse, according to the retrieval of the 579,450-word academic corpus, it was found that 原因 (cause) was used in 578 cases, while 因为 (because) only appeared in 290 cases. It can be seen that causal nouns appear more often in written language, especially in official and objective academic discourse. By contrast, causal conjunctions are distributed in both spoken and written language, but are less used in academic discourse.

According to [6, 13], there is an obvious tendency of nominalization in written language, especially in academic discourse. That is, static nouns and formal verbs are more frequently used in written language. In the other words, verbs are more colloquial. Since conjunctions are mainly used to connect the relationship between sentences, when using the causal conjunction "because" to state the causal relationship, there are two sentences used to express cause-effect. However, causal nouns tend to encode causal events into sentences and act as subjects, objects or attributives, so they are more in line with the requirements of nominalization in written discourse.

In addition, the postposed causal clauses are more subjective, which are usually embodied in the negative, modal, comparison and emphasis [11]. However, the causal events (content information) of causal nouns are less subjective as syntactic constituent. Compared with causal conjunctions, causal relationships marked by causal nouns are more objective. Therefore, it is easy to appear in written discourse and academic discourse.

4.2 Information Adjustment Function

Causal nouns can not only state the causal relationship, but also adjust the type of information through the syntactic configuration of effect information and content information. For example, when the information is encoded as attributes, the speaker intentionally treats it as background information. Correspondently the other information in the causal relationship is regarded as focus. For example:

(27) 因此, 以改变过错行为为目的的惩罚一旦出现, 人会本能地采取对立的情绪和对抗的行动。这是在实践中惩罚比奖励更难掌控和取得良好教育效果的内在原因。

Therefore, once the punishment for the purpose of changing wrongful behavior appears, one will instinctively take opposing emotions and confrontational actions. This is the inherent *reason* why punishment is more difficult than reward to achieve good educational effect in practice.

As shown in (27), in the sentence where 原因 (cause) is located, the focus is the judgment that *this* refers to, which is the content information. While the effect encoded as an attribute is the known information. Similarly, when information is encoded into the object, it becomes the focus, such as (28).

(28) 这并不是曾国藩独创的, 但是为什么惟独湘军能成大事呢?原故就在于曾国藩所加的那点组织和训练。

It is not Zeng Guofan's original creation, but why is it that only the Xiang Army can achieve great goals? The *reason* lies in the organization and training that Zeng Guofan added.

When the effect is used as the subject, the sentence appears in the form of an existential sentence. Meanwhile, the causal noun is indefinite. The indefinite causal noun can elicit the speaker's expectation for the followings, therefore the causal noun can activate a pragmatic expectation:

(29) 采用"SOS" 信号作为船舶遇难的呼救是有一番来由的。

There is a *reason* for using the "SOS" signal as a distress call for a ship.

Finally, the difference between causal nouns and conjunctions is that conjunctions connect two components and require both cause and effect events in the causal relationship to appear in discourse. However, causal nouns have no such requirement. As shown in Table 1, the content information of causal nouns is not necessary. Therefore, the causal noun can be used for the statement of the effect with unclear causal relationship, such as (30). So we find that causal nouns can adjust the elaborate extent of information.

(30) 般投资者不知就里, 在恐惧心理下, 又只好盲目跟进, 不问情由, 竞相抛售, 从而使股价跌得更惨。

Ordinary investors do not know where to go, and under the fear, they have to follow up blindly, regardless of the reason, and compete to sell, thus making the stock price fall even worse.

5 Conclusion

Causal nouns can be associated with two types of information, namely the content information the effect information. These two types of information can occupy various syntactic positions in the sentences and contexts. This paper firstly explains the definition of content information and effect information of causal nouns, and put forward the syntactic verification conditions for the distinction between the two. Then by describing the distribution and combination of content information and effect information in discourse and sentences, it is found that there are obvious differences of syntactic configuration between the content information and effect information of causal nouns. By comparing with the causal conjunction 因为 (because), causal nouns demonstrate special pragmatic functions. They tend to appear in formal written styles such as academic discourse. Moreover, they can realize the allocation of foreground and background information in terms of information adjustment. Besides, causal nouns are usually used to adjust the amount of information and arouse the listener expects.

Acknowledgements. I am grateful to the anonymous reviewers of CLSW2022 for helpful suggestions and comments. This research was supported by the National Social Science Fund of China under grant No. 21CYY032. All errors remain my own.

References

1. Lv, S.: Collected Works of Lv Shuxiang I [吕叔湘文集·第一卷]. Commercial Press, Beijing (1990). (In Chinese)
2. Shen, J.: Transferred reference and metonymy[转指与转喻]. Contemp. Linguist. [当代语言学] **1**, 1–9 (1999). (In Chinese)
3. Jiang, Y.: Enantiosemy of "Yuangu" in Mandarin Chinese: From the perspective of lexicalization ["缘故"词义双重对立现象的词汇化溯因]. J. Donghua Univ. [东南大学学报] **2**, 208–211 (2007). (In Chinese)
4. Kou, X., Yuan, Y.: The selectional restriction between event attribute nouns and the self-designation de-constructions [论事件属性名词与自指"的"字结构的选择限制]. Contemp. Linguist. [当代语言学] **3**, 396–418 (2017). (In Chinese)
5. Zhu, B., Lou, S.: Assignment of cause or result inside the combined attributes of "Yuangu" ["缘故"组合式定语的因果赋值]. Chinese Linguist. [汉语学报] **3**, 57–66 (2019). (In Chinese)
6. Kou, X.: The discourse functions of shell nouns in mandarin: a genre-based study in popular and professional science articles. In: Dong, M., Gu, Y., Hong, J.F. (eds.) Chinese Lexical Semantics. CLSW 2021. LNCS, vol. 13249, pp. 230–240. Springer, Cham (2022). https://doi.org/10.1007/978-3-031-06703-7_17
7. Schmid, H.-J.: English Abstract Nouns as Conceptual Shells. Mouton de Gruyter, Berlin (2000)
8. Flowerdew, J., Forest, R.: Signalling Nouns in English: A Corpus-Based Discourse Approach. Cambridge University Press, Cambridge (2015)
9. Wang, X.: A review of *resomptif anaphore* in text analysis [篇章分析中的概述回指]. Contemp. Linguist. [当代语言学] **3**, 301–306 (2012). (In Chinese)
10. Lu, S., Pan, H.: "NP de NP" nominal constructions and the "Hidden Predicate" account [从"NP的NP"名词短语结构看"谓词隐含"]. Lang. Learn. Res. [语言教学与研究] **3**, 46–58 (2019). (In Chinese)

11. Song, Z., Tao, H.: A comparative study of Chinese and English causal clause sequences in discourse [英汉因果复句顺序的话语分析与比较]. Chinese Linguist. [汉语学报] **4**, 61–71 (2008). (In Chinese)

12. Wu, Z., Lan, X.J.: The semantic prosody of "Youyu": evidence from corpora. In: Hong, J.F., Zhang, Y., Liu, P. (eds.) Chinese Lexical Semantics. CLSW 2019. LNCS, vol. 11831, pp. 654–660. Springer, Cham (2020). https://doi.org/10.1007/978-3-030-38189-9_66

13. Zhai, W.: An analysis of the linguistic features of chinese academic writing of humanities and social sciences category [汉语人文社科类学术写作语言特征分析]. Master Dissertation, Xiamen University (2018) (In Chinese)

Construction of Effective News Corpus in Commodity Futures Domain

Lingling Mu[1], Le Kang[2,3], Yintao Jia[1], Ning Zhao[1], Wenxin Li[1], Xiaoyang Feng[1], and Hongying Zan[1(✉)]

[1] School of Computer and Artificial Intelligence, Zhengzhou University, Zhengzhou 450001, China
{iellmu,iehyzan}@zzu.edu.cn
[2] School of Computer Science and Technology, Tsinghua University, Beijing 100084, China
kangle@tsinghua.edu.cn
[3] Zhengzhou Commodity Exchange, Zhengzhou 450004, China

Abstract. Effective news in the domain of commodity futures contains information about market analysis and operation suggestions, which has a significant impact on futures prices. It is of great significance for the supervision and risk prediction of the futures market to identify the effective news and analyze its correlation with the futures market. This paper collected cotton futures news from January 2020 to March 2021 from major Chinese websites, and manually annotated 5,025 news passages to construct effective news corpus FENC (Future Effective News Corpus), which includes 2,828 effective news. We used FENC to train effective news classification models based on pre-trained models. This paper also ensemble SOTA classification models to automatically identify the effective news from January 2020 to March 2021, and automatically constructed the extended effective news corpus FENC-E which includes 34,272 effective news and 30,211 non-effective news. FENC and FENC-E can be used for the effective news identification in the futures domain.

Keywords: Commodity futures · Effective news corpus · Text classification · Classification models

1 Introduction

With the rapid development of the Internet, the Internet has gradually replaced traditional media and has become the main way for futures investors to obtain information and perceive changes of futures market. The impact of Internet news on financial markets has become an important direction for behavioral finance research [1, 2]. The study found that online news has an impact on the futures and options market prices [3–5], which can be used to explain the reasons for the volatility of options and futures [6, 7]. More and more futures institutions have taken news indicators as an important reference for investment decisions; market supervisors use news to identify potential market risk information and capture abnormal trading clues. But in general, most news analysis

© The Author(s), under exclusive license to Springer Nature Switzerland AG 2023
Q. Su et al. (Eds.): CLSW 2022, LNAI 13495, pp. 103–111, 2023.
https://doi.org/10.1007/978-3-031-28953-8_9

applications in the futures are still in their infancy, the level of news analysis still needs to be further improved, and the application effect is far from ideal [8].

"Internet black mouth" [9] means that market participants with certain influence in the futures market, recommend their opinions or spread good and bad news through the Internet, self-media platforms and other channels after buying futures of related products to artificially induce uninformed investors to follow the trend of investment, and lead to panic in the market. This is a typical illegal behaviour in the securities and futures market, which not only seriously misleads the majority of investors, but also has a great impact on the fair market. It is a typical application scenario of public opinion analysis in the domain of futures market supervision.

This paper believes that when news like "Internet black mouth" contains market analysis and operation suggestions (as shown in Fig. 1, the red tokens are effective information), it will have psychological implications for readers and will affect readers' trading operations. This paper regards such news as effective news. Compared with other news, effective news has a greater impact on the futures market. Therefore, identifying the effective news and analyzing its correlation with the futures market is of great significance to the supervision and risk prediction of the futures market. Corpus is the basis of natural language process, and occupies an important position [10], so this paper constructs an effective news corpus for classifying the effective news.

本周弱势反弹概率较大，但上行空间不大，近期预计主力合约CF2009在11300-12000元/吨区间震荡概率较大。
〈p〉 操作建议。在全球疫情没有实质好转前，防疫仍然常态化，全球贸易环境因政治操控恶化，全球经济大幅下滑，棉花消费预计将在低位维持较长时间，棉花消费逐步恢复，棉花价格维持震荡、底部逐渐上抬的走势。纱厂可逢低阶段性采购，反弹上涨不宜追高。投机者可按区间震荡思路操作。

...It is expected that the main contract 2009 will fluctuate in the range of 11300-12000 yuan / ton in the near future.Operation suggestions. ...The cotton consumption is expected to remain low for a long time....Investors can do some operations according to the idea of range shock.

Fig. 1. Example of effective news annotation

Taking cotton futures as an example, this paper collected news related to cotton futures from platforms such as Sina Weibo and China Cotton Network during January 2020 to March 2021, manually annotated the news during June and October 2020 to construct a Commodity Futures Effective News Corpus (FENC) and trained classification models to recognize the effective news. The three best models were ensemble to predict the effectiveness of cotton news during January 2020 to March 2021 to construct a larger-scale effective news data corpus FENC-E.

2   Construction of FENC

2.1   Data Collection

This paper collected cotton futures news released by online platforms such as Sina Weibo, Sina Finance, Oriental Fortune, Toutiao, WeChat Official Account, and China

Cotton Network during January 2020 to March 2021. After removal of irrelevant data and deduplication, a total of 64,440 news passages were collected. The maximum sentence length, minimum sentence length and average sentence length (excluding numbers, spaces and punctuation marks) of news are 30,646, 2, 1,484.18 respectively. The median length is 879, and the most is 134. Among them, 41% of news articles are under 500 words in length, 43% of news articles are between 500 and 2,000 words in length. Most news articles are under 2,000 words in word length, and only 16% of news articles are over 2,000 words in length.

2.2 Annotation Specification

News categories are divided into two cases: effectiveness (0) and non-effectiveness (1). If the news content includes the text that describes market analysis, operation, and investment advices, it will be annotated as "effectiveness (0)". The red font in Fig. 1 includes operation and investment advice, so it is annotated as effective news. Effective news generally has effective keywords, as shown in Table 1. If there is only common knowledge or introductions and data descriptions of futures products in the news without market analysis, operation and investment advice, it will be annotated as "non-effectiveness (1)", as shown in Fig. 2.

Table 1. Effective keywords

预测未来会.../预计会.../预期... predict that the future will.../expected to...	重点关注.../重点留意... Focus on...
做空.../做多... Long... / Short...	操作上建议... Operation advice...
持有.../多单持有... Hold.../long hold...	观望... Wait...

非引导性新闻示例：华东、华中、东北市场中下旬成交亦有所减慢，下游消化自身存货为主，采购操作较为谨慎。华南市场需求较好，下游按需补库，生产企业库存整体仍呈削减趋势，原片价格稳步上调。西南、西北市场前期上涨较为缓慢，在需求良好、库存低位支撑下，中下旬部分生产企业价格仍有小幅上调。

Fig. 2. Example of noneffective news

2.3 Annotation

This paper manually annotated the news during June and October 2020, and constructed an effective manual annotation corpus FENC in the futures domain. In order to obtain high-quality data, annotation was done in a mode of iterative correction with multiple rounds to annotate and revise the specification. The overall process was divided into three stages: test annotation, formal annotation and spot-checking, as shown in Fig. 3.

Test Annotation Stage: Annotators were trained to familiarize themselves with the annotation process, learn preliminary annotation specifications in detail, and each annotator is assigned a small number of tasks to annotate. After this annotation phase, the annotators mainly understood the task and goal of the annotation. After discussing the existing inconsistencies in the annotated results, we improved the annotation specification and moved to the formal annotation phase.

Formal Annotation Stage: This stage adopted the mode of multiple rounds of iterative correction for annotation. Annotators worked in pairs to annotate the same set of news corpus. If there was any inconsistency in the annotation, the experts discussed the issue in a timely manner and updated or supplemented the annotation specification. Finally, the first annotator would confirm the annotated results and obtain the final result.

Spot-Checking Stage: Experts extracted a portion of the corpus from the second stage results to check whether it conformed to the annotation specification, modified the erroneous annotation, and constructed a refined annotated corpus.

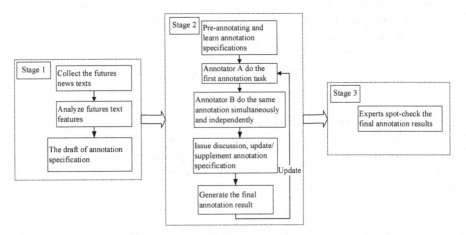

Fig. 3. The process of effective future news annotation

2.4 Data Analysis

After all the annotation work was completed, the consistency evaluation metric Kappa was used to measure consistency, such as formula (1–3):

$$K = \frac{P_0 - P_e}{1 - P_e} \tag{1}$$

$$P_0 = \frac{N_g}{n} \tag{2}$$

$$P_e = \frac{a_1 \times b_1 + a_2 \times b_2 ... + a_n \times b_n}{n^2} \tag{3}$$

where N_g is the number of the same annotated results of same data, n is the amount of total annotated news, a_i and b_i is the annotated results of two annotators for same data, respectively. The annotation consistency of the first two stages reaches 76.35%, and the annotation consistency of the second and third stages is about 80.14%, which is highly consistent according to Table 2.

Table 2. Annotation Consistency Evaluation Level

Results	Level
0.0–0.20	very low consistency
0.21–0.40	general consistency
0.41–0.60	medium consistency
0.61–0.80	high degree of consistency
0.81–1.0	almost exactly

Table 3. Statistics on the Result of Manual Annotation Effective News

Categories	Quantity			
	June	September	October	Total
Effective news	687	12	2287	2986
Non-effective news	598	38	3325	3961
Total	1285	60	6212	6947

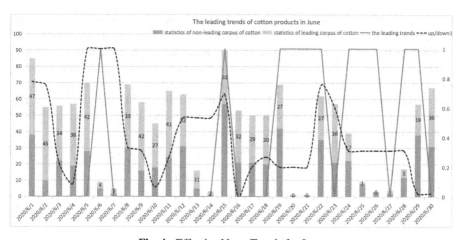

Fig. 4. Effective News Trends for June

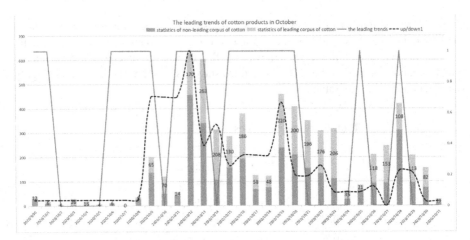

Fig. 5. Effective News Trends for October

The detailed information of annotated corpus is shown in Table 3, and the number of effective news and noneffective news is basically balanced. Statistics of news effectiveness trends from June 1st to June 30th and September 30th to October 31st are shown in Figs. 4 and 5. The visualizing method is as follows: Statistics the number of effective news and noneffective news per day during the interval time. If the number of effective news is greater than the number of noneffective news, the news published on this day is considered as effective. The secondary axis reflects the effective trend of the month, with 0 indicating effective and 1 indicating noneffective. As Fig. 4 and 5 indicate that before and after the effective news appeared, the futures market changed significantly.

3 Recognition of Effective News

Natural language process technique has obtained outstanding achievements in text classification, semantic understanding and other domain [11, 12]. In this paper, the effective news corpus is divided into train set and test set according to the ratio of 4:1, as shown in Table 4. The news effectiveness recognition task is regarded as a text classification task, and the accuracy rate (Acc), the precision rate (P) and the recall rate (R) are used as the evaluation metrics, as shown in formulas (4–7). In the formula, TP, TN, FP, and FN represent the number of true "non-effectiveness", true "effectiveness", false "non-effectiveness", and false "effectiveness" respectively.

$$Acc = \frac{TP + TN}{TP + TN + FP + FN}. \tag{4}$$

$$P = \frac{TN}{TN + FN}. \tag{5}$$

$$R = \frac{TN}{TN + FP}. \tag{6}$$

$$F1 = 2 * \frac{P * R}{P + R}. \qquad (7)$$

Table 4. FENC Effectiveness Distribution

	Total Corpus	Effectiveness	Non-effectiveness
Train	6040	2911	3129
Test	1507	674	833

3.1 Classification Models

The classification baseline models used in this paper are the pre-trained model BERT[1] (Bi-directional Encoder Representations from Transformer) [13], RoBERTa[1] [14] and Mengzi[2] [15]. Before classification, the original news was pre-processed, including removing punctuation, numbers, letters and stop words (using the stop word list of Harbin Institute of Technology), text segmentation and other operations.

BERT. This paper set the maximum sentence length of BERT to 512. While the average length of news in the dataset is 1,286, the original news needed to be pre-processed. First, removing the noise words in the news, such as "免责声明/disclaimer", "责任编辑/editor-in-chief" and other information irrelevant about futures analysis. And then intercepting the text with less than 512 words. After analyzing the dataset, it was found that most of the effective contents are in the second half of the news. Therefore, this paper reversely intercepts 512 words from the end of the de-noised text as the input to the model. In this paper, we used the BERT-base-Chinese model with 12 model layers, 768 hidden units and 12 attention heads, the learning rate is 2e-5, the training round is 3, the batch size = 3, and the total parameters are 110M.

RoBERTa. We adopted the chinese_roberta_wwm_ext_L-12_H-768_A-12 model sets the maximum sentence length of RoBERTa to 512, and used the same data processing method as the BERT model for text classification.

Mengzi. This paper adopted the Mengzi-bert-base-fin model, which is pre-trained on 20G financial news, announcements, research reports and other financial data. The number of model layers used in the experiment is 12, the learning rate is 5e-5, the number of hidden units is 768, the number of attention heads is 12, the training round is 3, the batch size = 3, and the total number of parameters is 103M.

---

[1] 1 https://github.com/ymcui/Chinese-BERT-wwm.
[2] 2 https://huggingface.co/Langboat/mengzi-bert-base-fin.

3.2 Results

The experiments in this article are carried out on the Ubuntu18.04 operating system, the CPU configuration is Intel i7-8750H, the GPU configuration is NVIDIA GTX-1080 (8G), the programming language used is Python3.6.9, and the deep learning framework is Tensorflow_gpu1.15.0, CUDA version is 10.0, cuDNN version is 7.4.

The results of the models in Sect. 3.1 under the above experimental environment are shown in Table 5.

Table 5. Effectiveness Classification Model Experiment Results

Model	P	F1	ACC
BERT	0.8593	0.9043	0.8818
BERT-HT	0.8913	0.9055	0.9006
BERT-T	0.9222	0.9062	0.9105
RoBERTa	0.8727	0.8656	0.8708
RoBERTa-T	0.8667	0.8154	0.8310
Mengzi-bert-base-fin	0.9354	0.8667	0.8796
Mengzi-bert-base-fin-T	0.8701	0.8775	0.8802

In Table 5, BERT-HT indicates that the input of the BERT model is the first 256 words of news and the tail of 256 words; the input of BERT-T is the tail of 512 words of news. Mengzi-bert-base-fin-T trains the model with news tail 512 words.

The results from Table 5 show that the three metrics of the BERT-T model with 512 words at the tail are better than other BERT models, which indicates that the BERT-based effectiveness classification model has a better effect on short news than long news. The reason is that the effectiveness-related content is mainly concentrated in the tail of the news. The Mengzi model has the highest classification accuracy. The reason should be that the corpus used in this paper is a news corpus in the domain of futures, which is closely related to the financial corpus used for Mengzi model pre-training.

3.3 Automatic Construction of Extended Efficient News Dataset FENC-E

According to the training results of Sect. 3.2, we integrate the three best models BERT-T, RoBERTa, Mengzi-bert-base-fin to predict the news from January 2021 to March 2021 to construct a larger scale effective news corpus FENC-E. The labels predicted by the models for the same data are converted into integers 0 (effective news) and 1 (noneffective news), respectively, and the three results are summed. If the sum is greater than or equal to 2, the final prediction result of this data is 1 (that is, this data is noneffective news), and if the sum is less than 2, the final prediction result for this data is set to 0 (that is, this data is effective news).

The consistency rate (Formula 1) between the prediction results and the manually annotated results of the news in June and October 2020 is 80.09%. According to the consistency evaluation level in Table 2, the prediction results and the manually annotated results are highly consistent. The FENC-E dataset includes a total of 34,272 validity news and 30,211 noneffective news.

4 Conclusion

Compared with other news, effective news has a greater impact on the futures market. Identifying the effective news and analyzing its correlation with the futures market is of great significance to the supervision and risk prediction of the futures market. This paper constructs an effective news corpus FENC and effective news recognition models, and integrates the three best-performing models to automatically construct an extended effective news corpus FENC-E, which provides a basis for market supervision and risk prediction in the futures domain.

References

1. Ouyang, Z., Li, H.: Research on the impact of internet news on financial markets: a literature review. Stat. Inf. Forum **34**(11), 122–128 (2019). (in Chinese)
2. Li, Z., Hu, Z.: The impact of internet news on financial asset prices: a literature review. Finan. Rev. **10**(04), 110–117+122 (2018). (in Chinese)
3. Yang, C., Gao, B., Yang, J.: Option pricing model with sentiment. Rev. Deriv. Res. **19**(2), 147–164 (2016). https://doi.org/10.1007/s11147-015-9118-3
4. Liu, C., Chou, R., Wang, G.: Investor sentiment and price discovery: evidence from the pricing dynamics between the futures and spot markets. J. Bank. Finan. **90**, 17–31 (2018)
5. Lin, R., Liu, Y.: Correlation analysis between public opinion index and futures market. Front. Trading Technol. **35**(2), 38–44 (2019). (in Chinese)
6. Gong, X., Lin, B.: The incremental information content of investor fear gauge for volatility forecasting in the crude oil futures market. Energy Econ. **74**, 370–386 (2018)
7. Seo, S., Kim, J.: The information content of option-implied information for volatility forecasting with investor sentiment. J. Bank. Finance **50**, 106–120 (2015)
8. Zhi, X., Xue, L., Zhao, H., Zhi, W.: Application of intelligent news analysis technology in the futures industry. Inf. Technol. Stand. (05):22–26+46 (2020). (in Chinese)
9. Jiang, D.: Improve laws and regulations to block the "black mouth" of the Internet. Securities Times (A01) (2018). (in Chinese)
10. Zan, H., Chen, J., Cheng, X., Mu, L.: Construction of word sense tagging corpus. In: Hong, J.-F., Su, Qi., Wu, J.-S. (eds.) CLSW 2018. LNCS (LNAI), vol. 11173, pp. 679–690. Springer, Cham (2018). https://doi.org/10.1007/978-3-030-04015-4_59
11. Zhang, Q., Mu, L., Zhang, K., Zan, H., Li, Y.: Research on question classification based on bi-lstm. In: Hong, J.-F., Su, Qi., Wu, J.-S. (eds.) CLSW 2018. LNCS (LNAI), vol. 11173, pp. 519–531. Springer, Cham (2018). https://doi.org/10.1007/978-3-030-04015-4_44
12. Mu, L., Cheng, X., Han, Y., Zan, H.: Word sense comparison between DCC and GKB. In: Hong, J.-F., Su, Qi., Wu, J.-S. (eds.) CLSW 2018. LNCS (LNAI), vol. 11173, pp. 772–788. Springer, Cham (2018). https://doi.org/10.1007/978-3-030-04015-4_67
13. Devlin, J., Chang, M., Lee, K., Toutanova, K.: Bert: pre-training of deep bidirectional transformers for language understanding. In: Proceedings of NAACL-HLT, Minneapolis, Minnesota, pp. 4171–4186 (2019)
14. Liu, Y., Ott, M., Goyal, N., et al.: Roberta: a robustly optimized bert pretraining approach. arXiv preprint arXiv:1907.11692 (2019)
15. Zhang, Z., Zhang, H., Chen, K., et al.: Mengzi: Towards Lightweight yet Ingenious Pre-trained Models for Chinese. arXiv preprint arXiv:2110.06696 (2021)

MSDD: A Multimodal Language Dateset for Stance Detection

Mengyang Hu[1], Pengyuan Liu[1,2(✉)], Weikang Wang[3], Hu Zhang[1], and Chengxiao Lin[1]

[1] School of Information Science, Beijing Language and Culture University, Beijing, China
liupengyuan@pku.edu.cn
[2] Chinese National Language Monitoring and Research Center (Print Media), Beijing, China
[3] Shanghai University of Finance and Economics, Shanghai, China
wwk@163.sufe.edu.cn

Abstract. Stance Detection is the task of automatically determining whether the author of a text is positive, negative, or neutral towards a given target. Correct detecting stance is conducive to false news detection, claim validation, and argument search. Detecting stance from certain types of conversation, especially multimodal conversation is an interesting problem which has not been carefully explored. In social interaction, people usually express their stance on instance, which is produced in a multimodal manner, through the usage of words (text), gestures (video) and prosodic cues (audio). Stance detection is an established research area in NLP, but in a multimodal context it is an understudied area. In this paper, we present MSDD, a novel multimodal dataset for stance detection, to explore multimodal language for expressing stance in conversation. We conducted a series of experiments on MSDD, and the result shows that multimodal information indeed improves the dialogue stance detection to some extent, but the fusion of the multimodal language needs to be enhanced.

Keywords: Multimodal dataset · Conversation · Stance detection

1 Introduction

Stance detection is the extraction of a subject's reaction to a claim made by a primary actor. Many tasks in life require the participation of dialogue stance detection, such as user behavior detection, multi-modal interaction, dialogue generation, etc. [1].

Stances involves multimodal communicative channels including effective use of words (text), accompanying gestures (vision) and sounds (acoustic), and the stances expressed by these three channels may not even be consistent [2]. The two sides of the dialogue usually do not express their stances with simple "yes" or "no", and the analysis of stances should be taken into consideration in the

© The Author(s), under exclusive license to Springer Nature Switzerland AG 2023
Q. Su et al. (Eds.): CLSW 2022, LNAI 13495, pp. 112–124, 2023.
https://doi.org/10.1007/978-3-031-28953-8_10

context of the conversation. In addition, the interlocutors may use rhetorical means such as exaggeration, sarcasm and humor to strengthen or conceal their stances in the process of dialogue, and the views expressed by these means are often very complex [3,4]. For example, Fig. 1 provides two cases of our dataset. In the first case, the language information of the speaker Rajesh has nothing to do with Champagne. It only indicates the position of Champagne. It does not directly express a position on the subject of "starting with champagne a little early". However, combining the smiling facial expressions of the characters and the cheerful tone of voice, we can conclude that the speaker is happy to drink champagne, and does not feel that drinking champagne is too early, which means, expressing a negative stance towards "drinking champagne too early". Also, in the second case, the speaker responded with a rhetorical question, but combined with a smiling face and a positive tone, we can determine that the speaker has a positive attitude towards "do you want to meet her". In both cases, there is always a need to combine multiple modalities with each other, which shows the importance of multiple modalities for stance detection tasks.

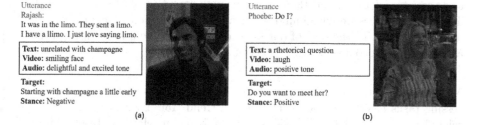

Fig. 1. Two cases of our dataset

However, most of the previous work in stance detection was carried out on social media textual data [5]. Detecting stance from conversation, especially in multimodal conversation has not been carefully explored. In this paper, we explore the role of multimodality and conversational context in stance detection and introduce a new resource to further enable research. More specifically, our paper makes the following contributions: (1) We create a new dataset, MSDD, for multimodal stance research with high-quality annotations, including both multimodal and conversational context features; (2) We exemplify various scenarios where incongruity in stance is noticeable across different modalities, consequently stressing the role of multimodal approaches to solve this problem; (3) We introduce several baselines and show that multimodal models are significantly more effective when compared to their unimodal variants; and (4) We also provide preceding turns in the dialogue which act as context information. Consequently, we surmise that this property of MSDD leads to a new sub-task for future work: stance detection in conversational context.

2   Related Work

Automated stance detection has gained increased interest in recent years. It is a widely studied linguistic device whose significance is seen in dialogue understanding and generation research. This work is connected to areas in stance detection and multimodal analysis.

Stance Detection: Stance detection [6] has been among active areas of research in natural language processing, and it can be mutually assisted with many other tasks, such as false news detection [7], rumor verification [8] and sentiment intensity analysis [7]. Conforti et al. [9] released WT–WT, a large, expert-annotated Twitter stance detection dataset, which is the first resource for stance in the financial domain, also further raise the challenge of cross-domain entertainment. Xu et al. [10] proposed cross-target position detection task. Zhang et al. [11] used external knowledge (semantic and emotional vocabulary) as a bridge to achieve knowledge transfer between different targets. Although stance detection has received enough attention, the existing research focuses on cross-domain and cross-target tasks, and there is not enough attention at the data level [12]. The only resources we have found so far are focused on multi-language [13] and image level [14]. To the best of our knowledge, ours is the first work to propose a resource on video-level stance detection.

Multimodal Analysis: Multi-modal research in various natural language processing tasks has become a recent research trend [15]. There are a lot of work related to multi-modality. In this paper, we focus on related datasets. Shin et al. [5] targeted multimodal sentiment analysis and showed how to use multimodal information to enhance the analysis of unstructured data on social media. Zadeh et al. [15] collected monologue videos on YouTube, and proposed a sentiment classification dataset CMU-MOSEI for review videos. Poria et al. [16] proposed the emotion classification task Meld for conversational videos. Hasan et al. [3] proposed a humor detection data set based on a TED talk, and Sharma et al. [17] published a dataset, annotated memes from various sources on the Internet to tackle Internet humor. Castro et al. [4] proposed a dataset of multimodal sarcasm detection. The above datasets all represent the auxiliary role of multimodal for various NLP tasks. However, as far as we know, there is no multimodal dataset containing text, video and acoustic for the stance detection task. This is also one of our original intention for proposing this dataset.

3   Dataset

To promote the exploration of multi-modal dialogue position detection, we present a new dataset, consisting of video, audio and text modality. In the following subsections, we first discuss data acquisition, then followed by annotation and statistics as well as qualitative aspects.

3.1 Data Acquisition

The task of dialogue position detection requires a large number of characters and rich dialogue forms. Scenario TV dramas often have many characters and various forms of dialogue, which are more in line with our real daily life. Following this train of thought, we chose two classic and famous TV series, "Friends" and "The Big Bang Theory", as our data source.

At first, we collected the whole episodes of these two shows from the Internet. But for labeling, the dataset needs to be sliced in the unit of dialogue. So we cut the video manually by watching the episodes. Specifically, we first capture the start and end time of the dialogue segment in the episode by manually watching the episode. Then we use the ffmpeg-based scripts to cut the complete videos into corresponding slices. In addition, these video clips are not only stored for visual modal features, but also used to obtain audio data. For the text part, due to the short time and small granularity of video clips, we chose iFLYTEK's voice dictation to convert audio data into text data, and use video subtitles to double check. The overall process is shown in Fig. 2.

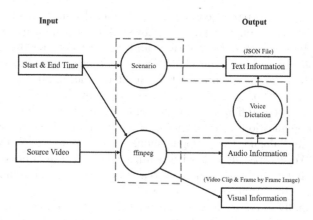

Fig. 2. Technical flow chart of original video processing

Eventually, a total of 1296 dialogue videos were collected in our experiment, of which 632 video clips were selected from the 1-7 seasons of "The Big Bang Theory", and 664 were from the 1-5 seasons of "Friends".

3.2 Annotation Process

We went through our labeling process in three steps: preparation, construction and revision. First, In the process of preparation we selected a few episodes for the trial labeling and formulated labeling specifications. Then the construction process is formally annotated by the above annotation specification. At last, we conducted the cross-checking for the revision part, which contains the videos themselves, scripts, subtitle files, text data in the preceding text, and so on. The annotation is carried out by two graduate student who have participated in the formulation of labeling specifications. One of them is responsible for the labeling of "The Big Bang Theory" and the other is "Friends". Each annotator performs an independent labeling process. Figure 3 shows the whole annotation process.

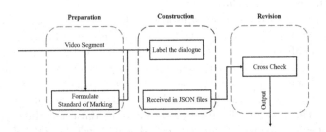

Fig. 3. Technical flow chart of original video processing

For the preparation part, we analyzed and labeled some extracted clips, and completed the annotation standard as follows: Opinion sentences can be words that do not directly express a position, and need to be judged based on the meaning of the sentence or the expression and tone of the character; Opinion sentences can be very short, with no limit on the number of words, even "Great.", "Yeah.", "No."; Opinion sentences can be ironic, that is, the speaker's actual point of view is different from the point of view in the language; Opinion sentences can be questions or even rhetorical questions; If there are two different positions in the dialogue, the dialogue should be marked as two pieces of data at this time. We selected 20 clips with definite labels for consistency check. The result shows that there was good consistency between the two annotators (the accuracy of the two annotators reached 85%).

In our formally annotation, the information about utterances were recorded in JSON format. Table 1 shows the meanings of each utterance record. Here, we

Table 1. The name and meaning of annotated objects in the dataset.

Name	Meaning
Utterance	Statements to express one's position in the dialogue
Utterance_Speaker	Speaker expressing the position in the dialogue
Context	The context of the position statement
Context_Speaker	Speakers expressing the context of the position sentence Utterance_Speaker is not involved
Show	The source of the dialogue BBT = The Big Bang Theory, F = Friends
Target	Participant's goal of the position
Stance	The position of the speaker

refer to the work of 12 to expand the meaning of utterance. It is worth noting that the "Target" can be an actual entity, such as "sushi" and "wind chimes", it can also be a specific event, such as "mind if I start", "Came into my apartment last night" and so on.

For revision, when the annotation completed, the two annotators will cross check each other's content by random sampling. We have also double-checked the labeling results of each annotator every two days to ensure the quality of the dataset. After all these steps, we got a total of 1296 video clips in our dataset, including 609 video clips that are labeled as positive, 635 video clips are labeled as negative, and the other 52 video clips are annotated as neutral.

Figure 1 shows an example of our annotation process. This example comes from the first episode of "The Big Bang Theory", which is the sixth episode of the episode, so we gave it the serial number 1_1_6. In this conversation, Leonard is the position expresser, and Penny is the dialogue participant, so the Utterance_Speaker is Leonard, the Context_Speaker is Penny, and the Context, as is shown in this screenshot, is what Penny said, "Why don"t you put some clothes on...", the Utterance is Leonard's reaction, "Really? Great.". Obviously, in this example the main content of the dialogue is Penny treat Leonard to dinner, so the Target is "dinner is on me". And by the clues of Leonard's words, we can see that Leonard is happy with this decision, so the Stance should be marked as "Positive". As shown in the bottom of Fig. 4, after the recording is completed, all the labeled items will generate JSON data items for recording and reading of the baseline model experiment.

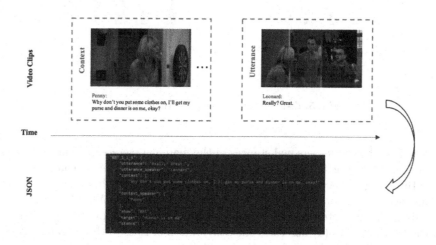

Fig. 4. An example of annotation.

3.3   Qualitative Aspects

Figure 1 provides two cases where stance is expressed through the combination between multiple modalities. In the first case, the language information of the speaker Rajesh has nothing to do with Champagne. It only indicates the position of Champagne. It does not directly express a position on the subject of "starting with champagne a little early". However, combining the smiling facial expressions of the characters and the cheerful tone of voice, we can conclude that the speaker is happy to drink champagne, and does not feel that drinking champagne is too early, which means, expressing a negative stance towards drinking champagne too early. Also, in the second case, the speaker responded with a rhetorical question, but combined with a smiling face and a positive tone, we can determine that the speaker has a positive attitude towards "do you want to meet her". In both cases, there is always a need to combine multiple modalities with each other, which shows the importance of multiple modalities for stance detection tasks.

3.4   Dataset Statistics

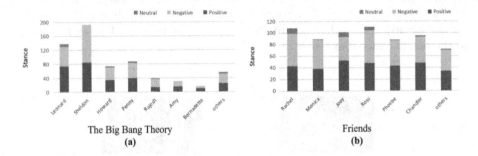

The Big Bang Theory
(a)

Friends
(b)

Fig. 5. distribution of roles and their stances

Figure 5(a) shows the personal stances of the main characters in "The Big Bang Theory", while Fig. 5(b) refers to "Friends". Among the main characters on The Big Bang Theory, Leonard and Sheldon have the most data, with 331 data items, accounting for 52.37% of the total data in this part. While in "Friends," the six main characters had an average amount of data, accounting for 84.81% of the total. Figure 6(a) describes the distribution of roles in the overall dataset. Combining Figs. 5 and Figs. 6, we can find that the proportion of each protagonist in the two dramas has basically reached more than 6%, and the total proportion reaches 90%. This is because these characters appear more often and have more dialogues, so there is more chance for the plot of dialogue with stance expression.

Figure 6(b) depicts the distribution of stances in the overall dataset. We found that the data of neutral stance was significantly less than that of the other two positions, the positive position and negative position accounted for 96% of

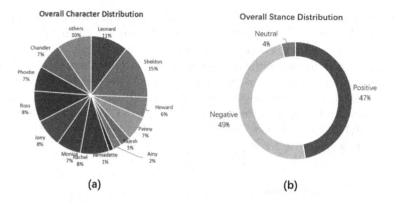

Fig. 6. overall characters and stances distribution

the total. We assume that is because in the TV series mainly featuring dialogue between characters, the dialogue often contains discussion or contradictory topics in order to promote the development of the plot. Characters rarely sidestep or obfuscate topics with neutral replies like "I don't know."

4   Features Extraction

Baseline model in this work is composed of two parts: feature extraction layer and linear classification layer. In the feature extraction layer, we input the segmented data fragments into Bert [18] for the text mode, the Librosa [19] feature extraction model for acoustic mode and the RESNET152 [21] for visual mode respectively according to the type of modes to obtain the data features of the three modes. Each segment of the conversation will have its corresponding data characteristics retrieved one by one according to the sequence number in the JSON file. These data features will be input into the linear classification layer based on Softmax classification for training and testing as required, and a series of parameters will be obtained to evaluate the training results. We obtain several learning features from the three modalities included in our dataset. For each modality, the process to extract these features are as followed:

Text Feature: We use Bert [18] to extract the features of textual utterance. Bert [18] provides a sentence representation $u_t \in \mathbb{R}^{d_t}$ for each utterance u, and we use the average of last four transformer layers of the first token ([CLS]) in the utterance. The modal we use here is Bert-Base, and the size of utterance representation (d_t) is 768.

Speech Feature: For audio modality, we need to obtain the speech features of each Utterance sentence in the dataset, and obtain information related to pitch, intonation, and other tone-specific details of the speaker. We utilize the popular speech-processing library Librosa [19] to process each utterance acoustic as a time series signal at first, which the sampling rate of sound signals is unified

44100 Hz for input. Then we use REPET-SIM method provided in Librosa [19] to separate the human voice and the environmental voice, and output part of the human voice to reduce the effect of environmental noise. Finally, we segment the audio signal into windows without overlap, in which the acoustic can be divided into fixed-length representations, and output MFCC, Mel Spectrogram, Spectral Centroid, and dynamic features corresponding to MFCC and Mel Spectrogram. All the extracted features are connected to form a 283 dimensional joint representation (d_a) for each window. We also calculate the average across the window segments: $u_a = \frac{1}{d_w}(\sum_i u_i^a) \in \mathbb{R}^{d_a}$.

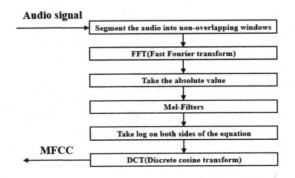

Fig. 7. Mel Frequency Cepstral Coefficents.

Taking MFCC (Mel Frequency Cepstral Coefficents) as an example, the process of outputting MFCC is shown in Fig. 7.

Video Feature: For the video modality, we use the pool5 layer of the pre-trained ResNet-152 [20] image classification model to extract visual features for each of the f frames in the utterance video. After pre-processing such as resizing, center-cropping and normalization, we take the mean value of the final 2048 dimensional feature vector u_i^v for each frame: $u_v = \frac{1}{f}(\sum_i u_i^v) \in \mathbb{R}^{d_v}$ as the visual representation of each utterance, which is the same averaging strategy as with the other modalities.

5   Experiments

In order to explore the role of multimodality in stance detection, we conduct multiple experiments to analyze the influence of each modality in the dataset on the effect of the baseline model on the dialogue stance detection.

5.1   Experimental Setup

In this work, we prepared two methods to test the performance of the dataset under different circumstances. In the first classification method, the training set will be created in a random stratification method to ensure that the label distribution in the training set is more even. In this method, the speaker in the test set may appear in the training set. We call this method speaker-dependent setting. The second method restricts the occurrence of the same speaker in the training set and the test set. We call this method speaker-independent setting. Compared with the first method, speaker-independent setting simulates the situation of conversational position detection in a completely unfamiliar environment, so it is more challenging. In our experiment, we use the data from "The Big Bang Theory" as the training set, and the data from "Friends" as the test set. In this way, the speakers in the training set and the test set are independent of each other.

During our experiments, we use precision, recall and F-score as the main evaluation metrics, weighted across all the positive, negative and neutral classes (the weights are gained based on the class ratios).

5.2 Baselines

We use Softmax classifier as the primary baseline for our experiments. Softmax classifier is one of the popular linear classifiers, which is suitable for multiple classification tasks. SVM is also commonly used in classification tasks, but it is more used for dichotomy problems. In our work, the stances of speakers can be positive, negative and neutral, which belongs to multiple classification tasks. Therefore, we chose Softmax to carry out the experiments.

We input the multi-modality features into Softmax classifier to map the features to values within the range $(0, 1)$, and make the sum of these values to be 1, which is to transform the classification problem into a probability problem. In the output, we select the target with the highest probability and take it as the result of classification.

5.3 Results and Discussion

Table 2. Speaker-dependent setup. Note: T = text, A = audio, V = video

Modality	Precision	Recall	F-score
T	0.749	0.767	0.748
A	0.447	0.471	0.390
V	0.441	0.455	0.440
T+A	0.746	0.764	0.745
T+V	0.721	0.742	0.724
A+V	0.452	0.467	0.450
T+A+V	0.714	0.736	0.718

The results of speaker-dependence setting are presented in Table 2. Compared with the acousticand visual information modality alone or the combination of the two modalities, the combined use of multiple modalities shows a better effect, and the classification accuracy of the baseline model is improved. However, compared with the text modality alone, the combination of multiple modalities reduces the accuracy of model classification. Through analysis, we believe that this is because there are many interferences in the original data during feature extraction, such as laughter in the acoustic information and text blocking in the video information, and these interferences are completely removed by filtering. Therefore, the characteristics of acousticand video modes are greatly affected, and the accuracy of acousticand video modes will also be reduced.

Table 3 presents the experimental results of the model under the speaker independent setting. Under this setting, the accuracy of acousticand visual modal data is still not ideal. However, compared with the speaker-dependent setting, the situation of independent speakers is more challenging. The new participants in the test set need a more universal model, which is also more in line with the situation of unfamiliar conversational scenes in daily life. Whether the speaker is independent has less effect on the method that uses acousticand visual modes; However, it has a greater impact on the method using text mode, and the accuracy of the method has been significantly reduced. It can be concluded that the use of acoustic mode and visual mode in dialogue stance detection will help to improve the adaptability of position detection model.

Table 3. Speaker-independence setup. Note: T = text, A = audio, V = video

Modality	Precision	Recall	F-score
T	0.729	0.759	0.741
A	0.466	0.489	0.473
V	0.502	0.486	0.408
T+A	0.624	0.649	0.635
T+V	0.671	0.650	0.619
A+V	0.475	0.490	0.476
T+A+V	0.592	0.615	0.603

6   Conclusion

In this paper, we present a novel multimodal dataset for stance detection called MSDD. By showing multiple examples from our dataset, we demonstrate the need for multimodal learning for stance detection. Consequently, we developed models that utilize three different modalities, including text, speech and visual signals. We use a series of baselines to evaluate our dataset, the results show that multimodal information indeed improve the dialogue stance detection to some extent, but the characteristics of the three modals are not well integrated. In the future, we will further explore multi-modal dialogue stance detection by expanding the data scale and seek for the better methods.

Acknowledgement. Support by Beijing Natural Science Foundation (4192057), Science Foundation of Beijing Language and Culture University (the Fundamental Research Funds for the Central Universities: 21YJ040005) and Beijing Language and Culture University Chinese and Foreign Postgraduate Innovation Fund Project (22YCX165).

References

1. AlDayel, A., Magdy, W.: Stance detection on social media: state of the art and trends. Inf. Process. Manag. **58**(4), 102597 (2021)
2. Zadeh, A., et al.: Multimodal sentiment intensity analysis in videos: facial gestures and verbal messages. IEEE Intell. Syst. **31**(6), 82–88 (2016)
3. Hasan, M.K., et al.: UR-FUNNY: a multimodal language dataset for understanding humor. arXiv preprint arXiv:1904.06618 (2019)
4. Castro, S., et al.: Towards multimodal sarcasm detection (an_Obviously_ perfect paper). arXiv preprint arXiv:1906.01815 (2019)
5. Shin, D., et al.: Enhancing social media analysis with visual data analytics: a deep learning approach. MIS Q. **44**(4), 1459–1492 (2020)
6. Mohammad, S., et al.: SemEval-2016 task 6: detecting stance in tweets. In: Proceedings of the 10th International Workshop on Semantic Evaluation (SemEval-2016) (2016)
7. Pomerleau, D., Rao, D.: Fake news challenge (2017)
8. Aker, A., Zubiaga, A., Bontcheva, K., Kolliakou, A., Procter, R., Liakata, M.: Stance classification in out-of-domain rumours: a case study around mental health disorders. In: Ciampaglia, G.L., Mashhadi, A., Yasseri, T. (eds.) SocInfo 2017. LNCS, vol. 10540, pp. 53–64. Springer, Cham (2017). https://doi.org/10.1007/978-3-319-67256-4_6
9. Conforti, C., et al.: Will-they-won't-they: a very large dataset for stance detection on Twitter. arXiv preprint arXiv:2005.00388 (2020)
10. Xu, C., et al.: Cross-target stance classification with self-attention networks. arXiv preprint arXiv:1805.06593 (2018)
11. Zhang, B., et al.: Enhancing cross-target stance detection with transferable semantic-emotion knowledge. In: Proceedings of the 58th Annual Meeting of the Association for Computational Linguistics (2020)
12. Küçük, D., Can, F.: Stance detection: a survey. ACM Comput. Surv. (CSUR) **53**(1), 1–37 (2020)
13. Cignarella, A.T., et al.: SardiStance@ EVALITA2020: overview of the task on stance detection in Italian tweets. In: EVALITA 2020 Seventh Evaluation Campaign of Natural Language Processing and Speech Tools for Italian. CEUR (2020)
14. Taulé, M., et al.: Overview of the task on multimodal stance detection in tweets on catalan# 1oct referendum. In: IberEval@ SEPLN (2018)
15. Zadeh, A.A.B., et al.: Multimodal language analysis in the wild: CMU-MOSEI dataset and interpretable dynamic fusion graph. In: Proceedings of the 56th Annual Meeting of the Association for Computational Linguistics (Volume 1: Long Papers) (2018)
16. Poria, S., et al.: MELD: a multimodal multi-party dataset for emotion recognition in conversations. arXiv preprint arXiv:1810.02508 (2018)
17. Sharma, C., et al.: SemEval-2020 task 8: memotion analysis-the visuo-lingual metaphor! arXiv preprint arXiv:2008.03781 (2020)

18. Devlin, J., et al.: BERT: pre-training of deep bidirectional transformers for language understanding. arXiv preprint arXiv:1810.04805 (2018)
19. McFee, B., et al.: librosa: audio and music signal analysis in Python. In: Proceedings of the 14th Python in Science Conference, vol. 8 (2015)
20. He, K., et al.: Deep residual learning for image recognition. In: Proceedings of the IEEE Conference on Computer Vision and Pattern Recognition (2016)
21. Tripathy, S., Swarnkar, T.: A comparative analysis on filtering techniques used in preprocessing of mammogram image. In: Pati, B., Panigrahi, C.R., Buyya, R., Li, K.-C. (eds.) Advanced Computing and Intelligent Engineering. AISC, vol. 1082, pp. 455–464. Springer, Singapore (2020). https://doi.org/10.1007/978-981-15-1081-6_39

Novel Lexical Semantic Change
and Interactivization

Meichun Liu, Yuyan Liang[(✉)], and Yuwei Wan

Department of Linguistics and Translation, City University of Hong Kong, 83 Tat Chee Avenue,
Kowloon Tong, Kowloon, Hong Kong, China
Yuyaliang2-c@my.cityu.edu.hk

Abstract. The study aims to explore newly arising lexical semantic changes that demonstrate an interesting tendency of semantic shifts towards highly interactive and socially impactive meanings. A number of such changes are provided with a focus on the novel cases where an abstract noun or an attributive adjective is used as a transitive verb in a causative-transitive construction (e.g., *tā nèihán wǒ le* 他内涵我了 'He covertly satirized me.'). A constructional analysis is proposed to account for the form-meaning mapping principles in the novel usage patterns that show a consistent tendency of semantic shift from less interactive to more interactive meanings. This tendency of 'interactivization' is evidenced in the changes from non-verbal to verbal and intransitive to transitive uses, detailed with a case study of the grammatical distributions of *nèihán*内涵 'inner quality' over two different time periods. The findings ultimately contribute to both interactional linguistics and Chinese lexical semantic studies in highlighting the observed trend of interactivization in lexical semantic changes under the popular use of social media that enhances the subtlety and complexity of human interaction.

Keywords: Novel usage · Interactional linguistics · Interactivization · Semantic extension

1 Introduction

This study looks into the interesting phenomena of novel lexical semantic changes within the framework of interactional linguistics. It investigates the specific cases of using an abstract noun or attributive adjective in a causative transitive pattern, as in *měihǎo nǐ de lǚchéng* 美好你的旅程 'Make your trip wonderful" and *tā nèihán wǒ le* 他内涵我了 'He satirized me'. A constructional account is provided to explicate the form-meaning mapping principles in the new usage patterns that encode highly interactive and socially impactive meanings. It is proposed that the newly occurring lexical changes demonstrate a general tendency of semantic shift from less to more interactive meanings, i.e., a trend of *interactivization*, as proposed in [1].

Previous studies in interactive linguistics focus more on how grammar emerges from interaction in discourse. [2] argued that the structure of a language is temporal, emergent and disputed. Unlike the rigid set of rules, the grammar of language "comes

© The Author(s), under exclusive license to Springer Nature Switzerland AG 2023
Q. Su et al. (Eds.): CLSW 2022, LNAI 13495, pp. 125–138, 2023.
https://doi.org/10.1007/978-3-031-28953-8_11

out of discourse and is shaped by discourse as much as it shapes discourse in an on-going process". This view of emergent grammar suggested that the structure in a language is constantly changing in actual use. The motivation lies in the cognitive and communicative demands for producing coherent discourse [3–7]. In line with such notions, a great number of works concentrated on the relationship between patterns of language use and structures of social action [8–11]. However, few studies explored lexical semantic issues from the perspective of interactional linguistics. This study examines a set of newly arising lexical semantic changes that show a general tendency of shifting from less to more interactive meanings, which is termed as "interactivization". The following examples from [1] serve to illustrate the six types of semantic changes towards higher degrees of interactivization:

(1) From intransitive to transitive use:

a. *zhàndòujī zài kōngzhōng lǐngháng*

战斗机 在 空中 领航

'The fighter takes the lead in the air.'

b. gōngsī lǐngháng xīn fāzhǎn.

公司 领航 新 发展.

'The company leads new development.'

(2) From affecting an inanimate object to a human object:

a. nǎniēzhè jiànshìqíng.

拿捏这件事情.

'Manipulate this matter.'

b. nǎniēzhège rén.

拿捏这个 人.

'Manipulate this person.'

(3) From a VO compound, to Compound+object, and Compound+ double object

a. wǒ zài yuànzilǐ bá cǎo.

我 在 院子里拔草.

'I'm pulling weeds in the yard.'

b. bácǎo yǎshīlándài.

拔草雅诗兰黛.

'Cancel the shopping plan of Estee Lauder product.'

c. bácǎonǐ yǎshīlándài.

拔草你 雅诗兰黛.

'Cancel the shopping plan of this Estee Lauder product.'

(4) From an adjective to a causative transitive verb:

a. nǐdeyuànwànghěn měihǎo.

你的愿望很 美好.

'Your wishes are good.'

b. měihǎo nǐde lǚchéng.

美好 你的 旅程.

'Make your journey wonderful.'

(5) From an emotion verb to a speech verb with intended manipulation

a. Emotion verb:

wǒ gǎndào ānwèi.

我 感到 安慰。

'I felt comforted.'

b. Speech verb:

wǒ ānwèi tā bié huīxīn yīqiè dōuyǒu xīwàng.

我 安慰 他: "别 灰心!一切 都有 希望。".

'I comforted him: "Don't be discouraged! There is hope for everything.'

(6) From physical contact to verbal contact with intended manipulation

a. Physical contact verb:

wǒ qiāodǎ zhuōzi.

我 敲打 桌子.

'I hit the table.'

b. Verbal contact verb:

lǎoshī jīngcháng qiāodǎ wǒ yào jìngxiàxīnlái zuòxuéshù.

老师 经常 敲打 我 要 静下心来 做学术.

'Teachers often exhort me to do academics calmly.'

Besides the six types mentioned in [1], there is another type of novel lexical semantic change that uses an abstract noun as a transitive verb, as shown below:

(7) From an abstract noun to a transitive verb:

a. *yīnyáng shì zhōngguó chuántǒngzhéxuédeyīzhǒngguānniàn*

阴阳 是 中国 传统哲学的一种观念.

'Yin Yang is a concept in traditional Chinese philosophy.'

b. *yǒuhuà shuōhuà nǐ bié yīnyáng wǒ*

有话 说话, 你 别阴阳 我.

'Say what you want to say directly, do not be ironic.'

In (7), The meaning of yīnyáng 阴阳 'Ying Yang' has changed from referring to a traditional Chinese philosophical thought as in (7a), to encoding a verbal delivery of passive-aggressive attack to another person. It is quite surprising that the abstract noun has been recently used as a transitive verb.

All the above examples show that the novel usages involve lexical semantic shifts from low interactivity to high interactivity as realized with varied syntactic patterns from low transitivity to high transitivity, from affecting an inanimate object to a human object, from an adjectival to causative use, from an abstract noun to a transitive verb, and taking one object to take two objects. In other words, the semantic change is manifested in syntactic realizations.

The observations serve as the foundation for the current investigation, which focuses on the change of an adjective or a noun to a transitive verb, as illustrated in (4) and (7) respectively. With a corpus-based approach, it aims to provide a constructional analysis by explicating the form-meaning reassociation in the novel usages, based on natural utterances collected from Weibo, a social platform in China.

2 Literature Review

The novel usages under study have been touched upon in previous literature, but little has been done to account for the linguistic properties involved in the observed changes from a constructional perspective, let alone the functional motivations for such novel changes.

2.1 Previous Studies on Adjective-Causative Alternation

Previous research has presented two opposing viewpoints on the cross-categorial use of an adjective in the "adjective + object" pattern. Some scholars claimed that the shift of part of speech from an adjective to a transitive verb is transient and heavily depends on the context [12, 13]. Other scholars, on the other hand, argued that when an adjective precedes an object, it becomes a transitive verb given its syntactic properties as a full-fledged verb [14–16].

To demonstrate that an adjective can be employed as a verb, [16] collected 100 examples of adjectives-to-verb conversion in non-business slogans and categorized them into four constructional categories, one of which is the adjective-causative alternation. In this alternation, an adjective can be used as the main predicate in the causative construction, denoting a causal change on the affected object. This type of usage is most commonly found in slogans, which is attributed to the strategy of cognitive economy. However, no explanation is given to the linguistic details in such changes, nor to the motivation for the semantic extension.

2.2 Previous Studies on Noun-TransitiveV Alternation

It is generally recognized that in ancient Chinese, nouns were often used as verbs; but in modern Chinese, such changes are seldom found. [17] observed that the occurrences of yǔ 雨 'rain' as a verb in four ancient texts are relatively similar (31 vs. 34). [18] pointed out that the conversion of a noun into a verb appears commonly as a rhetorical device in ancient writings. In contrast, such conversions, if any, occur mostly in the spoken variety of Modern Chinese. In our observation, there appears to be a trend of changing a noun to a transitive verb in the novel usages of social media.

In order to explore what is involved in the lexical semantic changes and how interaction works for these changes, this study will address three main questions: 1) What are the syntactic and semantic characteristics of the adjective-to-causativeV alternation and the noun-to-transitiveV alternation? 2) What types of adjectives and nouns can go into the alternations? 3) What are the motivations for the adjective-causative alteration and noun-transitive alternation? Our observation and analysis are based on natural utterances from Weibo dataset (2011–2022) and we provide a constructional analysis from the perspective of interactional linguistics, which will be introduced in the next section.

2.3 Interactional Linguistics and Usage-Based Approach

The present study adopts the theoretical premises in Interactional Linguistics and Usage-based Approach by focusing on the interactive need in language use. Interactional linguistics is an approach to describing linguistic structures and meanings as a resource for social interaction. Previous studies within the framework focus mainly on discourse analysis and interactional sociolinguistics, including the sequential organization of turns of utterances [19–22], the prosodic features [23, 24] and interactional meanings in conversation [25, 26]. Interactional linguistics also suggests that grammar should be observed in actual use and the motivations for linguistic patterns are derived from the cognitive and communicative demands for producing coherent discourse. In line with this assumption, the current study investigates the semantic changes of words in their actual usage and considers communicative demand as an important motivation for semantic changes.

Usage-based Approach takes the view that language structure is not fixed but dynamic and fluid. Language constraints are probabilistic and largely shaped by communicative needs in actual use. The repetition of frequently-occurring linguistic patterns is an important determinant of semantic change [27, 28]. The theory provides an important theoretical basis for this study in explaining lexical semantic changes; that is, language is as a product of human creation in a broad social context and frequency is a key factor in semantic change.

In line with the theoretical premises of interactive linguistics and usage-based approach, the study explores the novel lexical semantic changes, based on naturally occurring data in Chinese social media.

3 Database and Method

To effectively identify the cases of adjective-causative alternation and noun-transitive V alteration, naturally occurring utterances in Weibo (micro-blog), a new popular and influential social platform, are used as the database in this study. The primary dataset is provided by NLPIR [29] as it is the largest available public data collection. This database includes about 5 million blogs and their meta data, such as blogs publishing time. According to our statistics, there are about 2.5 billion characters in the blogs over the six years of publishing time, from 2009 to 2014. Though the Weibo database has not been updated recently, it is large enough to provide sufficient data for our research.

Besides, to provide a diachronic comparison over two periods of time, an additional database is built for a case study of the newly arising target word *nèihán* 内涵 'inner quality/covert message'. To compare its grammatical distributions, two sub-datasets were compiled, each with 500 sentences randomly extracted from Weibo in 2009–14 and 2018–22, respectively. The two sub-datasets allow a contrastive comparison of the distributional variations of *nèihán* 内涵 across the two different time periods. Please see details in Sect. 5.

Since it may not be feasible to manually exhaust all the concerned patterns of adjective-causative and noun-transitiveV, automatic tools are applied to help with extracting relevant examples. Firstly, the blogs are preprocessed by LAC [30] with functions such as sentence segmentation and pos tagging. The verbs, nouns and adjectives with frequency > 100 are recorded in three collections respectively as the first step. To extract the target instances, POS tags are utilized for initial selection. Since categorial changes are the main concern of the study, the target words are chosen only when they occur in both non-verbal and verbal categories. Secondly, we use LTP [31], an open-source neural-based toolkit, to implement dependency parsing on each sentence. If a candidate appears in the verb-object (*sòng* 送 'send' in *wǒ sòng tā yīshù huā* 我送她一束花 'I sent her a bouquet of flowers') or as a pivotal V (*qǐng* 请 'treat' in *tā qǐng wǒ chīfàn* 他请我吃饭 'He treats me to lunch'), the candidate and corresponding sentence will be recorded in files. After this step, 1075 adjective-causative alternations and 999 noun-transitive alternations as candidates are collected. But there are also many unwanted noises, for example, the adjective *wánshàn* 完善 'complete' has long been used as a causative verb. Hence, it is not included. By manually checking each recorded candidate and its usage, the final set of data is determined for investigating the adjective-causative/noun-transitive alternations with novel semantic changes.

4 Emerging Changes: From Non-verbal to Verbal Usage

4.1 The Adjective-Causative Alternation

This section focus on the adjective-derived changes that convert a gradable adjective to a transitive verb. In total, 127 tokens of adjective-causative alternation are obtained. All of them are evaluative adjectives, which display the causative-transitive alternation, such as *měihǎo* 美好 'delightful', *jīngxǐ* 惊喜 'surprise', *qīngxīn* 清新 'fresh', *jīngcǎi* 精彩 'wonderful', *guānghuá* 光滑 'smooth', *qīngchè* 清澈 'clear', *wēnnuǎn* 温暖 'warm', *chéngshú* 成熟 'mature', *róuhé* 柔和 'soft', *jiǎndān* 简单 'simple'. Below are some examples of such shifting adjectives:

(8) yīwǎn zhūdùtāng wēnnuǎn nǐdewèi

一碗 猪肚汤, 温暖 你的胃。

'A bowl of pork belly soup will warm your stomach.'

(9) fēnxiǎng wēihuódòng jīngxǐ nǐ de shēnghuó.

分享 微活动, 惊喜 你 的 生活!

'Share micro-events and surprise your life!'.

(10) xīngchén qīngchèle míshīdeyǎn.

星辰 清澈 了 迷失的眼。

'The star makes the lost eye clear'

In general, these adjectives can be used in four major constructions:

(11) Attributive use before a noun:

mǎjiāqídejīngcǎirénshēng ràng wǒ xiànmù le.

马嘉祺的<u>精彩</u>人生 让 我 羡慕 了.

'Ma Jiaqi's wonderful life makes me envious.'

(12) Intransitive predicative use:

wǒde rénshēng yǐjīng zúgòu jīngcǎi le.

我的人生已经 足够 <u>精彩</u> 了.

'My life is good enough.'

(13) Marked causative use with a causative marker ling/rang/shi/jiao:

Xièxiènǐmen ràng wǒderénshēng jīngcǎi le yīxiē.

谢谢你们, 让 我的人生<u>精彩</u> 了 <u>一些</u>.

'Thank you for making my life better.'

(14) Unmarked causative-transitive use:

dúshū jīngcǎi le wǒderénshēng!

读书<u>精彩</u> 了 我的人生!

'Reading makes my life wonderful!'.

It is clear that *jīngcǎi* 'wonderful' is an evaluative adjective that can be used as an attribute modifying a noun or as a stative predicate, as in (11–12). It may also be used in the causative construction with an overt causative marker *ràng.* as in (13), while (14) illustrates the more recent use of *jīngcǎi* as a transitive V in the unmarked causative-transitive pattern. This novel usage pattern signals a re-association of form and meaning, which can be captured by the postulation of a new construction in Mandarin, as detailed below.

This novel usage in (14) above is semantically related to the marked causative construction in (13) as they both involve a causative meaning. The constructional shift from the marked to the unmarked causative is accompanied with the semantic change of *jīngcǎi* from denoting an attributive quality to denoting a change of state into the quality, i.e., caused to be wonderful. The newly arising construction can be analyzed as follows:

(15) The Adjective-derived Causative-transitive Construction (ACTC)

FORM: NP1 VAdjective-derived NP2

MEANING: The Subject-NP$_1$ serves as a Causer that causes the Object-NP$_2$ to change into the quality denoted by the adjectival meaning of the V

Example: *dúshū jīngcǎi le wǒderénshēng!* 读书<u>精彩</u>了我的人生!

'Reading makes my life wonderful!'

In sum, the Construction profiles a change of state or resultative state on the affected object that manifests the attributive quality originally denoted by the adjectival root.

4.2 The Noun-transitiveV Alternation

This section will focus on the noun-derived lexical semantic changes that converts an originally nominal lexeme to verbal uses. In the dataset, it found that eight commonly-occurring nouns can be used as transitive verbs, with a semantic change to denote a verbal interaction, including *sīxìn* 私信 'private message', *pínglùn* 评论 'comment', *wēixìn* 微信 'WeChat', *wàimài* 外卖 'order delivery', *ǒuxiàng* 偶像 'idol', *héxié* 和谐 'harmony', *nèihán* 内涵 'inner quality', and *huǒ* 火 'fire'. Below are examples for the last three target words, which are considered to undergo more recent changes:

(16) Nouns used as a transitive verb:

a. *xiūdé zài wēibóshàng húshuō! xiǎoxīn wǒ héxiéle nǐ*

休得 在 微博上 胡说! 小心 我 和谐了你。

'Don't talk nonsense on Weibo! Otherwise, I will block (harmonize) you.'

b. *bǎoluó nèihán hādēng.*

保罗 内涵 哈登。

'Paul covertly ironized Harden.'

c. *yīyèzhījiān píngtái huǒle liúlìlì.*

一夜之间 平台 火了 刘 俐俐.

'Overnight, the platform made Liu Lili become popular.'

These examples show that a rather abstract noun is used as an unmarked transitive verb followed directly by an affected object, indicating some sort of an impactive change on object. In view of semantic-to-syntactic change, the Noun-derived Transitive-Impactive Construction is proposed to capture the novel usage pattern, as specified below:

(17) The Noun-derived Transitive-Impactive Construction (NTIC)

FORM: NP1 + $V_{Noun-derived}$ + NP2

MEANING: The Subject-NP1 delivers an act of verbal interaction that renders an impact on the Object-NP2 in a way pertaining to the meaning of the nominal root

Example: *bǎoluó nèihán hādēng* 保罗内涵哈登 'Paul covertly ironized Harden.'

This Construction may account for the re-association of form and meaning in the novel usage pattern that shows the grammatical shift from a noun to a transitive verb with the corresponding semantic shift. To further explore the process of such a constructional change, a detailed case study of the keyword *nèihán* 内涵 'inner quality' is provided below, which demonstrates the most-recently arising change observed in the corpus.

5 A Case Study of *nèihán* 内涵 'Inner Quality/Covert Message'

To give a detailed analysis of the uses of *nèihán* 'covert quality', a sub-corpus was built that include a total of 1000 sentences containing the keyword *nèihán*内涵from two separate time periods of Weibo dataset (2009–2014 vs. 2018–2022). For each period, 500 sentences with the keyword are randomly selected. The two sub-datasets are built for a contrastive comparison of the uses of the keyword in two different time periods. The distributional variations between the two time periods are shown below in Table 1. It is noticed that the percentage of the verbal use of *nèihán* 内涵 has increased significantly over time, along with the decrease of its nominal use:

Table 1. The overall syntactic distribution of *nèihán*.

Grammatical roles	%	
	2009–2014	2018–2022
Noun	90%	46%
Intransitive verb	7%	19%
Transitive verb	3%	35%

In the earlier period, from 2009–2014, *nèihán* 内涵is mainly used as a noun, accounting for 90% of the total sample. The nominal use originally denotes an inner quality of a person or an object as in (18a), occupying 73%. The rest of the proportion in nominal use denotes covert obscene information or graph, normally appearing in a compound, such as *nèihán-tú*内涵图 'a porno graph' in (18b). Further derived from the nominal sense of obscene information, *nèihán* 内涵gets to be used as an intransitive verb indicating the inclusion of something indecent, normally related to sexual innuendo, as in (18c).

(18) From an abstract noun to an intransitive verb with semantic change in 2009-2014:

a. as a N denoting inner quality (73%):

tā hěn yǒu nèihán

他很 有 内涵。

'He is a person with inner-wisdom.'

b. as a N denoting covert obscene information (17%):

zuìqiángdàde nèihán-tú zhī yī míngbáide shízài shì tài xié'è le

最强大的 内涵图 之一, 明白的 实在 是 太邪恶 了!

'It is one of the most indecent pictures. So evil to understand!'

c. as an intransitive V denoting pervert:

zhème kāifàng de dòngzuò me dìyīzhāngtú nèihán le

这么 开放 的 动作么?!第一张图 内涵 了。

'Such an open posture? ! The first picture contains the meaning of obscene.'

Compared to the intransitive use (7%), the transitive use of *nèihán* as shown in (19a) below is even lower in frequency (3%). However, few years later in 2018–22, the transitive use of *nèihán* has grown significantly from 3% to 35%, with the impactive sense denoting the indirect and subtle verbal attack to different objects, as in (18a-c).

(19) A transitive verb with newly arising meaning in 2018-2022:

a. as a transitive V to human O:

tā nèihán wǒ le

他内涵 我 了。

'He indirectly satirized me.'

b. as a transitive V to animate O:

zhēnnīdefěnsī lián dàxióngmāo dōu nèihán

珍妮的粉丝 连 大熊猫 都 内涵。

'Jenny's fans even indirectly satirized pandas.'

c. as a transitive V to inanimate O:

jiějiě yīzhízàinèihán zhōngguónánzúdeshībàisài

姐姐 一直在内涵 中国男足的失败赛。

'My sister has been indirectly satirizing the failure of the Chinese men's

football team.'

It is clear that the noun *nèihán* 内涵 'inner quality' has undergone a lexical semantic change from denoting the positive inner quality to denoting covert message, which specifically refers to covert obscene information at the first stage, then extends to an indirect, non-obvious verbal act to attack, criticize, or impact a target, encoded as the direct object. The following pie charts show the semantic change within the two time periods (Fig. 1).

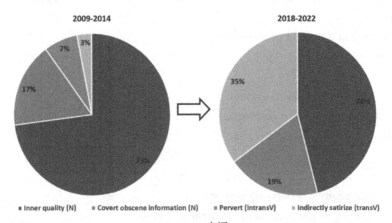

Fig. 1 The semantic change of *nèihán* 内涵 in 2009–2014 and 2018–2022

Interestingly, the specific nominal sense of covert obscene information/graph and its relevant intransitive use for the inclusion of pervert graphs tend to disappear in 2018–2022. Instead, the general sense of containing a covert message (not necessarily 'porno') is derived for the verbal use of *nèihán* 内涵, appearing in 2018–2022, with a relatively higher frequency increase for the transitive use (35%). Along with the lexical semantic change of *nèihán*, other abstract nouns such as *yīnyáng* 'Yin-yang' have also shown such a shift, which motivates the postulation of the new construction NTIC, as spelled out in (17). The Construction may be realized in two alternative forms, unmarked transitive and *bèi*-passive, as shown in (20). Both conveys the meaning that a deliberating Agent-subject delivers a verbal act of indirect attack, teasing or criticism to impact the affected Patient-Object (normally human) in a subtle and opaque manner.

(20) The transitive and the passive constructional patterns.

Constr. Pattern	Form-meaning mapping	Example
Transitive	Form: NP$_1$ + V + NP$_2$ Meaning: Actor + V + Theme	朱小姐狠狠内涵了国内竞技氛围。 'Miss Zhu indirectly satirized the domestic competitive atmosphere.'
Passive	Form: NP$_1$ + Passive marker *bèi* + NP$_2$ + V Meaning: Patient + Passive marker + Actor + V	我竟然被他内涵到了。 'I was insulted by his indirect satire.'

The semantic-to-syntactic change also involves a shift in evaluative polarit, whereby the originally positive sense of the noun *nèihán*内涵, referring to the inner quality/knowledge/wisdom of a person, is first extended to a rather negative meaning of obscene message, and then to a more general sense of covert message with a rather mean and derogative purpose. This shift also shows how words are manipulated to express interactive meanings in the social media, a tendency of interactivization in semantic change, as proposed in [1].

6   Summary and Discussion

The novel usage patterns in the Adjective-Causative alternation and Noun-TransitiveV alternation indicate that semantic shifts tend to go from less interactive to more interactive meanings. In the Adjective-Causative alternation, an evaluative adjective appears in the unmarked causative-transitive construction, which profiles the caused change into the attributive state denoted by the adjective, such as *jīngcǎi*精彩 'making it wonderful'. In the Noun-TransitiveV alternation, the semantic change is from nominal to intransitive use and then to highly transitive and affective use, such as *nèihán*内涵, as a representative case.

Based on the observed tendencies of semantic changes, it is confirmed that recent lexical semantic shifts occur along with the trend of interactivization, which may be motivated by the intensive degree and extensive range of interaction in social media. The ways lexical meanings change echo and respond to the intense communicative need in the digital era. The meaning-making process occurs in social interaction, which is viewed as "the primordial site for the use and the development of language" [32], even though it is virtual social interaction on the Internet. It also reflects linguistic creativity as new lexical meanings emerge with accompanied syntactical behavior. The use of readily available adjectives as causative verbs in the Adjective-derived Causative-Transitive Construction specified in (15) seems to manifest the economy principle in language use, which suggests speakers tend to use shorter forms in speaking with the least effort [33]. Furthermore, the increased need of human interaction in social media brings about the necessary change toward highly transitive forms, such as the Noun-derived Transitive-Impactive Construction in (17), which represents the intended manipulation of interpersonal relations through verbal interaction.

However, the vitality and persistence of the emerging usages remain uncertain, given the changeability and dynamics of social media interaction. The emergence of the new meanings is motivated by communicative need, linguistic creativity, and cognitive transfer under the shared social context and interactive rubrics. Nevertheless, as [34] says, "the dynamics of social interaction are simply too complex and unpredictable to be managed with anything else but an adaptive inventory of resources." The adaptive inventory is constantly shaped by the complexity and flexibility of interaction that are bound to be unpredictable in giving rise to specific new meanings. For instance, the usage of *nèihán* 内涵 denoting covert obscene graphs has been rarely seen after 2018.

Nevertheless, a general tendency of semantic change from less interactive to more interactive meanings seems to be in place, as illustrated repeatedly in the novel usages of words.

The analysis from the perspective of interactional linguistics has already provided an understanding of how people deploy linguistic resources in meaning-making in studies of discourse analysis. This study further extends the core tenets of Interactional Linguistics to lexical semantic issues in Mandarin Chinese, showing that semantic shifts are under the influence of interactivization.

7   Conclusion

This study explores the novel usages found in popular social media that involve lexical semantic changes of adjectives and nouns into transitive verbs with a causative or impactive meaning. Based on Weibo data, two major cases of novel changes are identified and constructional accounts are provided to account for the form-meaning re-associations underlying the observed changes. From the perspective of interactional linguistics, the novel usage patterns under study are taken to be instances of emerging lexical semantic changes demonstrating the general tendency of interactivization from low interactive to high interactive meanings. It ultimately shows that lexical semantic developments may also be motivated by interactional mechanisms under the popular and massive use of social media. With regard to the method of building a database, automatic tools are utilized to help detect the target candidates that may have undergone novel changes. Given the limitations of automatic selection, manual checking and editing follow to ensure accurate coverage of the target words. A detailed case study of the most recent meaning change in the uses of the word *nèihán* 'inner quality' is provided to show its progressive process of change from nominal to verbal uses over two different periods of time. The distributional skewing indicates that the word has been indeed used more frequently as a transitive or intransitive verb in Weibo, reinforcing the tendency of semantic changes from less interactive to more interactive meanings. Further works are recommended to explore other possible patterns of lexical semantic changes under the influence of interactivization in different speech communities.

References

1. Liu, M.C., He, T.C., Xue, S.R.: Cross-categorial extension and interactivization. Invited talk from Renmin University, Beijing, China, June 2021
2. Hopper, P.: Emergent grammar. Linguistics Society. In: Annual Meeting of the Berkeley, vol. 13, pp. 139–157, September 1987
3. Givón, T.: From discourse to syntax: grammar as a processing strategy. In: Givón, T. (Eds.) Series: Syntax and Semantics (1979)
4. Chafe, W.L.: The pear stories: cognitive, cultural, and linguistic aspects of narrative production. Adv. Disc. Process. 3 (1980)
5. Dubois, D. J. Fuzzy Sets and Systems: Theory and Applications. Academic Press (1980)
6. Hopper, P.J., Thompson, S.A.: Transitivity in grammar and discourse. Language, 251–299 (1980)
7. Hopper, P.: Emergent grammar. In: Annual Meeting of the Berkeley Linguistics Society, vol. 13, pp. 139–157, September 1987
8. Sacks, H., Schegloff, E.A., Jefferson, G.: A simplest systematics for the organization of turn taking for conversation. In: Studies in the Organization of Conversational Interaction, pp. 7–55 (1978)
9. Goodwin, C.: Conversational organization. Interaction between Speakers and Hearers (1981)
10. Pomerantz, A.: Agreeing and disagreeing with assessments: some features of pre-ferred/dispreferred turn shaped (1984)
11. Mazeland, H., Huiskes, M.: Dutch 'but'as a sequential conjunction. Stud. Interact. Linguist. **10**, 141–169 (2001)
12. Wang, L.: History of Chinese Grammar, pp. 102–104. The Commercial Press, Beijing (1998)
13. Xing, Fuyi. Word Recognition and Difficulty, pp. 52–138. The Commercial Press, Beijing (2003)
14. Lu, S.: A study of the usage of monophonic adjectives. Chinese Lang. 2 (1984)
15. Zhu, D.: Zhu Dexi's Collected Works, vol. 1: Grammar Lecture Notes Grammar Answer to Quantifiers and Pronouns (1999)
16. Yang, D.: A cognitive study of adjective verbs in Chinese non-commercial slogans, Hunan Normal University (2017)
17. Cai, J.: On the use of nouns as verbs. Lang. Teach. Res. 4 (1985)
18. Bojiang, Z.: Functional explanation of word usage. Chinese Lang. **5**, 339–346 (1994)
19. Selting, M., Couper-Kuhlen, E. (eds.) Studies in interactional linguistics (2001)
20. Steensig, J.: Notes on turn-construction methods in Danish and Turkish conversation. In: Selting, M., Couper-Kuhlen, E. (eds.), pp. pp. 259–286. Studies in interactional linguistics (2001)
21. Lindström, A.: Language as social action. Grammar, prosody, and interaction in Swedish conversation. Dissertaton, Uppsala (1999)
22. Helasvuo, M.-L.: Syntax in the making: the emergence of syntactic units in Finnish conversation. Benjamins (2001)
23. Zellers, M., Ogden, R.: Exploring interactional features with prosodic patterns. Lang. Speech **57**(3), 285–309 (2014)

24. Selting, M.: On the interplay of syntax and prosody in the construction of turn constructional units and turns in conversation. Pragmatics **6**, 357–388 (1996)

25. Östman, J.-O.: You know. A discourse functional approach. Benjamins (1981)

26. Hakulinen, A., Selting, M. (eds.) Syntax and lexis in conversation. Benjamins (2005)

27. Bybee, J.: From usage to grammar: the mind's response to repetition. Language **82**(4), 711–733 (2006)

28. Bybee, J.L.: Usage-based theory and exemplar representations of constructions. In Hoffmann, T., Trousdale, G. (Eds.) The Oxford Handbook of Construction Grammar. Oxford University Press (2013)

29. Zhang, H.P.: Web (2018). http://www.nlpir.org/wordpress/download/weibo.7z Accessed 31 Jan

30. Jiao, Z.Y., Sun, S.Q., Ke, S.: Chinese Lexical Analysis with Deep Bi-GRU-CRF Network. arXiv preprint arXiv:1807.01882 (2018)

31. Che, W.X., Feng, Y.L., Qin, L.B., Liu, T.: N-LTP: An Open-source Neural Chinese Language Technology Platform with Pretrained Models. arXiv preprintarXiv:2009.11616 (2020)

32. Schegloff, E.A.: Turn organization: one intersection of grammar and interaction. In: Ochs, E., Schegloff, E.A., Thompson, S.A. (Eds.) Interaction and Grammar, pp. 52–133 (1996b)

33. 邓云华. 白解红. 张晓. 英汉转类词的认知研究.《外语研究》**6**, 17–20 (2009)

34. Selting, M., Couper-Kuhlen, E. (Eds.) Studies in Interactional. Linguistics, vol. 10. John Benjamins Publishing. (2001)

The Phonetic Types, Mechanism, and Motivation of Syllable Contraction of "Numerals + Ge" in Henan Dialect

Yanmin Qiao(✉)

School of Liberal Arts, Nanjing University, Nanjing 210023, Jiangsu, China
josieqiaoyanmin@sina.com

Abstract. The pronunciation of numerals "one" to "ten", "ji" and the classifiers "ge" are investigated in 65 counties in Henan province. What's more mechanism and motivation of syllable contraction of "numerals + ge" are discussed. The rusults show that: the pronunciation of "numerals + ge" in Henan dialect, has three different types. The first type: "ge" keeps its integrity, which remains in the southern part of Henan; the second type: the consonant[k] of "ge" is lost, and numerals and "ge" are still two syllables, which are distributed in the central part of Henan; the third is to form a syllable, which is mainly concentrated in Jin dialect areas in northern Henan and its surrounding areas. The process is: two independent syllables → the consonant[k] of "ge" is lost → a syllable with a long vowel → a normal syllable.

The priority levels of different numerals combined with "ge" in the same dialect are: one, two, three > seven, several, four, ten, five, eight > six, nine.

The syllable contraction of different numerals and "ge" occurs at different stages of the vowel evolution of "ge". In Wuzhi dialect, the vowel of "ge" may be *a while combination; In Xingyang dialect, it may be *ɔ; in Luoyang typle, it may be *o; and Jiyuan, Huojia, and Anyang dialects, it may be *ɤ/ə. Border zones often take many forms. The geographical distribution shows that the vowel of "ge" had a historical evolution of a → ɔ → o → ə/ɤ, which was left over due to the unbalanced development of various points.

There are several reasons for the syllable contraction of numerals and "ge". Firstly, "ge" does not have the function of quantity. Secondly, the classifiers "ge" is generalized in Henan dialect. Thirdly, usage frequency and combination play an important role in communication. Numerals and "ge" are often used frequently. Lastly, the Principle of "one pronunciation, one meaning" Promotes the merge of numerals and "ge".

Keywords: "numerals + ge" · Syllable contraction · Jin dialect · Official dialect in Central China

This study was funded by the following projects: "A Study on the Contact Evolution between Jianghuai Mandarin and Its Surrounding Dialects and Database Construction (19ZDA307)" and "A Study on Dialect Use and Variation of Urban Adolescents from the Perspective of Language Contact –A Case Study of Shanghai, Nanjing and Hangzhou (17YJC740084)".

© The Author(s), under exclusive license to Springer Nature Switzerland AG 2023
Q. Su et al. (Eds.): CLSW 2022, LNAI 13495, pp. 139–160, 2023.
https://doi.org/10.1007/978-3-031-28953-8_12

1 Introduction

In Mandarin, when the numerals are "liang(*two*)" or "san(*three*)", and the classifiers are "ge", the numerals are combined with "ge", and the numerals change their pronunciations into [lia] and [sa] separately. However, in Henan dialect, the numerals "one" to "ten" and "several" can be combined with the classifiers "ge". Such as:

(1) Wo   chi   le   **[yo]**_{yi ge}   pingguo.   (Neihuang county)

　　I   ate   particle   one   apple.

　　I ate one apple.

(2) Wo   chi   le   **[yɔ]**_{yi ge}   mo.   (Xingyang county)

　　I   ate   particle   one   steamed bun.

　　I   ate   one   steamed bun.

(3) Wo   mai   le   **[suo]**_{si ge}   baozi.   (Luoyang city)

　　I   bought   particle   four   steamed stuffed buns.

　　I   bought   four steamed stuffed buns.

(4) Yi hui er gongfu, ni   dou   chi **[lua]**_{liu ge}   xiao   baozi a.   (Yanshi county)

　　After a while,   you   ate   six   small   steamed stuffed buns.

　　After a while, you ate   six   small   steamed buns.

(5) Wo   mai^D   **/lyr¹³/**_{liu ge}   xiangjiao.(Huojia county)

　　wo   mai   particle   six   bananas.

　　I   bought   six   bananas.

(6) Ni cai chi   **/tɕʰyo⁴²/**_{qi ge}   bianshi ya!   (Mianchi county)

　　you only   ate   seven   dumplings.

　　You   ate   only   seven   dumplings.

(7) Wo mai   le   **/pɑ²⁴/**_{ba ge}   pingguo.   (Xun county)

　　I   bought particle   eight   apples.

　　I   bought   eight   apples.

(8) Ni   cai   chi   **/tɕyo⁵¹/**_{jiu ge}   jiaozi ya!(Jiyuan county)

　　you   only   ate   nine   dumplings.

　　You ate only nine   dumplings.

(9) Wo chi   le   **/suo⁵³/**_{shi ge} jiaozi .(gongyi county)

　　I   ate   particle   ten   dumplings.

　　I   ate   ten dumplings.

(10) Wo chi hao **/tɕyo³¹/**_{ji ge} jiaozi le.(xin'an county)

　　I   ate   seven   dumplings.

　　I   ate   seven   dumplings.

At the same time, if the current pronunciation of numerals and the current pronunciation[1] of "ge" are combined, the current pronunciation can not get in many dialects, such as: Jiaozuo city, Jiyuan city, Qinyang county, Huojia county, Xinxiang city, Wuzhi county, Boai county. For examples:

　　In Xingyang county: If we make the current pronunciation of "yi[i¹³]" and "ge[kɤ⁵¹]" merged, we couldn't get the pronunciation of [yo⁴²].

　　Luoyang city: if we make the current pronunciation of "si[sɿ ³¹]" and "ge[kɤ⁵¹]" merged, we couldn't get the pronunciation of [suo⁵¹].

---

[1] The current pronunciation means that the pronunciation is used by people now.

Mianchi city: if we make the current pronunciation of "qi[tɕ^{h}i^{55}]" and "ge[kɤ^{31}]" merged, we couldn't get the pronunciation of [tɕ^{h}yo^{42}].

In addition, in some dialects, the consonant of "ge" falls off and does not form a syllable contraction in the process of speech, such as:

(11) ni   jiujiu   ke zhen duo a, ni dou you [tɕi^{51} ɵə^{0}] $_{qi\ ge}$ jiujiu ya! (Xinmi county)

  you   uncles   so many,   you have seven uncles.

  you have so many uncles,   and you have seven uncles.

(12) wo chi lou [pɑ^{52} ɵə^{0}] $_{ba\ ge}$ jiaozi.(Kaifeng xian)

  I ate particle eight dumplings.

  I ate eight dumplings.

At present, scholars make the research of this phenomenon focusing on two aspects.firstly, describing dialect syllable contraction phenomenon, such as Huojia dialect (He 1989), Xingyang dialect (Wang 1994), Xinxiang county dialect (Xie 2006), Jiaxian dialect (Chen 2007), Hua county dialect (Liu 2004), Dengfeng dialect (Fang 2012), Luoyang dialect (Xu 2016), Xinmi dialect (Mengyang 2019), Linzhou dialect (Wu and Guo 2019) and the syllable contraction in central north China official dialect (Sun 2014.a). Secondly, analyzing the syllable contraction mechanism. e.g., Yuen Ren Chao (1927/1980), Jiang, Lansheng (1994), Feng, Chuntian (2002), Liu, Xiangbai (2004), Zhu, Ligang (2017) etc., all of which disscuss how liang(two) and san(three) are merged with "ge". However, scholars have different views at present.

When "two" and "three" are combined with "ge" separately, Yuen Ren Chao (1927/1980) speculated that the process of syllable contraction are that:

liaŋ + kɤ → liaŋgə → liãə → liãa → lia.

san + kɤ → saŋ kɤ → sangə → sãə → sãa → sa.

Lin Tao, Wang Lijia (1992) and Liu Xiangbai (2004) also believed that the process is that the initial consonant of "ge" is lost and weak reading is ə, and then produce syllable contraction. For example:

	even read modulation	light sounds	syllable contraction ,lose the tail of vowel
u+kɤ	→u+kɤ	→u ə	→uə
i^{55}+kɤ^{51}	→i^{35} kɤ^{51}	→i^{35} ə	→i^{35}
liaŋ^{214}+kɤ^{51}	→liaŋ^{214} kɤ^{51}	→liaŋ^{214} ə	→lia^{214}
san^{55}+kɤ^{51}	→san^{55} kɤ^{51}	→san^{55} ə	→sa^{55}

So this paper investigates the pronunciation of "numerals + ge" in 65 dialect points of Henan Province, analyzing the process of the syllable contraction of "numerals + ge". And the reasons of syllable contraction. For the convenience of discussion, all of the syllables do not mark with tone.

2 The Syllable Contraction Types, Dialect Distribution, and Historical Stage of "numerals+ge"

2.1 The Syllable Contraction Types and Dialect Distribution

In the process of speech, the pronunciation forms of "numerals + ge" have three types in Henan dialect. **Type one:** The consonant of ''ge'' do not fall off, that is to say, the numerals and ''ge'' do not merge, and they are read separately. **Type two:** the consonant

[k]of "ge" falls off, maintaining the weak-reading form, and it does not merge with the numerals, which is two syllables. This is called continuous-reading aphasia. In some dialects, when the consonant [k] of "ge" falls off, the vowel is affected by the preceding word, resulting in producing the medial vowel of [i], [u]or [z]. **Type three**: the consonant [k]of "ge" falls off, and then the vowels of "ge" are merged with the numerals, changing two syllables into a syllable.

2.1.1 Type One: Maintain Its Original Syllable

Type one: except "one, two, and three" can be combined with "ge", the other numerals do not merge with "ge" during the process of speech, which is represented by "-" in the following tables. This phenomenon is mainly distributed in the south of Henan, as shown in the following Table 1.

Table 1. The pronunciation of "numerals + ge" in Guanzhong dialect regions, Yantai dialect regions, luoxiang dialect regions, shangfu dialect regions, xinbeng dialect regions

Dialect regions	Dialect places	yi ge (one)	liang ge (two)	san ge (three)	si ge (four)	wu ge (five)	liu ge (six)	qi ge (seven)	ba ge (eight)	jiu ge (nine)	shi ge (ten)	ji ge (several)
Guan zhong regions	Lingbao	yo	lia	sa	—2	—	—	—	—	—	—	—
	Sanmenxia	yo	—	—	—	—	—	—	—	—	—	—
	Shan xian	—	—	—	—	—	—	—	—	—	—	—
Luosongregions	Lushi county	yo	lia	sa	—	—	—	—	—	—	—	—
Zheng kai regions	Minquan	yo	lia	sa	—	—	—	—	—	—	—	—
Yanhe regions	fanxian	—	—	—	—	—	—	—	—	—	—	—
Luo xiang regions	Xiangcheng	yo	lia	sa	—	—	—	—	—	—	—	—
	Huai yang	—	lia	sa	—	—	—	—	—	—	—	—
	Zheng yang	yo	lia	sa	—	—	—	—	—	—	—	—
	Queshan	yo	lia	sa	—	—	—	—	—	—	—	—
	Shangcai	yo	lia	sa	—	—	—	—	—	—	—	—
Shangfu regions	Yong cheng	—	lia	sa	—	—	—	—	—	—	—	—

(continued)

2 "—" means that The consonant of "ge" does not fall off, that is to say, the numerals and "ge" do not merge, and they are read separately.

Table 1. (*continued*)

Dialect regions	Dialect places	yi ge (one)	liang ge (two)	san ge (three)	si ge (four)	wu ge (five)	liu ge (six)	qi ge (seven)	ba ge (eight)	jiu ge (nine)	shi ge (ten)	ji ge (several)
	Suixian	yo	lia	sa	—	—	—	—	—	—	—	—
	Luyi	—	lia	sa	—	—	—	—	—	—	—	—
	Zhe cheng	—	—	—	—	—	—	—	—	—	—	—
	Taikang	yo	lia	sa								
Nanlu regions	Fang cheng	yo	lia	sa	—	—	—	—	—	—	—	—
	Neixiang	yo	lia	sa	—	—	—	—	—	—	—	—
	Deng zhou	—	—	—	—	—	—	—	—	—	—	—
Xinbeng regions	Tongbai	yo	lia	sa	—	—	—	—	—	—	—	—
	Xinyagn	—	—	—	—	—	—	—	—	—	—	—
	Xixian		lia	sa	—	—	—	—	—	—	—	—
	Shang cheng	—	lia	sa	—	—	—	—	—	—	—	—
	Guang shan	—	—	—	—	—	—	—	—	—	—	—
	Huaibin	—										—

2.1.2 Type Two: Lost Consonant

This phenomenon is mainly distributed in the central part of Henan, as shown in the following Table 2.

It can be seen from the table above, the consonant of "ge" all fall off in "si ge(four), wu ge(five), liu ge(six), qi ge(severn), jiu ge(nine), shi ge(ten)", but no syllable contraction is formed in Zhengzhou, Kaifeng County, Neihuang, Qingfeng and Xiping. Even in Kaifeng County and Qingfeng County, the "ba ge(eight)" is also in the stage of continuous aphasia.

After falling off the consonant of "ge", there are two forms of pronunciation. Type one: only the consonant of "ge" falls off. Type two: after the consonant of "ge" falls off, it is affected by the previous word to produce a medial vowel of [i], [u] or [z]. For example, in Kaifeng county and Neihuang county, in the phrase of "qi ge(seven), ji ge(several)", they will produce the vowel of [i], while in the phrase of "wu ge(five), liu ge(six), jiu ge(nine)", they will produce the medial vowel of [u]. Meanwhile in Neihuang county, in the phrase of "si ge(four), shi ge(ten)", they will produce the medial vowel of [z].

Table 2. The pronunciation of "numerals + ge" in Zhengkai dialect regions and Nanlu dialect regions

Dialect places		ba ge (eight)	qi ge (seven)	ji ge (several)	si ge (four)	shi ge (ten)	wu ge (five)	liu ge (six)	jiu ge (nine)
zheng kai regions	Zhengzhou	pa	tɕʰi Øo	tɕi Øo	sɿ Øo	ʂʅ Øo	u Øo	liou Øuo	tɕiou Øuo
	Kaifeng couty	pa Øə	tɕʰi Øiə	tɕi Øiə	sɿ Øə	ʂʅ Øə	u Øuə	liəu Øuə	tɕiəu Øuə
	Neihuang	pa	tɕʰi Øio	tɕi Øio	sɿ zɣ	ʂʅ zɣ	u Øuo	liou Øuo	tɕiou Øuo
	Qingfeng	pa Øə	tɕʰi Øə	—	—	ʂʅ Øə	u Øə	liou Øə	tɕiou Øə
Nan lu regions	Xiping	pa kɣ	tɕʰi Øə	tɕi Øə	sɿ Øə	ʂʅ Øə	u Øə	liou Øuə	tɕ iou Øuə

2.1.3 Type Two: Syllable Contraction

The phenomenon of syllable contraction is mainly distributed in the northern part of Henan, After combing, according to the different vowels at the end of the syllable, it is divied into Wuzhi type, Xingyang type, Luoyang type and Jiyuan type.

(1) Wuzhi type

In Wuzhi dialect, after the combination of numerals and "ge", the final vowel is [ɑ], and a long vowel. As shown in the table below.

Table 3. The Pronunciation of "numerals +ge" in Wuzhi Dialect

dialect places	yi ge (one)	qi ge (seven)	ji ge (several)	wu ge (five)	liu ge (six)	jiu ge (nine)	si ge (four)	shi ge (ten)	liang ge (two)	san ge (three)	ba ge (eight)
Wuzhi	y:o/ i:ɑ	tɕʰi:ɑ	tɕi:ɑ	u:ɑ	lu:ɑ	tɕyo:uɑ	sɿ:ɑ	ʂl:ɑ	liɑ	sɑ	pʌ

(2) Xingyang type

In Xingyang, except for "liang ge(two), san ge(three)", after the combination of the other numerals and "ge", the final vowel is [ɔ]and a long vowel. As shown in the table below.

(3) Luoyang type

Luoyang type is mainly distributed in Luoyang and its surrounding areas, including Yanshi, Xin'an county, Yiyang and Gongyi, and so on. Among Luoyang type, numerals and "ge" form a combination, and the final vowel is [o], except for "liang ge(two), san

Table 4. The Pronunciation of "numerals +ge" in Xingyang Dialect

dialect places	yi ge (one)	qi ge (seven)	ji ge (several)	wu ge (five)	liu ge (six)	jiu ge (nine)	si ge (four)	shi ge (ten)	liang ge (two)	san ge (three)	ba ge (eight)
Xingyang	yɔ	tsʰiːɔ	tɕiːɔ	uːɔ	liouːɔ	tɕiouːɔ	sıːɔ	ʂɫːɔ	lia	sa	pa

ge(three), pa ge(eight)". Luoyang type can also be divided into two types: A and B. As shown in the table below.

Table 5. The Pronunciation of "numerals +ge" in Luanchuan, Luoyang, Yanshi, Xin'an Gongyi

	Dialect places	yi ge (one)	qi ge (seven)	ji ge (several)	wu ge (five)	liu ge (six)	jiu ge (nine)	si ge (four)	shi ge (ten)	liang ge (two)	san ge (three)	ba ge (eight)
A	Luanchuang	yo	tɕʰio	tɕyo	uo	luo	tɕyo	so	ʂo	lia	sa	pa
B	Luoyang	yo	tɕʰyo	tɕyo	uo	luo	tɕyo	suo	ʂuo	lia	sa	pa
	Yanshi	yo	tɕʰyo	tɕyo	uo	luo	tɕyo	suo	ʂuo	lia	sa	pa
	Xin'an	yo	tɕʰyo	tɕyo	uo	luo	tɕyo	suo	ʂuo	lia	sa	pa
	Yiyang	yo	tɕʰyo	tɕyo	uo	luo		suo	ʂuo	lia	sa	pa
	Gongyi	yo	tɕʰyo	tɕyo	uo	—	tɕyo	suo	ʂuo	lia	sa	pa

The difference between type A and type B is that the pronunciation of qi ge(seven) is [tɕʰio] in type A, while type B is [tɕʰyo]. At the same time, The combined sounds of "si ge, shi ge" are [so], [ʂo], while type B is [suo], [ʂuo].

(4) Jiyuan type

In Jiyuan type, the last vowel after the combination is [ə], which is concentrated in northern Henan including Jiyuan, Qinyang, Wenxian, Boai, Jiaozuo, Huojia, Huixian, as well as Fengqiu, Changyuan, and other places. We subdivide it into two types: A and B. As shown in the Table 6 below.

It can be seen from the above table that, the final vowel after the combination of other numerals and "ge" is [ə] or [ɤ], in addition to "liang ge(two), ang e(three), ba ge(eight)". But there are also differences among different dialects. Such as, after the combination of "liu ge(six)", the pronunciation is [luə] in type A, while type B reads [lyə].

2.2 The Syllable Contraction of Historical Stages of "Numerals + ge"

Wang Hongjun (1999: 201) pointed out that the combination of two syllables generally goes through the process of "two normal syllables → a normal syllable + soft tone

Table 6. The Pronunciation of "numerals +ge" in Jiyuan, Qinyang, Wenxian, Boai, Luoning, Huojia, Fengqiu, Changyuan

	Dialect places	yi ge (one)	qi ge (seven)	ji ge (several)	wu ge (five)	liu ge (six)	jiu ge (nine)	si ge (four)	shi ge (ten)	liang ge (two)	san ge (three)	ba ge (eight)
A	Jiyuan	iə	tɕʰiə	tɕiə	uə	luə	tɕyə	sə	ʂə	lia	sa	pa
	Qinyang	iə	tɕʰiə	tɕiə	uə	luə	tɕyə	sə	ʂə	lia	sa	pa
	Wenxian	iə/yo	tɕʰiə	tɕiə	uə	luə	tɕyə	sə	ʂə	lia	sa	pa
	Boai	iə	tɕʰiə	tɕiə	—	luə	—	sə	—	lia	sa	pa
	Luoning	iə	tɕʰiə	tɕiə	uə	luə	tɕ yə	sə	ʂə	lia	sa	pa
B	Huojia	yɣ	tɕʰiɣ	tɕiɣ	uɣ	lyɣ	tɕyɣ	sʅ ɣ	sʅ ɣ	lia	sa	pa
	Fengqiu	yə	tɕʰiə	tɕiə	uə	—	tɕyə	sə	ʂə	lia	sa	pa
	Changyuan	yə	tɕʰiə	tɕiə	ŋə	lyə	tɕyə	sʅ ə	ʂʅə	lia	sa	pa

→ a long syllable → a normal syllable". The synchronic geographical distribution reflects the diachronic phonetic evolution. From the pronunciation form of the synchronic geographical distribution of "numerals + ge" in Henan dialect, we can see the historical track of "numerals + ge". The pronunciation of "numerals + ge" have their own syllables in Guanzhong dialect areas, Yantai dialect areas, Luoxiang dialect areas, Shangfu dialect areas, Xinbeng dialect areas and so on. That is to say, "numerals + ge" is still in two normal syllable stages, which is the stage that the combination has not yet begun. The consonant [k]of "ge" in Zhengkai dialect areas and Nanlu dialects dialect areas are lost, which is the first stage in the process of phonetic integration. In Wuzhi dialect and Xingyang dialect, the consonant [k] of " ge" is lost, and then the finals and the front words are combined into a long syllable, which is the second stage, namely the long syllable stage. In Jiyuan type and Luoyang type, the numerals and "ge" are merged into a normal syllable, and the long sound disappears. This is the last stage of combination. What is more, the combination of two syllables are completed. In other words, the combination of the numerals and "ge" experienced the followed stages: two normal syllables → the consonant [k] of "ge" loss → a long syllable → a normal syllable.

On the one hand, the development of various dialects is uneven. Some dialects have completed the combination of numerals and "ge", and some are still in development. For example, Jiyuan type and Luoyang type have developed rapidly and have completed the combination. Xiping in Nanlu dialect areas, Qingfeng County, Neihuang County, and Kaifeng County in Zheng Kai dialect areas are still in the stage of the loss of consonant [k] of "ge". Therefore, the core areas of the syllable contraction is Jin dialect in Northern Henan radiating from the core areas to the surrounding areas. The Luosong dialect areas of Zhongyuan Mandarin are close to the Jin dialect areas, so the combination of syllables develops rapidly. The Zhengkai dialect areas of Zhongyuan Mandarin are a little far from the core area, so it develops slowly. Xin Beng dialect areas, Guanzhong dialect areas, Yantai dialect areas, Luoxiang dialect areas, and Shangfu dialect areas are all far away from the core area, so it develops the slowest. On the other hand, in the same dialect, when different numerals merge with "ge", the degree is not balanced. Some have completed the syllable contraction, and some have not. Such as:

Table 7. The Pronunciation of "numerals +ge" in Dengfeng, Xinmi, Xinzheng, Huixian, Anyang, Linzhou, Tangyin, Qixian

	Dialect places	yi ge (one)	qi ge (seven)	ji ge (several)	wu ge (five)	liu ge (six)	jiu ge (nine)	si ge (four)	shi ge (ten)	liang ge (two)	san ge (three)	ba ge (eight)
Zheng kai dialect areas	Dengfeng	yo	tɕʰyo	tɕyo	uə	—	tɕiəu / Øə	sə	ʂə	lia	sa	pa Øə
	Xinmi	yo	tɕʰi Øə	tɕiə	uə	lyə	tɕiou / Øə	sɿ ə	ʂʐ ə	lia	sa	pa Øə
	Xinzheng	yo	tɕʰiə	tɕiə	uə	liou / Øuə	tɕyə	sɿ ə	ʂʐ ə	lia	sa	pa
Yubei jin dialect areas	Huixian	yə	tɕʰiə	tɕiə	uə	liou / Øuə	tɕiou / Øuə	sə	ʂə	lia	sa	pa
	Anyang	yə	tɕʰiə	tɕiə	uə	liou / Øuə	tɕiou / Øuə	sə	ʂə	lia	sa	pa
	Linzhou	yə	tɕʰiə	tɕiə	uə	liou / Øuə	tɕiou / Øuə	sə	ʂə	liɔ	sɔ	pɔ
	Tangyin	yə	tɕʰiə	tɕiə	uə	liou / Øuə	tɕiou / Øuə	sə	ʂə	lia	sa	pa
	Qixian	yə	tɕʰiə	tɕiə	uə	liou / Øuə	tɕyə	sə	—	lia	sa	pa

It can be seen from the above Table 7. that in the Dengfeng, Xinmi and Xinzheng dialects of Zheng Kai dialect areas, "yi ge, liang ge, san ge,si ge, wu ge, qi ge, shi ge, and ji ge (several)" have complete the combination, while "liu ge, jiu ge" have not finished the process.

In Huixian, Anyang, Linzhou, Tangyin, Qixian, and other dialects of Jin dialect in northern Henan, "liu" and "jiu" have not been combined with "ge", which is still in the stage of the loss of consonant [k], and the vowel of "ge" are affected by the preceding words, resulting in [u] medial vowel (Fig. 1).

The number of different numerals combined with ''ge" in 65 dialects is counted as shown in the Table 8 below.

It can be seen from the above table that due to the high use frequency of ''yi ge, liang ge, san ge", the number of syllable contractions is dominant and the proportion is the highest. The number of ''liu ge" and ''jiu ge" is small, and the proportion is low. The number of ''si ge, wu ge, shi ge, ji ge, ba ge" is equivalent.

Therefore, when different numerals are combined with ''ge", the priority of forming a combination is:

yi ge,liang ge,san ge > qi ge,ji ge,si ge,shi ge,wu ge,ba ge > liu ge,jiu ge.

Table 8. Statistical table of " numerals + ge " in Henan dialect (In the following table, "quantity of syllable contraction" means the number of numerals can be combined with "ge" in the dialect investigated in this paper; the "proportion of syllable contraction" refers to the proportion of numerals can be combined with "ge".)

numerals + ge	Quantity of syllable contraction	Proportion of syllable contraction
yi ge (one)	50	76.9%
liang ge (two)	52	80%
san ge(three)	49	80%
si ge (four)	34	52.3%
wu ge (five)	34	52.3%
liu ge (six)	18	27.7%
qi ge(seven)	30	46.1%
ba ge (eight)	30	46.1%
jiu ge (nine)	14	21.5%
shi ge (ten)	27	41.5%
ji ge ((several)	30	46.2%

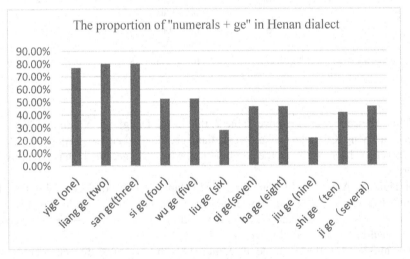

Fig. 1. The proportion of "numerals + ge" in Henan dialect

3   The Generating Process of Syllable Contraction of "numerals and ge"

As has been analyzed above, the first stage of syllable contraction is the falling off of the consonant [k] of "ge", which has reached a consensus in academia, but there are still two problems. First, how does the consonant [k] fall off? Yuen Ren Chao (1927)

believed that [k] was lost after becoming a voice sound [g], that is to say: k > g > Ø. Kong, Xiangqing (2005) believed that [k] first became a voiced sound [g], and then was assimilated into [ŋ], that is to say: k > g > ŋ > Ø, and then lost. Zhu Ligang (2017) believed that after [k] became a voiced sound[g], it was further weakened into [ɣ] by the influence of language flow, and then lost, that is to say:k > g > ɣ > Ø. They are all possible. Second, after [k]is lost, what specific changes have taken place to the syllable of numeral and the vowel of ''ge'', is it lost, combined, or fusion?

In most dialect areas of Henan Province, ''liang ge(two), san ge(three), ba ge(eight)'' have formed the syllable contraction, and the main vowel after syllable contraction is [a], which is quite different from the syllable contraction of other numerals and ''ge''. Therefore, in this paper, the ''yi ge, si ge, wu ge, liu ge, qi ge, jiu ge, ji ge'' is divided into a group, and ''liang ge, san ge, ba ge'' is divided into the other group.

3.1   The Process of Syllable Contraction of "YI GE, SI GE, WU Ge, Liu Ge, Qi Ge, Jiu Ge, Ji Ge"

3.1.1   The Process of Syllable Contraction of Wuzhi Type and Xinyang Type

According to Table 3, after the syllable contraction in Wuzhi type and Xingyang type, the last vowel is [a] and [ɔ] respectively, so it is speculated that when the numerals are combined with ''ge'', the final vowel of ''ge'' is[*a]and [*ɔ] respectively. After the syllable contraction, it is a long vowel, which is in the early stages of sound in Wuzhi type and Xingyang type. In Xingyang dialect, when ''yi(one)'' is combined with ''ge'', the form of syllable contraction is [yɔ]. Because [i] is affected by the round vowel [ɔ], it changed into [yɔ]. In Wuzhi dialect, when ''yi'' is combined with ''ge'', the form of syllable contraction is [yo], which should be affected by the surrounding dialects. In Wuzhi dialect, when ''jiu(nine)'' is combined with ''ge'', the form of syllable contraction is [tɕyo:ua]. According to the form, it is believed that it may be affected by the previous word vowel [u], resulting in producing the [u] media vowel. Therefore, it is speculated that when ''wu(five)'' and ''liu(six)'' are combined with ''ge'', they may be affected by the preceding words and also produce the media vowel[u]. The specific process of syllable contraction is as follows:

	Wuzhi type	Xingyang type
yi ge(one)	i + *a → i a → iːa	i + *ɔ → i ɔ → iɔ → yɔ
qi ge(seven)	tɕʰi + *a → tɕʰi a → tɕʰiːa	tsʰi + *ɔ → tsʰi ɔ → tsʰiːɔ
ji ge(several)	tɕi + *a → tɕi a → tɕiːa	tɕi + *ɔ → tɕi ɔ → tɕiːɔ
si ge(four)	sๅ + *a → sๅ a → sๅ ːa	sๅ + *ɔ → sๅ ɔ → sๅ ːɔ
shi ge(ten)	sๅ + *a → sๅ a → sๅ ːa	ʂๅ + *ɔ → ʂๅ ɔ → ʂๅ ːɔ
wu ge(five)	u + *a → u a → u ua → uːa	u + *ɔ → u ɔ → uɔ
liu ge(six)	lu + *a → lu a → lu ua → luːa	liou + *ɔ → liou ɔ → liouːɔ
jiu ge(nine)	tɕiou + *a → tɕ yo ua → tɕ yo:ua	tɕiou + *ɔ → tɕiou ɔ → tɕiouːɔ

3.1.2 The Process of Syllable Contraction of Luoyang Type

Table 4 shows that the final vowel is [o] after the syllable contraction. According to Table 5, in Luanchuan dialect, the form of syllable contraction of "qi ge(seven),si ge(four),shi ge(ten)" are [tɕʰio],[so],[ʂ o] respectively, it is speculated that the vowel of "ge" maybe [*o]. The process of syllable contraction is:

qi ge(seven): tɕʰi+*o→tɕʰi   o→tɕʰio

si ge(four): sɿ+*o→sɿ   o→so

shi ge(ten): ʂl+*o→ʂl   o→ʂo

Because the vowel of "yi" is [i], when it is combined with [*o], it is usually assimilated into [y] by the round [o], then the form of syllable contraction is changed into [yo]. That is to say:

i + *ko → i + o → io → yo.

In Luoyang, Yanshi, Xin'an, Yiyang, Gongyi, and other dialects, the form of syllable contraction of "qi ge, ji ge (several) " are [tɕʰyo],[tɕyo] respectively, and the process of syllable contraction is the same as the process of syllable contraction of "yi ge".In Luanchuan dialect, the vowel of syllable contraction of "qi ge" is [io], which is the predecessor of [yo].

In Luoyang, Yanshi, Xin'an, Yiyang, Gongyi, and other dialects, the form of syllable contraction of "si ge, shi ge" are [suo] and [ʂ uo]. Because during the process of the syllable contraction, affected by the round vowel of [o], it produced the [u] medial vowel, and then form the vowel of [uo]. That is to say:

si ge(four): sɿ+*o→sɿ   o→so→suo

shi ge(ten): ʂɿ+*o→ʂɿ   o→ʂo→ʂuo

The process of syllable contraction of "wu ge, liu ge, jiu ge" is relatively simple, and the vowel of "ge" is affected by the preceding word, resulting in producing [u] medial vowel or directly combing. That is to say:

Wu ge(five): u+*o→u   uo→uo   u+*o→u   o→uo

Liu ge(six): lu+*o→lu   uo→luo   lu+*o→lu   o→luo

When jiu(nine) is combined with "ge", the syllable [iouo] does not exist in the local dialect phonology, so [i]and [u]are combined into [y] firstly, namely:

jiu ge(nine): tɕiou + *o → tɕiouo → tɕyo.

Therefore, in Luoyang type, when numbers are combined with "ge", the vowel of "ge" may be [*o].

in Luanchuan dialect, the main vowel of "yi ge, qi ge, ji ge(several)" is all [i], but the vowel of form of syllable contraction of "qi ge" is [io], not [yo]. While the vowel of the form of syllable contraction of " yi ge, ji ge" is [yo], indicating that the evolution is not synchronous within the dialect.

3.1.3 The Process of Syllable Contraction of Jiyuan Type

The pronunciation of yi(one), liu(six) and qi(seven) all have laryngeal plug tails, when yi(one), liu(six), and qi(seven) are combined with "ge", they lose the laryngeal plug tails firstly and then the two syllables are combined. The syllable contraction is as follows:

yi ge(one): i?+*ə/*ɣ→i+*ə/*ɣ→iə→i+ə→iə

qi ge(seven): tɕʰi?+*ə/*ɣ→tɕʰi+*ə/*ɣ→tɕʰi+ə→tɕʰiə

ji ge(several): tɕi+*ə/*ɣ→tɕi+*ə/*ɣ→tɕi+ə→tɕiə

si ge(four): sɿ+*ə/*ɣ→sɿ+ə→sɿə→sə

shi ge(ten): ʂʅ+*ə/*ɣ→ʂʅ+kə→ʂʅə

wu ge(five): u+*ə/*ɣ→u+ə→uə

liu ge(six): lu?+*ə/*ɣ→lu+ə→lu uə→luə

When jiu(nine) is combined with "ge", [i] and [u] are formed into [y] firstly. Namely: jiu ge(nine): tɕiou + *ə/*ɣ → tɕiou + ə → tɕiou ə → tɕ iouə → tɕyə.

In Huojia dialect and Changyuan dialect, the form of syllable contraction of "liu ge" is [lyɣ]or [lyə], which is different from [luə] in Jiyuan dialect. Because in Huojia dialect the syllable of "liu(six)" is [liou], when [liou] is combined with "ge", [i] is combined with [u] into [y].

liu ge(six): liou + *ə → liou uə → liuə → lyə.

In Huojia, Changyuan, and other dialects, the syllable of contraction of "yi ge(one)" is [yə] or [yɣ], which is different from [iə] in type A. The reason is that it may be affected by the surrounding dialects.

In Changyuan dialect, the form of syllable contraction of "wu ge(five)" is [ŋə⁵⁴]. The consonant of [ŋə⁵⁴] is [ŋ], which is the retention of ancient pronunciation, similar to [ŋuə⁵⁵] in Xunxian dialect and [ŋə⁵⁴] in Huaxian dialect.

In the boundary zone, evolution is often asynchronous (Table 9).

Table 9. The form of syllable contraction of "numerals and ge" in some boundary areas

Dialect places	yi ge (one)	qi ge (seven)	ji ge (several)	si ge (four)	shi ge (ten)
Ruzhou	yo	tsʰyo tsʰiɛ	tɕyo tɕiɛ	suo sɿ ɣ sɣ	ʂɣ
Mianchi	yo	tɕ ʰiə	tɕyo	suo	ʂə
Ruyang	yo	tɕʰyo	tɕiə	sɿ ə	ʂʅə
Yuanyang	yo	tɕʰiɔ	tɕyo	suo	ʂuo

Ruzhou dialect belongs to the Nanlu dialect areas in the Official dialect in Central China, geographically adjacent to Yichuan county in Luosong dialect areas and Dengfeng county in Zhengkai dialect areas. There are two forms of syllable contraction of "qi ge, ji ge", that is [yo] or [iɛ] in Ruzhou dialect. In Ruzhou dialect, there are three forms of the syllable contraction of "si ge", namely [suo] ﹅ [sɿ ɣ], and [sɣ]. Mianchi dialect belongs to the Luosong dialect areas of Official Speech in Central China. In Mianchi dialect, the main vowels of "qi" and "ji" both are [i], however, the form of syllable contraction of "qi ge" is [tɕ ʰiə], while the form of syllable contraction of "ji ge" is [tɕʰyə]. In Luoyang type, the vowel of syllable contraction of "qi ge" and "ji ge" both are [yo]. In Luoyang type, the vowel of syllable contraction of 'si ge(four)" and "shi ge(ten)" both are [uo]. While in Mianchi dialect, the vowel of syllable contraction of "si ge" and "shi ge" are not consistent. The form of syllable contraction of "si ge" is [suo], and the form of syllable contraction of "shi ge" is [ʂ ə]. Ruyang belongs to the South Lu dialect areas of Official Speech in Central China. Geographically, it is close to Ruzhou City, but the forms of syllable contraction of "qi ge" and "ji ge" are also inconsistent. In Yuanyang dialect, the vowel of syllable contraction of "qi ge" is [iɔ], while the vowel of syllable contraction of "ji ge(several) " is [yɔ], and their vowels are inconsistent (Table 10).

For example, Xinxiang County, Xun County, Hua County:

Table 10. The pronunciation of "numberals + ge" in Xinxiang County, Xun County, and Hua County in the border areas

Dialect places	yi ge (one)	wu ge (five)	liu ge (six)	jiu ge (nine)	qi ge (seven)	ji ge (several)	si ge (four)	shi ge (ten)
Xinxiang county	yɔ	uɔ	liɔ	tɕiɔ	tɕ ʰiə	tɕ iə	s̩ ɤ	ʂ ə
Xun county	yɔ	ŋuə	liɔ	tɕiɔ	tɕ ʰiɛ	tɕiɛ	s̩ ə	ʂ̩ ə
Hua county	yɔ	ŋə	liɔ	tɕiɔ	tɕ ʰiɛ	tɕiɛ	s̩ ə	ʂ̩ ə

In Xinxiang county dialect, after combination, the main vowel of "yi ge, wu ge, liu ge, jiu ge" is [ɔ], while the main vowel of "qi ge, ji ge, si ge, shi ge" is [ə]. In Xunxian dialect and Huaxian dialect, after combination, the main vowel of "yi ge, liu ge, jiu ge" is [ɔ], while the main vowel of "qi ge, ji ge" is [ɛ] and the main vowel of "si ge, shi ge" is [ə]. Therefore, due to the influence of surrounding dialects, the evolution of the border areas may not be synchronized.

In all, due to the vowel of "ge" is different, when numerals are combined with "ge", so the forms of syllable contraction are different. That is to say, different numerals are combined with "ge" is not synchronized. Different forms of syllable contraction belong to different historical levels. After combination, if the main vowel of the syllable is [a], the combination occurred in the early stage. If the main vowel of the syllable is [ɔ], the combination occurred in the second stage. If the main vowel of the syllable is [o], the combination occurred in the third stage. And if the main vowel of the syllable is [ə] or [ɤ], its combination occurred belongs to the last stage. The geographical distribution reflects that the vowel of " ge " has experienced the evolution: a → ɔ → o → ə/ɤ, which remains due to the unbalanced development of different dialect places. Wuzhi type develops the slowest, and then Xingyang, Luoyang, and Jiyuan types develop fast. Its evolution is still moving forward.

3.2   The Process of Syllable Contraction of "Liang Ge, San Ge, Ba Ge"

From the above analysis, it can be seen that when the numerals are combined with "ge", the vowel of "ge" is different in different dialects in Henan Province, some are [a], some are [ɔ], some are [o], some are [ə] or [ɤ]. But the pronunciation of the syllable contraction of "liang ge(two), san ge(three), ba ge(eight)" has strong consistency in Henan dialect. As follows:

numerals + ge	pronunciation	dialect places
liang ge (two)	lia	Lingbao, Lushi county, Xiangcheng, Zhengyang, Queshan, Yongcheng, Luyi, Suixian, Tongbai, Xixian, Shangcheng, Jiyuan, Qinyang, Wenxian, Boai, Xinxiang county, Huojia, Qixian, Huixian, Anyang, Tangyin, Luanchuan, Luoyang, Yanshi, Xin'an, Yiyang, Mianchi, Luoning, Zhengzhou, Gongyi, Xingyang, Xinzheng, Xinmi, Dengfeng, Qingfeng county, Neihuang, Huaxian, Xunxian, Yuanyang, Changyuan, Minquan, Ruyang, Ruzhou, Jiaxian, Fangcheng, Neixiang, Xiping
	liɔ	Linzhou
san ge (three)	sa	Lingbao, Lushi county, Xiangcheng, Zhengyang, Queshan, Yongcheng, Luyi, Suixian, Tongbai, Xixian, Shangcheng, Jiyuan, Qinyang, Wenxian, Boai, Xinxiang county, Huojia, Qixian, Huixian, Anyang, Tangyin, Luanchuan, Luoyang, Yanshi, Xin'an, Yiyang, Mianchi, Luoning, Zhengzhou, Gongyi, Xingyang, Xinzheng, Xinmi, Dengfeng, Qingfeng county, Neihuang, Huaxian, Xunxian, Yuanyang, Changyuan, Minquan, Ruyang, Ruzhou, Jiaxian, Fangcheng, Neixiang, Xiping
	sɔ	Linzhou
ba ge (eight)	pa Øə	Kai feng county, dengfeng, xinmi, qingfeng
	pa	Lingbao, Lushi county, Xiangcheng, Zhengyang, Queshan, Yongcheng, Luyi, Suixian, Tongbai, Xixian, Shangcheng, Jiyuan, Qinyang, Wenxian, Boai, Xinxiang county, Huojia, Qixian, Huixian, Anyang, Tangyin, Luanchuan, Luoyang, Yanshi, Xin'an, Yiyang, Mianchi, Luoning, Zhengzhou, Gongyi, Xingyang, Xinzheng, neihuang, Xuaxian, Xunxian, Yuanyang, Changyuan, Minquan, Ruyang, Ruzhou, Jiaxian, Fangcheng, Neixiang, Xipingxian
	pɔ	Linzhou

From the table above, it can be seen that "liang ge(two), san ge(three)" have finished the syllable contraction, which is read as [lia] and [sa] in most dialects of Henan Province. However, it is more special in Linzhou dialect, which is read as [liɔ³¹²] and [sɔ³¹²] respectively. In Jin dialect of the northern Henan, the pronunciation "ba" has the laryngeal plug tail, including [pʌʔ²³](Jiyuan)、[paʔ³³](Huojia)、[pʌʔ³³](Linzhou) and so on. In Zhongyuan Mandarin areas, "ba" does not have the laryngeal plug tail. But regardless of having the laryngeal plug tail, the pronunciation of syllable contraction of "ba ge" is [pa]. Especially, in Linzhou dialect, the pronunciation of syllable contraction of "ba ge" is [pɔ] and [pa Øə] in Kaifeng county.

According to Table 4, in Xingyang dialect, After the numeral "yi, si, wu, liu, qi, jiu, ji" are combined with "ge", the last vowel of the syllable contraction is all [ɔ], while, the last vowel of the syllable contraction of "liang ge(two), san ge(three), ba ge(eight)" is [a].It is inconsistent. The same as Jiyuan type and Luoyang type. Why?

According to the above analysis, in Xingyang dialect, when numerals are combined with "ge", the vowel of "ge" may be [*ɔ]. It is assumed that, in Xingyang dialect, when "two, three, and eight" are combined with "ge", the vowel of "ge" may be [*ɔ], and then the process of syllable contraction is as follows:

liaŋ+*kɔ→liaŋ+gɔ→liaŋ+ŋɔ→liaŋ　ŋɔ→lia　ɔ→liaɔ

saŋ+*kɔ→saŋ+kɔ→saŋ+gɔ→saŋ+ŋɔ→sa　ɔ→saɔ

pa+*kɔ→pa+gɔ→pa+ɔ→pa　ɔ→paɔ

As a matter of fact, the pronunciation of the syllable contraction of "liang ge, san ge, ba ge" are [lia], [sa], [pa], not [liaɔ], [saɔ], [paɔ]. When the vowel of "ge" is [o], so is it.

Accordingly, it is speculated that, when "two, three, eight" are combined with "ge", the vowel of "ge", may be undergoing two changes after the consonant of "ge" is lost. One is that, before the combination, the vowel of "ge" becomes [a], and then it merges with the front word. The other is that the vowel of "ge" falls off in the process of syllable contraction.

The first possibility is that when "two, three and eight" are combined with "ge", after consonant[k] of "ge" is lost, the vowel is affected by the front word, assimilated into [a], and then fused with the front word. To "liang" and "san", [a] is nasalized as [ã] firstly, and then the vowel of "ge" is assimilated into [a] by [ã], and then fusion occurs. The combination of "ba" and "ge" is simple. Firstly, the consonant[k] of "ge" is lost and then the vowel is assimilated into [a]. That is to say:

liaŋ + kv³ → liaŋ gv → liaŋ ŋv → liã v → liã a → lia.
san + kv → san gv → saŋ ŋv → sã v → sã a → sa.
pa + kv → pa gv → pa v → pa a → pa.

In Shandong dialects around Henan Province, the pronunciation of syllable contraction of "ba ge" has [pa iə], [pa ia], [pa a], etc. (Feng 2002).

The second possibility is that since "liang" and "san" have nasal endings, the variant form of "ge" is not easy to be independent, they fall off directly. The process of syllable contraction is as follows:

liaŋ+kv→liaŋ　gv→liaŋ　v→liaŋ→lia

san+kv→san　gv→saŋ　gv→san　v→sa

pa+kv→pa　gv→pa　v→pa

Today, in Kaifeng County, Dengfeng County, and Xinmi Dialect, the pronunciation of "ba ge " is [pa Øə]. The consonant[k] of "ge" falls off and vowels weaken. Because of its weakness of [ə], it is also possible to lose in the process of fast reading.

---

³ Here the "v" represents the vowel may be [a]、[ɔ]、[o]、[ɤ] or [ə]. The same as below.

It is worth noting that in Jin dialect of northern Henan, the pronunciation of "ba" has the laryngeal plug tail. So when "ba" is combined with "ge", firstly the laryngeal plug tail loss, and then combined.

Jiaxian: pa^{24} pa^{31} (ba ge)

Xingyang: pa^{13} pa^{42} (ba ge)

Luoyang: pa^{24} pa^{42} (ba ge)

Mianchi: pa^{55} pa^{42} (ba ge)

In Linzhou dialect, after the combination, the main vowels of "liang ge, san ge, ba ge" is [ɔ],not [a]. Because in Linzhou dialect, in mid-ancient, the main vowel of words in xian she and shan she evolved into [a], and the main vowel of words in guo she evolved into [ɔ].In Linzhou dialect, the pronunciation of "liang ge, san ge, ba ge" are [liɔ^{312}],[sɔ^{312}],[pɔ^{312}] respectively.

4 The Motivation of Combination of Numerals and "Ge" in Henan Dialect

Why can numerals and quantifiers be combined in Henan dialect when quantifiers are individual quantifiers? The reasons are as follows:

4.1 "ge" Does not Have the Quantify Function

The classification of individual quantifiers in Chinese Mandarin is mainly reflected in that some quantifiers are classified by shape. For example, "yi gen huanggua (a cucumber)", "yi li mi(a grain of rice)", "yi zhang zhuozi(a table)" and "yi liang che(a car)", the differences in individual quantifiers highlight their different images. In Henan dialect, the individual quantifier "ge" is generalized. The quantifier "ge" has been unable to highlight the image of things and gradually becomes redundant components. Driven by the principle of language economy, the quantifier "ge" may be weakened, and they are combined with numerals.

"The quantifiers are usually connected with numerals in front and nouns in latter, thus they three definitely will have relations. Therefore, we say that the "unit quantifier" in quantifiers is focused on the numerals, playing as calculating; the "individual quantifier " in quantifiers focuses on nouns and acting as adjectives." [1] Structurally, "Individual quantifiers are closely combined with nouns because they focus on the form and do not play a quantitative role. Individual quantifiers are just 'symbolic' quantifiers, so even if omitted, it does not affect the integrity of the structure and the clarity of the meaning. Thus, the combination of individual quantifiers and numerals is less stable than other quantifiers" [2]. Dong Xiufang (2013), also believed that "Chinese individual quantifiers belong to grammatical functions and have little to do with specific measures" [3].

While measuring quantifiers, collective quantifiers, container quantifiers, temporary quantifiers, etc., are a dominant quantization means. With the function of quantifiers, these quantifiers must appear. Such as in English, there are not many individual quanti-fiers involved in the measurement, but there are quantifiers, collective quantifiers, con-tainer quantifiers, etc. Like: "a cup of milk" "a herd of cattle". Xu Xijian (1987) pointed out that there must be quantifier words while using as measuring, currency unit, collective unit, volume unit, utensil capacity unit, time unit, action, and behavior in Jingpo language.

4.2 Generalization of classifiers "ge" in Henan dialect

In Henan dialect, the individual classifiers "ge" is generalized. The individual quantifiers "ben, liang, strip, gen, ba" in Mandarin, etc., can all use one classifiers "ge" instead in the areas of Jin Dialect in Northern Henan, Zheng Kai dialect areas, and Luo Song dialect areas of speaking Zhongyuan official language. Meanwhile, numerals are combined with "ge".

It can modify common nouns, abstract nouns, proper nouns, etc. Like:

(13) Wo zheng qi che lei, [iə]yi ge che tu ran ting wo qian mian, cha dian er Zhuang zhu wo.(Jiyuan)

While I am riding, a car suddenly stops in front of me and almost knock me down.

(14) Wushi duo sui le, ta cai xun zhe [iə]yi ge xifu.(Boai)

He finally gets married at around the age of 50.

(15) Ni jiujiu ke zhen duo, ni dou you [tɕʰiə]qi ge jiujiu a! (Qinyang)

You have seven uncles, so many! (Qinyang)

(16) Wo jia mei san lai, wo xiang qu mai [lia]liang ge san fang jia yong. (Yanshi)

I don't have any umbrellas at home, I want to buy one or two.(Yanshi)

(17) Deng [sa]san ge zhongtou mei deng zhe ta, wo zou lai. wo yi zou, ta dou qu lai, ni shuo qi ren bu qi ren.(Xin'an)

I've waited for three hours but failed to meet him. As soon as I leave, he arrives, which makes me furious.

(18) Yi zhongwu lai , [iə]yi ge wenti dou mei chuli liao, bai pao lai lai. (Jiaozuo)

It is already half a day, but failing to solve problems even one problem, is a waste of time.

(19) [iə]Yi ge xuanxuan dou gou chouren lai, you lai yi. (Huixian)

I have enough of having one child Xuanxuan, and here is one more. (Huixian)

(20) Wo kan ni shang [iə]yi ge zhengda dou gou nan lai, ni hai xiang shang beida lei. (Wenxian)

I wonder if you can go to Zhengzhou University, not to mention Peking University.

Example (13)-(20) "[iə] che, [iə] xifu, [tɕʰiə] uncles, [lia] umbrellas, [sa] zhongtou, [iə] wenti, [iə] xuanxuan, [iə] zhengda" is essentially a combination of numerals and quantifiers, equivalent to "yi ge che(one car)","yi ge xifu(on wife)" "qi ge jiujiu(seven uncles)", "liang ge san(two umbrellas)", "san ge xiaoshi(three hours) ", "yi ge wenti(one question)", "yi ge xuanxuan(one xuanxuan)", "yi ge zhengda(one zhengda)" in mandarin.

Nouns can be omitted if mentioned previously, like:

(21) *ni you na xie shu lei, ni cai gei wo [iə] yi ge (Jiyuan)*

You have so many books, but only one for me.

(22) *[sə] si ge dou gou lai, bu yong gei wo na duo. (Qinyang)*

Four is enough, I don't need more.

When the numeral is "one" and the classifiers is an individual quantifier, it forms the structure of "nouns + one", emphasizing the nature and the numeral also will pronounce together.

(23) *Ta dou shi lao shi gedan [iə] yi ge. (Jiyuan)*

He is a person as honest as stone.

(24) *Lan qianbao [iə] yi ge, diu dou diu lai ba, you sha xin teng lei.(Jiyuan)*

No need to waste time feeling distressed about the lost ragged wallet.

Example (23) "as honest as stone" means "he is an honest man". Example (15) In the same way. Here, the predicate part should be "numeral + quantifier + nouns", but change to "nouns + numeral + quantifier" in Jiyuan dialect, where the number word is " one", the quantifier is individual quantifiers, the numerals and quantifier combine together, become "nouns + one" structure.

4.3 Usage Frequency and Combination Play an Important Role in Communication

Numerals and quantifiers always are together. Numbers, quantifiers, and nouns are often used together, which is frequently used in spoken language. According to the characteristics of the human cognitive model, people can understand the entire paragraph meaning after pragmatic inference on the local symbolic information of the combination of common paragraphs. "Psychological experiments show that the more familiar things people are, the more they ignore the details" [4]. "When the reduction and wear of the form do not bring about any difficulties in meaning recognition, it will make it possible to weaken and fall off the phonetic form in the article, and eventually merge pronunciation" [5].

(25) *Jin ge xia wu wo yi hui er chi [sə] si ge pingguo, chi tai duo lai, xia wu la du, bu de jin. (Jiyuan)*

I ate four apples this afternoon, too much to get ill and have loose bowels.

Example (25) The emphasis point of this sentence is the number of apples eaten is "four", so the omission of "ge" will not bring difficulties in understanding it.

4.4 The Principle of "One Pronunciation, One Meaning" Promotes the Merge of Numerals and Quantifiers

Since the quantifier "ge" does not have the function of measuring, assume that the quantifier "ge" disappears completely, and "numeral" is not combined with "ge", what will be the result? Let's look at an example firstly, such as:

(26) *Wo si jiu ren ke hao lei. (Jiyuan)*

My fourth uncle is very nice .

or: all of my four uncles are very nice.

Example (26), here "four" can represent my fourth uncle, or there are four uncles, two different meanings, both read [sʅ ^{24}], which will cause ambiguity. Therefore, when expressing quantity, the phonetic form of the quantifier "ge" cannot be lost, but on grammatical function "ge" does not have measuring function, so combine pronunciation becomes possible.

For another example, when "numerical words + time words" form expressing time points and time periods, individual quantifiers have the function of distinguishing different meanings in Mandarin of the modern Chinese language. For example, "May" refers to the time point, and "five months" refers to the period. In the Henan Jiyuan dialect, when expressing the time point and time period, the form is the same, both express as "May". If the form is the same, there will be ambiguity. so in communication, it is distinguished by the phonetic form, and the "five" and "ge" are merge pronunciation when referring to the time period.

(27) [u²¹³]yue ˌfugong fuchan lai. (Jiyuan)

We will resume to work and production in May.

(28) Wo yixai zai jia dai you [uə⁵¹] yue. (Jiyuan)

I've stayed at home for five months.

Example (28), if the pronunciation is [uə⁵¹], it means a period.

Therefore, the principle of "one pronunciation and one meaning" promotes that "ge" cannot completely disappear. Although "ge" does not have the function of measuring, it has a distinguished meaning when combine with numerals.

5 Conclusion

From the perspective of synchronicity, the pronunciation forms of syllable contraction of "numerals + ge" in Henan dialect, have three different types while continuous reading. The first type: numerals are not combined with "ge". The second type: the consonant of "ge" get starts to weaken and fall off, which is the first stage of syllable contraction. The third type: numerals are combined with "ge", and the two syllables are changed into a syllable. That is to say: it experienced the process: two independent syllables → the loss of consonant[k] of "ge" → a syllable with a logn vowel → a normal syllable.

In Henan dialect, the speed of syllable contraction is not synchronized in different regions. Dialects in the areas of Guanzhong, Yantai, Luoxiang, Shangfu, Xinbao, where speak official dialect, developed a little slow; but dialects in zhengkai dialect ares and nanlu dialect areas, etc.are still in the stage of aphonic pronunciation, Jin dialect in northern Henan province developed rapidly, where most areas have already completed the combination. But the development is not balanced even in the same dialect area. The priority levels are: one, two, three > seven, several, four, ten, five, eight > six, nine.

It is speculated that the phonetic form of the quantifier "ge" has multiple synchronic variations according to the forms of syllable contraction. These synchronic variations indicate that the combination of different numerals and "ge" occurs in different stages of the consonant evolution of "ge".In Wuzhi dialect, the consonant of "ge" may be [*a] while combination; In Xingyang dialect, it may be [*ɔ]; In Luoyang type, it may be

[*o]; and in Jiyuan, Huojia, and Anyang, it may be [*ɤ/ə]. Border zones often take many forms. The geographical distribution shows that the consonant of "ge" had experienced the historical evolution: a → ɔ → o → ə/ɤ, which was left over due to the unbalanced development of various points.

In the process of synthesizing, the consonant [k]of "ge" is weakened due to continuous reading, so that it falls off, which is the precondition of synthesizing. For the remaining syllable components of "ge", it may change as splicing, fusion, or falling off. When the numerals are "two, three, eight", the vowel of "ge" is assimilated into [a] under the influence of the preceding word, and then merges with the preceding syllable; or the vowel of "ge" falls off directly. When the numerals are "one, seven, ji(several), four, ten, five, six, nine", "ge" is influenced by the preceding character to produce a medial vowel of [i], [u] or [z], and then merges or merges with the preceding character syllable. The combination of "numeral + ge" is not formed by the inverse method of taking the initial of the front word and the vowel of the latter word, but by the loss of the middle consonant, the combination or fusion of vowels to one syllable.

The reason why the combination is formed is that, for generalization of the quantifier "ge" in Henan dialect, the classifiers "ge" does not have the function of measuring, and thus the grammatical function is weakened, which leads to the weakening and falling off of the consnant of "ge" in the phonetic form. In addition, numerals and quantifiers always be used together to modify the nouns. In communication, the focus of semantic information is "numerals" and "nouns". The abrasion of "ge " will not bring understanding difficulties in semantic recognition. Language economic principles also drive quantitative combination.

The syllable contraction of "numerals + ge" is mainly distributed in Jin dialect in the northern province and its surrounding areas, and the distribution range is more consistent with the distribution area of Z-suffixation in Henan dialect.

The rhyme of Z-suffixation change is also a syllable contraction in essence. Is it the Z-suffixation change that promotes the process of the syllable contraction of "numerals + ge" combination, or is the syllable contraction of "numerals + ge" that promotes the Z-suffixation? This article won't do the analysis for the time being and will analyze it in another article.

References

Guo, S.: A New Probe into Chinese Grammar and Rhetoric. Commercial Press, Beijing (1979). (in Chinese)

Situ, Y.: On the expressive function of chinese individual quantifiers. J. Shantou Univ. **01**, 31–36 (1991). (in Chinese)

Dong, X.: Internal differences of individual quantifiers in modern Chinese. Chinese Teach. World. **01**, 18–26 (2013). (in Chinese)

Dong, X.: The Derivation and Development of Chinese Disyllabic Words (Revised Edition), p.46 Commercial Press, Beijing (2011). (in Chinese)

Sun, H.: Research on the Phenomenon of Mandarin Chinese in the Central Plains. Doctoral Dissertation of Shaanxi Normal University, p. 240 (2014). (in Chinese)

He, W.: Research on Huojia Dialect. The Commercial Press, Beijing (1989). (in Chinese)

Wang, S.: Divided-sound words and sound compound words in Xingyang (Guangwu) Dialect. Stud. Lang. Linguist. **01**, 160–165 (1994). (in Chinese)

Xu, Q.: On the types of chinese dialect syllable contraction——also on the phenomenon of luoyang dialect syllable contraction. J. Xinjiang Univ. **44**(02), 146–150 (2016). (in Chinese)

Wei, M.: Research on the phenomenon of syllable contraction of Xinmi Dialect in Henan. J. Jinzhong Univ. **36**(06), 73–78 (2019). (in Chinese)

Wu, X., Guo, Q.: The phenomenon of phonetci changes in the "Numeral+ge" structure of Linzhou Dialect. Mod. Chinese. **04**, 82–86 (2019). (in Chinese)

Chao, Y.: Two, three, four er, eight er. Originally published in "The Eastern Miscellany", Vol. 24, No. 12, 1927, From Linguistics Essays by Zhao Yuanren's, pp. 240–246. The Commercial Press, Beijing (2002). (in Chinese)

Jiang, L.: Characteristics of Beijing Dialect in Late Qing Dynasty Reflected in《Yanjing Women's Language》. Linguist. Res. **04**, 15–19 (1994). (in Chinese)

Feng, C.: Some problems on the compound words "two" and "three" -- Also on Chao Yuanren's theory of "aphasia". Stud. Lang. Linguist. **02**, 38–44 (2002). (in Chinese)

Liu, X.: An analysis of the "one + nouns" structural analysis of Beijing Dialect. Stud. Chinese Lang. **01**, 36–39 (2004). (in Chinese)

Zhu, L.: On phonetic weakening constraints in connected speech-a case study of Beijing Mandarin "Numeral+ge". Chinese Lang. Learn. **05**, 62–69 (2017). (in Chinese)

Li, X.: Research on Neihuang Dialect in Henan. China Social Sciences Press, Beijing (2016). (in Chinese)

Cao, R.: A Study on phonetic changes of Kaifeng Dialect. Master's degree thesis of Tianjin Normal University (2016). (in Chinese)

Liu, X.: Analysis on the Phenomenon of syllable contraction in xinmi dialect. Cult. Educ. Mater. **34**, 44–48 (2016). (in Chinese)

Shao, W.: Henan Zhi·Dialect. Henan People's Publishing Press, Zhengzhou (1991). (in Chinese)

Song, X.: The phonetic formation rules of sound compound words in Xinmi dialect. Master's degree thesis of Zhengzhou University (2017). (in Chinese)

Feng, X.: Noun Rhyming in Wuzhi (Xihuafeng) Dialect. Master's degree thesis of Beijing Language and 20 Culture University (2008). (in Chinese)

Kong, X.: The Combination of two syllables in Xinji Dailect. Nankai Linguist. **02**, 110–116 (2005). (in Chinese)

Wang, H.: Non-Linear Phonology of Chinese. Peking University Press, Beijing (1999). (in chinese)

Wang, X.: The combination of numerals and "ge" in the northern Mandarin dialect of Chinese. Nankai Linguist. **02**, 77–87 (2014). (in Chinese

A Hybrid Account of the Expressivity in Mandarin Nominals

Fan Liu$^{(\boxtimes)}$

School of Liberal Arts, Auhui Normal University, Wuhu 241003, China
fanliu_ling@foxmail.com

Abstract. This study provides a hybrid account of the Mandarin "*ni ge* NP" structure. It is the expressivity that yields its syntactic and semantic effects. In the descriptive dimension, *ge* serves as a relation function that builds a similarity relation between the hearer and the property that the NP denotes, which explains that NPs cannot co-refer with a possible discourse participant in many cases. In the expressive dimension, *ge* conveys the speaker's subjective judgments, which correctly predicts its resistance to an honorific form as well as the semantic restrictions.

Keywords: Nominals · *ni ge* NP · Expressivity · Hybrid semantics · Mandarin Chinese

1 Introduction

This paper proposes a formal account of the expressivity of Mandarin nominal expressions under the framework of hybrid semantics. Our case in point is the nominal structure "*ni ge* NP" in Mandarin Chinese, as illustrated in (1) and (2).

(1) **Ni ge zhu** hai mei qichuang.

you GE pig still not get.up

'You pig still not get up.'

(2) **Ni ge siren**, kuai lai bang wo.

you GE dead.man, quick come helpme.

'You dead man, come over here to help.'

Previous analyses, such as [1], treat the highlighted expressions in (1) and (2) as appositive structures. These nominal expressions aforementioned, nevertheless, have demonstrated several idiosyncratic properties that are quite different from typical Mandarin appositives. On the one hand, in terms of syntax, it is generally assumed that Mandarin nominal expressions have a canonical sequence like [Numeral + Classifier + Noun]. Notwithstanding, the numeral *yi* 'one', which is supposed to be omitted, cannot be reduced in the corresponding positions in (1) and (2). See the test below:

© The Author(s), under exclusive license to Springer Nature Switzerland AG 2023

Q. Su et al. (Eds.): CLSW 2022, LNAI 13495, pp. 161–168, 2023.
https://doi.org/10.1007/978-3-031-28953-8_13

(3) a. #ni **yi**ge zhu.

you one GE pig

'you as a pig'

b. #ni **yi** ge siren

you one GE dead.man

'you as a dead man'

On the other hand, semantically speaking, the traditional truth-conditional semantics fails to capture the meaning of "*ni ge* NP" structures in (1) and (2). Since the hearer must not be a pig or a dead man according to the context, *ni* 'you' cannot built a coreferential relation with the following items, which additionally makes the appositive solution like (3) directly rule out.

In brief, this "*ni ge* NP" pattern, as far as we have seen, has not been fully explained in the current literature. Yet the properties of the component *ge* involved not have received a convincing treatment. This paper aims at diagnosing the expressive effects of *ge* in the "*ni ge* NP" structures. In the following sections, we will present a novel solution to the semantics of *ge*, and assume that *ge* is actually an operator rather than a classifier. The rest of the paper proceeds as follows: Sect. 2 lays out some empirical generalizations of the "*ni ge* NP" structures. Section 3 provides a formal hybrid analysis. Section 4 concludes.

2   Some Empirical Generalizations

2.1   Unsubstitutivity

Unlike the typical appositives, the components involved in the "*ni ge* NP" pattern cannot be substituted with other counterparts. First, the pronoun must be the second singular *ni* 'you'. Even the honorific form cannot be accepted in the "*ni ge* NP" structure, as (4) shows. However, both examples are grammatical in a common appositive pattern, like (5).

(4) a. **ni** ge da jiaoshou

you GE big professor

'you big professor'

b. *****nin** ge da jiaoshou

you.HON GE big professor

Int: 'dear you big professor'

(5) a. **ni** yi wei da jiaoshou

you one CL big professor

'you as a big professor'

b. **nin** yi wei da jiaoshou

you.HON one CL big professor

'dear you as a big professor'

Additionally, the element between *ni* and the NP can must be the sole *ge*, rather than other possibilities, such as *yi ge* 'one GE' or *zhe ge* 'this GE'. See the tests in (3) and (6) respectively.

(6) Hao ni (*zhe) ge Laowang!

well you (*this) GE Laowang.

'How dare you, Laowang?'.

2.2 Semantic Restrictions

The second property worth noting is that the NPs involved demonstrate various semantic restrictions. The nominals that are not permitted in the typical appositives, such as *Shengdanjie* 'Christmas' and *Xiangling Sao* 'Sister Xianglin', but nonetheless can occur in the *"ni ge* NP" structure. Consider:

(7) a. *Hao ni yi ge **Shengdanjie**!

well you one GE Christmas.

Int. 'What a bad Christmas!'

b. Hao ni ge **Shengdanjie**!

well you GE Christmas.

'What a bad Christmas!'.

(8) a. ??Ni yi ge **Xianglin Sao**!

you one GE Sister Xianglin.

Int. 'You as a Sister Xianglin!'

b. Ni ge **Xianglins Sao**!

you GE Sister Xianglin.

'You Sister Xianglin!'.

The contrast between (7) and (8) again supports that the *"ni ge* NP" structure cannot be treated as the omitted form of the appositive *"ni yi ge* NP", hence the appositive proposal is ruled out. Moreover, from the syntax perspective, since the NPs involved must combine with the so-called classifier *ge* at the very beginning, it requires further exploration the mechanism that *ge* can merge with the NPs in (7b) and (8b), rather than in (7a) and (8a).

2.3 Compound Complexity

Another point related to semantic restrictions is that the NPs in the *"ni ge* NP" structure, despite of its unselective property already shown in (7) and (8), cannot be simplex nouns. See the contrast below:

(9) a. Ni ge **gou dongxi**!

you GE dog stuff.

'You dog!'.

b. *Ni ge **dongxi**!

you GE stuff.

Int. 'You (as) stuff!'.

(10) a. Ni ge **nanren** jiujie sha?

you GE male.person struggle what.

'What are you man struggling with?'.

b. * Ni ge **ren** jiujie sha?

you GE person struggle what.

Int.'What are you person struggling with?'.

In (9) and (10), *gou dongxi* 'dog stuff' and *nanren* 'male person' are compounds and thus are well accepted, while the corresponding simplex words *dongxi* 'stuff' and *ren* 'person' are not grammatical. That creates a logical paradox: the compound actually denotes the subset that the simplex refers to, see (11). As a result, the items that denote the subset are allowed, while the simplex word with a larger extension leads to ungrammaticality.

(11) a. [[*gou dongxi*]] $\subseteq$ [[*dongxi*]]

$\lambda x[\text{dog.stuff}(x)] \subseteq \lambda x[\text{stuff}(x)]$

b. [[*nanren*]] $\subseteq$ [[*ren*]]

$\lambda x[\text{male.person}(x)] \subseteq \lambda x[\text{person}(x)]$

2.4 Interim Summary

To recap, the "*ni ge* NP" pattern has some complex properties. First, the components involved cannot be substituted with other counterparts. Second, the NPs demonstrate the different semantic restrictions from the relevant appositive forms. Last, the NPs cannot be simplex nouns. So far, all of the three issues introduced above remain unexplained in previous literature concerning the "*ni ge* NP" structure. In the next section, we will develop a formal account for such properties in hybrid semantics.

3   A Hybrid Account

3.1   Diagnosing the Expressivity

The syntactic-semantic effects of the "*ni ge* NP" structure have placed it in parallel with the so-called expressive vocatives. Take English and German for example in (12) and (13) respectively.

(12) a. You idiot!   b. You bastard!

c. You linguist!   d. You philosopher! (English).

(13) a. Du Arschloch!'you asshole' b. Du Student! 'you student'.

c. Du Student hältst den Zustand sicher für angemessen.

you student hold the state surely as adequate.

'You (damn) student surely consider the state as adequate.'(German).

As is already observed by [2, 4, 5] and many others, cases like (12) and (13) receive a reading that expresses the speaker's negative attitude toward the following NP; that is, an innocent expression like *linguist* in (12c) receives an expressive flavor and has to be interpreted as some kind of insult similar to the use of a proper expressive like *idoit* in (12a).

Along with this approach, it is natural to assume that Mandarin "*ni ge* NP" structure contributes to the expressivity as well. This prediction is supported by the following arguments. First, the NPs involved do not only carry a truth-conditional meaning. Expressions such as *gou dongxi* 'dog stuff' in (9a) and *tu zaizi* 'rabbit cub', can naturally occur in the structure, while the hearer is not possible to be an animal.

Second, higher degree of subjectivity can increase the structure's legibility. More evaluative the NPs are, more grammatical the whole structures will be. That is, when combining with subjective modifiers, "*ni ge* NP" can be uttered felicitously; when co-occur with a simplex NP, the structure presents contradictory effect. Compare (10b) with the examples below:

(14) a. Ni ge wangenfuyide ren!

you GE ungrateful DE person.

'You ungrateful person!'.

b. Ni ge mei gutoude ren.

you GE not bone DE person.

'You servile person!'.

Third, an expressive item is always tied to the situation of utterance and thus is nondisplaceable. See the examples from [5]. All these cases below show that the negative attitude toward Kresge that the speaker displays by his/her use of *damn* still holds, even if the rest of the content does not necessarily do so.

(15) a. The damn Kresge isn't late for work. #He's a good guy.

b. That damn Kresge was late for work yesterday. #But he's not damn today, because today he was on time.

c. Sue says that that damn Kresge should be fired. #I think he's a good guy.

d. Sue believes that that damn Kresge should be fired. #I think he's a good guy.

e. Maybe that damn Kresge will be late again. #But if not, he's a good guy.

f. #If that damn Kresge arrives on time, he should be fired for being so mean.

Back to the Mandarin structure, the emotional status conveyed by "*ni ge* NP" behaves similarly in this respect. Consider:

(16) Ni ge hunzhang dongxi jintian mei chidao, #ni zhenhao.

you GE bastard stuff today not late, you really good.

'You bastard aren't late for work. #You're a good guy.'

Based on the aforementioned evidence, we argue that the *"ni ge* NP" structure conveys a negative attitude towards the hearer, and exhibits the expressivity feature of nondisplaceability. Hence it can be naturally treated as an expressive structure. A proposal will be provide in Sect. 3.2 to deal with the issue.

3.2 Semantic Derivation

Although the expressivity phenomenon has implicitly been acknowledged in the semantic literature, it has not received a satisfying analysis until a multidimensional approach. Along with this approach, the expressive items such as *damn* and *fucking*, are generally supposed to carry subjective attitudes. Take (17) for example. As *fucking* expresses the speaker's negative attitude towards the state of the sate of affairs under discussion, the semantics can be represented as (18). (cf. [2–4], a.o.)

(17) *John isn't fucking clam.

(18) a. At-issue content: $\neg(\mathbf{calm(John)})$.

b. Conventional implicature content: the speaker expresses a negative attitude at John being clam.

c. Conventional implicature's preposition: $\mathbf{calm(John)}$.

The most fundamental assumption of classical multidimensional semantics is that meanings operate on different dimensions. An utterance may express both an at-issue (truth-conditional) content in the descriptive dimension and a conventional implicature in the expressive dimension. This assumption, in recent studies, has been further developed into a hybrid approach. (cf. [4, 5], a.o.)

To capture (19), a more comprehensive system has been built like (20). The derivation begins by applying the lexical insertion rule (LxL) to each of the lexical expressions. After this, *damn* is first combined with *Daniel* via multidimensional application (MA). The resulting *u*-proposition is then stored into the third dimension by an application of use-conditional elimination (UE), before the resulting expression becomes the argument of is dancing in a final step, again via MA.

(19) That damn Daniel is dancing. (cf. [4]: 153).

(20)

$$
\cfrac{
\cfrac{damn}{I_e \blacklozenge \mathbf{damn} : \langle e, u \rangle \bullet U} \text{ LxL} \quad \cfrac{\cfrac{Daniel}{\mathbf{daniel} : e \blacklozenge \mathbf{daniel} : e \bullet U} \text{ LxL}}{\cfrac{\mathbf{daniel} : e \blacklozenge \mathbf{damn(daniel)} : u \bullet U}{\mathbf{daniel} : e \blacklozenge \mathbf{daniel} : e \bullet \mathbf{damn(daniel)} : u} \text{ UE}} \text{ MA}
\quad
\cfrac{is\ dancing}{\mathbf{dance} : \langle e, t \rangle \blacklozenge \mathbf{dance} : \langle e, t \rangle \bullet U} \text{ LxL}
}{
\mathbf{dance(daniel)} : t \blacklozenge \mathbf{dance(daniel)} : t \bullet \mathbf{damn(daniel)} : u
} \text{ MA}
$$

Since this hybrid approach can account for the property of speaker linking and nondisplaceability, especially inspired by this proposal and the well-explained cases adopted in Mandarin Chinese (e.g. [6–8], a.o.), we specified the *"ni ge* NP" structure as a functional mixed use-conditional item.

(21) ni ge jiaoshou

you GE professor

'you professor'

Take (21) for example, the key point of the derivation is to identify how *ge* contributes its sematic content to the whole structure. At first glance, *ge* in the *"ni ge* NP" structure can be naturally treated as a typical classifier, since it occurs in a nominal expression and followed by a NP. However, as Sect. 2 demonstrates before, *ge* can combine with a proper noun in this pattern, while according to [1], the typical classifier is generally not allowed to be followed by proper noun. Hence it is reasonable to doubt whether *ge* in the *"ni ge* NP" structure has the homogeneity with the classifier *ge* in a canonical sequence like [Numeral + Classifier + Noun]. Under the framework of hybrid semantics, we argue that the special *ge* here no longer functions as a classifier, but serves as a relation function that builds a similarity relation between the hearer and the property that the NP denotes in the descriptive dimension. Moreover, to capture the expressivity of the whole structure, *ge* additionally conveys the speaker's subjective judgment in the expressive dimension (cf. [9, 10]). The general lexical entry for *ge* in Mandarin *"ni ge* NP" patter is provided as (22).

(22) $[[ge]] = \lambda P_{<e,t>}\lambda x[R_c(P, y) \wedge y = g(i)] \blacklozenge \lambda x.$negative-attitude (x, y)

(22) states that *ge* takes a property P as its argument, yield a meaning that builds a similarity relation between the hearer y and the property P that the NP denotes, which explains that NPs cannot co-refer with a possible discourse participant in example (1) and (2). And the variable y will be reduced by the discourse index g(i) in the subsequent derivation.

Adopting the updated compositional system of [4] with [2]'s bullet '•' and [3]'s diamond '♦', we propose that *ge* is combined with the NP, which is *jiaoshou* 'professor' in (21), through MA. The neutral use-conditional U is added as the third dimension, explaining the neutral usage of *jiaoshou* 'professor'. In the end, *ni* 'you' will be inserted via LxL to satisfy the discourse index *g(i)*. See:

(23)

$$\frac{\dfrac{ge}{\lambda P_{<e,t>}\lambda x[R_c(P, y)\wedge y=g(i)] \blacklozenge \lambda x.\textbf{negative-attitude } (x, y)}\text{LxL} \quad \dfrac{jiaoshou}{\lambda x.\textbf{professor}(x)}\text{LxL}}{\dfrac{\lambda x[R_c(\textbf{professor}, y)\wedge y=g(i)] \blacklozenge \lambda x.\textbf{negative-attitude } (x, y):<e,u>}{\lambda x[R_c(\textbf{professor}, y)\wedge y=g(i)] \bullet \lambda x.\textbf{negative-attitude } (x, y):<e,u>}\text{UE}}\text{MA}$$

The present analysis reaps three immediate advantages. First, the unsubstitutivity of the *"ni ge* NP" pattern, as shown in (4), can be predicted. It is the speaker's subjective judgment that *ge* conveys led to its resistance to an honorific form like *nin*. Second, since *ge* in the structure does not serve as a classifier, it exhibits different semantic restrictions from the canonical nominal sequence [Numeral + Classifier + Noun]. Thus the examples like (7) and (8) follow naturally. Third, the proposal intuitively captures the compound complexity of the NPs involved. As simplex nouns cannot be mapped in a similarity relation that is demonstrated in (22), the expressions like *dongxi* 'stuff' and *ren* 'person' in (9) and (10) are consequentially ruled out.

4 Conclusion

To conclude, this paper has demonstrated the syntactic and semantic effects of Mandarin *"ni ge* NP" structure. We argue that it is the expressivity that leads to these effects. In the descriptive dimension, *ge* serves as a relation function that builds a similarity relation between the hearer and the property that the NP denotes which explains that NPs cannot co-refer with a possible discourse participant in many cases. In the expressive dimension, *ge* conveys the speaker's subjective judgment, and thus its resistance to an honorific form as well as the semantic restrictions, are readily captured.

Acknowledgments. I would like to extend my deepest gratitude to the anonymous reviewers and the editors for helpful suggestions and comments on earlier versions of this paper. This work is financially supported by the National Social Science Foundation of China under grant #21CYY028. The author alone is responsible for any errors and mistakes in this paper.

References

1. Huang, C.-T., Li, A., Li, Y.: The Syntax of Chinese. Cambridge University Press, Cambridge (2009)
2. Potts, C.: The Logic of Conventional Implicature. Oxford University Press, Oxford (2005)
3. McCready, E.: Varieties of conventional implicature. Semant. Pragmat. **3**, 1–57 (2010). https://doi.org/10.3765/sp.3.8
4. Gutzmann, D.: Use-Conditional Meaning. Oxford University Press, Oxford (2015)
5. Gutzmann, D.: The Grammar of Expressivity. Oxford University Press, Oxford (2019)
6. Luo, Q., Wang, Y.: A contrastive analysis of hen and ting in Chinese. In: Lu, Q., Gao, H.H. (eds.) Chinese Lexical Semantics, vol. 9332, pp. 33–41. LNCS. Springer International Publishing, Cham (2015).https://doi.org/10.1007/978-3-319-27194-1_4
7. Luo, Q., Wang, Y.: When degree meets evaluativity: a multidimensional semantics for the ad-adjectival modifier hǎo 'well' in Mandarin Chinese. In: Dong, M., et al. (Eds.) Chinese Lexical Semantics, CLSW 2016. LNCS, vol. 10085, pp. 472–482. Springer International Publishing Cham (2016)https://doi.org/10.1007/978-3-319-49508-8_45
8. Luo, Q., Liu, F.: The expressive content of the ad-adjectival tai 'too' in Mandarin Chinese: Evidence from large online corpora. In: Hong, J.-F., Su, Q., Wu, J.-S. (eds.) Chinese Lexical Semantics. LNCS (LNAI), vol. 11173, pp. 311–320. Springer, Cham (2018). https://doi.org/10.1007/978-3-030-04015-4_26
9. Liu, F., Luo, Q.: Gradability, subjectivity and the semantics of the adjectival zhen 'real' and jia 'fake' in Mandarin. In: Hong, J.-F., Zhang, Y., Liu, P. (eds.) Chinese Lexical Semantics. LNCS (LNAI), vol. 11831, pp. 165–172. Springer, Cham (2020). https://doi.org/10.1007/978-3-030-38189-9_17
10. Xie, Z., Luo, Q.: Degree intensifiers as expressives in Mandarin Chinese. Lang. Linguist. **20**(2), 256–281 (2021). https://doi.org/10.1075/lali.00033.xie

The Relationship Between the Emphatic Meaning and the Adversative Meaning from the Perspective of Linguistic Typology: The Cases of Chinese *Kě* and *Jiùshì*

Wei Bian[(✉)] [iD]

Department of Chinese Language and Literature, School of Humanities, Tsinghua University, Beijing, China
bianweithu@163.com

Abstract. Regarding the relationship between the emphatic meaning and the adversative meaning, most previous studies focused on a single multifunctional word in a single language and failed to systematically classify the relationship. From the perspective of linguistic typology, this paper takes the semantic evolution of the Chinese multifunctional words *kě* and *jiùshì* as examples, combined with materials in English, German, French, Spanish and Korean. It is concluded that the four types of relationship between the emphatic meaning and the adversative meaning are: direct relationship>indirect relationship>weak relationship (specific context)>ambiguous relationship. On this basis, it is further proved that from the emphatic meaning direct to the adversative meaning is a universal semantic evolution path, which is unidirectional, and the evolution condition is "exceeding expectations" meaning. The evolution mechanisms include absorption of contextual meaning, inference and generalization. The evolution from the adversative meaning to the emphatic meaning may be a special usage in a specific context, and its use is limited, which is not grammaticalization, and does not pose a challenge to the hypothesis of unidirectionality.

Keywords: Emphatic Meaning · Adversative Meaning · *Kě* · *Jiùshì* · Linguistic typology · Semantic change

1 Introduction

In Chinese, some emphatic markers can also be used as adversative markers. Take *kě* and *jiùshì* for example:

  （1） a.这个苹果可好吃了。
      Zhè gè píngguǒ kě hǎochī le.
      DEM CLF apple very delicious CRS
      'This apple is very delicious.'

© The Author(s), under exclusive license to Springer Nature Switzerland AG 2023
Q. Su et al. (Eds.): CLSW 2022, LNAI 13495, pp. 169–185, 2023.
https://doi.org/10.1007/978-3-031-28953-8_14

b. 这个苹果不大，可很好吃。

Zhè   gè   píngguǒ bú   dà,   kě   hěn   hǎochī.
DEM   CLF   apple   NEG   big   but   very delicious
'This apple is not big, but it is delicious.'

(2) a. 我现在就是想吃苹果，别的水果不吃。

Wǒ   xiànzài jiùshì xiǎng chī píngguǒ, biéde shǔiguǒ bù   chī.
1SG   now   just   want eat apple   other fruit   NEG   eat
'I just want to eat apples now, not other fruits.'

b. 我想吃苹果，就是附近没有卖。

Wǒ   xiǎng chī píngguǒ, jiùshì fùjìn   méiyǒu mài.
1SG   want eat apple   but   nearby NEG   sold
'I want to eat apples, but they are not sold nearby.'

In examples (1a) and (2a), both *kě* and *jiùshì* are emphatic adverbs. However, in examples (1b) and (2b), *kě* and *jiùshì* are both adversative conjunctions. What is the relationship between emphatic markers and adversative markers? Does this linguistic phenomenon have cross-linguistic manifestations? What are the paths and mechanisms of semantic evolution? This paper selects *kě* and *jiùshì* to analyze in combination with other languages.

Regarding the relationship between emphatic marker and adversative marker, most previous studies have focused on case descriptions. For example, *kě*, Xi Jia [1] analyzed the evolution path of *kě*: rhetorical question marker > emphatic marker > adversative marker. Zhang Lili [2] argued that both the emphatic adverb and the persistent interrogative adverb can be the sources of the adversative usage of *kě*. Different from the multifunctional viewpoints of others, Zhang Xiusong [3] believed that the modal adverb *kě* has only a central meaning, i.e. to profile the (mis)match between the objective affair and the subjective expectation.

There is also a lot of discussion about the semantic function of *kě*. Zhang Wangxi and Li Huimin [4] believed that the core semantic function of the adverb *kě* is to highlight [expectation]. Wang Yingxian [5] pointed out that the contrasting meaning contained in the sentence formed by the adverb *kě* exists between the subjective cognition of the listener and the objective fact stated by the speaker. Zhang Lili [2] believed that the key reason why the emphatic adverb *kě* can enter the adversative context is that it has a reminder function.

Regarding *jiùshì*, Zhang Yisheng [6] maintained that the adversative usage of *jiùshì* developed from the usage of pointing out exceptions. Chen Li [7] and Sun Yaping [8] believed that the evolution path of *jiùshì* is: confirmation usage > emphatic usage > exclusive usage > adversative usage. Bian Wei [9] discussed the evolution of *jiùshì* when comparing the differences between 纵予连词 *zòngyǔ* conjunctions 'conjunctions for hypotheses and concessions' 就是 *jiùshì* and 就算 *jiùsuàn*. It is believed that *jiùshì* is developed from the adverbial phrase into a modal adverb through grammaticalization and lexicalization, and further into the *zòngyǔ* conjunction through grammaticalization. However, that paper did not discuss the use of *jiùshì* as an adversative conjunction, and we will discuss it further. There is a common evolutionary path from exclusive to adversative meaning, and Winterstein [10] provided a good discussion of this evolution from diachronic and cross-linguistic perspective, but didn't analyze it in connection with emphatic meaning.

Few previous studies have analyzed the relationship between emphatic usage and adversative usage from a typological point of view, nor have they classified their relationship, so these studies are not systematic and universal enough. This paper takes the diachronic changes of *kě* and *jiùshì* in Chinese as examples, and combines materials in five languages, including English, German, French, Spanish and Korean. We classify different relations, summarize the semantic change path, and explore the conditions, directions and mechanisms of semantic change.

2 Two Chinese Cases from the Emphatic Meaning to the Adversative Meaning

There are two relationships between the emphatic marker and the adversative marker: from emphatic usage to adversative usage and from adversative usage to emphatic usage. The two Chinese words in this section are of the former type, but the evolution of *kě* is directly from emphatic usage to adversative usage, and the relationship is closer; the evolution of *jiùshì* is from emphatic usage to exclusive usage and then to adversative usage, which belongs to indirect association.[1]

As for the situation from adversative usage to emphatic usage, it is rare in Chinese. Li Xiaojun [11] mentioned that 却 *què* and 倒 *dào* have the adversative usages first and then the emphatic usages. But in fact, there is a lot of controversy in the academic circles. For example, Zhang Lili [12] argued that *dào* developed from the modal adverb to the adversative adverb, and *què* is also not from the adversative usage to the emphatic usage. Therefore, this paper focuses on the development from emphatic usage to adversative usage.

2.1 The Semantic Change of *Kě*

Kě was originally a verb, with the meaning of permission in the early stage, such as example (3), and further extended to the meaning of "suitable", such as example (4):

（3）小子鸣鼓而攻之可也。

Xiǎozǐ	*míng*	*gǔ*	*ér*	*gōng*	*zhī*	*kě*	*yě.*
2PL	beat	drum	and	attack	3SG	permit	CRS

---

[1] The evolutions of *kě* and *jiùshì* in this paper mainly refer to the existing research results, and the differences between *kě* and *kěshì* (可是) can be referred to Zhang Lili [2]. We don't discuss *kěshì* anymore. Because the research goal of this paper is not to analyze the semantic change of cases in detail, but to find the laws of semantic change across languages.

（4）其味相反，而皆可于口。

Qí   wèi   xiāngfǎn,   ér   jiē   kě   yú   kǒu.
3PL.GEN taste opposite   but   both   suit for   taste
'They taste different, but they are both delicious.' （《庄子·天运》）

Xi Jia [1] pointed out that since the Han Dynasty (202 B.C.–220 A.D.), due to the influence of context, *kě* was used as an adverb, which produced rhetorical usage similar to难道*nán dào* 'rhetorical question marker' and岂*qǐ* 'rhetorical question marker'. The example sentence is quoted as follows:

（5）出一美言善行而天下从之, 或见一恶意丑事而万民违, 可不慎乎!

Chū   yī   měiyán   shànxíng ér   tiānxià   cóng zhī, huò jiàn
do   one good.word beneficence so everyone follow it   or   see
yī   èyì   chǒushì ér   wànmín   wéi,   kě   bú   shèn   hū!
one   spite scandal so   everyone disobey Q   NEG   cautious SFP
'If you do good words and deeds, everyone will learn from you; if you do bad things, everyone will disobey. Shouldn't you be cautious?'   （《新论》）

In the Han Dynasty, *kě* was often used in conjunction with negative words such as 不*bù* 'no' and 无*wú* 'without'. In the Tang Dynasty (618 A.D.–907 A.D.), the use of *kě* to express rhetorical meaning was very common, and it could get rid of negative words and modal particle at the end of sentences, as the following example illustrates:

（6）二百年来霸王业，可知今日是丘墟。

èr   bǎi   nián   lái bàwángyè, kě   zhī   jīnrì   shì   qiūxū.
two   hundred year   hegemony   Q   know   today COP   ruins
'How could he know that the hegemony he has achieved in the past two hundred years has turned into ruins?'   （皮日休《南阳》）

Xi Jia [1] believed that *kě* in the Tang Dynasty derived the emphatic meaning from the rhetorical meaning, and its questioning tone weakened and disappeared. In fact, emphatic usage is the pragmatic purpose of rhetorical usage. Zhang Lili [13] cited some examples of the adverb *kě* in Tang poetry, and we quote one of them as follows:[2]

（7）老方却归来，收拾可丁丁。

Lǎo   fāng   què   guīlái,   shōushi   kě   dīngdīng.
old   already again return   collection really rare
'I was able to return to my hometown when I was old, but the scriptures I have collected are really rare.'   （孟郊《读经》）

She believed that *kě* here expresses 'really' and is an emphatic adverb.

When *kě* is in the position of contextual cohesion and plays a role in strengthening the tone, it expresses the adversative meaning while emphasizing the latter clause or the

---

[2] The usage of *kě* as a modal adverb in the Tang Dynasty was not common, and was mainly distributed in Tang poetry.

following phrase, which is equivalent to 却*què* 'but'. This adversative usage was used in the Tang Dynasty:

（8）石状虽如帻，山形可类鸡。

Shí   zhuàng   sūi   rú   zé,   shān   xíng   kě   lèi   jī.
rock   shape   although   like   hat   mountain shape   but   like   chicken
'Although the rocks on the mountain look like hats, the overall shape is like a chicken.'
（韦庄《鸡公帻》）

（9）相见情已深，未语可知心。

Xiāng   jiàn   qíng   yǐ   shēn,   wèi   yǔ   kě   zhī   xīn.
each.other see   feeling already deep   NEG   speak   but   know mind
'The two have deep feelings for each other, even if they don't talk to each other, they know each other.'   （李白《相逢行》）

Example (8) is an example of a transitional stage, there are two interpretations, *kě* can be understood as 'but' or 'really'. Some examples of *kě* expressing adversative meaning after the Tang Dynasty are quoted from Zhang Lili [2]:

（10）他将毒药放在汤里，可着我拿过去与你吃。

Tā   jiāng   dúyào   fàng zài   tāng   lǐ,   kě   zhúo   wǒ   ná-guò-qù
3SG   OBJ   poison   put into   soup   inside   but   let   1SG   take-DIR-DIR_ITITIVE

yǔ   nǐ   chī.
give 2SG eat
'He put poison in the soup, but let me take it for you to eat.' （关汉卿《感天动地窦娥冤》）

（11）贾母笑道："这么着也好，可就只忒苦了宝丫头了。"

Jiǎmǔ   xiào   dào: "zhèmezhāo   yěhǎo,   kě   jiù   zhǐ   tuī
Lady   smile   say   so   all.right   but   just   only   too

kǔ   le   bǎoyātou   le."
suffer PRT   Baochai   CRS
'The Lady Dowager smiled and said, "That's all right, but it's just too hard for Baochai."'
（《红楼梦》第九十六回）

Through the above analysis, the semantic change of *kě* is summarized as follows: rhetorical meaning > emphatic meaning > adversative meaning. As for the motives and mechanisms of evolution, Xi Jia [1] believed that the emphatic usage is the pragmatic purpose of rhetorical usage, and the emphatic meaning can help express the adversative meaning. When it is used in the syntactic position of cohesion and transition, it is easy to develop adversative meaning. Zhang Lili [2], based on the investigation of Yuan Dynasty opera materials and "A Dream of Red Mansions", believed that the key to entering the adversative context of *kě* is that it has a reminder function. In the usage of commenting, presenting facts, opening new topics, *kě* with the function of reminder can form an adversative relationship with the previous text.

2.2   The Semantic Change of *Jiùshì*

In the pre-Qin period (before 221 B.C.), *jiù* was mainly used as a verb, which means to go and approach. For example:

（12）主人就东阶，客就西阶。
    Zhǔrén jiù   dōng jiē, kè   jiù   xī   jiē.
    host   head.for east step guest head.for west step
    'The host goes to the east step, and the guest goes to the west step.' (《礼记·曲礼》)

Zhang Lili [14] pointed out that the emphatic adverb *jiù* first appeared in Zhao Qi's annotation to MengZi in the Eastern Han Dynasty (25 A.D.–220 A.D.):

（13）一战胜齐，遂有南阳，然且不可。
    Yí   zhàn shèng qí, suì yǒu   nányáng, rán qiě bù kě.
    one fight defeat state thus occupy city   but even NEG appropriate
    'Even if you defeat Qi in one fight and thus get Nanyang, it still shouldn't be done.' (《孟子·告子下》)

赵岐注："就使慎子能为鲁一战，取齐南阳之地，且犹不可。"
    Zhàoqí zhù: " jiù   shǐ shènzǐ néng wèi lǔ yí zhàn,
    ZhaoQi annotate exactly let ShenZi can   for state one fight
    qǔ   qí   nányáng zhī dì,   qiě yóu bù kě. "
    occupy state city   GEN land but still NEG appropriate
    'Zhao Qi annotated: "Even if Shen Zi was allowed to lead Lu State to war and obtained the land of Nanyang in Qi State, it would still be inappropriate to do so."'

The *jiù* in the example is the emphatic adverb. 就使*jiùshǐ* is formed by combining the adverb *jiù* and the causal verb *shǐ*.

During the Wei, Jin, Southern and Northern Dynasties (220 A.D.–589 A.D.), the usages of preposition, adverb, and conjunction of *jiù* appeared at the same time. We focus on the adverb. Example (14) is quoted from Zhang Lili [14], in which *jiù* is the emphatic adverb.

（14）就如张衡思侔造化、郭象言类悬河，不自劳苦，何由至此。
    Jiù rú   zhānghéng sī   móu zàohuà, guōxiàng yán lèi xuánhé,
    just like ZhangHeng ingenuity like nature GuoXiang speech like river
    bù zì láokǔ, héyóu zhì cǐ?
    NEG from diligent wherever reach such
    'Just like Zhang Heng has deep thoughts like nature, Guo Xiang speaks fluently like a river, if they are not diligent and hardworking, how can they reach such a level?'
    (《南齐书·王僧虔/寂列传》)

Zhang Yisheng [6] pointed out that probably in the Song (960 A.D.–1279 A.D.) and Yuan Dynasties (1271 A.D.–1368 A.D.), *jiù* and *shì* began to be used together, and they were originally phrases expressing judgment. For example (15), *jiùshì* means judgment.

（15）一个汉子从外面过来，就是那郭排军。

Yí   gè   hànzi   cóng   wàimiàn   guòlái,   jiù   shì   nà   guōpáijūn.
one   CLF   man   from   outside   come.over just   COP   DEM   Guopaijun
'A man came from outside, that is Guo Paijun.'   （《碾玉观音》下）

The *jiùshì* used to express judgment is often followed by noun phrases. With the expansion of functions, it can also be connected to predicate components or clauses, thus developing into a mood adverb expressing the emphatic meaning. For example:

（16）刚刚讨药的这人，就是救那婆子的。

Gānggāng tǎo   yào   de   zhè   rén,   jiùshì   jiù   nà   pózi   de.
Just.now   demand medicine GEN DEM man   exactly save DEM woman SFP
'The person who just asked for medicine is to save the old woman.'（《窦娥冤》第二折）

（17）喝的莎塔八，跌倒就是睡。

Hē   de   shātǎbā,   diēdǎo   jiùshì   shuì.
Drink AUX   drunk   fall   exactly   sleep
'He got drunk and fell down and just slept on the ground.'
（关汉卿《邓夫人苦痛哭存孝》）

Example (16) can be seen as an example of a transitional phase, which has two interpretations. It can be understood as a judgment, referring to the person mentioned above, *jiùshì* is the adverbial-verb phrase; it can also be understood as emphasizing the act of "saving the woman", *jiùshì* is an adverb. The *jiùshì* in example (17) no longer expresses judgment, but emphasizes "sleep".

Regarding the relationship between emphatic usage and exclusive usage, Chen Li [7] believed that emphatic meaning is used to direct the speaker's attention to a certain range, which is an exclusive usage relative to the overall range. For example:

（18）老人道："十一郎要见亡夫人，就是今夜罢了。"

Lǎorén dào: "shíyīláng   yào   jiàn   wáng   fūren,   jiùshì   jīnyè   bà le."
Old.man say ShiYilang want.to see   deceased wife   only   tonight CRS
'The old man said, "Shi Yilang wants to see his deceased wife, and the time is tonight."'
（《初刻拍案惊奇》卷二十三 1627A.D.）

Chen Li [7] believed that there are two explanations for *jiùshì*: exclusive adverb or emphatic adverb. It can be seen that they are closely related. When emphatic usage is on a specific object, action or range, there is an exclusive meaning. She believed that the use case for *jiùshì* to represent an adversative meaning was not much more until the Qing Dynasty (1636 A.D.–1912 A.D.). For example:

（19）刘姥姥道："还都好，就是今年左边的槽牙活动了。"
Liúlǎolao dào: "hái dōu hǎo, jiùshì jīnnián zuǒbiān de cáoyá huódòng le."
Granny.Liu say still all good but this.year left.side GEN back.teeth loose CRS
Granny Liu said, "It's all good, but this year one of my back teeth on the left side has come
loose."   （《红楼梦》第三十九回）

The *jiùshì* in the sentence indicates the adversative meaning, but from another angle, it can also be understood as the exclusive meaning. Compared with the situation before *jiùshì*, only these situations are different.

Regarding the conditions for the development of *Jiùshì* from the exclusive meaning to the adversative meaning, Zhang Yisheng [6] pointed out: in order to explain the preceding item P, "*jiùshì* X" can be used to demonstrate and explain. When the object listed by the speaker is some kind of exception, the purpose of the speaker pointing out the exception is to further supplement and amend P, so that the adversative relationship will be derived between "*jiùshì* X" and P. In a word, the evolution path of *jiùshì* is: confirmation usage>emphatic usage>exclusive usage>adversative usage. There is an indirect connection between emphatic usage and adversative usage.

On the whole, *kě* and *jiùshì* both change from emphatic usage to adversative usage, although the development of *jiùshì* has an intermediate stage of exclusive usage. Previous studies have discussed the two terms as different types. We choose to combine them, as on the one hand, it helps to refine the evolution path from emphatic meaning to adversative meaning from a macro perspective; on the other hand, it helps to better examine the close relationship between emphatic usage, exclusive usage and adversative usage.[3]

3 A Cross-Linguistic Examination of the Relationship Between the Emphatic Meaning and the Adversative Meaning

This section selects five languages to investigate, including English, German, French, Spanish, and Korean, to explore whether there are some linguistic elements which have both the emphatic usage and the adversative usage, and analyze the relationships between the two usages.[4]

We can use the etymological dictionary to look up the original meaning and the current common meaning of the words. Judging the relationship between the emphatic usage and the adversative usage in three steps: Firstly, we need to find words with the emphatic usage and the adversative usage, and analyze their original meanings. If the original meaning has the emphatic usage, it means that there is a shift from the emphatic usage to the adversative usage, but the intermediate stage is still unclear. If the original meaning is not related to the high degree or the emphatic usage, it means that the emphatic usage may come later than the adversative usage. Secondly, we examine the

---

[3] In order to have stronger operability and semantic relevance, this paper restricts the indirect connection to only one different category between two semantic categories.

[4] The selection of typological language samples needs to consider the balanced distribution of language families and regions. Among the selected languages, English and German belong to the Germanic languages, and French and Spanish belong to the Romance languages. The family of Korean is still controversial.

relationships between the various meanings and observe the process of semantic change. Finally, we observe whether the usages of emphatic adverbs are restricted. If there is no emphatic usage in the original meaning, and the emphatic usage is only used in limited circumstances, such emphatic usage may be brought about by context or construction.

3.1 Two Meanings of English *But*

According to the Online Etymology Dictionary, *but* is derived from Old English *butan, buton* "unless; with the exception of; without, outside," from West Germanic *be-utan, a compound of *be- "by" (see by) + *utana "out, outside; from without," from *ut* "out" (see out (adv.)). Not used as a conjunction until late Old English, "on the contrary." Senses attested in early Middle English include "however, yet; no more than."[5]

From the etymological explanation, it can be seen that the adversative usage of *but* comes from the exclusive usage. This is similar to the Chinese *Jiùshì*. In the Oxford Dictionaries, the adversative usage of *but* is as follows:

（20） *By   the   end   of   the   day,   we   were   tired   but   happy.*
      PRE ART   end   PRE   ART   day   3PL   COP-PST   tired   but   happy
      'At the end of the day, we were tired but happy.'

In addition to the adversative usage, *but* also has the emphatic usage, but the usage conditions are limited, and it needs to be used before repeated words, such as the example in the New Oxford Dictionary:

（21） *Nothing,   but   nothing   would   make   him   change   his   mind.*
      Nothing,   but   nothing   would   CAUS   2SG change   2SGR   mind
      'Nothing, absolutely nothing, would change his mind.'

It can be seen that *but* is directly transformed from the exclusive usage to the adversative usage, while the emphatic usage may be generated in the construction where words appear repeatedly, and its usage is not universal.

3.2 Two Meanings of German *Aber*

The original meaning of *aber* is "emphatically, repeatedly", used as an adverb, and in this sense it was replaced by *wieder* ("again") in the 16th century. Only in some combinations today, like *aber und aber(mals)* ("again"). Later, *aber* has the usage of strengthening assertion, confirming to be true, expressing surprise, etc., which is further developed into adversative conjunctions.[6] Example (22) indicates the usage of emphatic adverb, and example (23) indicates the usage of adversative conjunction:

---

[5] The English etymological query URL for *but* is https://www.etymonline.com/search?q=but.
[6] The German etymological query URL for *aber* is https://www.dwds.de/wb/aber#1.

(22) *Das   ist   aber   wunderbar!*
This   COP   very   wonderful
'This is awesome!'

(23) *Er   ist   zwar   alt,   aber   noch   rüstig.*
3SG   COP   though   old   but   still   energetic
'Although he is old, he is still very energetic.'

It can be seen that the German *aber* is developed from emphatic adverb to adversative conjunction, which is similar to the Chinese *kě*.

3.3 Two Meanings of French *Mais*

The etymology of the French *mais* is the Latin adverb *magis*, which means "more; to a greater extent", which is closer to the emphatic meaning, because the enhancement of the degree is also an emphatic usage.[7]

The adverb *mais* is often located at the beginning of a sentence and plays a role in strengthening the mood. For example, in the New Century French-Chinese Dictionary:

(24) *Mais   non,   ce   n' est   pas   lui.*
indeed   NEG   this   NEG COP   NEG   3SG。
'It really wasn't him.'

There is also a kind of emphasis used in conjunction with interjections, etc., to emphasize the answer or exclamation, such as: Eh *mais*! (Ah!).

The adversative usage of *mais* is more common, like:

(25) *Elle   est   riche,   mai   avare.*
3SG   COP   rich   but   stingy
'She is rich but stingy.'

In general, the French *mais* also changes from the emphatic meaning to the adversative meaning, which is similar to the Chinese *kě*.

3.4 Two Meanings of Spanish *Pero*

Spanish *pero* is derived from Latin *per* ("for") + *hoc* ("tanto, so much").[8] *Pero* is used at the beginning of a sentence to strengthen the mood, such as (26), and later developed the adversative usage, such as (27):

---

[7] The French etymological query URL for mais is http://www.frdic.com/dicts/fr/mais.

[8] The Spanish etymological query URL for pero is http://www.esdict.cn/dicts/es/pero.

（26）*Pero ¡qué   hermosa noche!*
FOC   how   beautiful night
'What a beautiful night!'

（27）*La   casa es   pequeña, pero cómoda.*
ART   room COP   small   but   comfortable
'The room is small but comfortable.'

In general, the Spanish *pero* is also from the emphatic meaning to the adversative meaning.

3.5 Two Meanings of Korean 나*(na)*

Longchao Korean-Chinese Dictionary notes: 나 (particle) is used after nominal, adverb or predicate whose last syllable is a vowel to express the emphatic meaning.[9] For example:

（28）무슨 보배 나 얻은 것처럼 그 책 을 좋아했다.
Museum   bobae   na   eod-eun geoscheoleom   geu
ART   treasure AUX   get   AUX   DEM
Chaeg-eul   joh-ahaess-da
Book-ACC   like-PST-DECL
'He liked the book very much, as if he had some kind of treasure.'

There is also a usage of 나, which is used as a connective ending, used after the stem of the last syllable is a vowel or "ㄹ" or after the word ending "-시-", to express opposition or adversativity, such as example (29). It can also be used after the stem of an adjective, often in the form of "-나- ㄴ" for the emphatic meaning. For example (30):

（29）이 옷 은 고우 나 좀 비싸다.
I   os-eun   gou   na   jom   bissa-da
DEM   dress-TOP beautiful REL a.little expensive-DECL。
'This dress is very beautiful, but a little expensive.'

（30）머 나 먼 길
Meo   na   meon   gil
far   REL   far   way
'very long way'

Since the etymology of the Korean word 나 has not been found, 나 itself is an adhesive component and cannot be used independently. Let's put it under the ambiguous relationship type for now.

To sum up, the relationship types of the emphatic meaning and the adversative meaning in different languages can be summarized as Table 1:

---

[9] The query URL for Korean 나 is https://www.youdao.com/result?word=%EB%82%98&lang=ko.

Table 1. Relationship types of the emphatic meaning and the adversative meaning.

	Chinese		English	German	French	Spanish	Korean
	kě	*jiùshì*	*but*	*aber*	*mais*	*pero*	ㄴ *(na)*
Direct relationship	+			+	+	+	
Indirect relationship		+					
Weak relationship			+				
Ambiguous relationship							+

It can be seen from the table that the path from the emphatic usage directly to the adversative usage is the most common, and the other three types need to expand the language sample, which needs to be further investigated by another paper. So next we mainly discuss the semantic change law of direct relationship.

4 The Law of Semantic Change from the Emphatic Meaning to the Adversative Meaning

It has been confirmed above that it is a common path to develop directly from the emphatic usage to the adversative usage.[10] It's worth thinking about further: why does this process take place? Is there unidirectionality? How did it happen? These questions correspond to the conditions, direction and mechanisms of the change from the emphatic meaning to the adversative meaning.

4.1 Conditions from the Emphatic Meaning to the Adversative Meaning

This section mainly analyzes the similarities and differences between the emphatic meaning and the adversative meaning in order to explore the conditions for semantic change. Taking the differences in the emphatic usage and the adversative usage of *kě* as an example, Zhang Lili [2] distinguished three usages of *kě* from three aspects: syntactic position, sentence pattern and subjectivity. As shown in the Table 2:

---

[10] According to the distribution in Table 1, we find that there is a general path from the emphatic usage directly to the adversative usage. At the same time, we also acknowledge that there are weak relationships that arise in specific contexts, as well as unclear etymology and evolutionary paths. But this does not negate the preceding general path, just as the unidirectionality of grammaticalization cannot be negated for some special cases.

Table 2. The classification of three usages of *kě*.

	Classification criteria	Emphatic adverb	Adversative adverb	Adversative conjunction
kě	Syntactic position	After the subject	After the subject	Before the subject
	Sentence pattern	Simple sentence	General adversative complex sentence	Typical adversative complex sentence
	Subjectivity	With subjective mood	With subjective mood	Without subjective mood

In the table above, the adversative usage corresponds to the adversative adverb and the adversative conjunction respectively. Here we mainly compare the emphatic adverb usage of *kě* and its more typical usage of adversative conjunction. It is not difficult to see that their differences are mainly in syntax, and the subjectivity of them is also related to syntax. Therefore, in order to find the connection between the two usages, we have to look for commonalities in terms of semantics.

Regarding the core semantic function of the adverb *kě*, it is mentioned in the preface: Zhang Wangxi and Li Huimin [4] believed that *kě* has the function of highlighting the expectation; Wang Yingxian [5] focused on its contrastive meaning, and Zhang Lili [2] believed that it has reminder function. These are actually related. Since the objective situation is different from the highlighted expectation, there will be contrast meaning, and the purpose of contrast is sometimes to remind the listener to pay attention to something. Although these functions are related, the levels are different.

It's worth thinking about: what is the core semantic basis behind these usages? We might as well jump out of the analysis of the case of *kě* and combine the sentences in German, French and Spanish, we will find that the meaning of "exceeding expectations" is a semantic gene that develops from the emphatic meaning to the adversative meaning. "Exceeding expectations" here includes "exceeding expectations of degree" and "exceeding expectations about facts".[11] Emphatic usage can include the above two types, with a certain degree of subjectivity, followed by predicate components; however, the adversative usage mainly corresponds to "exceeding expectations about facts", generally has no subjectivity, and is mostly used in adversative sentences, where the adversative marker represents the logical semantic relationship between clauses. This core meaning is also suitable for explaining *kě*:

---

[11] "Exceeding expectations" here is not exactly the same as counter-expectation. "Exceeding expectations of degree" expresses a subjectivity, which is related to the emphatic usage. "Exceeding expectations about facts" and counter-expectation are related, highlighting the contrast between the expectations of common sense reasoning and the expectations of the hearer.

（31）　这个苹果我可吃不下。
Zhè   gè   píngguǒ   wǒ   kě   chī   bú   xià.
DEM   CLF   apple   1SG   actually   eat   NEG   up
'I can't eat this apple anymore.'

（32）　这个苹果可红，可甜了。
Zhè   gè   píngguǒ   kě   hóng,   kě   tián   le.
DEM   CLF   apple   very   red   very   sweet   CRS
'This apple is very red and sweet.'

（33）　这个苹果可红，可不太甜。
Zhè   gè   píngguǒ   kě   hong,   kě   bú   tài   tián.
DEM   CLF   apple   very   red   but   NEG   very   sweet
'This apple is very red, but not very sweet.'

In example (31), there is such an exceeding expectation: others believe that I can eat the apple up, but I actually feel full or have a small appetite to eat it. Example (32) is the speaker's subjective opinion that the apple's redness and sweetness exceed the general expectations. In example (33), usually red apples would be very sweet, but it actually exceeds the factual expectation and is not sweet, which represents the adversative usage.

Lü Shuxiang [15] pointed out that the occurrence of the adversative meaning is mostly because one thing triggers some kind of expectation, while another event exceeds this expectation, so there is a kind of adversativity in psychology. It can be seen that "exceeding expectations" is the link between the adversative meaning and the emphatic meaning, but the objects are different, some are of degree, some are of fact. This may also explain why words such as Chinese非常*fēicháng* 'very' and English *very*, which also express the emphatic meaning, do not have the adversative usage, because they have nothing to do with expectation.

4.2   The Direction from the Emphatic Meaning to the Adversative Meaning

From the above, it can be found that the evolution direction from the emphatic meaning to the adversative meaning is more common, and the opposite direction rarely occurs. According to our investigation, there are also cases where there is the adversative usage first, followed by the emphatic usage, but the emphatic usage is limited, only in specific sentence patterns and constructions. It is difficult to say that it has experienced grammaticalization, so there is no challenge to the unidirectionality of grammaticalization, such as English *but*.

The factors that affect the direction of this semantic change are as follows: On the one hand, it is the influence of the unidirectionality of grammaticalization. In terms of the decategorialization of grammaticalization, this evolution conforms to the categoriality. Hopper [16] pointed out that there is such a cline: major category (>intermediate category)>minor category. In this schema the major categories are noun and verb (categories that are relatively "open" lexically), and minor categories include preposition, conjunction, auxiliary verb, pronoun, and demonstrative (relatively "closed" categories). Adjectives and adverbs comprise an intermediate degree between the major and minor categories. Words such as *kě*, *mais* and *aber* have evolved from emphatic adverbs to adversative conjunctions, and their evolution direction conforms to the categoriality. On the other hand, from the perspective of the sentence patterns, it also conforms to the expansion from simple sentence to complex sentence. From the point of view of the collocation objects of words, it also conforms to the expansion of words such as adjectives to larger language units such as phrases and clauses.

4.3 Mechanisms from the Emphatic Meaning to the Adversative Meaning

Bybee et al. [17] believed that there are five basic mechanisms of semantic change, namely metaphorical extension, inference, generalization, harmony and absorption of contextual meaning.

We argue that in the evolution from the emphatic meaning to the adversative meaning, the main mechanisms are absorption of contextual meaning, inference, and generalization. Because metaphorical extension is suitable for lexical meaning and grammatical meaning closer to the lexical end, while inference is suitable for more grammatical or more abstract meaning. In addition, adversative conjunctions are often located between two clauses and are greatly affected by the context, so there will also be absorption of contextual meaning. Generalization is also reflected. From the usage of emphatic adverbs to adversative conjunctions, the collocation and use of words has been expanded to a certain extent, and it is no longer limited to subjective expressions.

First, let's look at the role of absorption of contextual meaning. The absorption of context means that a language form absorbs the meaning of the context in which it is used for a long time, and gradually normalizes it and becomes a conventional meaning. Zhang Lili [2] believed that the key to the transformation of the emphatic adverb into the adversative adverb lies in the adversative context. Wang Yingxian [5] believed that for *kě* in declarative sentences, the context reflecting the contrastive relationship is the key. The statements of adversative and contrastive contexts have merit, but do not reflect their connection to emphatic meaning. We believe that the context of "explicit exceeding expectations about facts" is more appropriate. Here "explicit" means that in a complex sentence, the expectation can be seen from the previous clause. While "implicit exceeding expectations about facts" mostly refers to the situation in a simple sentence. The meaning of *kě* is closer to "exceeding expectations of degree" at the beginning. When *kě* is between clauses, it highlights the difference between the preceding and following clauses, and is used for "exceeding expectations about facts" to express the adversative meaning.

Secondly, inference is also an important mechanism. Bybee et al. [17] argued that meaning from the context that was not originally present can inhere in a gram as the result of inference. The frequent use of a gram in a particular context, as we have seen, can lead to the inference that that context is actually part of the meaning of the gram. *kě* acquires the meaning of "exceeding expectations about facts" through the absorption of context. When it frequently appears in adversative complex sentences, people will regard this contextual meaning as part of the meaning of *kě* itself, so through inference, *kě* went from "exceeding expectations of degree" to "exceeding expectations about facts", and the use of the adversative conjunction of *kě* has been fixed.

Finally, there is the effect of the generalization mechanism. Bybee et al. [17] believed that generalization is the loss of specific features of meaning with the consequent expansion of appropriate contexts of use for a gram. Taking *kě* as an example, in the process of developing from an emphatic adverb to an adversative conjunction, on the one hand, the subjectivity is worn away and the subjective mood is lost; on the other hand, the syntactic collocation is expanded. It extends from a position within a simple sentence to a position between two clauses. Sentences containing *kě* expand from simple sentences to complex sentences. French *mais* is the same: its subjectivity is worn away; *mais* is often used as a modal adverb at the beginning of a sentence, and when used as an adversative conjunction, it extends into the middle of two clauses.

5 Conclusion

From the perspective of language typology, this paper discusses the use of the same linguistic form to express the emphatic meaning and the adversative meaning, taking the semantic change of the Chinese multifunctional words *kě* and *jiùshì* as an example, and analyzing the semantic changes with materials in five other languages. According to the closeness of the relationship, we can summarize four types of relationship between the emphatic meaning and the adversative meaning, which can be divided into: direct relationship>indirect relationship>weak relationship (specific context)>ambiguous relationship. On this basis, it is further proved that the transition from the emphatic meaning to the adversative meaning is a general law of semantic change. The evolution condition is that it needs to have the meaning of "exceeding expectations", the direction of evolution is unidirectional, and the evolution mechanism includes absorption of context, inference and generalization.

This paper plays an important role in the analysis of the multi-functionality of words and the exploration of the law of semantic change in different categories. In terms of depth, it analyzes the generation of multi-functionality of words from the perspective of diachronic evolution; in terms of breadth, the case analysis is promoted to the induction of general evolution paths through the perspective of typology.

Acknowledgments. I am grateful to the anonymous reviewers of CLSW 2022 for helpful suggestions and comments. The work was supported by the China Scholarship Council's public joint training program for doctoral students (File No. 202106210175).

References

1. Xi, J.: Probe into origin of adverb "ke"'s adversative function. Stud. Lang. Linguist. **2**, 80–83 (2003). (in Chinese)
2. Zhang, L.L.: A comprehensive discussion on the formation of the adversatives "ke" and "keshi." J. Chinese Lit. Natl. Cheng Kung Univ. **54**, 167–206 (2016). (in Chinese)
3. Zhang, X.S.: A study on the emergence of the grammatical meaning of "ke" as a mood adverb. J. Jiangsu Normal Univ. (Philos. Soc. Sci. Edn.). **4**, 125–134 (2016). (in Chinese)
4. Zhang, W.X., Li, H.M.: Interlocution contexts and inter-subjectivity of the adverb "ke." Lang. Teach. Linguist. Stud. **2**, 1–8 (2009). (in Chinese)

5. Wang, Y.X.: Contrast and emphasis: an essay on the modal adverb ke in declarative sentences. Lang. Teach. Linguist. Stud. **2**, 83–91 (2015). (in Chinese)
6. Zhang, Y.S.: The coherent functions of jiùshì in text and the evolution of its grammaticalization. Chinese Teach. World. **3**, 80–90 (2002). (in Chinese)
7. Chen, L.: The diachronic study of Chinese adversative category, pp. 198–210. Hunan Normal University, Changsha (2012). (in Chinese)
8. Sun, Y.P.: The study of the origin of Chinese adversatives, pp. 58–60. Jiangxi Normal University, Nanchang (2017). (in Chinese)
9. Bian W.: The Differences Between *Jiùshì* and *Jiùsuàn* as Conjunctions and Their Formation Mechanisms. In: CLSW2021, LNAI, vol. 13249, pp. 144–159 (2022)
10. Winterstein, G.: From exclusive to adversative meaning: A diachronic and cross-linguistic perspective. Paper presented at the workshop: researching pragmatic particles in communication: cognitive, argumentative and social dimensions, Norwegian University of Science and Technology, Trondheim, Norway, May 2016
11. Li, X.J.: The Lexicon of grammaticalization in Chinese, pp. 113–114. China Social Sciences Press, Beijing (2021). (in Chinese)
12. Zhang, L.L.: The historical development and performance of the adversative adverbs fan, que and dao. Chinese Stud. **4**, 253–288 (2011). (in Chinese)
13. Zhang, L.L.: The formation of the emphatic adverb Ke in Mandarin. Tsing Hua J. Chinese Stud. **1**, 1–44 (2017). (in Chinese)
14. Zhang, L.L.: The formation of the concessive conditionals Ji Bian and Jiu. Humanitas Taiwanica **71**, 99–145 (2009). (in Chinese)
15. Lü, S.X.: Essentials of Chinese Gramma, pp. 476–483. The Commercial Press, Beijing (1982). (in Chinese)
16. Hopper, P.J., Traugott, E.C.: Grammaticalization. Cambridge University Press, Cambridge (2003). https://doi.org/10.1017/CBO9781139165525
17. Bybee, J., Perkins, R., Pagliuca, W.: The Evolution of Grammar—Tense, Aspect, and Modality in the Languages of the World, pp. 281–302. University of Chicago Press, Chicago (1994)

Research on the Semantic Map
of Multifunctional Morpheme Cong

Huijie Zhuang(⊠)

School of Culture and Communication, Central University of Finance and Economics,
Beijing 100098, China
zhuanghuijie2006@126.com

Abstract. In this paper, the multifunction morpheme of Chinese word "Cong(从)" is comprehensively researched, and then the diachronic semantic evolution and synchronic dialect distribution are combined to discuss the semantic evolution of "Cong(从)" by using the semantic map method. The semantic implication of "Cong(从)" in the diachronic evolution and the mechanism of its evolution are deeply explored. It is pointed out that "Cong(从)" in some dialects is semantically discontinuous. But from a diachronic perspective, these semantic functions are all related, and in fact Chinese dialect vocabulary has both commonality and its own uniqueness. When the multifunctional morphemes of Chinese dialects are investigated from a synchronic perspective, it is very necessary to combine the diachronic semantic evolution research, otherwise it may not be possible to clarify the true relationship between the various semantic functions of the multifunctional word.

Keywords: "Cong(从)" · Grammaticalization · Semantic Evolution · Semantic map

1 Forword

In Mandarin Chinese, "Cong(从)" is a multifunctional morpheme that can be used a verb, preposition and adverb. In dialects, "Cong(从)" also has some functions that do not exist in Mandarin, such as the meaning of disposal, locative and along. The existing works mostly focused on the grammaticalization of "Cong(从)", and the diachronic studies and dialect studies are separated. Different from these works, in this paper the diachronic semantic evolution and synchronic dialect distribution are combined to discuss the semantic evolution of "Cong(从)" by using the semantic map method, furthermore, the semantic function, diachronic evolution and the internal evolution mechanism

This work was supported by the major projects of the National Philosophy and Social Science Foundation of China "Interactive Research on Rhetoric, Vocabulary and Grammar in the Vision of Big Language (20&ZD298)", "Research on the Thesaurus and Diachronic Evolution of Commonly Used Words in Modern Chinese (11&ZD125)" and the projects of Central University of Finance and Economics "New Exploration on the Reform and Practice of Aesthetic Education in Finance and Economics Colleges (020851622002)".

© The Author(s), under exclusive license to Springer Nature Switzerland AG 2023
Q. Su et al. (Eds.): CLSW 2022, LNAI 13495, pp. 186–207, 2023.
https://doi.org/10.1007/978-3-031-28953-8_15

are deeply explored. Semantic map is an effective analysis method to investigate the differences and commonalities of lexical semantic function association patterns, which is helpful for us to deeply investigate and elaborate the semantic evolution of "Cong(从)".

2   Function Entries and Synchronic Semantic Investigation of "Cong(从)"

Based on the function definitions in "Modern Chinese Dictionary" and "Modern Chinese Eight Hundred Words", the existing research results and the dialect survey materials, in this paper, the 13 function entries of "Cong(从)" are selected as follows: follow, obey, always, comitative, according to, human source, locative source, time source, state source, via, locative, range and along. Referring to the existing research results, the semantic function of each entry with example sentences is explained as follows.

A. Follow, to walk or proceed in accordance with. 若有宾客, 则从后。(《周礼·天官冢 宰》)
B. Obey, to follow the commands or guidance of. 对此事我真是力不从心啊。
C. Always, adverb with the meaning of "at all times, forever". 他上学从没迟到过。
D. Comitative preposition, followed by another participant of the action. 伴从嫁 。(Fuzhou dialect)
E. According to, preposition. 从这方面来看他不是什么好人。
F. Human source preposition, followed by the human object that is the source of the action. 你从他要一点吧。(Baoding Dialect)
G. Locative source preposition, followed by the locative source of the action. 从校门 往北走便是中央主楼。
H. Time source preposition, followed by the starting time of the action. 北京的天气 从五月份开始就热了起来。
I. State source preposition, followed by the starting state of the action. 从老师成为 朋友。
J. Via preposition, followed by the route or place that the action passes through. 我 从田里小路那边来的。
K. Locative preposition, followed by the route or place. 小林从学校吃的饭。
L. Range, adverb, represent the whole extent of the durability for action. 从历史的长 河里。
M. Along, preposition. 从河边走。

Based on the above definitions, the semantic functions of "Cong(从)" in 21 Chinese dialects are investigated, which are listed in Table 1.

According to the dialect survey in Table 1, there are many different semantic functions in different dialects, and the initial verbs meaning has disappeared in many dialects, therefore, the relationships between the semantic functions of "Cong(从)" cannot be established from the actual usage in Chinese dialects. Based on the diachronic semantic investigation of "Cong(从)" and the grammaticalization and semantic evolution path, the connection of these semantic functions will be established from the diachronic perspective, then the synchronic semantic map will be drawn using the dialect data, and finally the diachronic conceptual space will be validated.

Table 1. The semantic functions of "Cong(从)" in Chinese dialects.

Dialect	Verb		Adverb	Preposition											Source
	Follow	Obey	Always	Comitative	According o	Human source	Locative source	Time source	State source	Via	Locative	Range	Along	
Standard mandarin	+	+	+		+		+	+	+	+		+		Modern Chinese Dictionary
Baoding		+	+		+	+	+	+	+	+	+	+		Investigated by author
Jinan							+	+			+	+		Dialect Dictionary
Rongcheng		+	+		+		+	+	+	+	+	+		Investigated by author
Chengdu			+				+	+	+	+		+		Dialect Dictionary
Guiyang							+	+	+	+		+		Dialect Dictionary
Wulumuqi			+				+	+		+	+	+		Dialect Dictionary
Yinchuan			+		+			+		+		+		Dialect Dictionary
Yanan		+	+				+	+	+		+			Investigated by author
Xi'an			+				+	+	+	+		+		Investigated by author

(continued)

Table 1. (*continued*)

Dialect	Verb		Adverb	Preposition											Source
	Follow	Obey	Always	Comitative	According o	Human source	Locative source	Time source	State source	Via	Locative	Range	Along	
Yangzhou			+				+	+		+				Dialect Dictionary
Linwu			+		+	+	+	+	+	+		+		Investigated by author
Liuzhou							+	+	+	+	+	+		Dialect Dictionary
Danyang			+				+	+		+		+		Dialect Dictionary
Jinhua			+					+				+		Dialect Dictionary
Changsha							+	+		+				Dialect Dictionary
Suzhou							+	+		+		+		Investigated by author

(*continued*)

Table 1. (*continued*)

Dialect	Verb		Adverb	Preposition											Source
	Follow	Obey	Always	Comitative	According o	Human source	Locative source	Time source	State source	Via	Locative	Range	Along	
Xuzhou								+						Dialect Dictionary
Nanchang			+				+	+	+			+		Dialect Dictionary
Pingxiang								+				+		Dialect Dictionary
Fuzhou		+		+										Dialect Dictionary
Nanning			+				+							Dialect Dictionary

Note that, the dialect dictionary in Table 1 is the reference of Rong Li [1]

3 Function Entries and Diachronic Semantic Investigation of "Cong(从)"

3.1 Semantic Function of "Cong(从)" in Ancient Chinese

"Cong(从)" is already a preposition in the Pre-Qin Period. Beijia Ma [2] pointed out that the characteristics of the Chinese preposition in the Pre-Qin and Han dynasties are: "One preposition has multiple functions, and one function is performed by multiple prepositions. It can be summarized as 'the number of the preposition is less, and the functions are more'". This can show that, "Cong(从)" already has a high degree of grammaticalization in Ancient Chinese.

In 《说文·从部》, "從, 相听也", "从, 随行也". "Cong(從)" and "Cong(从)" are ancient and modern words respectively, which both have the meaning of "follow". In the Pre-Qin Period, the meanings of "obey" and "lead" have been derived from the basic meaning of "follow", and "Cong(从)" has been grammaticalized as a preposition, indicating locative source, state source, time source, via, range and human source, etc. For example,

(1) 主人与客让登,主人先登, 客从之, 拾级聚足, 连步以上。(《礼记·曲礼》) (follow).
   The meaning of "obey" is generated by the original [+follow] semantic sememe contained in action, which is derived from the subjective will of "following" the opinions of others through metaphors.
(2) 强言霸说于曹伯, 曹伯从之, 乃背晋而奸宋。(《左传·哀公七年》) (obey).
   Thus, the relationship between "follow" and "obey" can firstly be established.
   In this period, "Cong(从)" also often appeared in the serial verb sentences pattern of "NP1 + V1(从) + NP2 + V2 + (O)", such as,
(3) 昔臣习于知伯, 是以佐之, 非能贤也。请从伯游。(《左传·襄公十三年》) (follow).
(4) 先帝后宫非有子者, 出焉不宜。皆令从死, 死者甚众。(《史记·秦始皇本纪》) (follow/ comitative).

In (3), V1 "Cong(从)" still contains verb meaning and cannot be regarded as a preposition. The sememe of the verb "follow" is: [+follow after] [+do something together] (the relationship between NP1 and NP2 are a master-slave relationship) [+run] [+displacement] [+path]. In (4), the verb meaning of V1 "Cong(从)" has been weakened, and the semantic function can be considered as the middle state of verb and preposition. For example, "从死" in (4) can be interpreted as "to die together or follow to die", although the sememes still contain [+follow after] [+do something together], but this only involves "sequence in time" and "NP1 the coordinator of the same action", the sememes of [+displacement] [+path] have completely disappeared. In the function entries of "Cong(从)", it has been introduced that comitative preposition is usually followed by another participant of the action, which is equivalent to "and, with". V1 "Cong(从)" in (4) already has the semantic function of "comitative", however, this kind of use case was quite rare in Ancient Chinese, and it often brought the difficulties in distinguishing between verbs and prepositions. So, the "comitative" semantic function has not developed greatly due to the constraints of language economy. As we all know, the serial verb construction is a prerequisite for grammaticalization, but the grammaticalization does not necessarily occur with the only prerequisite, the possibility of semantic metaphor must be added, besides, the grammaticalization will not cause the understanding difficulties in daily life. Fuxiang Wu[3] has investigated the grammaticalization of function word "with" in the history of Chinese language, and he pointed out that the "follow" function can be grammaticalized into the "comitative" function. Lansheng Jiang[4] pointed out that, the accompanying verb itself contains the lexical meaning of "together, jointly", and the evolution of comitative preposition only changes the lexical meaning into the grammatical meaning. Based on the above analysis, the association between "follow" and "comitative" can be established.

In the whole Ancient Chinese Period, the most verb semantic function of "Cong(从)" is "follow", and the second is "obey". The preposition functions, from most to least, are locative source, range, via, time source, state source, according to, human source and along. The detailed literature survey results are shown in Table 2.

According to the literature corpus survey, the preposition function of "Cong(从)" has appeared in the inscriptions on oracle bones and on bronze in Early Ancient Chinese. At the beginning, prepositions often have a single function, and the number of the objects they take is small. However, with the development of language and diversity of expression semantics, the structure of sentences has become more and more complex. And the components followed by prepositions have become more and more, the scope of objects of prepositions has expanded, which has also made the functions of prepositions to become more and more refined. The connections between multiple functions of "Cong(从)" can be further discussed from the following objects.

The "via" function of "Cong(从)" has the sememes of [+accompanying] [+running] [+displacement] [+path], and the following objects are mostly "the sign of road or place", further the verbs V2 followed are mostly operational or orientational, such as "come", "go", "enter" and so on. For example:

(5) 丙戌, 单子从阪道, 刘子从尹道伐尹。(《左传·昭公二十三年》)(via).

Beijia Ma[2] pointed out that the "follow" function of "Cong(从)" can mean, "People and people or people and things always follow each other, that is, the subject and the object are always together. When the subject passes through a place, people and places also always follow. The subjects develop from accompanying people to accompanying space". The "locative source" function that means it is followed by the locative source of the action, has been extended from the "via" function of "Cong(从)", furthermore, the "locative" function is extended. The "locative source" function has the sememes of [+running][+position][+displacement][+starting point], and the following objects are mostly nouns, pronouns, and noun phrases that express location, further the V2 followed are mostly verbs with tendency or movement (running), such as "come", "enter" and so on. For example:

(6) 孔子之弟子从远方来者, 孔子荷杖而问之曰: ......(《吕氏春秋·孟冬纪》) (locative source).

The objects that follow "Cong(从)" with "time source" semantic function are mostly time nouns or pronouns that means time source. For example, in (7) "是" in "从是而

Table 2. The semantic functions of "Cong(从)" in Ancient Chinese

Literaure	Verb		Preposition								
	Follow	Obey	Via	Locative source	Time source	State source	Locative	Range	According to	Human source
尚书	9	26								
诗经	18	12								
周易	9	14								
仪礼	102	38	1							
周礼	22	12								
礼记	54	61		3			1	1		
春秋公羊传	20	21								
春秋谷梁传	14	16								
左传	188	284	5	3	1		1	1		
国语	48	88			1		1			
战国策	53	45		13	2	2	1	6	3	
论语	7	14			3					
孟子	13	18		1						
墨子	17	26		8				6		
庄子	15	19		2						
荀子	13	64		4		1				
韩非子	25	39		11	2	1	2	1	1	
吕氏春秋	22	24	1	14	12	2		1	6	
老子		1								
商君书	6	6								
管子	47	62	1	9		1	1	2	1	
晏子	26	19	2	3				2		
孙子	3	4						1		
大戴	24	23		2		2				
韩诗外传	27	23	1	5	1		1	3		
吴子	2	8		1						
尉缭	2	8						1		
六韬	3	4		4			1	1	2	

(continued)

Table 2. (*continued*)

Literaure	Verb		Preposition							
	Follow	Obey	Via	Locative source	Time source	State source	Locative	Range	According to	Human source
司马法	1	1								
慎子	1	4	1	1						
通玄真经	11	17		2	1			1		
关尹子	2	5								
鹖冠子	10	5		3	1	1		4	1	
邓析子	2	3								
孝经		2								
素问	29	76	7	18		3	10	10		
灵枢	1	7	29	38		4		21	4	
孔子家语	38	51		1			1		1	
孔丛子	15	9		1				1		
史记	469	199	35	136	8	3	8	22	10	2
新语	3	5								
春秋繁露	6	31	1	8				5	1	
淮南子	27	36	2	19	1	5	5	8	3	
新序	21	27		13		1	1	2	4	
说苑	47	53	5	17			1	1	2	
新书	18	21								
马王堆汉墓帛书	2	6		4				3		
睡虎地秦墓竹简	4	8								
Sum	1496	1545	90	344	34	26	35	104	39	2

不睦" means the iconic time of the event "三十二年春, 宣王伐鲁, 立孝公", and the detailed sentence is as follows,

(7) 三十二年春, 宣王伐鲁, 立孝公, 诸侯从是而不睦。(《国语·周语上》) (time source).

Considering the projection mode of semantic metaphor from space to time, the association between the "follow", "via", "time source" and "locative source" can be established.

The small changes of the V2 verbs followed "Cong(从)" is that displacement verbs [+running] are expanded to non-displacement verbs, such as "see", "talk", "dwell". For examples,

(8) 晋灵公不君, 厚敛以雕墙。从台上弹人, 而观其辟丸也。(《左传·宣公二年》) (locative).

With the change of the V2 verbs followed "Cong(从)", the preposition function is expanded to "locative" function, that is, it has the sememes of [+accompanying] [-running] [-displacement] [+place]. Therefore, the association between the "via" and "locative" can be established. The objects that follow the "Cong(从)" with the "state source" semantic function are mostly adjectives or nouns used as adjectives. For example, in (9) "冥冥" is used to describe the state of "昏暗".

(9) 从冥冥见照照, 犹尚肆然而喜, 又况出室坐堂, 见日月光乎!(《淮南子·卷二十泰族训》) (state source).

According to the semantic change from content words to function words, "state source" can only originate from "locative source" rather than "time source" with more function semantics, so the association between the "locative source" and "state source" can be established. The "range" function has the sememes of [+space] or [+time], and the following objects are mostly location nouns, time nouns, etc., further the V2 followed are mostly "Zhi(至)" or "Dao(到)". For example:

(10) 从此以东, 梁地十余城皆恐, 莫肯下矣。(《史记·项羽本纪》)(range).

The space range function or time range function can be derived from the "accompanying in space" function of "Cong(从)", so the association between the "via" and "range" can be established. The objects that follow the "human source" function are the specific object of "ask for", mostly referring to human nouns, further the V2 followed is generally a verb with the meaning of "ask for", such as "Dai(贷)", "Shi(贳)", etc. The whole sentence expresses the semantic of "ask for" or "beg". For example,

(11) 从昆弟假贷, 犹足为生, 何至自苦如此。(《史记•司马相如列传》)(human source).

Refer to the semantic map of "comitative – human direction – human source" with the meaning of "connect" in Huijie Zhuang[5]. According to the semantic function of "Cong(从)" in this period, the "human direction" function is missing. Considering the extension of semantic function, the association between the "comitative" and "human source" can be firstly established, which will be verified later. The objects that follow the "according to" function are mostly tools, methods, conditions, etc., which are used to realize the action, and the V2 followed are mostly speculative verbs. For example,

(12) 孺子容三年而为三兆, 凭从此之见, 若问三人之贤与不贤, 所未敢识也。(《孔子家语·好生第十》) (according to).

The "according to" function of "Cong(从)" can be derived from the verb function "obey", which has the possibility of semantic metaphor. Hongfeng He [6] pointed out that, the "accompanying" developed the preposition usage of "depending on", and the verb with the meaning of "follow" has the sememes of [+follow][+accompanying] [+path], and [+accompanying] sememe will be grammaticalized as a preposition with the [+obey]. We believe that, the "accompanying" function of "Cong(从)" is first weaken into the verb with the meaning of "obey", and then the [+obey] function gradually increase, finally, "Cong(从)" is grammaticalized as "according to" preposition. Therefore, the association between the "obey" and "according to" is established.

Based on the above analysis, in the Pre-Qin Period the objects that follow the verb "Cong(从)" continued to expand, from objects of people to objects of things, and then to locative objects and time object and so on. The conceptual space of "Cong(从)" in Ancient Chinese Period can be drawn as follow (Fig. 1):

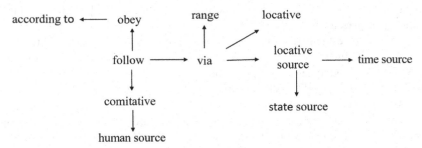

Fig. 1. The conceptual space of "Cong(从)" in Ancient Chinese Period.

3.2 Semantic Function of "Cong(从)" in Middle Chinese

In the period of middle Chinese, the verb function of "Cong(从)" has decreased compared with the Ancient Chinese Period, and the usage cases with the prepositions function have increased rapidly. The prepositions function of "locative source" and "according to" are mostly used. In this period, the same semantic functions as the ones in the previous period are "locative source", "time source", "state source", "via", "locative", "range", "human source" and so on. In this period, the core function has always been "locative source", the cases with "according to" function are less. The specific literature surveys are shown in Table 3:

In Wei Jin Southern and Northern Dynasties Period, with the expansion of the objects that follow "Cong(从)", the preposition usages of "according to" gradually increased. The following objects of "according to" function are mostly state adjectives or nouns such as tools and methods. Literature examples are as follows:

(13) 务在宽恕, 罪疑从轻。(《三国志•魏书•王朗传》) (according to).
The "human source" function of "Cong(从)" first appeared in the Western Han Dynasty, and developed in Wei Jin Dynasty. However, the following object NP2 was limited to nouns referring to people, and V2 was limited to the verbs with the meaning of "seeking", due to the restriction of semantics of NP2 and V2, the "human source" function did not develop further in the following period.
(14) 亭长从人借牛而不肯还之, 牛主讼于恭。(《后汉书•鲁恭传》)(human source).
Compared with the ancient Chinese period, the semantic functions of "locative end-point", "human direction" and "always" of "Cong(从)" have appeared in the Middle Chinese, for example:
(15) 道德清净, 佛与正觉, 无所从来、无所从去、亦无所住。(《彼岸而光赞经》卷八)(locative endpoint).
In Buddhist scriptures, there are often usage cases of "无所从来, 无所从去". Due to the symmetry of rhythm and pragmatics, the "locative source" function has reduced the new relative "locative endpoint" function. Therefore, the association between "locative

Table 3. The semantic functions of "Cong(从)" in Middle Chinese

Literature	Verb		Preposition											
	Follow	Obey	Comitative	Via	Locative source	Time source	State source	Locative	Locative endpoint	Range	According to	Human source	Human direction	Along
抱朴子内篇	20	9		1	10	1	2	2		4	3			
世说新语	11	19	1	4	17			3		3	2	3		
新校搜神记	39	9		5	41	1	1	4		3	3	4	1	
洛阳伽蓝记	7	5		2	16		1	1		1	1			
颜氏家训	4	6			2		1							
道行般若经	26	9		3	95	4	33	14	4	14	95	2	1	
佛说兜沙经		0			12						1			
阿门佛国经	2	1		1	16	1		2		4	1			
佛说遗日摩尼宝经	1	0		1	7		2	1		2	6		1	
佛说般舟三昧经	4	0			7	1					3			
般舟三昧经	11	3		1	24	1	3	1	2	2	20			

(continued)

Table 3. (*continued*)

Literature	Verb		Preposition											
	Follow	Obey	Comitative	Via	Locative source	Time source	State source	Locative	Locative endpoint	Range	According to	Human source	Human direction	Along
文殊师利问菩萨署经	7	9			1		1	1		1	10			
法镜经	2	1			2		1				3	3		
佛说菩萨本业经	1	0		1	1		1				3			
阿含口解十二因缘经	3	4			4		3			1	26	1		
中本起经	17	2		2	15		1	2		5	12			
修行本起经	6	1		3	9		1	1		3	5			
梵摩渝经		1					1				1			
大明度经	18	2		2	59	1	18	9		10	55		1	
了本生死经		0					4				23			
佛说四愿经		0					1							
六度集经	28	33			7		3	1		2	4	8	1	

(continued)

Table 3. (*continued*)

Literaure	Verb		Preposition											
	Follow	Obey	Comitative	Via	Locative source	Time source	State source	Locative	Locative endpoint	Range	According to	Human source	Human direction	Along
生经	17	27		6	40		1	1		2	14	8	1	
佛说普曜经	21	7		1	35	1	19	1		14	48			
光赞经	15	19			48	17	13	12	13	11	40	1		
大楼炭经	6	1		12	34	14	9	4		5	27		1	1
阿育王传	19	7		2	15	2	7	1		6	8	1		
出曜经	45	38		15	107	9	35	14	3	69	69	8	6	1
大庄严论经	6	6		4	30	3	9	3		6	24	2	5	1
妙法莲华经	24	3			47	7	10	2		6	10			
悲华经	10	0		4	16		11	2		4	8	10	4	
百喻经	1	1		1	7		3				10	1		
佛本行集经	85	17		31	395	53	64	103	1	49	74	45	17	

(*continued*)

200   H. Zhuang

Table 3. (*continued*)

Literature	Verb		Preposition											
	Follow	Obey	Comitative	Via	Locative source	Time source	State source	Locative	Locative endpoint	Range	According to	Human source	Human direction	Along
佛说他真陀罗所问问如来三昧经	3	6		5	30	1	6	1	2	6	19		1	
佛说阿阇世王经	20	12		3	40		6	1	2	3	34	3	6	1
齐民要术	7	4		4	18	1	1			18	4			
Sum	519	271	1	116	1227	123	282	190	27	260	707	105	47	4

source" and "locative endpoint" is established. In addition, "Cong(从)" has the "human direction" function, such as,

(16) 舍利弗从其众会言: "是事微妙, 快乃知是。"(《佛说阿 阇世王经》卷下) (human direction).

Referring to the conceptual space of "connect" meaning in Huijie Zhuang [5], the association between "comitative" and "locative direction" can be established.

"Conglai(从来)" is a time adverb with semantic function of "always". In the literature of Table 3, there are 25 cases of "Conglai(从来)" in the corpus, but only two cases have the function of "always". For example,

(17) 昔苏峻事公, 于白石祠中祈福, 许赛其牛。从来未解。(《搜神记》卷九) (always).

(18) "颛顼"字项当为许录反, 错作许缘反, 遂谓朝士言: "从来谬音'专旭'当音'专翻'耳。"(《颜氏家训·勉学第八》)(always).

In academia, there are many discussions on the lexicalization of "Conglai(从来)". For example, Beijia Ma [2] and Yinfeng Liang [7] have discussed "Conglai(从来)" from different perspectives in Chinese history, and they all believed that time adverb "Conglai(从来)" originated from the structure of "Suoconglai(所从来)", which first appeared in Wei Jin Southern and Northern Dynasties Period. From the "action source" function with the meaning of "come from some places", "Suoconglai(所从来)" is extended to the "time source" function. Combined with the grammaticalization of "Lai(来)", "Conglai(从来)" becomes time adverb, semantically representing the previous state.

So, the association between "time source" and "always" can be established, and finally the conceptual space of "Cong(从)" in Middle Chinese Period can be drawn as follow (Fig. 2):

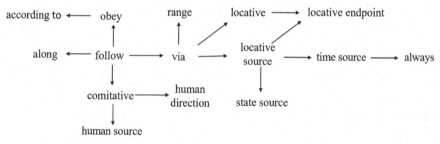

Fig. 2 The conceptual space of "Cong(从)" in Middle Chinese Period.

3.3 Semantic Function of "Cong(从)" in Early Modern Chinese

In the early modern Chinese period, the "follow" function of "Cong(从)" have been further reduced, and the preposition function has decreased compared with that in Middle Chinese period. Among these function, "locative source" is still its core function, and the function cases of "time source", "range" and "via" have slightly increased. However, the function cases of "state source", "locative", "human source", "human direction" and

Table 4. The semantic functions of "Cong(从)" in Early Modern Chinese

Literature	Verb		Adverb	Preposition								
	Follow	Obey	Always	Via	Locative source	Time source	State source	Locative	Range	According to	Human source	Human direction
敦煌变文集新书	27	36	6	17	75	6	11	2	23	24	8	2
祖堂集	10	21	5	8	134	7	5	2	7	18	4	7
大唐三藏取经诗话	2	1		2	3	1	1					
新刊大宋宣和遗事	11	21	1		4	2						
五代史平话	21	24		12	12	4	2	2		3		
全相平话五种	21	63		1	13	2			5	2		
关汉卿戏曲集	2	5			1	1	1		5			
元刊杂剧三十种	4	17	1		14	7	3	1	13	4		
老乞大谚解		0			4	2			2			
朴通事谚解		1			2	1			1			
永乐大典戏文三种	2	2			3	3	1		4	2		
水浒传	19	40	1	99	302	21	19	5	38	17		
西游记	22	35	3	22	111	1	10	2	24	6		

(continued)

Table 4. (*continued*)

Literature	Verb		Adverb	Preposition									
	Follow	Obey	Always	Via	Locative source	Time source	State source	Locative	Range	According to	Human source	Human direction
金瓶梅	8	7	2	23	181	79	9	11	30	5		1
平妖传	3	12	10	9	61	3	16	2	18	2		1
醒世姻缘传	22	24	28	34	263	105	25	30	90	16	1	3
儒林外史	5	2	13	24	98	13	4	4	18	2		3
红楼梦	5	26	55	32	194	27	20	15	57	119		6
岐路灯	23	18	21	15	115	62	7	2	5	91		
Sum	207	18	146	298	1590	91	133	78	340	21	13	23

"according to" have decreased, and the functions of "locative end", "things direction" and "along" have disappeared. The specific literature survey is shown in Table 4:

The following objects of the "locative source" function are mostly location nouns, and V2 is a directional verb with the sememes of [+direction] [+displacement]. The following objects of the "locative" function are location information nouns, but the V2 is mostly verbs without the displacement, such as:

(19)　且说张横将引三二百人，从芦苇中间……直到寨边。(《水浒传》第六十四回) (locative).

The following objects of the "state source" are mostly state nouns such as "dream" and "drunk", and V2 is mostly a verb that means state changes, such as:

(20)　王陵台刀南伴　斫，将士初从梦里惊。(《敦煌变文集·汉将王陵变文》)　(state source).

It is worth noting that, from the appearance of "according to" function to the Qing Dynasty, the "according to" function did not become its core semantic function. Yet, in early modern Chinese period the "according to" function cases of "Cong(从)" have greatly increased, "Cong(从)" can not only indicate the based-on standard of the action, but also constitute the structure of "从……(上/来)看/说/讲" indicating that it is based on a certain aspect of the situation. On the whole, the conceptual space of "Cong(从)" in this period is the same as that in the Middle Chinese.

4 Synchronic Semantic Mapping of "Cong(从)"

Based on the diachronic conceptual space, the synchronic semantic mapping of Chinese dialect "Cong(从)" is drawn according to the statistics in Table 1 as follows (Figs. 3–5).

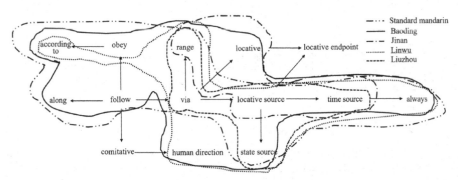

Fig. 3 The semantic mapping of "Cong(从)" (1)

From Figs. 4 and 5, the functional nodes of "Cong(从)" in Jinhua, Pingxiang, Fuzhou, and Nanning dialects are not continuous. Although "Cong(从)" in Modern Chinese has lost its meaning as a content word, it is very strange that the functional nodes of "Cong(从)" in multiple dialects violate the semantic map continuity criterion. This phenomenon cannot be explained from the dialect data in synchronic level, however, it can be well

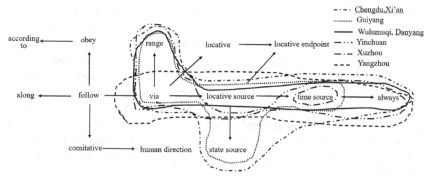

Fig. 4 The semantic mapping of "Cong(从)" (2)

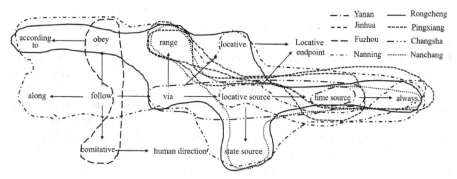

Fig. 5 The semantic mapping of "Cong(从)" (3)

explained from the diachronic semantic evolution of "Cong(从)". It can be said that, the semantic functions of the different Chinese dialect "Cong(从)" are inherited from the Chinese in different historical periods and different regions. Different regions have different choices of the multiple semantic functions, so the semantic chains in some dialects are not continuous. However, from a diachronic perspective, these semantic functions are all related. It can be said that, the Chinese dialect vocabulary has both commonality and its own uniqueness.

5 Conclusions

Haspelmath[8] pointed out that in the diachronic process, a vocabulary cannot arbitrarily generate new functions that are not directly related to its existing functions, the new functions should be gradually expanded step by step. However, in Chinese dialects, there is a phenomenon that the different functions of the same vocabulary such as "Cong(从)" appear to be far apart in conceptual space. From a synchronic perspective, the multifunctional morphemes of Chinese vocabulary do not seem to have continuity in semantic functions, but from a diachronic perspective, there must be cognitive connections between different functional nodes. This kind of semantic evolution in diachronic level causes the diversity of semantic functions in the synchronic level.

This anti-continuity characteristic of "Cong(从)" is worthy of our attention. The semantic functions in synchronic level are the product of diachronic evolution. The functions in synchronic level can be the product of different stage in diachronic evolution, and they can also be some semantic functions of other words in the dialect system, of course they can also be an arbitrary choice of dialect vocabulary for diachronic semantic function. Therefore, when the multifunctional morphemes of Chinese dialects are investigated from a synchronic perspective, it is very necessary to combine the diachronic semantic evolution research, otherwise it may not be possible to clarify the true relationship between the various semantic functions of the multifunctional word.

From the diachronic and synchronic comparison of the semantic function of "Cong(从)", it can be seen that:

(1) The semantic functions of some words can be decreased in the diachronic semantic evolution, and the disappearance of certain functions may cause semantic discontinuity, which is the cross-chain phenomenon in the synchronic level. During the diachronic semantic evolution, the connection between some functional nodes is broken. This phenomenon does not mean that there is no connection between these nodes, and it could be caused by the semantic choice of some specific symbolic form, which are one of the reasons for the lateral relationship. The semantic map method is a powerful tool to explain the lateral relationship. The diachronic evolution research based on the semantic field can provide a new perspective for the phenomenon that violates semantic map continuity criterion, and most of the discontinuity in semantic map can be verified by the implicit or disappeared connection of one semantic function node in the history of languages. Therefore, if the functional nodes are not connected in the dialect semantic map, diachronic research should be considered. In theory, the evolution of the semantic function is the one from the existing functional nodes to the adjacent functional nodes in the conceptual space, and it is almost impossible to jump directly from a functional node to a distant functional node without direct connection. The broken chain phenomenon of "Cong(从)" indicates that there may be a discontinuity in the semantic map of Chinese dialects, and this discontinuity may be cut off by other words.

(2) The diachronic evolution of a word can be first analyzed by the semantic map method, then synchronic semantic connection of polysemy can be well explained, and the diachronic semantic connection can help to explain the reasons for the semantic transfer in the past synchronic semantic map.

(3) The functional nodes of "Cong(从)" in semantic map can help lexicographers to determine the lexical meaning of "Cong(从)" more reasonably, and also provide reference for lexical interpretation for ancient Chinese translation and Chinese and foreign language translation.

In this paper, the research on "Cong(从)" combines the diachronic semantic evolution and synchronic dialect distribution, and makes up for the deficiency of the simple synchronic dialect distribution through diachronic materials research. This kind of research is a supplement to the theory of the semantic map model and has methodological significance. The existing research on semantic map method is often based on synchronic different dialects or different languages, however, the synchronic language patterns are the result of diachronic evolution that may lead to the disappearance of intermediate connections. If the construction of semantic maps does not take diachronic evolution into account, it is possible that the two semantic associations without direct connection are incorrectly linked in order to avoid discontinuity in semantic maps.

References

1. Li, R.: Dictionary of Modern Chinese Dialects. Jiangsu Education Press, Nangjing (2002)
2. Ma, B.: Modern Chinese Prepositions. Zhonghua Publishing House, Beijing (2002). (in Chinese)
3. Wu, F.: A typological study of grammaticalization of the comitative preposition in Chinese language. Stud. Chinese Lang. **01**, 43–58+96 (2003). (in Chinese)
4. Jiang, L.: Sources, paths, and types of the grammaticalization of Chinese conjunction prepositions. Stud. Chinese Lang. **04**, 291–308+383 (2012). (in Chinese)
5. Zhuang, H.: Research on the Diachronic Semantic Map of Chinese Verbs Lian(连) and Jie(接). Int. J. Knowl. Lang. Process. **2**(11), 35–47 (2020)
6. He, H.: On the semantic category of relying-on-meaning preposition in Chinese. Yangtze River Acad. **01**, 112–120 (2015). (in Chinese)
7. Liang, Y.: The study of the prepositions in Zutangji. Bull. Linguist. Stud. 196–216+346 (2009). (in Chinese)
8. Martin, H.: The geometry of grammatical meaning: semantic maps and cross-linguistic comparison. In: Tomasello, M. (ed.) The new psychology of language, vol. 2, pp. 211–243. Erlbaum, New York (2003)

Aspectuality and Subjectivity of *Le* in Chinese Conditionals

Vincent Jixin Wang[(⊠)] and Huahung Yuan

Zhejiang International Studies University, Hangzhou, China
loewenzahn@126.com

Abstract. In this paper, we explore the sematic-pragmatic function of *le* in con-ditionals. Based on relevant diagnostics, we argue that *le* in the antecedent (le_{ant}) merely has the scope over VPs in the antecedent with the semantics of perfectivity, whereas *le* in the consequent (le_{con}) serves as a hybrid marker which relates the aspectual meaning "change of state" to the subjectivity reflected in the speaker's epistemic expectation. This accounts for whether a conditional is interpreted as counterfactual or hypothetical, as well as for specific moods triggered by le_{con}.

Keywords: *Le* · Aspectuality · Subjectivity · Chinese conditionals · Epistemic expectation

1 Introduction

Most Chinese linguists distinguish two kinds of particle *le*: Le_1 is attached to verbs and gives rise to terminative or completive meaning, while le_2 appears sentence-finally and scopes over the proposition (see [1–5] etc.). Especially, le_2 is considered as multi-functional: It relates a current result-state to the speech time, and hence possesses the function of the perfect aspect in English, on the other hand it can also trigger special modal readings such as "contrary to expectation" (see [6, 7]). In [8] and [9], le_2 is regarded as a kind of grammatical ingredients for counterfactuality in Chinese, because the appearance of le_2 in Chinese conditionals is often associated with the counterfactual reading, as discussed in [10, 11] among others:

(1)   要有电，灯就会亮了。
       yào yǒu diàn,   dēng jiù huì liàng le
       if   have electricity light then will light up LE
       'If there were electricity, the light would light up.'

However, le_2 is neither a sufficient nor a necessary condition for interpreting a Chinese conditional as counterfactual: (1) can obtain a hypothetical meaning in the context, where the addressee is lack of such a knowledge and the speaker is trying to make him convinced of it. The previous studies do not elaborate on the proper semantic-pragmatic contributions *le* makes to conditionals. For example, (2a) without sentence-final *le* can

© The Author(s), under exclusive license to Springer Nature Switzerland AG 2023
Q. Su et al. (Eds.): CLSW 2022, LNAI 13495, pp. 208–220, 2023.
https://doi.org/10.1007/978-3-031-28953-8_16

be embedded under *wo bu renwei* ('I do not think') which conveys the inconsistency with the expectation of the speaker, while (1) not:

(2)   a. 要有电，灯就会亮
         yào yǒu diàn, dēng jiù huì liàng
         if   have   electricity   light then will   light up
         'If there were electricity, the light would light up.'
      b. 我不认为，要是有电，灯就会亮。
         wǒ bù rènwéi, yàoshì yǒu diàn, dēng jiù huì liàng
         I neg think   if   have electricity light then will light up
         'I don't think if there is electricity, the light will light up.'
      c. #我不认为，要是有电，灯就会亮了。
         #wǒ bù rènwéi, yàoshì yǒu diàn, dēng jiù huì liàng le

This reflects the fact that *le* expresses a positive expectation of the speaker, conflicting with the semantics of the embedding phrase.

In this paper, we label two syntactically distinct *le*s as le_{ant} (*le* in the antecedent) and le_{con} (*le* in the consequent), respectively, and focus on le_{con}. We argue that le_{ant} shows the function as a pure aspectual marker, while le_{con} takes the whole conditional as its argument and serves as a hybrid aspectual-modal marker.[1] In a nutshell, le_{con} relates what [2] called "currently relevant state" to the subjectivity established by it (e.g., expectation of the speaker): The change of state referring to the past is regularly opposed to speaker's expectation to the currently relevant state, which regularly establishes a negative (e.g., regrettable, reproachful) mood. However, the non-past one frequently accords with the epistemic expectation of the speaker, hence the triggered mood may signal the emphasis of speaker's positive stance which causes further speech acts (e.g., suggestions, agreements etc.). This captures the function of le_{con} in both of counterfactual and hypothetical conditionals properly.

The paper is structured as follows: The second part provides evidence for distinct functions of le_{ant} and le_{con}. In Sect. 3, we deal with the twofold function of le_{con} and the corresponding relation between aspectuality and subjectivity imposed on *le*-conditionals. The conclusion is obtained in Sect. 4.

2   Two *les* in Conditionals

The particle *le* can appear either in the antecedent or in the consequent of a conditional, or even in both:

---

[1] We do not discuss whether the sentence-final *le* is indeed a merge of le_1 and le_2, as proposed in [1] and [3].

(3)   a. 如果下雨了，地上就会变湿。
        rúguǒxià-yǔ-le,   dì-shàng jiù huì biàn shī
        if   fall-rain-Acc ground-on then will become wet
        'If it rains, the ground will get wet.'
     b. 如果下雨了，地上就会变湿了。
        rúguǒxià-yǔ-le, dì-shàng jiù huì biàn shī le
        if   fall-rain-Acc ground-on then will become wet le
     c. 如果下雨，地上就会变湿。
        rúguǒxià-yǔ   dì-shàng   jiù   huì   biàn   shī
        if   fall-rain ground-on   then will become wet
     d. 如果下雨，地上就会变湿了。
        rúguǒxià-yǔ   dì-shàng   jiù   huì   biàn   shī le
        if   fall-rain-Acc ground-on then will become wet le

The interpretations seem to vary with whether le_{con} (co-)occurs, but not le_{ant}: le_{ant} merely indicates the happening of the raining event relative to a specific time (e.g., a time point in the future), which must temporally proceed the realization of the event encoded by the consequent. The semantics of conditional per se requires such a temporal ordering, thus the (non-)appearance of le_{ant} normally do not change the aspectual meaning of relative anteriority in the antecedent.

In case of the occurrence of le_{con}, however, le_{con} highlights that the speaker assigns an assessment with subjectively high probability to the conditional proposition, if comparing (3b, d) with (3a, c).[2] Hence, (3b, d) can be embedded under expressions indicating high probability or the positive expectation of the speaker, but are incompatible with those claiming low probability or inconsistency with expectations:

(4)   a. 很可能/我认为，如果下雨 (了)，地上就会变湿了。
        hěn kěnéng /wǒ rènwéi, rúguǒxià-yǔ (le), dì-shàng jiù huì biàn shī le
        very possible I think if fall-rain-Acc ground-on then will become wet LE
        'It is possible/I think that if it rains, the ground will get wet.'
     b. #不太可能/我不认为，如果下雨 (了)，地上就会变湿了。
        bù tài kěnéng /wǒ bù rènwéi, rúguǒxià-yǔ (le), dì-shàng jiù huì biàn shī le
        neg too possible I neg think if fall-rain-Acc ground-on then will become
        wet LE
        Intended: 'It is less possible/ I don't think if it rains, the ground will get
        wet.'
     c. 很可能/我认为/不太可能/我不认为如果下雨 (了)，地上就会变湿。
        hěn kě néng /wǒ rèn wéi/ bù tài kě néng /wǒ bù rènwéi rúguǒxià-yǔ (le),
        very possible I   think neg too possible I neg think if   fall-rain-Acc
        dì-shàng jiù huì biàn shī
        ground-on then will become wet LE
        'It is possible/I think/ It is less possible/ I don't think that if it rains, the
        ground will get wet.'

___
[2] Clearly, (3b) and (3d) can be interpreted counterfactually. We leave this issue in Sect. 3.

Note that the subjectivity mentioned above is not manifested in le_{ant}. (5) demonstrates the invalid implication, due to le_{ant}'s lack of subjective function:

(5)　　如果下雨了，地上就会变湿了。↛ 很可能/我认为会下雨。

　　　rúguǒ xià-yǔ (le), dì-shàng jiù huì biàn shī le ↛ *hěn kě néng /wǒ rèn wéi huì xià-yǔ*
　　　if -rain-Acc ground-on then will become wet LE very possible I　think *huì xià-yǔ*

On the other hand, the scope of le_{con} should include the whole conditional rather than prima facie the consequent:

(6)　　a. 如果下雨 (了)，地上就会变湿了。↛ 很可能/我认为地上会变湿。

　　　rúguǒ xià-yǔ (le), dì-shàng jiù huì biàn shī le
　　　if　-rain-Acc ground-on then will become wet LE
　　　↛ *hěn kě néng /wǒ rèn wéi dì-shàng jiù huì biàn shī*
　　　very possible I　think ground-on then will become wet LE

　　　b. 如果下雨 (了)，地上就会变湿了。

　　　rúguǒ xià-yǔ (le), dì-shàng jiù huì biàn shī le
　　　dì-shàng jiù huì biàn shī Acc ground-on then will become wet LE
　　　→ 很可能/我认为，如果下雨 (了)，地上就会变湿。

　　　↛ *hěn kě néng /wǒ rèn wéi, rúguǒ xià-yǔ (le), dì-shàng jiù huì biàn shī*
　　　very possible I　think　if　fall-rain-Acc ground-on then will become wet
　　　'It is possible/I think that if it rains, the ground will get wet.'

Since we treat le_{ant} as an aspectual marker, it is syntactically located at the head of the AspP. However, le_{con} encodes the meaning of subjectivity with respect to the assessment of the speaker to a proposition. This leads to the assumption that le_{con} patterns with sentence-final particles such as *ne, ya* etc., which represent a specific attitude of the speaker, and is hence base-generated at the head of CP. Following the "split CP" analysis in [12], we propose le_{con} occupies the head of Attitude CP ($CP_{attitude}$). Accordingly, the syntactic structure for (5) can be reflected in (7):

(7)　　$[_{CPattitude}[_{TopP}$ [如果 $[_{AspP}[_{vP}$ 下雨] $le_{ant}]$] $[_{Top'}$ $[_{TP}$ 地上就会变湿]]] $le_{con}]$
　　　$[_{CPattitude}[_{TopP}$ [*rúguǒ* $[_{AspP}[_{vP}$ *xià-yǔ*] $le_{ant}]$] $[_{Top'}$ $[_{TP}$ *dì-shàng jiù huì biàn*]]] $le_{con}]$

Summing up: le_{ant} scopes over VPs in the antecedent and patterns with le_1 indicating the perfectivity, whereas le_{con} has its scope over the conditional and reveals a specific subjectivity connected with the expectation of the speaker, as elaborated in Sect. 3.

3　le_{con} as Hybrid Marker

In this section, we focus on the semantic-pragmatic meaning caused by le_{con}, given that le_{con} scopes over the whole conditional and exhibits the syntactic property of completing a sentence as sentence-final particle ([13]). We provide further linguistic evidences which illustrate that le_{con} fulfills indeed the twofold function of aspectuality and subjectivity.

Moreover, the two functions relate each other in a systematic way. Hence, we treat le_{con} as a hybrid marker.

3.1 Aspectuality: Change of State

As pointed out in [2, 7, 14] etc., sentence-final *le* (*le₂*) semantically refers to "change of state", logically from $\neg p$ to p, which typically results from the realization of an involved event.[3] Note that le_{con} in conditionals also share this aspectual property:

(5)　　a. 我若继续上课，明年可以毕业了。(胡适：四十自述。)
　　　　　wǒ ruò jìxù shàng kè, míngnián kěyǐ bìyè le
　　　　　I　if continue take course next-year can graduate LE
　　　　　'If I continue to take courses, I can graduate next year. '
　　　　b. 重复的机会如果出现了，那么他就是一个巨大的幸运者了。
　　　　　zhòngfù-de jīhuì rúguǒ chūxiàn le, nàme tā jiù shì (张炜：你在高原)
　　　　　repeat-de chance if appear Acc　then he then be
　　　　　yī-gè jùdà-de xìngyùn-zhě le
　　　　　one-Cl giant luck-person LE
　　　　　'If the opportunity of repetition appears, he will be a giant lucky person.'
　　　　c. 要是你早这么做了，就不会像现在这样不知该怎样回答本杰的问题
　　　　　了。(阿瑟·黑利：超载)
　　　　　yàoshì nǐ zǎo zhème zuò-le, jiù bù huì xiàng xiànzài zhèyàng
　　　　　if you early this do-Acc then neg will alike now this
　　　　　bù zhī gāi zěnyàng huídá běnjié de wèntí le
　　　　　neg know should how answer Benjie of question LE
　　　　　'If you had done so, it wouldn't have happened to you that you don't know how to respond to Benjie's question.'

In (8b), for example, the state that at this moment he is not yet a lucky guy will be transferred into the opposite one, provided that the repeated chance has taken place. Basically, the occurrence of the currently relevant state causally depends on the realization of the event expressed by the antecedent. As a result, the reference time (e.g., the time in which the event in the antecedent has been realized) anchored by le_{con} can refer to either a future time point (as in (8a, b)) or a past time point (as in (8c)). We briefly conclude that the aspectual meaning manifested in "change of state" is an inherent semantic property of le_{con} in conditionals.

3.2 Subjectivity: Expectation of the Speaker

The other prominent function of le_{con} concerns subjectivity, which mainly relates to the expectation of the speaker, or more precisely *the epistemic expectation with subjectively high probability* in terminology of [15]. In other words, when le_{con} appears at the end of the conditional, it conveys that the conditional proposition is anchored in the epistemic

---

[3] [14] defines this aspectual function as "relative past/perfectivity" and further distinguishes two kinds of *le₂*, which is less relevant here.

state of the speaker and corresponds with what he normally expects. Consequently, le_{con} shows the following properties of subjectivity:

First, le_{con} can never be attached sentence-finally, when the involved conditional is incompatible with the subjective evaluation or expectation. Relevance conditionals such as (9a, b) and Chinese bare conditionals like (9c, d) reject the attachment of le_{con}, since in the former case, the antecedent specifies the circumstances in which the consequent is relevant, whereas the latter explored in [16] is formalized in term of universal quantifiers and semantically has the flavor of necessity.

(9)　　a. 如果你饿了，冰箱里有三明治（＊了）。
　　　　　*rúguǒ nǐ è-le, bīngxiāng-lǐ yǒu sānmíngzhì (*le)*
　　　　　if　　you hungry-Acc refrigerator in have sandwich LE
　　　　　'If you are hungry, there is sandwich in the refrigerator.'
　　　　b. 如果你想知道，其实张三才是凶手（＊了）。
　　　　　*rúguǒ nǐ xiǎng zhīdào ， qíshí Zhāngsān cái shì xiōngshǒu (*le)*
　　　　　if you want know in fact Z.S then be murderer
　　　　　'I you want to know, in fact, Zhangsan is the murder.'
　　　　c. 谁说不，谁就会被批评（＊了）。
　　　　　*shuí shuō bù, shuí jiù huì bèi pīpíng(*le)*
　　　　　who say neg who then will PS criticize LE
　　　　　'Anyone who says no will be criticized.'
　　　　d. 谁演谁，谁就像谁（＊了）。
　　　　　*shuí yǎn shuí, shuí jiù xiàng shuí (*le)*
　　　　　who play who who then resemble wo LE
　　　　　'Anyone who plays the role of a certain figure will resemble to that one.'

However, when an evaluative expression appears in the consequent of a bare conditional, the whole sentence seems to be compatible with le_{con}, as shown in (10).[4] In such a situation, the flavor of necessity is lexically cancelled, due to the subjective assessment associated with the semantics of evaluative expressions per se.

(10)　　谁买中概股了，谁就倒霉了。
　　　　shuí mǎ zhōnggài-gǔ le, shuí jiù dǎoméi le
　　　　who buy China Concepts Stocks Acc who then misfortune LE
　　　　'Anyone who bought China Concepts Stocks will be misfortune.'

In contrast to (9), in factual conditionals such as (11), where someone other than the speaker believes the proposition expressed by the antecedent to be true, le_{con} seems to be indispensable. In this case, the speaker utters his expectation from the perspective of the addressee, which generally leads to the performance of a specific speech act such as suggestion for the addressee or agreement with his evaluation:

---

[4] We are very thankful to an anonymous reviewer for this example.

(6)   A: 这本书太无聊了！
       Zhè-běn shū tài wúliáo le!
       This-Cl book too boring LE
       'This book is too boring (to read)'
       B: 我没看过，但是，如果这本书真这么无聊，
       wǒ méi kàn-guò, dànshì, rúguǒ zhè-běn shū zhēn zhème wúliáo
       I neg read-EXP but   if   this-Cl book truly such boring
       #那你不必再继续阅读/那你不必再继续阅读了。
       #nà nǐ bù bì zài jìxù yuèdú /nà nǐ bù bì zài jìxù yuèdú le
       then you neg must again continue read then neg must continue read LE
       'I didn't read it. But, if it is so boring, you don't need to keep reading it.'

Second, as shown in (2) and (4), as well as in (12), *le*-conditionals cannot be embedded under phrases such as *wo bu renwei/juede/xiangxin, juebu/butai keneng* etc., since *le*$_{con}$ marks the epistemic expectation of the speaker with relatively high probability:

(12)   a. #我不信/不认为/不确定/怀疑，如果营养太多，肠胃就吸收不好了。
        #wǒ bù xìn /wǒ bù rènwéi/ bù quèdìng /huáiyí, rúguǒ yíngyǎng tài duō,
        I neg believe I neg think   Neg sure   doubt if nutrition too much
        cháng wèi jiù xīshōu bù-hǎo le
        intestine stomach then absorb neg good LE
        Intended: 'I don't believe/I don't think/I am incertain/I doubt that if one
        takes in too much nutrition, his intestine and stomach will not absorb well.'
        b. #不太可能/绝不可能，如果明天放晴，他就会去打球了。
        #bù tài kěnéng /jué bù kěnéng, rúguǒ míngtiān fàng qíng, tā jiù huì qù dǎqiú le
        Neg too possible /absolutely neg possible if tomorrow put sunny he then will go play ball LE
        Intended: 'It is less possible/ it is not absolutely possible that if it is sunny
        tomorrow, he will go to play balls.'

Third, the subjectivity imposed on *le*$_{con}$ consistently signifies special kinds of mood with respect to the speaker. We argue that the meaning of a positive expectation is fundamentally related to subjectivity in case of *le*$_{con}$, hence speaker-oriented adverbials such as *dique ruci, tanbai shuo, laoshi shuo* etc. are compatible with both of counterfactual and hypothetical *le*-conditionals as shown in (13). On the other hand, some adverbials with a negative emotional meaning (regrettable, reproachful etc.) are mainly combined with counterfactual *le*-conditionals, but not with hypothetical *le*-conditionals, while adverbials specifying positive emotions generally only match hypothetical *le*-conditionals, as demonstrated in (14) and (15), respectively:

(13)   a. 的确如此/坦白说/老实说，如果刚才 11 号上场，比赛就赢了。
         dequè rúcǐ /tǎnbái shuō /lǎoshí shuō,
         Indeed   frankly speaking
         rúguǒ gāngcái 11 hào shàngchǎng, bǐsài jiù yíng le
         if just eleven number take-the-field game then win LE
         'Indeed/Frankly speaking, if No.11 had taken the field, they would have
         won the game.'
         b. 的确如此/坦白说/老实说，如果待会儿 11 号上场，比赛就会赢了。
         dequè rúcǐ /tǎnbái shuō /lǎoshí shuō,
         Indeed   frankly speaking
         rúguǒ dàihuì 11 hào shàngchǎng, bǐsài jiù yíng le
         if later eleven number take-the-field game then win LE
         'Indeed/frankly speaking, if No. 11 take the field, they will win the game.'

(14)   a. 很遗憾/太可惜了，如果刚才 11 号上场，比赛就赢了。
         hěn yíhàn de shì /tài kěxī le,
         regretfully too pity Acc
         yàoshì gāngcái 11 hào shàngchǎng, bǐsài jiù yíng le
         if just eleven number take-the-field game then win LE
         'Regretfully, /It's a pity that if No.11 had taken the field, they would have
         won the game.'
         b. #很遗憾/太可惜了，如果待会儿 11 号上场，比赛就会赢了。
         # hěn yíhàn de shì /tài kěxī le, yàoshì dàihuì 11 hào shàngchǎng, bǐsài jiù yíng le
         regretfully too pity Acc if later eleven number take-the-field game then win LE

(15)   a. 幸运的是/令人期待的是，如果他这次考试通过，就可以晋升了。
         xìngyùn de shì /lìng rén qīdài de shì,
         Fortunately   let person expect of be
         rúguǒ tā zhè-cì   kǎoshì tōngguò, jiù   kěyǐ   jìnshēng   le
         if   he this-time   exam pass-Exp then can   promote LE
         'Fortunately,/ It is expected that if he pass this exam, he can promote. '
         b. #幸运的是/令人期待的是，如果他那次考试通过了，就可以晋升了。
         #xìngyùn de shì /lìng rén qīdài de shì,
         Fortunately   let person expect of be
         rúguǒ tā zhè-cì   kǎoshì tōngguò   le, jiù   kěyǐ jìnshēng le
         if   he that-time exam   pass-Exp Acc then can   promote LE'
         Intended: 'Fortunately, / It is expected that if he had passed that exam, he
         could have promoted.'

Note that it is not *le*$_{con}$ alone that determines whether the involved *le*-conditional generates a positive or negative mood. In case that the content of the conditional conveys a negative issue according to the public common sense as in (16), a negative adverbial turned out to be available for hypothetical *le*-conditionals, while a positive one can modify counterfactual *le*-conditionals:

(16)   a. 幸运的是/很庆幸，如果我那时再晚一点出发，就赶不上火车了。
          xìngyùn de shì/ hěn qìngxìng,
          Fortunately   very fortunately,
          rúguǒ wǒ nà-shí zài wǎn-yīdiǎn chfā, jiù gǎn-bù-shàng huǒchē le
          if   I   that-while again later-a bit depart then catch-neg-up train LE
          'Fortunately, if I had departed a little later at that time, I would have
          missed the train.'
          (Counterfactual reading, but a positive mood)
        b. 很遗憾/可惜，如果这种情况持续下去，他估计活不过今年了。
          hěn yíhàn de shì/ kěxī,
          regretfully   pity
          rúguǒ zhè-zhǒng qíngkuàng chíxù xià-qù, tā gūjì huó bù guò jīnnián le
          if   this sort condition continue down   he possible live neg pass this-year LE
          'Regretfully, / It is a pity that if this condition continues, it is possible
          that he cannot survive over the end of this year.'
          (hypothetical reading, but a negative mood)

Therefore, contextual factors or world knowledge also play a significant role in producing a specific mood. Nevertheless, the subjective meaning of le_{con} is inherently fixed:
In either case, the ultimate reading results from the epistemic expectation of the speaker
to the conditional proposition, depending on whether le_{con} relates the consistency of
expectation (hypothetical reading) or counter-expectation (counterfactual reading) to
the whole conditional (s. 3.3). Moreover, by means of a corpus-based analysis, [17]
point out that there exists a strong tendence that especially the counterfactuality is generally associated with uttering exclamations. With respect to the counter-expectation,
the uttered exclamation normally reflects a negative mood.

In summary, we conclude that le_{con} ascribes subjectivity to the involved conditional,
which leads back to the speaker's epistemic expectation to the proposition encoded by
the conditional. Furthermore, this expectation is basically assigned with relative high
probability. Next, we investigate how the aspectual meaning of le_{con} is related to the
subjectivity generating a plausible interpretation of *le*-conditionals.

3.3   Combining Aspectuality with Subjectivity

Based on the treatment of le_{con} as a hybrid marker, we propose that the currently relevant state encoded in *le*-conditionals is situated in the epistemic expectation of the
speaker. This explains how the counterfactual or hypothetical reading of *le*-conditionals
is generated. Consider the following examples:

(17)　a. 如果你认真学习，那时早就考上大学了。

rúguǒ nǐ rènzhēn xuéxí, nà-shí   zǎo   jiù   kǎo-shàng   dàxué   le

if   you serious learn   that-while early then examine up university LE

'If you had studied seriously, you would have passed the entrance exam to universities at that time.'

　　b. 如果你认真学习，明年就可以上大学了。

rúguǒ nǐ rènzhēn xuéxí, míngnián   jiù kǎo-shàng dàxué   le

if   you serious learn   next year then exam up   university LE

'If you study seriously, you will go to university next year.'

Basically, the aspectuality of le_{con} refers either to a change of state in the past where the currently relevant state maintains from a past time point as in (17a), or to one in the non-past where the state will genuinely come about relative to a future time as in (17b). In the former case, the realized state in the actual world is contrary to the speaker's expectation. By means of le_{con}-attachment, the speaker emphasizes the incompatibility of his epistemic expectation with the contrasting actual state available to him, which leads to the counterfactual reading. In the latter case, however, the speaker solely predicts that normally the result state would turn out to be true, since the causal dependence of the consequent on the antecedent, together with the change of state, is consistent with the speaker's epistemic expectation.

Note that the derivation of the counterfactual or hypothetical interpretation of a *le*-conditional is based on the pragmatic process, since it is evaluated relative to the speaker's epistemic expectation, not to the actual world. Therefore, (17) can be corrected by the response of the addressee:[5]

(18)　　a. A: 如果你认真学习，那时早就考上大学了。

rúguǒ nǐ rènzhēn xuéxí, nàshí zǎo jiù kǎo-shàng dàxué le

if you serious learn that-while early then examine up university LE

'If you had studied seriously, you would have passed the entrance exam to universities at that time.'

　　　B: 你忘了？我早就大学毕业了。

nǐ wàng le? wǒ zǎo jiù dàxué bìyè le

you forget Acc I early then university graduate LE

'Did you forget? I have graduated from the university. '

　　　b. A: 如果你认真学习，明年就可以上大学了。

rúguǒ nǐ rènzhēn xuéxí, míngnián zǎo jiù kǎo-shàng dàxué le

if you serious learn next year then exam up university LE

'If you study seriously, you will go to university next year.'

　　　B: 实际上，我没有考大学的资格。

shíjìshàng, wǒ méi-yǒu kǎo dàxué de zīgé

in fact   I neg have exam university of qualification

'In fact, I don't have the qualification for the entrance exam to universities.'

---

[5] Examples in (18) indeed reflect the communicative function of le_2 "correction of the wrong assumption" proposed in [2].

Finally, according to [17], it is frequently observed that a specific mood is licensed by the subjectivity encoded by le_{con}. The counterfactual reading results from the counter-expectation, thus is often associated with a negative mood of the speaker, whereas the hypothetical reading usually explicates the speaker's positive stance (e.g., assessment) to the conditional proposition, which can be exemplified as agreement with the addressee's opinion or further suggestions for the addressee.

The aspectual-subjective correlation of le_{con} is summarized in the following table (Table 1):

Table 1 .

	Dimension I:	Aspectuality
le_{con}	Reference to past	Reference to non-past
Dimension II:	Counterfactual	Hypothetical
Subjectivity (the speaker's epistemic expectation with relative high probability)	Negative mood (e.g., regrettable, reproachful etc.)	The speaker's positive stance to the conditional proposition (e.g., agreement, suggestion ect.)

Accordingly, we formalize the following truth condition for le-conditionals:

(19) $[\![le_{con}([\![\varphi \to \phi]\!])]\!]^{\alpha, w_@, t^*} = 1 iff.$:

(i) $\forall w', t \left[\begin{array}{c} (w'Rw_@ \wedge w', t \in \mathcal{E}_{\alpha,t^*}) \to \\ (\varphi(w', t) \subseteq \phi(w', t)) \end{array} \right], if \neg(t < t^*),$ or

(ii) $\forall w', t \left[\begin{array}{c} (w'Rw_@ \wedge w', t \notin \mathcal{E}_{\alpha,t^*}) \to \\ (\neg\varphi(w', t) \wedge \neg\phi(w', t)) \end{array} \right], if (t < t^*)$

Our proposal is that the meaning of le-conditionals must be evaluated relative to three essential parameters: the speaker itself (α), the world of assessment ($w_@$) and the speech time (t^*).[6] The truth condition is then divided into two parts: If under the condition for all tuples w', t satisfying that t does not temporally proceeds the speech time and the accessibility relation $w'Rw_@$ holds, $\varphi(w', t)$ implies $\phi(w', t)$, then the relevant world-time-pair is located in the epistemic expectation of the speaker α at t^* ($\mathcal{E}_{\alpha,t^*}$). If $\neg\varphi \wedge \neg\phi$ holds under the condition for all tuples w', t with $w'Rw_@$, but $t < t^*$, then the involved world-time-pair is not included in $\mathcal{E}_{\alpha,t^*}$. . Obviously, (i) captures the hypothetical reading of le-conditionals and (ii) the counterfactual reading.

4   Conclusion

In this paper, we examine the semantic-pragmatic function of le in conditionals. We distinguish between le_{ant} and le_{con} by arguing that the former patterns with le_1 which can

---

[6] WE adopt partially the relativist semantics proposed in [18]. Note that the world of assessment is defined as the world where the speaker makes his assessment or evaluation to state of affairs, based on his epistemic state. It should not be identified with the actual world.

only scopes over VPs in the antecedent and delivers the semantics of perfectivity, whereas the latter should be treated as a hybrid marker assigning the meaning "change of state" and subjectivity to the whole conditional. Essentially, the epistemic expectation of the speaker with relative high probability underlies the subjectivity encoded by le_{con}. As a result, the aspectuality-subjectivity-correlation captures whether a conditional is interpreted as counterfactual of hypothetical, depending on whether the time point where the change of state occurs temporally proceeds the speech time. Basically, the hypothetical reading indicates the consistency of the conditional proposition with the epistemic expectation of the speaker, whereas the counterfactual reading is caused by the counter-expectation. The proposed treatment also accounts for the fact that the counterfactual reading is regularly associated with negative moods and the hypothetical reading can emphasize the speaker's positive stance companied with further performance of speech acts.

References

1. Chao, Y.-R.: A Grammar of Spoken Chinese. University of California Press, Berkeley (1968)
2. Li, C., Thompson, S.: Mandarin Chinese: A Functional Reference Grammar. University of California, Berkeley (1981)
3. Zhu, D.-X.: Lectures on Grammar. The Commercial Press, Beijing (1982). (in Chinese)
4. Smith, C.S.: The Parameter of Aspect, 2nd edn. Kluwer Academic Publishers, Dordrecht (1997)
5. Soh, H.-L.: Aspect. In: Huang, C.-T., Li, Y.-H., Simpson A. (eds.): The Handbook of Chinese Linguistics, pp. 126–155. Wiley, Blackwell (2014)
6. Ljungqvist, M.: Le, guo and zhe in Mandarin Chinese: a relevance-theoretic account. J. East Asian Linguis. **16**, 193–235 (2007)
7. Soh, H.-L.: Speaker presupposition and Mandarin Chinese sentence-final -le: a unified analysis of the "change of state" and the "contrary to expectation" reading. Nat. Lang. Linguist. Theory **27**, 623–657 (2009)
8. Wang, Y.-Y., Jiang, Y.: The ingredients of counterfactuality in Chinese. In: Yan, J. (ed.) Approaching Formal Pragmatics, Chapter 9. Shanghai Educational Publishing House (2011). (in Chinese)
9. Wang, Y.-Y.: The Ingredients of Counterfactuality in Mandarin Chinese. Dissertation at the Hong Kong Polytechnic University (2012)
10. Chen, G.-H.: A comparison between english and chinese hypothetical conditionals. Foreign Lang. Teach. Res. **73**, 10–19 (1988). (in Chinese)
11. Jiang, Y.: On the counterfactual reading of Chinese conditionals. In: Zhang, B. (ed.) Studies and Investigations on Chinese Grammar 10, pp. 257–279. The Commercial Press, Beijing (2000) (in Chinese)
12. Paul, W.: Why particles are not particular: Sentence-final particles in Chinese as heads of a split CP. Studia Linguistica **68**(1), 77–115 (2014)
13. Zhang, N.-N.: Sentence-final aspect particles as finite markers in Mandarin Chinese. Linguistics **57**, 967–1023 (2019)
14. Fan, X.-L.: On the difference of aspectuality and verbal phases in le_2. Linguistic Science **20**(01), 60–75 (2021). (in Chinese)
15. Chen, Z.-Y., Wang, M.-Y.: The cognitive modal of expectation and its type – on a series of Phenomena related to *jing(ran)/pian(pian)*. In: Language Teaching and Linguistic Studies, pp. 48–63. (in Chinese)
16. Cheng, L., Huang, C.-T.: Two types of donkey sentences. Nat. Lang. Linguist. Theory **14**, 121–163 (1996)

17. Zhang, Y., Chen, Z.-Y.: Chinese counterfactual conditional sentences and non-factual conditional sentences. Chin. Linguist. **3**, 42–59 (2020). (in Chinese)
18. Lasersohn, P.: Subjectivity and Perspective in Truth-Theoretic Semantics. Oxford University Press, New York (2017)

Research on the Phenomenon of Tone Sandhi of BB in ABB-Pattern Adjectives from the Perspective of Coercion Effects

Huilu Luo[1] and Zuoyan Song[1,2]($\boxtimes$)

[1] Department of Chinese Language and Literature, Peking University, Beijing, China
meszy@pku.edu.cn
[2] Center for Chinese Linguistics, Beijing, China

Abstract. The tone of BB is one of the concerns of phonetic studies of ABB, and previous studies have noticed that the tone of BB is mostly yinping or becomes yinping, but there is still a lack of research on the variation law and reasons of BB's tone. By comparing the tones of BB in "Modern Chinese Dictionary (1996 edition)" and "Modern Chinese Dictionary (2015 edition)", we found that the tone sandhi of BB is related to the part of speech of BB, with a high proportion of non-adjectival BB's tones changing to yinping, and adjectival BB tending to be pronounced in the original tones. The descriptive meaning also influences the tone sandhi of BB, and BBs with lower descriptivity tend to change to yinping. We suggest that coercion effects are the main reason for BB changing tones, and components whose semantics do not meet the requirements of construction are phonetically coerced.

Keywords: ABB-pattern adjectives · BB tones sandhi pattern · Yinping · Part of speech of BB · Coercion effects

1 Introduction

ABB-pattern adjectives are productive schema constructions that usually consist of a monosyllabic adjectival morpheme A and an overlapping morpheme BB (e.g., 红彤彤 hong2 "red" tong1tong1 and 甜腻腻 tian2 "sweet" ni4ni4). There are also a few noun morphemes and verb morphemes with BB forming ABB (e.g., 油汪汪 you2 "oil" wang1wang1 and 笑哈哈 xiao4 "smile" ha1ha1). Lv [1] termed this form "the vivid form of adjectives", and some linguists [2–4] pointed out that ABB-pattern adjectives have significant descriptive effects. The function of ABB is to describe the state, the semantic meaning of which is "the state related to A", and BB complements the state by describing more characteristics related to the trait of A. For example, 白 bai2 means "white", and 白茫茫 bai2mang2mang2 describes "an endless white", while 茫茫has the semantic meaning of "without borders, unable to see clearly" which is a description of the spatial distribution of the trait "white", bringing to mind an endless white color.

This project is supported by National Social Science Funds of China (Major Programe, Grant No. 21 & ZD310). We would like to extend our sincere thanks.

© The Author(s), under exclusive license to Springer Nature Switzerland AG 2023
Q. Su et al. (Eds.): CLSW 2022, LNAI 13495, pp. 221–232, 2023.
https://doi.org/10.1007/978-3-031-28953-8_17

In terms of phonetic form, scholars paid more attention to the tone of BB. Lv [1] noticed that BB in spoken Beijing dialect is commonly pronounced in yinping (e.g., 慢腾腾 *man4* "slow" *teng1teng1* and 沉甸甸 *chen2* 'heavy' *dian1dian1*). Through quantitative research, Cao [5] argued that BBs with yinping are overwhelmingly dominant, with 95 out of 160 BBs being yinping, and BBs whose tones are not yinping tend to be turned into yinping. Li [6] counted ABBs in *"Eight Hundred Words of Modern Chinese"* and *"Modern Chinese Dictionary* (1996 Edition)" and found that more than 60% of BBs are yinping. Further, Li [6] pointed out that ABB-pattern adjectives are generally words describing sound, color, and dynamics, and words with yinping can more vividly depict the rapidity of sound, the intensity of color, and the intensity of dynamics with the help of high-pitched sound.

Previous studies on the rules and reasons for tone sandhi of BB are relatively few. Li [7] argued that there is no rule for when the tones of BB are changed and when they are not. Ma [8] pointed out that to achieve the vividness of description and expression, the tone needs to be raised when vocalizing, and the pitch of yinping is the highest in Mandarin Chinese. Therefore, for the purpose of "vividness", the tone of BB tends to be yinping in spoken language. In addition, Ma [8] argued that BBs that are compound-word morphemes and whose meaning are related to A are generally pronounced in their original tones (e.g., 白晃晃 *bai2* "white" *huang3huang3*), while BBs that are non-word morphemes or are compound-word morphemes but whose meaning is not related to A must be pronounced yinping (e.g., 沉甸甸 *chen2* "heavy" *dian1dian1*).

Ma's [8] discussion of the relationship between semantics and tones in ABB provides some inspiration for this research, while there are some limitations. First, Ma [8] only examined 16 ABBs that are read their original tones (non-yinping), lacking a comprehensive grasp of ABBs whose BBs do not change their tones. Furthermore, the correlation of the semantics of A and BB cannot explain all the patterns of tone sandhi of BB. For example, in A_{color}BB, according to Ma's [8] hypothesis, in "蓝盈盈 *lan2* 'blue' *ying2ying2*, 绿莹莹 *lv4* 'green' *ying2ying2*, 绿茸茸 *lv4* 'green' *rong2rong2*" and "碧油油 *bi4* 'bluish green' *you1you1*, 黑油油 *hei1* 'black' *you1you1*, 绿油油 *lv4* 'green' *you1you1*, 乌油油 *wu1* 'black' *you1you1*", both BBs and As are semantically related and the tone of BBs should not be changed. However, in the actual spoken language, the BBs in first group do not alter their tones, but the BB in second group is often altered. In addition, there are some BBs in A_{color}BB that are not semantically related to A, such as "沉沉 *chen2chen2*, 茫茫 *mang2mang2*" in "黑沉沉 *hei1* 'black' *chen2chen2*, 黑茫茫 *hei1* 'black' *mang2mang2*", but the tones of these BBs do not change.

Fang [9] argued that ABBs with negative meanings do not undergo tone sandhi, which is due to the fact that the high-pitched tone sandhi of duplicated components is correlated with diminutive expressions, while negative words hardly have diminutive meaning and therefore the tone sandhi do not occur. In fact, the diminutive meaning is not a necessary condition for the tone sandhi of ABB (e.g., 汗淋淋 *han4* "sweat" *lin1lin1*, 黑油油 *hei1* "black" *you1you1* and 热腾腾 *re4* "hot" *teng1teng1*). Besides, not all ABBs pronounced with the original tone carry negative meanings. To sum up, the diminutive meaning does not provide a general explanation for the tonal sandhi of BB.

There are two different views on the trend of tone sandhi of BB. One view is that the BB in ABB is commonly pronounced in yinping. According to [10], "the reduplicated suffixes of monosyllabic adjectives are pronounced as 55 tones, regardless of the original tone of the words" (e.g., 软绵绵 *ruan3* "soft" *mian2mian2*, 直挺挺 *zhi2* "straight" *ting3ting3* and 沉甸甸 *chen2* "heavy" *dian1dian1*). Another view is that not all non-yinping BBs are pronounced as yinping, and that the tone sandhi trend of BB is weakening. Li [7] examined the tones of BBs in the three *Modern Chinese Dictionaries* and pointed out that BBs are generally read in their original tones, and the original tones are mostly yinping. In addition, there are fewer non-yinping BBs annotated as original tones in *Modern Chinese Dictionary* (1978 Edition), the number of such BBs increases in *Modern Chinese Dictionary* (1989 Edition), and the number of non-yinping BBs annotated as original tones in *Modern Chinese Dictionary* (1996 Edition) is a bit more. It can be seen that the tones of BBs gradually changed from being read yinping to the original tones [7]. Lin [11], Li [12] and Mou [13] also argued that there is a non-sandhi trend of BB in ABB-pattern adjectives.

Based on previous studies, this paper introduces the Construction Grammar Theory to research the phenomenon, laws and causes of BB's tone sandhi in ABB. Integrity is the core of the CG, and construction is a gestalt, a conventional form-meaning/function pair. Form includes phonetic, morphological and syntactic features, and meaning includes semantic, function, pragmatic and other information. Booij [14] proposed Construction Morphology, introducing the construction method to the analysis of lexical internal structure. For some features in words that are difficult to depict by rules, CM tends to provide reasonable explanations. Constructions as a whole affect the form and meaning of constituents, and Hilpert [15] pointed out that sometimes there are cases where words and constructions are incompatible, when coercion effects occur. Under the coercion effects, the meaning of the word changes in the constructional context. Michaelis [16] proposed the principle of coercion effects, which states that "If a lexical item is semantically incompatible with its morphological-syntactic environment, the meaning of the item is consistent with the meaning of the embedded structure." Song [17] pointed out that CG emphasizes the top-down, whole-to-part research of constructions, and that the meaning and function of the whole should be defined before the meaning and function of the components can be defined, and that the components cannot be studied in isolation.

This paper aims to collect ABB-pattern adjectives included in *Modern Chinese Dictionary* (2015 Edition), examine the tones and tone sandhi of BBs in them, and compare them with ABBs in *Modern Chinese Dictionary* (1996 Edition) to study the characteristics and trends of the tone sandhi of ABB. In both dictionaries, it is clearly stated that the reduplicated forms are annotated according to the actual pronunciation, such as 沉甸甸, which is annotated as *chéndiāndiān* according to its actual pronunciation in the spoken language. Therefore, like [7], this paper holds the view that the phonetic annotations of *Modern Chinese Dictionary* can generally reflect the actual pronunciation of ABBs. In the process of research, CM helps to explore the pattern of tone sandhi of BB, and coercion effects can provide a more generalized theoretical explanation for it.

2 BB'S Tone Sandhi Pattern

2.1 Characteristics of BB'S Tone Sandhi

In previous studies on the tone sandhi of BB, although there are controversies about whether all of BBs are changed to yinping and the variation of the proportion of tone sandhi, there is a consensus among scholars that the direction of tone sandhi is from non-yinping to yinping. On the basis of this consensus, we will further examine the characteristics and patterns of tone sandhi of BB.

The *Modern Chinese Dictionary* (2015 Edition) (abbreviated as the 2015 edition below) contains 224 ABB-pattern adjectives, and there are 137 ABBs in which the original tones of BBs are yinping, accounting for 61.2%, indicating that the BBs originally in yinping still occupy a large proportion. There are 26 ABBs with BBs turning into yinping, accounting for 11.6%, of which 7 are directly annotated as yinping and 19 are annotated as yinping in additional spoken pronunciation. In addition, there are 61 ABBs with non-yinping BBs being noted as the original tones, accounting for 27.2%.

We compared the findings of Li's [7] examination of BB's tones in *Modern Chinese Dictionary* (1996 Edition) (abbreviated as the 1996 edition below) with the 2015 edition, and obtained the following table (Table 1).

Table 1. Comparison of the Annotations of BB in the 1996 and 2015 Editions

	Annotated tone	yinping		non-yinping	Total Number
	Original tone	yinping	non-yinping	non-yinping	
the 1996 Edition	Qty	118	37	36	191
	Percentage	61.8%	19.4%	18.8%	100%
	Total	81.2%		18.8%	100%
the 2015 edition	Qty	137	26	61	224
	Percentage	61.2%	11.6%	27.2%	100%
	Total	72.8%		27.2%	100%

As can be seen from the table, the proportion of adjectives with BB originally toned in yinping in the 2015 Edition is basically the same as that in the 1996 edition. The total percentage of ABBs with BBs annotated as yinping was 81.2% in the 1996 edition, while the percentage of these ABBs in the 2015 edition had decreased, but still accounted for a large percentage, 72.8%. Compared to the 1996 edition, the 2015 edition shows a rise in the number of BBs pronounced in non-yinping tones, which is mainly influenced by the 15 ABBs re-annotated in their original tones. In terms of phonetic form, most BBs are yinping tones, which is still a typical feature of ABB construction. However, not all non-yinping BBs change their tones, and the proportion of non-yinping BBs that change their tones decreased. Under what conditions does a BB in non-yinping change its tone? And under what conditions does it retain its original tone? Is there a regularity in the tonal sandhi of BB, and what is the internal motivation for this change? What is the reason for the decrease of the proportion of such tone sandhi? To address these questions, the present study further examines the factors influencing the tone sandhi of BB.

2.2 Influencing Factors of BB'S Tone Sandhi

We counted the tone sandhi of ABB (non-yinping) and the part of speech of BB in the 2015 edition, and drew a token frequency table (Table 2) of tone sandhi of ABB and a type frequency table (Table 3) of tone sandhi of BB (non-yinping).

Table 2. Statistics of the Token Frequency of ABB's Tone Sandhi in the 2015 Edition

Part of speech	ABB with BB changed to yinping	Qty	ABB with BB not changed to yinping	Qty	Total	Tone sandhi percentage
Nominal	沉甸甸, 黑洞洞, 黑油油, 绿油油, 乌油油, 亮堂堂, 乱蓬蓬, 黑糊糊, 黏糊糊, 血糊糊, 文绉绉	11	赤条条, 空洞洞, 孤零零	3	14	79%
Verbal	汗淋淋, 乱腾腾, 慢腾腾, 热腾腾, 湿淋淋, 湿漉漉, 水淋淋, 血淋淋, 直瞪瞪, 直愣愣, 黄澄澄	11	空荡荡, 空落落, 圆滚滚, 白晃晃, 明晃晃, 金晃晃, 光闪闪, 金闪闪, 亮闪闪, 明闪闪, 暖融融, 平展展	12	23	48%
Adjectiv-al	黑黝黝, 红彤彤	2	白皑皑, 白茫茫, 白蒙蒙, 赤裸裸, 恶狠狠, 光灿灿, 黑沉沉, 黑茫茫, 黑蒙蒙, 红艳艳, 黄灿灿, 灰沉沉, 灰蒙蒙, 火辣辣, 金灿灿, 金煌煌, 蓝盈盈, 蓝莹莹, 懒洋洋, 乐陶陶, 泪涟涟, 绿茸茸, 绿莹莹, 毛茸茸, 闷沉沉1, 闷沉沉2, 密麻麻, 暖洋洋, 气昂昂, 气鼓鼓, 清泠泠, 清凌凌, 热辣辣, 软绵绵, 甜腻腻, 雾沉沉, 雾茫茫, 雾蒙蒙, 喜洋洋, 喜盈盈, 香馥馥, 笑吟吟, 笑盈盈, 阴沉沉, 圆鼓鼓, 直挺挺	46	48	4%
Onomat-opoeia	噗碌碌	1		0	1	100%
Other	骨碌碌	1		0	1	100%
Total		26		61	87	

Table 3. Statistics of the Type Frequency of Non-yinping BB's Tone Sandhi in the 2015 Edition

Part of speech	BB turning into yinping	Qty	BB not turning into yinping	Qty	Total	Tone sandhi percentage
Nominal	甸甸, 洞洞[a], 油油, 堂堂, 蓬蓬, 糊糊, 绉绉	7	条条, 洞洞, 零零	3	10	70%
Verbal	淋淋, 腾腾, 漉漉, 瞪瞪, 愣愣, 澄澄	6	荡荡, 落落, 滚滚, 晃晃, 闪闪, 融融, 展展	7	13	46%
Adjectival	黝黝, 彤彤[b]	2	皑皑, 茫茫, 蒙蒙, 裸裸, 狠狠, 灿灿, 沉沉, 艳艳, 辣辣, 煌煌, 盈盈, 莹莹, 洋洋, 陶陶, 涟涟, 茸茸, 麻麻, 昂昂, 鼓鼓, 泠泠, 凌凌, 绵绵, 腻腻, 馥馥, 吟吟, 挺挺	26	28	7%
Onomatopoeia	碌碌[c]	1		0	1	100%
Other	碌碌	1		0	1	100%
Total		17		36	53	

[a]Because of the difference in the tone sandhi of 黑洞洞 hei1dong1dong1 and 空洞洞 kong1dong4dong4, they are listed separately in this table.
[b]We suggest that the tones of 黑黝黝 hei1you1you1 and 红彤彤 hong2tong1tong1 are likely to be influenced by the pronunciations of ABBs (黑幽幽 hei1you1you1, 红通通 hong2tong1tong1), which have similar semantics, same consonants and vowels, and can be used interchangeably. This assumption remains to be further confirmed.
[c]The 碌碌 lu1lu1 in 噗碌碌 pu1lu1lu1 is an onomatopoeic word, and the word 骨碌 gu1lu0 in 骨碌碌 gu1lu1lu1 is a two-alliterated word. The two 碌碌 are different in part of speech, so they are separated.

The tables show that there is a correlation between the tone sandhi of BB and the part of speech of BB. Among ABBs with tone sandhi, 24 ABBs with non-adjectival BBs (92%) are found, among which noun BBs and verb BBs are predominant, and only 2 cases (8%) of adjectival BBs are found. Among 60 ABBs whose BBs are non-yinping and do not change tones, 46 of them have adjectival BBs, accounting for 75% of the total. In ABB_N, there are 11 words that are changed in tone, and only 3 words are not changed. The proportion of tone sandhi in ABB_N is 79%, and that in ABBV is 48%, while ABB_A has the lowest proportion of tone sandhi at 4% (Table 2).

There are 53 non-yinping BBs in the 2015 edition, including 10 nominal BBs, 13 verbal BBs, 28 adjectival BBs, 1 onomatopoeic BB and 1 BB of other part of speech. In terms of the type frequency of tone sandhi, BB_N is 70%, BB_V is 46%, and BB_A still has the lowest type frequency at 7%. The type frequencies of all three types of BBs turning into yinping is comparable to the token frequencies of the ABBs composed of them, which shows that the pattern of tone sandhi of BBs is related to the part of speech of them. To summarize, non-adjectival BBs have a high proportion of tone sandhi, while adjectival BBs tend to be pronounced in their original tones instead of being changed to yinping.

3 Analysis on the Motivation of Tone Sandhi of BB Under Coercion Effects

Constructions are conventional form-meaning pairs, and phonetic features are one of the forms of constructions. Reduplicated constructions in Chinese Mandarin have some commonalities in tone, and there are also relatively fixed tone sandhi patterns in Chinese dialects.

According to [1], the second A of AABB adjectives is generally pronounced yinping in the spoken Beijing dialect, and the BB in AABB is also often pronounced yinping in spoken language (e.g., 慢慢腾腾 *man4man4teng1teng1* and 干干净净 *gan1gan1jing1jing1*). Xu [18] argued that for AABB adjectives commonly used in spoken language, regardless of their original tones, BBs will be basically changed to yinping, while AABB adjectives, generally used as written words, basically do not undergo tone sandhi. Li [6] pointed out that most of BBs in ABB are yinping, and also mentioned that BBs in the complete reduplication AABB are often pronounced as yinping in the spoken language. Li [19] pointed out that the second syllable of ABB in Qinyang dialect is mostly pronounced as neutral tone, and the third syllable is pronounced as yangping[1]. Luo [20], who examined the reduplicated patterns in Xiangfan dialect, mentioned that the second syllable B of "ABBer" and ABB is pronounced as neutral tone, and the third syllable "B(er)" is mostly pronounced as yinping (24 tone). Ma [21] summarized the tone pattern of BB in the Harbin dialect as "neutral tone + yinping". Fang [9] pointed out that high-pitched tonalization is a common tone sandhi trend in Chinese dialects, and that "AAer", a reduplicated adverb, and "ABBer", which is used as adverbial, both undergo yinping tone sandhi in Beijing dialect. Furthermore, Fang [9] argued that the high-pitched tone form has the effect of highlighting the subjective attitude of the speaker. According to previous research, it is not difficult to find that the duplication of adjectives in Chinese Mandarin and dialects have their own fixed tone sandhi patterns, and yinping and yinpingization are the typical phonetic features of some reduplicated adjectives in Chinese Mandarin and some dialects.

Peng [22] mentioned that the instance with the highest textual frequency is usually considered as construction paradigm, and the difference between the instance and construction paradigm affects the degree of marginality of the instance. We used the BCC multi-domain corpus to search 224 ABB-pattern adjectives in the 2015 edition and retrieved 177,851 instances. In 60% of these words (106401), the original tone of BB is yinping. It can be seen that BB in yinping is a typical phonetic feature of ABB, and ABB$_{yinping}$ can be regarded as a paradigm of ABB construction.

In terms of meaning and function, the function of ABB is to describe the state, the descriptive meaning is its basic meaning, and the meaning of ABB can be understood

---

[1] In Mandarin Chinese, the pitch of yangping is 35.

as "the state associated to A". Liu [3] and Shao [4] pointed out that ABB has an obvious descriptive function compared with A, AB and BA. According to Zhang [23], the meaning of ABB is vivid, which does not focus on the accuracy of expressions, but focuses on increasing the vividness of language, evoking people's association through images. For example, 黑洞洞 *hei1dong1dong1*, 黑沉沉 *hei1chen2chen2* and 黑黝黝 *hei1you1you1* will make people associate with various characteristics related to 黑 *hei1* "black". Zhao [24] argued that the added meaning of BB is the main source of ABB's descriptivity. Thus, adjectival morphemes expressing traits are the typical constituents of ABB. The descriptive meaning of ABB and the phonetic feature of BB are matched. In exploring the reasons for the reduplicated parts of ABB to be pronounced in yinping, Ma [8] suggested that in order to make the semantics more vivid, the tone needs to be raised, and yinping has the highest pitch.

Constructions as a whole impact the semantics and forms of constituents, and there are coercion effects on non-typical constituents' meaning and form, changing them into typical meaning and form. Hilpert [15] stated that morphological constructions exhibit coercion effects during word formation, polishing the semantics of non-conforming constituents to enable them to enter the construction. Due to coercion effects, the meaning of noun constituents is turned into "the typical trait of the noun refers to", while the meaning of verb constituents is transformed into "the trait of an action or the feeling it brings". For example, the noun 冰 *bing1* "ice" in 冷冰冰 *leng3* "cold" *bing1bing1* is used to "cold like ice", and the meaning of the verb绷 *beng1* "stretch tight" in紧绷绷 *jin3* "tight" *beng1beng1* is coerced to "the tightened or tensioned state".

Coercion effects are not only on the semantic but also on the phonetic form. When BB$_N$ and BB$_V$ that are not yinping form a construction, they tend to alter their tones to yinping. Coercion effects are the intrinsic motivation for the changes of tones of BBs. The non-yinping adjectival BBs are of attribute, with strong descriptive features which are typical in semantics of ABB, so they are less phonetically coerced and do not need to change their tones (e.g., 白皑皑*bai2* "white" *ai2ai2*, 恶狠狠 *e4* "fierce" *hen3hen3* and 闷沉沉 *men1/4 chen2chen2*). The semantic distance between the words composed of BBn/v and the prototype of the construction is large because BBn and BBv do not have the function of directly characterizing the trait. In order to make the constituents conform more to the requirements of the construction, not only the semantic meanings of BBs are coerced, but also the tones are coerced to the typical tone of BB. For example, 绿油油 *lv4* "green" *you1you1* describes "thick green and shiny" and 绿莹莹 *lv4* "green" *ying2ying2* describes "green and crystal", where the tones of 油油 and 莹莹 are both yangping. In spoken language, the tone of 油油 becomes yinping, while 莹莹 is still pronounced in yangping. We argue that this difference in tones is caused by the different coercion effects of the two BBs. 油 *you2* "oil" is a noun morpheme, which is an untypical constituent. In order to satisfy the constituent requirement of ABB construction, the meaning of 油 is coerced to the meaning of "shiny", which is related to the property of oil, and the tone is also coerced to yinping. 莹 is an adjectival morpheme with the meaning of "shiny and transparent", which complements the trait related to 绿 and meets the semantic requirements of the components in ABB, so it is pronounced in its original tone in ABB.

In fact, the phenomenon of tone sandhi of BB can be regarded as a phonetic compensation mechanism. Constructions are conventional form-meaning pairs, and the phonetic features of instances whose meaning features are far from the prototype of constructions are more affected by the coercion effects, making them closer to the typical forms of constructions.

The coercion of tones of BB by ABB is not only related to the part of speech of BB, but also influenced by the specific semantics of BB. For example, the word 条 *tiao2* in 赤条条 *chi4* "bare" *tiao2tiao2* is a noun morpheme, but it is still pronounced in yangping. The semantic meaning of 条 is "something long and thin", or it is used as a quantifier to modify things that are long and thin. Although 条 is a noun morpheme, the shape of the thing it refers to is very obvious, and its descriptivity is more prominent than other noun morphemes, with certain figurativeness and vividness. 条 is relatively more in line with the semantic requirements of ABB, so the tone of 条 is not coerced to yinping. The words 晃 *huang3* and 闪 *shan3* are verbal morphemes, both meaning " to sparkle", and in ABB they mean "sparkling". Although the two morphemes are verbal, the semantics of them directly highlight the attribute of "sparkling", and their tones are also not changed. The 碌碌 in 骨碌碌 has no lexical meaning. According to [25],骨碌 is the reduplication form of the noun 毂 *hu1/3* "the log in the center of the wheel" after the phonetic change, and 骨碌 is the way to write it when it is used as a verb, and when it is used as a noun, it is written as 轱辘 *gu1lu1*. For this reason,骨碌 is a two-alliterated word, and 碌 has no morpheme meaning, so when it enters ABB, the tone is changed to yinping under the coercion effects. Some BBs in the process of grammaticalization (e.g., 腾腾 *teng2teng2* and 糊糊 *hu2hu2*), will be more coerced in phonetic form as the collocation range expands and the degree of semantic bleaching becomes higher, and they will be pronounced in yinping.

Overall, the strong correlation between the tone sandhi and the part of speech of BB, and the influence of descriptivity of BB on BB's tones are due to the fact that the intrinsic motivation of the tone sandhi of BB is the coercion effects of ABB. Coercion effects will polish some forms in the instances that break the constraints of constructions and do not meet the requirements of prototypes of constructions, so that these instances are still within the limits allowed by the constructions.

4   Reasons for Some BBs not Changing Tones

In ABB, the BB tones change to yinping, which is the result of the coercion effects on BB phonetic form. Also, we should note that the variation in tones of BBs is also influenced by similar or related forms.

The essay counted the ABBs whose BBs (non-yinping) are both annotated as original tones in the 1996 and 2015 editions and those whose BBs (non-yinping) are annotated as yinping tones in the 1996 edition and changed to original tones in the 2015 edition and analyzed the reasons why these BBs are not or no longer changed to yinping. There are 12 ABBs annotated with original tones (non-yinping) in both editions, and 15 ABBs changed to original tones (non-yinping) in the 2015 edition (Table 4). The semantics of most BBs that did not change tones in the 2015 edition are descriptive, which satisfies to some extent the semantic requirements of ABB constructions for components (e.g., 赤条

条 *chi4* "bare" *tiao2tiao2*, 光闪闪 *guang1* "light" *shan3shan3*, 明晃晃 *ming2* "bright" *huang3huang3*, 热辣辣 *re4* "hot" *la4la4*).

The corresponding forms of ABB, such as AB and BA, also affect the tone sandhi of BB. The pronunciation of BB will be influenced by the corresponding forms of ABB that are used frequently, which weakens coercion effects of phonetic forms. The word 空洞洞 *kong1* "empty" *dong4dong4*, where BB is a noun morpheme, and the words 空荡荡 *kong1* "empty" *dang4dang4* and 空落落 *kong1* "empty" *luo4luo4*, where BBs are verb morphemes, both have AB or BA forms (空洞 *kong1dong4*, 空荡 *kong1dang4* and 落空 *luo4kong1*) with similar meanings to them. These corresponding forms are high-frequency words in daily life, and some of them are more commonly used than the ABBs. We searched 空洞 *kong1dong4*, 空荡 *kong1dang4* and 落空 *luo4kong1* in the BCC multi-domain corpus, and the frequencies are 7597, 962, and 4387 in order, while the corresponding ABBs occur 185, 4292, and 504 times, respectively. These ABBs are influenced by the corresponding forms, and the BBs are not changed in tones. In addition to 空洞洞, 空荡荡 and 空落落, the pronunciations of 平展展 *ping2* "flat" *zhan3zhan3* and 圆滚滚 *yuan2* "round" *gun3gun3* are also affected by their corresponding forms 平展 *ping2zhan3* and 滚圆 *gun3yuan2*.

Table 4. Statistics of ABB with Unchanged Tones

	ABB	Qty
Note original tones in both editions[a]	赤条条, 空洞洞, 孤零零[b], 空荡荡, 空落落, 圆滚滚, 光闪闪, 金闪闪, 亮闪闪, 明闪闪, 暖融融, 平展展	12
Change to original tones in 2015 edition	白晃晃, 明晃晃, 金晃晃, 金煌煌, 毛茸茸, 绿茸茸, 清凌凌, 热辣辣, 火辣辣, 软绵绵, 蓝盈盈, 绿莹莹, 懒洋洋, 笑吟吟, 雾茫茫	15

[a]Since the adjectival BB pronounced in the original tone conforms to the rules of coercion effects, only instances of the non-adjectival BB pronounced in the original tone are listed in the table.
[b]According to the author's personal sense of speech, the 零零 *ling2ling2* in 孤零零 *gu1* "alone" *ling1ling1* should be pronounced in yinping tone in spoken language, but whether this sense of speech is universal or not needs to be further examined.

5   Conclusion

The tones of BBs are mostly yinping, which is a distinctive phonetic feature of ABB construction, and the coercion effects can change the tones of BBs to a typical yinping tone. There is a pattern of which BBs will be changed and which BBs will retain non-yinping tones. Whether or not a non-yinping BB is changed depends on whether or not the part of speech and semantics of the BB meet the requirements of ABB construction for the components.

By examining tones of BBs in Modern Chinese Dictionary (2015 Edition), we found that adjectival BBs are not easily coerced by the construction, while the tones of nominal and verbal BBs are usually changed to yinping under the coercion effects. ABB-pattern adjectives are state adjectives, whose function is to describe the state. The semantics of ABB is "the state associated to A", which has strong vividness and descriptivity. Therefore, ABB requires the constituents to be properties or states, and adjectival morphemes are the typical components of ABB. The nominal morphemes and verbal morphemes denote reference and statement respectively, which do not meet the semantic requirements of ABB and are coerced by the construction when entering it. Coercion effects are not only affected on constituents' semantics, but also on phonetic forms. The atypical BBs' tones are changed to yinping under the coercion effects, and this phonetic coercion can be regarded as a compensatory mechanism. Nominal morphemes and verbal morphemes with strong semantic descriptivity (e.g., 条条 tiao2tiao2 and晃晃 huang3huang3) do not undergo tone sandhi because they can satisfy the semantic requirements of ABB to a certain extent and are less coerced phonetically.

To sum up, the coercion effects are the main influencing factors of the tone sandhi of BB. Besides, the tone of BB is also influenced by the pronunciations of high frequency corresponding forms such as AB and BA. The few examples of constructions that seem to be incompatible with the pattern of tone sandhi do not actually affect the overall mechanism of tone sandhi of BB under the coercion effects. Furthermore, since the tone sandhi is mostly seen in colloquialism, it remains to be further explored whether the trend of tone sandhi is influenced by factors such as the popularity of Mandarin and the narrowing of the difference between written and spoken languages. The pitches of tones, typical tones and tone sandhi patterns of ABB in Chinese dialects may be different from those in Chinese Mandarin. For example, the Yinping in Shaoxing is a falling tone, and after the tone sandhi, the latter B of ABB is a falling tone, while the former B is mostly a rising tone [26]. Therefore, the tone sandhi of ABB in Chinese dialects should be further examined.

References

1. Lv, S.X.: Xiandai hanyu babai ci (The Eight Hundred Words of Modern Chinese). Commercial Press (1980)
2. Zhu, D.X.: Xiandai hanyu yufa yanjiu (A Study of Modern Chinese Grammar). The Commercial Press (1980). https://doi.org/10.26549/jxffcxysj.v3i16.6253
3. Liu, D.Q.: Suzhou fangyan chongdie shi yanjiu (The study of Reduplicated Forms in Suzhou Dialect). Stud. Lang. Linguist. 1, 7–28 (1986)
4. Shao, J.M.: ABB shi xingrongci dongtai yanjiu (the Dynamic Study of ABB pattern Adjectives). Chin. Teach. World 1, 19–26 (1990)
5. Cao, R.F.: Putonghua ABB shi xingrongci de dingliang fenxi (Quantitative Analysis of ABB-Pattern Adjectives in Mandarin). Linguist. Res. 3, 22–25 (1995)
6. Li, Y.: Chongdie xingrongci biandiao wenti de kaocha (Examination of the Tone Sandhi of Reduplicated Adjectives). J. Shaoguan Univ. 11, 14–20 (2001)
7. Li, Z.J.: ABB shi xingrongci zhong BB zhuyin de shengdiao wenti (The Issue of Tone of BB's Annotation in ABB-Pattern Adjectives). Lang. Plann. 12, 2–6 (1998)
8. Ma, Z.W.: Xingrongci ABB shi de shengdiao duyin kaocha (the Study on the Tone of the Adjective Pattern of ABB). Nankai Linguist. 2, 55–61+165 (2006)
9. Fang, M.: Beijinghua erhua ciyu yinping biandiao de yufa yiyi (The Morphsyntactic Significance of the Tone Sandhi in Words with the Diminutive Suffix in Beijing Mandarin). Essays Linguist. 1, 33–51 (2015)

10. Huang, B.R.: Xiandai hanyu shang zengding 2 ban (Modern Chinese Volume 1 Updated 2nd Edition). Higher Education Press (1997). https://doi.org/10.32629/mef.v1i2.19

11. Lin, L.: Tan xingrongci ABB chongdie xingshi de duyin (Discussion of the Pronunciation of the Reduplicated Forms of the Adjective ABB). Lang. Plann. **12**, 22–25 (1992)

12. Li, X.M.: Danyinjie xingrongci dieyin houzhui du 55 diao bian (Discussion of the Mono-syllabic Adjectival Reduplicated Suffix Pronounced 55 Pitch). Stud. Chin. Lang. **2**, 137–138 (2000)

13. Mou, X.M.: Guanyu ABB shi xingrongci de duyin (The Pronunciation of ABB-Pattern Adjectives). Lang. Plann. **2**, 26 (2001). https://doi.org/10.3969/j.issn.1001-8476.2001.02.020

14. Booij, G.: Construction morphology. Lang. Linguist. Compass **4**(7), 543–555 (2010). https://doi.org/10.1111/j.1749-818X.2010.00213.x

15. Hilpert, M., Zhang, G.H.: Goushi yufa jiaocheng: goushi yufa jiqi zai yingyu zhong de yingyong (Construction grammar and its application to English). Peking University Press (2016). https://doi.org/10.32629/er.v3i5.2697

16. Michaelis, L.A.: Type shifting in construction grammar: an integrated approach to aspectual coercion. Cogn. Linguist. **15**(1), 1–67 (2004). https://doi.org/10.1515/cogl.2004.001

17. Song, Z.Y.: Jiyu goushi lilun yu wuxing jiegou de dongming dingzhong fuheci yanjiu—cong dongci shijiao dao mingci shijiao (A Study on Modifier-head VN Compounds Based on Construction Grammar and Qualia Structure: From Verb-perspective to Noun-perspective). Chin. Teach. World **36**(01), 33–48 (2022)

18. Xu, J.K.: Xiandai hanyu xingrongci chongdie xingshi AABB biandiao guilv diaocha (A Survey of Modern Chinese Adjectival Reduplication Pattern AABB Tone Sandhi Law). Hunan Normal University (2012). https://doi.org/10.7666/d.y2149291

19. Li, Y.M.: Biyanghua xingzhixingrongci de chongdie ji youguan de jielv wenti (Reduplication of Qualitative Adjectives and Related Rhythmic Issues in Biyang Dialect). Stud. Lang. Linguist. **1**, 18–27 (1996)

20. Luo, Z.Q.: Xiangfan fangyan de chongdie shi (Reduplicated Forms in Xiangfan Dialect). Dialect **1**, 82–89 (2002)

21. Ma, B.: Hanyu zhuangtaici cizhui jiqi leixingxue tezheng (Chinese State Affixes and Their Typology Features). Central Univ. Nationalities (2007). https://doi.org/10.7666/d.y1050000

22. Peng, R.: Tushixing goushi de bianjie: bianyuan gouli he bianyi gouli (On the Marginal Instances and Mutating Instances of Schematic Construtions). Chin. Teach. World **34**(03), 339–353 (2020)

23. Zhang, M.L.: Jindai hanyu houzhui xingrongci cidian (A Dictionary of Modern Chinese Suffixed Adjectives). Guizhou Education Press, Guiyang (2001). https://doi.org/10.1515/glochi-2015-1015

24. Zhao, Q.: Tonggan yinyu shijiao de xiandai hanyu ABB shi zhuangtai xingrongci (ABB-Pattern State Adjectives in Mandarin: A Study from the Perspective of Synaesthetic Metaphor). Chin. Teach. World **35**(02), 206–219 (2021)

25. Shi, Q.: Hanyu xingrongci chongdie xingshi de lishi fazhan (A Study On the Historical Development of Reduplication Patterns of Chinese Adjectives). The Commercial Press (2010)

26. Wang, B., Du, Y., Yang, L.: A study of the characteristics of ABB-type adjectives in Shaoxing dialect. In: Hong, J.-F., Zhang, Y., Liu, P. (eds.) CLSW 2019. LNCS (LNAI), vol. 11831, pp. 102–109. Springer, Cham (2020). https://doi.org/10.1007/978-3-030-38189-9_10

Extracting Concepts and Semantic Associates for Teaching Tang 300 Poems to L2 Learners

Yanlin Li[(⊠)] ⓘ and Chu-Ren Huang ⓘ

The Hong Kong Polytechnic University, Hong Kong, China
yanlin.li@connect.polyu.hk, churen.huang@polyu.edu.hk

Abstract. This research aims to explore the possibility of extracting language concepts and semantic associates through the diachronic construction of cross-linguistic knowledge resources based on the framework of an existing fine-grained ontological system developed by the Sinica BOW Tang 300 poems project. The authors attempt to provide language educators with a different perspective of instructional design by understanding and meeting L2 learners' needs through the in-depth analysis of massive bilingual language data. It is hoped that synergized linguistic knowledge net(s) could better facilitate L2 Chinese language teaching and learning.

Keywords: Small domain ontology · Cross-linguistic knowledge · Concept knowledge · Semantic associates

1 Introduction

Ontology is the study of how human knowledge system is represented and organized [1, 2]. Such an emergent discipline illustrates the basic concepts in human knowledge systems and demonstrates the relations of these concepts by showing how the concepts are organized. Gruber also discussed the design of ontologies and its use, especially in the context of computational representation for knowledge sharing, which allows computers to directly process the semantic content online [3]. In the field of language and lexicon, ontological studies mainly focused on mapping the linguistic system to the ontological system logically with the lexical semantic relations, such as hypernym–hyponym which demonstrates the superclass–subclass relation and holonym–meronym which shows the whole–part or entity–constituent relation [2, 4].

Atchison points out that human's mental lexicon, containing phonologically and semantically related lexical items, is developed when learning new words [5]. However, the mental lexicon is organized in a complex manner rather than what is like in the dictionary. Thus, the traditional way of language resource development like purely building dictionary for language learning could no longer meet the needs of L2 learners in the development of their second mental lexicon. A more synergized knowledge net which not only providing word senses, but also connecting conceptual knowledge across languages is in demand for second language education [6]. Moreover, studies show that the second mental lexicon that learners developed during second language acquisition

© The Author(s), under exclusive license to Springer Nature Switzerland AG 2023
Q. Su et al. (Eds.): CLSW 2022, LNAI 13495, pp. 233–243, 2023.
https://doi.org/10.1007/978-3-031-28953-8_18

is stored separately from the first mental lexicon, and it can shrink as the age grows [7, 8]. That is to say, a more comprehensive bilingual lexical knowledge system should be developed reflecting the second mental lexicon as well as linking to L1 as much as possible for learners to acquire a second language from a young age.

Therefore, the purpose of this study is to identify the concept knowledge that second language learners gained from authentic language materials in their first language (L1) at a young age (lower primary school years). With the identified learner-familiar concepts, the authors hope to further explore the possibility of extracting semantic resources according to those learner-familiar concepts through cross-linguistic knowledge resources based on the frameworks of the existing fine-grained ontological systems for the purposes of second language (L2) teaching and learning. Based on the rationale, a framework is developed according to the existing structure developed by the Sinica BOW Tang 300 poems project, in which the upper part of the ontology is mapped to SUMO (The Suggested Upper Merged Ontology by IEEE), and the lower part is extended by using the ImageNet Synset search. WordNet and Oxford Elementary learner's English Chinese dictionary are used for searching the missing relations in both the upper and the lower parts. Furthermore, a diachronic comparison is conducted between the Sinica BOW Tang 300 Poems domain ontology and the newly built modern Chinese cartoon domain ontology. The comparison aims to explore the possibility of extracting semantic resource for L2 language teaching and learning by identifying the connecting same concept knowledge of L1 that student gains from the authentic language materials. This paper attempts to give an insight to the relevant Chinese or bilingual ontological knowledge nets and their pedagogical implications in Chinese language teaching and learning.

2 Constructing a Small Domain Ontology

There are abundant cross-linguistic knowledge resources in the world academia. Taking Sinica BOW as an example, Sinica BOW stands for the Academia Sinica Bilingual Ontological Wordnet developed by the Institute of Linguistics and the Institute of Information Science of Academia Sinica. It integrates three main resources which are WordNet, SUMO (Suggested Upper Merged Ontology), and the English-Chinese Translation Equivalents Database (ECTED). Such a combination of ontology and WordNet assigns each linguistic form a precise location in the taxonomy, and clarifies the relation between the conceptual classification and its linguistic instantiation, as well as facilitated a genuine cross-lingual access of knowledge. The built-in versatile function in the bilingual system allows queries for either English or Chinese. And the logical structure with the embedded WordNet and SUMO knowledge allows user to get either conceptual nodes or the ontology. In addition, domain information provides users with knowledge in another dimension. To further explore the possibility of applying the system modal to domain knowledge representation, Huang et al. applied the modal to build small domain ontology in the study entitled Sinica BOW Tang 300 Poems project [9]. The study has shed the light on the application of the bilingual ontological system and showed the possibilities of the empirical use in the field of second language education. The initial rationale of the Sinica BOW Tang Poem project was to adopt SUMO as the framework for ontological representations, and to use Wordnet as a lexical knowledgebase to provide the natural interface between the domain lexica and SUMO and supplement the knowledge. Since Sinica BOW bridged up both SUMO ontology and WordNET, it was used as the primary referential knowledgebase in the study. The research team collected domain lexicon from a target collection of texts (Tang 300 poems), and mapped them to the SUMO ontology. With regard to domain selection, the team followed the two criteria: (1) the selected items should play roughly equivalent roles in the knowledge backgrounds of the target ontology and the reference ontology (i.e. our contemporary ontology); (2) the selected items should be empirically verifiable with lexical resources supporting the target ontology.

Tang 300 poems, commonly used in L1 Chinese young learners' learning materials, are adopted as the preliminary language resources for this study. However, understanding those ancient verses is not an easy task for the L2 learners, who do not have enough background knowledge of Chinese language. How could language teachers introduce the Tang 300 poems to L2 Chinese learners? Would it be easier for L2 learners to start with some verses including the concepts that they have already gained from L1? To answer these questions, a comparable corpus with massive language data from bilingual cartoon subtitles is built to identify learners' L1 knowledge base as well as to connect them to the concepts from Tang 300 poems. Given that cartoon watching is one of the most common out-of-school language activities young learners engage in which includes abundant concrete concepts, e.g. animal characters, bilingual cartoon subtitles with massive language data are selected for constructing the comparable corpus so as to connect learners' L1 knowledge base in this preliminary study.

This pilot study adopts Huang et al.'s approach to construct small domain ontology, also known as non-standard ontology. Furthermore, the framework is tailored to match the needs of L2 young learners of Chinese based upon the original design of Sinica BOW. By following the refined structure, the work of mapping lexical data to ontology is carried out accordingly. Firstly, as the preparation, a comparable corpus for L2 young learners of Chinese is built to serve as the text resources for domain resources database. Secondly, a pilot experiment is conducted on constructing a small domain ontology by using Sinica BOW as the primary referential resource. Animal words from the corpus, which are concrete concepts, are selected for this pilot study to map with the existing animal domain ontology from Sinica BOW Tang Poems project. Such a comparison of the concrete concepts, which L2 young leaners are familiar with, could serve as a good starting point for the learners to expand their knowledge net.

To start with, each lexical item is assigned a unique correct Chinese English sense and its corresponding English Chinese synset. Items mapped through Sinica BOW to a SUMO conceptual node. When mapping items, the principles of item mapping in Tang 300 poems project are utilized: (1) if there is no exact match, WordNet is consulted to establish lexical semantic relation between a lexical item and SUMO; (2) if the match is found, lexical items are assigned to an appropriate SUMO node.

Since SUMO, as an upper ontology, only provides rough-grained upper classification, and WordNet does not include all relations for such a hierarchical conceptual network [4, 10]. ImageNet is adopted for looking up the lower levelled ontological nodes, which are not included in SUMO and WordNet. ImageNet is an image database organized and constructed upon the WordNet hierarchy in which images are used to illustrate each synset from WordNet (only nouns in the current version) [11]. Figure 1 shows the adopted framework of constructing small domain ontologies which is developed based on the original resource and structure of Sinica BOW by adding ImageNet to the three main resources— WordNet, SUMO and the English-Chinese Translation Equivalents Database. In the newly built animal domain ontology, 68 animal words are identified from the bilingual cartoon resources and are mapped to the 22 upper ontology nodes.

Lancsbox [12], a recent data processing tool developed by Lancaster University, is used to review the contexts of the chosen animal words to filter out the incorrect word sense(s). With the careful analysis of findings from the semi-automatically built ontology, semantic knowledge with their pedagogical implication is found for the further construction of small ontology for language learning.

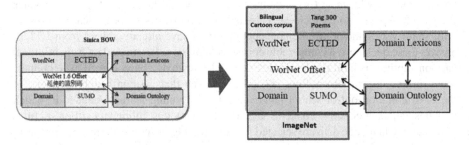

Fig. 1. The resource and structure of constructing small domain ontologies

3   A Diachronic Comparison

3.1   Animal Words and Upper Ontology Nodes

This study examines the ontology nodes by comprehensively comparing the newly built animal domain ontology with Sinica BOW Tang poem animal domain ontology. The mapping identifies links of 19 existing upper ontology nodes from Sinica BOW Tang 300 Poems which includes arachnid, canine, feline, carnivore, hoofed mammal, bird, insect, primate, reptile, rodent, warm blooded vertebrate, aquatic mammal, cold blooded vertebrate, xenarthra, marsupial, mollusk, fish, ape, worm (see Table 1).

It also identifies 3 newly added nodes in the cartoon corpus: (1) 兔类 (Lagomorpha) which links to the word *bunny* 兔子 tùzi with the frequency of 9 in the texts; (2) 浣熊科动物 (Procyonid) linking to *raccoon* 浣熊 huànxióng with the frequency of 7 in the texts; and (3) 恐龙 (Dinosaur) which links to *tyrannosaurus* 暴龙 bàolóng with the frequency of 1 in the texts.

Table 1. Direct upper ontological nodes linking to the 68 identified animal nouns

Upper Ontological Nodes
1   蜘蛛类（arachnid）
2   犬科动物（canine）
3   猫科动物（feline）
4   肉食性动物（carnivore）
5   有蹄哺乳动物（hoofed mammal）
6   鸟类（bird）
7   昆虫类（insect）
8   灵长类（primate）
9   兔类 (Lagomorpha)
10   爬行动物（reptile）
11   啮齿动物（rodent）
12   浣熊科动物（Procyonid）
13   温血脊椎动物（warm blooded vertebrate）
14   水栖/海洋哺乳动物（aquatic mammal）
15   冷血脊椎动物（cold blooded vertebrate）
16   贫齿类（Xenarthra）
17   有袋类（marsupial）
18   软体动物（mollusk）
19   鱼类（fish）
20   猿（ape）
21   蠕虫（worm）
22   恐龙 （dinosaur）

3.2   Identifying Similarities and Differences

As mentioned in the resource preparation part, one of the main reasons for choosing "animal" domain is to compare the results and ontological nodes with the animal ontological structures in the Sinica BOW Tang 300 Poems project. Under the shared ontological system, there are both similarities and differences among animal hyponyms. Obviously, most of the animal words in Tang Poems are monosyllabic words, others are disyllabic words. Unlike the Tang poems, multi-syllabic words and compound words are used more in the modern cartoon language texts. There are 16 animal concepts appear in both Tang poems and the cartoon collection including complete overlaps as well as partial overlaps with variation (see Table 2 below). The complete overlaps are *bear* 熊 xióng, *horse* 马 mǎ, *goose* 鹅 é, *wolf* 狼 láng, *chicken* 鸡 jī, *butterfly* 蝴蝶 húdié, *bat* 蝙蝠 biānfú, *eagle* 鹰 yīng, *peacock* 孔雀 kǒngquè. The partial overlaps, on the other hand, could be further divided into two sub-categories. One group is the partial overlap of Chinese expressions with shared Chinese character(s), and the other group is the same English concept with complete different Chinese names.

The first sub-category contains the animals such as *tiger* and *firefly*. Tiger is called 虎 hǔ in Tang poems and 老虎 lǎohǔ in the cartoon corpus. Similarly, *firefly* is called 萤 yíng in Tang poem and 萤火虫 yínghuǒchóng in the cartoon corpus. 虎 hǔ and 萤 yíng are the shared part in both ontological systems. This is very representative that ancient Chinese people tends to use single character which contains the main semantic information to name the animals. On the contrary, modern Chinese animal names add more detailed supports to the description of the animals. 老虎 lǎohǔ *tiger*, for instance, contains the prefix 老 lǎo in front of 虎 hǔ in more modern context. The original meaning of the word 老 is old. However, when 老 is used as a prefix, it no longer contains its meaning of old in most contexts. Instead, Zhu and Huang's book [13] entitled *A Student Grammar of Chinese* summaries that the prefix *lǎo* takes on the following meanings: 1) familiarity or seniority or respect like 老师 lǎoshī *teacher* and 老板 lǎobǎn *boss*; 2) a casual and informal meaning such as 老婆 lǎopó *wife* and 老公 lǎogōng *husband*; or 3) animals like 老虎 lǎohǔ *tiger* and 老鼠 lǎoshǔ *mouse*.

Table 2. Overlaps with the Sinica Bow Tang 300 Poems

	Animal	动物名称	Radical	Tang Poem	上层分类1
1	Spider	蜘蛛	虫	蟢子	蜘蛛类 (arachnid)
2	Dog	狗	犭	犬	犬科动物 (canine)
3	Bear	熊	灬	熊	肉食性动物 (carnivore)
4	Horse	马	马	马	有蹄哺乳动物 (hoofed mammal)
5	Goose	鹅	鸟	鹅	鸟类 (bird)
6	Wolf	狼	犭	狼	犬科动物 (canine)
7	Chicken	鸡	鸟	鸡	鸟类 (bird)
8	butterfly	蝴蝶	虫	蝴蝶	昆虫类 (insect)
9	Bat	蝙蝠	虫	蝙蝠	啮齿动物 (rodent)
10	Tiger	老虎	虍	虎	猫科动物 (feline)
11	Eagle	鹰	鸟	鹰	鸟类 (bird)
12	Firefly	萤火虫	艹, 虫	萤	昆虫类 (insect)
13	Turtle	乌龟	刀	鳖	爬行动物 (reptile)
14	Cobra	眼镜蛇	虫	蛇	爬行动物 (reptile)
15	Gorilla	大猩猩	犭	猩	猿 (ape)
16	Peacock	孔雀	隹	孔雀	鸟类 (bird)

The second sub-category includes "spider". It is called 蟢子 *xǐzi* in Tang poems, whereas in modern Chinese cartoon, it is called 蜘蛛 *zhīzhū*. Similarly, "dog" is called 犬 *quǎn* in Tang poems, whereas 狗 *gǒu* is used in the modern cartoon texts. Another example is "turtle", 鳖 *biē* is used in Tang poems whereas乌龟 *wūguī* is used in the modern cartoon corpus. Unlike the first sub-category, these animal names do not share any of the same character(s), but they are conveying same meanings and concepts.

The diachronic comparison of the animal ontologies from the two different studies brings educators with some new perspectives of Chinese second language teaching. On the one hand, teachers could take advantage of the conceptual knowledges that learners obtain from the daily watch of the cartoon and making direct links to the Tang poem teaching with the animal names with no variants like 马 horse, 鹅 goose, and 鸡 chicken. On the other hand, it would be helpful it the teacher to take good use of the variants for introducing language knowledge. For instance, tiger would be a good example for teachers to introduce the usage of prefix 老 *lǎo* by comparing 虎 *hǔ* in the poems with 老虎 *lǎohǔ* in modern cartoon. Like spider and firefly to arouse students' attention with the cultural background knowledge. Further and deeper discussions need to be involved in terms of the pedagogical framework of introducing Chinese Tang poems to the L2 young learners. The following section will give an in-depth discussion of those identical concepts.

3.3 Analysis on the Identical Concepts with Exactly Same Expressions in Chinese

Given complete overlaps of animal words are identified in both Tang poem and modern cartoon ontological structures, an in-depth examination on these identical concepts is conducted to find out the relationship between those animal words and the co-occurred animal words used in both genres.

Among the animal names with no variants, four of them 鸡 jī *chicken*, 孔雀 kǒngquè *peacock*, 鹰 yīng *eagle*, 鹅 é *goose* are cohyponyms under the hypernym "bird"; three others are mammals, but under different sub-ontological nodes: 马 horse under "hoofed mammal", 熊 bear under "carnivore" and 狼 wolf under "canine" is also under "carnivore".

Under the domain node of bird, it is found that the word 鸡 jī *chicken* has a closer semantic relation with 犬 quǎn *dog* in the Tang poems. For instance, the poet 王维 Wang Wei depicted the peacefulness of village life with the verse日出云中鸡犬喧 rì chū yún zhōng jī quǎn xuān *The sun rises through clouds, roosters crow and dogs bark in the village*. Although chicken and dogs are not co-hyponyms sharing the same hypernym, they are two of most common farm animals in cottages. The use of the two animals as representative elements provides a vivid mental image of village life. Unlike the poem by Wang Wei, the association of chicken and dogs by poet 杜甫Du Fu functions figuratively, the verse 况复秦兵耐苦战, 被驱不异犬与鸡 kuàng fù qín bīng nài kǔzhàn, bèi qū bù yì quǎn yǔ jī shows soldiers battling hardly are like dogs and chicken being caught up on to the battlefield. It indicates metaphorically that the soldiers are powerless and helpless in the war.

In the modern cartoon corpus, two animals co-occur with 鸡 jī *chicken* in the same sentence: 秃鹫 tūjiù *vulture* and 猴子 hóuzi *monkey*. Obviously, vulture and chicken are under the same domain of "bird" which shares more commonality. Unlike the co-hyponyms, chicken and monkey, which have less in common, pair up to function as exaggeration in the context 就像一只脸像猴子的鸡 *like a chicken with face of a monkey*.

Under the mammal words, only one co-occurred word pair 狼 *wolf* and 豺 *jackal* is found in Tang poems, whereas no word pair found in the modern cartoon corpus. In Tang poems, the poet 李白 Li Bai used the two animals as a pair metaphorically in the verse 所守或匪亲, 化为狼与豺 suǒ shǒu huò fěi qīn, huà wéi láng yǔ chái to indicate that whoever garrisons the daunting route to the region of Shu is either a bandit gangs or someone brutal like a wolf or a jackal.

蝙蝠 *bat* is the only word under the hypernym of "rodent" with complete overlaps in both ontological structures. However, no co-occurred animal word is found in Tang poem. Bat only pairs up with another animal 考拉 *koala* in the modern cartoon context as a neologism 考拉蝙蝠 *koala-bat*, a newly created character in cartoon which does not exist in the reality.

To further examine the extracted semantic resources, WebVectors, an online prediction-based word embeddings tool to serve distributional semantic models, is adopted for the comparison [14]. The semantic relations between words are reflected by semantic vectors according to co-occurrence distribution of works in the huge amounts of raw linguistic training data from Wikipedia. Two-dimensional map is generated to visualize the positions of the words in the semantic space. In this paper, the semantic relation generated from WebVectors is used as benchmarking data for comparative analysis of identical animal concepts in both Tang Poem and the modern cartoon domain ontological structures. Figure 2 illustrates *wolf* 狼 láng with its immediate neighbors are of the same radicals 犭. Moreover, among the co-occurred animal word pairs, only the pair of *wolf-jackal* shows relevantly higher semantic associate level at 0.614 with the similarity threshold at 0.6.

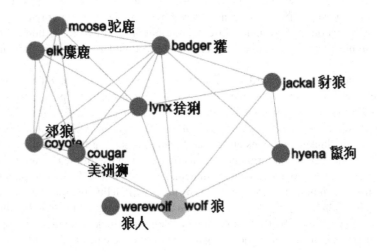

- 李白《蜀道难》所守或匪亲, 化为狼与豺。*(狼 wolf-豺 jackal)*

Fig. 2. Semantic associates for wolf with a relevant sample stanza from Tang poems (computed on English Wikipedia)

However, Fig. 3 interprets the semantic relation of the words in a different angle using t-SNE [15] with Chinese conceptual classification by radials. The algorithm calculates a similarity measure between pairs of all the nine animal names which are identical in both domain ontologies plus the four co-occurred animal words in both the high dimensional space and in the low dimensional space. Although the analyzed nine animal words are relatively scattered, *wolf-jackal, chicken-dog, bat-koala* appear to share more similarities. This finding helps explain why those concepts tends to be used together. Expect for *bat-koala*, a neologism, used as an animal character for a modern cartoon story, the first two pairs, *wolf-jackal* and *chicken-dog,* seem to simply reflect the conventionalization (lexicalization) of the terms. The words *wolf and jackal* are highly correlated both in English and Chinese. And the *chicken-dog* pair, in fact, reflects the fact that these are two of the most prominent domesticized animals that figure prominently in agricultural societies and are often associated with the same context. This is probably the prototypical motif in Chinese poetry with chicken or dog, such as the idiom 鸡犬相闻 jīquǎn xiāngwén which means *roosters crow and dogs bark.* There are even more examples of chicken or dog used alone but typically associating the sound of the animal to houses in the village or other cozy and welcoming environments such as 鸡鸣jī míng and 报晓 bàoxiǎo in Tang poems which both mean *roosters crow.* Sounds of chicken and dogs are obviously also frequent motifs in children's literature in English as well. In particular, those co-occurred animal concepts tend to embody metaphorical meanings by constructing "simulations" through sensory modalities of bodily experiences [16].

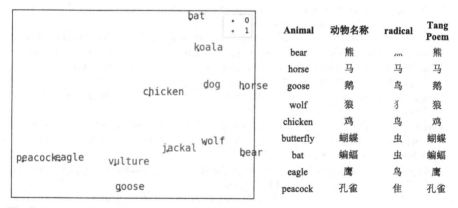

Fig. 3. Visual representation of word relations using t-SNE with the nine identical animal Chinese concepts classified by radials

4   Conclusion

This pilot study achieves to build an "animal" domain ontology with the cross-linguistic lexical resources for L2 young learners of Chinese. By comparing newly built domain ontology with the existing Tang Poem animal domain ontology, it is found that both lexical structures share most of the same upper ontology nodes, only a few additional nodes found in the modern cartoon corpus. More importantly, it is clear that complete overlaps, partially overlaps, variation are all found by examining the animal concepts. As a pedagogical implication, it would be easier for L2 young learners to start learning Tang Poems with the context including the animal concepts gained from their L1 knowledge base. On the one hand, it is worth noticing that some animal words in the context with literal meaning would be easier to comprehend than those of metaphorical meaning. On the other hand, language educators could take advantage of the embodied stimulations of different sensory modalities to better facilitate L2 learners to grasp the animal concepts with metaphorical meanings. Although this is only a small-scale preliminary study, it provides language educators different perspective to understand and meet L2 learners' needs and hopefully to facilitate writing and storytelling. Further construction of the ontological structure would be helpful to verify the current findings and expand the knowledge net of concepts and semantic associates systematically.

References

1. Prévot, L., Huang, C.R., Calzolari, N., Gangemi, A., Lenci, A., Oltramari, A.: Ontology and the lexicon: a multi-disciplinary perspective. In: Huang, C.R., Calzolari, N, Gangemi, A., Lenci, A., Oltramari, A., Prévot, L. (eds.) Ontology and the Lexicon: A Natural Language Processing Perspective, pp. 3–24. Cambridge: Cambridge University Press (2010)
2. Huang, C.R.: Notes on Chinese grammar and ontology: the endurant/perdurant dichotomy and Mandarin DM compounds. Lingua Sinica 1(1), 1–22 (2015)
3. Gruber, T.: Toward principles for the design of ontologies used for knowledge sharing. Int. J. Hum. Comput. Stud. 43(5–6), 907–928 (1995)
4. Pease, A., Fellbaum, A.: Formal ontology as interlingua: the SUMO and WordNet linking project and GlobalWordNet. In: Huang, C.R., Calzolari, N, Gangemi, A., Lenci, A., Oltramari, A., Prévot, L. (eds.) Ontology and the Lexicon: A Natural Language Processing Perspective, pp. 25–35. Cambridge: Cambridge University Press ((2010)
5. Aitchison, J.: Words in the Mind: An Introduction to the Mental Lexicon. Blackwell, Malden (2003)
6. Huang, C.R.: From Synergy to knowledge: corpus as a natural format for integrating multiple educational resources. In: The 4th National Natural Language Processing Symposium, the Philippines. De LaSalle University, Manila (2007)
7. Jiang, N.: Lexical representation and development in a second language. Appl. Linguis. 21, 47–77 (2000). https://doi.org/10.1093/applin/21.1.47
8. Takashima, H., Yamada, J.: Shrinkage of the mental lexicon of Kanji in an elderly Japanese woman: the effect of a 10-year passage of time. J. Cross Cult. Gerontol. 25(1), 105–115 (2010). https://doi.org/10.1007/s10823-009-9106-x.PMID19957202
9. Huang, C.R., Lo, F.J., Chang, R.Y. Chang, S.: Sinica BOW and 300 Tang Poems: an overview of a bilingual ontological Wordnet and its application to a small ontology of Tang poetry. In: Workshop on Possibilities of a Knowledgebase of Tang Civilization. Institute for Research in Humanities, Kyoto University, pp. 20–21 (2004)
10. Niles, I., Pease, A.: Linking lexicons and ontologies: mapping wordnet to the suggested upper merged ontology. In: Proceedings of the IEEE International Conference on Information and Knowledge Engineering. (IKE 2003), Las Vegas, Nevada (2003)
11. Deng, J., Dong, W., Socher, R., Li, L.J., Li, K., Fei-Fei, L. ImageNet: a large-scale hierarchical image database. In: 2009 IEEE Conference on Computer Vision and Pattern Recognition, IEEE, pp. 248–255 (2009)

12. Brezina, V., Weill-Tessier, P., McEnery, A. #LancsBox v. 5.x. [software] (2020). http://corpora.lancs.ac.uk/lancsbox
13. Zhu, Y.P., Huang, C.R. A Student Grammar of Chinese. Cambridge University Press (In Press, 2020)
14. Kutuzov, A., Elizaveta K.: WebVectors: a toolkit for building web interfaces for vector semantic models. In: International Conference on Analysis of Images, Social Networks and Texts. Springer, Cham (2016)
15. Van der Maaten, L., Hinton, G. Visualizing high-dimensional data using t-SNE. J. Mach. Learn. Res. 9(Nov), 2579–2605 (2008)
16. Barsalou, L.W.: Perceptions of perceptual symbols. Behav. Brain Sci. 22(4). 637–660 (1999)

Tracing Lexical Semantic Change with Distributional Semantics: Change and Stability

Jing Chen$^{(\boxtimes)}$, Bo Peng, and Chu-Ren Huang

Department of Chinese and Bilingual Studies, The Hong Kong Polytechnic University, Yuk Choi Road 11, Hung Hom, Kowloon, Hong Kong, China
jing95.chen@connect.polyu.hk, {peng-bo.peng,churen.huang}@polyu.edu.hk

Abstract. Recent studies suggest an increasing interest in detecting lexical semantic changes in the context of distributional semantics. However, most proposals have been implemented with English datasets but not much with Chinese data. This paper thus presents an exploratory study using the popular Skip-gram models and post-processing operations to obtain historical word embeddings, testing whether methods in fashion could capture lexical semantic change in Chinese historical texts. Our results demonstrate a positive answer to this question by suggesting interesting cases which may have undergone the process of meaning generalization and shown competence among homographs. Additionally, our analysis also indicates that social contexts play an important role in lexical semantic change.

Keywords: Lexical semantic change · Diachronic word embeddings · Social context

1 Introduction

Lexical semantic change, studying how lexical meanings have changed over time, has long been discussed in the linguistics community. Historical linguists are mostly concerned with how to conceptualize individual meaning changes into different types of mechanisms, [1–4], and also how to reveal the regularities and constraints in the process of lexical semantic change [5–7].

With the recent advance in the field of natural language processing and the availability of large historical corpora, recent studies situating lexical semantic change at the intersection of linguistics and computer science bring new insights to this ever-young topic. It also serves as a promising methodology to supplement traditional linguistic findings with more empirical evidence from large-scale data [8–13].

Over the past two decades, a growing number of proposals exploiting statistical and computational methods have been put forward and implemented to detect and evaluate lexical semantic change in historical texts [8,11,12,14,15]. Among these proposed methods, most make use of diachronic word embeddings

© The Author(s), under exclusive license to Springer Nature Switzerland AG 2023
Q. Su et al. (Eds.): CLSW 2022, LNAI 13495, pp. 244–252, 2023.
https://doi.org/10.1007/978-3-031-28953-8_19

to detect the meaning changes [16–19]. However, current work is mainly conducted for English [11–13], while much fewer attempts have been made for Chinese data [20,21].

This paper serves as an exploratory study on Chinese lexical semantic change, testing whether the predominant method could work in Chinese texts. We trained static word embeddings on People's Daily to obtain word embeddings for four intervals from 1953 to 2003, respectively. The word embeddings are post-processed to align semantic spaces between two adjacent intervals and are then quantified by how far they have moved in the shared space. Our results suggest interesting cases that underwent meaning changes from 1953 to 2003, such as '推出' and '加盟', and that experienced competence among homographs for dominant usages, such as '帅' and ''机制'. Besides, we briefly discussed the impact of social contexts on meaning change.

The remainder of this paper is organized as follows. Section 2 briefly summarizes studies exploiting computational approaches to detect lexical semantic changes and then situates our work with previous findings. In Sect. 3, we introduce our data and method. Section 4 describes and also discusses the preliminary results. This paper ends up with a brief conclusion and further steps for our work.

2 Related Work

We have witnessed an increasing number of papers statistically investigating lexical semantic change over the past twenty years. These contemporary works on semantic change roughly relied on two indicators: frequency and distribution. The frequency-based analysis holds a basic idea that changed meaning could be a possible reason for frequency fluctuation [15,16]. For example, the sudden frequency rise of *gay* in the 1980s does have an underlying meaning change, from 'happy' to 'homosexual'. Compared to frequency signals, distributional information provides more direct evidence to identify meaning change. Simply put, the distribution-based methods generally take the change of context information of target words in diachronic corpora as an approximation of meaning change [22,23].

The distribution-based methods later become predominant and a variety of distributional proposals have been implemented to model meaning change over time [11,14,19]. Earlier work exploits co-occurrence matrices to record co-occurrence patterns and then directly makes comparisons between target intervals [24,25]. Later, the arrival of word2vec revolutionized the method of word representations with significant improvements in precision and efficiency [9] and also spurred the study of using distributional models to detect semantic change. The workflow of applying static word embeddings to semantic change typically is 1)first training individual word embeddings on diachronic corpora for time-sliced intervals, and 2) then post-processing word embeddings by projecting embeddings living in different periods onto the same space for further comparison [11,16,18,19].

Table 1. Overview of four subcorpora: *C1, C2, C3, and C4*

Periods	Word tokens(million)	Word types(million)
C1	164	1.15
C2	98	0.58
C3	155	1.26
C4	176	1.28

Word2vec models generally train one vector for a single word form, which does not differentiate the possible senses of each word. Meanwhile, some proposals, such as state-of-the-art BERT models [26], take this task to a sense-level detection by training different embeddings for different senses. For example, [27] obtain representations for each occurrence of target words using BERT models [26], then clustered them into different usage types making use of the K-Means clustering algorithm, and then measured semantic change with multiple metrics. Other models, but less widely used, such as topic-based analysis, K nearest neighbor analysis, and ensemble models, have also been put forward in existing studies [28–30]. However, the recent SemEval2020 shared task1 working on unsupervised lexical semantic change detection surprisingly indicated that static neural embeddings outperformed other paradigms in both two subtasks: whether a word's meaning changed and to what extent a word's meaning changed [13].

3   Methodology

Building on the insightful findings from previous studies, this paper, as an exploratory study, investigates Chinese lexical semantic change using static neural embeddings, firstly.

Corpora. Detecting lexical semantic change requires the target corpus containing temporal information. Our dataset is a 50-year dataset collected from *People's Daily*, one of the most popular newspapers in China, spanning from 1953 to 2003. To our knowledge, this is the largest dataset with the longest time span that is publicly free to all texts. To continuously monitor lexical semantic change and to cover the most critical milestones in the Chinese history of these 50 years, we split the dataset into four roughly equal periods: from 1953 to 1966 (*C1*), from 1967 to 1978 (*C2*), from 1979 to 1991 (*C3*), from 1992 to 2003 (*C4*).

Preprocessing. We first conduct data cleaning, such as removing all website links, blank lines, and other non-character signs, like '#, $, %, *'. We then exploit *Thulac*[1] package for word segmentation. The statistics of the preprocessed corpora are presented in Table 1.

---

[1] Thulac, THU lexical analyzer for Chinese. More information could be accessed via https://github.com/thunlp/THULAC-Python.

Shared Vocabulary. The varying sizes for each subcorpora and errors introduced by word segmentation necessitate a normalization of raw frequencies into measures such as instances per million. We assume that words with a normalized frequency larger than 1 are adopted in the lexicon for each subcorpus. To track the change in word usage over the four periods, we first built a shared vocabulary V by intersecting four wordlists for four subcorpora[2], which has a capacity of 12,548 words (see Table 2).

Table 2. Normalized words in each period and the shared vocabulary

	C1	C2	C3	C4
Words	20, 378	18, 576	24, 564	25, 028
Shared vocabulary	12, 548			

Training Models. In line with previous findings, we investigated lexical semantic change with static neural word embeddings in this paper. Such a detection system generally takes three components: a model for semantic representations, an alignment technique, and a change measure [13]. We first train static word embeddings for each subcorpus using the two most popular models, both CBOW and Skip-gram models [9]. We then evaluate the quality of word embeddings using the biggest Chinese word similarity benchmark dataset *COS960* [31]. The results suggest that word embeddings trained by Skip-gram models have higher correlation scores, around 0.5[3] (p <0.01), which are supposed to provide a better basis for further processing.

Post-Processing. We then selected word embeddings trained by Skipgram models for post-processing by aligning every two consecutive models into a shared space using the Orthogonal Procrustes algorithm [18,19], such as projecting the C2 model onto C1's space, and making vectors between two adjacent intervals comparable. C1 and C2 intervals are also aligned as we expect that longer time intervals would capture more statistically salient meaning changes.

4 Results and Discussion

By projecting word embeddings for target intervals onto the same semantic space, we could speculate semantic change by measuring cosine similarities between word embeddings for the same word living in different time intervals. The larger the cosine similarity, the more consistent its contexts across the compared intervals, and possibly the more stable its meaning. On the contrary, the

---

[2] Nouns referring to institutions and places, numbers, quantifiers, and exclamation words are removed as stop words.

[3] Considering the scale of raw data and the loss of word pairs in each subcorpus, as well as the relation between 'cosine similarity' and 'true similarity', we assume the correlation score here is reasonable.

smaller its cosine similarity, the more possible a word that has changed its meaning.

Our work builds on the intuition that radical social events may bring about significant lexicon changes [32]. Relying on this intuition, we design four roughly equal parts, covering the most important milestones from 1953 to 2003, for comparison and to estimate whether significant semantic changes occurred in resonance with substantial social changes. For our analysis, we first evaluate this question by assessing lexical semantic change between every two consecutive intervals by calculating cosine similarities for each word in the shared vocabulary. Since semantic change is in nature cumulative, we also align the first interval $C1$ approximately representing word usage in the 50s with the last interval $C4$ approximately representing word usage in the 90s for comparison, which enables us to identify words whose meanings have changed, statistically.

4.1 Interval Comparisons

We compare words in terms of semantic change across every two adjacent intervals by calculating and ranking their cosine similarities. Statistics is presented in Table 3.

If words whose cosine similarities are less than 0.5 are deemed as having significant meaning changes across the discussed intervals, results indicate that most words in the shared vocabulary stay relatively stable across the adjacent intervals, as much fewer words have a score within the range of 0.0 to 0.5, with 1.1% of words for the C1C2 interval, 1.89% for the C2C3 interval, and 0.2% for the C3C4 interval.

Among these three compared groups, the C2C3 interval seems to have more significant changes, while the C3C4 interval has fewer words statistically showing meaning changes. The C2C3 interval roughly represents the time of the Cultural Revolution (the C2 period) and the first 10 years of the Reform and Opening-up (the C3 period), which could be reasonably regarded as a time that underwent radical social changes in the history of Modern China. We also note that the division between C3 and C4 is out of practical considerations, keeping the length of each interval as much equal as possible, and there are no as significant milestones as C2 and C3 in the C4 interval. Therefore, the C3C4 interval is regarded as a period of history with fewer major social changes.

From the statistics here, we speculate that there is a higher correlating possibility between radical social changes and significant lexical semantic changes, which means that social contexts have significant impacts on lexical meaning changes, even for a common vocabulary.

4.2 Word Comparisons

To satisfy the curiosity of whether historical word embeddings capture any meaning changes sensitive to native speakers, we take the C1C4 interval for comparison with the intuition that the longer the time, the easier the changed words could be identified.

Table 3. The number of words on different scales of cosine similarities

	C1C2	C2C3	C3C4	C1C4
[0.0, 0.3)	1	3	0	8
[0.3, 0.4)	9	29	3	62
[0.4, 0.5)	128	204	19	305
[0.5, 0.6)	659	1060	136	1296
[0.6, 0.7)	3246	4324	965	4490
[0.7, 1.0]	8505	6928	11425	6387

In the C1C4 group, we first take words whose similarity score is lower than 0.3 as target words for further investigation. At the risk of oversimplifying, we extract the top nearest neighbors of these target words for preliminary discussions(see Table 4).

Table 4. Changed words with their cosine similarities and nearest neighbors in each period

Word	Cosine similarities	Nearest neighbours C1	C4
越共	0.2049	越盟；共军；叛乱	农德孟；杜梅；阮文
推出	0.2110	推出手；推开；推出去	面世；面市；问世
南越	0.2758	印度支那；败局；泰国；西贡	亡基；辽代；谒；观音堂
机制	0.2786	链霉素；合霉素；青霉素；人造胶	机制型；新机制；体制；制度化
帅	0.2899	尧舜；挂帅；穆桂英；诸葛	陈子华；程潜；关生；王子健
加盟	0.2910	边疆区；乌克兰共和国；土库曼共和国	现加盟；加盟站；加盟制

Our results demonstrated that the first sixth words of the eight target words, '越共', '推出', '南越', '机制', '帅', '加盟', have shown interesting usage shifts from 1953 to 2003, which further suggest two possible tendencies: generalization, and competence among homographs from dominant usages.

Neighboring words of '推出' are more concrete action verbs in *C1*, while its neighbors are more abstract in *C4* mostly referring to the launch of new products. Similarly, the neighboring words of '加盟' in the *C1* period mostly are countries, and its usage predominantly relates to accessing an influential organization. However, its dominant usage drifted to *franchise-related* concepts, such as stores, in the *C4* period.

The detected words, '南越', '越共', '机制', '帅',are homographs that are competing for dominance in two periods, respectively. For the term '南越', the dominant meaning is highly correlated with the Vietnam War (1955–1975) in the *C1* period. More crucially, the need to refer to Vietnam in terms of two separate entities by the north and south is, in fact, the consequence of the geopolitical situation during the Vietnam war, i.e., Vietnam was divided into two countries to the north and south. The duration of the Vietnam War coincides with the period between C1 and C2. However, the southern Vietnam government in Saigon no longer exists in C4, which cannot compete for the original meaning of '南越', a historical state in Chinese history.

This is corroborated by the changes of '越共', 'the Vietcong, the Vietnam communist party'. The C1 period is during the height of the Vietnam War, and the collocates of '越共' are historically situated, such as its predecessor '越盟', 'Viet Minh', and its role in the war such as '共军', '叛乱', which are underlying its roles as a belligerent in the Vietnam War. During the C4 period, the fight for independence and the Vietnam War were both past histories. Therefore, the term keeps the basic referential meaning of the party and hence is often used close to the characteristics of the party, such as the names of its leaders, '农德孟' and '杜梅'. These are interesting cases of usage drifts that indicate the necessity of contextualizing changes in social and historical environments.

Also, the word '机制', is used more frequently for the synthesis products, such as penicillin, in period *C1*. However, it refers more generally to the operating system of an organization or the market in *C4*. The term '帅' was predominantly used as the supreme commander in the period *C1* but was used more frequently as an adjective *handsome* in *C4*.

This is an open question of how social contexts influence word meaning in historical texts. Another related and more fundamental issue is now how to define nominal meanings. Note that nouns having endurant meanings refer to continuants and their denoting meanings do not change over time.

5   Conclusions

This paper exploits Skip-gram models with post-processing operations to obtain diachronic word embeddings to detect lexical semantic changes from 1953 to 2003. As an exploratory study, we briefly discussed the impact of social changes on meaning changes based on this 50-year newspaper dataset.

While we haven't extensively discussed how meaning has changed in a finer-grained time interval, our results still demonstrate a positive answer to the question of whether the predominant diachronic word embeddings could capture any meaning changes in Chinese data.

Due to the lack of evaluation datasets for the detection task, we leave our detection results under quantitative evaluation at the current stage. In addition, this paper generally focuses on whether and to what extent a word has changed, but does not step into the question of which sense(s) has changed. These questions are served as research tasks in the near future.

References

1. Bloomfield, L.: Language. Rinehart & Winston, Holt, New York (1933)
2. Ullmann, S.: The Principles of Semantics. Glasgow University Publications, Edinburgh

3. Bréal, M., Cust, N., Postgate, J.P.: Semantics: Studies in the Science of Meaning
4. Geeraerts, D.: Diachronic Prototype Semantics: A Contribution to Historical Lexicology. Oxford Studies in Lexicography, Oxford (1997)
5. De Saussure, F.: Course in General Linguistics. Columbia University Press, Columbia (2011)
6. Traugott, E.C., Dasher, R.B.: Regularity in Semantic Change. Cambridge Studies in Linguistics, Cambridge (2002)
7. Zhao, Q., Huang, C.-R., Long, Y.: Synaesthesia in Chinese: a corpus-based study on gustatory adjectives in mandarin. Linguistics 56(5), 1167–1194 (2018)
8. Michel, J., et al.: Quantitative analysis of culture using millions of digitized books. Science 331(6014), 176–182 (2011)
9. Mikolov, T., Chen, K., Corrado, G., Dean, J.: Efficient estimation of word representations in vector space (2013)
10. Devlin, J., Chang, M.W., Lee, K., Toutanova, K.: Pre-training of deep bidirectional transformers for language understanding, Bert (2019)
11. Tahmasebi, N., Borin, L., Jatowt, A.: Survey of computational approaches to lexical semantic change (2019)
12. Kutuzov, A., Øvrelid, L., Szymanski, T., Velldal, E.: Diachronic word embeddings and semantic shifts: a survey (2018)
13. Schlechtweg, D., McGillivray, B., Hengchen, S., Dubossarsky, H., Tahmasebi, N.: SemEval-2020 task 1: unsupervised lexical semantic change detection. In: Proceedings of the Fourteenth Workshop on Semantic Evaluation, Barcelona, December 2020. International Committee for Computational Linguistics (2020)
14. Sagi, E., Kaufmann, S., Clark, B.: Semantic density analysis: comparing word meaning across time and phonetic space. In: Proceedings of the EACL 2009 Workshop on GEMS: Geometrical Models of Natural Language Semantics, pp. 104–111, March 2009
15. Hilpert, M., Gries, S.: Assessing frequency changes in multistage diachronic corpora: applications for historical corpus linguistics and the study of language acquisition. Literary Linguist. Comput. 24, 385–401 (2009)
16. Kulkarni, V., Al-Rfou, R., Perozzi, B., Skiena, S.: Statistically significant detection of linguistic change (2014)
17. Kim, Y., Chiu, Y.-I., Hanaki, K., Hegde, D., Petrov, S.: Temporal analysis of language through neural language models (2014)
18. Hamilton, W.L., Leskovec, J., Jurafsky, D.: Cultural shift or linguistic drift? comparing two computational measures of semantic change. In: Proceedings of the 2016 Conference on Empirical Methods in Natural Language Processing, Austin, Texas, Association for Computational Linguistics, November 2016
19. Hamilton, W.L., Leskovec, J., Jurafsky, D.: Diachronic word embeddings reveal statistical laws of semantic change (2018)
20. Tang, X., Qu, W., Chen, X.: Semantic change computation: a successive approach. In: Cao, L., et al. (eds.) BSI/BSIC -2013. LNCS (LNAI), vol. 8178, pp. 68–81. Springer, Cham (2013). https://doi.org/10.1007/978-3-319-04048-6_7
21. Tang, X., Qu, W., Chen, X.: Semantic change computation: a successive approach. World Wide Web 19, 375–415 (2016). https://doi.org/10.1007/s11280-014-0316-y
22. Harris, Z.S.: Distributional structure. Word 10(2–3), 146–162 (1954)
23. Firth, J.R.: A synopsis of linguistic theory, 1930–1955 (1957)
24. Gulordava, K., Baroni, M.: A distributional similarity approach to the detection of semantic change in the Google Books ngram corpus. In: Proceedings of the GEMS 2011 Workshop on GEometrical Models of Natural Language Semantics, Edinburgh, UK, Association for Computational Linguistics, July 2011

25. Rodda, M.A., Senaldi, M., Lenci, A.: Panta rei: tracking semantic change with distributional semantics in ancient Greek. Italian J. Comput. Linguist. **3**, 11–24 (2017)

26. Devlin, J., Chang, M., Lee, K., Toutanova, K.: BERT: pre-training of deep bidirectional transformers for language understanding. In: Proceedings of the 2019 Conference of the North American Chapter of the Association for Computational Linguistics: Human Language Technologies, Volume 1 (Long and Short Papers), Minneapolis, Minnesota, Association for Computational Linguistics, June 2019

27. Giulianelli, M., Del Tredici, M., Fernández, R.: Analysing lexical semantic change with contextualised word representations. In: Proceedings of the 58th Annual Meeting of the Association for Computational Linguistics, Association for Computational Linguistics, July 2020

28. Wijaya, D.T., Yeniterzi, R.: Understanding semantic change of words over centuries. In: Proceedings of the 2011 International Workshop on DETecting and Exploiting Cultural DiversiTy on the Social Web, DETECT 2011, pp. 35–40, New York, Association for Computing Machinery (2011)

29. Gonen, H., Jawahar, G., Seddah, D., Goldberg, Y.: Simple, interpretable and stable method for detecting words with usage change across corpora. In: Proceedings of the 58th Annual Meeting of the Association for Computational Linguistics, Association for Computational Linguistics, July 2020

30. Gruppi, M., Adali, S., Chen, P.: Schme at semeval-2020 task 1: a model ensemble for detecting lexical semantic change (2020)

31. Huang, J., Qi, F., Yang, C., Liu, Z., Sun, M.: COS960: a Chinese word similarity dataset of 960 word Pairs. arXiv preprint arXiv:1906.00247 (2019)

32. Diao, Y.: The Development and Reform of Mainland Chinese in the New Era. Hung Yeh Publishing, Taibei (1995)

A Study on the Recovery of Omitted Constituents in Chinese Elliptical Sentences

Han Yan[1,2], Yiran Zhao[1,2], Peipei Sun[1,2], and Yanqiu Shao[1,2(✉)]

[1] College of Information Sciences, Beijing Language and Culture University, Beijing, China
[2] National Language Resources Monitoring and Research Center (CNLR) Print Media Language Branch, Beijing, China
yqshao163@163.com

Abstract. Rule-based processing of an elliptical sentence corpus and the construction of a dataset is the basis for various elliptical recovery tasks. We clarify the scope of Chinese elliptical sentences from a linguistic point of view, manually annotate the existing elliptical corpus, and construct a dataset for elliptical recovery. Moreover, we address the problems of different criteria for judging ellipsis and different degrees of fineness in recovering elliptical components in the manual annotation process and study the criteria for recovering elliptical components of Chinese elliptical sentences based on the needs of elliptical recovery tasks and the operability of computers. The linguistic explanation provides a reference for the dataset's expansion in the subsequent tasks of omission position detection and omission-referent disambiguation.

Keywords: Ellipsis recovery · Elliptical sentence · Elliptical constituent · Semantic role

1 Introduction

Ellipsis is a vital topic in linguistics. Traditional linguistics focuses on explaining ellipsis from the cognitive perspective. The study of ellipsis in traditional Chinese linguistics began with Ma [1], followed by Li [2], who proposed that ellipsis is the omission of substantive words that serve as syntactic components, such as subjects and objects. Then Lv [3] analyzed the way of omission. Moreover, Lv [4] developed relevant theories. Furthermore, Wang Wei-Hsien broadened the exploration and deepen the study of ellipsis based on the "Three Flats" theory [6]. Since the 1980 s Wang [7], Zhu [8] and Chen [9] have further compared and distinguished ellipsis with zero-anaphora, implication, hint, and other ellipsis phenomena, broadening the exploration and study of ellipsis. Liu [5] focused on the structure "X+de(的) " in modern Chinese, exploring and confirming the presuppositional role of "de(的) " in pragmatics.

Computational linguistics focuses on solving the obstacles brought by omissions to Chinese information processing tasks in engineering practice.

© The Author(s), under exclusive license to Springer Nature Switzerland AG 2023
Q. Su et al. (Eds.): CLSW 2022, LNAI 13495, pp. 253–264, 2023.
https://doi.org/10.1007/978-3-031-28953-8_20

Cao et al. [10] proposed an empty anaphora resolution in semantic ellipsis based on a hierarchy of linguistic components. Yin et al. [11] proposed a semantic-based omission determination approach from the syntactic meaning and built an omission recovery model at the semantic level. Huang et al. [12] analyzed and introduced the relevant parsing methods for zero anaphora from a linguistic perspective. Jiang et al. [13] systematically compared the domestic and international research methods of zero anaphora and pointed out the factors that limit the study of zero-anaphora resolution. Zheng et al. [14] proposed a multi-attention fusion model toward the comprehension of short Chinese text.

Traditional linguistics studies the phenomenon of modern Chinese omission mainly by way of introspection, while computational linguistics focuses on presenting the methods and results of omission recovery. This paper focus on the recovery of omission components in Chinese texts. We first present information about the size and content of our corpus and the construction of the dataset. Then we elaborate the rules for corpus annotation, including clarifying the definition of the omission phenomenon in this study and determining the scope of omission recovery and providing a linguistic explanation for the restoration of omissions to be studied. Finally, we present our future tasks and related work to be carried out based on the dataset for sentence-level Chinese ellipsis resolution.

2   Ellipsis Corpus Extraction and Annotation

Our study for elliptical sentences is based on an existing corpus of semantic dependency graphs. The aim is to improve the accuracy of the dependency analyzer in analyzing the corpus through a targeted study of Chinese omission.

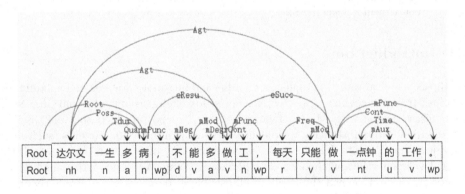

Fig. 1. The semantic dependency graph

Semantic dependency analysis focuses on the semantic relationships among constituents and emphasizes that a component with multiple parent nodes is called a multi-parent node in a dependency graph. [15]. The characteristic of

multi-parent nodes makes itself an essential manifestation of the omission phenomenon in semantic dependency graphs, so multi-parent nodes usually represent the omission of semantic components (Fig. 1). In the sentence "达尔文一生
多病,不能多做工,每天只能做一点钟的工作。 (Darwin was sick all his life and
could not do much work, and could only do one hour of work a day.)", "达尔
文(Darwin) " is a multi-parent node. "多病(was sick) " "做工(do work) " and
"做(do) " are its three parent nodes. The semantic role of "达尔文(Darwin) " is
omitted twice in the next two clauses and needs to be recovered.

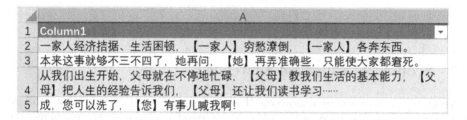

Fig. 2. The recovered text

The scale of the existing semantic dependency graph corpus is 21,729 sentences, from which we screened and extracted a total of 3,476 sentences of actual
text containing omissions as the raw material we need to annotate. Inside brack-
ets "【】" are the omitted components that are restored (Fig. 2). These texts cover
formal and informal genres, including news, novels, plays and textbooks. The
annotators annotated the 3476-sentence corpus for recovery and constructed an
elliptical sentence corpus of size 3057 sentences, with 1774 sentences restored
from news and 471 from novels, 233 sentences restored from plays, 579 sentences
restored from textbooks.

Based on the elliptical sentence corpus, we construct a dataset of ellipsis
recovery and explain the details of the recovery of omitted constituents from a
linguistic perspective to serve the subsequent tasks of ellipsis recovery in Chinese
text such as an ellipsis position detection and an ellipsis anaphora resolution.
The final result is a Chinese text omission elimination dataset with a size of
3057 sentences (Fig. 3). Recovered-omission components marked with "【】" in
Fig. 2 correspond to "content" in Fig. 3, and "index" indicates the position of an
elliptical constituent. For example, in the first sentence, "index:13" indicates that
there is an omission immediately following the 13th character. And "content:一
家人 " means that the elliptical content is "一家人 ".

In the process of annotation, for the ongoing task of Chinese text omission disambiguation, we define the omission phenomenon under study and make
trade-offs for the omitted components to be recovered; combined with linguistic
theories, we organize and elaborate the necessary annotation specifications.

{"uuid": "news_1701", "text": "一家人经济拮据、生活困顿，穷愁潦倒，各奔东西。",
                    "targets": [{"index": "13", "content": "一家人"},
                                {"index": "18", "content": "一家人"}]}
{"uuid": "novel_423", "text": "本来这事就够不三不四了，她再问，再弄准确些，只能使大家都窘死。",
                    "targets": [{"index": "16", "content": "她"}]}
{"uuid": "edu_444", "text": "从我们出生开始，父母就在不停地忙碌，教我们生活的基本能力，
                            把人生的经验告诉我们，还让我们读书学习....",
                    "targets": [{"index": "18", "content": "父母"},
                                {"index": "29", "content": "父母"},
                                {"index": "40", "content": "父母"}]}
{"uuid": "play_256", "text": "成，您可以洗了，有事儿喊我啊！",
                    "targets": [{"index": "8", "content": "您"}]}

Fig. 3. The ellipsis-recovered database

3 Scoping of Elliptical Sentence

An ellipsis is an approach to access the concise expression and the clear understanding. According to Wang Wei-Hsien's "Three Flats" theory, the phenomenon of ellipsis can be specifically explained as syntactic ellipsis, semantic ellipsis and pragmatics ellipsis. The ellipsis studied in this paper belongs to the category of pragmatics. And based on the theory, the following paper identifies and summarizes the relevant concepts of ellipsis, and clarifies the scope of the research on ellipsis.

3.1 Ellipsis

Syntactic Ellipsis. Syntactic ellipsis is the deletion of syntactic components, mainly including the Ingredient-Nested structure, the Predicate-Coherent structure. In e.g.(1,2), "推选(elected) " and "当(be) ", "转(turned) " and "看(looked) " share the same subject argument "他(him) " and "他(He) " separately.

(1) 咱们推选他当主席。 (*Ingredient-Nested structure*)
    (We elected him to be the chairman.)
(2) 他转过身来看了我一眼。 (*Predicate-Coherent structure*)
    (He turned and looked at me.)

It can be found that syntactic ellipsis exists in the deep semantic structure, which requires deep syntactic analysis to obtain the elliptical syntactic components.

Semantic Ellipsis. Semantic ellipsis is also called intentional ellipsis, mainly including Implication, Hint, and "De(的) "-structure. As presented in e.g.3, the judgment verb is omitted. The answer in e.g.4 implies, "I don't know what time it is". In e.g.5, a human entity is lacking.

(3) 今天周六。 (*Implication*)
    (Today is Saturday.)

(4) -几点了? -我没带手表。 (*Hint*)
(-What's the time? -I don't have a watch.)
(5) 他是卖菜的。 (*"De(的)"-structure*)
(He is a vegetable seller.)

In sum, the syntactic ellipsis and semantic ellipsis are both deep structural ellipsis, and the omission of constituent is achieved in the process of transferring from the deep structure to the surface structure [16].

Pragmatics Ellipsis. Pragmatics ellipsis is a direct deletion in the surface structure whose elliptical constituents can be recalled from the context [17]. The pragmatics ellipsis includes but is not limited to zero-anaphora which is an inherited ellipsis, and the omitted constituents are mainly the dominant component of the predicate verb and the subject in the non-verb predicate statement [18] as examples shown below.

(6) [她 $_1$] 自从城里回来后 , [$\varnothing_1$]^1 整天心神不安。
(She has been distracted all day since returning from the city.)
(7) 他有个[弟弟 $_1$], [$\varnothing_1$]打工去了。
(He has a younger brother who went to work.)

3.2 The Definition of Ellipsis in Our Work

In this research, we define the phenomenon of ellipsis based on Shao Jing-Min's [19] view from the perspective of Wang Wei-Hsien's "Three Flats" theory. An ellipsis is a sentence that is bounded by periods or question marks–and caused by the contextual constraints in the pragmatic category. We can explicitly recover the elliptical discourse components with the contextual cues, and the meanings of sentences do not change.

4 Linguistic Explanation for the Recovery of Omitted Components

The annotation process specified complex issues in linguistics, such as generalized-topic structures, which are not to be investigated. Pauses between subjects and predicates due to sentence length are not symbols of omission. The definite article attached to the main clause is restored together regardless of its length. Omitted elements in an adverbial-predicate structure are added beyond the structure instead of being directly attached to the main clause by insertion. The linguistic explanations are elaborated in the following subsections.

---

^{1} [$\varnothing_1$] indicates an omission whose equivalent could be found before or behind itself in the sentence.

4.1   The Generalized Topic Structure

If one or more subject-predicate structures are nested within a sentence and omitted as a whole at different positions in the same sentence, we adopt the view that such a subject-predicate structure is a "generalized topic" [20] and we don't treat it as an ellipsis.

(8) 台湾必须从「经济发展至上」的迷思中跳脱，[∅]² 才是真正永续经营之道。
   (Taiwan must break away from the myth of "economic development first" to truly run a sustainable business.)

(9) 站长在网上是不介入讨论的公正者，[∅]也养成我「耳朵不轻」的好习惯。
   (The webmaster is an impartial person who does not intervene in discussions on the Internet, which develops a good habit of mine.)

(10) 海云不懂音乐，[∅]正如她不懂世上绝大部分事物一样，但她也听出卡罗弹得多么半调子。
    (Haiyun didn't understand music, just as she didn't understand the vast majority of things in the world, but she could hear how half-tuned Carlo was playing.)

In the above set of sentences, the first clause is a subject-predicate structure acting as a generalized topic whose content is a complete event, and the second clause illustrates the first one semantically. The sentence is a typical generalized topic structure consisting of two clauses and we do not regard them as an ellipsis.

4.2   The Subject-Omission and the Non-Subject Structure

The prototype of the subject-omission is the subject-predicate sentence, and there is an explicit declarative relationship between the subject and the predicate. The non-subject sentence is not lacking a subject structurally but is indistinguishable between subject and predicate. So we need to distinguish between subject omission and non-subject one when making a judgment of the presence or absence of ellipsis in a sentence.

(11) [∅₁]面对国际，[台北 ₁]的压力很大。
    (In the face of international situation, Taipei is under great pressure.)

(12) [∅]环视周围，许多人在遇到事业瓶颈时，会兴起改行转业的念头。
    (Looking around, when many people encounter bottlenecks in their careers, they will have the idea of changing careers.)

The first clause in e.g.11 is a subject-predicate structure with the subject role, 台北 (Taipei), omitted. Therefore the subject of a subject-deficient sentence is only omitted due to restrictions or cues of context, thus it can be restored exactly in semantic.

---

² [∅] indicates a position in the text where an elliptical component may be considered to be added but is not needed.

In contrast, the first clause in e.g.12 is independent of context and is less restricted by other clauses. The subject in front of "环视(Looking) " is too abstract to specify. Pragmatically this is a speech act, which is communication between author and reader and is an essential expression of the interpersonal interaction function of language. Therefore, it is unabridged and does not require completion.

4.3   Complex Subject Roles

The complex subject role of a noun structure modified by multiple determiners usually occupies a clause format separately, with the other predicate parts appearing in sequence after the subject role.

(13) [在台湾黑暗山区与云雾对话百万年的桧木 $_1$], 不畏湿气 , [Ø$_1$]千年不朽。
      (The Hinoki who has communicated with cloud and fog in the dark mountainous area of Taiwan for one million years, is not afraid of moisture and is immortal for thousands of years.)
(14) [社经地位高、资源丰富的人 $_1$], 面临危机时「抗压性」比一般人强 , [Ø$_1$]解套的管道也多。
      (People with high socio-economic status and rich resources are more resistant than the average person when facing a crisis, and have more channels to unwind.)
(15) [许多孜孜兀兀、好不容易干到主管的老先生们 $_1$], 往往看不惯年轻一代的率性与散漫 , [Ø$_1$]殊不知新世代的创意和冲劲可能就从这种漫不在乎中迸发。
      (Many old gentlemen who are diligent and have finally managed to be in charge often dislike the recklessness and sloppyness of the younger generation, but they do not know that the creativity and drive of the new generation may burst out of this indifference.)

The first clause of the e.g.13 is a complex subject role, with a comma separating it in tone rather than semantically. If removed, the complex subject forms a typical subject-predicate structure with the first predicate "不畏(not afraid of) ". The subject "社经地位高、资源丰富的人 (People with high socioeconomic status and rich resources)" is the subject of "面临(face) " in the e.g.14, the phrase "许多孜孜兀兀、好不容易干到主管的老先生们 (Many old gentlemen who are diligent and have finally managed to be in charge)" is the subject of "看不惯(dislike) " in the e.g.15. Therefore, when the complex subject-role occupies the position of a single clause and is followed by multiple clauses, we recover the omitted subject-role for the second clause containing a predicate constituent.

4.4   Complex Central Arguments

The complex central argument in omitted constituent annotation means that the predicative constituent is preceded by a peripheral semantic role for modification and is syntactically represented as an adverbial-predicate structure.

The peripheral semantic role, which represents time, room, method, and tool, is usually in the position of adverbial, dependent on the central argument that represents the action and behavior. When the central semantic role is lacking in the central argument, it needs to be reinstated beyond the peripheral semantic role. When a central semantic role preceding central arguments is omitted, the central semantic role needs to be complemented beyond a peripheral semantic role.

(16) [Ø$_1$]从田园造景作起,继而[钟建志 $_1$]接触陶艺。
(Starting from garden landscaping, Zhong Jianzhi took up ceramics.)

(17) [Ø$_1$]四岁开始学英文, 学校的英文课对[她 $_1$]来说太简单。
(For her, who started learning English at the age of four, English classes at school were too easy.)

In the e.g.16, the first clause is an adverbial-predicate structure. The prepositional phrase "从田园造景(from garden landscaping)" which acts as the adverbial, is a peripheral semantic role suggesting the starting point of the event and is a modifier of the central argument "作起(Starting)". And "钟建志(Zhong Jianzhi)", which was omitted in advance, needs to be restored before "从田园造景作起(Starting from pastoral landscaping)". In the following sentence, according to the conventions of Chinese expressions, the omitted subject "她(she)" in the first clause should be added in front of the time component "四岁(at the age of four)".

The closeness between subjects and predicates is lower than that between adverbials and predicates, so the central semantic role and the action behavior are independent of each other, and the closeness between the two is weak. The peripheral semantic role played by the adverbial has a strong dependence on the central argument.

(18) a. [红桧种子 $_1$]彷佛有着神秘力量 , [Ø$_1$]在严苛的大自然中长成坚韧的通天巨木。
b.[红桧种子 $_1$]彷佛有着神秘力量, 在严苛的大自然中 [Ø$_1$]长成坚韧的通天巨木。
(The red juniper seeds seem to have a mysterious power to grow into a tough, giant tree in the harsh nature.)

Exceptionally, when the peripheral semantic role acting as an adverbial in the adverbial-predicate structure is not very closely related semantically to the pivotal argument element, the elliptical semantic role is positioned relatively freely and can be added before the gerund or can be inserted in the middle of the gerund structure. The peripheral semantic role generally includes time, space, or state, which indicates a range rather than defining a specific spot as the peripheral semantic role in the above example does.

We uniformly fill the elliptical components outside the peripheral semantic roles in the annotation process to facilitate computer operation. When a complex central argument element is formed due to modification or description by a peripheral semantic role, its omitted subject role is to be complemented beyond the peripheral semantic role.

4.5   Complex Subject-Predicate Structures

The structure between the subject and the predicate within the subject-predicate structure is loose, and there can be pauses or other components inserted between the subject and the predicate. Due to the looseness of the subject-predicate structure and the diversity of insertable components, the different components inserted will produce different omissions, and we will need to make different recoveries.

The Intervention of Peripheral Semantic Actors Does Not Form an Ellipsis. The omitted subject role is to be complemented outside the peripheral semantic role. However, there is no omission between a subject role and one action, and they are just separated by the peripheral semantic role when the peripheral semantic role intervenes between the subject-predicate structure.

(19) [邓相扬]基于地利之便，[Ø]得以长期记录邵族的宗教祭典。
      (Deng Xiangyang was able to record the religious rituals of the Shao people for a long time based on the convenience of the location.)
(20) [环保署]也针对油污处理、船体移除、渔民损失赔偿，[Ø]估计所需金额。
      (The EPA also estimated the amount needed for oil treatment, hull removal, and compensation for fishermen's losses.)

In the above sentences, the peripheral semantic role "地利之便 (the convenience of the location)" is introduced by the preposition "基于(based on) ", then intervenes between the subject role "邓相杨 (Deng Xiangyang)" and the verbal structure with "记录(record) " as the central thesis element. Although the comma separates the two parts, the comma here only serves as a marker for the intonational pause, and the two parts are combined into a single sentence structure, with the whole sentence being a complete sentence without omission.

The Intervention of Multiple Actions Forms an Ellipsis. Another situation of complex subject-predicate structure is that the sentence internally contains several verbal components representing multiple behavioral actions. Each of them acts as the central argument of each clause connected by conjunctions, contributing to sharing the same subject role, thus developing an elliptical sentence.

(21) [创业者 1]都会建立自己的经营团队，而且 [Ø1]几乎都是从以自己为中心的同心圆开始，[Ø1]逐步向外拓展人脉。
      (Entrepreneurs build their operating teams, and almost always start with concentric circles centered on themselves and gradually expand their networks outward.)
(22) [Ø1]为了提高国片制片量，[电影基金会 1]提议政府设立「国片辅导金」。
      (To increase the number of national films produced, the Film Foundation proposed to the government to set up a "National Film Coaching Grant".)

(23) [扁柏 $_1$]与红桧树型各异 , [Ø$_1$]笔直通天 , [Ø$_1$]含有较多油脂 , [Ø$_1$]可以提炼
出芳香精油。
(The cypress tree is different from the red cypress tree in shape, but the
cypress tree is straight and contains more oil, from which can be extracted
the aromatic oil.)

For example, e.g.21 is connected by a coordinating conjunction "而且(and) ",
and e.g.22 is connected by a non-coordinating conjunction "为了(for) ". Sometimes coordinating conjunctions can also be omitted, as presented in e.g.23, and
the omitted elements are considered recoverable ones.

4.6   Other Elliptical Constituents

The other elliptical components are mainly modifiers such as attributes and
adverbials. In Chinese texts, complements are more flexible than attributes and
adverbials, and there are fewer cases of complement ellipsis, so complements
are not considered in the scope of ellipsis recovery in this research. According to
linguistics ontology theory, attributes and adverbials can be further distinguished
into restrictive and descriptive categories. Based on the fact that "restrictive"
and "descriptive" are too subjective to make a clear boundary between them,
we stipulate that in a sentence, when the exact modifier-center phrase is used
again without the modifier, all the omitted modifiers should be recovered. In
addition, to ensure semantic integrity, all the attributives before the head are
supplemented regardless of length, as shown in examples.

(24) 后来他发现[这个56岁的男人 $_1$]真的有毛病 , [Ø$_1$]真的能为电影里的死死活
活痛不欲生。
(Later he found out that there was something wrong with this 56-year-old
man, and that he could ache for the dead and alive in the movie.)
(25) 后来我慢慢体会到[这片大地的古老 $_1$], [Ø$_1$]很适合表达现代人的孤独感。
(Later on, I slowly realized the antiquity of this land, which is very suitable
to express the loneliness of modern people.)

In the e.g.24, the definite-center structure of the second clause, i.e., "这个56岁
的男人(the 56-year-old man) ", is omitted by the previous hint. In the recovery process, we recover not only the main clause but also the definite article "这个56岁
的(this 56-year-old) ", although it is possible to complete the sentence by recovering only the main clause. Similarly, in the e.g.25, we restore the definite-center
structure as the subject, i.e., "这片大地的古老(the oldness of this earth) ".

5   Conclusion

Ellipsis recovery is an essential task for Chinese natural language processing.
We extract and filter the sentences containing omissions based on the existing
semantic dependency graph corpus, restore the complete semantics by manual
annotation, build the dataset, and give a linguistic interpretation of the rules

adopted in the annotation process. This work defines the elliptical sentence in the pragmatic category and distinguishes the general topic structure, the subject-omission, and the non-subject structure. Moreover, the research involves the determination and recovery of ellipsis under the intervention of complex subject roles, complex central arguments, and peripheral semantic roles.

On the well-constructed dataset, we will define the tasks of elliptical position detection and elliptical referent disambiguation. Specifically, we model omitted position detection as a sequence annotation task to detect which position in a sentence is omitted and omitted referent disambiguation as a relation extraction task to find out the referent objects of omitted positions in a sentence. We will then make the dataset publicly available to facilitate the methodological evaluation of the current task or definition of other tasks by other related researchers and jointly provide methodological-level references for improving the performance of automatic question and answer and machine translation in natural language processing.

We will also work on expanding the size of the corpus, refining the classification within the core semantic roles, giving more attention to the omission of non-core semantic components in Chinese texts, and expanding and improving the recovery rules based on engineering reality better to serve the analysis and automatic expression of semantics. We expect that our work will help improve the accuracy of semantic dependency analysis and better assist tasks involving natural language processing such as automatic question and answer, machine translation, and event extraction.

Acknowledgments. We thank the anonymous reviewers for their insightful comments. This work was supported by the National Natural Science Foundation of China (61872402), the Humanities and Social Science Project of the Ministry of Education (17YJAZH068),Science Foundation of Beijing Language and Culture University (supported by "the Fundamental Research Funds for the Central Universities") (18ZDJ03), and supported by the Fundamental Research Funds for the Central Universities, and the Research Funds of Beijing Language and Culture University(22YCX055).

References

1. Ma, J.Z.: Ma's Grammar, 1st edn. The Commercial Press, ShangHai (1989). (In Chinese)
2. Li, J.X.: Newly Written National Languages Act, 1st edn. The Commercial Press, ShangHai (1924). (In Chinese)
3. Lv, S.X.: The Essentials of Chinese Grammar, 1st edn. The Commercial Press, ShangHai (1947). (In Chinese)
4. Lv, S.X.: Problems of Chinese Grammar Analysis, 1st edn. The Commercial Press, BeiJing (1979). (In Chinese)
5. jingyao, L.: Nominal marker "de" in modern Chinese and its role of marking presupposition. In: Liu, M., Kit, C., Su, Q. (eds.) CLSW 2020. LNCS (LNAI), vol. 12278, pp. 34–40. Springer, Cham (2021). https://doi.org/10.1007/978-3-030-81197-6_3
6. Wang, W.X.: Study of ellipsis. Stud. Chinese Lang. **6**, 409–415 (1985). (In Chinese)

7. Wang, L.: Outline of Chinese grammar, 1st edn. Shanghai Education Press, Shang-Hai (1982). (In Chinese)
8. Zhu, K.Y.: Ellipsis and hint. J. Henan Univ. (Philos. Soc. Sci. Edn) **5**, 92–97 (1987). (In Chinese). https://doi.org/10.15991/j.cnki.411028.1987.05.020
9. Chen, P.: A discourse analysis of the Chinese zero anaphora. Stud. Chinese Lang. **5**, 363 (1987). (In Chinese)
10. Cao, J., Zhou, J.Y., Xiao, C.X.: Chinese empty anaphora resolution based on semantic construction analysis. Nat. Sci. J. Xiangtan Univ. **23**(4), 28–33 (2001)
11. Yin, H., Xu, W., Zhao, K., Dang, J.: Ellipsis recovering study based on concept model. Comput. Eng. **33**(22), 229–231+237 (2007)
12. Huang, X., Zhang, K.L.: Zero anaphora in Chinese-the state of art. J. Chinese Inf. Process. **23**(4), 10–15 (2009)
13. Jiang, Y.R., Zhang, Y.Y., Mao, T., Zhang Y.S: A survey of chinese zero anaphora resolution. J. Chin. Inf. Process. **34**(3), 1–12 (2020)
14. Zheng, J., Kong, F., zhou, G.D.: A study of ellipsis recovery for short text comprehension. J. Chin. Inf. Process. **34**(4), 77–84 (2020)
15. Zheng, L.J., Shao, Y.Q., Yang, E.H.: Analysis of the non-projective phenomenon in Chinese semantic dependency graph. J. Chin. Inf. Process. **28**(6), 41–47 (2014)
16. Wang, W.X.: Study of ellipsis. Stud. Chin. Lang. **6**, 409–415 (1985). (In Chinese)
17. Zheng, Y.H.: A study on the nature and norm of elliptical sentences **2**, 12–19+3 (1998). (In Chinese) https://doi.org/10.16499/j.cnki.1003-5397.1998.02.002
18. Chen, P.: A discourse analysis of the Chinese zero anaphora. Stud. Chin. Lang. **5**, 363 (1987). (In Chinese)
19. Shao, J.M.: A new explanation of "elliptical sentences" and "non-subject-predicate sentences". Lang. Study **7**, 26–28 (1991)
20. Song, R.: Stream model of generalized topic structure in Chinese text. Stud. Chin. Lang. **6**, 483–494+575 (2013)

Recognition of Disyllabic Intransitive Verbs and Study on Disyllabic Intransitive Verbs Taking Objects Based on Structure Retrieval

Shufan Zhou[1(✉)], Chengwen Wang[2], and Endong Xun[1]

[1] Beijing Language and Culture University, Beijing, China
zhshf9797@163.com
[2] Peking University, Beijing, China

Abstract. Verb-object constructions have always been the focus of Chinese gram-mar research. In Chinese, it has been agreed that transitive verbs take objects, while intransitive verbs taking objects are often confusing. There are very few studies addressing intransitive verbs taking objects. In particular, no investigations have been carried out on the quantitative analysis of the ability of disyllabic intransitive verbs taking objects of different structures and object semantics. Therefore, this study focused on the phenomenon of disyllabic intransitive verbs taking objects and made use of large-scale corpus to investigate the disyllabic intransitive verbs and their objects in order to enrich the understanding of unconventional verb-object constructions in the language. It first proposed a semantic role classification sys-tem on the basis of previous studies, and defined the word structure types, as the basis for judging the verb structure types and object semantic types in intransi-tive verb with object structure. Based on the BCC corpus, this study analyzed the top 4237 high-frequency disyllabic verbs in the fifth edition of Modern Chinese Dictionary. It used structure retrieval to complete the recognition of intransitive verb and its object acquisition, and artificially identified the verb structure types and object semantic roles. It was found that verb-object intransitive verbs have the strongest ability to take objects and the role of "quantity" is the semantic role that most often serves as the object of disyllabic intransitive verbs.

Keywords: Disyllabic intransitive verbs · Non-object objects · Structure types · Semantic roles · Structure retrieval

1 Introduction

In modern Chinese syntax, "Verbs occupy an indisputable position as the core of orga-nization" [1]. Therefore, verbs have always been the focus of research in the Chinese language field. There is the classical dichotomy of transitive and intransitive in the classi-fications of verbs. Traditional grammar simply holds that transitive verbs can take objects and intransitive verbs can not. However, with the development of language, intransitive

© The Author(s), under exclusive license to Springer Nature Switzerland AG 2023
Q. Su et al. (Eds.): CLSW 2022, LNAI 13495, pp. 265–282, 2023.
https://doi.org/10.1007/978-3-031-28953-8_21

verbs tend to take non-object[1] objects, such as '聚首北京' (jùshǒu běijīng, 'gather in Beijing'), '捐躯沙场' (juānqū shāchǎng, 'die on the battlefield'), '移民加拿大' (yímín jiānádà, 'immigrate to Canada') and so on.

Most existing studies have addressed the phenomenon of intransitive verbs taking objects through individual cases, without comprehensively and systematically studying the syntactic and semantic characteristics of intransitive verbs taking objects based on large-scale empirical corpus. On the one hand, the semantic types of the objects taken by intransitive verbs lack systematic recognition; on the other hand, intransitive verbs that can take objects are not limited to the monosyllabic verbs that some scholars have pointed out. Many disyllabic intransitive verbs in Chinese also have the ability to take objects. Starting from the perspective of disyllabic supplemented by the analysis of the structural types of words, it is of value to comprehensively investigate the ability of intransitive verbs to take objects. Therefore, this study set out to examine the structure of disyllabic intransitive verbs with non-object objects. Based on corpus analyses, the structural types of disyllabic intransitive verbs and the semantic roles of their objects in this structure were investigated quantitatively.

Empirical research based on statistical analysis of corpus provides a new research approach for analyzing such unconventional verb-object structure in Chinese grammar, and the conclusions drawn are more reliable than the introspective or case-by-case studies. The investigation on the tendency of the type of verb structure and the semantic role of the object based on quantitative analysis will also enrich the understanding of the realization of the intransitive verb with object structure, which will enrich the theoretical research of Chinese unconventional verb-object structure and at the same time have high practical value.

2 Research Status

There have been many studies on intransitive verbs with objects in the field of Chinese. Some scholars focus on the semantic features of objects and divide the objects of intransitive verbs from the semantic perspective. Zhao [2] believed that the objects of intransitive verbs are limited to the following types: self-object denoting momentum and time, the destination of the action, the point of origin of the action, the inverted subject which means "existential", the inverted subject which means "coming" and "appearing", the inverted subject which means "leave" and "disappear". Zhu [3] divided the objects of intransitive verbs into objects that represent time or degree, locative objects that represent the end point of motion, and existential objects that represent existence, appearance and disappearance. Guo[4] pointed out that, from the perspective of semantic types, intransitive verbs are abundant in objects, and they are beyond counting, and some objects are also difficult to be accurately classified from semantic types.

---

[1] Lin et al. once put forward in the "Modern Chinese Verb Dictionary" that "looking at the object from the back of the verb, the verbs are divided into two categories, those with object are called transitive verbs, and those without object are called intransitive verbs". This paper adopts the definition of intransitive verb and object by Lin et al., among which the object specifically includes patient, objective and result, and the non-object includes semantic roles except the patient, objective and result.

Some scholars have analyzed intransitive verbs which can take objects. Zhang [5] and Sun [6] et al. analyzed the intransitive verbs that take objects from the perspective of the number of syllables. They believed that intransitive verbs that can take objects have a tendency to be syllable restricted, and they are all monosyllabic. Guo [4] investigated intransitive verbs that take objects from the perspective of style, semantics, pragmatics and prosody. He pointed out that intransitive verbs that can take objects are frequently used verbs in spoken English, but have a wider range in newspaper style; they express human actions, behaviors, or emotions; they are the type of verbs that are most easily remembered; they are mainly monosyllabic. Diao [7], Gao [8], Liu [9], Zhang [10], Zhu [11] et al. analyzed the intransitive verbs that take objects from the perspective of the structural types of verbs, held that verb-object verbs with objects are particularly typical in the phenomenon of intransitive verbs becoming transitive. Based on the analysis of the collected use cases, they summarized the grammar conditions, semantic conditions and the development trend of "verb-object verb + object".

Existing research on the structure of intransitive verbs with objects in Chinese academic circles mostly focuses on case research and theoretical research. At the same time, it can also be found that the research topic needs to be further carried out: (1) In terms of the semantic characteristics of the objects taken by intransitive verbs, scholars generally believe that the semantic role of the objects carried by intransitive verbs cannot be object, but they have different opinions on the specific semantic roles of the objects. Due to the lack of quantitative analysis, there is still no general consensus on the semantic roles of the objects taken by intransitive verbs. (2) Up to now, there are many perspectives on intransitive verbs that take objects, and some scholars focus on verb-object intransitive verbs with object, little is known about the difference in the ability of intransitive verbs to take objects between intransitive verbs of the verb-object type and intransitive verbs of other structural types.

This study was an attempt to examine the structure of disyllabic intransitive verbs with objects. Firstly, according to the previous studies on semantic roles and word structure types, the semantic role system and word structure type system were developed to serve the subsequent classification of verb structure types and object semantic types. Secondly, disyllabic intransitive verb recognition and object acquisition were carried out based on structure retrieval technology. Finally, in view of the obtained corpus of disyllabic intransitive verbs with objects, the structural types of verbs and semantic roles of objects were identified, and on the basis of the identification results, the differences in the ability of verbs with different structural types to take objects and the tendency characteristics of object semantics in the phenomenon of disyllabic intransitive verbs with objects were summarized.

3   The Identification Basis of Object Semantic Roles and Verb Structure Types

This part clarifies the semantic role system and the word structure types, which subsequently serve as the basis for the identification of the object semantic roles and the verb structure types in the structure of intransitive verbs with objects.

3.1 Semantic Role System

At present, the semantic role classification systems established by the Chinese academic circle all directly refer to the practices of case grammar and valency grammar. The Chinese case relation system established by Lin et al. [12] is a very influential and representative system, which has three levels. The first level is character and situation. The second level is centered around the core of predicate verb, which consists of seven elements: subject, object, adjoiner, system, dependence, environment and basis-reason. The third level is the further classification of the seven elements, the subject is divided into three cases: agent, possessor, theme; the object is divided into three cases: patient, objective and result; the adjoiner is divided into three cases: dative, partner, benchmark; the system is divided into three cases: relative, ofpart and quantity; the dependence is divided into three cases: instrument, material, method; the environment is divided into four cases: scope, location, time, direction; the basis-reason is divided into three cases: accordance, cause and purpose. There are 22 cases in total, which provide a good foundation for the in-depth study of Chinese semantic roles. In Lin [12] and Yuan [13]'s description of the semantic role classification system, in addition to semantic interpretation, each case also lists the corresponding prepositional case markers.

In this study, the naming of semantic roles mainly adopted the explanation from Lin et al. [12], and the "direction" case was supplemented by "locative source" and "target destination" mentioned by Yuan [13]. "Locative source" refers to the place where the action and behavior begin, and "target destination" refers to the place where the action and behavior end. As for the specific identification of semantic roles, this study not only considered the semantic characteristics of each role, but also used the prepositional case markers for transformation analysis. In order to make the result of semantic role identification more accurate, based on the prepositional case markers mentioned by Lin and Yuan, referring to the research of Fang [14] and Yu [15] et al., this paper formulated the prepositional case markers used in the subsequent object semantic role identification. The semantic role system after fusion and corresponding prepositional case markers are shown in Table 1.

3.2 Verb Structure Types

In terms of the structural types of words, Huang and Liao [16] firstly divided compound words into composite, overlapping and additive, among which composite words include five structural types: union, partial positive, supplementary, verb-object and subject-predicate. The structure type of overlapping words is overlapping type, and the additive words include prefix type and suffix type. The identification of verb structure in this paper was based on the standards of Huang and Liao [16]; eight structural types were selected as the types of structure division of intransitive verbs that take objects subsequently: union, partial positive, supplementary, verb-object and subject-predicate, overlapping, prefix and suffix.

Table 1. Semantic role system and corresponding prepositional case markers.

Semantic role system		Prepositional case markers
subject	agent	被(bèi), 由(yóu), 让(ràng), 给(gěi), 归(guī), 叫(jiào)
	theme	
	possessor	
object	patient	把(bǎ), 将(jiāng)
	objective	把(bǎ)
	result	把(bǎ), 将(jiāng)
adjoiner	dative	给(gěi), 向(xiàng), 替(tì), 代(dài), 跟(gēn), 和(hé), 为(wèi), 当着(dāngzhe), 对(duì), 对于(duìyú), 于(yú), 管(guǎn), 就(jiù), 向着(xiàngzhe), 针对(zhēnduì), 面对(miànduì), 冲(chòng), 对着(duìzhe)
	partner	跟(gēn), 连(lián), 和(hé), 同(tóng), 与(yǔ), 随(suí), 像(xiàng)
	benchmark	比(bǐ), 比着(bǐzhe), 较(jiào)
system	relative	
	ofpart	
	quantity	
dependence	instrument	用(yòng), 拿(ná), 以(yǐ), 靠(kào)
	material	用(yòng), 拿(ná), 由(yóu), 把(bǎ)
	method	用(yòng), 以(yǐ), 拿(ná), 经(jīng), 靠(kào)
environment	scope	关于(guānyú), 就 (...问题) (jiù(...wèntí)), 在 (...方面、...上、...情况下、...条件下、...过程中) (zài(...fāngmiàn,...shàng,....qíngkuàng xià,...tiáojiàn xià,...guòchéng zhōng)), 围绕(wéirào)
	time	在(zài), 于(yú), 趁(chèn), 乘(chéng), 当(dāng), 赶(gǎn), 到(dào), 待(dài), 直到(zhídào), 等(děng), 至(zhì), 临(lín), 由(yóu), 自(zì), 从(cóng), 打(dǎ), 打从(dǎcóng), 经(jīng), 经过(jīngguò)
	location	在(zài), 于(yú), 当(dāng), 经(jīng), 经过(jīngguò), 临(lín), 顺着(shùnzhe), 沿(yán), 沿着(yánzhe), 挨(āi)
	locative source	从(cóng), 自(zì), 打(dǎ), 打从(dǎcóng), 由(yóu)
	target destination	到(dào), 至(zhì), 往(wǎng), 向(xiàng), 朝(cháo), 奔(bèn), 对着(duìzhe)

(*continued*)

Table 1. (*continued*)

Semantic role system		Prepositional case markers
basis-reason	accordance	按(àn), 照(zhào), 按照(ànzhào), 遵照(zūnzhào), 依照(yīzhào), 依(yī), 据(jù), 依据(yījù), 根据(gēnjù), 论(lùn), 靠(kào), 凭(píng), 借(jiè), 凭借(píngjiè), 以(yǐ), 本着(běnzhe), 比着(bǐzhe), 循着(xúnzhe), 沿(yán), 基于(jīyú), 鉴于(jiànyú)
	cause	因为(yīnwèi), 因(yīn), 为(wèi), 以(yǐ), 由(yóu), 由于(yóuyú), 出于(chūyú)
	purpose	为(wèi), 为着(wèizhe), 奔(bèn)

4 Data Foundation

4.1 Dictionary Resources and Corpus Resources

The disyllabic verbs examined in this paper were selected from the entry of disyllabic verbs in Modern Chinese Dictionary (5th Edition). There are 15,891 disyllabic verbs in Modern Chinese Dictionary (5th Edition). Considering the workload, this study obtained the word frequency table of disyllabic verbs in Modern Chinese Dictionary based on BCC (Beijing Language and Culture University Modern Chinese Corpus) [17]. According to the frequency, the first 4237[2] high-frequency disyllabic verbs were selected as the basis for the recognition of intransitive verbs that take objects.

The identification of disyllabic intransitive verbs and the acquisition of their objects were based on the structure retrieval function of BCC. Judging whether a verb is transitive or not and extracting the object of a verb requires full use of syntactic structure and functional information. Structure retrieval can effectively support the retrieval needs based on the nature and function of language units, thereby helping to identify intransitive verbs and obtain objects. The corpus in the BCC structure retrieval system is derived from the Chinese Syntactic Structure Treebank constructed by Lu et al. [18]. The Treebank is syntactically represented as chunked phrase structure trees (see Fig. 1), including three types of chunks: syntactic constituent chunks that form the basic structure of sentences, cohesive chunks that act as cohesive contexts, and auxiliary chunks that express additional semantics. The Treebank tags mainly include chunk property tags, chunk function and purpose tags, and sentence boundary tags (see Table 2). 1–4 in Table 2 are the chunk property tags. NP, VP, and UNK are mainly used to describe the nominality or predicate of the subject, the object, the whole predicate and the core predicate. NULL is used to uniformly mark the chunking properties of other constituents. 5–9 in Table 2 are the function tags of the chunk, which describes the syntactic roles of the chunk units in terms of syntax. 10–11 in Table 2 are the purpose tags of the chunk, which describes the connection function and the tone function of the chunk units from the discourse function and interpersonal function. 12–15 in Table 2 are the tags of sentence boundaries and levels.

---

[2] Select high frequency disyllabic verbs according to Zipf's law.

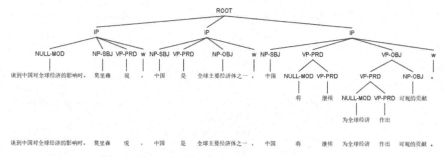

Fig. 1. Example of a chunked phrase structure tree.

Table 2. Treebank tag sets.

Serial number	Symbol	Tag type	Serial number	Symbol	Tag type	Serial number	Symbol	Tag type
1	VP	predicate chunk	6	NPRE	nominal predicate	11	AUX	auxiliary chunk
2	NP	nominal chunk	7	MOD	adverbial, complement	12	ROOT	single sentence or complex sentence
3	UNK	chunk that predicates juxtaposed with nouns	8	SBJ	subject	13	IP	complete clause
4	NULL	other property chunk	9	OBJ	object	14	HLP	one-member sentence or fragment
5	PRD	predicate	10	CON	cohesive chunk	15	W	punctuation

4.2 BCC Structure Retrieval System

BCC designs and implements a powerful query language (BCC search strategy). Users select the corpus, input the search strategy, and then can query the language fragments that conform to the search strategy. According to user needs, BCC designs retrievals with two different functions, simple retrieval and complex retrieval (structure retrieval). Among them, complex retrieval can improve the accuracy of extraction results by restricting parts of speech and length, and can also realize instantiated retrieval of the vocabulary in the same search strategy, thereby improving retrieval efficiency. Therefore, this paper chose complex retrieval on the query. The retrieval statement is in the form of "Query{Condition}Operation", "Query" is the query unit, "Condition" is used to limit the query unit on condition or output, and "Operation" mainly counts the frequency or context of the query unit. The specific composition of search strategy is described in Table 3.

Table 3. Composition description of the search strategy.

Search strategy	Constitution	Description	Example
Query	character or string	Chinese and English characters or strings	'被', '打击'
	part of speech symbol	Consistent with Peking University's part-of-speech tagging symbols	a, d, v, n, r, p, q, u, m, w
	~	Represents any word	'提高 ~' can match '提高水平'
	*	Indicates a clutch within a clause	'见*面' can match '见个面'
	phrase type symbol	The phrase type symbol adopts the tag symbol in the Chinese Syntactic Structure Treebank, in the form of lTag*Tagl	"INP-OBJ*NP-OBJI" represents a nominal object chunk
	()	"()" is enclosed outside the constituent unit inside the search strategy. The components in the i-th "()" are represented by "$i"	'把*(n)' captures the noun 'n'. '$1' is the noun 'n'
Condition	length restriction	len($1) = 2	'把*(n){len($1) = 2}' means that the length of the noun is 2
	content restriction	$1! = [着 著 向]	'朝(~)背后(v){$1! = [着著向]}' means that the word after '朝' cannot be '着', '著' or '向'
	output restriction	"print($i)" outputs the content in the i-th "()", if there is no print statement, the search result of the entire search strategy is output by default	'把*(n){print($1)' to output the noun 'n'
Operation	Freq	Output the frequency of the query unit	Item Freq
	Context	Output the context of the query unit	Context

4.3   Recognition of Disyllabic Intransitive Verbs and Acquisition of Their Objects

In order to identify intransitive verbs and obtain their objects from these 4237 disyllabic verbs, this study constructed a series of structural search strategies based on language rules. In Table 4, only the search strategies used in this paper are listed. For details, please refer to the Baidu Netdisk link[3].

Table 4. Search strategy for extracting object and object components.

Serial number	Search strategy
1	IVP-PRD*VerbVP-PRDIINP-OBJ*(~)NP-OBJI{print($1)}Freq
2	INULL-MOD*把*(n)NULL-MODIIVP-PRD*VerbVP-PRDI{print($1)}Freq
3	INULL-MOD*将*(n)NULL-MODIIVP-PRD*VerbVP-PRDI{print($1)}Freq
4	INP-SBJ*(~)NP-SBJIIVP-PRD*被*nVerbVP-PRDI{print($1)}Freq
5	INP-SBJ*(~)NP-SBJIIVP-PRD*由*nVerbVP-PRDI{print($1)}Freq

In Table 4, search strategy 1 realizes the object extraction of verbs. Search strategies 2–5 realize the extraction of the object components of verbs through the typical syntactic environment of the object, *Bǎ*(把) construction and *Bèi*(被) construction. 4237 verbs were traversed to replace "Verb" in the search strategy, and then the object or object component of the verb were extracted.

After that, the object instances of search strategy 1 and the results of search strategies 2–5 can be intersected to determine whether the verb is transitive or not. If a certain verb obtains a large number of instances through search strategy 1, and the instances cannot appear in *Bǎ*(把) construction and *Bèi*(被) construction, it proves that the verb is an intransitive verb that takes a non-object component. In the actual operation process, in order to ensure the typicality and universality of a certain usage, this study only regarded language instances with a frequency greater than 10 extracted by the search strategy as valid use cases. For each specific verb, which search strategy can be used to extract the results that meet the retrieval requirements, the corresponding verb is marked with the corresponding "Query id". The specific test process is shown in Fig. 2.

As shown in Fig. 2, when the verb does not have the Query1 tag, it is considered as an intransitive verb without object. When the verb has the Query1 tag but not Query2–5 tag, it means that the verb can take object but it does not have object argument, this study considers the verb to be an intransitive verb that can take non-object object. When the verb is marked with Query1 and marked with Query2–5, it means that the verb can take object and has object argument, and the verb is considered a transitive verb. Taking the verb '久违' (*jiǔwéi*, 'long absence') as an example, the retrieval results and markings are now explained in Table 5.

---

[3] https://pan.baidu.com/doc/share/bNya85m~do4LfI8OkIn07g-590695225
099967.(password:jgfd).

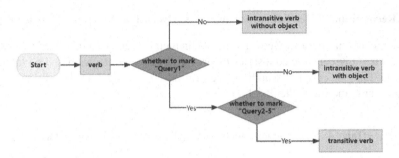

Fig. 2. Intransitive Verb Test Process.

Table 5. The retrieval results and markings related to '久违' (*jiǔwéi*, 'long absence').

Serial number	Search strategy	Retrieval results	Tag
1	IVP-PRD*久 违VP-PRDIINP-OBJ*(~)NP-OBJI{print($1)}Freq	'官场 21' '故国 15' '舞台 11' …	Query1
2	INULL-MOD*把*(n)NULL-MODIIVP-PRD*久 违VP-PRDI{print($1)}Freq	none	
3	INULL-MOD*将*(n)NULL-MODIIVP-PRD*久 违VP-PRDI{print($1)}Freq	none	
4	INP-SBJ*(~)NP-SBJIIVP-PRD*被*n久 违VP-PRDI{print($1)}Freq	none	
5	INP-SBJ*(~)NP-SBJIIVP-PRD*由*n久 违VP-PRDI{print($1)}Freq	none	

As shown in Table 5, the verb '久违' (*jiǔwéi*, 'long absence') is marked with Query1, but not with Query2–5, so '久违' (*jiǔwéi*, 'long absence') is determined as an intransitive verb with object. The statistical results for 4237 disyllabic verbs are shown in Table 6.

Table 6. Verb type and verb quantity statistics.

Verb type	Quantity
transitive verbs	2408
intransitive verb without object	524
intransitive verb with object	1305

5 Econometric Analysis of Disyllabic Intransitive Verbs with Object Structure

In order to investigate the tendency characteristics of disyllabic intransitive verbs with object structure in the choice of verb structure types and object semantic roles, this study used the obtained data of 1305 disyllabic intransitive verbs that take objects and their objects as the basis, using a combination of introspection and data analysis, artificially identified the structural types of verbs and the semantic roles that their objects can play. The certification process adopted the method of "two-two processing and third-party audit" to ensure the quality of certification. Finally, after the consistency check, the consistency rate of the identification of the structural type of the verb and the semantic role that its object can play remained above 70%.

After artificial identification of verb structure types and object semantic roles, it was found that 7 types of verb structure types and 16 types of object semantic roles can be contained in disyllabic intransitive verbs with object structure. The following will describe the data in detail from the two aspects of verb structure type and object semantic role.

5.1 The Structural Types of Intransitive Verbs with Object

In addition to single-morpheme words[4], all intransitive verbs that can take objects in this paper actually included seven structural types: subject-predicate, verb-object, partial positive, union, supplementary, suffix and overlapping. E.g:

a. 明帝崇祯自缢煤山 (subject-predicate type)
   Míngdì chóngzhēn zìyì méishān
   'Ming emperor Chongzhen hanged himself in the coal mountain'

b. 银泰牵手阿里巴巴 (verb-object type)
   Yíntài qiānshǒu ālǐ bābā
   'Intime joins hands with Alibaba'

c. 姚明久别赛场 (partial positive type)
   Yáomíng jiǔbié sàichǎng
   'Yao Ming is away from the court for a long time'

---

[4] In the data of disyllabic intransitive verbs and their objects in this paper, there are 5 single-morpheme words appearing as intransitive verbs, including '腻歪' (*nìwai*, 'disgusted'), '溜达' (*liūda*, 'walk'), '咆哮' (*páoxiào*, 'roar'), '辗转' (*zhǎnzhuǎn*, 'move') and '团圆'(*tuányuán*, 'reunion'), three of which can take objects, namely '溜达', '咆哮' and '辗转'. Examples of them with objects are '自己溜达公园' (*zìjǐ liūda gōngyuán*, 'walk in the park by myself', '巨狮咆哮山谷' (*jùshī páoxiào shāngǔ*, 'the lion roars the valley', and '民警辗转交城、文水等地' (*mínjǐng zhǎnzhuǎn jiāochéng, wénshuǐ děng dì*, 'police moved in Jiaocheng County, Wenshui County and other places').

d. 她往返重庆和温州两地 (union type)
   Tā wǎngfǎn chóngqìng hé wēnzhōu liǎngdì
   'She travels between Chongqing and Wenzhou'

e. 追车人这款日系SUV看齐宝马奔驰 (supplementary type)
   Zhuīchērén zhèkuǎn rìxì SUV kànqí bǎomǎ bēnchí
   'Car chaser, this Japanese SUV is on par with BMW and Mercedes-Benz'

f. 玩家进化精灵 (suffix type)
   Wánjiā jìnhuà jīnglíng
   'The player makes the sprite evolve'

g. 知识分子嚷嚷两句 (overlapping type)
   Zhīshì fènzǐ rāngrang liǎngjù
   'Intellectual shouts'

Based on these seven structural types, this study further conducted a statistical analysis on the intransitive verbs with object in the data. Figure 3 shows the proportion of the number of intransitive verbs with object in each structure type.

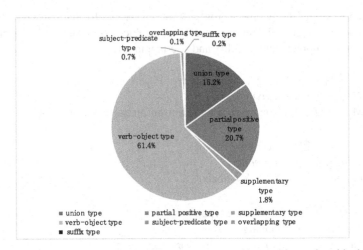

Fig. 3. Statistics on the distribution of structure types of intransitive verbs with object.

As shown in Fig. 3, although the intransitive verbs of the seven structural types of subject-predicate type, verb-object type, partial positive type, union type, supplementary type, suffix type and overlapping type can all carry objects, their abilities to carry objects are different. The verb-object intransitive verbs account for 61.4% of all the intransitive verbs with object, and the ability to take the object is the strongest. On the one hand, the total number of verb-object intransitive verbs is quite large, with a total of 1214. On the other hand, these verb-object intransitive verbs (799 in total) that can take objects tend to be more grammaticalized, such as '首' (*shǒu*, 'head') in the '聚首' (*jùshǒu*, 'gathering') does not reflect the original meaning, but expresses the meaning of "gathering" together with '聚' (*jù*, 'gather') as a whole. Followed by partial positive and union intransitive verbs, accounting for 20.7% and 15.2% respectively. Supplementary, subject-predicate, suffix and overlapping intransitive verbs have poor ability to take objects, among which the proportion of overlapping intransitive verbs is even only 0.1%, such intransitive verbs often have a strong colloquialism, such as '嚷嚷' (*rāngrang*, 'shout').

5.2   The Semantic Role of the Object of Intransitive Verbs

According to statistics, 16 semantic roles can appear in the object position of intransitive verbs, including quantity, location, locative source, target destination, time, instrument, material, method, accordance, cause, purpose, scope, dative, partner, theme, agent. E.g:

a. 新线铺轨**7935**公里 (quantity)
  Xīnxiàn pūguǐ 7935 gōnglǐ
  '7935 kilometers of track laying on the new line'

b. "黄埔学生军"驰骋沙场 (location)
  Huángpǔ xuéshēngjūn chíchěng shāchǎng
  'Whampoa Student Army gallops on the battlefield'

c. 小男孩逃脱死神的魔掌 (locative source)
  Xiǎo nánhái táotuō sǐshén de mózhǎng
  'Little boy escapes the clutches of death'

d. 焰火洒落人间 (target destination)
  Yànhuǒ sǎluò rénjiān
  'Fireworks spilled over the world'

e. 二人厮守终生 (time)
  Èrrén sīshǒu zhōngshēng
  'The two stay together forever'

f. 我举例一部纯文学的作品 (instrument)
  Wǒ jǔlì yībù chún wénxué de zuòpǐn
  'I give an example of a work of pure literature'

g. 我们沐浴阳光 (material)
  Wǒmen mùyù yángguāng
  'We bathe in sunshine'

h. 他自居名士 (method)
  Tā zìjū míngshì
  'He calls himself a celebrity'

i. 先生写生山水 (accordance)
    Xiānsheng xiěshēng shānshuǐ
    'He sketches landscape'

j. 小蝶吃醋若楠跟大宝的关系 (cause)
    Xiǎodié chīcù ruònán gēn dàbǎo de guānxi
    'Xiaodie is jealous of Ruonan's relationship with Dabao'

k. 克林顿角逐总统宝座 (purpose)
    Kèlíndùn juézhú zǒngtǒng bǎozuò
    'Clinton's run for the presidency'

l. 马宝山与杨部长打赌马八一当兵的事 (scope)
    Mǎbǎoshān yǔ yángbùzhǎng dǎdǔ mǎbāyī dāngbīng de shì
    'Ma Baoshan and Minister Yang make a bet on Ma Bayi's military service'

m. 田畴献策曹操 (dative)
    Tiánchóu xiàncè cáocāo
    'Tian Chou offers advice to Cao Cao'

n. 佟俊约会张倩 (partner)
    Tóngjùn yuēhuì zhāngqiàn
    'Tong Jun dates Zhang Qian'

o. 双腿积聚脂肪 (theme)
    Shuāngtuǐ jījù zhīfáng
    'Fat accumulates in legs'

p. 动物园里逃走**30**多只猛兽 (agent)
    Dòngwùyuánlǐ táozǒu 30duōzhī měngshòu
    'More than 30 beasts escaped from zoo'

Based on these 16 semantic roles, this study further conducted a statistical analysis of the semantic roles of objects carried by intransitive verbs in the data. The proportion of various semantic roles played by objects carried by intransitive verbs is shown in Fig. 4.

As shown in Fig. 4, in the structure of intransitive verbs with objects observed in this paper, the priority series of semantic roles serving as objects are: quantity > dative > location > partner > theme > target destination > agent > locative source > scope > cause > time > material = purpose > method = instrument > accordance. Among them, "quantity" accounts for the largest proportion, as high as 27.0%, which has a strong relationship with the expressions of momentum and time in discourse communication. The proportion of "dative", "location" and "partner" is next, all above 10.0%. The "theme", "target destination", "agent", "locative source", "scope", "cause", "time", "material", "purpose", "method", "instrument" and "accordance" account for

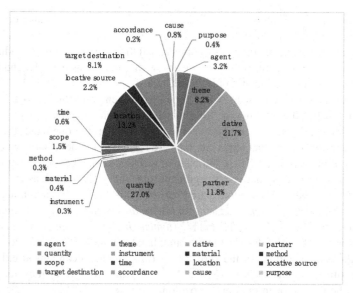

Fig. 4. Statistics on the distribution of semantic roles played by the objects of intransitive verbs.

about 26.2% in total, carrying a large part of the semantics with nearly one-third of the number, although the respective proportions of these semantic roles are not large.

In addition, the annotation results of 1305 disyllabic intransitive verbs with object and their objects show that some intransitive verbs can only take objects of one semantic role, and some in different contexts can take objects of more than one semantic role. The distribution of disyllabic intransitive verbs with object and the number of semantic types of objects they can take is briefly illustrated in Fig. 5[5].

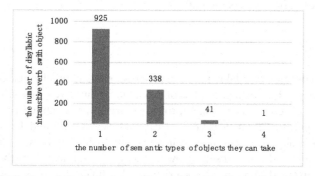

Fig. 5. The distribution of disyllabic intransitive verbs with object and the number of semantic types of objects they can take.

---

[5] For the specific distribution of the number of verbs with different semantic types of objects, see the Baidu Netdisk link: https://pan.baidu.com/s/1ysqQVNBORdzJ-Ca50GnfQg (password: alhz).

As shown in Fig. 5, among these 1305 verbs, 925 verbs can only take objects with a single semantic role, and the other 380 verbs can take objects with multiple semantic roles. The number of semantic types of objects and the number of corresponding disyllabic intransitive verbs conform to the power-law distribution as a whole, and there are more verbs with fewer semantic objects in Chinese. At the same time, the number of disyllabic intransitive verbs with object with various semantic roles also accounts for nearly one third of the total number of disyllabic intransitive verbs with object in this paper, and their existence also reflects some problems. On the one hand, the types of semantic roles of objects that verbs can take are related to the necessary semantic role framework of the verb itself. These intransitive verbs that can take objects with multiple semantic roles have many necessary argument roles themselves, such as the necessary roles of '争执' (*zhēngzhí*, 'dispute') are "partner" and "cause", so it can appear both in '土豪女争执服务员' (*tǔháonǚ zhēngzhí fúwùyuán*, 'local tyrant female quarrel with waiter') and in '她们争执日记的所有权' (*tāmen zhēngzhí rìjì de suǒyǒuquán*, 'their quarrel over ownership of diary'). On the other hand, Chinese grammar is complex and flexible, the role "location" of the verb '聚集' (*jùjí*, 'gather') can appear either in the subject position, such as '河畔聚集游玩人员' (*hépàn jùjí yóuwán rényuán*, 'tourists gather by the river'), or in the object position, such as '几千名韩国市民聚集首尔广场' (*jǐqiānmíng hánguó shìmín jùjí shǒu'ěr guǎngchǎng*, 'thousands of South Korean citizens gather in Seoul Plaza'), the former's object position is "agent", the object position of the latter is "location". In addition, some intransitive verbs also have ambiguity, such as the verb '取经' (*qǔjīng*, 'learn from scriptures'). '取经' (*qǔjīng*, 'learn from scriptures') can take the object with the semantic role of "dative", such as '张云龙取经总裁专业户刘恺威' (*zhāngyúnlóng qǔjīng zǒngcái zhuānyèhù liúkǎiwēi*, 'Zhang Yunlong learns from Liu Kaiwei, a professional who plays the role of president'), or take the object with the semantic role of "target destination", such as '唐玄奘取经西竺' (*tángxuánzàng qǔjīng xīzhú*, 'Tang Xuanzang went to Xizhu to learn Buddhist scriptures'). It is the existence of these factors that constitutes the richness of object semantics in the modern Chinese verb-object structure.

6 Conclusion

This study recognized disyllabic intransitive verbs and acquired their objects based on structural retrieval. Based on the corpus of disyllabic intransitive verbs with objects, the structural types of verbs and the semantic roles of objects were identified, providing large-scale data support for the analysis of the structural types of verbs and the determination of the semantic roles of objects in the structure of intransitive verbs with objects. At the same time, the identification results show that disyllabic intransitive verbs with object structure tend to manifest certain characteristics in the choice of object semantic roles and verb structure types, which can provide new ideas for the syntactic semantics research of unconventional verb-object structure in modern Chinese.

However, this study also has some shortcomings. Firstly, due to limited manpower, it only selected some disyllabic verb entries in the Modern Chinese Dictionary (5th Edition) as the object of investigation of intransitive verbs in this paper, and the scope of investigation needs to be further expanded. Secondly, it has to be noted that the limitation of the semantic constraints of the treebank chunk tags may affect the accuracy of intransitive verb recognition to a certain extent. Finally, there is still much room for improvement in the consistency rate of manual identification of verb structure types and object semantic roles.

Future work can identify disyllabic intransitive verbs according to all disyllabic verb entries in Modern Chinese Dictionary (5th Edition), improve the design of search strategy to improve the accuracy of intransitive verb recognition. At the same time, the consistency rate of manual identification can be increased to improve the accuracy of the analysis of verb structure types and object semantic roles in the structure of disyllabic intransitive verbs with objects.

Acknowledgments. This study was supported by Project supported by The National Natural Science Foundation of China, "Study on the Characterization and Generation Method of Chinese Parataxis Graph" (No.62076038), BLCU Supported Project for Young Researchers Program (supported by the Fundamental Research Funds for the Central Universities) (22YCX044), and Project funded by China Postdoctoral Science Foundation (2022M710246).

References

1. Xing, F.: Chinese Grammar. Northeast Normal University Press, Changchun (1996). (in Chinese)
2. Zhao, Y.: Grammar of Spoken Chinese. The Commercial Press, Beijing (2005). (in Chinese)
3. Zhu, D.: Lectures on Grammar. The Commercial Press, Beijing (2005). (in Chinese)
4. Guo, J.: Try to talk about the phenomenon of intransitive verbs with objects such as "fly to Shanghai." Stud. Chin. Lang. **05**, 337–346 (1999). (in Chinese)
5. Zhang, Y.: A Study of The Acceptor Object Sentence in Modern Chinese. Xuelin Press, Shanghai (2004). (in Chinese)
6. Sun, T.: Research on The Realization Mode and Permission Mechanism of Non-core Argument in Modern Chinese. Publishing house of Chinese and western, Shanghai (2019). (in Chinese)
7. Diao, Y.: Also talk about "verb-object verb + object" form. Lang. Plann. **06**, 39–41 (1998). (in Chinese)
8. Gao, G.: Collocation rules of "verb-object verb + object." Lang. Plann. **06**, 36–38 (1998). (in Chinese)
9. Liu, Y., Li, J.: The transformation form of "verb-object verb + object" and the semantic type of object. J. Jianghan Univ. **05**, 44–48 (1998). (in Chinese)
10. Zhang, B.: The condition and development trend of "verb-object structure + object." Res. Ancient Chin. Lang. **03**, 2–6 (1999). (in Chinese)
11. Zhu, J., Sheng, X.: On the formation of verb-object structure with object format. Chin. Lang. Learn. **03**, 37–42 (2008). (in Chinese)
12. Lin, X., Wang, L., Sun, D.: A Dictionary of Chinese Verbs. Beijing Language and Culture Institute Press, Beijing (1994). (in Chinese)
13. Yuan, Y.: On the hierarchical relation and semantic features of the thematic roles in Chinese. Chin. Teach. World **03**, 10–22+2 (2002). (in Chinese)
14. Fang, Q.: A Dictionary of Modern Chinese Prepositions. The Commercial Press, Beijing (2017). (in Chinese)
15. Yu, S., Zhu, X., Wang, H.: A Detailed Explanation of Modern Chinese Grammatical Information Dictionary. Tsinghua University Press, Beijing (2003). (in Chinese)

16. Huang, B., Liao, X.: Modern Chinese (Revised sixth Edition) (Volume 1). Higher Education Press, Beijing (2017). (in Chinese)
17. Xun, E., Rao, G., Xiao, X., Zang, J.: The development of BCC corpus in the context of big data. Corpus Linguist. **01**, 93–109+118 (2016). (in Chinese)
18. Lu, L., Jiao, H., Li, M., Xun, E.: A discourse-base Chinese chunkbank. Acta Automatica Sinica. 1–12 (2021). http://kns.cnki.net/kcms/detail/11.2109.TP.20200521.1558.007.html. (in Chinese)

The Introduction of Positive Position in "V$_{Wish}$ + VP$_{neg}$" and Its Pragmatic Consequences

Chen Ju[1(✉)] and Yulin Yuan[2]

[1] Department of Chinese Language and Literature, Peking University, Beijing, China
juchen727@163.com
[2] Department of Chinese Language and Literature, University of Macau, Avenida da Universidade, Taipa, Macau, China
yuanyl@pku.edu.cn

Abstract. When verbs about wish are followed by a negative clause, the positive attitude within these verbs is often suppressed. The sentence cannot express a "pure" wish, but rather express concern or curse. In interactive communication, negation always introduces a corresponding positive position into the dialogue. The introduction and emphasis on the possibility of negative things violates the Pollyanna principle; hence, breaks "the maxim of quantity"; and finally makes the sentence imply concern and even curse.

Keywords: Wish · Negation · Engagement System · The Maxim of Quantity · Pollyanna Principle

1 Introduction

In Chinese Mandarin, as a speech act, wishing are often expressed with a lexical mark, followed by a verbal object. Zhou [1] classifies wishes into typical and atypical forms. The typical forms include *X (wish marker) + S*, *NP + X + S* and *Adv + X + S*, while the atypical forms include *X + AP*, *X + NP*, *X......X* and *Ø + S*. All wish markers can enter typical forms, while atypical forms can only accommodate some of them. Zhou also classifies wish markers into typical markers and atypical markers, based on wishing features within the words: Typical wish markers include *Zhù* (祝 'wish') *Yuàn*(愿 'wish') *Zhùyuàn*(祝愿 'wish') and *Zhùfú*(祝福 'bless'), while atypical markers include *Xīwàng*(希望 'hope') and *Ràng*(让 'let').

As can be seen, typical wish markers are verbs that specifically express good wishes, while atypical wish markers are capable of expressing other meanings in addition to good wishes. We refer to the typical wish markers as wish verbs, and discuss wishes expressed with these verbs in this paper.

We found that a wish verb is often followed by an affirmative clause rather than an equivalent negative form:[1]

---

[1] This project is supported by Research & Development Grant for Chair Professor (CPG2022–00032-FAH) and Start-up Research Grant (SRG2022–00011-FAH). We would like to extend our sincere thanks. Abbreviations used throughout in this paper: SG = single; NEG = negation; PREP = preposition; AUX = auxiliary; PL = plural.

© The Author(s), under exclusive license to Springer Nature Switzerland AG 2023
Q. Su et al. (Eds.): CLSW 2022, LNAI 13495, pp. 283–294, 2023.
https://doi.org/10.1007/978-3-031-28953-8_22

(1) 衷心　　　祝愿　　　赛事　　　　成功。
Zhōngxīn zhùyuàn sàishì   chénggōng.
sincerely wish   tournament succeed
'Wish the tournament to succeed sincerely.'

(2) 祝　你　一路　　　平安。
Zhù nǐ yīlù   píng'ān
wish 2SG all the way safe
'Wish you safe all the way.'

If we change these object clauses above into negative forms, the sentence would be unnatural in ordinary context:

(1') ?衷心　　　祝愿　　　赛事　　　不要　失败。
Zhōngxīn zhùyuàn sàishì   bùyào shībài.
sincerely wish   tournament NEG   fail
'Wish the tournament not to fail sincerely.'

(2') ?祝　你　一路上　　　不要　出　　意外。
Zhù nǐ yīlùshàng bùyào chū   yìwài
wish 2SG all the way NEG   happen accident
'Wish you not to meet any accident all the way.'

赛事不要失败 'tournament do not fail' is semantically similar to 赛事成功 'tournament succeed'; and it is the same with 一路上不要出意外 'not to meet any accident all the way' and 一路平安 'a safe journey'. However, when people use wish verbs to conduct a wishing speech act, they would use the affirmative form rather than the negative one.

In everyday communication, "$V_{wish} + VP_{neg}$" can even imply a negative meaning, which express curse and is contrary to a good wish. A post on a Douban group and its popular response can be an example:[2]

---

[2] The group called *hahahahahahahahahahaha*. It is a group to post jokes. All the members in this group can post or reply to posts in the group; and everyone who see the posts or responses can "like" them, to express their agreement.

(3) **Title** My husband sent a New Year's Eve wish to his leader, keeping up with the times.
Body paragraph The whole message was very succinct, just ten words:
"祝 您 在 新 的 一 年 不 得病。"
zhù nín zài xīn de yī nián bù débìng
wish 2SG PREP new AUX one year NEG get ill
'Wish you not to get ill in the new year.'
When I found out it, it was too late. He sent this message to every leader that he added
WeChat friend with.
......
Although this is reasonable, it sounds really weird.
Response
A: Why didn't he say
"祝 身体 健康"
zhù shēntǐ jiànkāng
wish body health
'Wish you good health.'
hahahahahahahahahaha. [326 likes]
B: Dose he want to resign smoothly after the New Year? [155 likes]
C: How is this different from saying,
"祝 你们 两口子 不 离婚"
zhù nǐmen liǎngkǒuzi bù líhūn
wish 2PLU couple NEG divorce
'Wish you two not to get divorced.'
when a couple gets married? [155 likes]

This wish was sent during Chinese New Year, when the spread of COVID-19 was accelerating. At this time, the wish 祝您在新的一年不生病 'wish you not to get ill in the new year' was sent in a "right" time. However, this kind of wish was posted as a joke and was thought to be "really weird". The three comments that received the most likes also showed how people feel about this wish: On the one hand, a negative clause is a weird way to express wishes. It is more appropriate to use the affirmative form to express the same meaning. On the other hand, the negative form may imply a curse, so that sending it to a leader is an act of resigning. The negative form 祝你们两口子不离婚'Wish you two not to get divorced' also implies a curse, and is therefore thought to be no different from 祝您在新的一年不生病 'wish you not to get ill in the new year'.

As can be seen above, a wish verb with a negative object clause is restricted in a conversation. Is it true that wish verbs cannot take any negative clause? Why is a wish verb difficult to followed by a negative object clause? Why can a wish with negative form express curse?

2 Different Meanings of "V$_{Wish}$ + VP$_{neg}$"

In Chinese Mandarin, there are several negative operators, such as 不 'no/not', 没/没有 'no/not'. 没/没有 'no/not' is used to "illustrate the action or state did not appear until the speaker speaks" [2], which means that this operator is associate with past tense. Obviously, a wish is associate with the future. Therefore, all our examples are negated by 不 'no/not'.

In general, a wish verb with an affirmative object clause is used much more frequently than "$V_{wish} + VP_{neg}$". Only typical forms of wishing can accept a negative object clause:

(4) a. 祝 好！— ＊祝 不 坏！(X+AP)
    zhù hǎo   zhù bù huài
    wish good   wish NEG bad
    'Wish you good!' 'Wish you not bad!'

b. 祝 永结同心   XX 贺
   zhù yǒngjiétóngxīn   XX hè
   wish a harmonious union lasting forever   XX congratulate
   'Wish you a harmonious union lasting forever! Congratulated from XX'
   —? 祝 永   不 离婚 XX 贺 (X......X)
   zhù yǒng   bù líhūn XX hè
   wish forever NEG divorce XX congratulate
   'Wish you never get divorced. Congratulated from XX'

c. 生日 快乐！— ＊生日   不   难过！(∅+S)
   shēngrì kuàilè   shēngrì bù nánguò
   birthday happy   birthday NEG sad
   'Happy birthday!' 'Not sad birthday!'

For these forms that can accept negative object clauses, there are three kinds of cases in which a wish verb followed by a negative object clause can still keep natural and express a good wish:

(i) When there is a corresponding affirmative form in the context:
(5) 祝 你 百 病 全 消 不 生病！
    zhù nǐ bǎi bìng quán xiāo bù shēngbìng
    wish 2SG hundred disease all disappear NEG get ill
    'Wish you be free from all diseases and not to get ill.'
(6) 祝 今天 结婚 的 人，一辈子 不 离婚，相互
    zhù jīntiān jiéhūn de rén, yíbèizi bù líhūn xiānghù
    wish today marry AUX people whole life NEG divorce each other
    扶持 到 老。
    fúchí dào lǎo
    support until old age
    'Wish those who get married today not to get divorced for the whole life and support each other into old age.'

In these examples above, 百病全消 'be free from all diseases' is basically equivalent with 不生病 'not to get ill'; 相互扶持到老 'support each other into old age' is also basically equivalent with一辈子不离婚 'not to get divorced for the whole life'. In this kind of cases, the negative object clause sets up for the corresponding affirmative form. The sentence is natural and only express good wishes.

(ii) When there is no corresponding affirmative object clause of the negative ones in the language:

(7)

新	的	一	年，	祝	大家	出门	不	晕车！
xīn	de	yī	nián	zhù	dàjiā	chūmén	bù	yūnchē
new	AUX	one	year	wish	everyone	go out	NEG	carsick

'In the new year, wish everyone not to get carsick when traveling!'

(8)

祝	你	今年	回家	不	被	催婚。
zhù	nǐ	jīnnián	huíjiā	bù	bèi	cuīhūn
wish	2SG	this year	go home	NEG	PREP	rush into marriage

'Wish you go home this year without being rushed into marriage.'

In these examples above, there is no common affirmative form that has the same meaning with不晕车 'no to get carsick' and不被催婚 'no to be rushed into marriage' in Mandarin. Therefore, if one wants to express this kind of wishes, this person would have to choose a negative object clause. In this case, a wish verb can also be followed by a negative object clause naturally and express only good wishes.

(iii) When there is an element that expresses eternality (e.g.永、永远'forever') or universality (e.g. 百'hundred'、万'ten thousand'):

(9)

祝	你	百	病	不	侵。
zhù	nǐ	bǎi	bìng	bù	qīn
wish	2SG	hundred	disease	NEG	invade

'Wish you not to get invaded by any diseases.'

(10)

愿	友谊	的	链条	永	不	生锈。
yuàn	yǒuyì	de	liàntiáo	yǒng	bù	shēngxiù
wish	friendship	AUX	chain	forever	NEG	rust

'Wish the chains of friendship never rust ever.'

In the two examples above, the negative object clauses do have their corresponding affirmative counterparts (e.g.百病不侵 'not to get invaded by any diseases' with身体健康 'be good health';不生锈 'not to be rust' with 常新 'always new'), and the affirmative counterparts does not appear in the context. If we remove 百 'hundred' or 永 'forever', the meaning of the sentence will change:

(9') 祝　你　　不　　生病。
zhù nǐ　　bù　　shēngbìng
wish 2SG NEG get ill
'Wish you not to get ill.'

(10') 愿　友谊　　　的　　链条　　不　　生锈。
yuàn yǒuyì　de　liàntiáo bù　shēngxiù
wish friendship AUX chain　NEG rust
'Wish the chains of friendship not to rust.'

In the two examples above, the sentences seem to imply the concerns of the speaker: the speaker gave the wishes, while at the same time worried that "you might be ill" or "the chains of friendship might rust".

This sense of concern, between wish and curse, is common in our communication:

(11) It is not easy to do this, but I hope that authors and readers will help us.

也　　祝愿　　我们　　自己 不要　　丧失　　信心
yě　 zhùyuàn women zìjǐ bùyào sàngshī xìnxīn
And wish　1PLU　self NEG　lose　faith
'And wish us not to lose faith.'

(12) We should have greater faith

I have been reading every issue of *Dushu* for a year or two. Whenever I talk to my friends about "the spread of culture", I always recommend it. Today, however, I was disappointed. In the "Post-Editorial Ramble" of the ninth issue of 1987, the editor said, 也祝愿我们自己不要丧失信心"and wish us not to lose faith". I feel uncomfortable reading it. Whether or not a magazine has vitality depends on the faith of its editorial staffs.

我　是　唯　愿　《读书》的　　编辑　　先生　　们　先
wǒ　shì wéi yàun dúshū de　biānjí xiānshēng men xiān
1SG be only wish *Dushu* AUX editorial sir　PLU before

有　更　大 的　信心,
yǒu gèng dà de　xìnxīn
have more big AUX faith
'I only wish the editors of *Dushu* to have greater faith first,'

then go into the new year with their readers. *Laojiu* cannot disappear!

Both examples above are taken from the magazine *Dushu*. In (11), the editor end with a negative wish 也祝愿我们自己不要丧失信心 'and wish us not to lose faith' in the "Post-Editorial Ramble" part. (12) was showed in the following year's issue of *Dushu*. It was a letter from a reader of that magazine, which was a response to the article in (11). The editor added a title to this reader's letter: "We should have greater faith". Clearly, for this reader, the wish verb followed by the negative object clause was not simply an expression of good wish, but also implied a concern of the speaker (i.e., the editor) about the possibility that "we may lose faith". This was why the reader felt "uncomfortable". The reader then used an affirmative object clause to express the wish for the editors:有更大的信心 'have greater faith'.

Because of this implicature, a wish verb followed by a negative clause can sometimes express imperative and the speech act of wishing is transformed into requesting:

(13) 我　　衷心　　　祝愿　　　你们　　在　　逐渐　　成熟　　　的
　　　wǒ　　zhōngxīn　zhùyuàn　nǐmen　zài　zhújiàn　chéngshú　de
　　　1SG　sincerely　wish　　　2PLU　PREP　gradually　mature　　AUX

同时　　　　不要　　失去　　童心。
tóngshí　　bùyào　shīqù　tóngxín
the same time　NEG　lose　childlike spirit

'I sincerely wish you not to lose your childlike spirit as you are gradually becoming mature.'

The example above implied the speaker's concern that "you will lose your childlike spirit as you are gradually becoming mature". The speaker wanted the listener "not to lose the childlike spirit", and euphemistically expressed the imperative.

Another element that influences the meaning of a wish is the degree of negativity. Compare the three sentences below:

(14) a. 祝　你　一路　　平安。
　　　 Zhù　nǐ　yīlù　　píng'ān
　　　 wish　2SG　all the way　safe
　　　 'Wish you safe all the way.'

b. 祝　你　一路上　　不要　遇到　麻烦。
　　 Zhù　nǐ　yīlùshàng　bùyào　yùdào　máfán
　　 wish　2SG　all the way　NEG　meet　trouble
　　 'Wish you not to meet any trouble all the way.'

c. 祝　你　一路上　　不要　被　撞　死。
　　 Zhù　nǐ　yīlùshàng　bùyào　bèi　zhuàng　sǐ
　　 wish　2SG　all the way　NEG　PREP　crash　die
　　 'Wish you not to be killed by a car crash.'

In (14a), the object clause is affirmative and the whole sentence expresses only good wish. In (14b) and (14c), the two object clauses are both negative. Comparing (14b) and (14c), "be killed by a car crash" in (14c) is much more serious than "meet trouble" in (14b). Therefore, (14c) can obviously imply a curse, which is opposite to a wish; while (14b) just imply concern.

If the content of the negative object clause has a close connection to the context, even if the clause is not strongly negative, it would express curse. As we can see in the example we mentioned in (3):

(15) 祝　您　在　新　的　一　年　不　得病。
　　　zhù nín zài xīn de yī nián bù débìng
　　　wish 2SG PREP new AUX one year NEG get ill
　　　'Wish you not to get ill in the new year.'

(16) 祝　你们　两口子　不　离婚
　　　zhù nǐmen liǎngkǒuzi bù líhūn
　　　wish 2PLU couple　　NEG divorce
　　　'Wish you two not to get divorced.'

(15) and (16) is excerpted from (3). If we look at these two sentences without any context, although the sense of wish is weakened, the sense of curse is not very strong either. However, if we put (15) in the time when COVID-19 is spreading, or put (16) in the time when the speaker is in a wedding, these sentences will imply curse.

In general, except in three special cases we mentioned above, where "$V_{wish} + VP_{neg}$" can express "pure" wish, this combination usually has negative implicature apart from its literal meaning. When the degree of negativity is rather low, the literal meaning of the wish verb is suppressed and the sentence expresses a sense of concern that the wish will not be fulfilled. When the degree of negativity is rather high, or the meaning has a close connection to the context, the sentence will go into the opposite direction of the literal meaning, expressing curse.

3   The Introduction of Positive Position by Negation

Why does "$V_{wish} + VP_{neg}$" often express negative meaning in everyday life? We believe this is related to the role that negation plays in communicative interaction.

Martin & White[3] refined the engagement system in their appraisal theory. They divided engagement system into monogloss and heterogloss. There are two directions of heterogloss: contract and expand. Denial is a type of contract, which includes deny and counter. And negation (such as no, didn't, never, etc.) is a kind of deny. They pointed out that "Negation is a resource for introducing the alternative positive position into the dialogue, and hence acknowledging it, so as to reject it. Thus in these dialogistic terms, the negative is not the simple logical opposite of the positive, since the negative necessarily carries with it the positive, while the positive does not reciprocally carry the negative, or at least not typically." Shen[4] also pointed out that the information conveyed by affirmative and negative sentences is different. Affirmative sentences convey information by "telling the listener P when the listener didn't know about P", whereas negative sentences convey information by "denying or refuting P when the listener may believe P or is familiar with P".

This kind of introduction is not only found in independent negative expressions, but is also retained when the clause embedded under a wish verb. When this kind of introduction is combined with the meaning of a wish verb, a negative pragmatic effect is produced:

(17) 祝愿　　我们　　不要　　丧失　　信心。
zhùyuàn women bùyào sàngshī xìnxīn
wish 1PLU NEG lose faith
'Wish us not to lose faith.'

The core meaning of wish verbs is to express a "good hope". Therefore, the object clause of a wish verb should express: (1) positive, good event or state; (2) an event or state that is associated with future tense, having a possibility of being realized. On this basis, the wish verb and the object clause combine to express the subject's attitude of wishing for the event or state to be realized. The semantic structure of (17) can then be analyzed into the following two layers:

① 'Not to lose faith' may take place (and the event or state is positive).

② The subject is willing for 'not to lose faith' to happen.

However, because of the introduction of the negative form, there is a further layer being carried:

(①) 'lose faith' may take place.

Since the negative object clause expresses a positive event or state, the corresponding affirmative is necessarily a rather negative one that the subject wishes not to achieve. In other words, "V_{wish} + VP_{neg}" always introduces a possibility of a negative event or state into the context. However, if a wish verb is followed by an affirmative object clause, the sentence won't have a negative introduction:

(18) 祝愿　　我们　　保持　　信心。
zhùyuàn women bǎochí xìnxīn
wish 1PLU keep faith
'Wish us keep our faith.'

Since the unmarked affirmative form does not introduce a corresponding negative form necessarily, the sentence contains only two layers of meaning.

① 'keep our faith' may take place (and the event or state is positive).

② The subject is willing for 'keep our faith' to happen.

As can be seen above, when the speaker uses an affirmative object clause, the possibility of the negative state being realized is not introduced.

According to "maxim of quantity" of Grice [5], in a conversation, the speaker should try to make the contribution as informative as is required but no more informative than is required. In the case of wishing, the speaker's purpose is to please the listener and strengthen the relationship between them. In an affirmative form, the speaker raises only the possibility of the wish being fulfilled, which is as informative as the context requires. However, in a negative form, the speaker not only raises the possibility of the fulfilment of the wish, but also introduces the possibility of a negative event. This kind of introduction is clearly more informative than the context requires. When the speaker chooses the negative form deliberately, rather than the affirmative one, it is clear that the speaker is not merely expressing a "pure" wish, but also emphasizing the possibility of a negative event. This combination of these two attitudes then becomes a natural way to express concern, suppressing the positive meaning of wish verbs.

The likelihood of a negative event occurring in real world also influences the meaning of "V_{wish} + VP_{neg}". If the negative event is likely to take place, it is relatively natural to remind the existence of such a probability. On the contrary, if the negative event is not likely to take place, reminding the existence of such a probability is completely violate the "maxim of quantity" and thus implies a curse:

> (19) 祝   你   不要   死于非命。
>   zhù nǐ bùyào sǐyúfēimìng
>   wish 2SG NEG   die unnaturally
>   'Wish you not to die an unnaturally death.'

If both the speaker and the listener are in wartime, in which people are likely to be killed, the speaker can say (19) just to express concern. However, if the speaker says (19) in a peaceful moment, the emphasis on the possibility of "die an unnaturally death" will become a curse. Generally speaking, the more negative an event is, the less likely it is to occur in reality. Therefore, the higher the degree of negativity, the more thoroughly the wish is suppressed and the stronger the curse-meaning.

In the context of wishing, the negative form introduces unnecessary information into the conversation, intentionally violating the "maxim of quantity" and creating a misalignment between the wish and the context. The rhetorical effect of irony is achieved by the misalignment.[3] Tu [6] pointed out that irony is essentially a kind of contrary: "The essence of irony lies in the semantic clash or tension between the category to which the proposition relates and the context." The context of wishing is often positive, in which the wishing act expresses the speaker's positive hopes and conveys a positive attitude. The semantics and the attitude of the discourse are matched to the context. However, the negative form of wishing implies a possibility of a negative event, creating a tension between the negative information and the positive context, prompting the listener to seek a different interpretation from the usual wish. The more negative the information implied by the wish, the more pronounced the tension between discourse and context, the higher the degree of irony, and the more a wish moves towards a negative curse.

This could further explain our observation. When the likelihood of a negative event occurring in real world is high, the context is not as positive, the emotional tension between the context and the negative form is not as strong; the irony is not as pronounced; and the sentence can express only the positive wish. When the likelihood of a negative event occurring in real world is low, the context is more positive; the emotional tension between the context and the negative information is strong; and the sentence will express concern or even curse. If the context is strongly related to the content of "V_{wish} + VP_{neg}", the tension between the negative implication and the context is extremely strong, and the sentence expresses curse (e.g., a wedding ceremony in which the speaker wishes the couple not to get divorced). Under this pragmatic mechanism, the meaning of a wish verb is suppressed.

When the object clause contains a component denoting eternality or universality, the speaker completely negates the possibility of the negative event taking place. In this way,

---

[3] Thanks to the anonymous reviewer for pointing this out.

the negative emotion is considerably weakened, the tension with the positive context is reduced and the ironic effect is eliminated. The sentence then can express "pure" wish.

4 Conclusion

We discussed the case of a wish verb followed by a negative object clause. The negative object clause always introduces the possibility of a negative event occurring (i.e., the presence of the corresponding affirmative). In the context of wishing, this introduction is more informative than the context required. By violating the "maxim of quantity", the negative implication suppresses the original positive meaning of the wish verb. The sentence then often expresses concern or even curse. The speaker's deliberate violation of the "maxim of quantity" creates a tension between the negative meaning and the positive context, producing an ironic effect. The more pronounced this tension is, the higher the degree of irony, and the more the sentence tends to express negative concern or even curse.

Under this pragmatic mechanism, only in a small number of cases can "V$_{wish}$ + VP$_{neg}$" express only positive wishes. Sometimes, the speaker has to choose a negative object clause because there is not a corresponding affirmative one. More often, the speaker expresses "pure" wishes by dissolving the negative meaning being introduced: (i) There is an affirmative form to set up or supply for the negative one, dissipating the negative implication; (ii) There is an element denoting eternality or universality, which strengthens the negation and dissipates the possibility of a negative event occurring; (iii) The context is not as positive and the tension between the context and the content of the sentence is not strong.[4]

What is behind the mechanism is also related to the human psyche. In social life, people often unconsciously follow the Pollyanna Hypothesis proposed by Boucher & Osgood [7]. People always tend to talk about the positive side of life (the good things, the good qualities) and to reject the negative side [8]. When people make a wish, they also follow this tendency, they tend to talk about the possibility of positive events and avoid introducing negative ones. With this pragmatic motivation, the introduction of a negative event becomes an overload of information, in contrast to the positive context, and thus suppresses the original positive meaning of the wish verb. The sentence then develops a sense of concern or even curse.

References

1. Zhou, X.J.: The form and meaning characteristics of congratulatory speech. J. Hubei Normal Univ. (Philos. Soc. Sci.) **26**(3), 68–71 (2006). (in Chinese)

---

[4] Usually, if an event can only be expressed by negative forms ($\neg$q), then the corresponding q is often an event with a high probability of occurrence. For example, for不被催婚 'be rushed into marriage' ($\neg$q), it is difficult to find an equivalent affirmative expression. In real life, people of marriageable age who are not married are often rushed to marry (q), and the probability of q is very high. Therefore, when we say "wish you not to be rushed into marriage", we are often in a rather negative context, and the tension between context and discourse is no strong.

2. Xiao, S.: Comparison and analysis between Chinese and african languages in the usage of negative words. In: Liu, P., Su, Q. (eds.) CLSW 2013. LNCS (LNAI), vol. 8229, pp. 275–287. Springer, Heidelberg (2013). https://doi.org/10.1007/978-3-642-45185-0_30

3. Martin, R., White, P.: The Language of Evaluation: Appraisal in English. Palgrave Macmillan, London (2005)

4. Shen, J.X.: Asymmetry and Markedness Theory. Jiangxi Education Publishing Housing, Nanchang (1999). (in Chinese)

5. Grice, P.: Logic and conversation. In: Cole, P., Jerry, L.M. (eds.) Speech Acts, pp. 41–58. Academic Press, New York (1975)

6. Tu, J.: A cognitive study of irony. Foreign Lang. Res. (2), 7–9+73 (2004). (in Chinese)

7. Boucher, J., Osgood, C.E., The Pollyanna hypothesis. J. Verbal Behav. (8), 1–8 (1969)

8. Yuan, Y.L.: On the implicit negation hidden in Chadianer and its grammatical effects. Stud. Lang. Linguist. 33(2), 54–64 (2013). (in Chinese)

A Grammatical Study of Chinese Counter-Expectation Marker *"Jìngrán"* -in Comparison with Korean Counter-Expectation Marker *"-tani"*

Qingcong Shan(✉)

Shanghai International Studies University, Shanghai 201620, China
shanqingcong@163.com

Abstract. The Chinese accidental commentary adverb *"Jìngrán"* and Korean conjunction ending *"-tani"* fall within the scope of typical counter-expectation markers in Chinese and Korean. The two mainly show that what happens objectively is contrary to expectations, which then express the emotion of surprise. Despite the fact that *"Jìngrán"* and *"-tani"* are known as typical counter- expectation markers in their languages, respectively, the two are not completely opposite to each other in terms of grammar, and differences are available between the two in syntax, semantics, and pragmatics. With the assistance of corpus, this study mainly starts from the perspective of language comparison, so as to carry out analysis on the characteristics of Chinese and Korean counter- expectation markers *"Jìngrán"* and *"-tani"* in the three planes of grammar research, and it can draw the conclusions as follows initially. At the level of syntactic, Chinese *"Jìngrán"* can appear at the beginning and in the middle of a sentence. With regard to Korean *"-tani"*, it can appear in the middle or at the end of a sentence. Concerning the types of expectation semantic, both Chinese and Korean-related expressions can be employed in the expression of a single expectation type, and the self-expectation types are great in number. However, Chinese *"Jìngrán"* can mark the types of compound expectation, with a variety of types. Korean *"-tani"* generally does not mark the types of compound expectation, and the types are relatively simple. At the level of pragmatics, Chinese *"Jìngrán"* generally lays emphasis on post-information, and "post-positioned focus" is more than "pre-positioned focus".

Keywords: Counter-expectation marker · *Jìngrán* · *-tani* · Counter-expectation category · Chinese-Korean comparison

1 Introduction

Counter-expectation categories have diverse methods of expression in different languages. Counter-expectation categories can be conducted either through explicit grammatical means, such as adverbs, modal particles, discourse markers of negation/transition/interrogation, and specific sentence patterns, or through relatively implicit forms such as specific context and information domain in interaction of discourse.

© The Author(s), under exclusive license to Springer Nature Switzerland AG 2023
Q. Su et al. (Eds.): CLSW 2022, LNAI 13495, pp. 295–311, 2023.
https://doi.org/10.1007/978-3-031-28953-8_23

This paper mainly makes comparison between both the similarities and differences in *"Jìngrán"* and *"-tani"*, which are known as Chinese and Korean counter-expectation markers respectively, from the perspective of Chinese and Korean languages. Therefore, this paper mainly attaches importance to the three issues as follows:

(1) What are the features of the Chinese and Korean counter-expectation markers *"Jìngrán"* and *"-tani"* in the aspects of syntactics, semantics, and pragmatics?

(2) What are the differences and similarities between the Chinese and Korean counter-expectation markers *"Jìngrán"* and *"-tani"* in the aspects of syntactics, semantics, and pragmatics?

(3) What Are the Motives for the Similarities and Differences Between the Chinese and Korean Counter-Expectation Markers *"JìNgrán"* and *"-tani"* at Different Levels?

2 Literature Review

The main research paradigms proposed by Chinese and Korean academic circles in the research of *"Jìng(rán)"* and *"-tani"* will be briefly reviewed. With multiple research perspectives employed by Chinese academic circles in the study on *"Jìngrán"* are very diverse and in-depth.

The research on counter-expectation related to *"Jìngrán"* mainly includes the studies conducted by Qiang [1], Shan [2, 3], Li and Zheng [4] etc. Qiang [1] carried out analysis on the counter-expectation situation, before dividing it into counter-indefinite expectation and counter-specific expectation, before the analysis on the fact that *"Jìngrán"* has factual features. However, the factuality of proposition is passively perceived by the speaker, and it is situated at a low status in terms of information territory and information entitlement. Shan [2, 3] analyzed the function of counter-expectation shown by *"Jìngrán"*, the accidental commentary adverb, which mainly includes the expression of the speaker's counter-expectation psychology. In the process, what is conveyed is the speaker's expectation, or the speaker's inference of the recipient's expectation, or the social groups' shared expectations with the speaker included. *"Jìngrán/Guǒrán"* are related to the semantic expression pattern of "expectation-result", but there are similarities and differences in the methods of expression and semantic relationships. Li and Zheng [4] made comparison between the grammatical meanings of *"Jìngrán"* and *"Jūrán"*, before proposing the statement that the unexpected meaning of the two was brought about by the counter-expectation context, and *"Jìngrán"* has the meaning of finality in terms of time, while *"Jūrán"* retains the meaning of being sound and safe. The latter has a stronger tone, but there are differences and overlaps between the two, which can be interchanged conditionally.

The research on *"-tani"* in the academic circle of Korean mainly lays emphasis on the semantic classification of *"-tani"*, regarding *"-tani"* as a marker of suddenness. Regarding the research on the semantic classification of *"-tani"*, most scholars regard *"-tani"* as a kind of semantic, but Kang [5] divided the usage of *"-tani"* into three parts, which are specifically *"-tani$_1$"* used in the sentences of echo interrogative, *"-tani$_2$"* in rhetorical interrogative sentences, and *"-tani$_3$"* in exclamatory sentences. He mainly analyzes the formation grammatical features, semantic and pragmatic features and unexpectedness of the three usages of "*-tani*". In the aspect of unexpectedness, "*-tani*" which is a modified interrogative sentence of an exclamatory sentence shows subordinate semantics, which is unexpected, and it reflects the immediate response of the speaker, which has the nature of strong counter-expectation. The "*-tani*" of the rhetorical question shows the fact that the speaker has no relevant expectations.

3 The Syntactic Similarities and Differences between the Chinese and Korean Counter-Expectation Markers "*Jìngrán*" and "*-tani*"

Through the statistics about 300 pieces of Chinese corpora, it is found that "*Jìngrán*", the Chinese counter-expectation marker, can appear both at the beginning or in the middle of a sentence, but not at the end of the sentence. Moreover, modal verbs such as "*huì*", "*néng*", "*yào*", or "*gǎn*", as well as related verb-final expressions including "*kàndǒng*", "*dǒngdé*" and "*wàngjì*" would appear in related example sentences. The specific statistics are shown in the figure as follows (Table 1):

Table 1. The Syntactic Distribution of Chinese Counter-Expectation Marker "*Jìngrán*"

Syntactic position	Type	Specific classification	Frequency	Proportion
At the beginning of the sentence	Modal verb expression	*Huì*	12	4%
		Néng	8	2.67%
		Yào	3	1%
		Gǎn	2	0.67%
		Verb-complement structure	9	3%
	General expression		80	26.67%
In the middle of the sentence	Modal verb expression	*Huì*	5	1.67%
		Néng	8	2.67%
		Yào	5	1.67%
		Gǎn	5	1.67%
		Verb-complement structure	8	2.67%
	General expression		155	51.67%
Total			300	100%

From the table listed above, we can see that "*Jìngrán*" can be located at the beginning, or in the middle, of a sentence, among which it is mostly located in the middle part of the sentence—it appears at the position for 186 times and accounts for 62% of the total. The phrase appears at the beginning of the sentence for 114 times, accounting for 38%.

Moreover, both the appearance at the two positions is used in combination with multi-functional modal adverbs such as *"huì"*, *"néng"*, *"yào"*, *"gǎn"*, and, interestingly, the number and proportion of its combination with multi-functional modal expressions when *"Jìngrán"* is located at the beginning of a sentence are higher than that of the situation when *"Jìngrán"* is located in the middle of a sentence. Specific examples are as follows:

(1) "醒醒吧! 对方是吸血鬼!<u>竟然</u>要去帮一个吸血鬼......本无法想象是一年前, 站在我们前面打倒了那个怪物的圣女说的话!"

  'Xǐngxǐngba! Duìfāng shì xīxuèguǐ! **Jìngrán** *yàoqù bāng yígè xīxuèguǐ......běn wúfǎxiǎngxiàng shì yìniánqián, zhànzai wǒmen qiánmian dǎdǎole nàge guaìwu de shèngnǚ shuōde huà!'*

  "Wake up! The other party is a vampire! To help a vampire......**I can't imagine** what the saint who stood in front of us and defeated that monster said a year ago!"'

(2) 有人敲门, 这么晚了, 是谁?我到大门口去开了门, 出我意料之外, <u>竟然</u>是何书桓! 他刚走怎么又来了?

  Yǒurén qiāomén, zhème wǎn le, shì shuí? Wǒ dào dàménkǒu qù kaīle mén, chū wǒ yìliàozhīwaì, **jìngrán** *shì héshūhuán! Tā gāng zǒu zěnmē yòu laí le?*

  Someone knocked on the door, it's so late, who is it? I went to the gate to open it, and **to my surprise**, it was He Shuhuan! Why did he come again just after he left?

(3) 嫒怜也是个业余的模特儿, 看多了俊俏的男人, 却第一次发现男人<u>竟然</u>能俊美得如此具有侵略性。

  Aàlián yěshì ge yèyú de mótèer, kànduōle jùnqiào de nánrén, què dìyīcì fāxiàn nánrén **jìngrán** *néng jùnměi de rúcǐ jùyǒu qīnlüèxìng.*

  Ai Lian is also an amateur model. She has seen a lot of handsome men, but for the first time, she found that men can be so handsome and aggressive.

(4) 梅蒂张口结舌地望着他, 气他<u>竟然</u>敢扯这么一个大谎, 又高兴他真的希望她会相信他。

  Méidì zhāngkǒujiéshé de wàngzhe tā, qì tā **jìngrán** *gǎn chě zhème yígè dàhuǎng, yòu gāoxìng tā zhēnde xīwàng tā huì xiāngxìn tā.*

  Maddy stared at him dumbfounded, angry that he dared to tell such a big lie, and glad that he hoped she would believe him.

In the examples mentioned above, *"Jìngrán"* in the Examples (1) and (2) is located at the beginning of the sentence to match with a functional modal adverb, which indicates the speaker's incomprehension, dissuasion, and surprise at the actors' behaviors without knowing the truth; *"Jìngrán"* in the Examples (3) and (4) is located in the middle of the sentences to collocate with modal adverb, indicating that although the speaker has some experience of something, he has the emotion of surprise and astonishment when the current situation is a new situation which goes beyond previous experience. In other words, even though *"Jìngrán"* indicates counter-expectation, the emotion of surprise is produced when it is triggered by different situational conditions (Table 2).

Table 2. The Syntactic Distribution of Korean Counter-Expectation Marker "*-tani*"

Syntactic position	Type	Frequency	Proportion
At the beginning of the sentence	*-go it(tani)-* (progressive aspect connective ending + *tani*)	10	3.33%
	-at/ot/yot(tani)- (Past tense connective ending + *tani*)	49	16.33%
	-eul su it/op/(tani)- (Connective ending expresses competence + *tani*)	12	4%
	-get(tani)- (Future tense/speculation connective ending + *tani*)	5	1.67%
	No special marker	63	21%
At the end of the sentence	Interrogative sentence in the sentence	21	7%
	Non-Interrogative sentence (dverb ahead)	34	11.33%
	Non-Interrogative sentence (no adverb ahead)	106	35.33%
Total		300	99.99%

Different from the Chinese "*Jìngrán*", the Korean phrase "*-tani*" can be employed in the middle and at the end of a sentence, rather than at the beginning of a sentence. Moreover, it is mostly used at the end of a sentence.

First of all, when "*-tani*" is located in the middle of a sentence, its successive expressions are more characteristic—they are usually preceded by "*-go it-*", "*-at/ot/yot-*" or "*-eul su it/op-*" which shows ability, and "*-get-*" which expresses willingness, etc. Among them, the "*-at/ot/yot-*" which expresses the past appear more frequently, accounting for 16.33%. The expressions following "*-tani*" are more regular, and they are usually used to express negative comments or emotions, such as "*antakkaun ir*", "*oiga optta*", and "*simgakan il*", etc. The property of counter-expectation possessed by these expressions are not obvious, and it is more about the evaluation of antecedent events.

(5) 경찰도 치안수요가 크게 늘 것으로 판단하고 있으나 병력증원이나 새로운 장 비 도입 등은 예산확보 등의 뒷받침이 필요해 엄두도 못 내고 있<u>다니</u> 안타까운 일이 다.

*gyongchaldo chiansuyoga keuge neul kkoseuro pandanhago isseuna byongnyokjjeungwonina saeroun jang bidoip deungeun yesanhwakppo deunge dwitppachimi piryohae omdudo mot naego itt**tani** antakkaun irida.*

The police also believe that the demand for security will increase significantly, but, unfortunately, they cannot **even** think about increasing the number of troops or introducing new equipment because they need to secure a budget.

(6) 그의 구속 여부를 둘러싸고 검찰 수뇌부와 수사팀이 무려 4시간30분 동안이 나 격론을 벌였다니 어려움에 처한 검찰의 적나라한 실상을 보는 것 같아 안 N럽고 답답하기만 하다.

geue gusok yobureul dulrossago gomchal sunwebuwa susatimi muryo nesigansamsipppun dongani na gyongnoneul boryotttani oryoume chohan gomchare jongnarahan silssangeul boneun got gata an sseuropkko dapttapagiman hada.

The prosecution's leadership and the investigation team had a fierce debate for as long as four and a half hours over whether he was arrested or not, which makes me feel sorry and frustrated as if I am seeing the stark reality of the prosecution in need.

Secondly, when "*-tani*" is employed as a final word at the end of a sentence, it is a typical counter-expectation expression which shows the unexpected and surprising semantics of "*Jìngrán*" or "*Jūrán*". These expressions can be further subdivided in accordance with the typical characteristics shown by their sentence patterns and vocabulary. For example, in the usage at the end of a sentence, "*-tani*" is often used in interrogative sentences to constitute the form of "*VP + -tani?*". In other words, the speaker seeks further confirmation from the other party with a sense of uncertainty at the same time of expressing surprise and uncertainty. In the expression of non-interrogative sentences, the expression of adverbs which co-occur with "*-tani*" is more prominent. It can be preliminarily believed that they fall within the scope of a separate category, which means that "*iroke*", "*geuroke*", "*ijeya*", "*nandeopssi*"often appears before "*-tani*", to distinguish them from non-interrogative expression without the markers of adverbs.

(7) 조금전까지도 불량배로 여기던 남자하고 단둘이 마주 앉아 밥을 먹다니?

jogeumjonkkajido bulryangbaero yogidon namjahago danduri maju anja babeul mokttani.

Do you sit down and eat dinner with the man you considered a rogue until a while ago?

(8) 참아내는 것이 약간의 불편이거나 눌러 삼키면 대강 가라앉는 것이려니 여겼는 데, 이렇게 멍들어버리다니.

chamanaeneun gosi yakkkane bulpyonigona nulro samkimyon daegang garaanneun gosiryoni yogyonneunde iroke mongdeuroboritani.

I thought it was going to be a little uncomfortable to put up with, or that it would subside if I swallowed it, but it bruised like this.

4   The Similarities and Differences in the Types of the Expectation Semantic of "*Jìngrán*" and "*-tani*"

Regarding the semantic types of expectation markers, our predecessors have made different kinds of classifications. According to the classification of expectations by Chen and Wang [6], expectations can be further subdivided into at least five types in accordance with the difference in cognitive subjects: (a) self-expectation, which means the speaker's expectation of things and is also known as the "speaker's expectation"; (b) others' expectation, which means the expectation from a person other than the speaker engaged in the process of conversation, who may be the listener or a third party. It is also known as "listener's expectation", and "third party's expectation", etc.; (c) common sense expectation, which refers to the knowledge related to social psychology, such as common sense, customs, laws, and regulations available in the society with the cognitive subjects denoting the "society" or "people" that the class refers to, and they are composed of many single cognitive subjects who are also known as "conventional expectation", "normative expectation", and "shared normalcy", etc.; (d) the expectation from preceding text, which means relevant knowledge in the text that is inferred from the information by the preceding sentences; (e) (behavior) subject expectation, which means the purpose for the act to be achieved before the act set up by the subject (usually the agent) of the behavior described in the text.

Because type (d) is mainly derived from common sense expectations, type (c), this paper mainly considers the combination of the two as the same type, named common sense expectations, while type (e), (behavior) subject expectations, attaches importance to the distinction between internal and external subjects which is expected to occur in the current discourse. We preliminarily hold the view that it is compatible with self-expectation and others' expectations. To ensure the relative clarity of the type, this paper mainly uses "self-expectation", "others' expectation", and "conventional-expectation" as the main semantic types of Chinese "*Jìngrán*" and Korean "*-tani*", analyzes the expectations involved in the two Chinese and Korean corpora based on the three types of expectation. Statistical analysis is carried out on the types, and concrete results in Table 3 and Table 4 can be obtained.

Table 3. The Expectation Semantic Types of Chinese Counter-Expectation Marker "*Jìngrán*"

Expectation Type	Specific classification	Frequency	Proportion
Single expectation type	Self-expectation	168	56%
	Others' expectation	55	18.33%
	Common sense expectation	20	6.67%
Compound expectation type	Self-expectation + common sense expectation	23	7.67%
	Others' expectation + common sense expectation	15	5%
	Others' expectation + self-expectation	19	6.33%
Total		300	100%

Firstly, it can be observed from the above-listed table that the Chinese counter-expectation marker "*Jìngrán*" can be used to mark not only a single type of expectation but also a compound type of expectation. Among the single type of expectation, the type of self-expectation is the greatest in number, which appears a total of 168 times, accounting for 56%, followed by others' expectation (55 times, 18.33%) and expectation of the common type (20 times, 6.67%), for example:

(9) 我不知道博尔术这个名字竟然会引起你这么大的反应!

    *Wǒ bùzhīdào bóěrshù zhège míngzi **jìngrán** huì yǐnqǐ nǐ zhème dà de fǎnyìng!*

    I didn't know the name Borsch **would** cause such a big reaction from you!

(10) 梅蒂张口结舌地望着他, 气他竟然敢扯这么一个大谎, 又高兴他真的希望她会相信他。

    *Méidì zhāngkǒujiéshé de wàngzhe tā, qì tā **jìngrán** gǎn chě zhème yígè dàhuǎng, yòu gāoxìng tā zhēnde xīwàng tā huì xiāngxìn tā.*

    Maddy stared at him dumbfounded, angry that he dared to tell such a big lie, and glad that he hoped she would believe him.

(11) 天色已经尽黑, 接近庄口, 竟然无人发现他这位熟客, 他也看不见庄内的人, 也不见灯光。

    *Tiānsè yǐjīng jìn hēi, jiējìn zhuāngkǒu, **jìngrán** wúrén fāxiàn tā zhèwèi shúkè, tā yě kànbújiàn zhuāngnèi de rén, yě bújiàn dēngguāng.*

    It was already dark, and close to Zhuangkou, no one found him as a regular customer, and he could not see the people in the village, or the lights.

In the example sentences above, the expectation types indicated by "*Jìngrán*" are the three types including self-expectation, others' expectation, and common-sense expectation. In example (9), the speaker is the first person "I", and "I" don't know whether the listener knows about "Boer". In such circumstance, there is no relevant presupposition, or the speaker tacitly assumes that the listener knows the "Boer technique", but the reality is that the listener does not know it. Hence, the difference in the information structure between the two is formed, and therefore it is easy to convey the effect which counters the speakers' self-expectation. In Example (10), the speaker (Metti) failed to expect that 'he lied', but he actually "told a big lie", which was opposite to the speaker's cognition. Moreover, the degree of magnitude exists, which leads to counter- others' expectations. In Example (11), according to general common sense of the society, "when it is dark, this regular customer should be found when approaching the village", but the reality is that by the end of the day, no one found this regular customer, which is counter-common sense expectation.

In addition to the single counter-expectation type in the prompt sentence, "*Jìngrán*" can also be used to indicate a type of compound expectation. The corpus of this paper mainly deals with "self-expectation + common sense expectation", "others' expectation + common sense expectation", and the type of "others' expectation + self-expectation", for example:

(12) 查四道:"七年不是一个短日子, 一个住在扬州城这么热闹地方的人, 竟然搬到百家 集那么僻静的地方去, 不是有些奇怪么?"

*Zhāsì dào: "qīnián búshì yígè duǎn rìzi, yígè zhùzài yángzhōuchéng zhème rènào dìfāng de rén, **jìngrán** bāndào bǎijiājí nàme pìjìng de dìfāng qù, búshì yǒuxiē qíguài me?"*

Cha Sidao: "Seven years is not a short period. Isn't it strange that a person who lives in such a lively place in Yangzhou City **should** move to a secluded place like Baijiaji?"

(13) 五大高手<u>竟然</u>没有一个人看到他是何时闪出去的?如何闪出去的?

*Wǔdà gāoshǒu **jìngrán** méiyǒu yígèrén kàndào tā shì héshí shǎnchūqù de? Héshí shǎnchūqù de?*

Not one of the five masters saw when he flashes out? How did he flash out?

(14) 一大早老妈的电话!老妈说真的不舍得我一个人在家, 讲着讲着<u>竟然</u>哭起来 了!我也想他们!

*Yídàzǎo lǎomā de diànhuà! Lǎomā shuō zhēnde shěbùdé wǒ yígèrén zàijiā,jiǎngzhejiǎngzhe **jìngrán** kūqǐlái le! Wǒ yě xiǎng tāmen!*

My mom's phone call early in the morning! My mom said she didn't want me to be at home alone, and **even** started crying while talking! I miss them too!

In the above-mentioned example, *"Jìngrán"* indicates three compound counter-expectation expressions of "self-expectation + common sense expectation", "others' expectation + common sense expectation", "others' expectation + self-expectation", which means that they are equipped with different types of expectation attributes. In Example (12), for "Zha Si", it was beyond his expectation that a person who lived in a lively and prosperous place moved to a very secluded place, and this situation also went against common senses, which means that there was no existence of special circumstances, and it is rare for someone to move from a lively place to a secluded place. In Example (13), none of the "five masters" saw his flashing out, which is another counter expectation, and as a master, one was supposed to have the capability of seeing the way of a person's flashing out, which can be recognized as common sense in the society. But reality is deviated from this common perception, and therefore there are also two combinations of expectation in this context. In Example (14), "Mom" and "I" cried on the phone, which was beyond expectation, as far as I or "Mom" was concerned. In other words, "I" did not expect "Mom" to cry, which is a counter self-expectation. "Mom" might fail to control her emotions and cried during the phone call, which is a counter others' expectation. That is to say, in the same context, different types of expectations may appear for different subjects.

In comparison with the diverse types of expectation semantic of *"Jìngrán"*, the type of expectation semantic for Korean *"-tani"* is relatively single. In accordance with our statistical corpus, Korean *"-tani"* is mainly a single type of expectation, and there is no compound type of expectation. Moreover, a single type is a self-expectation type, and the number of types of others' expectation is extremely limited.

(15) 세상에,심장병으로 ɴ러지셨다는데 수술을 거부하시<u>다니</u>!

sesangesimjangppyongeuro sseurojisyotttaneunde susureul gobuhasitani!

Oh, my God, you refused surgery when you collapsed from a heart attack!

Table 4. The Expectation Semantic Types of Korean Counter-Expectation Marker "-*tani*"

Expectation Type	Specific classification	Frequency	Proportion
Single expectation type	Self-expectation	289	96.33%
	Others' expectation	8	2.67%
	Common sense expectation	3	1%
Total		300	100%

(16) 아키코는 "이 조그만 법률사무소에서 네 명 가운데 세 명이 노인과 함께 생활하고 있다니 믿기지가 않는다"고 말한다.

*akikoneuni jogeuman bomnyulsamusoeso ne myong gaunde se myongi noingwa hamkke saenghwal hago itt**tani** mitkkijiga anneundago malhanda.*

Akiko says, "I can't believe that three out of four people in this small law firm are living with old people."

(17) 양이 음을 따르다니.

*yang-i eum-eul ttaleu**tani**.*

Yang follows yin.

It can be found through the observation of the above examples that the Korean '-*tani*' mainly means that the speaker feels a sense of being beyond expectation and surprise due to the occurrence of something that is contrary to his expectation. In the counter self-expectation expression of Example (15), the speaker expects that the man may be in need of surgery upon seeing a very serious situation such as a person's fainting due to a heart attack. But, in fact, the person refuses to accept surgery, which goes against the speaker's judgment and expectation on the basis of facts, and expresses the speaker's surprise. In Example (16), the others' expectation expresses an expectation or emotion. She holds the view that in a small law firm, it is rather difficult to understand that three-quarters of the people live with the elderly, which is difficult for young people to understand, and thus she makes an unbelievable evaluation, expressing the speaker's surprise. In Example (17), "Yang" follows "Yin", which does not conform to the common sense that "Yin" follows "Yang", and it belongs to the situation of counter common-sense expectation.

5 The Pragmatic Similarity and Differences of Chinese and Korean Counter-Expectation Marker "*Jìngrán*" and "-*tani*"

Regarding the analysis on the pragmatic function of "*Jìngrán*", Luo [7] conducted a more in-depth analysis on the aspects including the functions of information, text, and expression. Here, we mainly make comparison between related expressions in Chinese and Korean with the help of the standard for the type of information function of "*Jìngrán*" in the theory proposed by Luo [7]. It is mainly composed of three criteria: the function of contrast background, the function of reverse preset, and the function of highlighting focus. However, because the "function of contrast background" and the "function of reverse preset" often overlap, this study will temporarily combine the two into one contrast parameter, namely the "contrast function". The pragmatic comparison of "*Jìngrán*" and "*-tani*" is mainly carried out in this part from the two aspects— "the function of contrast" and "the function of highlighting focus".

First of all, with regard to the function of comparison, it mainly deals with the comparison between the preset information and the actual information, so as to figure out whether the expression of the comparison information has close relationship with whether there are suggestive words in related expressions. In other words, in some expressions, what exists between the explicit event A and implicit event B is the expression about the comparison of promoting information which is similar to "originally though" or "initially thought", while no similar expression is available in some sentences. At the time, the contrast between events is directly expressed in an implicit form (Table 5).

Table 5. Comparison of the Contrast Functions of Chinese "*Jìngrán*" and Korean "*-tani*"

Type	Explicit contrast		Implicit contrast		Total
Parameter	Frequency	Proportion	Frequency	Proportion	
Chinese "*Jìngrán*"	14	4.67%	286	95.33%	300 (100%)
Korean "*-tani*"	95	31.67%	205	68.33%	300 (100%)

From the above table, it can be learned that, in terms of the similarity, related expressions in Chinese and Korean can both indicate explicit and implicit contrasts of events, and implicit contrasts, rather than explicit contrasts, are available in both Chinese and Korean. In terms of differences, Korean "*-tani*" has more explicit contrast than Chinese, while Chinese "*Jìngrán*" has more implicit contrast than Korean. Relevant examples are listed as follows.

(18) 水柳茫然接过礼盒, 他为什么要把这东西送给她?想不到她竟然睡了两天, 但他为何不等她?

   Shuǐliǔ mángrán jiēguò lǐhé, tā wèishěnme yào bǎ zhè dōngxi sònggěitā? Xiǎngbúdào tā jìngrán shuì le liǎngtiān, dàn tā wèihé bùděng tā?

   Shuiliu took the gift box in a daze, why did he give this to her? **Unexpectedly**, she slept for two days, but why didn't he wait for her?

(19) "我不知道博尔术这个名字竟然会引起你这么大的反应!"

   Wǒ bùzhīdào bóěrshù zhègè míngzi jìngrán huì yǐnqǐ nǐ zhème dà de fǎnyìng!

   I didn't know the name Borsch **would** cause such a big reaction from you!

(20) "자네가 이런 일을 하다니 뜻밖이야."

   janega iron ireul hatani tteutppakkiya.

   "It's a surprise that you're doing this."

(21) 이렇게 순해 보이는 사람을 의심하<u>다니</u>.
*iroke sunhae boineun sarameul uisimha<u>**tani**</u>.*
I can't believe you're suspicious of someone who looks so gentle.

In Example (18), before *"Jìngrán"*, there are often markers of explicit contrast, such as "beyond expectation" and "unexpectedness", indicating explicit contrast, which means that the speaker or the actor has shown a clearer expectation or speculation about the event and stated the expected event which occurs objectively under the assistance of *"Jìngrán"*. In Example (19), there is no similar explicit expression, but relevant expression is hidden in the sentences, and the relatively implicit expression of event can be activated with the help from encyclopedic knowledge with the aim of forming a contrast. In Example (20), the explicit contrast of Korean *"-tani"* mainly means that when *"-tani"* is used in a sentence, it expresses the contrast with the assistance from relatively explicit markers such as *"tteutppakkida"*, and the contrast is often shown through clear information of evaluation. In Example (21), there is no explicit marker or an expression which is similar to this marker, but the implicit contrast is expressed directly employing the semantic meaning of implication. For instance, "the person who looks very docile should not be gentle" is an implicit semantic in contrast to it.

Secondly, in terms of the function of focus, "focus" is the part which the speaker desires the hearer to pay attention to the most, and its essence is a pragmatic concept with the function of discourse. It is pointed out by Luo [7] that the modal adverb of *"Jìngrán"* has a more obvious role in highlighting the focus, and it is equipped with the function of highlighting the following components. Since the Chinese *"Jìngrán"* has the function of highlighting the focus, then is its position which highlights the focus in the front or at the back? Does the Korean *"-tani"* have a similar function? If it has such function, what are the similarities and differences in terms of the focus? According to the review of the corpus, preliminary data can be obtained as follows (Table 6):

Table 6. Comparison of the Focus Position of Chinese *"Jìngrán"* and Korean *"-tani"*

Type	Front focus		Back focus		Total
Parameter	Frequency	Proportion	Frequency	Proportion	
Chinese "Jìngrán"	52	17.33%	248	82.67%	300 (100%)
Korean "-tani"	180	60%	120	40%	300 (100%)

It can be seen from the above-mentioned table that in terms of similarity, the expressions related to Chinese and Korean have a certain function of prompting the focus, but in terms of differences, it is indicated by related expressions in Chinese and Korean that obvious differences are available in the position and proportion of the focus. Chinese *"Jìngrán"*, as a sensitive word indicating the focus of a sentence, is usually the case that it lays emphasis on the post-information, because post-information usually falls within the scope of [-common sense] [+accidental] new information, which is the key point which the speaker wants to highlight. For instance,

(22) 忽然一人拉住她的臂膀, 苏婉儿回头一看, <u>竟然</u>是唐尚礼。

Hūrán yìrén lāzhù tā de bìbǎng,sūwǎnér huítóu yíkàn, **jìngrán** *shì tángshànglǐ.*

Suddenly someone grabbed her arm, Su Wan'er looked back and saw that it was Tang Shangli.

(23) 有种族倾向的阿肯色州长为了阻止 9 名黑人学生上学, <u>竟然</u>派国民警卫队(相当于武警)占领了小石城中心高中。

Yǒu zhǒngzhú qīngxiàng de ākěnsè zhōuzhǎng wèile zǔzhǐ jiǔmíng hēirén xuéshēng shàngxué, **jìngrán** *pài guómín jǐngwèiduì(xiāngdāngyú wǔjǐng) zhànlǐng le xiǎoshíchéng zhōngxīn gāozhōng.*

The racially inclined governor of Arkansas sent the National Guard (equivalent to the armed police) to occupy Little Rock Central High School to prevent nine black students from going to school.

In Examples (22) and (23), "*Jìngrán*" introduces the following information "Tang Shangli" and "dispatching the National Guard" as the focus of the sentence, and they are the new information that deviates from the speaker's expectations, as well as the new information component which the speaker wants to convey to the hearer. Especially when "*Jìngrán*" is located at the beginning of a sentence, the focus is usually post-positioned, and therefore the focus distribution of Chinese "*Jìngrán*" shows more "post-positioned focus" than "pre-positioned focus". On the contrary, the distribution of Korean "*-tani*" shows a distribution of mirror image, where there is generally more "front-positioned focus" than "post-positioned focus", which is closely related to the position of "*-tani*", the position of focus indicated by "*-tani*" at the end of the sentence suggests that the position of focus is easier to be pre-positioned; while the "*-tani*" in the middle of the sentence has the possibility of pre-positioning and post-positioning.

(24) 꼭 해결하야 할 사업이 있는 것도 아닌데 그까짓 어린 녀석 하나를 만나려고 일 부러 그 먼 길을 가<u>다니</u>!

*kkok haegyolhaya hal saobi inneun gottto aninde geukkajit orin nyosok hanareul mannaryogo ilburo geu mon gireul ga**tani**!*

I don't have a business to work on, but I'm going all the way to meet a little guy like that!

(25) 아키코는"이 조그만 법률사무소에서 네 명 가운데 세 명이 노인과 함께 생활하 고 있<u>다니</u> 믿기지가 않는다"고 말한다.

*akikoneuni jogeuman bomnyulsamusoeso ne myong gaunde se myongi noingwa hamkke saenghwal hago itt**tani** mitkkijiga anneundago malhanda.*

Akiko says, "I can't believe that three out of four people in this small law firm are living with old people."

The basic proposition of "*-tani*" at the end of the sentence, as well as the characteristics of the preposition and postposition shown by "*-tani*" in the sentence, determines that the type of focus preposition shown by Korean-related expressions is more prominent.

6 Comparison between Chinese and Korean Counter-Expectation Markers *"Jìngrán"* and *"-tani"*

In the above context, a comparative analysis on the syntactic, semantic, and pragmatic dimensions of the Chinese *"Jìngrán"* and Korean *"-tani"* is mainly conducted. The similarities and differences between the two are initially summarized as follows:

Firstly, at the level of syntactic, concerning the similarity, both *"Jìngrán"* and *"-tani"* in Chinese and Korean can appear in sentences and can be employed through the combination with modal adverbs or antecedent endings which express ability. With regard to the difference, (1) Chinese *"Jìngrán"* can appear at the beginning of a sentence, rather than at the end of a sentence. Korean *"-tani"* can be used at the end of a sentence, but it cannot appear at the beginning of a sentence. Moreover, its being used at the end of a sentence occupies a large proportion. (2) The proportion of Chinese *"Jìngrán"* in the middle of the sentence is greater than that at the beginning of the sentence, and it is mostly used in combination with multi-functional modal adverbs in the sentence. The expression of Korean *"-tani"* in the sentences is more characteristic—they are often preceded by expressions of antecedent suffix which expresses tense or ability and they are often followed by the expressions of negative evaluation or emotion. Additionally, the Korean *"-tani"* located at the end of a sentence is a typical counter-expectation expression. In the commonly used interrogative sentences, it constitutes *"VP + -tani"*, and its co-occurrence with adverb expressions is more prominent in non-interrogative expressions.

Secondly, at the level of semantic, with regard to similarities, both *"Jìngrán"* and *"-tani"* in Chinese and Korean can express a single type of expectation, and self-expectation accounts for the largest proportion. In the aspect of difference, the Chinese counter-expectation marker *"Jìngrán"* can mark expectation of compound types, with diverse types. However, the Korean counter-expectation marker *"-tani"* cannot mark compound types of expectation, and the types are relatively single.

Thirdly, the similarities are mainly analyzed from the aspects of contrast function and focus position at the pragmatic level. Both related expressions in Chinese and Korean can indicate the explicit and implicit contrast of events, and both Chinese and Korean are mainly dominated by implicit contrast. In contrast, explicit contrast is relatively few in number. Chinese and Korean-related expressions all have a certain function of indicating the focus. With regard to the differences, Chinese *"Jìngrán"* generally lays emphasis on post-positioned information, and the "post-positioned focus" is more than "pre-positioned focus". Korean *"-tani"* usually attaches importance to pre-information, with more "pre-positioned focus" than "post-positioned focus".

7 The Reasons for Similarities and Differences between Chinese and Korean Counter-expectation Markers *"Jìngrán"* and *"-tani"*

The reasons for the similarities and differences between Chinese and Korean counter-expectation markers *"Jìngrán"* and *"-tani"* mentioned above can be primarily explained through the three aspects, including language type, subjectivity, and information structure.

First of all, the syntactic differences between related expressions in Chinese and Korean have close connection with the language type of Chinese and Korean. The component of function words in Chinese is one of the important means in the expression of grammar and the speaker's emotion and attitude. The same is true for "*Jìngrán*" as an expression of the nature of an adverb. Generally speaking, it can only play its due role at the beginning of a sentence and in the middle of a sentence. However, it cannot appear at the end of a sentence to function as the completion marker of a sentence; while "*-tani*" can appear in the middle of a sentence or at the end of a sentence, rather than at the end of a sentence, which is related to its suffix attribute.

Secondly, with regard to the differences in the types of expectation semantic in related expressions in Chinese and Korean, they have close relationship with subjectivity. According to the view of Traugott (1999), counter-expectation is actually a representation of the speaker's "point of view", and thus it is regarded as a manifestation of the "subjectivity" of language, which refers to the fact that the speaker expresses his position, attitude, and emotion while uttering the words. At the same time, the speaker leaves a mark of "self" in the discourse. People's expectations of an event can be shown from different aspects—not only from the speaker himself, but also from the perspective of other participants in relevant context. More than that, it can even be conducted from the perspective of a third party that is beyond the context. However, in the selection process of different "viewpoints", the counter-expectation from one's perspective is the most direct, convenient, and economical expression, and it is also supposed to be the most unmarked expression.

However, Chinese and Korean have different characteristics in some types of compound expression, and it is closely related to the characteristics of expression shown by respective language. Chinese-related expressions allow the roles played by each participant in the context to be flexible by mostly using flexible word order and function words, and thus the range of options for listeners or readers is wider. Expectation inferences can be made from various aspects or positions. On the contrary, Korean is often expressed with the assistance from related suffixes, and it is less flexible than Chinese. However, the establishment of types related to expectation is relatively fixed. It is less likely for the types of combination to cross between expectation types and they are mostly presented in the form of self-expectation.

Thirdly, the pragmatic differences between the expressions related to Chinese and Korean mainly have close relationship with the information structure. The behavioral information that usually indicates the occurrence of an event before "*Jìngrán*" in Chinese is regarded as known information. The speaker or the expectation subject would infer the occurrence of an event under the indication or foreshadowing of known information. However, this event is usually hidden in the sentence and may not be manifested in the sentence. However, an event actually happening in reality is an event that deviates from the expected inference, which means the new information that the subject wants to emphasize, so that relevant information or focus is mostly post-positioned. On the contrary, the expressions related to Korean mostly appear in the middle or at the end of the sentence. When they are located in the middle of the sentence, it is rather obvious that the attribute of expectation is not strong, and most of them refer to the evaluation or attitude towards the previous event. The new information or focus of relevant expression are likely to be pre-positioned or post-positioned. When related expression is located at the end of the sentence, its attribute of expectation is strong, falling within the scope of typical expectation expression. However, when related expression is located at the end of the sentence, the new information or focus of related expression is mostly the previous component expressed immediately at the end of the sentence, and it is also the new information or focuses which the intended subject aims to lay emphasis on.

8 Conclusion

This paper mainly makes comparison between the syntax, semantics, and pragmatics of the Chinese counter-expectation marker "*Jìngrán*" and the Korean counter-expectation marker "*-tani*" using some example sentences from the corpus, followed by the analysis and summary of the characteristics, similarities, and differences in the expression of the two. Moreover, a preliminary analysis of the reasons for the similarities and differences is conducted.

Firstly, at the syntactic level, with regard to the similarities, both the Chinese counter-expectation marker "*Jìngrán*" and the Korean counter-expectation marker "*-tani*" can appear in the sentences, and both of them can be employed in combination with modal adverbs and word endings expressing ability. When it comes to the differences, Chinese-related expressions can occur at the beginning of a sentence, rather than at the end of a sentence, while Korean-related expressions can appear at the end of a sentence rather than at the beginning of a sentence, with its appearance at the end of the sentence occupying a greater proportion.

Secondly, at the level the types of expectation semantic, with regard to the similarities, both Chinese and Korean-related expressions have a single type of expectation, and there are many types of self-expectation. Concerning the differences, Chinese-related expressions can mark compound types of expectation, and there are various types. However, Korean-related expressions generally do not mark compound types of expectation, and the types are relatively single.

Thirdly, at the level of pragmatics, regarding the similarities, related expressions in both Chinese and Korean can indicate the explicit and implicit contrasts of events, and implicit contrasts occupy a large proportion in both of them. Moreover, related expressions have the function of indicating the focus. Concerning the differences, Chinese-related expressions generally lay emphasis on post-positioned information, while Korean-related expressions generally attach importance to pre-positioned information.

Fourth, in terms of the motives that result in the above-mentioned similarities and differences, we have initially analyzed three main reasons: with regard to syntax, it is mainly related to the language types of the two languages, and the adverb attribute of the Chinese "*Jìngrán*" and the Korean "*-tani*" influence their distributions in sentences, respectively. Regarding the types of expectation semantics, it mainly has relationship with subjectivity. In terms of pragmatics, it mainly has close relationship with the structure of language information.

References

1. Qiang, X.N.: Non-specific and specific expectations in counter-expectation situations: a case study of "Jìngrán" and "Piānpiān". J. Stud. Chin. Lang. (6), 675–689+767 (2020). (in Chinese)
2. Shan, W.: Research on the Expectation-Deviating Expressions in Modern Chinese. Ph.D. thesis, Jilin University (2017). (in Chinese)
3. Shan, W.: A study on the counter-expectation function of the mirative commentary adverb "*Jìngrán*". J. Sinogram Cult. **17**, 41–44 (2021). (in Chinese)
4. Li, B.Z., Zheng, S.M.J.: The grammatical meaning of "*Jìngrán*" and "*Jūrán*". J. Chin. Lang. Lear. **3**, 56–64 (2021). (in Chinese)
5. Kang, K.Y.: Three uses of the Korean ending "*-tani*". J. Korean Semant. **69**(3), 219–251 (2020). (in Korean)
6. Chen, Z.Y., Wang, M.Y.: The Cognitive Model of Expectation and its Types: On a Series of Phenomena related to *Jìngrán/Piānpiān*. J. Lang. Teach. Linguist. Stud. **5**, 48–63 (2021). (in Chinese)
7. Luo, S.L.: A Pragmatic Function Analysis on Modality Adverbs of "*Jìngrán*" Category. Master. Thesis, Guangxi Normal University (2007). (in Chinese)

Variations in Alternative Pattern of Light Verb Construction Between Taiwan and Mainland Mandarin

Menghan Jiang[1]([✉])[ID] and Chu-Ren Huang[2][ID]

[1] Shenzhen MSU-BIT University, Shenzhen, China
menghan.jiang@connect.polyu.hk
[2] The Hong Kong Polytechnic University, Hung Hom, Hong Kong, China
churen.huang@polyu.edu.hk

Abstract. In this study, we examine the variations in the alternative pattern of light verb construction between Taiwan and Mainland Mandarin, based on a large-scale comparable corpora statistical approach. The results show that these two variants display significant differences in preference for introducing the theme of the taken complement of the light verb, and Taiwan light verb significantly favors two specific alternations: e.g., 进行对可行性研究 *jinxing dui kexingxing yanjiu*, 进行研究可行性 *jinxing yanjiu kexingxing* 'to conduct research on practicability'. Moreover, we have also shown that some linguistic factors influence the alternations' choices: e.g., the complexity of the theme. Based on the observations, we further argue that the specific alternations in Taiwan indicate the different syntactic types of light verb complements in the two language variations.

Keywords: Corpus-Based Approach · Light Verb Construction · Language Variation

1 Introduction

In modern Chinese, there exists a kind of semantically bleached verb which is called the light verb (the most typically used ones are 进行/加以/做/搞/从事 *jinxing/jiayi/zuo/gao/cong* 'proceed/inflict/do/do/engage'). They are similar to English light verbs (e.g., take rest, give advice, [1]) in the sense that the predicative content mainly comes from its taken complement (e.g., [2]), while the light verb itself may only contribute aspectual information, without containing any eventive information [3]. For example, for the construction 进行讨论 *jinxing taolun* proceed_discuss 'to discuss', the predicative information all comes from the complement 讨论 *taolun* 'discuss', while the light verb 进行 *jinxing* 'proceed' itself only contributes information about event shape and indicates the event type that the event of 'discuss' is an activity which has a duration/process.

Due to the semantic impoverishment of the light verb, the taken complement of the light verb is always verbal (e.g., 研究 *yanjiu* 'research' in 进行研究 *jinxing yanjiu* proceed_research 'to conduct research'). In that sense, if the verbal complement

© The Author(s), under exclusive license to Springer Nature Switzerland AG 2023
Q. Su et al. (Eds.): CLSW 2022, LNAI 13495, pp. 312–322, 2023.
https://doi.org/10.1007/978-3-031-28953-8_24

contains two arguments, it is natural for it to have another theme (whether internal or external). For example, in the construction 进行研究*jinxing yanjiu* proceed_research 'to conduct research', 研究*yanjiu* 'research' is a two-argument predicate, it can have a theme (e.g., 可行性*kexingxing* 'practicability'). According to previous studies (e.g., [4]), the most frequent pattern is the prepositional structure such as 对可行性进行研究*dui kexingxing jinxing yanjiu* for_practicability_proceed_research 'to conduct research on practicability' [4]. However, we have observed that there are different alternative patterns to introduce the theme of the verbal object in the corpus data. For example, for the light verb进行*jinxing* in Mainland, there are mainly three alternations to introduce the theme of the verbal complement, as shown in 1), 2), and 3):

1) 对可行性进行研究
     dui kexingxing jinxing yanjiu
     for_practicability_proceed_research
     'to conduct research on practicability'

2) 进行可行性研究
     jinxing kexingxing yanjiu
     proceed_practicability_research
     'to·conduct research on practicability'

3) 进行 (对) 可行性的研究.
     jinxing (dui) kexingxing de yanjiu
     proceed_(for)_practicability_DE_research
     'to conduct research on practicability'

In 1), the theme is introduced by a prepositional structure and appears before the light verb. For 2), the theme is used as a modifier of the taken complement. For 3), the prepositional structure (对 可行性 *dui kexingxing*) appears between the light verb and the taken complement, and the taken complement is nominalized and marked with 的 *de*.

Moreover, variation differences in alternative patterns between Mainland and Taiwan Mandarin have also been observed in the corpus. Besides the three alternations shown above, another two alternative constructions have also been found in the Taiwan corpus.

4) 进行对可行性研究
     jinxing dui kexingxing yanjiu
     proceed_for_practicability_research
     to conduct research on practicability'

5) 进行 研究 可行性
     jinxing yanjiu kexingxing
     proceed_research_practiciability
     'to conduct research on practicability'

For 4), the prepositional structure appears between the light verb and the taken complement (without 的 *de*). For 5), the taken complement can be followed directly by the theme. These two alternative constructions cannot be accepted by Mainland Mandarin speakers, nor can they be detected in the Mainland corpus.

2 Research Question and Methodology

Based on the observations, we address two research questions: (1) Empirically and statistically, is there any distributional difference between Mainland and Taiwan in terms of their alternative choices? (2) What factors are influencing their alternation choices?

In this study, we investigate the most typical light verb进行*jinxing* [4]. We collect 111 and 119 tokes of 进行*jinxing*, from Mainland Mandarin and Taiwan Mandarin, respectively. We further annotate the alternation types for each token in each variant. The five alternations are shown in Table 1.

The corpus we use is the Annotated Chinese Gigaword corpus which was collected and available from LDC and contains over 1.1 billion Chinese words, with 700 million characters from Taiwan Central News Agency and 400 million characters from Mainland Xinhua News Agency [5].

Table 1. Alternations of light verb constructions

	Description	Examples
Type 1 PP_LV_H	Prepositional structure appears before light verb	对可行性进行研究 *dui kexingxing jinxing yanjiu* for_practicability_proceed_research 'to conduct research on practicability'
Type 2 LV_NP_H	Theme as a modifier appears between light verb and complement	进行可行性研究 *jinxing kexingxing yanjiu* proceed_practicability_research 'to conduct research on practicability'
Type 3 LV_NP_ DE_H	Prepositional structure appears between light verb and taken complement with DE	进行 (对) 可行性的研究 *jinxing (dui) kexingxing de yanjiu* proceed_(for)_practicability_DE_research 'to conduct research on practicability'
Type 4 LV_PP_ H	Prepositional structure appears between light verb and taken complement	进行对可行性研究 *jinxing dui kexingxing yanjiu* proceed_for_practicability_research 'to conduct research on practicability'
Type 5 LV_H_NP	Theme can directly follow light verb complement	进行研究可行性 *jinxing yanjiu kexingxing* proceed_research_practiciability 'to conduct research on practicability'

Previous studies on Chinese light verb constructions showed that light verbs can take either a noun or a verb as an object, as long as it contains eventive information (e.g.,

[6]). This fact poses serious challenges in determining the actual categorical status of the so-called deverbal nouns in Chinese light verb constructions, as they do not bear any morphological markers for their categorical status. Type 1, the most commonly adopted construction, is such a case where the preposed PP is linked to the predicate-argument structure of the head (H), which could either be a noun or a verb. Type 2 and Type 3, on the other hand, can be analyzed as having the top-level structure of LV_NP, where the eventive complement is combined to form NP with the H. The nominal status is further evidenced by DE marking it as the head of a relative clause (Type 3), and it is taking a Pre-Head NP argument (Type 2). Type 4 takes a pre-Head PP argument and Type 5 takes a post-Head argument, both are consistent with the head being a verb.

3 Data Analyses

3.1 The First Research Question

The distribution of each alternation in each variety is shown in Fig. 1. We can see that Type 4 and Type 5 are only detected in Taiwan data.

We further use the chi-square test to investigate whether the distribution differences have statistical significance or not. As shown in Table 2, the results (Standardized Pearson residuals e_{ij} are transformed into signs [7]. The "+" ($e_{ij} > 2$) can be interpreted as a statistically significant overuse of the light verb with the factor, while "−" ($e_{ij} < -2$) shows a statistically significant underuse of the light verb with the factor. The "0" (e_{ij} [−2,2]) indicates a lack of statistical significance.

The results indicate that 进行 *jinxing* in Mainland Mandarin prefers alternation Type 1: such as in 6). While in Taiwan Mandarin, 进行 *jinxing* is favored by Type 2 (as in 7)), Type 4 (as in 8–9)), and Type 5 (10–12)).

6) 对政策进行调控
   dui zhengce jinxing tiaokong
   for_policy_proceed_regulate
   'to regulate policy'

7) 环保学家反对毫无限制地在此地区进行森林砍伐
   haunbaoxuejia fandui haowuxianzhi de zai cidiqu jinxing senlin kanfa
   Environmentalist_oppose_unrestricted_in_this_area_deforestation
   'Environmentalists oppose unrestricted deforestation in this area'

8) 进行对市政府工务部门质询
   jinxing dui shizhengfu gongwu bumen zhixun
   proceed_for_municipal government_works department_inquiry
   'to conduct inquiries to the municipal government works department'

9) 利用基因分子新的鲸鱼研究方法进行对鲸鱼研究
   liyong jiyunfenzi xinde jingyu yanjjiu fangfa jinxing dui jingyu yanjiu
   utilize_genetic molecule_new_research_method_proceed_for_whale_research
   'to conduct research on whales using new whale research genetic molecule methods'

10) 进行研制高级复合材料减速板
     jinxing yanzhi gaoji fuhe cailiao jiansuban
     proceed_develop_advanced_composite_material_speed brake
     'to develop advanced composite material speed brake'

11) 开始进行处理教育预算
     kaishi jinxing chuli jiaoyu yusuan
     start_proceed_process_education_budget
     'to start processing education budget'

12) 进行调整自用车辆税费
     jinxing tiaozheng ziyong cheliang feishui
     proceed_adjust_own-use_vehicle_tax fee
     'to adjust taxes and fees for own-use vehicles'

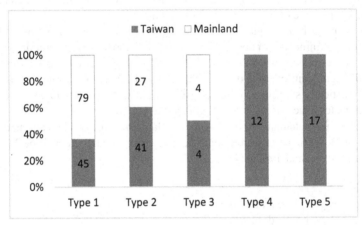

Fig. 1. Frequency distribution of 进行 *jinxing* in two varieties

Table 2. Result of Chi-square test for 进行 *jinxing* in two varieties

	Type 1	Type 2	Type 3	Type 4	Type 5
Taiwan 进行 *jinxing*	–	+	0	+	+
Mainland 进行 *jinxing*	+	–	0	–	–

We have observed significant differences in word order preference between Mainland and Taiwan Mandarin. For the light verb 进行 *jinxing*, the theme in Taiwan Mandarin prefers to appear after the light verb (either appears between the light verb and the complement or follows the complement), while the theme in Mainland Mandarin significantly prefers to appear before the light verb.

3.2 The Second Research Question

3.2.1 Factors Influence the Syntactic Choices

In this section, we aim to answer the second question: what factors can influence syntactic choices?

We annotate all the tokens of 进行 *jinxing* (230 tokens = 111 + 119) in both Mainland and Taiwan Mandarin, with some potential factors which may influence the syntactic choices among different alternations, as shown in Table 3. These factors were chosen from the previous researches [8–12], and also based on our observations. To facilitate the annotation procedure, we simplified these variables to binary values: Yes or No. The annotator is a trained expert in Chinese linguistics, and the reliability and validity of the annotation have been tested.

With the fully annotated data, the Chi-square test is conducted to examine the significance of the co-occurrence of each feature with each alternation. Both Mainland and Taiwan 进行 *jinxing* only show significance with Type 1 and 2.

The results (Table 4) show that for 进行 *jinxing* in both Mainland Taiwan Mandarin, complex theme (as in 13)), animate theme (as in 14)) and proper noun theme (as in 15)) prefer to occur in Type 1 alternation. The main variation differences between Mainland and Taiwan are: 1) the complex complement tends to be shown in Type 1 alternation in Mainland Mandarin, while the complexity of complement does not affect the alternation choice in Taiwan Mandarin. 2) pronominal theme significantly prefers Type 1 in Mainland Mandarin, while no significance has been observed in Taiwan Mandarin for this feature.

13) 对 复杂 景物 和简单 景物 进行 跟踪
    dui   fuza   jingwu   he   jiandan   jingwu   jinxing   genzong
    for_complex_scene_and_simple_scene_proceed_trace
    'to trace the complex and simple scene'

14) 对 妇女 进行 检测
    dui funü jinxing jiance
    for_female_proceed_test
    'to test on female'

15) 与 美国 进行 对话
    yu meiguo jinxing duihua
    with_America_proceed_dialogue
    'to have a dialogue with America'

Table 3. Potential factors to influence the syntactic choices

Feature	Examples of Yes	Examples of No
complexity of the theme (whether the theme has a modifier)	对落后的工厂生产技术进行改造 *dui luohou de gongchan shengchan jishu jinxing gaizao* for_backward_DE_factory_production_technology_proceed_improve 'to improve the backward factory production technology'	对技术进行改造 *dui jishu jinxing gaizao* for_technology_proceed_improve 'to improve the technology'
complexity of the taken complement (whether the complement has a modifier)	进行对政策长期深入的贯彻 *jinxing dui zhengce changqi shenru de guanche* proceed_for_policy_long-term_in-depth_DE_implement 'proceed with a long-term in-depth implementation of the policy'	进行对政策的贯彻 *jinxing dui zhengce de guanche* proceed_for_policy_DE_implement 'to implement the policy'
Animacy of theme (whether the theme is animate)	对陈庆辉进行调查 *dui chenqinghui jinxing diaocha* for_Chenqinghui_proceed_investigate 'to investigate Chen Qinghui'	对可行性进行研究 *dui kexingxing jinxing yanjiu* for_practicability_inflict_research 'to conduct research on practicability'
pronominality of the theme (whether the theme is a pronoun)	为此进行协商 *wei ci jinxing xieshang* for_this_proceed_negotiate 'to negotiate about this issue'	对报告进行汇总 *dui baogao jinxing huizong* for_report_proceed_summarize 'to summarize the report'
Whether the theme is a proper noun	对陈庆辉进行调查 *dui chenqinghui jinxing diaocha* for_Chenqinghui_proceed_investigate 'to investigate Chen Qinghui'	对男性进行检测 *dui nanxing jinxing jiance* for_male_proceed_test 'to test on male'

Table 4. Chi-square test results for syntactic choice of Mainland and Taiwan 进行 *jinxing*

Factors	Mainland 进行 *jinxing*		Taiwan 进行 *jinxing*	
	Type 1	Type 2	Type 1	Type 2
Attribute of theme	+	−	+	−
Attribute of complement	+	−	0	0
Animacy of theme	+	−	+	−
Proper noun	+	−	+	−
Pronominality of theme	+	−	0	0

3.2.2   Correlation Between Alternation Choice and Length of Theme

As observed in Sect. 3.2.1, the complexity of the theme significantly correlated with the syntactic choice. In this section, we further investigate the correlation between the length of the theme and different alternations, by a Kruskal-Wallis test [13]. We also use Dunn's procedure with a Bonferroni correction [14] for multiple comparisons.

The results in both Mainland and Taiwan Mandarin show that the length of theme for Type 1 alternation is significantly higher than the other alternations ($\chi^2 = 11.406$, $p = 0.01$, $\chi^2 = 26.971$, $p < 0.001$). This finding confirms that the complexity of the theme is a crucial factor that influences syntactic choices. In particular, complex themes (themes with attributes and are relatively longer) tend to appear before the light verb (the Type 1 alternation), while the simple theme is more likely to appear in the post-light verb position.

4   Discussion

We have observed that Mainland Mandarin and Taiwan Mandarin differ in introducing the theme of the event. Mainland Mandarin show favors in Type 1, while Taiwan Mandarin significantly prefers two specific types: Type 4 and Type 5. We argue that these two specific types of alternations indicate the different syntactic types of light verb complements in Mainland and Taiwan.

Previous studies have numbers of debates on the syntactic type of the taken complements of light verbs. Some studies consider the taken complement as a 名动词/动名词 *ming dongci/dong mingci* 'nominal verb', which has both nominal and verbal properties (e.g., [3, 15]), while others hold the opinion that the complement has already been transferred from the original verb to a typical noun through the process of nominalization (e.g., [16, 17]).

According to our observations from the corpora data, we argue that there are different types of taken complements ([6]) in Taiwan and Mainland. The taken complements as 研究 *yanjiu* 'research' in 进行可行性研究 *jinxing kexingxing yanjiu* and 进行研究可行性 *jinxing yanjiu kexingxing* belong to different syntactic types: deverbal and typical verb. We will illustrate this issue in detail.

The study of Shi [18] differentiates two kinds of eventive phrases which can appear in the object position. He argues that due to its internal nominal structure and the typical nominal syntactic behavior, 保护*baohu* 'protect' in sentence 16a should be considered as a Noun (can be modified by attribute). In contrast, in sentence 16b, 保护 *baohu* 'protect' here has syntactic behavior of verbs (e.g., can take object and complement). The whole phrase 保护环境 *baohu huanjing* protect_environment 'protect the environment' has the verbal internal structure (V-O structure) and can be used as a predicate as in 我们要保护环境 *women yao baohu huanjing* we_need_protect_environment 'We need to protect the environment' [18].

16) a. 我们需要注意环境保护。
    women xuyao zhuyi huanjing baohu
    we_need_pay attention to_environment_protect
    'We need to pay attention to environmental protection.'
    b. 我们需要注意保护环境。
    women xuyao zhuyi baohu huanjing
    we_need_pay attention to_protect_environment
    'We need to pay attention to environmental protection.'

For light verb constructions, the variation differences we have observed in our data can be well classified by this standard. For the usage of Mainland light verb construction, the theme can only appear before the eventive complement, either before the light verb (17a) (Type 1) or between the light verb and the taken complement with DE (17b) (Type 2), which shows the typical properties of a Noun.

17) a. 对可行性进行研究
    dui kexingxing jinxing yanjiu
    for_practicability_proceed_research
    'to conduct research on practicability'
    b. 进行可行性的研究
    jinxing kexingxing yanjiu
    proceed_practicability_research
    'to conduct research on practicability'

However, in Taiwan-specific usage, the object 研究 *yanjiu* 'research' can be followed by the theme 可行性 *kexingxing* 'practicability' (18a), which shows that 研究 *yanjiu* here remains the property of a regular verb of taking another object. Moreover, 研究可行性 *yanjiu kexingxing* as a VO phrase is considered as a VP in the sense that it has the verbal internal structure (V-O structure) and can be used as a predicate (政府研究可行性 *zhengfu yanjiu kexingxing* government_research_practiciability 'the government conducts research on practiciability'). Furthermore, the whole VO phrase as a VP can be modified by adverbial (18b). Hence, we use "VP" to distinguish it from a de-verbalized Nominal Phrase (可行性的研究 *kexingxing de yanjiu* 'research on practiciability').

18) a. 进行研究可行性
    jinxing yanjiukexingxing
    proceed_research_practiciability
    'to conduct research on practicability'

b. 政府目前正对有关项目进行研究可行性
zhengfu muqian zheng dui youguan xiangmu jinxing yanjiu kexingxing
Government_now_being_for_related_project_proceed_research_practiciability
'Now the government is conducting practicability research for related projects.'

In this regard, we adopt the analyses of Shi [18] and consider the 研究 *yanjiu* in Mainland usage as a deverbal noun that has been transferred from the verb through the process of de-verbalization. While in Taiwan-specific usage, 研究 *yanjiu* keeps the verbal characteristic of taking another object (as in 18a). Moreover, we have also found in Taiwan usages, that when eventive complement is modified by a prepositional structure, DE is not always necessary (19), Type 4 alternation.

19)   进行 对可行性研究
      jinxing duikexingxingyanjiu
      proceed_for_practicability_research
      'to conduct research on practicability'

While in Mainland, in this context, DE has to appear to license the sentence (e.g., 进行对可行性的研究 *jinxing dui kexingxing de yanjiu*). As prepositional structure cannot modify an NP directly without DE (e.g., [19]), what we found in Taiwan data is another piece of evidence to prove that the taken complement in Taiwan usage is a verb.

Therefore, we conclude as the taken complement in Taiwan Mandarin shown in Type 4 and Type 5 alternations should be considered a verb, while in Mainland usage the taken complement of light verb is a deverbal noun.

5   Conclusion

In this study, we have observed the differences in alternative choices in introducing the theme of the event between Mainland and Taiwan Mandarin. The theme in Taiwan Mandarin prefers to appear after the light verb (either appears between the light verb and the complement or follows the complement), while in Mainland Mandarin, the theme significantly prefers to appear before the light verb.

For the factors that may influence the syntactic choices, for light verb 进行 *jinxing* in both varieties, the theme's complexity significantly correlates with their syntactic choices. In particular, the complex and animate themes prefer to occur before the light verb for both Mainland and Taiwan light verbs.

Based on the distributional variations between Taiwan and Mainland Mandarin, we further argue that the taken complements in different alternations belong to different syntactic types. The complement in Mainland alternations can be considered as a deverbal noun that has undergone the process of de-verbalization. While in Taiwan specific alternations, the taken complement should be considered as a typical verb. The whole phrase taken by 进行 *jinxing* is a verbal phrase.

References

1. Jespersen, O.: A Modern English Grammar on Historical Principles. Part VI, Morphology. George Allen and Unwin Ltd, London (1965)
2. Zhu, D.X.: Xiandai Shumian Hanyu li de Xuhua Dongci he Mingdongci (Dummy Verbs and NV in Modern Chinese). J. Peking Univ. (Humanities and Social Sciences) **5**, 1–6 (1985)
3. Jiang, M., Huang, C.R.: A comparable corpus-based study of three DO verbs in varieties of mandarin. In: Chinese Lexical Semantics: 19th Workshop, CLSW 2018, Revised Selected Papers, vol. 11173, p. 147. Springer(2018)
4. Cai, W.L.: 'Jingxing' Daibin Wenti (Issues on the Complement of 'jinxing'). Chin. Lang. Learn. **3**, 7–11 (1982)
5. Huang, C.R.: Tagged Chinese Gigaword Version 2.0. Lexical Data Consortium, University of Pennsylvania, Philadelphia. ISBN 1-58563-516-2(2009)
6. Jiang, M., Shi, D., Huang, C.R.: Transitivity in light verb variations in Mandarin Chinese– a comparable corpus-based statistical approach. In: Proceedings of the 30th Pacific Asia Conference on Language, Information and Computation, pp. 459–468 (2016)
7. Agresti, A., Kateri, M.: Categorical Data Analysis, pp. 206–208. Springer, Berlin Heidelberg (2011)
8. Bresnan, J.: Is syntactic knowledge probabilistic? Experiments with the English dative alternation. Roots: Linguistics in search of its evidential base, pp. 75–96 (2007)
9. Bresnan, J., Cueni, A., Nikitina, T., Baayen, R.H.: Predicting the dative alternation. Cognitive Foundations of Interpretation, pp. 69–94 (2007)
10. Bresnan, J., Hay, J.: Gradient grammar: an effect of animacy on the syntax of give in New Zealand and American English. Lingua **118**(2), 245–259 (2008)
11. Bresnan, J., Ford, M.: Predicting syntax: Processing dative constructions in American and Australian varieties of English. Language **86**(1), 168–213 (2010)
12. Jiang, M., Huang, C.R.: Transitivity variations in mandarin VO compounds—a comparable corpus-based approach. In: Chinese Lexical Semantics: 18th Workshop, CLSW 2017, Revised Selected Papers, pp. 564–575. Springer (2017)
13. Test, K.-W.: In: The Concise Encyclopedia of Statistics. Springer, New York, NY (2008)
14. Dunn, O.J.: Multiple comparisons using rank sums. Technometrics **6**, 241–252 (1964)
15. Chen, N.P.: Xiandai Hanyu Mingcilei de Kuoda (The Expansion of Modern Chinese Noun Class). Zhongguo Yuwen **5**, 379–389 (1987)
16. Xiao, F.: 'Jinxing' (On light verb jinxing). Chinese Knowledge (1955)
17. Li, L.D.: Xiandai Hanyu Dongci (Verbs in Modern Chinese). China Social Science Press, Beijing (1990)
18. Shi, D.X.: Mingci he Mingcixing Chengfen (Nouns and Nominals). Peking University Press (2011)
19. Huang, B.R., Liao, X.D.: Xiandai Hanyu (Modern Chinese). Beijing Higher Education Press (2007)

Responses to Questions in Mandarin Chinese

Jiun-shiung Wu[(✉)] [iD]

Institute of Linguistics, National Chung Cheng University, Minhsiung, Chiayi County, Taiwan
Lngwujs@ccu.edu.tw

Abstract. This paper presents the result of a preliminary examination on responses to *ma* questions and *A-not-A* questions in Mandarin Chinese. We recognize five types: predicate response, *shì* response, *duì* response, *yǒu* response and *huì* response. Only the first three can function as felicitous positive responses to positive *ma* questions, instead of *A-not-A* questions. This difference is attributed to the confirmation-seeking vs. information-seeking distinction of question types. Only predicate- and *huì* responses can serve as felicitous negative responses to positive *ma* questions, rather than *A-not-A* questions. This discrepancy is ascribed to the negative connotation carried by *bù shì/bù duì*. As for negative *ma* questions, agreement with a negative proposition under inquiry can be expressed by *shì*- and *duì* responses, since they state confirmation of the negative proposition. However, disagreeing with a negative proposition under question can hardly be done, except by predicate responses, because double-negatives are psycho-linguistically more expensive and therefore strongly dispreferred.

Keywords: Responses to questions · Questions · Semantics · Mandarin Chinese

1 Introduction

Responses to questions in Mandarin Chinese (for short, Chinese) has attracted few linguists' attention, if any. However, this shortage is not because responses to questions are a simple phenomenon and do not deserve attention. Rather, it is a very complicated linguistic phenomenon, which calls for detailed examination. This paper presents the result of a preliminary study on this phenomenon.

Answers to English polar questions, regardless of whether positive or negative, behave in a similar way, as illustrated below.

(1) A: Does John exercise every day?
     B: Yes, he does./No, he does not.

(2) A: Doesn't John exercise every day?
     B: Yes, he does./No, he does not.

(1) and (2) reveal that, if the fact is that John exercises every day, then the answer is *Yes, he does*; if the fact is that John does not exercise every day, then the response is *No, he does not*. It does not matter whether the question itself is positive or negative.

© The Author(s), under exclusive license to Springer Nature Switzerland AG 2023
Q. Su et al. (Eds.): CLSW 2022, LNAI 13495, pp. 323–336, 2023.
https://doi.org/10.1007/978-3-031-28953-8_25

There are different ways to categorize questions in Chinese. [1] states, in Chapter 18, four types: (i) question-word question, (ii) disjunctive questions, (iii) tag question and (iv) particle question. [2] also presents four kinds in Chapter 7: (i) *ye-no* questions, (ii) disjunctive questions, (iii) *A-not-A* questions and (iv) *wh*-questions. [3] tells two types apart: (i) confirmation-seeking questions and (ii) information-seeking questions. See examples below.

(3) a. Zhāngsān chī-le   shéme?

   Zhangsan eat-Pfv[1]   what

   'What did Zhangsan eat?'

   b. Zhāngsān xǐhuān   píngguǒ háishì   xiāngjiāo?

   Zhangsan like   apple   or   banana

   'Does Zhangsan like apples or bananas?'

   c. Zhāngsān xǐ-bù-xǐhuān   xiāngjiāo?

   Zhangsan like-not-like   banana

   Does Zhangsan like bananas (or not)?'

   d. Zhāngsān xǐhuān   xiāngjiāo   ma?

   angsan   like   banana   Q

   'Does Zhangsan like bananas?'

(3a) is in the category of question-word questions in [1] and of *wh*-questions in [2]. (3b) is treated as a disjunctive question in both [1, 2]. (3c) is considered a particle question in [1] and a *yes-no* question in [2]. (3d) is regarded as a confirmation-seeking question and (3a–c) information-seeking, as proposed in [3].

In this paper, we examine how particle questions, referred to as *ma* questions later,[2] and *A-not-A* questions are responded. I show that the classification of question plays a significant role in how *ma* questions and *A-not-A* questions are responded. These two types of questions are usually considered counterparts of English *yes-no* questions and it seems to make sense to expect that they can be responded in the same way. However, the picture is far more complicated. Let's look at some examples below.

---

[1] The abbreviations used in this paper include: EPI for an epistemic modal, Pfv for a perfective aspect marker, Prc for a sentential particle, Q for an interrogative particle.

[2] Sentence-final particles in Chinese can serve different functions, e.g. [4]. There are at least two sentence-final particles in Chinese, i.e. *ne* and *ba*, which can present a question. In this paper, we focus on *ma* only.

(4) Q: Nǐ   è   ma?
you   hungry   Q
'Are you hungry?'
A: è/   shì, wǒ è/   duì,   wǒ è/   #yǒu,   wǒ è/
Hungry/ yes, I   hungry/ right,   I   hungry/ #have, I   hungry/
?huì, wǒ è.
?EPI   I   hungry
"Yes, I am.'
A': bù è/   #bùshì, wǒ bù è/   #bù   duì, wǒ bù è/
Not hungry/ #no   I   not hungry/ #not   right I   not hungry/
?méiyǒu, wǒ bù è/   bù   huì, wǒ bù   è
not.have I   not hungry/ not EPI I   not hungry
'No, I am not.'

(5) Q: Nǐ è-bù-è?
you hungry-not-hungry
'Are you hungry (or not)?'
A: è/   #shì, wǒ è/   #duì,   wǒ è/   #yǒu,   wǒ è/
Hungry/ yes, I   hungry/ right,   I   hungry/ #have, I   hungry/
?huì, wǒ è.
?EPI   I   hungry
'Yes, I am.'
A': bù è/   #bùshì, wǒ bù è/   #bù   duì, wǒ bù è/
Not hungry/ #no   I   not hungry/ #not   right I   not hungry/
#méiyǒu, wǒ bù è/   ?bù   huì, wǒ bù è
#not.have I   not hungry/ ?not EPI I   not hungry
'No, I am not.'

As we can see above, *ma* questions and *A-not-A* questions can be responded in different ways. We identify five types of responses among the responses in (4) and (5): (i) predicate response, where the predicate in a question is identified as a response, (ii) *shì* response, where *shì* 'be' is used, (iii) *duì* response, where *duì* 'correct' is adopted, (iv) *yǒu* response, where *yǒu* 'have' is utilized,and (v) *huì* response, where *huì* 'EPI' is relied on.

In (4) and (5), A represents positive responses, whereas A' stand for negative ones. (4) and (5) show the following. For *ma* questions such as in (4), felicitous positive responses are: predicate response, *shì* response, and *duì* response, while *huì* response is marginal and *yǒu* response is infelicitous.

On the other hand, concerning *A-not-A* questions, the only felicitous response is the predicate response. *Huì* response is marginal while *shì-, duì-* and *yǒu* responses are all infelicitous.

Regarding negative responses, for *ma* questions, only predicate- and *huì* responses are felicitous, but the *shì-, duì-* and *yǒu* responses are not. As for *A-not-A* questions, only predicate response is legitimate and *hui* response is marginal, while the other three are not good.

Given the variety concerning positive and negative responses to *ma* questions and *A-not-A* questions, a satisfactory explanation for this variety is clearly required. In this paper, I present an analysis of this variety. I argue that the classification of questions into confirmation-seeking and information-seeking shed light on how these two types of questions are responded.

This paper is organized as follows. Section 2 is a literature review, where previous studies on responses to questions, i.e. [5, 6], are reviewed. In Sect. 3, I present an analysis for the diversity of responses to *ma* questions and *A-not-A* questions. Section 4 concludes this paper.

2 Literature Review

In this section, we review studies on dynamic semantics of questions. I show that the dynamic semantics proposed based on the traditional proposition set account of questions and cannot explain the different ways respond to *ma* questions and *A-not-A* questions as briefly shown in Sect. 1 and a careful examination of the responses is called for.

[5] examines an enlightening issue. They note that, in certain languages, an assertion and a polar question can be answered in the identical way. For example,

(6) Anne: Sam is home.
    Ben: Yes/Yeah, he's home./No, he isn't home.(= 2, p83, [5])

(7) Anne: Is Sam home?
    Ben: Yes/Yeah, he's home./No, he isn't home.(= 3, ibid)

(6) and (7) show that the same response, i.e. *yes, he's home* or *no, he isn't home*, can answer a declarative sentence as in (6) and an interrogative sentence as in (7). [5] suggests that the semantics of a declarative sentence and of an interrogative sentence share a great extent so as for the same response to be felicitous to these two types of sentences. [5] proposes semantics of a declarative sentence and of a polar question as follows:

(8) $A(S[D], a, K_i) = K_o$ such that:
   (i) $DC_{a,o} = DC_{a,i} \cup \{p\}$
   (ii) $T_o = push(<S[D]; \{p\}>, T_i)$
   (iii) $ps_o = ps_i \overline{\cup} \{p\}$

(9) $PQ(S[I], K_i) = K_o$ such that:
   (i) $T_o = push(<S[I]; \{p, \neg p\}>, T_i)$
   (ii) $ps_o = ps_i \overline{\cup} \{p, \neg p\}$

A represents Assertion Operator. a is the author of the assertion. S[D] stands for the declarative sentence uttered. $K_{i, o}$ are input and output discourse structures. *DC* is discourse commitment. *ps* is projected set, which represents a future common ground. *T* is a Table, which stores issues to be resolved as the conversation proceeds. *push* is to insert information to a Table, similar to the function of *push* on a stack in push-down automata. **PQ** is a polar question operator.

With the information above, (8) and (9) can be explained. (8) says the following. An assertion updates the input discourse structure and produces an output one if three conditions are satisfied. First, the propositional content of the assertion *p* is added into the discourse commitment. Second, *p* is also pushed onto the Table, waiting for resolution. Third, *p* is also added into the future common ground.

On the other hand, (9) tells us the information below. A polar question operator updates the input discourse structure and produces an output one if two conditions are met. First, the semantics of the polar question, i.e. $\{p, \neg p\}$, is pushed onto the Table. Second, the semantics of the polar question is added into the future common ground.

As indicated by (8) and (9), generally speaking, the semantics of a declarative sentence or a polar question are pushed onto the Table and added to the input *ps* (Projected Set). Since uttering a declarative sentence is to propose to add its propositional content into DC, as suggested by [5], (8) follows accordingly. On the other hand, since the Hamblin-style semantics of questions is the set $\{p, \neg p\}$, it is natural that in (9) $\{p, \neg p\}$ are pushed onto the Table and added to ps_i. Because a polar question does not indicate the speaker's commitment, (9) does not say anything about updating DC_i.

[5] suggest that, in general, for an assertion and a polar question, confirmation means to add *p* to $DC_{a, i}$, and disconfirmation is to put $\neg p$ to $DC_{a, i}$. Given the similar dynamic semantics of an assertion and of a polar question, a general confirming move type and reversing (disconfirming) move type are proposed to work on (8) and (9) to confirm or disconfirm an assertion or a polar question.

[6] proposes Commitment Space Semantics to take care of the contextual effects and illocutionary force of questions. A commitment state is a set of propositions, which are accepted explicitly by the participants of a conversation up to the current moment. Commitment Space Developments (CSD) is a list of moves in the conversation as of the present time. CSD is represented as series of commitment states $< C_0, C_1, \dots C_n >$.

A polar question and its responses can be modeled using CSD as follows:

(10) a. $<\dots, C^*> + S_1$ to S_2: *Did I win the race?*

$= <\dots, C^*, [\{\sqrt{C}\} \cup C + S_2 \vdash \varphi \cup C + S_2 \vdash \neg\varphi]^{S_1}>$

b. $(10) + S_2$: *Yes* $= (10) + {}^{S_2} S_2 \vdash \varphi$

c. $(10) + S_2$: *No* $= (10) + {}^{S_2} S_2 \vdash \neg\varphi$

$<\dots, C^*>$ represents a CSD up to the current time. At this moment, S_1 asks S_2: Did I win the race? Asking a polar question, the speaker wishes the addressee to commit himself/herself to the truth of φ or of $\neg\varphi$, formalized as $S_2 \vdash \varphi$ and $S_2 \vdash \neg\varphi$. If S_2 responds with *yes*, then he/she is committed to the truth of φ, as in (10b). If S_2 says no, then he/she is committed to the truth of $\neg\varphi$, as in (10c).

[6] argues that the proposed semantics can take care of biased questions, such as *I won the race* with a rising intonation, which the participant of a conversation can only

continue with one legitimate move. This semantics can be captured as follows, where S_2 is no longer wished to be committed to the truth of $\neg \varphi$.

(11) $<..., C^*> + S_1$ to S_2: *I won the race?*

$= <..., C^*, [\{\sqrt{C}\} \cup C + S_2 \vdash \varphi]^{S_1}>$

Although these two studies focus on different aspects of responses to questions, they both rely on the proposal that the semantics of a polar question is the set $\{p, \neg p\}$, as proposed in [8–10]. While this so-called Hamblin-style semantics of question is very popular and can even be regarded as a "standard" theory of semantics of question, [5, 6] cannot be applied to the Chinese examples in (4) and (5) for the following reason. The responses to (4) and (5) are still from the set $\{p, \neg p\}$, but, the syntactic forms that confirm p or $\neg p$ vary from a *ma* question to an *A-not-A* question. This paper conducts a preliminary analysis of this variation.

3 Confirmation of a Proposition Inquired or Not

For the sake of explanation, (4) and (5) are repeated below as (12) and (13). Five types of responses are identified: predicate response, *shì* response, *duì* response, *yǒu* response and *huì* response. All of the five types have a negative version with the negator *bù* preceding them.

(12) Q: Nǐ   è   ma?
      you   hungry Q
      'Are you hungry?'
      A: è/   shì, wǒ è/   duì,   wǒ è/   #yǒu,   wǒ
      Hungry/ yes, I   hungry/ right, I   hungry/ #have, I
      è/   ?huì,   wǒ è.
      hungry/?EPI   I   hungry
      "Yes, I am.'
      A':bù è/   #bùshì, wǒ bù è/   #bù   duì,   wǒ bù
      Not hungry/#no   I   not hungry/ #not   right I   not
      è/   ?méiyǒu, wǒ bù è/   bù   huì, wǒ bù è
      hungry/?not.have I   not hungry/ not EPI I not hungry
      'No, I am not.'

(13) Q: Nǐ è-bù-è?

you hungry-not-hungry

A: è/   #shì, wǒ   è/   #duì,   wǒ   è/   #yǒu,   wǒ

Hungry/ yes,   I   hungry/   right,   I   hungry/ #have,   I

è/?huì, wǒ   è.

hungry/?EPI   I   hungry

'Yes, I am.'

A': bù   è/   #bùshì, wǒ   bù   è/   #bù   duì, wǒ   bù

Not   hungry/ #no   I   not hungry/ #not   right I   not

è/   #méiyǒu, wǒ bù   è/   ?bù   huì, wǒ bù   è

hungry/ #not.have I   not hungry/ ?not   EPI   I not   hungry

'No, I am not.'

Given the above abstraction over the responses, we can summarize the (in)felicitous and marginal responses in (12) and (13) below:

(14) Positive *ma* questions
   a. Positive responses

Predicate response	*Shì* response	*Duì* response	*Yǒu* response	*Huì* response
✓	✓	✓	#	?

   b. Negative responses

Predicate response	*Shì* response	*Duì* response	*Yǒu* response	*Huì* response
✓	#	#	?	✓

(15) a. Positive responses

Predicate response	*Shì* response	*Duì* response	*Yǒu* response	*Huì* response
✓	#	#	#	?

   b. Negative response

Predicate response	*Shì* response	*Duì* response	*Yǒu* response	*Huì* response
✓	#	#	#	?

(14) and (15) demonstrate two major patterns and two minor ones. The first major pattern is that predicate response works for both *ma* questions and *A-not-A* questions. The second major pattern is that responses that confirm the proposition under inquiry, i.e. *shì* response and *duì* response, are felicitous concerning *ma* questions, while they are infelicitous with respect to *A-not-A* questions. On the other hand, for positive *ma* questions, only the predicate responses and *huì* response is a legitimate negative response, while, for *A-not-A* questions, only predicate response is a legitimate negative response.

As for the minor patterns, the first is that *yǒu* response is infelicitous for both types of questions, and the second is that *huì* response is marginal except for when functioning as a negative response to a positive *ma* question.

Positive *ma* questions and *A-not-A* questions in (14) and (15) demonstrate a clear pattern. Predicate response, *shì* response, and *duì* response are felicitous, as positive responses, with respect to *ma* questions, but infelicitous regarding *A-not-A* questions.

[3] sheds light on the diversity in positive responses to positive *ma* questions and *A-not-A* questions. In a nutshell, [3] proposes the following. In Chinese, *ma* questions (a.k.a. particle questions or *yes-no* questions) is referred to as confirmation-seeking because the speaker utters a *ma* question for an addressee to confirm or disconfirm the proposition under inquiry. On the other hand, *A-not-A* questions, *wh*-questions and disjunctive questions are regarded as information-seeking because the speaker provides potential answers for an addressee to choose, in the sense that the potential answers are constrained by the question. For example, for an *A-not-A* question, an addressee is expected to choose *A* or *not A* as his/her answer to the question.

The fact that positive responses which confirms the proposition under inquiry, i.e. *shì-* and *duì* responses, are felicitous to positive *ma* questions but not to *A-not-A* questions converges with [3]: a confirmation-seeking question, i.e. a *ma* question, allows only responses which confirms or disconfirms a proposition under inquiry, whereas an information-seeking question, e.g. *A-not-A* questions, are not compatible with such responses.

Given the above explanation for positive responses, a question immediately arises: why are negative *shì-* and *duì* responses, which disconfirm a proposition under inquiry, infelicitous to a positive *ma* question, if a *ma* question is confirmation-seeking? The answer to this question may lie in that negative *shì-* and *duì* responses carry a negative connotation. By using *bù shì* or *bù duì*, the speaker is reporting a proposition being false and reporting a proposition being false is very often offensive. Due to this negative connotation, even though *bù shì* and *bù duì* disconfirm a proposition under inquiry, the negative connotation they carry prevent them from serving as a felicitous negative response to a positive *ma* question. It follows from an *A-not-A* question being information-seeking that *bù shì* and *bù duì* are infelicitous to an *A-not-A* question since these two responses disconfirm a proposition under inquiry, though with a negative connotation.

So, how can one respond to a positive *ma* question to disconfirm the proposition inquired in the question? It seems that *bù huì* 'not EPI' is a neutral negative response, which disconfirms a proposition without any negative connotation discussed above. Let's see one example.

(16) A: Jīntiā   hǎo   rè   a!
           Today   very   hot   Prc
           'It's so hot today!'
      B: Bù   huì   a!   Cāi   èr-shí-wǔ   dù   a!
           Not   EPI   Prc   only 25   degree   Prc
           'No, it is not. It's only 25 °C.'
      B': #huì   a/   duì   a!   zhēnde hěn   rè.
           #EPI   Prc/   right Prc   really   very   hot
           'Yes, it is.'

As we can see from (16), in order to express disagreement with A's statement, B uses *bù huì* 'not EPI', rather than *bù duì* 'not correct', which would connote a strong negative attitude on B's part. That is, *bù huì* 'not EPI' is a neutral negative response with no negative connotation. If one wishes to agree with A's statement, *duì* 'correct' can be used, but not *huì* 'EPI', because *huì* 'EPI' in its positive form only responds to a question containing epistemic *huì*.

Yǒu responses are interesting as well. They are infelicitous in (12) and (13), but they are felicitous in examples below.

(17) Q: Nǐ   yùndòng   ma?
           you   exercise   Q
           'Do you exercise?'
      A: Yǒu,   wǒ   yùndòng.
           Have,   I   exercise.
           'yes, I do.'
      A': Méiyǒu,   wǒ   bù   yùndòng.
           not.have   I   not   exercise
           'No, I do not.'

(18) Q: Nǐ   yùn-bù-yùndòng?
           you   exercise-not-exercise
           'Do you exercise (or not)?'
      A: Yǒu,   wǒ   yùndòng.
           Have,   I   exercise.
           'yes, I do.'
      A': Méiyǒu,   wǒ   bù`   yùndòng,
           not.have   I   not   exercise
           'No, I do not.'

The difference between *è* 'hungry' in (12) and (13) on the one hand and *nǐ yùndòng* 'you exercise' in (17) and (18) lies in that *è* 'hungray' is a stage-level predicate, which presents the state true of the subject for a (long or short) period of time, whereas *nǐ yùndòng* 'you exercise' is habitual and describes a characterizing reading, which is discussed in [16–20]. [21] discusses different readings of *ū* plus a situation in Taiwan Southern Min (for short, TSM), including a characterizing reading. *ū* is the TSM counterpart of *yǒu* in Chinese. At least in Chinese used in Taiwan (referred to as Taiwan Mandarin), *yǒu* can be extended to function as *ū* in TSM in the sense that *yǒu* plus a situation denotes a similar array of readings to TSM *ū*. This explains why *yǒu* and *méiyǒu* are felicitous responses to *nǐ yùndòng ma* 'you exercise Q', but not to *nǐ è ma* 'you hungry Q' since *ū* in TSM and *yǒu* in Chinese or, at least, Taiwan Mandarin cannot go with a stage-level state, such as *è* 'hungry', to produce a reading of the state true of the subject at the speech time.

Predicate response is felicitous, positive or negative alike, to positive *ma* questions and *A-not-A* questions because they provide information, which can be inferred to confirm or disconfirm a proposition under inquiry. For example, *è* 'hungry' or *bù è* 'not hungry' provide information, based on the *A-not-A* question in (13), and hence are felicitous as a response to an *A-not-A* question. On the other hand, responding *è* 'hungry' confirms the proposition inquired in(12), while responding *bù è* 'not hungry' disconfirms the proposition. As a result, *è* 'hungry' and *bù è* 'not hungry' are felicitous, as well, to a *ma* question.

The questions in (12) and (13) are positive. Let's look at the responses to negative *ma* questions. Please note that the responses to negative *ma* questions in Chinese, among other east Asian languages, are referred to as an *agreement/disagreement* system, such as [11–15], in the sense that a positive response means that the responder agrees with the negative proposition under inquiry, while a negative one indicates that the responder does not agree with the negative proposition under inquiry. Therefore, in the previous case the response is translated as *no* followed by a negative sentence in English, whereas in the latter the response is translated as *yes* followed by a positive sentence. See the examples below.

(19) Q: Nǐ   bù   è   ma?
    You   not   hungry   Q
    'Aren't you hungry?'
   A: è/   shì, wǒ bù è/   duì, wǒ   bù   è/   #yǒu,   wǒ
    hungry/ yes, I not è/   right,I   not   hungry/ #have,   I

    bù è/   #huì, wǒ   bù   è
    not hungry/ #EPI I   not   hungry
    'No, I am not.'
   A': Bù   è/   ?bùshì, wǒ   è/   ?bù   duì, wǒ è/
    not   hungry/ ?no,   I   hungry/ ?not   right, I   hungry
    ?méiyǒu,   wǒ bù è/   #bù   huì, wǒ   bù   è
    ?not.haveI not hungry/ #not   EPI,   I   not   hungry
    'Yes, I am.'

(20) Q: Nǐ   bù   yùndòng   ma?
       You   not   exercise   Q
       'Don't you exercise?'
    A: yùndòng/shì,   wǒ   bù   yùngdòng/ duì,   wǒ   bù   yùngdòng/
       exercise/yes,   I   not   exercise/   right, I   not   exercise
       #yǒu,   wǒ   bù   yùndòng/   #huì, wǒ   bù   yùngdòng.
       #have,   I   not   exercise/   #EPI, I   not   exercise
       'No, I don't.'
    A': bù   yùndòng/   bùshì,   wǒ   yùndòng/ bù   duì,   wǒ
       not   exercise/   no,   I   exercise/   not   right,   I
       yùngdòng/   ?méiyǒu,   wǒ   yùndòng/   #bù   huì,   wǒ   yùngdòng.
       exercise /   #not.have,   I   exercise/   #not EPI,   I   exercise
       'Yes, I do.'

As we can see from (19) and (20), the five types of responses discussed above for positive *ma* questions and *A-not-A* questions apply to the negative *ma* questions in (19) and (20) as well. The responses in A are those that agree with the negative question, while the ones in A' are those that disagree with the negative question. Moreover, *A-not-A* questions involve the negator *bù* and do not have a positive vs. negative distinction, and therefore are not discussed here. The linguistic facts demonstrated in (19) and (20) can be summarized below as below.

(21) Negative *ma* questions (19)
    a. Responses that agree with the negative question

Predicate response	*Shì* re-sponse	*Duì* re-sponse	*Yǒu* re-sponse	*Huì* re-sponse
✓	✓	✓	#	#

    b. Responses that disagree with the negative question

Predicate response	*Shì* re-sponse	*Duì* re-sponse	*Yǒu* re-sponse	*Huì* re-sponse
✓	?	?	?	#

(22) Negative *ma* questions (19)
    a. Responses that agree with the negative question

Predicate response	*Shì* re-sponse	*Duì* re-sponse	*Yǒu* re-sponse	*Huì* re-sponse
✓	✓	✓	#	#

    b. Responses that disagree with the negative question

Predicate response	*Shì* re-sponse	*Duì* re-sponse	*Yǒu* re-sponse	*Huì* re-sponse
✓	?	✓	?	#

The questions in (19) and (20) are negative *ma* questions. *è* 'hungry' in (19) is a stage-level state, while (20) denotes a habitual or characterizing reading. In terms of expressing agreement with the negative questions, predicate-, *shì-* and *duì* responses are felicitous, all of which express confirmation (of a negative proposition).

In terms of stating disagreement with the negative questions, a state-level state allows only a negative predicate response, but not the other four, i.e. *shì-*, *duì-*, *yǒu-*, and *huì* responses, while a question expressing a characterizing reading permits negative predicate responses and *bù duì*, but not with the other three.

The reason why, generally, only the negative predicate responses can express disagreement with negative questions is that disconfirmation of a negative proposition is confusing except for explicitly negating the predicate under inquiry. Processing negation takes more efforts than processing a positive sentence (see Sect. 1.1, [23]). Processing double-negative takes much more efforts. This is why disagreeing with a negative question by means of responses other than explicitly negating the predicate is preferably avoided.

There is also minor discrepancy with respect to negative *ma* questions in (19) and (20): *bù duì* is felicitous to (19), which expresses a characterizing reading, while it is infelicitous to (20), containing a stage-level predicate. *Bù duì* literally means 'not accurate', which tends to describe a permanent state of truth. A stage-level state presents a stage of a state, i.e. a relatively shorter span of a state, e.g. [22] and hence cannot be responded to by *bù duì*. On the other hand, a characterizing reading is one of the possible readings expressed by an individual-level predicate, which denotes a, more or less, permanent property and therefore is felicitous with respect to *bù duì*.

4 Conclusion

In this paper, I discuss responses to *ma* questions and *A-not-A* questions in Chinese. Five types of responses are identified: predicate responses, *shì* responses, *duì* responses, *yǒu* response and *huì* responses. As positive responses, predicate-, *shì-* and *duì* responses are felicitous to positive *ma* questions, but not to *A-not-A* questions.

This distinction relies on the dichotomy of questions proposed in [3]: a *ma* question is confirmation-seeking, while an *A-not-A* question is information seeking. Positive *shì-* and *duì* responses confirm the proposition under inquiry and therefore are felicitous, while they do not provide information required by an information-seeking question and as a result are not felicitous to *A-not-A* questions.

Bù shì and *bù duì* are infelicitous as a negative response to a positive *ma* question because they carry a negative connotation in the sense that they report a proposition being false, which is very often offensive. *Bù huì* 'not EPI' is a neutral negative response with no negative connotation and therefore is felicitous, as a negative response, to a positive polar question.

As for negative *ma* questions, predicate-, *shì-* and *duì* responses, all of which agree with a negative question are felicitous. Concerning disagreement with a negative question, generally, only negating the predicate under inquiry is felicitous. The other responses do not provide explicit negation of the predicate under inquiry and are more difficult to process psycholinguistically. Therefore, these responses are dispreferred as responses that disagree with a negative question.

But, *bù duì* is a felicitous response that expresses disagreement with a negative question, to a question denoting a characterizing reading, but not one with a stage-level state. This is because *bù duì* describes a permanent state of truth and is compatible with a characterizing reading, but not with a stage-level state.

This paper deals with 'form', but does not present a formal semantic account, cf. [24]. We will continue pursue this issue and attempt to provide a formal semantic/pragmatic account for this intriguing issue.

Acknowledgements. The research reported here is funded by Ministry of Science and Technology, Taiwan, under the grant number MOST 107-2410-H194-069. I hereby acknowledge MOST's financial support. I thank CLSW reviewers and audience for helpful comments and suggestions. All remaining errors are mine.

References

1. Li, C.N., Thompson, S.: Mandarin Chinese: A Functional Reference Grammar. University of California, Berlekey (1981)
2. Huang, J.C.-T., Li, A.Y.-H., Li, Y.: The Syntax of Chinese. Cambridge University, Cambridge (2009)
3. Her, O.-S., Che, D., Bodomo, A.: On a dichotomy of question types: a case study of Mandarin Chinese and Changsha Xiang. Linguis. Rev. **29**, 257–291 (2022)
4. Xiong, J.: A Deontic modal SFP in Chengdu Chinese. In Dong, M., Gu, Y., Hong, F. (eds.), Chinese Lexical Semantics: 22nd Workshop, CLSW 2021. LNAI 13249. pp. 160–171. Springer, Berlin (2022)
5. Farkas, D.F., Bruce, K.B.: On reacting to assertions and polar questions. J. Semant. **27**, 81–118 (2009)
6. Krifka, M.: Biased in commitment space semantics: declarative questions, negated questions and question tags. In: Proceedings of SALT 25. LSA, Washington D.C. (2015)
7. Krifka, M.: Response particles as propositional anaphors. In Proceedings of SALT 23, pp. 1–18. LSA, Washington D.C. (2013)
8. Leonard, H.C.: Questions in montague English. Found. Lang. **10**, 41–53 (1973)
9. Karttunen, L.: Syntax and semantics of questions. Linguist. Philos. **1**, 3–44 (1977)
10. Groenendijk, J., Martin, S.: Studies on the Semantics of questions and the Pragmatics of Answers. Ph.D. Dissertation. University of Amsterdam (1984)
11. Kuno, S.: The Structure of the Japanese Language. MIT Press, Cambridge MA (1973)
12. Pope, E.N.: Questions and Answers in English. Mouton, The Hague (1976)
13. Sadock, J., Zwicky, A.: Speech act distinctions in syntax. In: Shopen, T. (ed.) Language Typology and Syntactic Description, pp. 155–196. Cambridge University Press, Cambridge (1985)
14. Floyd, S., Villermet, M., Birchall, J.: Answers to polarity questions in South American languages. Paper presented at the AMAZÒNICAS VI. Leticia, Colombia (2016)
15. Holmberg, A.: The Syntax of Yes and No. Oxford University Press, Oxford (2016)
16. Comrie, B.: Aspect: An Introduction to the Study of Verbal Aspect and Related Problems. Cambridge University Press, Cambridge (1976)
17. Deo, A.: Tense and Aspect in Indo-Aryan Languages: Variation and Diachrony. Ph.D. Dissertation. Stanford University (2006)

18. Deo, A.: Temporal genericity and the contribution of imperfective marking. In: Proceedings of the 10th Symposium on Logic and Language, pp. 109–118. Research Institute for Linguistics, Hungarian Academy of Sciences and Theoretical Linguistics Program, Eöströs Loránd University, Budapest (2009)

19. Bybee, J., Dahl, Ö.: The creation of tense and aspect systems in the languages of the world. Stud. Lang. **13**, 51–103 (1989)

20. Bybee, J., Perkins, R., Pagliuca, W.: The Evolution of Grammar. Tense, Aspect and Modality in the Languages of the World. University of Chicago Press, Chicago (1994)

21. Wu, J.-S., Zheng, Z.-R.: Toward a unified semantics for $\bar{u}$ in $\bar{u}$ + situation in Taiwan Southern Min: A Modal-Aspectual Account. In Hong, J.-F., Su, Q., Wu, J.-S. (eds.) Chinese Lexical Semantics, 19th Workshop, CLSW 2018, LNAI, pp. 408–422. Springer, Berlin (2018)

22. Kratzer, A.: Stage-level and individual-level predicates. In: Carlson, G., Pelletier, J. (eds.) The Generic Book. University of Chicago Press, Chicago (1995)

23. Tien, Y.: Negating Processing: A Dynamic Pragmatic Account. Ph.D. Dissertation. University College London, London (2014)

24. Hsieh, H.: From form to meaning and to concept. In Dong, M., Lin, J., Tang, X. (eds.) Chinese Lexical Semantics: 17th Workshop, CLSW 2016, LNAI 10085. pp. 159–172. Springer, Switzerland (2016)

Semantic Dependency Analysis of Special Sentence Patterns in Ancient Chinese

Xuan Chen[1,2] and Yanqiu Shao[1,2(✉)]

[1] College of Information Sciences, Beijing Language and Culture University, Beijing, China
yqshao163@163.com
[2] National Language Resources Monitoring and Research Center (CNLR) Print Media Language Branch, Beijing, China

Abstract. With the development of natural language processing, automatic semantic analysis has attracted more and more attention. This research delineates the semantic dependency labeling rules of several kinds of special sentence patterns in ancient Chinese. And we compare the result of manual annotation with automatic semantic parser and put forward improvement methods to those poor results. This research can help to improve the semantic understanding of ancient Chinese, the translation of ancient Chinese and the perfomance of parser to a certain extent.

Keywords: Ancient Chinese · Special sentence pattern · Semantic dependency · Labeling rules

1 Introduction

So far, computer processing of natural language has successfully moved from the study of form to meaning. The development is the result of the failure of form sdudy to meet the requirement of accuracy, as well as determined by the nature of semantics itself. Semantic interpretation is very important in any language processing system because simple syntactic analysis using structural rules cannot deal with the fuzziness of natural language well. At present, there are still few researches on semantic dependency analysis in ancient Chinese. Therefore, we propose a whole set of semantic dependency graph annotation system in ancient Chinese based on parataxis of Chinese itself and the advantages of dependency analysis on processing language.

The research on semantic dependency of special sentence patterns in ancient Chinese is not only conducive to further understanding the internal structure of special sentence patterns such as elliptical sentences and passive sentences, but can also promote the semantic understanding of ancient Chinese by computers and the translation of ancient Chinese. From the practical level, this research is a valuable exploration and can provide relevant knowledge for the development of the automatic syntactic semantic parser.

© The Author(s), under exclusive license to Springer Nature Switzerland AG 2023
Q. Su et al. (Eds.): CLSW 2022, LNAI 13495, pp. 337–349, 2023.
https://doi.org/10.1007/978-3-031-28953-8_26

The research has four parts. Firstly, relevant work is briefly introduced. Secondly, the semantic dependency corpus of ancient Chinese and its labeling specification are briefly introduced. Thirdly, the labeling rules of various special sentence patterns in ancient Chinese are described and compared with the results of automatic labeling. Finally, the prospect of future work is put forward.

2 Related Works

Semantic Dependency Parsing (SDP) is a deeper-level way of expression of Chinese semantic based on Dependency Grammar (DG) [1]. It is a semantic analysis method that combines the dependency structure and semantic information in a sentence to better express the structure and implies meaning of a sentence. Semantic dependency analysis, based on dependency syntax, includes semantic dependency tree analysis and semantic dependency graph analysis [2]. At present, there are few studies on semantic dependency analysis of ancient Chinese. Based on the corpus of *the Twenty-Four Histories*, the database research team from Tianjin University has constructed a evaluation benchmark for the understanding of Classical Chinese based on crowd-sourced labeling system and a dataset C-CLUE [3]. It includes fine-grained Named Entity Recognition (NER) task and Relation Extraction (RE) task based on corresponding datasets. Wang (2014) [4] studied the automatic word segmentation in medieval Chinese and took the Book of Han as an example to discuss the method of word segmentation in ancient Chinese. There is little further research on semantic dependency analysis of special sentence patterns in ancient Chinese.

3 Semantic Dependency Graph Corpus of Ancient Chinese

At present, we have built a semantically dependent corpus of 3000 sentences of ancient Chinese, all of which are from *the Twenty-Four Histories*.

3.1 Labeling Rules

Our existing labeling rules are based on semantic dependency graph labeling guidelines on modern Chinese, which can be seen at "coarse-grained semantic relationship label instruction" from http://ir.hit.edu.cn/sdp2020ccl.

In addition to the basic annotation guidelines, we have also formulated corresponding detailed guidelines for proper nouns in ancient Chinese and polysyllabic words other than proper nouns to assist labeling. In computer information processing, proper nouns are mostly regarded as named entities and word segmentation units. In our guidelines we also regard a named entity as a word segmentation unit, whose POS labelling is NR. The dependency arc is labeled as mHc-NR with the parent node on the right of the named entity pointing to the left. Polysyllabic words whose meanings are closely combined except named entities are regarded as separate word segmentation units. These tags can be found in the examples of semantic dependency graph below.

3.2   Annotation Platform and Automatic Semantic Parser

In the process of corpus construction, we use the self-built online semantic dependency graph annotation platform and semantic parser. After the annotators log in to platform with their own accounts, the page displayed is shown in Fig. 1, which shows the result of automatic annotation. Manual correction can be made afterwards. In the dependency graph of Fig. 1, the first line is the segmentation result, which is divided by single character. The second line shows part of speech of each character, and the CTB part-of-speech tagging set is adopted. The main functions of the platform include correcting segmentation errors, correcting errors in POS labeling, semantic dependency relationship labeling, searching data by keyword and then annotating or correcting errors, and etc.

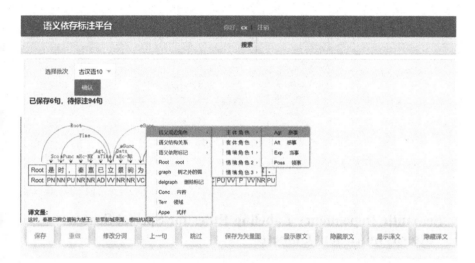

Fig. 1. Interface of annotation platform

The semantic dependency graph parser mentioned in this paper was proposed by Liu (2021) [5]. The parser model can be divided into sentence representation layer, word granularity feature fusion layer and typing layer. The sentence representation layer uses Bert and other pre-trained language models to obtain powerful semantic representation. The word granularity feature fusion includes taking the final character representation as the word representation and combining it with the features such as parts of speech and knowledge. And in the typing layer, the probability of forming an arc between words is given by biaffine classifier. The training data set is from Semeval-2016 task 9 [6].

The annotation results of our corpus are stored as CoNLL data format, with a total of ten columns, as shown in Table 1 below. The number in the first column represents the position of the character in the sentence. The second is character and punctuation, and the third column is the word prototype. In Chinese the second column has no difference with the third one. The fourth and fifth column are coarse-grained and fine-grained parts of speech respectively. The sixth is the syntactic feature, which is not used here and marked with an underscore. The seventh column is the ordinal number of the character's parent node, which also can be called its center character. The eighth is the semantic relationship between the node and its parent node. Columns 9 and 10 are not marked in our corpus.

Table 1. Storage forms of annotation result

1	上	上	NN	NN	–	2	Aft	–	–
2	疑	疑	VV	VV	–	0	Root	–	–
3	其	其	PN	PN	–	5	Exp	–	–
4	虚	虚	VA	VA	–	2	Cont	–	–
5	妄	妄	VA	VA	–	2	Cont	–	–
6	,	,	PU	PU	–	2	mPunc	–	–
7	以	以	P	P	–	9	mPrep	–	–
8	才	才	AD	AD	–	9	Desc	–	–
9	卿	卿	NN	NN	–	10	Pat	–	–
10	付	付	VV	VV	–	2	eSucc	–	–
11	廷	廷	NN	NN	–	12	mHc	–	–
12	尉	尉	NN	NN	–	10	Datv	–	–
13	辩	辩	VV	VV	–	10	ePurp	–	–
14	,	,	PU	PU	–	13	mPunc	–	–
15	以	以	P	P	–	16	mPrep	–	–
16	不	不	AD	AD	–	15	mNeg	–	–
17	实	实	VV	VV	–	13	eSucc	–	–
18	见	见	VV	VV	–	13	eSucc	–	–
19	原	原	NN	NN	–	18	Cont	–	–
20	。	。	PU	PU	–	18	mPunc	–	–

4 Semantic Dependency Labeling Rules for Special Sentence Patterns in Ancient Chinese

Referring to Liu (1991) [7], we divide ancient Chinese special sentence patterns into six categories: object preposition sentence, attribute postposition sentence, elliptical sentence, passive sentence, prepositional structure postposition sentence and determinative sentence. Then we will give description to each category. 600 sentences were randomly selected from our corpus and the frequency of occurrence of special sentence patterns was statistically analyzed. The results are as follows:

Therefore, it can be seen that special sentence patterns, especially elliptical sentences, account for a large proportion in ancient Chinese. So it is necessary to carry out analysis of special sentence patterns (Fig. 2).

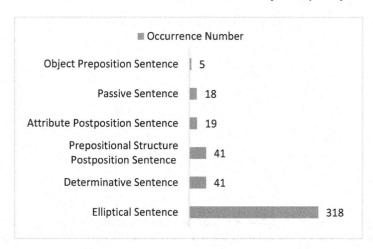

Fig. 2. Frequency of occurrence of special sentence patterns

4.1 Object Preposition Sentence

Under certain conditions, the object can be placed before the verb or preposition, which can be divided into two categories: negative pronoun object preposition and interrogative pronoun object preposition (Fig. 3).

(1) 至元中, 历仕为兰溪主簿, 尉获盗三十, 械徇诸市, 伯启以无左验, 未之信;

(During Zhi Yuan, he worked as the chief clerk of Lanxi. Once, a county lieutenant captured 30 thieves, and ordered them to parade with torture equipment. Bo Qi didn't believe it because of no evidence;)

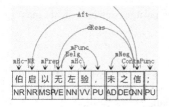

Fig. 3. Example of object preposition sentence with negative pronouns (after artificial correction)

To save space and for reading ease, we don't show complete sentences in the figures of semantic dependency graph examples (Table 2).

Table 2. Result of automatic annotation

24	伯	伯	NR	NR	–	25	mHc-NR	–	–
25	启	启	NR	NR	–	33	Agt	–	–
26	以	以	MSP	MSP	–	27	mPrep	–	–
27	无	无	VE	VE	–	29	mNeg	–	–
28	左	左	NN	NN	–	27	Loc	–	–
29	验	验	VV	VV	–	27	Belg	–	–
30	,	,	PU	PU	–	27	mPunc	–	–
31	未	未	AD	AD	–	33	mNeg	–	–
32	之	之	DEC	DEC	–	33	mMod	–	–
33	信	信	NN	NN	–	20	eAdvt	–	–
34	;	;	PU	PU	–	33	mPunc	–	–

Object preposition sentence with negative pronouns: in this sentence, "之" is the object of "信", and the normal sentence order should be "信之". "之" refers to the arrest of the thief above, as the content of "信", so it should be marked as the content of "信", labelled as Cont (Fig. 4).

(2) 罢酒出, 帝召袁盎诸大臣通经术者曰: 太后言如是, 何谓也?

(After the banquet, Emperor Jing summoned Yuan Ang and other ministers who were proficient in classics and asked: "What did the empress dowager mean by saying such words?").

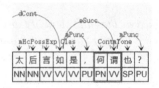

Fig. 4. Example of object preposition sentence with interrogative pronouns(after artificial correction)

Object preposition sentence with interrogative pronouns: in this sentence, "何" is the object of "谓". The normal sentence order should be "谓何". Therefore, we mark "何" as the content of "谓", labelled as Cont.

The existing semantic parser doesn't work well with how to mark object preposition, which is reflected in the failure to recognize the preposed object, so it cannot correctly annotate. For example, "之" in the above example is automatically labeled as a modality marker mMod; and "何" is automatically label as dCont, which is the demoted content of "曰" above, which is wrong.

4.2 Passive Sentence

A passive sentence is a sentence pattern with a passive relationship between the subject and the verb predicate. Common passive sentences in Classical Chinese mainly use mark words such as "于", and "为" to express passivity, and there are also passive sentences without mark words (Fig. 5).

(3) 上疑其虚妄, 以才卿付廷尉辩, 以不实见原。

(The emperor suspected that the charges were false and handed Xie Over to court officer for examination. And at last Xie was forgiven because the charges could not be confirmed.)

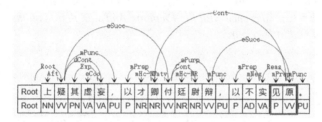

Fig. 5. Example of "见" passive sentence(after artificial correction)

In this sentence, "见" is a passive marker, expressing passivity, which is marked with preposition marker "mPrep" with dependency arc pointing from "原" to "见". "才卿" is the object of "原" and the person forgiven, so it is marked as the patient of "原", labelled as Pat (Fig. 6).

(4) 有猛密者, 地在缅境, 数为缅侵夺, 举族内徙, 有司居之户碗。

(A tribe called Mengmi, who lived in Myanmar, was harassed several times by The Burmese and relocated internally. Local officials let them live in Huwan.)

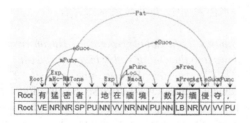

Fig. 6. Example of "为" passive sentence(after artificial correction)

In this sentence, "为" is a marker indicating passivity, which is marked as a preposition marker "mPrep" with dependency arc pointing from "缅" to "见". "猛密" is the object of "夺", the thing captured, so it is marked as the patient of "夺" the subject, labelled as Pat.

The existing semantic parser can recognize the marker words such as "为" in the labeling of passive sentences, but "见" is regarded as another content verb rather than a passive marker. Moreover, the passive semantic relationship between the receiver of the action and the verb has not been marked out, such as "才卿" and "原", "猛密" and "夺" mentioned above.

4.3   Elliptical Sentence

(5)   帝曾幸方山, 文晔大言求见, 申父功厚赏屈。

(When Emperor Gaozu visited Fangshan, Liu Wenye called out loudly on the side of the road to ask for an audience with the Emperor. And said that his father had done a lot of good but had little reward.)

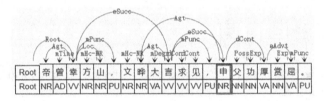

Fig. 7. Example of subject omission in elliptical sentence(after artificial correction)

Subject omission: in this sentence, the subject of "申" in the third clause is "文晔" in the second clause, and the semantic relationship between them should be marked, so the dependency arc should point from "申" to "文晔" and be marked as "Agt" (agent) (Fig. 7).

Predicate omission: normally, a sentence can have no subject, but must have a predicate. However, in ancient Chinese, predicates can be omitted as a minor part of language communication.

(6)   县九: 禄福, 呼蚕水出南羌中, 东北至会水入羌谷。

(There are nine counties: Lufu County, where the Hucan river originates from the southern Qiang and flows into the Qiang Valley in the northeast.)

In this sentence, "县九" means that there are nine counties, "县" is a noun, "九" is a quantifier, and the predicate between is omitted, so the quantifier "九" is marked as the central argument of this clause, to replace the role of predicate.

Object omission: in elliptical sentences of ancient Chinese, the omission of object is always something known to the speakers. In order to express more with few words without causing difficulties in understanding, the known information in language fragments is omitted while the new information is retained (Fig. 8).

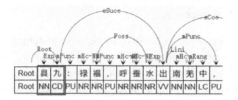

Fig. 8. Example of predicate omission in elliptical sentence(after artificial correction)

(7) 青龙中, 帝图讨辽东, 以俭有干策, 徙为幽州刺史, 加度辽将军, 使持节, 护乌丸校尉。

(During the Qinglong reign, Emperor Ming decided to launch a campaign against Liaodong region. Because Wu Qiujian had strategies and talents, he was appointed governor of Youzhou and awarded the title of General Du Liao. Besides, Emperor Ming let him hold the imperial ceremony and be Wuwan lieutenant.)

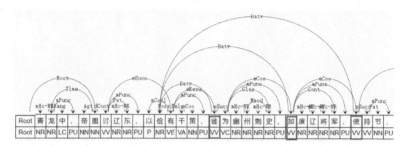

Fig. 9. Example of object omission in elliptical sentence(after artificial correction)

In this sentence, the verb "徙", "加" and "使" in the fourth, fifth and sixth clauses all omit the object "俭", so the semantic relationship between these verbs and the object should be marked out as Datv (dative), that is to say, "俭" is the dative of these three verbs (Fig. 9).

In elliptical sentences, automatic semantic parser can not recognize the subject and object omitted outside the clause, and thus cannot mark the semantic relationship (Fig. 10).

4.4 Determinative Sentence

A determinative sentence makes a positive or negative statement about some property of someone or something. In ancient Chinese, "者" and "也" are typically used as determinative words. According to *Ancient Chinese Dictionary* [8], "者" is used as a modal particle to introduce meaning of determination when in determinative sentences. According to *Ancient Chinese Dictionary Compiled by Li Wang* [9], when in determinative sentences, "者" is a modal particle to show pause. It can also be used at the end of the former clause in a compound sentence, leading to following explanation. As can be seen in this sentence: 吾妻之美我者, 私我也。*(My wife says I'm handsome because she's partial to me.)*

(8) 夫击瓮叩缶弹筝搏髀, 而歌呼呜呜快耳者, 真秦之声也;

(The earthen percussion, the bat, the zither, and the singing of babbling which are agreeable to ears are the authentic music of Qin.)

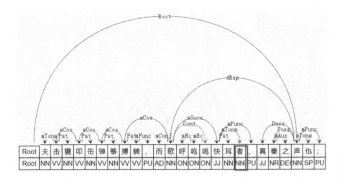

Fig. 10. Example of determinative sentence(after artificial correction)

In this sentence, "也" is the determinative word, labelled as tone marker, and its parent node is the center word of the clause. It is important to note that "者" is used as a pronoun in quite a few cases except as a modal particle. At this time it can be put after a predicate or predicate phrase to form a nominal structure, which needs to be labeled according to the specific situation. As in the following sentence, "者" is a pronoun meaning a certain type of people:

(9) 今秦王欲吞天下, 称帝而治, 此布衣驰骛之时而游说者之秋也。

(Now that the King wanted to annex states and declare himself emperor, it was a good time for political activists and lobbyists of humble birth to spread their ambitions.)

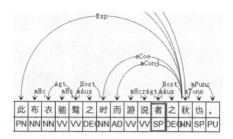

Fig. 11. Example of "者" as a pronoun

4.5 Attribute Postposition Sentence

In order to emphasize the attributive, the attributive can be placed after the central word (Fig. 11).

(10) 铁旗城后察昔折一烈率其族类部曲三千余户来附。

(Chaxi Zheyilie, who was behind Tieqi city, came to joined him with his clansman and more than three thousand subordinates.)

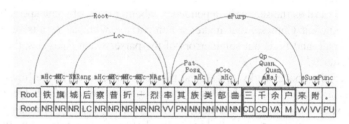

Fig. 12. Example of attribute postposition sentence

In this sentence, "三千余户" is used as a post attributive to modify the preceding "族类部曲" to indicatd the number. When labeling, the dependency arc points from "户" to "曲", the parent node of the modified component, and is marked as "Qp" (quantity phrase) (Fig. 12).

4.6 Prepositional Structure Postposition Sentence

In ancient Chinese, preposition structures are usually put after modified verbs or adjectives as a complement.

(11) 觇两督兵至, 尽伏精锐于林中, 阳驱诸贼自浮桥西渡。

(When they detected the arrival of the two governor's troops, they ambushed their best men into the woods, and pretended to lead the thieves across the pontoon bridge to the west of the river.)

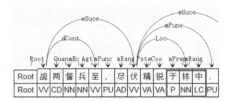

Fig. 13. Example of prepositional structure postposition sentence

In this sentence, "于林中" is placed after "伏精锐" to indicate the place where the action takes place. When marking, the dependency arc points from the verb "伏" to " 林", which indicates the place and is marked as "Loc" (location). "林" points to the prepositional marker "于" and is labeled as "mPrep"(prepositional marker) (Fig. 13).

Compared with the normal sentence order, the two special sentence patterns, attributive postposition and prepositional postposition, only change the syntactic position, but the semantic relationship is not affected, which has little influence on the automatic semantic parser.

5   Conclusion and Future Work

This paper describes the semantic dependency labeling rules of some special sentence patterns in ancient Chinese, and makes a comparison with the results of automatic semantic parser, and finds out some errors of the parser when analyzing these special sentence patterns.

However, the above works still stay at the descriptive level. In the future, we will take the research as a basis and add it to the existing model as knowledge and adjust it constantly, so as to improve the analysis ability of the existing semantic parser on special sentence patterns in ancient Chinese. In addition, there are still some fuzzy areas in labeling and standardization of semantic relations in ancient Chinese, and there is room for improvement in labeling consistency. How to use ancient Chinese expertise to develop more scientific labeling rules to guide labeling work is also the direction we need to work on in the future.

Acknowledgments. This research project is supported by the National Natural Science Foundation of China (61872402), the Humanities and Social Science Project of the Ministry of Education (17YJAZH068), Science Foundation of Beijing Language and Culture University (supported by "the Fundamental Research Funds for the Central Universities") (18ZDJ03).

References

1. Robinson, J.J.: Dependency structures and transformation rules. Language **46**(2), 259–285 (1970)
2. Yanqiu, S., Lijuan, Z.: Deep semantic analysis: from dependency tree to dependency graph. Int. J. Adv. Intell. (2016)

3. https://mp.weixin.qq.com/s/96mWqyvIuri2_jUSybwi-g
4. Jialing, W.: A case study of automatic word segmentation in middle Ancient Chinese taking the book of Han as example. Nanjing Normal University (2014)
5. Dianqing, L.: Improving Chinese semantic dependency graph with external knowledge. Beijing Language and Culture University (2021)
6. Che,W., Shao, Y., Liu, T., Ding, Y.: Semeval-2016 task 9: Chinese semantic dependency parsing. In: Proceedings of the 10th International Workshop on Semantic Evaluation, pp. 1074–1080 (2016)
7. Yongkang, L.: Classification and analysis of special sentence patterns in Ancient Chinese. Si Chuan People's Publishing House, Chengdu (1991)
8. Shuangdi, Z., Guoguang, Y.: Ancient Chinese Dictionary (1906). The Commercial Press, Beijing (2014)
9. Wang,L.: Ancient Chinese Dictionary Compiled by Li Wang, vol. 974. China Publishing House, Beijing (2000)

A Study on the Selection Mechanism of the Chinese Loan Words of the Same Signified with Different Signifiers

Wenqi Chen[1], Jiaming Gan[2(✉)], Xiaolei Gu[3], Jin Li[4], and Ruozhu Wang[5]

[1] China Mobile (Shanghai) Industrial Research Institute, Shanghai, China
[2] The Primary School Attached to Foshan Gaoming Cangjiang Middle School, Foshan, Guangdong, China
ganjiaming723@163.com
[3] Beijing Jingshan School, Beijing, China
[4] Qinhuangdao Tobacco Monopoly Bureau, Qinhuangdao, Hebei, China
[5] CSIC International Engineering Company Limited, Beijing, China

Abstract. "The Chinese loan words of the same signified with different signifiers" refers to the different words that denote the same object or concept from a foreign language in the process of borrowing foreign words because of the translation strategy or other factors. The coexistence of the loan words of the same signified with different signifiers is not in line with the economy of language, and in most cases, it will generate word competition, and eventually, some words will retain successfully, while the rest will be eliminated. In this paper, we take the Chinese loan words of the same signified with two signifiers in the late Qing Dynasty and Republican Periods as the object of study and use "An Etymological Glossary of Selected Modern Chinese Words" and "Modern Chinese Dictionary (7th edition)" as the research materials to establish a database. The study provides an in-depth analysis of the factors influencing one-word occupation from the perspectives of the translation strategy, morpheme meaning, the number of syllables, and the preference of Chinese characters. We find that expression clarity, form simplicity, and cultural adaptability play important roles in two-word competition. Words with clear expression, short length, and positive meaning are more likely to survive. This study focuses on the dynamic evolution of Chinese words, which has some significance and value in revealing the evolutionary pattern of Chinese vocabulary.

Keywords: Chinese loan words · Words of the same signified with different signifiers · Lexical competition · Word occupation · Translation strategies

1 Preface

Chinese has a long history of borrowing foreign words: first, the introduction of Buddhist vocabulary in the Han and Tang dynasties, second, the Eastward Transmission of Western Sciences in the late Qing Dynasty, and third, the influx of new words in the Reform and Opening up. The loan words that appeared in the late Qing Dynasty were unprecedented

© The Author(s), under exclusive license to Springer Nature Switzerland AG 2023
Q. Su et al. (Eds.): CLSW 2022, LNAI 13495, pp. 350–367, 2023.
https://doi.org/10.1007/978-3-031-28953-8_27

in terms of the large number, new content, and richness of translation strategies, which have a great impact on the development of Chinese and gave birth to a large number of loan words of the same signified with different signifiers.

Scholars have a clear definition of "the words of the same signified with different signifiers." According to Yang Shishou [1], it refers to the same or the same kind of objects with several different signifiers. Zhou Jian [2] defined it as the phenomenon of words with different signifiers for an object. There are both narrow and broad definitions of loan words in the academic world. Scholars who hold a narrow view of loan words believe that loan words refer to words of transliteration and words with transliteration features, but do not include words of free translation [3–5]. Scholars who hold a broad view of loan words affirm that words of free translation are also loan words [6–8]. In this paper, we take a broad view of loan words, so "the Chinese loan words of the same signified with different signifiers" can be defined as the different Chinese words expressing the same foreign word or concept produced in the process of borrowing foreign words.

According to the number of different signifiers, they can be classified as "the same signified with two signifiers", "the same signified with three signifiers", etc. This paper mainly focuses on the Chinese loan words of the same signified with two signifiers in the late Qing and Republican periods and tries to explore the selection mechanism of lexical competition.

At present, studies have been conducted to explore the competition of synonyms. Liu Xiaomei [9] pointed out that there are factors such as word form, semantic meaning, style, and novelty in the competition of synonyms. Based on a richer corpus, Song Zuoyan [10] found that whether words can win the competition depends on the economy principle of language. Words with semantic transparency, expression clarity, and conforming to the rhyme pattern of Chinese words are highly competitive. The semantic transparency and word length have the greatest influence on the competition. In recent years, some studies have conducted in-depth researches on the selection mechanism of loan words. Dang Jingpeng [11] argued that the reasons affecting the propensity of Chinese native speakers to choose loan words were as follows: in terms of linguistic features, the principle of fill-in-the-blank priority, the principle of form simplicity, the economy principle of language, and the principle of subject pattern matching; in terms of word use, the borrowing time, duration of use, frequency of use, and range of use of loan words. Some studies have already paid attention to the loan words of the same signified with different signifiers in the late Qing Dynasty. Liu Shantao [12] summarized the distribution status of them, including word vacancy, word complement, word occupation, word retirement, etc. Previous studies have mostly focused on the competition mechanism of synonyms within the ancient and modern Chinese system, while little has been done on the dynamic competition mechanism of loan words of the same signified with different signifiers in the important period.

Therefore, in this paper, we take the first tool book in China that specifically includes the newborn loan words in the late Qing and Republican periods, the Etymological Glossary of Selected Modern Chinese Words (edited by the Chinese Language Society of Hong Kong) [13], as a sample, and conduct a comprehensive investigation of the loan words of the same signified with two signifiers. By manually marking information such as translation strategy, morpheme meaning, the number of syllables, and the preference of Chinese characters, and then consulting the Modern Chinese Dictionary (7th ed.) [14], we build a word corpus to explore the occupation of the words and its factors.

2   Factors Influencing the Occupation of the Chinese Loan Words of the Same Signified with Two Signifiers

According to the statistics, a total of 979 groups of the loan words of the same signified with different signifiers are included in the Etymological Glossary of Selected Modern Chinese Words in Modern Chinese, among which 586 groups of the loan words of the same signified with two signifiers are included, accounting for about 60%. According to the retention of the 1172 words in the Modern Chinese Dictionary (7th ed.) [14], the results of a two-word competition can be divided into three situations: one-word occupation, co-occupation, and co-retirement.

Table 1. Two-word competition of the Chinese loan words of the same signified with different signifiers in the late Qing and Republican periods.

Competition results	Quantity (group)	Ratio	Example
One-word occupation	370	63.1%	灵感(líng gǎn, inspiration) / 烟士披里纯(yān shì pī lǐ chún, inspiration) → 灵感
Co- occupation	67	11.4%	发动机(fā dòng jī, engine) / 引擎(yǐn qíng, engine) → 发动机、引擎
Co-retirement	149	25.4%	节礼日(jié lǐ rì, Boxing Day) / 箱子日(xiāng zi rì, Boxing Day) → Ø

As can be seen from Table 1, in the two-word competition of Chinese loan words of the same signified with two signifiers, the result of one-word occupation takes up a larger proportion. This paper analyzes the reasons from the perspectives of translation strategy, morpheme meaning, the number of syllables, and the preference of Chinese characters.

2.1   Translation Strategies

Referring to the viewpoint of the Thesaurus Working Group of the Chinese Language and Literature Society of Hong Kong [8], we classify the 370 groups of loan words into the words of transliteration, the words with transliteration features (including the words of transliteration with the feature of free translation, the words of semi-transliteration and semi-free translation and the words of transliteration with interpretation), and the words of free translation. It was found that there were 41 groups of words that were influenced by the translation strategies leading to the one-word occupation, accounting for about 11.1%.

Specifically, there are seven types of opposites in the translation strategies, namely: "transliteration" vs "free translation", "transliteration" vs "transliteration with the feature of free translation", "transliteration" vs "semi-transliteration and semi-free translation", "transliteration" vs "transliteration with interpretation", "free translation" vs "transliteration with the feature of free translation", "free translation" vs "semi-transliteration and semi-free translation", "free translation" vs "transliteration with interpretation". The competition situation is shown in Table 2.

Table 2. The situation of the one-word occupation due to the translation strategies.

Opposing types of translation strategies		Quantity (group)	Occupation type	Quantity (pcs)	Ratio
Transliteration VS free translation		26	Free translation	26	100%
Transliteration VS Words with transliteration features	Transliteration VS Transliteration with the feature of free translation	4	Transliteration	1	25%
			Transliteration with the feature of free translation	3	75%
	Transliteration VS Semi-transliteration and semi-free translation	3	Semi-transliteration and semi-free translation	3	100%
	Transliteration VS Transliteration with interpretation	1	Transliteration with interpretation	1	100%
Free translation VS Words with transliteration features	Free translation VS Transliteration with the feature of free translation	1	Free translation	1	100%
	Free translation VS Semi-transliteration and semi-free translation	4	Free translation	2	50%
			Semi-transliteration and semi-free translation	2	50%
	Free translation VS Transliteration with interpretation	2	Free translation	2	100%

Among the 41 groups of Chinese loan words of the same signified with two signifiers, 26 groups are transliteration in opposition to free translation, all of which are successfully occupied by the words of free translation. For example, the words of free translation such as "导师 (dǎo shī, tutor)", "抵制(dǐ zhì, boycott)", "肥皂(féi zào, soap)", "灵感(líng gǎn, inspiration)" and "油橄榄(yóu gǎn lǎn, olive)" occupied, while the corresponding words of transliteration such as "丢德(diū dé, tutor)", "杯葛(bēi gé, boycott)", "色盆(sè pén, soap)", "烟士披里纯(yān shì pī lǐ chún, inspiration)" and "阿利袜(ā lì wà, olive)" were eliminated. In the competition between the 8 groups of transliteration and words with transliteration features, most of the latter occupied. For example, the word of semi-transliteration and semi-free translation "英寸(yīng cùn, inch)" replaced the word of transliteration "因制(yīn zhì, inch)". The "英(yīng, "in-")" of "英寸(yīng cùn, inch)" indicated both the pronunciation (in-) and the meaning (British), and "寸(cùn, "-ch")" also indicated both the pronunciation (-ch) and the meaning (a quantifier in China). Moreover, in the competition with the rest words with transliteration features, the words of transliteration were all eliminated, while the words of free translation showed a clear advantage.The words of free translation are evenly matched against the words of semi-transliteration and semi-free translation, e.g., "国际公制(guó jì gōng zhì, The metric system) (free translation) / 梅德测量法(méi dé cè liáng fǎ, The metric system) (semi-transliteration and semi-free translation) → 国际公制", "脑桥(nǎo qiáo, pons Varolii) (free translation) / 瓦罗尔氏桥(wǎ luó ěr shì qiáo, pons Varolii) (semi-transliteration and semi-free translation) → 脑桥", "摩托车(mó tuō chē, motor vehicle) (semi-transliteration and semi-free translation) / 机器脚踏车(jī qì jiǎo tà chē, motor vehicle) (free translation) → 摩托车", "乌托邦(wū tuō bang, Utopia) (semi-transliteration and semi-free translation) / 华严界(huá yán jiè, Utopia) (free translation) → 乌托邦". The words of free translation were all successful in competing with the words of transliteration with the feature of free translation and the words of transliteration with interpretation.

Table 3. The proportion of one-word occupation due to the translation strategies.

Translation strategy		Before the one-word occupation		After the one-word occupation		Retention ratio (Quantity $(pcs)_2$/ Quantity $(pcs)_1$)
		Quantity $(pcs)_1$	Ratio	Quantity $(pcs)_2$	Ratio	
Words of transliteration		34	41.5%	1	2.4%	2.9%
Words with transliteration features	Words of transliteration with the feature of free translation	5	6.1%	3	7.3%	60%
	Words of semi-transliteration and semi-free translation	7	8.5%	5	12.2%	71.4%
	Words of transliteration with interpretation	3	3.7%	1	2.4%	33.3%
Words of free translation		33	40.2%	31	75.6%	93.9%

As can be seen from Table 3, before the one-word occupation, the number of the words of transliteration is slightly larger than the number of the words of free translation and far larger than the words with transliteration features, which has an obvious advantage among all the translation strategies. After the one-word occupancy, the retention ratio of the words of transliteration is lowest, and the words of free translation is in a strong position. Combining Table 2 and Table 3, we can see that the rate of successful occupancy shows the following regular pattern: words of transliteration < words with transliteration features < words of free translation. In other words, in the competition of the loan words of the same signified with two signifiers, the less transliteration features (and the more free translation features) the words contain, the more advantages the words have in word occupation.

In the rapidly changing society of the late Qing Dynasty, the need for timeliness often made it too late for translators to create loan words in the form of free translation. Transliteration, as the most direct and convenient way to introduce foreign concepts, became one of the main types of loan words in the late Qing Dynasty. However, the disadvantages of transliteration are also obvious, as it regard Chinese characters and syllables as meaningless symbols. For example, the words of transliteration such as "西那多 (xī nà duō, senator)" and "玛得玛第加 (mǎ dé mǎ dì jiā, mathematics)" are difficult for Chinese native speakers to relate to "参议员 (cān yì yuán, senator)" and "数学 (shù xué, mathematics)".

In addition, during the late Qing and Republican periods, it was the Chinese dialects of the southeastern coastal areas that were used to translate foreign words earlier. However, the phonetic differences among dialects were so great that it was difficult for Mandarin monolingual speakers or speakers of a particular dialect to understand the words of transliteration from the phonetic systems of other dialects. For example, Shanghai people used to call "transformer" "方棚 (fāng péng, transformer)" because its English pronunciation is similar to that of the Shanghainese word "方棚(fāng péng, transformer)". For people who do not know Shanghainese, it is impossible to relate the word "方棚(fāng péng, transformer)" to the transformer in terms of pronunciation, form, or meaning. Therefore, some of the words of transliteration in the late Qing and Republican periods may be influenced by the dialect of the translator and have limitations that hinder understanding and communication, thus making it difficult for them to be in a dominant position in the competition with the words of free translation.

2.2 Morpheme Meaning

In the case of the same translation strategy, the morpheme meaning of the words has an important influence on whether the words can successfully occupy the position. According to statistics, there were 224 groups of words, accounting for 60.5% of the total number of the loan words of the same signified with two signifiers, which were influenced by morpheme meaning. In this paper, these words are divided into two cases: words with the same number of syllables but different partial morphemes, and words with a different number of syllables but the morphemes are in an inclusion relationship, as shown in Table 4.

As can be seen from Table 4, there are 195 groups of words with the same number of syllables but different partial morphemes. By comparing the differences between the morphemes, these words can be subdivided into the following 5 types.

Table 4. The situation of the one-word occupation due to the morpheme meaning.

Morpheme meaning performance	Quantity (group)	Type	Ratio
Words with the same number of syllables but different partial morphemes	195	Morpheme synonymy	87.1%
		Naming preference	
		Combination relationship	
		Generic-specific relationship	
		Passively retire	
Words with different numbers of syllables but the morphemes are in inclusion relationship	29	\	12.9%

Morpheme Synonymy. There are 66 groups with different morphemes but similar morpheme meanings, and the internal structure of each group is the same, with only one different morpheme. For example, "炸弹(zhà dàn, bomb) / 爆弹(bào dàn, bomb) → 炸弹", "挂桥(guà qiáo, drawbridge) / 吊桥(diào qiáo, drawbridge) → 吊桥", "赛跑(sài pǎo, race) / 赌跑(dǔ pǎo, race) → 赛跑", "离心力(lí xīn lì, centrifugal force) / 离中力(lí zhōng lì, centrifugal force) → 离心力", "下半旗(xià bàn qí, half-staff) / 落半旗(luò bàn qí, half-staff) → 下半旗". When the morpheme meanings are similar, the more accurately the morphemes express, the more competitive they are. Taking "炸(zhà, bomb)" and "爆(bào, bomb)" for example, both have the meaning of "suddenly break", but the former is more inclined to artificial, purposeful behavior, such as "炸药(zhà yào, explosive)" and "轰炸(hōng zhà, bombing)", while the latter is more inclined to the spontaneous situation without external force, such as "爆仓(bào cāng, blow up)" and "爆胎(bào tāi, puncture". Therefore, "炸弹(zhà dàn, bomb)" expresses the meaning more accurately than "爆弹(bào dàn, bomb)", so it can occupy the position.

In addition, this paper finds that there are 5 groups of words with differences in ancient-Chinese and vernacular features. One group is occupied by words with ancient-Chinese features, such as "色盲(sè máng, parachromatoblepsia) / 色瞎(sè xiā, color blindness) → 色盲", and 4 groups are occupied by words with vernacular features, such as "海狗(hǎi gǒu, fur seal) / 海犬(hǎi quǎn, fur seal) → 海狗", "三脚架(sān jiǎo jià, tripod) / 三足架(sān zú jià, tripod) → 三脚架", "仰泳(yǎng yǒng, backstroke) / 仰泅(yǎng qiú, backstroke) → 仰泳", "小写(xiǎo xiě, lowercase) / 小书(xiǎo shū, lowercase) → 小写". Therefore, we speculate that in the competition of the words of the same signified with two signifiers, when the morpheme meanings are close and there are ancient-Chinese features in opposition to vernacular features, the words with vernacular features have stronger competitiveness, so they are more likely to occupy the position in oral communication.

Naming Preference. When naming the same foreign object, the translators chose different focuses, resulting in the phenomenon of the same signified with different signifiers, and there are 34 groups of such cases. For example, "芥末(jiè mò, mustard) / 芥辣(jiè là, mustard) → 芥末", where "末(mò, powder)" focuses on the appearance of (powder) and "辣(là, pungent)" focuses on the smell (spicy). "经线(jīng xiàn, longitude) / 经

圆(jīng yuan, longitude) → 经线", where "线(xiàn, line)" focuses on the nature (arc, auxiliary line) and "圆(yuan, circle)" focuses on the appearance (circle). "盲字(máng zì, braille) / 凸字(tū zì, braille) → 盲字", where "盲(máng, blind)" focuses on the purpose (for blind people) and "凸(tū, convex)" focuses on the appearance (the letters are made up of raised dots with different arrangements). "时针(shí zhēn, clockwise) / 短针(duǎn zhēn, clockwise) → 时针", where "时(shí, hour)" focuses on the purpose (indicating hour) and "短(duǎn, short)" focuses on the relative length (the hour hand is the shortest compared to the minute and second hands).

On the whole, appearance, smell, etc. belong to the surface properties of objects, while nature, use, etc. belong to the inherent properties. Words are more likely to be retained when the morpheme gets to the essence of the object better. There is also a subjective-objective distinction within the surface properties of objects. Appearance is generally objective, while the smell is relatively subjective. When morphemes refer to objects from an objective perspective, they are more competitive than from a subjective perspective.

Combination Relationship. There are 5 groups of combination relations (whole-partial relations) between the opposing morphemes. Among them, 2 groups are occupied by words with the morpheme meaning of "whole": "雌雄同株(cí xióng tóng zhū, monoecious) /雌雄同本(cí xióng tóng běn, monoecious) → 雌雄同株" and "雌雄异株(cí xióng yì zhū, dioecism) / 雌雄异本(cí xióng yì běn, dioecism) → 雌雄异株". "本(běn, root)" generally refers to the stem or root of the plant, while "株(zhū, plant)" means the plant, and the stem or root is part of the whole plant.

There are 3 groups of words with the morpheme meaning of "partial" occupied: "定滑轮(dìng huá lún, fixed pulleys) / 定滑车(dìng huá chē, fixed pulleys) → 定滑轮", "动滑轮(dòng huá lún, moving pulleys) / 动滑车(dòng huá chē, moving pulleys) → 动滑轮" and "唐人街(táng rén jiē, Chinatown) / 唐人城(táng rén chéng, Chinatown) → 唐人街". In terms of distribution, words with a relatively "partial" meaning are slightly more heavily retained. These words are easier to retain because they have a smaller scope and conform to the principle of expression clarity. However, since the sample is too small, we can only make preliminary speculations and need more corroboration from the corpus.

Generic-Specific Relationship. There are 5 groups of generic-specific relations between opposing morphemes, all of which are occupied by words referring to the "specific concept" (i.e., with smaller extensions): "哺乳动物(bǔ rǔ dòng wù, mammal) / 哺乳生物(bǔ rǔ shēng wù, mammal) → 哺乳动物", "火成岩(huǒ chéng yán, igneous) / 火成石(huǒ chéng shí, igneous) → 火成岩", "海峡(hǎi xiá, strait) / 水峡(shuǐ xiá, strait) → 海峡", "外耳(wài ěr, external ear) / 外窍(wài qiào, external ear) → 外耳", and "中耳(zhōng ěr, middle ear) / 中窍(zhōng qiào, middle ear) → 中耳". According to the Modern Chinese Classification Dictionary [14], "动物(dòng wù, animal" is included in "生物(shēng wù, creature)", "岩(yán, cliff)" is included in "石(shí, stone)", "海(hǎi, sea)" is included in "水(shuǐ, water)", and "耳(ěr, ear)" is included in "窍(qiào, aperture)". Therefore, we tentatively infer that when words constituting generic-specific relations by morpheme meanings compete with each other, words with smaller morpheme extensions are more advantageous because they point more clearly.

Passively Retire. With the development of loan words, one may withdraw from the competition of the original concept and refer to other objects in later. There are 8 groups of words that fall into this case, such as "空气(kōng qì, air) / 生气(shēng qì, air) → 空气", "大副(dà fù, chief mate) / 大伙(dà huǒ, chief mate) → 大副", "发条(fā tiáo, clockwork) / 法条(fǎ tiáo, clockwork) → 发条", "气体(qì tǐ, gas) / 气质(qì zhì, gas) → 气体", and "相片(xiàng piàn, photo) / 照相(zhào xiàng, photo) → 相片".

The above 5 types are our initial classification of words with the same number of syllables but different partial morphemes. In addition, there is another kind of morpheme meaning performance, that is, words with a different number of syllables but the morphemes are in an inclusion relationship. There are 29 groups of words in this type, all of which are won by words with more syllables, such as "大陆岛(dà lù dǎo, mainland island) / 陆岛(lù dǎo, mainland island) → 大陆岛", "工程师(gōng chéng shī, engineer) / 工师(gōng shī, engineer) → 工程师", "化学变化(huà xué biàn huà, chemical change) / 化变(huà biàn, chemical change) → 化学变化", "人类学(rén lèi xué, anthropology) / 人学(rén xué, anthropology) → 人类学", "巡捕房(xún bǔ fang, chemical change (police station in former foreign concessions)) / 捕房(bǔ fang, chemical change (police station in former foreign concessions)) → 巡捕房", "蒸馏水(zhēng liú shuǐ, distilled water) / 蒸水(zhēng shuǐ, distilled water) → 蒸馏水", etc. This paper finds that under the condition that some of the morphemes are the same, people tend to choose words with a higher number of syllables (morphemes) to achieve semantic integrity. Since loan words in the late Qing and Republican periods were dominated by words denoting new objects and new concepts in fields such as science and technology, people needed new words that could convey more accurate information.

2.3   The Number of Syllables

The word length becomes the main factor affecting word occupancy when the translation strategies and morpheme meanings are more or less the same. According to statistics, there are 47 groups of words of the signified with two significers, accounting for about 12.7%, which are affected by word length. They have the following 7 types of syllable number oppositions.

Monosyllable vs Disyllable. There are 2 groups of this type of opposition, both of which are won by monosyllables. During the competition of the words of transliteration "打(dǎ, dozen)" and "打臣(dǎ chén, dozen)", "打(dǎ, dozen)" retained at the end. During the competition of the words of free translation "种(zhǒng, kinds)" and "种变(zhǒng biàn, kinds)", "种(zhǒng, kinds)" retained at the end. The word "打(dǎ, dozen)" is the unit of counting, and the word "种(zhǒng, kinds)" is the basic unit of the biological classification system. For the basic units, people often prefer short monosyllabic words, to achieve a convenient and quick effect in counting and enumeration.

Disyllable vs Tri-syllable. There are 35 groups of this type of opposition, all of which are won by disyllables. The predominance of disyllables is a feature of modern Chinese, which is also evident in the competition of loan words. For example, "蛋糕(dàn gāo, cake) / 鸡蛋糕(jī dàn gāo, cake) → 蛋糕", "周刊(zhōu kān, weekly) / 星期刊(xīng qī kān, weekly) → 周刊(zhōu kān, weekly)", "电车(diàn chē, tram) / 电气车(diàn qì chē, tram) → 电车", "地图(dì tú, map) / 地景图(dì jǐng tú, map) → 地图", "股骨(gǔ gǔ, thighbone) / 大腿骨(dà tuǐ gǔ, thighbone) → 股骨". The word "蛋糕(dàn gāo, cake)" uses the morpheme "蛋(dàn, egg)" as a representative form to express the meaning of "鸡蛋(jī dàn, egg)" and the word "周(zhōu, week)" is a short form of the synonym "星期(xīng qī, week)", which are then combined with another morpheme to form a disyllable. These words either use the abbreviated morpheme or select the short ones, then formed disyllables that are retained.

Disyllable vs Four-syllable. There are 2 groups of this type of opposition, both of which are won by disyllables. For example, "电扇(diàn shàn, electric fan) / 电气风扇(diàn qì fēng shàn, electric fan) → 电扇", "电扇(diàn shàn, electric fan)" takes a morpheme before and after the word "电气风扇(diàn qì fēng shàn, electric fan)", which is a common abbreviation method. After a long time and high frequency of use, "电扇(diàn shàn, electric fan)" gradually replaces "电气风扇(diàn qì fēng shàn, electric fan)".

Disyllable vs Six-syllable. This type has 1 group of opposites, and the disyllable wins. For example, "大使(dà shǐ, ambassador) / 特命全权大使(tè mìng quán quán dà shǐ, ambassador) → 大使". As people gradually understand and master this concept, the short one's advantages of brevity and ease of communication are more prominent, so it has been able to occupy the position, even though it is not as comprehensive as the longer one.

Tri-syllable vs Four-syllable. There are 6 groups of this type of opposition, all of which are won by tri-syllable words. For example, "打字机(dǎ zì jī, typewriter) / 打字机器(dǎ zì jī qì, typewriter) → 打字机", "机(jī, machine)" can represent the full meaning of "机器(jī qì, machine)", so "打字机(dǎ zì jī, typewriter)", which has fewer syllables, wins.

Four-syllable – Five-syllable. This type of opposition has one group, and the four-syllable word wins. For example, "解析几何(jiě xī jǐ hé, analytic geometry) / 几何解析学(jǐ hé jiě xī xué, analytic geometry) → 解析几何", the former can already express the general meaning, so the word with fewer syllables wins.

In the competition of the 47 groups of words, all of them are occupied by words with a shorter length. Table 5 shows that the proportions of monosyllables and disyllables are also much higher than that of the remaining multisyllabic words. This phenomenon is in line with the economy principle of language, which means that people tend to choose the least number of words that can satisfy both the speaker and the listener when communicating. The low success rate of four-, five-, and six-syllable words in occupancy is due to the long and awkward pronunciation. Loan words with shorter lengths can reduce the burden of memory, improve communication efficiency, and meet the requirements of both sides of communication to save time and effort. Therefore, in the competition between loan words of the same signified with different signifiers, the shorter words are more likely to successfully occupy the position in a group of words with approximately the same translation strategies and morpheme meaning.

Table 5. The proportion of one-word occupation due to the word length.

The number of syllables	Before the one-word occupation		After the one-word occupation		Retention ratio (Quantity (pcs)$_2$/ Quantity (pcs)$_1$)
	Quantity (pcs)$_1$	Ratio	Quantity (pcs)$_2$	Ratio	
Monosyllable	2	2.1%	2	4.3%	100%
Disyllable	40	42.6%	38	80.9%	95%
Tri-syllable	41	43.6%	6	12.8%	14.6%
Four-syllable	9	9.6%	1	2.1%	11.1%
Five-syllable	1	1.1%	0	0%	0%
Six-syllable	1	1.1%	0	0%	0%

2.4 The Preference of Chinese Characters

According to statistics, there are 9 groups of words with the same translation strategies but with different Chinese characters. Take the words of transliteration as examples, such as "铋(bì, bismuth) / 璧士密司(bì shì mì sī, bismuth) → 铋", "伏特(fú tè, volt) / 弗打(fú dǎ, volt) → 伏特", "咖喱(gā li, curry) / 架厘(jià lí, curry) → 咖喱", "可可(kě kě, cocoa) / 苛苛(kē kē, cocoa) → 可可", "卢布(lú bù, Ruble) / 罗卜(luó bǔ, Ruble) → 卢布", etc.

When foreign words are introduced, translators have different Chinese characters for the same object or concept, which is roughly influenced by two factors. One is the phonetic system of different dialects. Two words with different pronunciations in Mandarin may have the same or similar pronunciations in some dialects. In the late Qing and Republican periods, translators from different dialects used the phonetic system of their respective dialects to translate foreign words, selecting words with the same or similar pronunciation but different written forms. For example, in Cantonese, the morpheme "特(tè)" of "伏特(fú tè, volt)" and the morpheme "打(dǎ)" of "弗打(fú dǎ, volt)" have the same initial consonant and the similar pronunciation. The second is the angle of consideration of the character. Translators may consider the ideographic nature of Chinese characters to express the meaning of new objects and concepts. For example, in the case of "可可(kě kě, cocoa)" and "苛苛(kē kē, cocoa)", the former is probably considered from the characteristic of delicious taste, while the latter adopts a grass-headed character "苛(kē, harsh)", presumably from the perspective of botanical properties.

It can be seen from the words successfully occupied that due to the special characteristics of Chinese characters and the influence of traditional Chinese national cultural psychology and cognitive habits of thinking, people's preference of Chinese characters in translation roughly reflects the following principles.

The Principle of Simplification. Take "铋(bì, bismuth) / 璧士密司(bì shì mì sī, bismuth) → 铋" as an example, both "铋(bì, bismuth)" and "璧士密司(bì shì mì sī, bismuth)" are the transliteration of bismuth (Bi). On the one hand, people tend to use words that are easy to write, read and understand. "铋(bì, bismuth)" meets the requirements and is easier to use. On the other hand, Chinese speakers like to use objects they know to infer objects they do not know. The radical " 钅 (jīn, metal)" in "铋(bì, bismuth)" indicates the metal element, and "必(bì)" suggests the pronunciation. In the semantic field of the chemical metal element, other words such as "铜(tóng, copper)" and "铝(lǚ, aluminum)", are also composed of " 钅 (jīn, metal)" plus parts that suggest pronunciation. When people see the uncommon word "铋(bì, bismuth)", they can also roughly infer its pronunciation and its analogous meaning based on the familiar character "铜(tóng, copper)" and "铝(lǚ, aluminum)".

The Principle of Association. Chinese characters are ideographic characters, and Chinese people are accustomed to inferring the meaning of the word from the form of the Chinese character. When the meaning expressed by the Chinese character is closer to the concept referred to, the words are easy to retain. On the one hand, people tend to choose words that can be associated with the meaning of the original word through association. For example, the word "咖喱(gā li, curry)" is phonetically similar to the original foreign word, and even its radical "口(kǒu, mouth)" is associated with food, which is easily accepted by the public. On the other hand, the word chosen should avoid misleading associations, such as "罗卜(luó bǔ, Ruble)", which is easily associated with "萝卜(luó bo, turnip)" and other things not related to money, so it was eliminated.

The Principle of Seeking Luck and Avoiding Harm. The Chinese people are concerned with good fortune and avoid words that contain the meaning of violence and death, so the word competition often retains words that are popular among the Chinese. For example, in the eliminated words "弗打(fú dǎ, volt)" and "苛苛(kē kē, cocoa)", the character "打(dǎ)" and "苛(kē, harsh)" easily remind people of the words "打架(dǎ jià, fight)" and "严苛(yán kē, strict and harsh)" which have unpleasant meanings. "伏特(fú tè, volt)" are common Chinese characters used in transliteration, and "可可(kě kě, cocoa)" evokes beautiful associations such as "可爱(kě ài, lovely)", "可口(kě kǒu, delicious)" and "可人(kě rén, pleasing)", so they finally retained.

2.5 Other Situations

In this paper, words with the same translation strategy, different morpheme meanings, and word length are tentatively classified as "other situations". There are 49 groups of such cases.

Among these words, 29 groups are occupied by words with a shorter length. For example, "褐煤(hè méi, lignite) / 棕色煤(zōng sè méi, lignite) → 褐煤", "晚报(wǎn bào, evening paper) / 黄昏报(huáng hūn bào, evening paper) → 晚报", "榴弹(liú dàn, grenade) / 开花弹(kāi huā dàn, grenade) → 榴弹", "巩膜(gǒng mó, sclera) / 眼白衣(yǎn bái yī, sclera) → 巩膜". From the perspective of word formation, most words of the same signified with two signifiers have the same internal structure, which is mostly a modifier-head structure. On this basis, if the morphemes have similar meanings or the morphemes assume similar epistemic functions, the increase in the number of morphemes can be seen as a violation of the economy principle of Chinese vocabulary. Taking "褐煤(hè méi, lignite) / 棕色煤(zōng sè méi, lignite)" and "晚报(wǎn bào, evening paper) / 黄昏

报(huáng hūn bào, evening paper)" as examples, their internal structures are the same, and the meaning of "褐(hè, brown" and "棕色(zōng sè, brown" are similar; "晚(wǎn, evening)" and "黄昏(huáng hūn, dusk)" both refer to a later time of the day, i.e., both of them can take on the ideographic function, so the word that meets the economy principle prevails in this case. From the perspective of word creation, longer words are likely to be richer in rhetoric, especially those in metaphorical and metonymic forms. For example, the latter of the two groups of words, "榴弹(liú dàn, grenade) / 开花弹(kāi huā dàn, grenade)" and "巩膜(gǒng mó, sclera) / 眼白衣(yǎn bái yī, sclera) ", both of which use the metaphorical form to add imagery to the concept, have been eliminated because they do not meet the requirements of scientific terminology. Most of the loan words in the late Qing and Republican periods contain scientific concepts, so it is clear that rhetorical word creation did not have a competitive advantage in this period.

At the same time, 20 groups are occupied by longer words. For example, "压路机(yā lù jī, road roller) / 铁车(tiě chē, road roller) → 压路机", "五线谱(wǔ xiàn pǔ, stave) / 正谱(zhèng pǔ, stave) → 五线谱", "内斜视(nèi xié shì, esotropia) / 斗视(dòu shì, esotropia) → 内斜视", "民事诉讼(mín shì sù song, civil procedure) / 私诉(sī sù, civil procedure) → 民事诉讼". There are two cases of word occupancy by longer words. In one case, the number of morphemes is limited so that it does not fully reflect the characteristics of the concept referred to. For example, in the group of words "压路机(yā lù jī, road roller) / 铁车(tiě chē, road roller)", the morpheme "铁(tiě, iron)" chosen for "铁车(tiě chē, road roller)" emphasizes the material of the object, but does not show the essential characteristic. In contrast, the word "压路机(yā lù jī, road roller)" clearly indicates its function, which reflects the important feature of the reflected object as a tool. In the second case, it is eliminated due to ambiguity arising from morpheme variation. Fu Huaiqing [3] called the meaning of the lexical items summarized in the lexicon the common morpheme meaning, and the variation in the word formation (within the same meaning) the morpheme variation. For example, in the group of "民事诉讼(mín shì sù song, civil procedure) / 私诉(sī sù, civil procedure)", the word "私(sī, private)" in "私诉(sī sù, civil procedure)" originally means "personal, own, as opposed to the public". In the absence of the context of "私诉(sī sù, civil procedure)", it may be understood as "secretly". Based on the concept of "私诉(sī sù, civil procedure)", the two meanings of "personal" and "secretly" are related and can be linked to the act of litigation, which may lead to the variation of the morphemes. So the word "私诉(sī sù, civil procedure)" is eliminated because of its ambiguity.

3 Selection Mechanism of Chinese Loan Words of the Same Signified with Two Signifiers

There are internal and external factors influencing Chinese lexical competition. The internal factors mainly include lexical meaning, expression, and Chinese rhythmic patterns, while the external factors mainly include language contact, dialect influence, and artificial avoidance [10, 11, 15]. By analyzing the internal factors of the occupancy of Chinese loan words of the same signified with two signifiers during the late Qing and Republican periods, this paper finds that the expression clarity, form simplicity, and cultural adaptability of Chinese play an important role in the two-word competition.

Overall, loan words with clear expression, simple form, and positive connotations of Chinese characters were more easily accepted, used, and spread.

3.1 The Principle of Expression Clarity

The more accurate and transparent the meaning of loan words is, the easier it is to win in the competition. This principle is reflected in the translation strategies, the morpheme meanings, and the preference of Chinese characters.

Since the Chinese inherent morphemes are all monosyllabic and Chinese morphemes are generally recorded in units of characters, Chinese speakers assume in their minds and habits that every syllable and character in Chinese has a meaning. The fewer transliteration features (and the more free translation features) a word have, the more clearly the word's meaning reflects the concept and the easier the word is to retain. The free translation can make people guess or judge the meaning of the word from the word form, which is more in line with the principle of expression clarity than words with other translation strategies, thus becoming the "strong translation" in the word competition.

The principle of expression clarity is reflected in the focus, the scope, and the feature. This paper finds that the more the morpheme meaning focuses on the essential features of the object, the easier it is to retain. For example, "炸弹(zhà dàn, bomb) / 爆弹(bào dàn, bomb) → 炸弹", "炸(zhà, bomb)" and "爆(bào, bomb)" have the same meaning of "suddenly break", but there is a focus distinction between "artificial" and "spontaneous", the morpheme "炸(zhà, bomb)" is retained because it is more in line with the implied characteristics of the object. The morpheme is easy to retain if it is from an objective point of view, e.g. "芥末(jiè mò, mustard) / 芥辣(jiè là, mustard) → 芥末". Words with a small range of morpheme meanings are more competitive than words with a large range in competition, such as "定滑轮(dìng huá lún, fixed pulleys) / 定滑车(dìng huá chē, fixed pulleys) → 定滑轮" and "动滑轮(dòng huá lún, moving pulleys) / 动滑车(dòng huá chē, moving pulleys) → 动滑轮". Words with small extensions of morpheme meaning have a competitive advantage over words with large extensions, such as "哺乳动物(bǔ rǔ dòng wù, mammal) / 哺乳生物(bǔ rǔ shēng wù, mammal) → 哺乳动物" and "海峡(hǎi xiá, strait) / 水峡(shuǐ xiá, strait) → 海峡". Words with vernacular features are easier to occupy than words with ancient-Chinese features, e.g. "海狗(hǎi gǒu, fur seal) / 海犬(hǎi quǎn, fur seal) → 海狗" and "三脚架(sān jiǎo jià, tripod) / 三足架(sān zú jià, tripod) → 三脚架". In cases where the number of syllables is different but the morphemes are inclusion relation, words with a larger number of morphemes dominate due to higher semantic integrity, such as "工程师(gōng chéng shī, engineer) / 工师(gōng shī, engineer) → 工程师" and "蒸馏水(zhēng liú shuǐ, distilled water) / 蒸水(zhēng shuǐ, distilled water) → 蒸馏水". Especially in the late Qing and Republican periods, people were initially exposed to new objects and new concepts, and they demanded higher semantic integrity of words. If these elements contribute to a more specific point of view and a clearer, more complete expression of the word, the word will be more competitive.

The principle of association in the preference of Chinese characters is also one of the manifestations of expression clarity. The higher the transparency from morpheme meaning to word meaning is, the more advantageous the word is, and words that cause ambiguity by the wrong association are often eliminated. For example, "咖喱(gā li, curry) / 架厘(jià lí, curry) → 咖喱", the radical "口(kǒu, mouth)" is associated with the food category. Another example is "卢布(lú bù, Ruble) / 罗卜(luó bǔ, Ruble) → 卢布", where the word "罗卜(luó bǔ, Ruble)" is easily associated with "萝卜(luó bo, turnip)" in a misleading way. Since Chinese characters are ideographic, the easier it is to establish a connection between the meaning of a character or its parts and the meaning of the word, the clearer the meaning of the word will express, and the more easily it is accepted by the public.

3.2 The Principle of Form Simplicity

In language communication, people prefer words with simple forms, so words with short lengths and simple characters are more advantageous. Words with shorter lengths are efficient to pronounce and write, and words with simple characters are easier to remember.

In this paper, we found that loan words with fewer syllables are easier to retain. For example, "种(zhǒng, kinds) / 种变(zhǒng biàn, kinds) → 种", "蛋糕(dàn gāo, cake) / 鸡蛋糕(jī dàn gāo, cake) → 蛋糕", and "打字机(dǎ zì jī, typewriter) / 打字机器(dǎ zì jī qì, typewriter) → 打字机". In the two-word competition, the retention proportions of monosyllables and disyllables are above 90%, while the retention proportion of other multisyllabic words is below 20%. However, it is not the case that the shorter the word length is, the more competitive it is. The above monosyllables such as "种(zhǒng, kinds)" and "打(dǎ, dozen)" happen to be quantifiers, which tend to be monosyllabic in form and thus have a high success rate in occupancy. When words are in disyllabic form, they conform to the modern Chinese lexical rhyme pattern and are highly competitive.

In terms of Chinese characters, people tend to choose characters that are easy to write, read and understand, in line with the principle of form simplicity. This is especially true for scientific terms. For example, "铋(bì, bismuth) / 璧士密司(bì shì mì sī, bismuth) → 铋", as a chemical metal element word, the monosyllable "铋(bì, bismuth)" meets the requirement of simplicity. In addition, the radical " 钅 (jīn, metal)" suggests the meaning of the class, and the part "必(bì)" suggests the pronunciation, which is easy to remember and use.

3.3 The Principle of Cultural Adaptation

The choice of Chinese loan words of the same signified with different signifiers is also governed by the principle of cultural adaptation. The influence of traditional Chinese national cultural psychology and cognitive habits is reflected in the translation strategies and Chinese characters. The cultural cognitive psychology of the ethnic group shows a subjective consciousness that takes the native language as the coordinates of identity while transliteration take the original culture as the coordinates, so the Chinese people are more willing to accept free translation. In terms of Chinese characters, the Chinese people are concerned with the principle of seeking good fortune and avoiding harm and reject words containing negative meanings such as violence and death. For example, " 伏特(fú tè, volt) / 弗打(fú dǎ, volt) → 伏特", there are "to fight" and "to attack" in the original meaning of "弗打(fú dǎ, volt)". Another example is "可可(kě kě, cocoa) / 苛苛(kē kē, cocoa) → 可可", the original meaning of "苛(kē, harsh)" has the meaning of "harsh" and "tedious", which is not easily accepted by people. When the character is used appropriately and the meaning is elegant and beautiful, the word is easier to retain. Thus, it can be seen that the loan words were adapted to the local culture when they were introduced into Chinese, and words that did not conform to the principle of cultural adaptation were eliminated.

On the whole, the occupation result of two-word competition is the result of the competition of the translation strategy, the morpheme meaning, the number of syllables, the preference of Chinese characters, as well as the result of various mechanisms such as the principle of expression clarity, the principle of form simplicity, and the principle of cultural adaptation. Ideally, words that are successfully occupied can satisfy the expression clarity and meaning transparency, and at the same time achieve the simplicity of word form and use appropriate characters. In practice, it is difficult to combine clarity of expression and simplicity of form. The shortness of word length means the reduction of morphemes, which may affect the expression of meaning, so the principle of expression clarity takes priority. When the word length is different but the semantic functions are similar, the principle of form simplicity takes precedence. The result of this competition also reflects the economy principle of language: the words with the fewest characters that satisfy the speaker's expression and the listener's understanding have greater dominance in the competition.

4   Conclusion

This paper establishes a corpus of Chinese loan words of the same signified with different signifiers during the late Qing and Republican periods based on dictionaries, conducts a qualitative and quantitative study on 586 groups of words, and explores in depth the occupancy situation, influencing factors and selection mechanism of words from a dynamic perspective. By focusing on the influencing factors such as translation strategy, morpheme meaning, the number of syllables, and the preference of Chinese characters in the two-word competition, it is found that the selection mechanism of the two-word competition follows the principles of expression clarity, form simplicity, and cultural adaptation, and the results of occupation are generally the result of a combination of factors. It is found that loan words with clear expression, short word length, and positive connotations of Chinese characters are easily accepted and have the advantage in the word competition.

This study focuses on the dynamic evolution of Chinese words, which has some significance and value in revealing the evolutionary pattern of Chinese vocabulary. However, there are some shortcomings in this paper. The object of this paper is the phenomenon of word occupancy in the two-word competition of loan words in the late Qing and Republican periods, and the research on the co-occupation and co-retirement of words has not been covered. In addition, the influence of external factors on lexical competition also needs to be deepened.

References:

1. Yang, S.S.: The emergence of words of the same signified with different signifiers in old Chinese. J. Liaoning Univ. (Philos. Soc. Sci. Ed.) **5**, 72–74 (1991). (in Chinese)

2. Zhou, J.: A study on Chinese loan words of the same signified with different signifiers. Zhongguo Yuwen **04**, 277–281 (1997). (in Chinese)
3. Fu, H.Q.: Modern Chinese Vocabulary. Peking University Press, Beijing (1985). (in Chinese)
4. Gao, M.K., Liu, Z.T.: An Etymological Glossary of Selected Modern Chinese words. Language and Literature Press, Beijing (1958). (in Chinese)
5. Wang, L.: History of Chinese Lexicon. Commercial Press, Beijing (1993). (in Chinese)
6. Hu, X.Z.: A Dictionary of Loanwords. Tian Ma Press, Beijing (1936). (in Chinese)
7. Luo, C.P.: Language and Culture. Beijing Publishing Group, Beijing (1950). (in Chinese)
8. Thesaurus Working Group of the Chinese Language and Literature Society of Hong Kong, The Chinese Language Society of Hong Kong: The General Explanation of "Thesaurus of Foreign Concept Words", Thesaurus Construction Newsletter, vol. 1, Hong Kong (1993). (in Chinese)
9. Liu, X.M.: Investigation on distributing of synonymies from Neologisms of Mandarin of the present age. J. Coll. Chin. Lang. Cult. Jinan Univ. **04**, 87–96 (2015). https://doi.org/10.16131/j.cnki.cn44-1669/g4.2005.01.011. (in Chinese)
10. Song, Z.Y.: The competition of synonyms in Chinese Mandarin and its influencing factors. Appl. Linguis. **01**, 86–95 (2019). https://doi.org/10.16499/j.cnki.1003-5397.2019.01.012. (in Chinese)
11. Dang, J.P.: Investigation on the borrowing process and the mechanisms of Chinese loanwords originated from English. Graduate School of Chinese Academy of Social Science (2017). (in Chinese)
12. Liu, S.T.: A study on the lexical distribution of Chinese loan words of the same signified with different signifiers. Lang. Teach. Linguis. Stud. **04**, 87–96 (2017). (in Chinese)
13. The Chinese language society of Hong Kong: an etymological glossary of selected modern Chinese words. Publishing House of the Unabridged Chinese Dictionary, Hong Kong (2001). (in Chinese)
14. Dictionary Editorial Office, Institute of Linguistics, Chinese Academy of Social Sciences: Modern Chinese Dictionary (7th edition). Commercial Press, Beijing (2016). https://doi.org/10.16499/j.cnki.1003-5397.1993.03.011. (in Chinese)
15. Wang, W.H.: Study of the solidity of basic vocabulary and the reasons for its evolution. J. Chin. Stud. Xiamen Univ. (2015). (in Chinese)
16. Huang, H.Q.: Some issues of the study of loanwords in Chinese. Thesaurus Construction Newsletter (Hong Kong) (1994). (in Chinese)
17. Liu, R., Pan, G.S.: An investigation into the use of English-originated loanwords in the 6th edition of the contemporary Chinese dictionary. Appl. Linguis. **01**, 96–105 (2019). https://doi.org/10.16499/j.cnki.1003-5397.2019.01.013. (in Chinese)
18. Shi, Y.W.: Loanwords in Chinese. Commercial Press, Beijing (2000). (in Chinese)
19. Su, X.C.: A shortcut to learning about culture: the meaning of words (1994). (in Chinese)
20. Su, X.C.: A Thesaurus of Modern Chinese. Commercial Press, Beijing (2013). (in Chinese)
21. Wang, B., Shi, X.: On detection of synonyms between simplified Chinese of Mainland China and traditional Chinese of Taiwan: a semantic similarity method. In: Lu, Q., Gao, H. (eds.) Chinese Lexical Semantics. CLSW 2015. Lecture Notes in Computer Science, vol. 9332. Springer, Cham (2015). https://doi.org/10.1007/978-3-319-27194-1_10
22. Wang, L., Yu, S., Wang, H.: Construction of an online lexicon of Chinese loan words and phrases translated from English. In: Wu, Y., Hong, JF., Su, Q. (eds.) Chinese Lexical Semantics. CLSW 2017. Lecture Notes in Computer Science, vol. 10709. Springer, Cham (2018). https://doi.org/10.1007/978-3-319-73573-3_32
23. Yang, X.P.: A Study on Loanwords in Chinese. People's Publishing House in Shanghai, Shanghai (2007). (in Chinese)
24. Zhang, C.H.: The synergistic mechanism of new word formation. Appl. Linguis. **02**, 52–62 (2009). https://doi.org/10.16499/j.cnki.1003-5397.2009.02.004. (in Chinese)

25. Zhang, D.X.: The third wave: the introduction and regulation of loanwords. Appl. Linguis. **03**, 70–76 (1993). (in Chinese)
26. Dong, S., Xu, J., Huang, C.-R.: Angry thunder and vicious frost: remarks on the unaccusativity of Chinese weather verbs. In: Liu, M., Kit, C., Su, Qi. (eds.) CLSW 2020. LNCS (LNAI), vol. 12278, pp. 64–73. Springer, Cham (2021). https://doi.org/10.1007/978-3-030-81197-6_6
27. Zhu, D.X.: Grammar Handouts. Commercial Press, Beijing (1982). (in Chinese)

A Case Study on Scalar Ordering Relations of Chinese Adverbs

Sheng-Chun Wu and Huichen S. Hsiao(✉) ⓘ

Department of Chinese as a Second Language,
National Taiwan Normal University, Taipei, Taiwan
guin0816@gmail.com, huichen.hsiao@ntnu.edu.tw

Abstract. The present study aimed to investigate whether the scalar structure of adverbs resembles scalar adjectives in respect to their ordering relations. Due to the fact that ordering relations in prior studies have often been examined in terms of differentiating antonyms of the same scalar dimension, investigating scalar implicatures, or probing the relations of scalar terms and modifiers, the present study intended to examine the ordering relations of Chinese adverbs of three dimensions (time/frequency/degree), based on responses collected from native speakers of Chinese. The results of the experiments indicated that, regarding the temporal adverbs, the ordering relation based on their semantic strengths from weakest to strongest was *jiāngyào* < *kuàiyào* < *jiùyào* (All three adverbs in Mandarin refer to the proximity and shortness of time, and can be literally translated as "almost" or "nearly" in English). The ordering relation of the target frequency adverbs based on semantic strength was *ǒu'ěr* (occasionally) < *yǒushí* (sometimes) < *jīngcháng* (often). Meanwhile, the ordering relation of degree adverbs was *yǒudiǎn* (a little) < *hěn* (quite) < *shífēn* (very). Moreover, the results of the experiment revealed that the semantic strength of the adverb with the highest strength in each dimension was significantly stronger than that of the target adverbs. Lastly, One-way ANOVA analysis detected no significant difference in the semantic strengths of the target adverbs between the three dimensions. Thus, the results of the present research supported the findings of previous related studies, and further provided more diverse and complete insights to the scalar structure of Chinese adverbs.

Keywords: Scalar Structure · Ordering Relations · Scalar Adverbs · Temporal Adverbs · Frequency Adverbs · Degree Adverbs

1 Introduction

The current study intends to examine the ordering relations of Chinese adverbs of three different scalar dimensions (i.e., time, frequency, degree), based on their semantic strengths. According to Kennedy & McNally [1], the three crucial parameters used to distinguish different adjectival scales are "a set of degrees", which represent measurement values; "a dimension", which indicates the kind of measurement; and "an ordering relation" that distinguishes adjectival pairs of the same dimensions and degrees

© The Author(s), under exclusive license to Springer Nature Switzerland AG 2023
Q. Su et al. (Eds.): CLSW 2022, LNAI 13495, pp. 368–383, 2023.
https://doi.org/10.1007/978-3-031-28953-8_28

by expressing inverse ordering relations. Ordering relations are often used to differentiate antonyms that belong to the same dimension but have different semantic strengths (e.g., tall/short; empty/full). Nonetheless, to the best of our knowledge, previous studies on scalarity mostly concern certain classes of scalar expressions, including conjunctions < or, and > ([2, 3]), determiners < some, all > ([3–5]), and adjectives ([6–8]), whereas other classes of scalar terms or the types of the expressions are constantly overlooked ([9]). Bolinger [10] supports this view by claiming that gradability is a property not exclusively of adjectives, but also of nouns, verbs, prepositions, and adverbs. Not only should the discussion of scalar expressions involve more classes of words, it should also be extended to languages other than English ([1]). As a result, we use Chinese adverbs as materials to investigate their ordering relations in the current study.

In addition, previous related studies on scalar expressions mainly focus on the discussion of pragmatic scalar implicatures ([9, 11, 12]), or examine the combination of degree modifiers and scalar terms (cf. [7, 8]; [13]), while there are relatively fewer studies that aim to probe the ordering relations of adverbs from different dimensions based on the evaluation of their semantic strengths. Based on the findings of the previous research discussed above, the current study has two aims. First, in previous studies, ordering relations are mostly used to distinguish antonym pairs of the same scalar dimension ([1]), while in the present research, ordering relations are used to investigate the relation of strengths between Chinese adverbs from three different dimensions. Moreover, the majority of previous related studies concentrate on the pragmatic performance of certain classes of scalar expressions in certain languages. Therefore, it is rather crucial to examine the ordering relations of Chinese adverbs from three dimensions based on their semantic strengths. The results of our study will be further used to examine the relative ordering relations between the adverbs. This study incorporated the experimental approach used in van Tiel et al. [9] to investigate the relative distance between the target adverbs with the goal of unfolding their ordering relations. The research questions of this study are described as follows:

(1) Do the adverbs of the three scalar dimensions (time/frequency/degree) have different semantic strengths, and can they be framed as corresponding ordering relations accordingly?

(2) Within the three scalar dimensions, is the semantic strength of the adverbs used as the maximum reference point significantly higher than the scalar items that are examined in the experiment? Furthermore, is there a significant difference in the relative semantic strengths between the scalar items among the three scalar dimensions?

2 Literature Review

The basis of ordering in our research is based upon the semantic distance between the target adverbs. This research approach is inspired by previous studies performed by other scholars on the topic of scalarity (cf. [12] for a brief review). For instance, van Tiel et al. [9] and Zevakhina [12] both conducted experiments to investigate the distance of the semantic strength between different adjectival pairs based on participants' responses via Likert scales. In addition, both studies further investigated the relation between semantic distance and scalar implicature, and the results showed that these two are correlated. In other words, as the semantic distance between two words from the same dimension increases, scalar implicature is more likely to occur. On the other hand, Horn [3] used the entailment relations within the same classes of words as a standard to clarify the ordering relations of different classes of words that belong to the same dimension, including quantifiers (all, most, some), conjunctions (and, all), modals (must, should, may), adjectives (beautiful, pretty, attractive) and verbs (adore, love, like). Not only did Horn investigate the ordering relations of expressions in different classes, he also further discussed the negated meanings of words from different dimensions to examine their relations with scalar implicature. Before getting into the design of present experiment, below is a review of some relevant findings of prior studies on Chinese adverbs.

In terms of temporal adverbs, scholars have proposed a basic classification method based on their literal meanings and the co-occurring performance with other lexicons. For instance, Zhang [14] divided temporal adverbs into three subtypes: adverbs that indicate time, adverbs that indicate frequency, and adverbs that indicate order. Each of the subtypes can be further divided into subcategories. On the other hand, according to Lu & Ma [15], indefinite temporal adverbs can be further classified into three subtypes due to the phase of the adverbs. Moreover, Chen [16] and Ding [17] both attempted to categorize temporal adverbs; the former classified the three temporal adverbs *jiāngyào*, *kuàiyào* and *jiùyào* according to their individual semantic features. Chen [16] claimed that although these three temporal adverbs can all be used to express the shortness and urgency of time, the time range expressed by *jiāngyào* is the largest among the three, and therefore the extent of urgency expressed by *jiāngyào* is relatively low compared to *kuàiyào* and *jiùyào*. Furthermore, Lu [18] pointed out that *jiù* is a temporal adverb that indicates close conjunction. As a result, the degree of urgency of *jiùyào* is higher compared to those of *jiāngyào* and *kuàiyào*. Ding [17] analyzed the three temporal adverbs based on their co-occurrence with other lexicons. In the corpus of 3000 sentences that include temporal adverbs, the order of the temporal adverbs based on the frequency of co-occurrence with other lexicons (from highest to lowest) is *jiùyào*, *kuàiyào*, and *jiāngyào*. Ding further mentioned that *jiùyào* is most frequently used with adverbs expressing urgency such as *mǎshàng* (right away) and *lìkè* (immediately) to convey the urgent nature of the event. Thus, the ordering relation in terms of the shortness and urgency of the time between these three temporal adverbs (from highest to lowest) is *jiùyào*, *kuàiyào*, and *jiāngyào*.

In regard to frequency adverbs, researchers applied different standards for classification. For instance, Shi [19] divided frequency adverbs into three magnitudes (low frequency, middle frequency, and high frequency), with *chángcháng* (often) as the center of the scale. Also, based on literal meanings and whether the adverbs can be used in certain sentence structures, Ding [20] divided frequency adverbs into 5 subtypes, in which the frequency spans from extremely low, relatively low, medium, relatively high, to extremely high.

As for degree adverbs, Wang [21] divided them into two subcategories, relative degree adverbs and absolute degree adverbs, according to whether the object modified by the adverb is comparable with other objects. The general standard of absolute adverbs is not based on comparison with other objects, but on speakers' mental judgment of the semantic strength of the degree adverbs. In addition, according to Zhang [22], the standard of absolute degree adverbs is based on human experience and mental representation that is relatively more subjective compared to relative degree adverbs. In terms of the classification of absolute degree adverbs, Zhou [23] categorized them into three types, while Zhang [22] divided them into 4 subtypes, including extremely high, very high, semi-high and relatively low. Furthermore, Wu [24] referred to adverbs that cannot be placed in comparison sentence structures as "prototype comparison degree adverbs". In other words, although these degree adverbs cannot be compared in the literal sentence structure, they can still be graded as 4 subtypes by the proto-standard in the human mental lexicon.

In the present study, our prediction regarding the ordering relations of the target temporal adverbs is based on the findings of previous studies ([16, 17]). That is, the ordering relation in respect of the shortness and urgency of the time between these three temporal adverbs (from highest to lowest) should be *jiùyào*, *kuàiyào*, and *jiāngyào*. In terms of frequency adverbs, if the categorization by Ding [20] and Shi [19] truthfully reflects the relative semantic strength of the frequency adverbs, we expect the results of our study to be consistent with the current classification. In other words, the ordering relation in respect to the semantic strength between these three frequency adverbs (from highest to lowest) should be *jīngcháng*, *yǒushí*, and *ǒu'ěr*. As for degree adverbs, *tài* (too; most) is the maximum reference point by the three different classifications mentioned above ([22–24]), while *bù* (not) is the minimum reference point on the scale. As for the ordering relation of the three target degree adverbs in this experiment, our prediction is based on the classification of Wu [24]. The ordering relation in respect to the semantic strength between the target degree adverbs (from highest to lowest) should be *shífēn* (very), *hěn* (quite), *yǒudiǎn* (a little).

The present study differs from previous research in two aspects: (a) previous studies on scalar ordering relations rarely investigated the Chinese language and adverbs in general, and thus this study concentrates on the ordering relations of different classes of Chinese adverbs; (b) the results of present study are based on the analysis of Likert scale responses collected from native speakers of Chinese. Additionally, in order to address unresolved issues from previous studies, the adverbs of the three scalar dimensions in the present study are placed into ordering relations with controlled contextual elements.

3 Method

3.1 Participants

Three hundred and sixty-eight native speakers of Chinese were recruited to participate in this experiment, including 66 males and 302 females. The 3 lists used in this experiment had 159, 112, and 97 participants, respectively. The mean age of the participants was

23.7, and the majority of them were undergraduate and postgraduate students at the time of the study. The participants were recruited via a link attached to a post on social media, and 20 of them were randomly chosen to receive convenience store gift cards as a reward.

3.2 Materials

In the current experiment, for the target adverbs of the temporal scalar dimension, we used three synonymous temporal adverbs (i.e., *jiùyào, kuàiyào,* and *jiāngyào*) that are classified into the same subcategory which represents the temporal phase that has not yet occurred according to Ding [17]. Additionally, in the experiment we used *yǐjīng* (already) and *háiméi* (yet) as maximum and minimum reference points, respectively, to represent the maximal and minimal values on the temporal scale. In terms of frequency adverbs, the target adverbs are *ǒu'ěr* (occasionally), *yǒushí* (sometimes), and *jīngcháng* (often), which represent the values of relatively low, medium, and relatively high on the frequency scalar dimension ([19, 20]). Furthermore, we used *cóngwèi* (never) and *zǒngshì* (always) as minimal and maximal references to test where the three target frequency adverbs fall between them. In respect to the degree adverbs, based on the subtypes from semantically strong to weak categorized by Wu [24], we selected *shífēn* (very), *hěn* (quite), and *yǒudiǎn* (a little) as our target materials. In addition, *tài* (too; most) is used as the maximum reference point for the 3 different classifications ([22–24]), while *bù* (not) is used as the minimum reference point on the scale.

The experiment included three lists, each containing thirty questions. Each list consisted of 18 target questions and 12 filler questions involving non-gradable adverbs. Among the 18 target questions, 12 involved a comparison between one target adverb with either the maximum or minimum adverb of the same scalar dimension, while six involved comparisons between two target adverbs of the same scalar dimension. The 10th, 20th, and 30th questions consisted of questions that involved comparisons between the maximum and minimum reference adverbs from the 3 scalar dimensions, and were used to filter participants' responses. We presumed that answering these questions incorrectly might indicate a lack of attention or misunderstanding of the tasks. Thus, the responses of those who failed these questions were excluded from the data analysis. All questions were presented in random order in the 3 lists, with questions including the same adverbs but in opposite order of appearance distributed in another list.

3.3 Procedure

The experiment was conducted via an online questionnaire which only included multiple-choice questions. The participants had to compare two statements that included different scalar adverbs and decide which statement had stronger semantic strength, in addition to the relative difference in semantic strength between the two statements. The entire duration of the experiment was approximately five minutes.

After seeing the two statements with scalar adverbs and a follow-up related question, the participants had to answer the question by selecting the most proper number on a scale that ranged from -3 to 3 based on their linguistic intuition. In order to prevent the participants from changing their responses after answering latter questions, participants were instructed that they should not return to the previous questions. Further, to help the participants become more familiar with the experimental design and procedure, we administered 2 practice trials that did not involve the target adverbs (without providing the correct answers) before the actual experiment began. The following is one of the practice questions.

Please compare the two sentences below

(1) *Jīntiān shì wēnnuǎn de tiānqì.*
Today is warm DE weather
"Today's weather is warm."

(2) *Jīntiān shì nuǎnhuo de tiānqì.*
Today is warm DE weather
"Today's weather is warm."

Question: *Xiāng jiào yú dì yī jù, dì èr jù zhōng tiānqì de yánrè chéngdù shì fǒu gèng gāo? Rúguǒ rènwéi gèng gāo qǐng xuǎnzé 3 ; Rúguǒ rènwéi gèng dī zé xuǎnzé -3 ; Rúguǒ rènwéi chéngdù zài cǐ qūjiān zé zuò chū xiāng duìyìng de xuǎnzé.*

(lit. compared to the first sentence, is the degree of hotness higher in the second sentence? If you think the answer is higher, please select 3 on the scale; if you think the answer is lower, please select -3. If you think the answer is between the two ends, please select the corresponding number on the scale.)

	O	O	O	•	O	O	O	
gèng bù *wēnnuǎn* (less warm)	-3	-2	-1	0	1	2	3	*gèng* *wēnnuǎn* (warmer)

Fig. 1. Likert Scale Used in the Practice Question

3.4   Target Questions and Examples

The design of the present experiment is based on the study of van Tiel et al. [9], which used a 7-point Likert scale as a grading system (as in Fig. 1). The participants had to use the first statement as a reference and compare it with the semantic strength of the second statement. However, in the present study, we have modified this scale to range from −3 to 3, instead of 1 to 7. In addition, to prevent the participants from constantly selecting the neutral response, we removed the central item of the scale 0, so that the participants could only select between the remaining 6 numbers (−3, − 2, −1, 1, 2, 3). In other words, if the participants determined that the semantic strength of the second statement is weaker than the first sentence, they should select a value between − 3 and −1, depending on their linguistic intuition. By contrast, if the participants believed that the semantic strength of the second statement is stronger than the first statement, they should choose a value from 1 to 3 based on the perceived difference in semantic strength. Moreover, each question had a counterpart with the two adverbs appearing in opposite order, so that questions including the same adverbs but in opposite order of appearance were distributed in another list. The following is an example of the target question (Fig. 2).

Please compare the two sentences below

(1)   (2)
Zhè wèi tóngxué zǒngshì chuānzhe hēisè yīfu.   *Zhè wèi tóngxué jīngcháng chuānzhe hēisè yīfu.*
This CL student always wear   black clothes   *This CL student often   wear   black clothes*
"This student always dresses in black."   "This student often dresses in black."

Question: *Xiāng jiào yú dì yī jù, dì èr jù zhōng zhè wèi tóngxué chuān hēisè yīfu de pínlǜ shìfǒu gèng gāo?*
(lit. compared to the first sentence, is the frequency of the student dressing in black higher in the second sentence?)

	O	O	O	•	O	O	O	
gèng dī (lower)	-3	-2	-1	0	1	2	3	*gèng gāo* (higher)

Fig. 2. Likert Scale Used in the Target Question

3.5 Data Conversion

Before proceeding to the formal analysis, we first removed the responses of the participants who took the online experiment more than once. Next, we used the 10th, 20th, and 30th questions in the questionnaire (in which participants were asked to compare two statements that involved the maximum and minimum reference adverbs from 3 dimensions) as a reference to eliminate participants who answered these questions incorrectly, as the incorrect answers to these questions could suggest lack of attention or misunderstanding of the task. We presumed that the answers to these three questions ought to be the two ends of the scale (i.e., 3 or -3), and thus there were at least two potential reasons to explain why participants gave different answers, including the possibilities that participants did not concentrate during the experiment, and that they did not exhibit sufficient sensitivity to the relative semantic strengths of the adverbs. As a result, after eliminating the responses of the "unqualified" participants (N = 117), we used the remaining 251 responses (List 1: 112; List 2: 75; List 3: 64) for further analysis.

In regard to the approach of the analysis, due to the design of the experiment and the comparison between maximum and minimum reference adverbs, the distribution of the data collected appeared to be a non-normal distribution and non-parametric. In addition, when the questions included the comparison between target adverbs and the maximum (e.g., *yǐjīng/zǒngshì/tài*) or minimum (e.g., *háiméi/cóngwèi/bù*) reference adverbs, the participants were inclined to select items on both ends of the scale (i.e., $3/-3$) instead of the typical normal distribution. Nonetheless, according to the Central Limit Theorem, when the sample size is large enough, the means of the data would be approximately distributed. Therefore, in the present study we used a One-Sample *t*-Test to examine the means, *t*-values, and *p*-values to determine if there is a significant difference between the adverbs from the 3 scalar dimensions and sequence them in the ordering relation accordingly.

The analysis employed in the present experiment was a combination of a calculation of the means of each adverb comparison among target adverbs and between target adverbs and the maximum or minimum adverbs in the three scalar dimensions, which was obtained through dividing the sum of participants' responses on the comparison by the number of participants. A 2-tailed One-Sample t-Test was applied to probe whether the means of the comparisons differed significantly from the median of the scale. We hypothesized that if two adverbs had the same semantic strength, then the means of the participants' responses should be closer to the center of the scale (i.e., 0). Thus, we compared the means of each pair, and examined whether the means of each pair and the center of the scale differed significantly (i.e., $p < 0.05$). We used the means as a standard to determine whether there is a significant difference between the semantic strengths of the two target adverbs and whether there is an ordering relation. Moreover, there are two reasons why we used the comparison between two target adverbs rather than the comparison between the target adverb and the maximum and minimum adverb. First, after analyzing the responses of the participants, we noticed that when the question involved the maximum or minimum reference adverbs, the participants were prone to select the two ends of the scale (i.e., $3/-3$). Therefore, no significant difference could be reached among the adverb pairs. The other reason was that within the same dimension, the respective distance between each target adverb item and the maximum or minimum reference adverb was not equivalent. Therefore, the relative difference of intervals could not truthfully reflect the actual ordering relation of the target adverbs.

The approach used for determining the ordering relation of the target adverbs in present study is as follows: First, we compared three pairs of comparisons of the three target adverbs in each dimension. Next, we examined whether the means of each pair were above or below the center of the scale, and whether the means were significantly different from the center of the scale by calculating the means and t-value via One-Sample t-Test. Afterward, we used the means and p-values for each pair of comparisons to determine the ordering relation of the three target adverbs. Before the experiment began, according to previous studies, we had roughly predicted and classified the three target adverbs of each dimension into three scalar items (low/middle/high) based on their relative semantic strengths. Then, we examined the means and p-values of the three pairs of comparisons (low/middle; low/high; middle/high), and if the results showed that the means of all three pairs of comparisons were above the center of the scale with p-value < 0.05. We used figures to examine whether the results of our experiment on the ordering relations of the three target adverbs were consistent with our predictions based on the previous studies. Further, in order to investigate whether the three maximum reference adverbs from the three dimensions indeed had higher semantic strengths compared to the target adverbs, we also examined the means of the comparisons between the three maximum reference adverbs and the three target adverbs from the same dimension, respectively.

Moreover, another modification we made in terms of the scale is that we converted the scalar items on the original Likert scale ranging from -3 to 3, into a scale that ranged from 1 to 7 to the avoid difficulties in calculation and for the convenience of presentation. In other words, the central item of the original scale (i.e., 0) was replaced by the new central item (i.e., 4) of the converted scale. As a result, when comparing the semantic strengths of the adverbs, we investigated whether the means were above or below 4, and whether the p-value was below 0.05 to determine the ordering relation of the target adverbs in the 3 scalar dimensions.

In addition, to examine whether the adverbs' order of appearance had an effect on their ordering relations, we compared the questions which contained the same adverbs presented in a different order. Further, we used a Pearson correlation test to analyze the degree of correlation between the means of the two lists, in order to probe whether the order of the adverbs had a significant effect on participants' responses. In theory, if the participants select values on the scale based on the corresponding semantic strength of the adverbs, rather than the order of appearance of the adverbs, the responses from the two lists should appear to be highly correlated in the analysis. But proceeding to further analysis, we shall clarify the standard used in the present analysis in respect to the ordering relations of the adverbs from the two lists.

As mentioned in the previous discussion, in order to avoid confusion regarding the analysis or comprehension of the data, we converted the original scale (-3 to 3), to a new scale that ranged from 1 to 7. Furthermore, the set of questions that included the same pair of adverbs but presented in opposite order were distributed in the other two lists. For instance, for one set of questions, the adverbs that were expected to have lower semantic strength were in the first sentence, while the adverbs with higher expected semantic strength were in the second sentence. Thus, we expected that for this set of questions the means for each comparison would be higher than 4. On the other hand, for the other set of questions involving stronger adverbs in the first sentence and weaker adverbs in the second sentence, we expected that the means for each pair of comparisons would be below 4. However, in order to make the correlation and comparison between the 2 sets of questions easier to calculate and present, we adjusted the scale of the second set of questions, in which the maximal item (7) on the original scale became the minimal item (1), while the minimal item (1) became the maximal item (7), and the rest of the items on the scale were converted accordingly. With the above modifications, both sets of questions could be evaluated by the standard of whether the mean of each comparison was above 4.

4 Results

After analyzing the responses from the participants and examining the means of each adverb pair and the t-values and p-values of the One-Sample t-Test, we found that the results of the ordering relations between the target adverbs in three dimensions were consistent with our predictions. In the following sections, we further discuss the results of the three dimensions, the maximum reference adverbs in each dimension, the effect of the appearance order of the adverbs, and whether the semantic strengths between the members of each dimension are significantly different from those in other dimensions.

4.1 Temporal Adverbs (*jiāngyào/kuàiyào/jiùyào*)

The means of the three target temporal adverbs are shown in Table 1, in which the mean of *jiāngyào/kuàiyào* is 4.6; the mean of *jiāngyào/jiùyào* is 4.7, and the mean of *kuàiyào/jiùyào* is 4.83 (note that within each comparison in our data, the order of the adverbs divided by forward slashes reflects the order by which they appeared in the descriptions in the questionnaire).

Table 1. Comparisons Between Temporal Adverbs

	jiāngyào/ kuàiyào	*jiāngyào/ jiùyào*	*kuàiyào/ jiùyào*	*jiāngyào/ yǐjīng*	*kuàiyào/ yǐjīng*	*jiùyào/ yǐjīng*
N	75	64	75	75	64	112
mean[1]	4.6	4.7	4.83	6.79	6.72	6.56
SD	2.01	1.55	1.91	1.00	1.21	1.44
t-value	2.58	3.63	3.76	24.04	17.91	18.76
p-value	0.0118	0.0005	0.0003	< 0.00001	< 0.00001	< 0.00001

Not only were the means of all three pairs of comparison above the center of the scale (i.e., 4), the results of One-Sample t-Test also suggested that the difference in these pairs was significant, and thus could be used to determine the ordering relation of the target temporal adverbs. In addition, we also compared the three target temporal adverbs with the maximum reference adverb (i.e., *yǐjīng*), and the results demonstrated that the means for the three pairs of comparison were all above 6.5, indicating a significant difference. Therefore, according to the analysis of participants' responses, the results of the present experiment on the ordering relation of the three temporal adverbs supported the findings of previous studies. That is, the semantic strengths of the three temporal adverbs from weakest to strongest were *jiāngyào* < *kuàiyào* < *jiùyào*.

4.2 Frequency Adverbs (*ǒu'ěr/yǒushí/jīngcháng*)

In respect to the results of target frequency adverbs shown in Table 2, the means of the three pairs of comparisons between the target frequency adverbs were all above 4 (the mean of *ǒu'ěr/yǒushí* was 4.76; the mean of *ǒu'ěr/jīngcháng* was 6.8, and the mean of *yǒushí/jīngcháng* was 6.75). Furthermore, the results of One-Sample t-Test revealed that the means of the three pairs were significant. The analysis also demonstrated that the means of the comparisons between the three target frequency adverbs and the maximum reference adverb (i.e., *zǒngshì*) were all significantly higher than 4. Thus, based on the results, we concluded that the ordering relations of the three frequency adverbs supported the previous findings. In other words, the ordering relation of the target frequency adverbs based on the semantic strength from weakest to strongest was *ǒu'ěr* < *yǒushí* < *jīngcháng*.

---

[1] The mean is acquired through dividing the sum of participants' responses on the comparison by the number of participants.

Table 2. Comparisons Between Frequency Adverbs

	ǒu'ěr/ yǒushí	*ǒu'ěr/ jīngcháng*	*yǒushí/ jīngcháng*	*ǒu'ěr/ zǒngshì*	*yǒushí/ zǒngshì*	*jīngcháng/ zǒngshì*
N	75	64	75	75	64	112
mean	4.76	6.8	6.75	6.91	6.97	6.73
SD	1.87	0.44	0.79	0.60	0.18	0.86
t-value	3.51	50.52	30.11	42.19	135.43	33.65
p-value	0.0008	< 0.00001	< 0.00001	< 0.00001	< 0.00001	< 0.00001

4.3 Degree Adverbs (*yǒudiǎn/hěn/shífēn*)

Lastly, we used the same approach to analyze the ordering relation of the target degree adverbs. The results in Table 3 indicated that the means of the three pairs of comparison between the three target degree adverbs were all above 4 (the mean of *yǒudiǎn/hěn* was 6.72; the mean of *yǒudiǎn/shífēn* was 6.94, and the mean of *hěn/shífēn* was 5.19). Moreover, the results of One-Sample *t*-Test demonstrated that the means of the three pairs of comparisons were significantly higher than the center of the scale. In addition, after analyzing the comparison between the target degree adverbs and the maximum reference adverb (i.e., *tài*), the results indicated that the means were all significantly above 4. As a result, based on the results of the present experiment, we concluded that the ordering relation of the three target degree adverbs was consistent with our prediction and previous studies. The semantic strengths of the target degree adverbs from weakest to strongest were *yǒudiǎn* < *hěn* < *shífēn*.

Table 3. Comparisons between degree adverbs

	yǒudiǎn/hěn	*yǒudiǎn/shífēn*	*hěn/shífēn*	*yǒudiǎn/tài*	*hěn/tài*	*shífēn/tài*
N	75	64	75	75	64	112
mean	6.72	6.94	5.19	6.76	6.42	5.07
SD	1.02	0.24	1.67	0.77	0.91	2.11
t-value	23.07	96.32	6.17	31.11	21.41	5.37
p-value	< 0.00001	< 0.00001	< 0.00001	< 0.00001	< 0.00001	< 0.00001

4.4   The Semantic Strength of the Maximum Reference Adverbs

According to the findings of the present experiment, in the three scalar dimensions (i.e., time/ frequency/degree), the semantic strengths of the adverbs that served as the maximum reference items (i.e., *yǐjīng/zǒngshì/tài*) were demonstrated to be significantly stronger in comparison to the target adverbs ($p < 0.05$). Furthermore, excluding the pair of *shífēn/tài*, the means of the other pairs were all above 6.5, which were close to the upper end of the Likert scale. In other words, the results of the present experiment demonstrated that the three adverbs indeed had the highest semantic strengths in the three scalar dimensions, and could be used as the maximum reference items.

In respect to the adverbs' order of appearance, the analysis examined the degree of correlation between the means of the two sets of questions, which included the same adverbs but were presented in opposite order. Theoretically speaking, if the order of appearance does not have a significant effect on the ordering relations of the adverbs, the means of the two sets of question ought to appear highly correlated. On the contrary, if the order of appearance does have a significant effect on the participants' responses, the means of the two sets of questions should not reach significant correlation. In our analysis, we used the means of the comparisons within target adverbs, and between target adverbs and the maximum reference adverb in each dimension as materials. Thus, there were 18 means in each set of questions which included 3 within-target-adverb comparisons, plus 3 comparisons between target adverbs and the maximum reference adverb, in 3 dimensions. The two-tailed correlation test of the 18 means of the two sets of questions revealed that the correlation between the two sets was $R = 0.9548$ ($p < 0.00001$). Therefore, the results of the correlation test demonstrated that the means of the two sets of questions were highly correlated, indicating that the order of adverbs' appearance did not have a significant effect on the participants' responses. In other words, participants determined the ordering relations of the target adverbs based on their semantic strengths, rather than based on whether the target adverbs appeared in the first or the second statement in the questionnaire.

4.5   Discussion on the Difference in Semantic Strength Between Dimensions

In the following, we examined whether the difference in semantic strengths of the target adverbs differs significantly between the three dimensions. To address the question, we used One-Way ANOVA with dimension (or adverb type) as a variable, to compare whether the means of the six comparisons of adverbs (i.e., weak/middle; weak/strong; middle/strong; weak/maximum reference item; middle/maximum reference item; strong/maximum reference item) differed significantly between the three dimensions. This was done to examine whether the relative semantic distance in terms of semantic strengths between the target adverbs resemble each other. The results of the analysis in Table 4 suggested that the means of the target adverbs did not differ significantly between the three dimensions. In other words, between the three dimensions (time/frequency/degree), the difference in the semantic strengths of the target adverbs did not reach significance, which indicated that the ordering relations and the relative semantic distance based on target adverbs' semantic strengths among the three dimensions were consistent.

Table 4. Comparison of Means Between Dimensions

Source	SS	df	MS	
Between-treatments	1.8889	2	0.9445	$F = 1.08715$
Within-treatments	13.0313	15	0.8688	
Total	14.9202	17		

5 Discussion

The present study aimed to examine the ordering relations of the target adverbs of the three scalar dimensions (i.e., time/frequency/degree) based on their relative semantic strengths. Through probing the linguistic intuition of native Chinese speakers, we further examined whether the findings of the present research are consistent with the findings of previous studies. In addition to investigating the ordering relation of the adverbs of the three scalar dimensions, we examined whether the semantic strengths of the maximum reference adverb in each dimension were significantly higher than the target adverbs within the same dimension, and thus could serve as the maximum reference for scalar items.

First of all, the analysis of the present experiment was based on the means of the comparisons between the target adverbs, *t*-value and *p*-value of One-Sample *t*-Test to determine whether the ordering relations of the adverbs in the present study were consistent with previous findings. In terms of temporal adverbs, the results of the present study were consistent with the classification of Chen [16] and Ding [17], in which the ordering relation of the three target adverbs from weakest to strongest was determined as *jiāngyào* < *kuàiyào* < *jiùyào*. In regard to frequency adverbs, the findings of present experiment supported the results of Ding [20], in which the relative semantic strengths from weakest to strongest of the target frequency adverbs were *ǒu'ěr* < *yǒushí* < *jīngcháng*. Lastly, in respect to degree adverbs, the results of present study were in line with the findings of Wu [24]. That is, the semantic strengths of the target degree adverbs from weakest to strongest were determined to be *yǒudiǎn* < *hěn* < *shífēn*. In addition, through analyzing the means and *p*-values of One-Sample *t*-Test of the comparison between the maximum reference adverbs (i.e., *yījīng/zǒngshì/tài*) and the three target adverbs of the three scalar dimensions, the results demonstrated that the semantic strength of the maximum reference adverb was significantly higher than those of the three target adverbs from the same dimension, and thus could be used as the maximum reference scalar item.

In terms of the effect of the adverbs' order of appearance, by comparing the means of the 18 pairs of adverb-comparisons from two different sets of questions, the Pearson correlation test suggested that the degree of correlation between the means of the two sets of questions were highly correlated ($R = 0.9548$; p (2-tailed) < 0.00001). It was found that the order of the adverbs' appearance did not have a significant effect on the ordering relations. Last but not least, the results of One-way ANOVA indicated that the differences in semantic strengths of the target adverbs did not differ significantly between the three dimensions (time/frequency/degree).

6 Conclusion

Owing to the fact that prior studies on ordering relations and scalarity mainly focused on a limited range of languages and classes of words, the present study was aimed at investigating whether the ordering relations based on the relative strengths of scalar terms present in other languages and word classes were also existent in Chinese adverbs. In order to verify the findings of prior studies on the relative strengths of Chinese adverbs based on their literal meanings and their co-occurring performance with other lexicons, the current study employed a different approach by probing native Chinese speakers' linguistic intuition of the ordering relations of the target adverbs in regard to their semantic strengths in the three scalar dimensions (time/frequency/degree). The preliminary results not only supported the prior findings with respect to the ordering relations of the target Chinese adverbs in the three respective dimensions, but made further contributions by demonstrating that the relative semantic distance between the target pairs of adverbs was consistent across the three dimensions. Nevertheless, the scope of the present study only concerned three types of adverbs in Chinese, and future studies are anticipated to expand the range of dimensions and languages to better capture the scalar expressions of adverbs.

Acknowledgments. This research was supported by a National Science and Technology Council (NSTC) research grant (MOST 110–2410-H-003–040-). We would like to thank the reviewers for their comments and Anwei Yu for his proofreading. All errors are of course our sole responsibility.

Appendix: Experimental Materials and Question Lists

Temporal adverbs:

現在快要/將要九點了。
Xiànzài **kuàiyào/jiāngyào** jiǔdiǎn le
It is **almost** nine o'clock.

太陽快要/就要下山了。
Tàiyáng **kuàiyào/jiùyào** xiàshān le
The sun is **about** to set.

公車快要/已經來了。
Gōngchē **kuàiyào/yǐjīng** lái le
The bus **is about to/has already**
come.

報告將要/就要完成了。
Bàogào **jiāngyào/jiùyào** wánchéng le
The report is **almost** finished.

這棟建築將要/已經完工了。
Zhè dòng jiànzhù **jiāngyào/yǐjīng**
wángōng le
This construction of the building is
almost/already finished.

天就要/已經亮了。
Tiān **jiùyào/yǐjīng** liàng le
It is **almost/already** dawn.

弟弟還沒/快要回家了。
Dìdi **háiméi/kuàiyào** huíjiā le
My younger brother **has not/ is about to**
come home.

包裹還沒/將要抵達了。
Bāo guǒ **háiméi /jiāngyào** dǐ dá le
The parcel **has not/ is about to**
arrive.

頭髮還沒/就要染好了。
Tóufǎ **háiméi /jiùyào** rǎnhǎo le
The hair **has not been/ is about to be**
finished dyeing.

Frequency adverbs:

我們有時/偶爾一起吃午餐。
Wǒmen **yǒushí /ǒu'ěr** yī qǐ chī wǔ cān
We **sometimes/occasionally** have lunch
together.

這台機器有時/經常會故障。
Zhè tái jīqì **yǒushí /jīngcháng** huì gù
zhàng
The machine **sometimes/often** breaks
down.

他有時/總是會睡午覺。
Tā **yǒushí /zǒngshì** huì shuì wǔjiào
He **sometimes/always** takes naps.

他們偶爾/經常在這裡買東西。
Tāmen **ǒu'ěr /jīngcháng** zài zhèlǐ mǎi
dōngxī
They **occasionally/often** shop here.

他偶爾/總是化妝上學。
Tā **ǒu'ěr /zǒngshì** huàzhuāng shàngxué
He **occasionally/always** wears makeup to
school.

這位同學經常/總是穿著黑色衣服。
Zhè wèi tóngxué **jīngcháng /zǒngshì**
chuānzhe hēisè yīfú
This student **often/always** dresses in
black.

老師從未/有時生氣。
Lǎoshī **cóngwèi /yǒushí** shēng qì
The teacher is **never/sometimes** angry.

會議從未/偶爾準時開始。
Huìyì **cóngwèi /ǒu'ěr** zhǔnshí kāishǐ
The meeting **never/occasionally** starts on
time.

老闆從未/經常遲到。
Lǎobǎn **cóngwèi /jīngcháng** chídào
The boss is **never/often** late.

Degree adverbs:

他很/有點討厭上班。
Tā **hěn /yǒudiǎn** tǎoyàn shàngbān
He **quite** hates working/He hates
working **a little**.

今天天氣很/十分熱。
Jīntiān tiānqì **hěn / shífēn** rè
The weather today is **quite/very** hot.

他很/太喜歡這一位演員。
Tā **hěn /tài** xǐhuān zhè yī wèi
yǎnyuán
He **quite** likes the actor/He likes the
actor **too much**.

這款飲料有點/十分熱銷。
Zhè kuǎn yǐnliào **yǒudiǎn / shífēn** rè
xiāo
This beverage is **somewhat/very**
popular.

這裡平常有點/太少人來。
Zhèlǐ píngcháng **yǒudiǎn /tài** shǎo rén
lái
This place has **few people/barely** has
people.

這隻手機 cp 值十分/太高。
Zhè zhī shǒujī cp zhí **shífēn /tài** gāo
The good value for his phone is
quite/too high.

媽媽不/很喜歡聽音樂。
Māma **bù /hěn** xǐhuān tīng yīnyuè
Mom **doesn't/quite** like to listen to
music.

電梯不/有點壅擠。
Diàntī **bù /yǒudiǎn** yōngjǐ
The elevator is **not/a little** packed.

這輛車不/十分貴。
Zhè liàng chē **bù/shífēn** guì
The car is **not/very** expensive.

References

1. Kennedy, C., McNally, L.: Scale structure, degree modification, and the semantics of gradable predicates. Language 345–381 (2005)
2. Chemla, E., Spector, B.: Experimental evidence for embedded scalar implicatures. J. Semant. **28**, 359–400 (2011)
3. Horn, L. R.: On the Semantic Properties of Logical Operators in English. Distributed by Indiana University Linguistics Club Ph.D. thesis, UCLA (1972)

4. Marty, P., Chemla, E., Spector, B.: Interpreting numerals and scalar items under memory load. Lingua **133**, 152–163 (2013)
5. Papafragou, A., Musolino, J.: Scalar implicatures: experiments at the semantics-pragmatics interface. Cognition **86**(3), 253–282 (2003)
6. Beltrama, A., Xiang, M.: Is 'good' better than 'excellent'? An experimental investigation on scalar implicatures and gradable adjectives. In: Proceedings of Sinn und Bedeutung, vol. 17, pp. 81-98 (2013)
7. Frazier, L., Clifton, C., Jr., Stolterfoht, B.: Scale structure: Processing minimum standard and maximum standard scalar adjectives. Cognition **106**, 299–324 (2008)
8. Kamoen, N., Holleman, B., Nouwen, R., Sanders, T., van den Bergh, H.: Absolutely relative or relatively absolute? The linguistic behavior of gradable adjectives and degree modifiers. J. Pragmat. **43**, 3139–3151 (2011)
9. Van Tiel, B., Van Miltenburg, E., Zevakhina, N., Geurts, B.: Scalar diversity. J. Semant. **33**(1), 137–175 (2016)
10. Bolinger, D.L.M.: Degree words: By Dwight Bolinger. Mouton, Paris (1972)
11. Gotzner, N., Solt, S., Benz, A.: Scalar Diversity, Negative Strengthening, and Adjectival Semantics. Front. Psychol. **9**, 1659 (2018)
12. Zevakhina, N.: Strength and similarity of scalar alternatives. In: Proceedings of Sinn und Bedeutung, vol. 16 (2012)
13. Erman, B.: There is no such thing as a free combination: a usage-based study of specific construals in adverb-adjective combinations. Engl. Lang. Linguist. **18**, 109–132 (2014)
14. Zhang, Y.S.: Modern Chinese Adverb Research. Academia Press, Shanghai (2004)
15. Lu, J.M., Ma, Z.: The Theory of Modern Chinese Function Words. Language Press, Beijing (1999)
16. Chen, S.Q.: A comparative analysis of the Chinese time adverb "jiangyao" "jiuyao" "kuaiyao". Master's Thesis, Jiangxi Normal University, Nanchang (2018)
17. Ding, H.J.: The Multi-perspectives Analysis of "Jiang yao" "Jiuyao" "Kuaiyao" and Teaching Chinese as a Foreign Language. Master's Thesis, Central China Normal University, Wuhan (2019)
18. Lu, S.X.: Eight Hundred Words in Modern Chinese. Commercial Press, Beijing (2010)
19. Shi, J.S.: Semantic function research on modern Chinese adverbs. Doctoral Dissertation, Nankai University, Tianjin (2002)
20. Ding, S.J.: The Studies of Frequency Adverbs in Chinese. Master's thesis, Yanbian University, Jilin (2004)
21. Wang, L.: Modern Chinese Grammar. Commercial Press, Beijing (1985)
22. Zhang, G.B.: Relative degree adverbs and absolute degree adverbs. J. East China Normal Univ. **2**, 92–96 (1997)
23. Zhou, X.B.: A study of Chinese degree adverbs. Study Chin. Lang. **2**, 100–104 (1995)
24. Wu, L.H.: A study on the Combination of Degree Adverb in Mandarin Chinese, Doctoral Dissertation, Jinan University, Guangzhou (2006)

Study of Chinese Words in Diachronic Corpus of Newspaper

Zixi Li, Tianle Gao, Guojing Huang, and Gaoqi Rao[⊠]

Beijing Language and Culture University, Beijing, China
1192518975@qq.com, raogaoqi@blcu.edu.cn

Abstract. This research examines the vocabulary used in Chinese newspapers using a diachronic corpus spanning 77 years, from 1872 to 1949. The Zipfian distribution in word use can be observed in the corpus, and the top frequency of words varies dramatically throughout epochs. The frequency of word types and tokens exhibits an inverted V-shaped trend. In terms of word entropy, a similar tendency has been discovered. Words that existed only once in history do well in representing linguistic life in the period. At the same time, the proportion of new words in the entire corpus is decreasing, reflecting the steady stabilizing of word growth.

Keywords: Diachronic corpus · Language of newspapers · Word distribution · Word evolution

1 Introduction

No social or ideological shift occurs without leaving its mark on the language. China underwent a tremendous transformation between the end of the 19th and the start of the 21st century. Newspapers have also been the main source of information for tracking the change of language since they continuously document social life. *ShenBao*, which covers the period from 1872 to 1949 and spans 77 years, served as the basis for our diachronic corpus. Following data cleansing, word segmentation specification formulation, annotation platform construction, named entity recognition, and other preparatory steps, full-text retrieval and a formatted retrieval index (BCC index, Xun [1, 2]) were built to produce the corpus of contemporary Chinese newspapers, which would provide online service. The corpus, which is built on linguistic data and linguistic annotation, aims to further the study of history, journalism, and digital humanities while also examining the development of modern Chinese writing. In light of this, this study uses statistical analysis of the terminology used across time to try to understand the context of language change.

2 Related Research

2.1 Research on Diachronic Evolution of Modern Chinese Vocabulary

Vocabulary is the fastest growing and most direct aspect of the language subsystem that reflects social life. Most studies on the development of language focus on the causes and

© The Author(s), under exclusive license to Springer Nature Switzerland AG 2023
Q. Su et al. (Eds.): CLSW 2022, LNAI 13495, pp. 384–398, 2023.
https://doi.org/10.1007/978-3-031-28953-8_29

effects of change. From the perspective of change causes, the change of vocabulary is associated with reform movements, syntagmatic and paradigmatic relations within the system, and other components within the system. From the perspective of change results, it is primarily the emergence of new words, the demise of old words, and the replacement of words [3]. During the late Qing and early Ming dynasties, society underwent considerable changes and civilizations clashed violently, generating significant changes in language life, and lexical change in that period played a vital part in the construction of contemporary Chinese words. Macroscopically, the researchers from Beijing Normal University [4] conducted a quantitative analysis, which revealed that the vocabulary was significantly enhanced by the production of new terms, absorption of dialect words, literary works, and literal translation in the late Qing and early Ming dynasties, but the parallelism of various processes caused some confusion. Under the microscope, Yang [5], Zhang [6], and Liu [7] investigated new terms in the late Qing Dynasty and the early Republic of China.

2.2 Quantitative Research on Vocabulary Evolution

As multidisciplinary research has grown in popularity, linguistics has also introduced new technical tools to evaluate the language. The quantitative investigation of language has steadily developed, and the change of vocabulary has also been heavily impacted. Shi et al. [8] presented a more scientific and practical method for reflecting dynamic changes in newspapers by extracting vocabulary; Hou [9] discussed four calculating strategies in word measurement research: frequency, usage, generality, circulation, and conducting small-scale trials. Quantitative studies on vocabulary change are also relatively developed in modern times, as seen by two components of language monitoring and survey research. With the help of measuring tools and a huge corpus, the yearly "Report on the Living Conditions of the Chinese Language" explains how languages change over time and reflect societal trends; Yang [10], Liu [11], and Rao [12] demonstrated that word usage variations could infer shifts in societal life and the focus of ordinary people's concerns. However, the aforementioned quantitative research all concentrates on either short-term surveys or a single aspect.

2.3 Research on Newspaper Lexicon

Newspapers are intimately linked to social life, and their content reflects all parts of it. They serve as essential resources for linguistic study. The study of newspapers' language has received a lot of attention in academic circles due to their ongoing change, and the study of their vocabulary is likewise evolving constantly. The academics from Beijing Normal University [4] objectively studied the vernacular and classical Chinese grammatical aspects of "Ta Kung Pao" from the standpoint of style. The survey illustrates the change of both vernacular and classical Chinese from the May Fourth Movement to the establishment of the People's Republic of China. Zhao et al. [13] conducted a quantitative stylistic analysis of newspaper headline language during the Anti-Japanese War in terms of word length, word type ratio, vocabulary density, and part of speech distribution; Wang et al. [14] surveyed the use of Chinese characters and words in newspapers, radio and television, and on the Internet. Chang [15] conducted a categorization study on the new words produced in the 20 years from 1978 to 1998; Han [16] looked explored the associations between Chinese characters and words and popular keywords used in newspapers using the dynamic circulation. Zhao [17] summarized the features of historic terms, dialect words, and loanwords to demonstrate the variation of words in Hong Kong Chinese publications since the twentieth century. Feng [18] did a lexical study on *ShenBao* in the late Qing and the early Republic of China from four perspectives: morphology, word-building, word form, and the new meaning of new words. He also analyzed *ShenBao*'s lexical language features in the late Qing and the early Republic of China.

The selection of *ShenBao* as the starting point for researching the change of modern Chinese vocabulary is extremely convincing, and the study from the standpoint of measurement is also innovative.

3 Use of Chinese Vocabulary

3.1 The Standard for Word Segmentation

On account of *ShenBao*'s long duration and complicated internal properties, as well as certain existing participle specifications [19, 20], this participle specification adopts a preliminary plan to try to adapt to the characteristics of different periods of Chinese and applies to all periods of modern Chinese.

To ensure "internal consistency of norms" and the integrity of meanings while cutting down on the division, this study emphasizes the notion of "large words" in the division of words. "Large words" are the named entities, which are often categorized as one sub-word unit. "Internal consistency" means that all irregularities in the treatment of participles induced by the number of syllables are normalized. For example, pronouns and subsequent components are separated regardless of the syllable of the succeeding component ("每/天" and "每/分钟" are separated), and the word "所" needs to be segmented. To ensure the integrity of its meaning, the number of words, for example, is not cut, "三分之二", and so on; while adverbs are followed by verbs in the verb-adverbial structure, the separable verb-object verbs, etc., must be segmented. It aims to ensure that the segmentation is as fine as possible to fully reflect the changes in words.

The particular content of the syllogism specification contains ten aspects: named entities, terms, and proper names; numerical and quantitative phrases; temporal words; pronouns; additional, compound, imaginary words, disjunctive words, idioms, and familiar words; and the syllogism specification fitted to this stage of *ShenBao*'s research is determined from many views of the meaning of words and the way they are structured.

Specifically, in terms of named entities, personal names, the names of a person, place, or organization, whether ancient or modern, Chinese or foreign, are all integrated into one segmentation unit, such as "卡尔·马克思/nr" "美国加州旧金山/ns" and"国联/nt"; Brands, models, and trademarks should be segmented together, such as "派克III/nb/复印机"; the contents of newspapers, journals, books, archives, and book titles should be combined, such as "《儒林外史》/nb", and trademark naming parts and generic names such as "牌" and "号" should be combined, such as "哈德门/nb/香烟". Both proper names and scientific terms should be integrated into one segmentation unit, such as "马克思主义/nm". Numerals, such as "三分之二", shall not be segmented. Numerical phrases shall be segmented, such as "四百/余/元"; if the sequence relationship is expressed, it will not be segmented, such as "钢七连". Time words are divided into years, months, days, hours, minutes, and seconds, such as "四月/十四日". Pronouns followed by nouns, such as "每/天" "我/营" and "何/故" should be removed. Function words need to be segmented separately. Idioms, locutions, and other common words are classified as segmentation units. Furthermore, when the previous or subsequent components indicate a person's surname, name, or position, no segmentation shall be made, such as "前总统" "严公/nr" and "庄宋氏/nr"; the noun structure, consisting of the words "者" or "所", is separated from the other components, and the other parts are divided according to the standard of word segmentation, such as "居/中国/ns/者". On the compound side, the "noun + noun" or "adjective + noun" structure is frequently a segmented unit, such as "海勇" "军中" and "下等城"; the "tendency verb + the verb" structure is divided into a segmentation unit, such as "开建/口岸"; the "adverb + verb" structure needs to be segmented, such as "屡/摧/大寇". In terms of separable words, those that can insert an independent language component in the middle are all segmented, such as "立/不/住"; if the condensation is tight and there is no receiver or destination of action tendency following the tendency component, it is combined into a segmentation unit, such as "送去"; if each is a word when taken apart, and the receiver or destination of the tendency part is followed by the part of action tendency, it is usually divided into two parts, such as "拘/入/捕房".

In general, the segmentation specification follows the principles of corpus-based, the purpose of diachronic linguistic research, and the needs of quantitative research. It is envisaged that ShenBao's word segmentation specification, which is based on the corpus's own properties, will make measurement study more convenient.

3.2 Corpus Description

The observation of linguistic changes can be improved with a longer time horizon and a larger corpus. To better understand the development of modern Chinese, this research uses a statistical analysis of word usage in *ShenBao*. Figure 1 displays the fundamental statistical data from the Corpus of *ShenBao*, including punctuation and Arabic numbers.

The corpus scale of *ShenBao* fluctuated significantly, as shown in Fig. 1. The scale fell dramatically in a few years, including 1919, 1938, and 1945. There were 4758 fewer articles published overall in 1938. This was owing to the invasion of Japan, which caused *ShenBao* to cease publication and then resume it multiple times.

The corpus can be divided into five groups on the basis of significant historical periods: the late Qing Dynasty (1872–1911, LQD for short); the period of Northern Warlords' Governance (1912–1927, NWG for short); the period of Nationalist Governance (1928–1937, NG for short); the period of WWII (1938–1945); and the period of Civil War (1946–1949, CW for short). Figure 2 depicts the total scale and average annual scale of the corpus for each period.

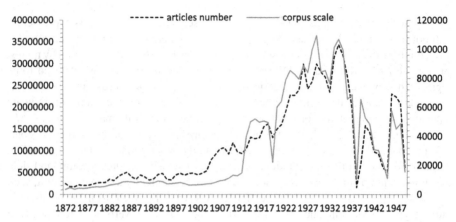

Fig. 1. The corpus scale and articles number of *ShenBao*

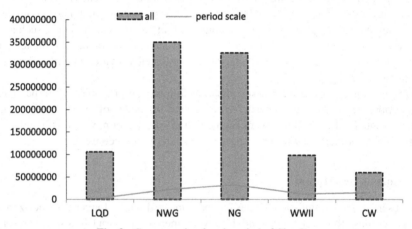

Fig. 2. Corpus scale of each period of *ShenBao*

Figure 1 and Fig. 2 show a reversed V-shaped trend: the period of Northern War-lords' Governance has the biggest corpus scale, followed by the period of Nationalist Governance, yet the average annual scale of the two periods is 10 million words differ-ent. During the Civil War, the corpus was at its smallest. The corpus scale was slightly greater in the late Qing Dynasty than in the period of WWII. During the period of WWII, the average annual scale of the corpus was nearly double that of the late Qing Dynasty. The length of reports expanded dramatically over time, as did the use of words.

3.3 Word Types and Tokens

Table 1 displays the statistical results of word types and tokens. There are no more than 6 million types in the corpus of 910 million words. Figure 3 depicts the distribution of word types and tokens on the time axis.

Table 1. Word use of *ShenBao*

Period	LQD	NWG	NG	WWII	CW	Total
Types	2127989	2488149	2541820	1226929	984796	5053572
Annual ave types	53200	508224	254182	153366	246199	64789
Tokens	97887916	317493736	298952886	90488468	55665308	860488314
Annual ave tokens	2447198	19843359	29895289	11311059	13916327	1103190

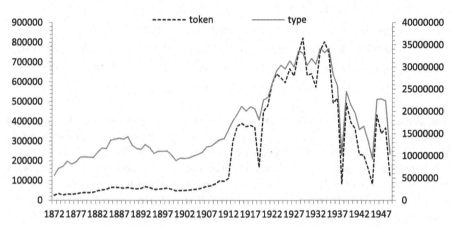

Fig. 3. Word tokens and types of *ShenBao*

Figure 3 illustrates that the general level of word usage in the newspaper has fluctuated since its inception in 1872, and the pattern of the number of word types and tokens is in a reversed V-shaped trend, with a similar trend in the time axis. There is no such thing as multiple word types and a small number of word tokens in a particular year, which implies a great diversity.

With 113,815 words, 1872 marked the year with the fewest word types overall. With 723,147 words, 1928 had the most words ever written. While the total number of word tokens climbed gradually over the late Qing Dynasty, the total number of word types rose dramatically. The number of word types doubled from its inception in the late 1880s. This was a byproduct of the Westernization movement, in which foreign ideas and objects were swiftly incorporated and words underwent a quick renewal. The Republic of China's foundation, which occurred during a time when Chinese polysyllabic words substantially increased and new concepts were consistently produced during the period of Nationalist Governance, reinforced this trend. In that year, Shanghai fell, forcing *ShenBao* to relocate to Hong Kong and Wuhan, which in turn influenced its readership. As a result, the start of the war was an unintended turning point in history.

As shown in Table 2, shared words between years account for 0.2% of all word types, while shared words between periods account for 5.03%. The difference between these two percentages indicates that the change in word usage is gradual and that words relating to the same things and acts are largely consistent throughout the same period.

Table 2. Shared words of *ShenBao*

Period		LQD	NWG	NG	WWII	CW	Total
Shared words among all years	types	17543					
	proportion	0.8%	0.7%	0.7%	1.4%	1.8%	0.3%
	tokens	60652639	176754788	142475406	42013468	25201471	447097772
	proportion	61.96%	55.67%	47.66%	46.43%	45.27%	51.96%
Shared words among all periods	types	374001					
	proportion	17.58%	15.03%	14.71%	30.48%	37.98%	7.4%
	tokens	87524976	296615232	278872914	84275213	51645038	798933373
	proportion	89.41%	93.42%	93.28%	93.13%	92.78%	92.85%

The actual use of shared words across years and periods is dominant: the number of shared words between years accounts for 57.95% of the total number of words, while the number of shared words between periods is as high as 93.77%.

A reversed V-shaped trend shows that the difference in the number of word types between the period of Northern Warlords' Governance and the period of Nationalist Governance is 201,454 words, and the period of WWII uses around 1,290,882 words less than the late Qing Dynasty and about 289,617 words more than the period of Civil War. *ShenBao* was in a chaotic stage in the late Qing Dynasty, with fewer pages and less substance, resulting in fewer word types and tokens, so there is an order of magnitude difference between that time and the subsequent two. In contrast, the number of word types and tokens during the period of WWII and the period of Civil War did not reach those of the late Qing Dynasty, indicating that the language situation in these two periods changed dramatically and was far less rich than before.

3.4 The Richness of Word Use

The Entropy of Words. Entropy is the measurement in bit, describing the complexity of a single independent signal system (Shannon, 2001). C_i is the ith word in the lexicon, n represents the lexicon length, and p refers to the proportion of a word by maximum likelihood estimation. The increase of the entropy represents the increase of the richness in language life. The entropy of words in each year is shown in Fig. 4.

$$\text{Entropy} = -\sum_{i=1, c_i \in C}^{i=n} p(c_i) log p(c_i) \tag{1}$$

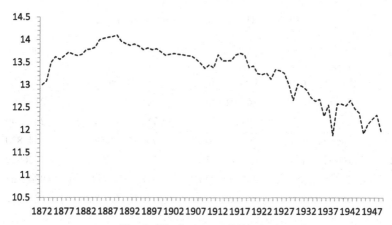

Fig. 4. Word entropy of *ShenBao*

In our work, the entropy is estimated using the annual corpus as an autonomous system, so there is no coherent relationship between years. Figure 4 depicts a reversed V-shaped pattern in word entropy. The highest entropy of words came in 1889 (14.10) and then oscillated down, reaching another modest peak in 1917 (13.70) and minimum values in 1938 (11.88) and 1945 (11.91). Despite changes over time, the word entropy declined progressively, indicating a decrease in the richness of word use. The distribution of word entropy follows the same pattern as the shift in the rate of emergence of new words (detailed in 4.7).

Zipfian Distribution in Word Use. A measurement of word distribution that shows the relationship between types and tokens. The words used to provide a Zipfian distribution, as seen in Table 3, with the majority of content consisting of a small number of high-frequency words. There is considerable disequilibrium among words in all periods. 26,460 words are sufficient to cover 80% of the corpus. On the contrary, 5,027,112 low-frequency terms account for only 1% of the corpus. The proportion of words required to achieve 80%, 90%, and 99% word usage in the late Qing Dynasty is larger than in previous periods. This indicates that the unevenness of word usage was slightly weaker in the late Qing Dynasty than in other time, indicating greater diversity in word usage. This phenomenon corresponds to the shifting of word types and tokens.

Table 3. The coverage of words of *ShenBao*

Period	80% Type Proportion	90% Type Proportion	99% Type Proportion	100% Type
LQD	33593 1.58%	105618 4.96%	1149110 54.00%	2127989
NWG	22990 0.92%	67723 2.72%	750958 30.18%	2488149
NG	18630 0.73%	60043 2.36%	796490 31.34%	2541820
WWII	16066 1.31%	49528 4.04%	522366 42.58%	1226929
CW	14920 1.52%	47235 4.80%	488431 49.60%	984796
Total	26460 0.52%	84252 1.67%	1159932 22.95%	5053572

3.5 Word Length

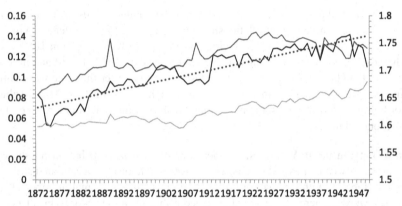

Fig. 5. The average word length and multi-word distribution of *ShenBao*

Figure 5 depicts the change in average word length of *ShenBao* from 1872 to 1949. All named entities, as well as punctuation, have been removed from this study. The black line depicts the overall word length trend, while the blue, red lines demonstrate the distribution of trisyllabic and tetrasyllabic words in proportion to the word types of species in that year and over time, with essentially the same tendency as the black dashed line. The trend line for word length is $y = 0.0017x + 1.6305$ with an R^2 of 0.8328, indicating that word length growth is close to a linear pattern, with an average word length increase of 0.17 words per decade. With the current word separation effect, the general trend is that word lengths become progressively longer over time and the fraction of multi-word words in the word list gradually increases. We can observe that in 1872, the word length was only around 1.65, but it climbed to about 1.75 around 1930 and then stabilized around that level. Trisyllabic words grew from 0.0829 to 0.1283, tetrasyllabic words increased from 0.0519 to 0.0956. The steady increase in word length represents an important characteristic of the transition from literary to typical vernacular, namely the diphthongization of monosyllabic words and the increasing number of multisyllabic words.

3.6 Word Used in One Period

Fig. 6. The words used in only one year of *ShenBao*

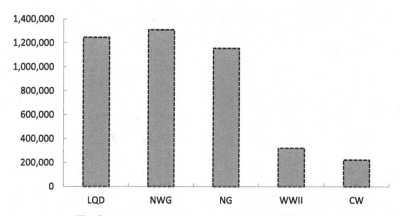

Fig. 7. The words used in only one period of *ShenBao*

A word that only appears in one text, or group of texts, or both, is referred to as a sole-used word. In this study, sole-used words, words that only appear in one year of the corpus and never appear in any other years, are used to describe the state of language use in each time period. Similarly, sole-used words in only one period are words that only appear in one year of the corpus and never appear in any other years. Overall, the amount of sole-used words exhibit a mixed growth pattern, with the number of sole-used words increasing considerably after the Republic. The three years with the most sole-used words are 1928, 1929, and 1935, with over 90,000 words each. There were English, personal, local, and trade names that corresponded to the Chinese translation in 1928, for example, such as "Busyligbt(别随拉脱)" "Rssen(罗司)" and "Oss(麦雷)". These are mostly nouns, with few verbs and adjectives.

The majority of the words used only one period appeared during the period of Northern Warlords' Governance, with the period of Civil War having the fewest sole-used words. In the late Qing Dynasty, the majority of the sole-used words were named entities, such as "王大臣钧鉴" "三等顾问官" and "何大令". The majority of the sole-used words used in the period of Northern Warlords' Governance were named entities, such as "秦陇复汉军大统领" "三角码头" and "铜锌合金", and so on. During the period of Nationalist Governance, new official names and place names appeared, such as "中央军事委员会主席" and "机关商场". The sole-used words during the period of WWII appeared in a great number of phonetic person names, such as "阿太米特" and "胡特勒", and certain chemical and biological terms, such as "金色葡萄球菌" and "有机汞", and so on. The majority of the sole-used words during the Civil War were people names, organizational names, and nouns with historical qualities, such as "善后事业委员会" "河西走廊" "工商辅导处" and "万能计算机". Table 4 shows the shared words during the period. The majority of the terms in the top ten frequencies are not particularly time-sensitive, while a tiny number of notional words in the top ten frequencies exhibit period features, such as "捕房" "太守" and "政府". Thus, it can be demonstrated that sole-used words are more indicative of a specific era's linguistic life than high-frequency words.

Table 4. 1st-10th shared words.

Period	1st-10th words	1st-10th notional words
LQD	之、有、而、以、各、等、为、其、将、在	有、为、捕房、中国、地方、办理、大令、太守、情形、知道
NWG	之、一、有、为、等、又、各、以、在、者	有、为、上海、下午、公司、上午、中国、代表、银行、北京
NG	之、的、一、在、为、有、及、等、二、三	为、有、上海、公司、下午、电话、上午、中国、代表、接洽
WWII	之、的、在、一、为、有、及、电话、与、又	为、有、电话、上海、公司、中国、声明、下午、遗失、日本
CW	的、之、在、一、为、及、有、又、二、是	为、有、电话、上海、公司、中国、下午、美国、政府、代表

3.7 New Words

Two approaches are used in this paper to count new words: Method A mandates that words that did not exist in any preceding year (since 1872) be counted as new words. Method B counts as new words that have not appeared in the previous five years. Since method A causes existing words to have a propensity to accumulate over time, the pace at which new words appear decreases with time. A comparison study was conducted concurrently to address this issue. The five years from 1872 to 1877 are the starting point for the analysis, and this research does not address the emergence of new words during that time. Figure 8 and Fig. 9 depict changes in the word types and new word frequency. The red and blue lines represent Method A and Method B, respectively.

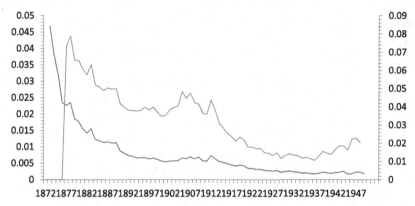

Fig. 8. Word frequency of new words in *ShenBao*

Fig. 9. Word types of new words in *ShenBao*

As illustrated in Fig. 8, new words account for a small share of overall word frequency, with all of them falling below 10%. Additionally, as time goes on, the percentage of new words in the corpus decreases, showing a tendency that is gradually waning. As a result of contact with Western society at the end of the Qing Dynasty, which required a significant number of named novelties and the subsequent gradual infiltration of these terms into the Chinese lexicon, this illustrates the process of vocabulary expansion from evident growth to gradual stabilization. According to Fig. 9, the quantity and frequency of new words climbed steadily starting in 1900, reaching a peak in 1921 with the greatest number of new variants, and then progressively dropping until about 1927. The new word types in this growth spike mostly comprise foreign nation names, regional names, newly founded organization names, rising business-related words, and so on.

Table 5. 1st-5th new words of high frequency.

Period	1st	2nd	3rd	4th	5th
1872–1882	堆入	光绪元年	保安公司	不留名	吃水
1883–1893	孤拔	急单	样张	附阅	淞隐漫录
1894–1904	义和拳	昭信股票	三门湾	司徒贻芬	自治公所
1905–1915	斐德兰	力森	美芬	盐政处	拳匪
1916–1926	太平洋会议	国务院	国务员	筹安会	上海学生联合会
1927–1937	抗日救国	五卅惨案	南京国民政府	补力多	五中全会
1938–1948	伪国	停战协定	全面抗战	散利痛	一二八事变
1949	地亚净片	马歇尔计划	市经济局	西藏中路	青年装

Table 6. 1st-5th new words of high frequency.

Period	1st	2nd	3rd	4th	5th
1872–1882	不留名	俄军	字册	广告	无名氏
1883–1893	孤拔	古今图书集成	急单	样张	附阅
1894–1904	倭奴	义和拳	昭信股票	三门湾	司徒贻芬
1905–1915	北伐	斐德兰	力森	美芬	盐政处
1916–1926	太平洋会议	国务院	国务员	筹安会	欧战
1927–1937	抗日救国	五卅惨案	甘一点	水泊梁山	南京国民政府
1938–1948	伪国	统一	停战协定	六中全会	全面抗战
1949	代总统	南京东路	地亚净片	民盟	四川北路

It can be observed that there is not a significant difference between the statistics of methods a and b in Tables 5 and 6, which display the 1st–5th new words in terms of frequency during the past 10 years. The terms "义和拳" and "拳匪" rose to the top of the new language around 1900, owing to the Gengzi Incident. The growing bourgeois regime and changes in the political environment resulted in a succession of changes in the nomenclature of organizations, leading to the emergence of the "国务院" "国务员" and "筹安会" and so on. As capitalist commerce flourished, the number of business-related phrases such as "地亚净片" and "青年装" increased. Though it is clear that the frequency of new words is declining, it is important to keep in mind that between 1900 and 1936, there was a double resurgence in the growth of word categories. These bounces should be the result of social movements, which also happen to occur at the same time as the social variables described above. As an illustration, the foundation of the Republican government was directly tied to the increase in the number of new word variants in 1912, both in terms of quantity and in terms of content. Even though there were fewer reports in 1938 and 1945, the following years (1939 and 1946) appear to have recovered from the prior year. As can be seen, new terms contain both timeliness and foreignness, and their emergence is directly tied to the current political and economic scene.

4 Conclusion

This article does a quantitative and in-depth investigation into how words are used, looking at word types, tokens, lengths, and changes in new terminology. Based on a statistical analysis of keywords used in *ShenBao*, this study investigates the changes in words used in newspapers over a 77-year period as well as the social changes that have occurred. The diphthongization of monophthong phrases is a crucial symptom of the transition from literary language to common vernacular that can be seen in the statistical data. The Chinese lexicon is steadily stabilizing as the percentage of new terms in the general corpus is declining, illustrating the gradual emergence of the modern Chinese lexicon. Due to the peculiarities of the *ShenBao* corpus, more progress in Chinese lexical distinction techniques research is required to gain a better understanding of word usage.

Acknowledgments. This paper is supported by MOE Funds of Humanity and Social Sciences "Quantitative Research on Words Usage in Newspaper since late Qing Dynasty" (20YJC740050).

References

1. Xun, E.-D., Rao, G.-Q., Xie, J.-L., Huang, Z.-E.: Diachronic retrieval for modern Chinese word: system construction and its application. J. China Inf. Process. **29**(03), 169–176 (2015). (In Chinese)
2. Xun, E.-D., Rao, G.-Q., Xiao, X.-Y., Zang, J.-J.: The construction of the BCC corpus in the age of big data. Corpus Linguist. **3**(1), 93–109 (2016). (In Chinese)
3. Ye, F.-S., Xu, T.-Q.: Linguistics' Outline (Revision), 2nd edn. Peking University Press, Beijing (2010). (In Chinese)
4. Chinese Teaching and Research Group, Chinese Department, Beijing Normal University.: The Changes and Development of Chinese Written Language Since the May 4th Movement. The Commercial Press, Beijing (1959). (In Chinese)
5. Yang, D.-Z.: The origin and development of "modern" neologisms as seen from new scientific terminologies in new novels of the period from late Qing dynasty to the republic of China. J. Shandong Univ. (Philos. Soc. Sci.) **01**, 147–153 (2007). (In Chinese)
6. Zhang, L.: New expressions and change in urban life focusing on Shanghai in late Qing dynasty (1843–1925). J. Shanghai Normal Univ. (Philos. Soc. Sci.) **03**, 110–115 (2008). (In Chinese)
7. Liu, X.-Y.: Research on neologism between the late Qing and the early republic of China. J. Hebei Univ. (Philos. Soc. Sci.) **40**(04), 55–59 (2015). (in Chinese)
8. Shi, Z.-Q., Zhang, P.: Comparative analysis of circulation lexicon and usage lexicon based on DCC dynamic circulation newspaper corpus. In: 8th National Joint Conference on Computational Linguistics on Proceedings, pp. 212–218. Tsinghua University Press, Beijing (2005). (In Chinese)
9. Hou, M.: Language monitoring and quantitative study of words. In: 25th Annual Conference of CIPSC on Proceedings, pp. 106–114. Tsinghua University Press, Beijing (2006). (In Chinese)
10. Su, X.-C., Yang, E.-H.: An analysis of the statistics of the Chinese vocabulary in 2005. J. Xiamen Univ. (Arts Soc. Sci.) **06**, 84–91 (2006). (In Chinese)

11. Liu, C.-Z., Qin, P.: A survey of idiom usage based on the DCC of Chinese mainstream newspapers. Appl. Linguist. **3**, 78–86 (2007). (In Chinese)
12. Rao, G.-Q., Li, Y.-M.: Extraction and investigation of modern Chinese long-lasting stable words based on 70 years newspaper corpus. J. Chinese Inf. Process. **6**, 49–58 (2016). (In Chinese)
13. Zhao, X., Gu, X.-Y.: A computational stylistic analysis on language of newspaper news headlines during the war of resistance against Japanese aggression: exemplified by xinhua daily and central daily news. Theory Modernization **05**, 114–119 (2015). (In Chinese)
14. Wang, T.-K., Hou, M., Yang, E.-H.: A survey on the use of Chinese characters in newspapers, radio and television, and the internet. Appl. Linguist. **1**, 29–37 (2007). (In Chinese)
15. Chang, Z.-B.: A brief analysis of the spreading of the new words and phrases in the new era among the newspapers and some other media. J. SJTU (Soc. Sci. Ed.) **04**, 97–101 (2001). (In Chinese)
16. Han, X.-J.: Research on Word Distribution of General Words and Relations among Characters Words and Phrases Based on Dynamic Circulating Corpus. Beijing Language and Culture University (2007). (In Chinese)
17. Zhao, R.-Q.: Language Variation of Chinese Newspapers in Hong Kong since the 20th century. Minzu University of China (2005). (In Chinese)
18. Feng, Z.: A Research on the Vocabulary of Shen Daily in the Period of Late Qing Dynasty and the Early Republic of China. Jilin University(2021). (In Chinese)
19. Yu, S.-W., Duan, H.-M., Zhu, X.-F., Sun, B.: The basic processing of contemporary Chinese corpus at Peking university Specification. J. China Inf. Process. **05**, 49–64 (2002). (In Chinese)
20. Yu, S.-W., Duan, H.-M., Zhu, X.-F., Sun, B.: The basic processing of contemporary Chinese corpus at peking university specification(sequel). J. China Inf. Process. **06**, 58–64 (2002). (In Chinese)

The Similarities and Differences of Thanks Responses between Native Speakers and Mandarin Teaching Materials in Taiwan

Chia-An Huang⬡ and Jia-Fei Hong(✉)⬡

National Taiwan Normal University, Taipei, Taiwan
{609840011,jiafeihong}@ntnu.edu.tw

Abstract. There is growing research on thanks responses in linguistics. However, there are still research gaps on thanks responses in varieties of Mandarin Chinese. To explore the similarities and differences between the arrangements of instructional materials of Teaching Chinese as a Second Language (TCSL) and the usage of native speakers, the present study uses Mandarin teaching materials, authentic materials collected from observation, and spoken corpus data to investigate the distribution of thanks response strategies used by native speakers of Mandarin in Taiwan. The results not only show reasons that possibly lead to differences between thanks responses in Mandarin teaching materials and the usage of native speakers, but also shed some light on the less explored aspects of thanks responses in the varieties of Modern Chinese.

Keywords: Thanks response · Taiwanese Mandarin · Authentic Materials

1 Introduction

Learning Mandarin has become an international trend in the 21st century. There is also growing comparative research on Mandarin Chinese and other languages. Under the premise of Taiwanese Mandarin as a variety under the umbrella of Modern Chinese [1], the present study addresses some communicative matters below that may arise when using Taiwanese Mandarin as the main medium of second language instruction.

In a broad sense, Bella [2] considers that language teaching materials generally put more emphasis on vocabulary and grammar points, while the transmission of pragmatic information is insufficient. Learners tend to grasp the examples teaching materials mention without understanding the culture behind the language, which in turn affects their interactions with native speakers. Eisenstein & Bodman [3] also state that learners' expressions are often constrained by their limited understanding of the socio-cultural aspects of the target language. Hence, if teaching materials are designed to effectively train second language learners, the real usage of native speakers cannot be ignored. However, in a narrow sense, there is a lot of room for research on the linguistics and teaching of Taiwanese Mandarin; the link between Taiwanese Mandarin teaching materials of the

© The Author(s), under exclusive license to Springer Nature Switzerland AG 2023
Q. Su et al. (Eds.): CLSW 2022, LNAI 13495, pp. 399–413, 2023.
https://doi.org/10.1007/978-3-031-28953-8_30

industry of Teaching Chinese as a Second Language (TCSL) and the usage by native speakers of Taiwanese Mandarin is still under active examination.[1]

Compared to other speech acts, the speech act of "thanks response" has yet to have its turn in the spotlight, let alone have research conducted on its usage in Taiwanese Mandarin. The present study takes Rüegg's [4] standpoint, viewing thanks responses as well-suited to examine the connection between Taiwanese teaching materials of TCSL (hereinafter referred to as Mandarin teaching materials) and the native speakers of Taiwanese Mandarin, in that "they are repetitively drilled into children by caretakers, and, as a result, directly reflect the societal values of the speaker." In order to understand whether Mandarin teaching materials reflect the usage of native speakers of Taiwanese Mandarin, the present study takes Taiwan as the research field, and proposes the following research questions. Firstly, what are the thanks response strategies arranged in Mandarin teaching materials? Secondly, what is the distribution of thanks response strategies that native speakers of Taiwanese Mandarin use in daily life? Thirdly, are the strategies presented in Mandarin teaching materials consistent with the usage of native speakers of Taiwanese Mandarin?

2 Literature Review

In her monograph, Aijmer [5] explains that thanks responses have fixed patterns that can be categorized. Edmondson & House [6] and Schneider [7] use the terms "ground" and "head move" to refer to the indispensable components that construct thanks responses. The present study here refers to these indispensable components as "head acts," which are included in the analysis.

As the name implies, "thanks responses" accompany and follow "thanks." Hence, these two speech acts form an adjacency pair, with the speech act of thanks as the first pair part, and the speech act of thanks response the second pair part. Kiesling [8] emphasizes that it is nearly impossible to predict the occasion the first pair part of an adjacency pair appears, but to be assumed that it can appear at any time. On the contrary, defining context is not that challengeable for the second pair part. Once the first pair part is positioned, whether there is a verbal response is clear. It is hence much easier to pinpoint thanks responses compared to the first pair part of thanks [9].

As of today, the related studies of thanks responses are mainly on varieties of English. Aijmer [5] and Schneider [7] were the first to categorize strategies of thanks responses, as listed in Table 1, and each strategy includes multiple realizations. Since both of them refer to each strategy by different letters, the present study continues to do so, as seen in Table 1.

According to Aijmer [5], the aim of strategy A is to balance the debt created by the thanker. Strategy B expresses the attitude that the thankee holds towards the favor s/he gave to others. The aims of strategy B and C are similar, whereas the latter is claimed to be used only in American English. Schneider [7] also refers to strategies of thanks responses as "Thanks Minimizers" (TM), viewing their use as a means to reduce the debts thankers bear from the expressions of thanks.

---

[1] In the present study, the industry of TCSL also includes teaching Chinese as a foreign (TCFL) or heritage language (TCHL).

Table 1. Strategies and realizations of thanks responses in varieties of English

Strategy	Realization
Minimizing the favour (strategy A)	That's okay; Okay
	No problem
	Don't mention it
Expressing pleasure (strategy B)	Great pleasure; Pleasure
Expressing appreciation of the addressee (strategy C)	You're welcome; Welcome
	Anytime; Sure
Returning thanks (strategy D)	Thanks
Acknowledging the thanks (strategy E)	Yeah

On the distribution of strategies, Aijmer [5] indicates that speakers of British English tend to use strategy A, and the discourse completion task (DCT) conducted by Schneider [7] verifies this opinion. In his study, the ratio of the use of strategy A in British English is apparently higher than that of American English and Irish English, whereas strategy C is found in American English and Irish English twice as much as in British English.

Based on the two above pioneer studies, several scholars have continued to expand the understanding of thanks responses. Farenkia [10] conducts DCT for Canadian English, and finds that native speakers of Canadian English have the highest use of strategy A, followed by strategy C. Furthermore, all the realizations are short. Bieswanger [11] compares Canadian English and American English via observation. The results show that speakers of Canadian English have the highest usage of strategy E, and the usage of strategy C in both research locations are higher than strategy A. Staley [9] focuses her research on restaurant service encounters between American servers and costumers. It is found that the use of strategy C is the most frequent, and strategy D ranks second in terms of frequency. In the abovementioned studies, the commonest thanks response strategy used in varieties of English is either strategy A or C.

Compared to English, varieties of Modern Chinese are much less explored; the classification of thanks response strategies is also different. Wang [12, 13] proposes a thanks-response model of Modern Chinese based on his empirical research in Chongqing, China. In his words, thanks responses of Modern Chinese are divided into "acceptance by acknowledgments (yìnguò jiēshòu xíng, 應諾接受型)," and "acceptance by using negatives (fǒudìng jiēshòu xíng, 否定接受型)." Native speakers of Modern Chinese accept thanks from others under these two strategies; the only difference is that the former directly accepts thanks, while the latter accepts thanks by using negative forms in realizations. Wang's [12] model is categorized in Table 2.

In Wang [12], native speakers of Modern Chinese have the largest use of "acceptance by using negatives." Among the realizations of this strategy, the frequency of "bú (yòng) xiè" (no need for thanks) is the most prominent. Wang [12] inspects the arrangements of Mandarin teaching materials and primary school textbooks in China, with the finding that both sources echo this phenomenon. The usage frequency of "bú (yòng) xiè" accounts for half of the realizations of thanks responses. However, Wang [12] considers that the

Table 2. Strategies and realizations of thanks responses in Modern Chinese

Strategy	Realization
Acceptance by acknowledgments	Okay (hǎo, 好)
	using onomatopoeia, e.g., Hmm (en, 嗯), Ah (ā, 啊), Uh (è, 呃), Um-Hum (m, 姆)
Acceptance by using negatives	No need for thanks (bú (yòng) xiè, 不(用)謝)
	You're welcome (búkèqì, 不客氣)
	It doesn't matter (méi guānxi, 沒關係)

prototypes of thanks responses of Modern Chinese contain both "*bú (yòng) xiè*" and "*búkèqì*" (you're welcome), in that the latter has a frequent use in his data, and is a must-learn realization by both learners and Chinese-speaking children.

Comparing varieties of English to Chinese, their strategies do not fully correspond to each other. In studies related to Mandarin Chinese, no token of strategy B is found, and although most of the realizations of "acceptance by using negatives" overlap with strategy A, "*búkèqì*" is most often associated with "You're welcome" of strategy C. However, if negatives imply passive rejections, it seems to contradict the meaning conveyed by strategy C, which is defined by Schneider [7] as, "I like you as a person." Due to the lack of studies on thanks responses of varieties of Chinese, it is difficult to juxtapose these two high-frequency realizations, and this contradiction will be further discussed in the following section.

Since the categorizations of varieties of English are relatively complete, the present study adopts the strategies performed on English to classify data. Moreover, in the sections of analysis and discussion, the present study provides its own perspective on the strategies of Modern Chinese based on Wang's [12, 13] foundation.

3 Methodology

In the literature reviewed in Sect. 2, Aijmer [5] conducts her research as a corpus-based study, with additional data collected from her own reading and those provided by native speakers. Schneider [7] and Farenkia [10] choose DCT, whereas Bieswanger [11], Wang [12, 13] and Staley [9] conduct observations to collect naturally occurring data from native speakers. From the perspective of authenticity, observation has the advantage of being least interfered by artificial design, hence, the present study adopted it as the research method, and the research process is as follows.

Foremostly, the present study selected three sets of influential Mandarin teaching materials published in Taiwan, and analyzed the distribution of thanks response strategies by positioning the first pair part of the adjacency pair. Secondly, carrying to Labov's [14] opinion of observing "how people speak when they are not being observed," the present study dealt with Taiwanese Mandarin native speakers' face-to-face interactions in their daily lives. The authentic materials used in this study (hereinafter referred to as observational data) were gathered from September 27th, 2021 to December 21st, 2021. In order to prevent negligence, observational data was recorded in the form of notes on the spot. The data of Mandarin teaching materials and observation were first calculated as tokens according to the occurrence of head acts. Then, tokens with shared properties were classified as the same type, and labeled according to these properties. Because the types were further categorized into the aforementioned five strategies (A-E) afterward, it was possible for one strategy to contain multiple types.

Due to the limited tokens of Mandarin teaching materials and observational data, the Spoken Corpus 2019 of the Corpus of Contemporary Taiwanese Mandarin (COCT) was referenced as another source. This corpus contains 1,300 episodes of TV programs produced in Taiwan from 2008 to 2019, with a cumulative word count of 39.45 million [15]. Similarly, the first pair part of the adjacency pair—in this case, the speech act of thanks—was used as the anchor of analyzing the distribution of its responses.

All TV programs can be divided into two types; one is closed-ended, and the other is open-ended. The former is equipped with fully-arranged scripts; meanwhile, some programs, in which hosts engage in conversation with guests, belong to the latter. Although open-ended programs do have scripts, there is a greater possibility of free expression. Since both types of programs are designed and implemented by native speakers, to some extent, the COCT Spoken Corpus 2019 simultaneously reflects native speakers' cognition towards "ought to be" and "to be (is)". The former is the data extracted from close-ended programs, with native speakers arranging dialogues based on appropriateness. The latter is the data extracted from open-ended programs, mirroring "actual face-to-face interactions," especially in the turn-taking of thanks and thanks responses. As for observational data, it reflects pure "is," belonging to natural reactions.

From the above two sources, the present study examines whether the thanks response strategies of Mandarin teaching materials are consistent with the usage of native speakers of Taiwanese Mandarin. If the arrangements of Mandarin teaching materials are similar to the observational and spoken corpus data, it can be assumed that the compilation of Mandarin teaching materials in terms of thanks responses is close to native speakers' daily usage. On the contrary, if there is a gap between these three sources, it can be assumed that the arrangements of Mandarin teaching materials in terms of thanks responses are inconsistent with native speakers' expressions, and there is also a gap between the "ought" and "is."

4 Data Analysis

In the present study, the speech act of thanks response is defined as the second pair part of the thanks-thanks response adjacency pair. Its realizations vary in terms of forms. Among all the possibilities, zero sign carries the meaning that no verbal speech forms, paralinguistic features nor body language are found in thanks responses [9, 12, 13]. Under the circumstances that it is difficult for Mandarin teaching materials to arrange responses including paralinguistic features and body language, zero sign in the present study simply represents "responses vacant," i.e., no verbal speech nor body language expressed in responding to thanks.[2]

---

[2] Martin & Zpaapvigna [16] make a clear distinction between paralanguage and body language, with the latter inclusive in the former. Wang [12, 13] directly uses paralanguage as a whole representation, whereas in the present study, these two terms are separated. In the observational data, only verbal speech forms and body language were recorded.

4.1 The Distribution of Thanks Responses Strategies in Mandarin Teaching Materials

In the three sets of Mandarin teaching materials, a total of 132 tokens were analyzed. After sorting, seven types were established as follows: "*kèqì*" (客氣, to be polite), "*nǎlǐ*" (哪裡, not a problem), "*búxiè*" (不謝, no need for thanks), "*méi shénme*" (沒什麼, nothing), "*yīnggāide*" (應該的, my duty), "*xièxie*" (謝謝, thanks) and "*wú*" (無, none). In line with related studies, the present study considers four of the seven types serving the same function of strategy A in Taiwanese Mandarin, which are "*nǎlǐ*" (not a problem), "*búxiè*" (no need for thanks), "*méi shénme*" (nothing) and "*yīnggāide*" (my duty). As for the type of "*xièxie*" (thanks), it is categorized into strategy D; and the type of "*wú*" (none) belongs to zero sign.

The only type left uncategorized is "*kèqì*" (to be polite). Most of its realizations are "*búkèqì*" (you're welcome), and it is overwhelmingly juxtaposed with "you're welcome" by the selected Mandarin teaching materials, search engine query results, and Chinese-English dictionaries. Therefore, it is tentatively classified into strategy C. According to Table 3, as a whole, the most frequently used strategy in Mandarin teaching materials is zero sign. Following are strategies C, A, and D.

Table 3. Distribution of thanks response strategies in Mandarin teaching materials

Strategy	Type	Token (head act)	
zero sign (82.5%)	wú (82.5%)	wú (無)	109 (82.5%)
		búkèqì (不客氣)	6 (4.5%)
strategy C (9.1%)	kèqì (9.1%)	bié (zhème) kèqì (別 (這麼)客氣)	4 (3.0%)
		tài kèqì (太客氣)	1 (0.8%)
		búbì kèqì (不必客氣)	1 (0.8%)
strategy A (6.9%)	nǎlǐ (3.0%)	nǎlǐ (哪裡)	4 (3.0%)
	búxiè (1.6%)	búxiè (不謝)	1 (0.8%)
		búbì xiè (不必謝)	1 (0.8%)
	méi shénme (1.5%)	méi shénme (沒什麼)	2 (1.5%)
	yīnggāide (0.8%)	yīnggāide (應該的)	1 (0.8%)
strategy D (1.5%)	xièxie (1.5%)	(yě) xièxie ((也)謝謝)	2 (1.5%)
Total (100.0%)	100.0%	–	132 (100.0%)

4.2 The Distribution of Thanks Response Strategies in Observational Data

The present study collected a total of 425 pieces of raw data from naturally occurring speech. After eliminating unsuitable ones, i.e., responses using body language only, 396 pieces of data were included in the analysis. Its distribution is shown in Table 4.

In Table 4, zero sign is the most frequently used strategy. Moreover, four new types appeared, which are "*búhuì*" (no), "*méishì*" (nothing), "*hǎo*" (okay) and "*en*" (hmm).

Table 4. Distribution of thanks response strategies in observational data

Strategy	Type	Token (head act)	
zero sign (41.4%)	wú (41.4%)	wú (無)	164 (41.4%)
strategy D (31.5%)	xièxie (31.5%)	xièxie (謝謝)	125 (31.5%)
strategy A (15.2%)	búhuì (13.1%)	búhuì (不會)	52 (13.1%)
	méishì (1.8%)	méishì (沒事)	7 (1.8%)
	nǎlǐ (0.3%)	nǎlǐ (哪裡)	1 (0.3%)
strategy C (6.6%)	kèqì (6.6%)	búkèqì (不客氣)	25 (6.3%)
		búyòng kèqì (不用客氣)	1 (0.3%)
strategy E (5.3%)	en (3.5%)	en (嗯)	14 (3.5%)
	hǎo (1.8%)	hǎo (好)	7 (1.8%)
Total (100.0%)	100.0%	–	396 (100.0%)

The former two types were categorized into strategy A, and the latter two were placed under strategy E. Excluding zero sign, the bulk of strategies found in the observational data is strategy D, followed by strategies A, C, and E.

4.3   The Distribution of Thanks Responses Strategies in Spoken Corpus

Based on the types established from Mandarin teaching materials and observational data, eight keywords were used to search thanks responses in the COCT Spoken Corpus 2019. These keywords, also known as the types were as follows, "*kèqì*" (to be polite), "*nǎlǐ*" (not a problem), "*búhuì*" (no), "*búxiè*" (no need to thank), "*méishì*" (nothing), "*méi shénme*" (nothing), "*yīnggāide*" (my duty) and "*xièxie*" (thanks). A total of 45, 435 pieces of raw data were found.

However, like many corpora, the COCT Spoken Corpus 2019 uses blank space to represent segments rather than conversational markers. The turn-taking is accordingly not clear, and causes difficulty in identifying pragmatic functions [17].[3] Therefore, the data were further selected in turn based on context, in which only identifiable pieces with explicit turn-taking were included in the analysis. At the end, a total of 633 pieces of data, including 727 tokens of thanks responses, were categorized and shown in Table 5.

Unlike Mandarin teaching materials and observational data, a spoken corpus lacking conversational markers was unable to include instances of zero sign. A purposive sampling was thus conducted. In terms of the order of strategies, the spoken corpus data is mainly based on strategy D, followed by strategies C and A.

---

[3] Due to this issue, the types of "*hǎo* (okay)" and "*en* (hmm)" with complex pragmatic functions were excluded from keywords to avoid bias.

Table 5. Distribution of thanks responses strategies in the COCT Spoken Corpus 2019

Strategy	Type	Token (head act)	
strategy D (46.5%)	xièxie (46.5%)	(yě) xièxie ((也)謝謝)	338 (46.5%)
		búkèqì (不客氣)	178 (24.5%)
		bú (yào/yòng) kèqì (不(要/用)客氣)	25 (3.4%)
strategy C (29.5%)	kèqì (29.5%)	bié (zhème) kèqì (別(這麼)客氣)	10 (1.4%)
		nǐ tài kèqì le (你太客氣了)	1 (0.1%)
		gànmá zhème kèqì (幹嘛這麼客氣)	1 (0.1%)
strategy A (24.0%)	búhuì (19.2%)	búhuì (不會)	139 (19.2%)
	nǎlǐ (2.5%)	nǎlǐ (哪裡)	18 (2.5%)
	yīnggāide (1.8%)	zhè shì yīnggāide ((這是)應該的)	13 (1.8%)
	méishì (0.4%)	méishì (沒事)	3 (0.4%)
	méi shénme (0.1%)	méi shénme (沒什麼)	1 (0.1%)
	búxiè (0.0%)	–	–
Total (100.0%)	100.0%	–	727 (100.0%)

5   General Discussion

After organizing data based on frequency of verbal speech forms, Mandarin teaching materials were found to have a tendency towards strategy C, while observational and spoken corpus data give priority to strategy D. In order to respond to the research questions, related discussion is divided into two subs for further exploration. The first part analyzes the distribution of strategies of the three sources, to examine whether there are differences between Taiwanese Mandarin and varieties of English. The second part explores the high frequency of strategy D in observational and spoken corpus data, and the high frequency of zero sign in Mandarin teaching materials and observational data.

5.1   The Distribution of Thanks Responses Strategies in Three Sources

Summarizing the data from Tables 3, 4 and 5, the overall ranking of strategies is shown in Table 6. At this stage, "*kèqì*" type was tentatively classified into strategy C, since its bulk realization of "*búkèqì*" is juxtaposed with "you're welcome." However, whether strategy C of English is equivalent to "*kèqì*" type of Mandarin Chinese remains unknown. The following examines if "*búkèqì*" and strategy C share similar meaning through an analysis of Chinese morphemes.

Disyllabic words are the mainstream in Chinese [18], however, Luo [19] finds the majority of new words trisyllabic. Under examination, features of trisyllabic combinations are as follows: (1) they can be condensed as words through lexicalization, but are

Table 6. Ranking of thanks response strategies in three sources

Ranking	Source		
	Mandarin teaching materials	Observational data	COCT Spoken corpus 2019
First	zero sign (82.5%)	zero sign (41.4%)	strategy D (46.5%)
Second	strategy C (9.1%)	strategy D (31.5%)	strategy C (29.5%)
Third	strategy A (6.9%)	strategy A (15.2%)	strategy A (24.0%)
Fourth	strategy D (1.5%)	strategy C (6.6%)	–
Fifth		strategy E (5.3%)	–

less likely to be included in dictionaries [20, 21]; (2) their formations are always unstable and imbalanced, in that their adopted patterns are either words or phrases [19].

Given that it is difficult to distinguish Chinese lexicalization without aspectual changes [22], even though "*búkèqì*" is viewed as undergoing its lexicalization [23, 24], and is categorized as idiomatic expression (IE) by all selected Mandarin teaching materials, its semantic meaning as a thanks response is yet to be included into any official definition [25]. It is accordingly not a fully recognized word, and its trisyllabic feature still gives room for the semantic independence of negative "*bù*" (no, don't).

Under the premise that (1) "*bù*" is able to independently negate the head, and (2) the head "*kèqì*" has commendatory sense [26], "*búkèqì*" is clearly at odds with the core of strategy C, which implies appreciation for a particular person [7]. Hence, whether "*búkèqì*" is a word or not, it is closer to strategy A, attempting to weaken the intensity of thanks by using negatives. Other tokens of the "*kèqì*" type also fall into this new category, in that they all contain morphemes with negative meaning. The distribution of thanks response strategies was thus reorganized in Table 7.

Table 7. Reordering of thanks responses strategies in three sources

Ranking	Source		
	Mandarin teaching materials	Observational data	COCT Spoken Corpus 2019
First	zero sign (82.5%)	zero sign (41.4%)	strategy A (53.5%)
Second	strategy A (16.0%)	strategy D (31.5%)	strategy D (46.7%)
Third	strategy D (1.5%)	strategy A (21.8%)	–
Fourth		strategy E (5.3%)	–

After dealing with strategy, further discussion goes on to type distribution. From Tables 3, 4 and 5, both observational and spoken corpus data contain the "*búhuì*" (no) type in strategy A, and it has a thriving performance in frequency. However, Mandarin teaching materials contain no use of this type. Moreover, although appearing in Mandarin teaching materials and marked as "commonly used in Taiwan," the type of "*búxiè*" (no need for thanks) does not show up in the observational nor spoken corpus data.

Even though "*búhuì*" has an intrinsic competitive edge on lexicalization owing to its disyllabic feature compared to "*búkèqì*," these two terms shall not be analyzed from the same perspective. As a thank represents a debt [27], a sense of apology for causing trouble is implied. "*Búhuì*" responds to that implicit sense since a modal verb can be negated and form a semantically-incomplete sentence alone only when there is already-known information to both interlocutors [28]. From Sect. 2, the already-known information is of course the unspoken debt. Since both interlocutors understand that "sorry for causing some trouble to you (bàoqiàn zàochéng máfán,抱歉造成麻煩)" is implied, and under the premise of modal verbs expressing subjective concepts [29], "*búhuì*" negates the possible guilt, thus alleviating the apologetic mood of the thanker.

The "*búhuì*" type makes up the bulk of strategy A in the observational data, with a frequency also quite high in the spoken corpus data, thus reflecting its frequent use by native speakers. Despite merging the variants of "*kèqì*" through the analysis of morphology, the ratio of "*búhuì*" in the data is still twice as much as "*búkèqì*." In the selected Mandarin teaching materials, this term is never used as a thanks response, nor is its pragmatic function in responding to thanks mentioned. It is a phenomenon that Wang [12, 13] does not observe, and a topic in Modern Chinese awaiting further explorion.

Consequently, in terms of the first and second research questions, in verbal speech forms, strategy A is the majority strategy presented in Mandarin teaching materials, whereas in both observational and spoken corpus data, strategy D is at the top. To illustrate the differences within the distribution of each strategy, the following subsection discusses the high frequency of strategy D and zero sign in the present data.

5.2   The Distribution of Strategy D and Zero Sign in Three Sources

The Usage of Strategy D in Observational and Spoken Corpus Data. According to Edmondson & House [6], Strategy D is a Feasible Option When Both Interlocuters Believe "They Are Benefited During the Encounter." Leech & Svartvik [30] Observe that Shop Keepers Often Return Thanks to Customers While Receiving Money. Staley [9] Finds that Strategy D is the Second Highest Strategy Used During Interactions Between Servers and Customers, Especially When Dealing with Payments in High-Class Restaurants. She Considers that It is Because Servers also Receive a Tip of 20% of the Total Consumption.

Edmondson & House [6], Leech & Svartvik [30] and Staley [9] all concentrate on societies dominated by varieties of English. It is accordingly possible for mutual benefits to appear during encounters associated with service. If the thanks responder is a shopkeeper, his/her benefit has a positive correlation with the amount of consumption. S/he is a direct beneficiary in that service encounter. On the other hand, if the thanks responder is a restaurant server in America, his/her income is highly dependent on tips. The higher-class the restaurant s/he serves at is, the more tips s/he can receive. The restaurant server is both a direct and indirect beneficiary in that service encounter.

This seems logical to illustrate the thanks responses from a customer's perspective. When they are thanked for seeking or buying something, due to their needs being fulfilled, strategy D can be used based on mutual benefit. However, from a server's perspective, when they receive thanks, their responses may not stem from mutual benefit alone, especially in Taiwan, a society dominated by Mandarin Chinese.

Taiwan has no tipping culture. Even though a "fixed 10% service fee" is gaining popularity, it is not paid to servers, but to the owners of restaurants or catering businesses. In other words, the amount of consumption and servers' income has low correlation, and the servers in Taiwan are thus less reliant on customers. For further discussion of this matter, please see example (1) extracted from observational data below.

(1) (Restaurant in hotel, ordering)
     Middle-aged customer, male: (orders) xièxie (hands the menu to server).
                                                            Thank you.
     Young server, female: (takes the menu) xièxie.
                                                            Thank you.

In example (1), the server will not receive any tip for her services, and her income is fixed. However, under the premise of a fixed salary, strategy D is still common in use in similar circumstances, which may lead to an assumption less associated with Edmondson & House [6], but with another definition—something related to duty.

According to Merritt [31], service encounters refer to the face-to-face interactions between servers and customers. The aim is to fulfill (1) the needs of the customer, and (2) the duty of the server to serve. Regardless of whether a money transaction is involved, once these two conditions are met, a service encounter is established.

63.9% of the observational data is associated with the context of service. One of the interlocutors has the identity of server, while the other interlocutor plays the role of customer. When their interactions fall within the scope of service duties, the usage of strategy D is high. That is, when responders are servers, they do not have to deduce the imbalance caused by the thanks, since it is their responsibility to fulfill the needs of customers. Choosing strategy D to convey an equivalent response and conclude the transaction is rather more appropriate.

However, other than obliged duty, the present study also finds mutual benefits implied in the spoken corpus data extracted from open-ended programs, such as dramas and talk shows, as example (2) shows.

(2) Host: jīntiān   fēicháng xièxie   Yùshān   diǎndī zuòzhě
          Today   very   thanks Mount Jade   tiny   author
          Lǐtáijūn   dàgē   lái   jiēshòu wǒmen
          person's name elder brother come receive   we
          de   fǎngwèn   xièxie nǐ
          DE   interview thanks you
"A big thanks to the author of *Tiny Things of Mount Jade*, Lee Tai-Chun, for partici-
pating in our interview today. Thank you."

     Guest: xièxie zhǔchírén
            Thanks   host
"Thank you, host."

As can be seen from example (2), the guest is a participant, and his/her intention and role are achieved via the help of the host. At the meantime, the host needs guests to participate in the program, and the guest also requires the opportunity to share their opinions and works. Hence, both mutual benefit and duty are implied, which explains that in Taiwan, strategy D is a feasible option under both of these two circumstances. However, most of the context related to duty and mutual benefit are replaced by zero sign in Mandarin teaching materials; only two pieces of data choose strategy D. One clearly shows mutual benefit, and the other implies obliged duty.

The Usage of Zero Sign in Observational Data and Mandarin Teaching Materials. Among the Strategies in Mandarin Teaching Materials and Observational Data, Zero Sign Dominates Over the Other Strategies. Similar Phenomena Only Occurred in Observation-Related Studies [9, 13].

The present study analyzes zero sign of Mandarin teaching materials as the first step, and finds it difficult to connect with Wang's [13] arguments, since the profiles of characters in Mandarin teaching materials are not concrete enough to distinguish any social factors. The high frequency of zero sign may be influenced by other conditions.

The present study considers two extra possible conditions. First, the verbal expressions in written forms put restrictions on turn-taking. The main purpose of Mandarin teaching materials is presenting appropriate occasions to use target vocabulary and grammar points, rather than intactly recording how turn-taking happens in daily life. That is to say, when the realization of thanks responses meets the need of target vocabulary or grammar points, the turn-taking has a higher chance to be realized.

The second possible condition is the cost of each thanks. In Wang's [13] research, the researcher played the role of thanker and asked for directions, in which a request was implied. The premise of thanks is the fulfillment of a favor. However, the arrangements of Mandarin teaching materials are far more complex. Besides the speech act of request, compliments, invitations, and wishes, etc., are all involved. Under the framework of the Politeness Principle [32], the cost cumulated in the interaction of Mandarin teaching materials and Wang's [13] is different, as Figs. 1 and 2 demonstrate.

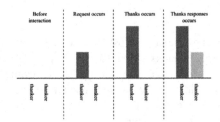

Fig. 1. The costs of interlocutors in Wang [30][4]

---

[4] Figures 1 and 2 are self-drawn schematic diagrams for the present study. The specific cost of each speech act depends on the context and all the social conditions at the time of interaction.

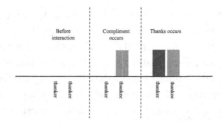

Fig. 2. The costs of interlocutors in Mandarin teaching materials

In Fig. 1, under the context of inquiry, the cost is cumulated on the side of the thanker; strategies other than zero sign can effectively shorten the imbalance. However, under the circumstance of compliment in Fig. 2, it is the thanker who is benefited. S/he thus proposes a thanks as response to the compliment. At this stage, the costs have been balanced. There is no need for a further response to thanks. Edmondson & House [6] and Schneider [7] also consider that TMs will not appear when the thanks, as an uptaker, is launched by a preceding *verbal* act, such as compliment (emphasis in original).

In the observational data, zero sign is concentrated in the context associated with service, in which thankees undertake the identity of server. Servers' working mode is mostly uninterrupted, and their burdens have a positive correlation with customer flows. At peak hours, servers may feel busy and tense, thus adopting zero sign as their responses to save time. Staley [9] also assumes that thanks in restaurants are highly repetitive, which implies less necessity to reply every single time, thus generating less responses.

According to the analysis and discussion, the arrangements of Mandarin teaching materials and the usage of native speakers of Taiwanese Mandarin are different. The former has less varied strategies than those found in the observational data. This has been verified by Bella [2], in which she finds that teaching materials often simplify native speakers' actual behavior. In the present study, it is also found that the distribution of type in each source is different, and realizations are functioned to reflect various intentions [33]. The reason is not only related to linguistic expressions, but also touches upon the socio-cultural aspects, as well as areas which previous studies have less explored.

6 Conclusion

Through the present study, it is shown that both Mandarin teaching materials and obser- vational data prefer strategy A, while under the circumstances related to duties or mutual benefit, strategy D is preferred for Taiwanese Mandarin native speakers.

Furthermore, the present study demonstrates the differences between Mandarin teaching materials and native speakers in terms of two aspects. One is owing to the lack of variety of strategies arranged in Mandarin teaching materials, and the other is due to the distribution of the types of strategies. Mandarin teaching materials overes- timate the frequency of the "*kèqì*" and "*búxiè*" types of strategy A, with the latter not found in the observational and spoken corpus data. While in the observational data, the frequency of the "*búhuì*" type is twice as much as the "*kèqì*" type. The open-ended programs in the spoken corpus data also demonstrate a blended use between the "*kèqì*" type and the "*búhuì*" type, which illustrates the complicated nature of thanks responses.

The present study attempts to sketch the thanks response strategies in Taiwan via the comparison of Mandarin teaching materials, observational data and spoken corpus data. It is highly expected that the gathering of all the outstanding studies together can build a systematic thanks response model of varieties of Chinese, and give a more close-to-native interpretation when discussing thanks responses in Taiwanese Mandarin.

Acknowledgements. . This study is supported by the National Science and Technology Council, Taiwan, R.O.C., under Grant no. MOST 110–2511-H-003 -034 -MY3. It is also supported by National Taiwan Normal University's Chinese Language and Technology Center. The center is funded by Taiwan's Ministry of Education (MOE), as part of the Featured Areas Research Center Program, under the Higher Education Sprout Project.

References

1. Su, H.-Y.: The indigenization and enregisterment of Taiwan Mandarin. Monumenta Taiwanica **17**, 1–35 (2018). https://doi.org/10.6242/twnica.201804_(17).0001. (In Chinese)
2. Bella, S.: Responding to thanks: Divergence between native speakers and FL learners of Greek and the consequences for establishing rapport. Glossologia **24**, 61–73 (2016)
3. Eisenstein, M., Bodman, J.: "I very appreciate": expressions of gratitude by native and non-native speakers of American English. Appl. Linguis. **7**(2), 167–185 (1986). https://doi.org/10.1093/applin/7.2.167
4. Rüegg, L.: Thanks responses in three socio-economic settings: a variational pragmatics approach. J. Pragmat. **71**, 17–30 (2014). https://doi.org/10.1016/j.pragma.2014.07.005
5. Aijmer, K.: Conversational Routines in English: Convention and Creativity. Longman, London; New York (1996)
6. Edmondson, W., House, J.: Let's talk and talk about it: a pedagogic interactional grammar of English. Urban and Schwarzenberg, München; Wien; Baltimore (1981)
7. Schneider, K. P.: No problem, you're welcome, anytime: responding to thanks in Ireland, England, and the USA. In: Barron, A., Schneider, K. P. (eds.) The pragmatics of Irish English, pp. 101–139. De Gruyter Mouton, Berlin, New York (2005). https://doi.org/10.1515/9783110898934.101
8. Kiesling, S.F.: Language Variation and Change. Edinburgh University Press, Edinburgh (2011)
9. Staley, L.: Socioeconomic pragmatic variation: speech acts and address forms in context. John Benjamins, Amsterdam; Philadelphia (2018)
10. Farenkia, B.M.: Face-saving strategies in responding to gratitude expressions: evidence from Canadian English. Int. J. Engl. Linguist. **2**(4), 1–11 (2012). https://doi.org/10.5539/ijel.v2n4p1
11. Bieswanger, M.: Variational pragmatics and responding to thanks—revisited. Multilingua **34**(4), 527–546 (2015). https://doi.org/10.1515/multi-2014-0106
12. Wang, C.-H.: Functional analysis of forms in Chinese thank-expressing replies. J. Jianghan Univ. (Humanit. Sci.) **26**(1), 79–83 (2007). (In Chinese)
13. Wang, C.-H.: A sociolinguistic exploration on the types and performance of Chinese responses to thanks. Lang. Teach. Linguist. Stud. **4**, 88–95 (2008). (In Chinese)
14. Labov, W.: Some principles of linguistic methodology. Lang. Soc. **1**(1), 97–120 (1972). https://doi.org/10.1017/S0047404500006576

15. National Academy for Educational Research (NAER): Taiwan huayuwen yuliaoku—huayuwen jiao yu xue de bibei gongju [Corpus of Contemporary Taiwanese Mandarin—A must-have tool for Mandarin teaching and learning]. NAER, Taipei (2021). (In Chinese)
16. Martin, J.R., Zappavigna, M.: Embodied meaning: a systemic functional perspective on paralanguage. Funct. Linguist. **6**(1), 1–33 (2019). https://doi.org/10.1186/s40554-018-0065-9
17. Hsieh, C.-L.: A Cross-Cultural Study of Chinese and English: Pragmatic Strategies in an Internet Society. Crane Publishing co. LTD, Taipei (2015). (In Chinese)
18. Feng, S.-L.: Lun hanyu de ziran yinbu [On "natural foot" in Chinese]. Stud. Chin. Lang. **1**, 40–47 (1998). (In Chinese)
19. Luo, J.: A structural and prosodic analysis of Trisyllabic new words. In: Dong, M.-H., Lin, J.-X., Tang, X.-R. (eds.) Chinese lexical semantics. CLSW 2016. LNCS, vol. 10085, pp. 120-127. Springer, Cham (2016). https://doi.org/10.1007/978-3-319-49508-8_12
20. Dong, X.-F.: Further grammaticalization of "shi": From functional word to word-internal element. Contemp. Linguist. **6**(1), 35–44 (2004). (In Chinese)
21. Wu, Y.-R., Biq, Y.-O.: Lexicalization of intensifiers: two X-shi constructions in spoken Mandarin. Chin. Lang. Discourse **2**(2), 168–197 (2011). https://doi.org/10.1075/cld.2.2.02yao
22. Dong, X.-F.: Lexicalization: Chinese 'bu' and its negative constructions. Contemp. Linguist. **5**(1), 12–24 (2003). (In Chinese)
23. Hu, Q.-G.: Bukeqi" and "bie keqi. J. Gannan Normal Univ. **5**, 49–53 (2009). (In Chinese)
24. Tang, X.-L.: Tan xiandai hanyu de yige duanyu "bukeqi" [On a phrase "bukeqi" in Modern Chinese]. J. Lang. Lit. Stud. **7**, 135–138 (2006). (In Chinese)
25. Revised Mandarin Chinese Dictionary. Page of bukeqi [not polite]. https://dict.revised.moe.edu.tw/dictView.jsp?ID=20776&word=%E4%B8%8D%E5%AE%A2%E6%B0%A3#searchL. Accessed 01 May 2021
26. Revised Mandarin Chinese Dictionary. Page of keqi [polite]. https://dict.revised.moe.edu.tw/dictView.jsp?ID=76428&q=1&word=%E5%AE%A2%E6%B0%A3#order1. Accessed 01 May 2021
27. Li, L.-N.: Hanyu "ganxie" yanyu xingwei yanjiu [On the speech act of thanks in Chinese]. Hubei Soc. Sci. **9**, 93–95 (2004). (In Chinese) https://doi.org/10.13660/j.cnki.42-1112/c.006750
28. Li, C.N., Thompson, S.A.: Mandarin Chinese: A Functional Reference Grammar. University of California Press, California (1981)
29. Jingyi, X.: A study on the expressions of modal particles of the suggestion function in Spoken Chinese. In: Hong, J.-F., Zhang, Y., Liu, P. (eds.) CLSW 2019. LNCS (LNAI), vol. 11831, pp. 94–101. Springer, Cham (2020). https://doi.org/10.1007/978-3-030-38189-9_9
30. Leech, G., Svartvik, J.: A Communicative Grammar of English, 2nd edn. Longman, London (1994)
31. Merritt, M.: On question following question in service encounters. Lang. Soc. **5**, 315–357 (1976). https://doi.org/10.1017/S0047404500007168
32. Leech, G.: Principles of pragmatics. Longman, London; New York (1983)
33. Zhang, K.-L., Mu, L.-L., Zan, H.-Y., Han, Y.-J., Sui, Z.-F.: Study on modality annotation framework of modern Chinese. In: Dong, M.-H., Lin, J.-X., Tang, X.-R. (eds.) Chinese Lexical Semantics. CLSW 2016. LNCS, vol. 10085, pp. 291–305. Springer, Cham (2016). https://doi.org/10.1007/978-3-319-49508-8_28

A Study on the Positional Relationship Between Preposition-Object Structures and Predicate Components in *Mozi* Based on Corpus

Jiqing Yang[1] and Yonghong Ke[1,2(✉)]

[1] Research Center for Folklore, Classics and Chinese Characters, Beijing Normal University, Beijing 100875, China
kyh@bnu.edu.cn
[2] Research Center for Collation and Standardization of Chinese Characters, Beijing, China

Abstract. When modifying the predicate components, the preposition-object structures in *Mozi* are mainly after predicate components, with relevant example sentences accounting for approximately 58.1% of the total. The prepositions that can appear only before predicate components are Wei(为), Cong(从), Yin(因), You(由), Yong(用), Yu(与) and Dang(当). The prepositions that can appear only after predicate components are Hu(乎/虖) and Zai(在). The prepositions that can appear both before and after predicate components are Yu(於), Yi(以), Zi(自), Yu(于) and Zhi(至). The preposition-object structures expressing space-time and involvement tend to be postpositive, while the preposition-object structures expressing method tend to be prepositive. Predicate components modified by preposition-object structures include words and phrases. When verb-object structures serve as the predicate, there is little difference between the number of prepositive and postpositive preposition-object structures. When other structures act as the predicate, the preposition-object structures are mainly postpositive. The most common number of syllables is two syllables (approximately 42.4%) when the preposition-object structure is prepositive and one syllable (approximately 57.3%) when the preposition-object structure is postpositive. Compared with *Zuozhuan*, the number of prepositive preposition-object structures in *Mozi* is increasing, which may reflect the change of Chinese means of expression from "abstract principles" to "iconic principles".

Keywords: *Mozi* · Preposition-object structures · Predicate component · Position

1 Introduction

The positional relationship of preposition-object structures and predicate components is an important topic in the research on Chinese word order. Yuen Ren Chao (1979)[1]

---

[1] "Preposition-object structures indicating where they are and where they are from can be placed after verbs rather than only before verbs" is "the only important difference between classical Chinese and vernacular", cf. Zhao Y.R.: A Grammar of Spoken Chinese. Commercial Press, Beijing (1979).

© The Author(s), under exclusive license to Springer Nature Switzerland AG 2023
Q. Su et al. (Eds.): CLSW 2022, LNAI 13495, pp. 414–431, 2023.
https://doi.org/10.1007/978-3-031-28953-8_31

and Wang Li [1] suggested that the position of the preposition-object structure in the contemporary age has changed significantly from its position in ancient times, and the synchronic investigation of the preposition-object structure's position is the basic work to study its diachronic change. Making statistics and comparisons on the number of prepositions and the frequency of preposition-object structures before and after predicate verbs or adjectives in *Zuozhuan* and *Shiji*, He Leshi [2] found that the use of postpositive preposition-object structures outweighs the use of prepositive preposition-object structures in *Zuozhuan*, which has been significantly reversed in *Shiji*, and therefore she speculated that the grammatical features from *Zuozhuan* to *Shiji* may have undergone remarkable changes. He Leshi [3] also compared the position of preposition-object structures in *Shishuoxinyu* and *Shiji*, *Dunhuang Bianwen* and *Shishuoxinyu*, *Guan Hanqing's drama collection* and *Dunhuang Bianwen* and further analyzed the changes in grammatical features. Jiang Shaoyu [4] argued that "Yu(于), Yu(於), Hu(乎), Zhu(诸) + location" phrases were after verbs in pre-Qin Chinese while they follow "the principle of temporal sequence" (PTS) in modern Chinese, which means the expression of the relationship between actions and locations in Chinese has changed from "abstract principles" to "iconic principles". Zhang Cheng [5] described the process of the word order change of prepositional phrases comprehensively and believed that the rise and disappearance of some prepositions, the meaning of prepositional phrases, and the development of VP structure were the reasons for the position change of prepositional phrases. Wang Hong-bin [6] and Liu Xiaojing [7] performed special analyses on preposition-object structures' positions in *Zuozhuan* and *Mencius*, respectively.

Mozi is an important piece of literature from the pre-Qin period, and it also is one of the most abundant works of pre-Qin scholars. Although the language style of *Mozi* is simple and unadorned, the Mohist covers a wide range of fields, which makes the content of *Mozi* informative and rich in language phenomena. At present, studies on *Mozi* mostly focus on its thought, while research on its language is limited. We cannot find comprehensive research on the positional relationship between preposition-object structures and predicate components in *Mozi*. The *Research on preposition of Mozi*, a master's thesis by Gao Yin [8], divided the prepositions of *Mozi* into seven categories in accordance with meaning: time, place, resort, reason and purpose, involvement, comparison and passivity. It also teased out typical prepositions such as Yi(以), Wei(为), Zi(自), Cong(从), You(由), Zhu(诸), Yong(用), Yin(因), Zhi(至), Hu(乎), Yu(于) and Yu(於). The differences between prepositions Yu(于) and Yu(於), the verb characteristics of prepositions, prepositional object preposing and ellipsis, and the fixed structure composition of prepositions also were discussed. This thesis mentioned the position of preposition-object structures but did not investigate them systematically and deeply. Moreover, some studies with the theme of pre-Qin Chinese word order use *Mozi* as one of the corpora, such as Zhang Cheng in *The Study of Exceptions in Position of Prepositional Phrases in Archaic Chinese* [9], Ma Lili in *A Study of Chinese Preposition "Yu"(于) and "Yu"(於) during pre-Qin Period* [10], Zhang Jie in *The Study of Special Word-order in pre-Qin Period Chinese by the Focus Theory* [11], etc., but there is no research on the positional relationship between preposition-object structures and predicate components in *Mozi*.

In these circumstances, this paper takes the text of *Mozi* as the corpus to conduct a comprehensive investigation on the positional relationship between the preposition-object structures and the predicate components of *Mozi*.

2 The Position of Preposition-Object Structures in Mozi

The term preposition-object structure refers to the linguistic unit composed of a preposition and its object. This paper focuses on the positional relationship between the preposition-object structures and the predicate components it modifies. Therefore, the preposition-object structures modifying sentences are not involved for the time being.

The predicate component is not simply confined to the predicate that states the subject in the sentence but also refers to the word or phrase whose function is to state. For example, "make their ambition achieved in the world and their fame spread in future generations" are two pivotal structures in Chinese, whose "achieve" and "spread" also are regarded as our research objects. When some preposition-object structures are used successively, the latter predicate component may be omitted because of the former, or only the latter verb is omitted. These two kinds of omissions are included in the research objects of this paper.

Prepositions in *Mozi* can be classified into three types, according to the preposition-object structures' positions: only before the predicate component, only after the predicate component, and both before and after the predicate component. Examples are as follows:

2.1 Prepositions that Appear Only Before the Predicate Components

There are seven prepositions in *Mozi* that appear only before the predicate components: Wei(为), Cong(从), Yin(因), You(由), Yong(用), Yu(与) and Dang(当).

1. Wei(为).

(1) 不为大国侮小国, 不为众庶侮鳏寡。《兼爱中》

bù wéi dà guó wǔ xiǎo guó, bù wéi zhòng shù wǔ guān guǎ。

Neg because big country bully small country, Neg because many many bully widower widow.

(King Wen of Zhou did not bully small countries because of Zhou's great strength, did not bully the few because of Zhou's richness.)

(2) 为人谋者不可不劝也。《节葬下》

wéi rén móu zhě bù kě bù quàn yě 。

for others plan thing must Neg can Neg encourage.

(Those who plan for others must encourage to do so.)

2. Cong(从).

(3) 必曰从恶人贼人生。《兼爱下》

bì yuē cóng è rén zéi rén shēng 。

must say from hate people injure people arise.

(Everyone will say that they arise from hating and injuring people.)

3. Yin(因).

(4) 因陵丘堀穴而处焉。《节用中》

yīn língqiū jué xué ér chù yān。

beside hill dig cave Conj live there.

(Human beings used to excavate caves beside hills and live there.)

(5) 因素出兵施伏。《备梯》

yīn sù chū bīng shī fú。

as normal dispatch troop make ambush.

(Dispatch troops and make ambushes as normal.)

4. Yong(用).

(6) 吾用此知之。《非命上》

wú yòng cǐ zhī zhī。

I because this know it.

(For this reason I know it.)

(7) 然则崇此害亦何用生哉?《兼爱中》

rán zé chóng cǐ hài yì hé yòng shēng zāi ?

this then investigate these disasters? what because arise Mod?

(In this case, let us investigate why these disasters arise.)

5. Cong(从).

(8) 民之为淫暴寇乱盗贼……由此止。《明鬼下》

mín zhī wéi yín bào kòu luàn dào zéi ……yóu cǐ zhǐ。

people do prostitution violence banditry rebellion thievery persecution…from then stop.

(People's prostitution, violence, banditry, rebellion, thievery and persecution…stop from then on.)

6. Yu(与).

(9) 子路进, 请曰: "何其与陈、蔡反也?"《非儒下》

zǐlù jìn, qǐng yuē: "hé qí yǔ chén 、 cài fǎn yě ?"。

Zi Lu come up, ask say, "Why you with Chen Cai different?".

(Zi Lu came up and asked, "Why do you behave differently with what you did in Chen and Cai?").

(10) 孔某与其门弟子闲坐。《非儒下》

kǒngmǒu yǔ qí mén dìzǐ xián zuò。

Confucius with his disciples idly sit.

(Confucius and his disciples sit idly.)

7. Dang(当).

(11) 昔者郑穆公当昼日中处乎庙。《明鬼下》

xīzhě zhèng mù gōng dāng zhòu rìzhōng chù hū miào。

past Zheng Mu duke in daytime noon be in temple.

(In the past, Duke of Zheng Mu was in the temple at noon.)

(12) 故当执有命者之言，不可不明辨。《非命上》

gù dāng zhí yǒu mìng zhě zhī yán, bú kě bú míng biàn。

so to uphold exist fate thing's words, Neg can Neg explicitly examine.

(So we should examine the words of fatalists explicitly.)

2.2 Prepositions that Appear Only After the Predicate Components

In *Mozi*, there are two prepositions that appear only after the predicate component: Hu(乎/虖) and Zai(在).

8. Hu(乎/虖).

(13) 人之生乎地上之无几何也，譬之犹驷驰而过隙也。《兼爱下》

rén zhī shēng hū dì shàng zhī wú jǐ hé yě, pì zhī yóu sì chí ér guò xì yě。

People live on earth not how much, compare it like four horses gallop Conj pass crevice.

(Man's life on earth is as brief as the passing of four horses glimpsed through a crevice in the wall.)

(14) 今也农夫之所以蚤出暮入，强乎耕稼树艺……《非命下》

jīn yě nóng fū zhī suǒ yǐ zǎo chū mù rù, qiáng hū gēng jià shù yì。

now Mod farmer's reason early go out evening return, diligent in farm cultivate plant plant...

(Now the reason why farmers go to work early and return late and they are diligent in farming cultivation and planting...).

9. Zai(在).

(15) 周人从者莫不见，远者莫不闻，著在周之春秋。《明鬼下》

zhōu rén cóng zhě mò bú jiàn, yuǎn zhě mò bú wén, zhe zài zhōu zhī chūnqiū。

Zhou people attend Nom none Neg see, distant Nom none Neg hear, write in Zhou's *Spring and Autumn Annals*.

(Among Zhou people, everybody attendant saw it and everybody in distant areas heard about it, and it was recorded in Zhou's *Spring and Autumn Annals.)*

2.3 Prepositions that Appear Before and After the Predicate Components

In *Mozi*, the prepositions Yu(於), Yi(以), Zi(自), Yu(于), Zhi(至) and their objects can appear both before and after the predicate components.

10. Yu(於).

(16) 虽子墨子之所谓兼者, 於文王取法焉。《兼爱下》

suī zǐmòzǐ zhī suǒ wèi jiān zhě, yú wénwáng qǔ fǎ yān 。

although Master *Mozi* call universal thing, from King Wen take model.

(The universal love advocated by Master Mozi is actually modeled after King Wen.)

(17) 耕柱子曰: "我毋俞於人乎?"《耕柱》

gēng zhù zǐ yuē: "wǒ wú yú yú rén hū ?".

Geng Zhu Master say, "I Neg better than people Mod".

(Master Geng Zhu said, "Am I better than others?").

11. Yi(以).

(18) 必以坚材为夫, 以利斧施之。《备穴》

bì yǐ jiān cái wéi fū, yǐ lì fǔ shī zhī.

must with strong material make shaft, with sharp axe add it.

(You must make the shaft with strong materials and add a sharp axe on it.)

(19) 饵鼠以虫, 非爱之也。《鲁问》

ěr shǔ yǐ chóng, fēi ài zhī yě.

bait rat with insect, Neg love them.

(Baiting rats with insects is not love for them.)

12. Zi(自),

(20) 若夫绳之引轱也, 是犹自舟中引横也。《经说下》

ruòfū shéng zhī yǐn gū yě, shì yóu zì zhōu zhōng yǐn héng yě.

Mod rope pull wheel Mod, like from boat in pull crossbar.

(Ropes pull the wheel, which is like pulling a crossbar of the boat.)

(21) 越王繄亏出自有遽, 始邦於越。《非攻下》

yuè wáng yīkuī chū zì yǒujù, shǐ bāng yú yuè.

Yue King Yi Kui come from Youju, begin country in Yue.

(The King of Yue came from Youju and established his country in Yue.)

13. Yu(于).

(22) 启乃淫溢康乐, 野于饮食……《非乐上》

qǐ nǎi yín yì kāng lè, yě yú yǐn shí.

Qi therefore prostitute, overdo happy happy wild in drink eat.

(Qi gave himself up to lust and indulgence. He ate and drank in the wild fields.)

(23) 诸加费不加于民利者, 圣王弗为。《节用中》

zhū jiā fèi bú jiā yú mín lì zhě, shèng wáng fú wéi.

every add expenditure Neg add to people benefit, sage king Neg do.

(Sage kings would never do what adds expenditures but doesn't add benefits to people.)

14. Zhi(至).

(24) 至今不废。《非攻下》

zhì jīn bú fèi.

to now Neg abolish.

(It has not been abolished until now.)

(25) 比至城者三表, 与城上烽燧相望。《号令》

bǐ zhì chéng zhě sān biǎo, yǔ chéng shàng fēng suì xiàng wàng.

close to rampart three pole, with rampart on beacon fire mutually look.

(There are three poles close to the rampart, in line with beacon fires on the rampart.)
The following Table 1 is an overview of the positions of prepositions in *Mozi*:

Table 1. Number of prepositions before and after predicate components in *Mozi*.

Preposition		Before the predicate component	After the predicate component	Total
Only before the predicate component	You(由)	2	0	2
	Dang(当)	3	0	3
	Yin(因)	5	0	5
	Yong(用)	6	0	6
	Cong(从)	6	0	6
	Wei(为)	32	0	32
	Yu(与)	34	0	34
Only after the predicate component	Hu(虖)	0	1	1
	Zai(在)	0	4	4
	Hu(乎)	0	113	113
Both before and after the predicate component	Yu(于)	1	35	36
	Zhi(至)	8	5	13
	Yu(於)	30	456	486
	Zi(自)	27	1	28
	Yi(以)	321	60	381
Total		475	675	1150

As the statistics of the example sentences show, there are 475 cases of the preposition-object structures before the predicate components and 675 cases of the preposition-object structures after the predicate components in *Mozi*. The proportion of the preposition-object structures before the predicate components is 41.3%, and the proportion of the preposition-object structures after the predicate components is 58.7%, accounting for the majority.

In conclusion, there are seven prepositions that can appear only before the predicate component: Wei(为), Cong(从), Yin(因), You(由), Yong(用), Yu(与) and Dang(当), while there are just two prepositions, Hu(乎/虖) and Zai(在), that can appear only after the predicate components. Although the number of prepositive prepositions outweighs the number of postpositive prepositions, the number of related example sentences is reversed: there are 94 use cases of prepositive prepositions, while there are 118 use cases of postpositive prepositions. In *Mozi*, the postpositive preposition-object structures are the majority.

3   The Relationship Between the Semantic Features of Preposition-Object Structures and Their Position

By the standard of semantic features, we divide preposition-object structures modifying predicate components into four categories: related matter, reason and virtue, which can be divided into subcategories (Table 2):

Table 2. Categories of preposition-object structures modifying predicate components.

Categories	Subcategories
Spatiotemporal	Space
	Time
Way	Mode
	Tool
	Accordance
	Material
	Starting point
Relation	Involvement
	Fields or situations
	Role
	Comparison
	Agent
	Patient
Cause	Reason
	Purpose or result

1. Space.

(26) 若立而为政乎国家。《尚同中》

ruò lì ér wéizhèng hū guó jiā 。

if assign and govern in country.

(If one is assigned to govern the country…).

(27) 道广三十步, 於城下夹阶者各二……於道之外为屏。《旗帜》

dào guǎng sān shí bù, yú chéng xià jiá jiē zhě gè èr ……yú dào zhī wài wéi píng 。

road wide 30 steps, at city down thing each two……at road's outside make barrier.

 (The road is 30 steps wide, and there are two wells on each side of the road under the city wall…. Make barriers outside the road.)

2. Time.

(28) 期以一日也, 及之则生, 不及则死。《鲁问》

qī yǐ yī rì yě, jí zhī zé shēng, bù jí zé sǐ 。

limit by one day Mod, reach them then live, Neg reach then die.

(If you can reach where they are within one day, they will survive, or they will die.)

(29) 自古及今未有能行之者也。《兼爱中》

zì gǔ jí jīn wèi yǒu néng háng zhī zhě yě 。

from ancient to today Neg be can do it thing Mod.

(From ancient times to today, there is no one who can do it.)

3. Mode.

(30) 以兼相爱、交相利之法易之。《兼爱中》

yǐ jiān xiàng ài 、 jiāo xiàng lì zhī fǎ yì zhī 。

with concurrently mutually love, associatively mutually benefit method change it.

(Change it with the method of universal love and mutual benefit.)

(31) 客攻以遂,《备城门》

kè gōng yǐ duí.

enemy attack by group.

(The enemy attack in groups.)

4. Tool.

(32) 君子不镜於水, 而镜於人。《非攻中》

jūn zǐ bù jìng yú shuǐ, ér jìng yú rén.

gentleman Neg mirror on water, but mirror on people.

(A gentleman does not take water as a mirror but takes a person as a mirror.)

(33) 饭於土塯, 啜於土形, 斗以酌。《节用中》

fàn yú tǔ liù, chuò yú tǔ xíng, dòu yǐ zhuó 。

eat with earthen bowel, sip with earthen cup, spoon with drink.

(They eat with earthen bowels, sip with earthen cups, and drink with wooden spoons.)

5. Accordance.

(34) 以德就列, 以官服事, 以劳殿赏。《尚贤上》

yǐ dé jiù liè, yǐ guān fú shì, yǐ láo diàn shǎng。

by virtue take position, by position undertake mission, by accomplishment determine emolument.

(A man's position was decided by his virtue, his missions by his position and his emolument by his accomplishment.)

(35) 自此观之, 乐非所以治天下也。《三辩》

zì cǐ guān zhī, lè fēi suǒyǐ zhì tiān xià yě.

from this see it, music Neg way govern world Mod.

(From this point of view, music is not the right method to govern a country.)

6. Material.

(36) 用 斲若松为穴户。《备穴》

yòng zǐ ruò sōng wéi xué hù.

with catalpa and pine make cave door.

(Build the caves' door with the timber of catalpa and pine.)

(37) 为颉皋, 必以坚材为夫。《备穴》

wéi jié gāo, bì yǐ jiān cái wéi fū.

make Jiegao, must with strong material make shaft.

(To fabricate Jiegao, you must make the shaft with strong materials.)

7. Starting point.

(38) 诸行赏罚及有治者, 必出於王公。《号令》

zhū háng shǎng fá jí yǒu zhì zhě, bì chū yú wánggōng.

all do reward punishment and make order Nom, must issue from governor.

(All rewards, punishments and orders must be issued by the governor.)

(39) 然则义何从出?《天志中》

ránzé yì hé cóng chū ?

then righteousness where from come?

(Then, where does the righteousness come from?).

8. Involvement.

(40) 故与人谋事, 先人得之; 与人举事, 先人成之。《尚同下》

gù yǔ rén móu shì, xiān rén dé zhī; yǔ rén jǔ shì, xiān rén chéng zhī.

therefore with others plan things, before others understand them; with others deal things, before others accomplish them.

(Therefore, when planning things with others, they will get it earlier than others; when dealing things with others, they will accomplish them earlier than others.)

(41) 上不利乎天, 中不利乎鬼, 下不利乎人。《天志中》

shàng bù lì hū tiān, zhōng bù lì hū guǐ, xià bù lì hū rén.

above Neg benefit to Heaven, middle Neg benefit to ghost, below Neg benefit to people.

(It isn't beneficial to Heaven above, to ghosts and spirits in the middle realm, and to the people below.)

9. Fields or situations.

(42) 况又有贤良之士厚乎德行, 辩乎言谈, 博乎道术者乎。《尚贤上》

kuàng yòu yǒu xián liáng zhī shì hòu hū dé xíng, biàn hū yán tán, bó hū dàoshù zhě hū.

let alone also exist sage virtuous people great in virtue behavior, eloquent in speech conversation, knowledgeable in principle method thing Mod.

(Let alone there also are sage and virtuous people who have great virtue and behavior, eloquent speech and conversation, enormous knowledge in principles and methods.)

(43) 故善为君者, 劳於论人, 而佚於治官。《所染》

gù shàn wéi jūn zhě, láo yú lùn rén, ér yì yú zhì guān.

therefore good be king thing, hard-working in evaluate people, yet leisurely in manage officials.

(Therefore, those who are good at being a king are hard-working in evaluating people, yet leisurely in managing officials.)

10. Role.[2]

(44) 无巧工不巧工, 皆以此五者为法。《法仪》

wú qiǎo gōng bù qiǎo gōng, jiē yǐ cǐ wǔ zhě wéi fǎ.

whether skillful worker Neg skillful worker, all with these five things as standard.

(Whether the worker is skillful or not, he will use these five items as standards.)

(45) 岂不以孔子为天子哉?《公孟》

qǐ bù yǐ kǒng zǐ wéi tiān zǐ zāi ?

Mod Neg with Confucius be the son of heaven Mod.

(Does that mean Confucius would be regarded as the son of Heaven?).

11. Comparison.

(46) 方今之时之以正长, 则本与古者异矣。《尚同中》

---

[2] Almost all Yi(以)-object structures expressing roles are "Yi(以)…Wei(为)" structures or "Yi(以)…Yi(以)Wei(为)" structures, whose meaning is "take… as…".

fāng jīn zhī shí zhī yǐ zhèngzhǎng, zé běn yǔ gǔ zhě yì yǐ。《shàng tóng zhōng 》
at present time elect governor, fundamentally from ancient Nom different.
(The governors at present are totally different from those in ancient times.)

(47) 非夫子, 则吾终身不知孔某之与白公同也。《非儒下》
fēi fū zǐ, zé wú zhōngshēn bù zhī kǒng mǒu zhī yǔ bái gōng tóng yě。《fēi rú xià 》
Neg you, then I all one's life Neg know Confucius with Bai Duke same Mod.
(But for you, I wouldn't know Confucius is just the same as Duke Bai throughout my life.)

12. Agent.

(48) 故国残身死, 为天下僇。《所染》
gù guó cán shēn sǐ, wéi tiān xià liáo。《suǒ rǎn 》
therefore country perish body die by world kill.
(Therefore, his country perished, and he was killed by people of the world.)

(49) 齐桓染於管仲、鲍叔, 晋文染於舅犯、高偃。《所染》
qí huán rǎn yú guǎnzhòng 、 bàoshū, jìn wén rǎn yú jiùfàn 、 gāoyǎn。《suǒ rǎn 》
Qi Huan dye by Guan Zhong and Bao Shu, Jin Wen dye by Jiu Fan and Gao Yan.
(Qi Huan was influenced by Guan Zhong and Bao Shu, Jin Wen was influenced by Jiu Fan and Gao Yan.)

13. Patient.

(50) 明乎顺天之意。《天志中》
míng hū shùn tiān zhī yì。《tiān zhì zhōng》
understand about follow Heaven's will.
(He understands that he should follow Heaven's will.)

(51) 盖尝尚观於圣王之事?《非命上》
hé cháng shàng guān yú shèng wáng zhī shì ?
why not try up examine at sage king's deed.
(Why not try examining this belief according to the deeds of sage kings?).

14. Reason.

(52) 不为大国侮小国, 不为众庶侮鳏寡。《兼爱中》
bù wéi dà guó wǔ xiǎo guó, bù wéi zhòng shù wǔ guān guǎ。
Neg because big country bully small country, Neg because many many bully widower widow.
(King Wen of Zhou did not bully small countries because of Zhou's great strength, did not bully the few because of Zhou's richness.)

(53) 天有邑人, 何用弗爱也?《天志上》
tiān yǒu yì rén, hé yòng fú ài yě ?
Heaven possess city people, what because Neg love Mod.
(Heaven possesses all people in the world, so how can he not love people?).

15. Purpose or result.

(54) 使从事乎一同天下之义。《尚同中》

shǐ cóng shì hū yī tóng tiān xià zhī yì.

make do in unify same world's righteousness.

(Make them work on unifying diverse views in the world.)

(55) 单财劳力毕归之於无用也。《辞过》

dān cái láo lì bì guī zhī yú wú yòng yě.

squander money waste manpower all concludes them with Neg use.

(Squandered money and wasted manpower are all finally useless.)

In terms of the semantic features of preposition-object structures, the number of preposition-object structures expressing space ranks first, with a total of 252 examples, of which 234 are postpositive; the number of preposition-object structures expressing involvement takes second place, with a total of 192 examples, of which 139 are postpositive; preposition-object structures expressing accordance has 164 examples, of which 160 are prepositive; and preposition-object structures expressing tool has 99 examples, of which 73 are prepositive. The specific data of the semantic features of preposition-object structures and their positions are shown in the following Table 3:

Table 3. Semantic features of preposition-object structures and their positions in *Mozi*.

Positions of preposition-object structures Sematic features of preposition-object structures		Before	After	Total
Spatiotemporal	Space	18	234	252
	Time	31	24	55
Way	Mode	31	11	42
	Tool	73	26	99
	Accordance	160	4	164
	Material	5	2	7
	Starting point	19	2	21
Relation	Involvement	53	139	192
	Fields or situations	1	68	69
	Role	26	0	26
	Comparison	19	62	81
	Agent	2	22	24
	Patient	15	47	62
Cause	Reason	30	13	43
	Purpose or result	0	18	18

By analyzing the relationship between semantic features and the position of preposition-object structures, we can see that semantic features influence the position of preposition-object structures: more than 60% of the preposition-object structures in the spatiotemporal category and relation category are after the predicate components, and even more than 90% of the preposition-object structures expressing place, agent, field or situation are after the predicate components. More than 60% of the preposition-object structures in the way category appear before the predicate components, and the prepositive preposition-object structures expressing accordance are more than 90%.

Hsin-1 Hsieh [12] proposed two kinds of principles for the combination and arrangement of language symbols—the iconic principles and the abstract principles". In the former, the combination and arrangement reflect the real situation, while the latter is not. And the two principles often compete with each other in one language. From the perspective of the positional relationship between the preposition-object structures and the predicate component, the abstract principles are more dominant in *Mozi*—preposition-object structures expressing time, field or situation, comparison and involvement are more likely to be after the predicate components, which is obviously not in accordance with the iconic principles.

4 The Relationship Between the Characteristics of Predicate Components and the Position of Preposition-Object Structures

4.1 Relationship Between Grammatical Features of Predicate Components and Preposition-Object Structures' Position

The grammatical structures of the predicate components modified by the preposition-object structures in *Mozi* are words and phrases; the words include monosyllabic words and polysyllabic words, and the phrases include verb-object phrases, modifier-head phrases, juxtaposition phrases, serial verb phrases, verb-complement phrases, etc.

1. Monosyllabic words.

(56) 怨结於民心。《修身》

yuàn jié yú mín xīn。

resentment form in people heart.

(Resentment is rooted in the hearts of the people.)

2. Polysyllabic words.[3]

(57) 与四邻诸侯交接。《尚贤中》

yǔ sì lín zhū hóu jiāo jiē。

with all neighbor feudal prince contact.

(Contact all the neighborhood feudal princes.)

3. Verb-object phrases.

---

[3] When determining whether a predicate component is a polysyllabic word, we also refers to Guirong Wang, Gaoqi Rao, and Endong Xun(2019).

(58) 百工为方以矩, 为圆以规, 直以绳, 正以县。《法仪》

bǎigōng wéi fāng yǐ jǔ, wéi yuán yǐ guī, zhí yǐ shéng, zhèng yǐ xiàn 。

Craftsmen draw square with square, draw circle with compasses, straight with line, perpendicular with pendulum.

(Craftsmen draw squares with a square and draw circles with a pair of compasses, draw straight lines with the carpenter's line and find the perpendicular by a pendulum.)[4]

4. Modifier-head phrase.

(59) 傅说被褐带索, 庸筑乎傅岩。《尚贤中》

fùyuè pī hè dài suǒ, yōng zhù hū fùyán.

Fu Yue wear coarse robe take rope, servant build at Fu Yan.

(Fu Yue once wore a coarse robe with ropes and worked as a servant to build the walls of Fu Yan.)

When Wu Ding discovered him, he promoted him and.

5. Parallel structure.

(60) 与之戮力同心。《尚贤中》

yǔ zhī lù lì tóng xīn.

with them join force one heart with them.

(Join forces and think in one mind with them.)

6. Serial verb phrase.

(61) 因素出兵施伏。《备梯》

yīn sù chū bīng shī fú 。

as normal dispatch troop make ambush.

(Dispatch troops and make ambushes as normal.)

7. Verb-complement phrases.

(62) 杂亓闲以镌、剑。《备梯》

zá qí jiān yǐ juān 、 jiàn 。《bèi tī 》

arrange them among with chopper sword.

(Arrange choppers and swords among them.)

We sum up the data of predicate components with different grammatical features and positions of preposition-object structures as follows (Table 4):

The table above shows that preposition-object structures in *Mozi* tend to appear after predicate components even though the grammatical features of predicate components are different. However, the verb-object structure is an exception with more prepositive preposition-object structures. We find 265 cases of 486 prepositive preposition-object structures that go together with verb-object phrases, accounting for 54.5%. One possible reason is that the structure of the verb-object phrases is relatively complex, and with the

---

[4] In (71), the verb "为" (draw) is omitted in "直以绳" (straight with line) and "正以县" (perpendicular with pendulum).

Table 4. Data of predicate components with different grammatical features and positions of preposition-object structures in *Mozi*.

Positions of preposition-object structures Grammatical features of predicate components		Before	After	Total
Word	Monosyllabic words	121	387	508
	(monosyllabic)[5]	0	3	3
	Disyllabic words	1	7	8
Phrase	Verb-object	305	200	505
	(verb-)object	0	2	2
	(verb-object)	0	1	1
	Modifier-head	26	57	83
	Juxtapose	8	15	23
	Serial verb	5	0	5
	Supplement	15	2	17

object in position after the verb, the preposition-object structure is compelled to take the position before the predicate component to make the sentence structure in balance, lest there are bulky components after the verb.

4.2 Relationship Between the Number of Predicate Components' Syllables and the Positions of Preposition-Object Structures

Analyzing the number of syllables of predicate components modified by preposition-object structures in *Mozi*, we find that the number of predicate components' syllables ranges widely, from 1 to 16. The following Table 5 displays the data clearly:

When the preposition-object structures are prepositive, the most common number of syllables of predicate components is 2, accounting for 42.4% of all prepositive cases; when the preposition-object structures are postpositive, the most common number of syllables of predicate components is 1, accounting for 57.3% of all postpositive cases. This difference is related to the prosodic characteristics of the Chinese language. Chinese often consists of 2 syllables to form a closer rhythm unit. When the predicate component is 1 syllable, the monosyllabic predicate component can be combined with the preposition to form a foot. At the same time, because the meaning of the preposition is relatively weak, this phonetic rhythm will not interfere with the semantic level, so the monosyllabic predicate component and the postpositive preposition-object structure form a common combination.

---

[5] In this table, parentheses indicate omission, (monosyllabic word) "means the monosyllabic word is omitted", (verb) object "means that the verb is omitted in verb-object phrases", and (verb object) "indicates the omission of verb-object phrases".

Table 5. Data on the number of predicate component syllables and the positions of preposition-object structures.

Positions of preposition-object structures Number of predicate components' syllables	Before	After	Total
0	2	3	0
1	120	386	1
2	206	189	2
3	55	53	3
4	21	21	4
5	20	12	5
6	20	7	6
7	7	1	7
8	6	0	8
9	6	0	9
10	2	0	10
11	2	2	11
12	3	0	12
13	2	0	13
16	2	0	16

5 Summary

In regard to a single preposition, the prepositions that appear only after the predicate components and the prepositions that can appear before and after the predicate components in *Mozi* and *Zuozhuan* have little difference, while the seven prepositions that appear only before the predicate components in *Mozi* have a small number of postpositive usages in *Zuozhuan*, such as:[6]

(63) 出因其资, 入用其宠, 饥食其粟。《僖公十五年》

chū yīn qí zī, rù yòng qí chǒng, jī shí qí sù 。《xī gōng shí wǔ nián 》

out by his patronage, in by his favor, hungry eat his millet.

(When I go out, I rely on his money. When I am in the country, I was supported by his favor. When I am hungry, I eat his food.)

(64) 立武由己,非由人也。《成公六年》

lì wǔ yóu jǐ, fēi yóu rén yě 。

establish military because oneself, Neg because others.

---

[6] See the data of *Zuozhuan*. Wang H.B.: A study on prepositions in *Chunqiu Zuozhuan*. Doctor, Fudan University (2003).

(Military achievements should be based on what you have done righteously rather than by others' inducement.)

According to Wang (2003), in general, 2366 preposition-object structures in *Zuozhuan* appear before the VP, accounting for approximately 33%, and 4799 preposition-object structures appear after the VP, accounting for approximately 67%. However, in *Mozi*, the proportion of the preposition-object structures has decreased to 58.1%, and the proportion of the preposition-object structures has increased, which may indicate that the Chinese expression has changed from the "abstract principles" to the "iconic principles".

Acknowledgments. This research is sponsored by the National Social Science Fund of China (No. 20BYY137).

References

1. Wang, L., Gao, H.S.: Zhonghua Book Company, Beijing (2015). (in Chinese)
2. He, L.S.: A comparison of the positions of preposition-object structures in Zuozhuan and Shiji. Stud. Lang. Linguist. **1**, 57–65 (1985). (in Chinese)
3. He L.S.: Hanyu Yufa Shi Duandai Zhuanshu Bijiao Yanjiu. Henan University Press, ZhengZhou (2007). (inChinese)
4. Jiang, S.Y.: Chouxiang Yuanze he Linmo Yuanze Zai Hanyu Yufa Shi Zhong De Titian. Res. Ancient Chinese Lang. **4**, 2–5 (1999). (in Chinese)
5. Zhang, C.: Historical Evolution of the Word-Order of Prepositional Phrases in Chinese. Beijing Language and Culture University Press, Beijing (2002). (in Chinese)
6. Wang, H.B.: A Study on Prepositions in Chunqiu Zuozhuan. Doctor, Fudan University, Shanghai (2003). (in Chinese)
7. Liu, X.J.: Study on Prepositions in Mencius. Master, Heilongjiang University, Harbin (2012). (in Chinese)
8. Gao, Y.: Research on Prepositions in Mozi. Master, Northeast Normal University, Changchun (2012). (in Chinese)
9. Zhang, C.: The study of exceptions in position of prepositional phrases in archaic Chinese. Stud. Lang. Linguist. **2**, 63–69 (2000). (in Chinese)
10. Ma, L.L.: A Study of Chinese Preposition "Yu"(于) and "Yu"(於) during pre-Qin Period. Master, Northeast Normal University, Changchun (2014). (in Chinese)
11. Zhang, J.: The Study of Special Word-order in pre-Qin Period Chinese by the Focus Theory. Master, Yunnan University, Kunming (2015). (in Chinese)
12. Hsin-1 Hsieh: Time and Imagery in Chinese (I). Foreign Linguist. **4**, 27–32 (1991). (in Chinese)

The First Step to Resolve the Centennial Controversy Over the Adverb *Dōu*: Classification

Hua Zhong[(⊠)] [iD]

Overseas Education College of Fujian Normal University, Fuzhou, China
jtingshan@163.com

Abstract. The Chinese adverb *dōu* (都) has been controversial for nearly a hundred years. How to classify *dōu* has always been an unsolved problem, and this is also the starting point of relevant research. After reviewing the existing classification views, this article examines the minimal difference between the tenable and untenable pairs of *dōu*$_a$ and *dōu*$_b$ sentences. Through their respective common conditions for the tenable sentences, we have found their opposite semantic cores that are their distinctive features: *Dōu*$_a$ has the semantics of plural eventualities, while *dōu*$_b$ has no. *Dōu*$_b$ has the procedural pragmatic meaning, in which the speaker judges that the occurrence or existence possibility of the eventuality described by the proposition is inferior to the expectation/normal, while *dōu*$_a$ has no. Thus it has been proved that the adverb *dōu* should be divided into two. Moreover, It is the first step to resolving the centennial controversy over the Adverb *dōu*.

Keywords: To classify the adverb *dōu* · *Dōu*$_a$ & *dōu*$_b$ · Semantic cores · Distinctive features

1 Introduction: Make Clear the Starting Point and Direction in the Dispute

The Chinese adverb *dōu* has been controversial for nearly a hundred years. How to classify it has been an unsolved problem, and this is also the starting point of related researche. Therefore, the following will review the classification views in the existing literature, compare their advantages and disadvantages, explain the author's view of the dichotomy of the adverb *dōu* and from the respective common conditions of all *dōu*$_a$ sentences and all *dōu*$_b$ sentences, clarify the distinctive features of *dōu*$_a$ and *dōu*$_b$ (see Zhong [1, 2]), and clarify how to classify the adverb *dōu*. It is the first step to resolving the centennial controversy over the adverb *dōu*, which lays a solid foundation for defining the semantic functions of different categories of *dōu*.

© The Author(s), under exclusive license to Springer Nature Switzerland AG 2023
Q. Su et al. (Eds.): CLSW 2022, LNAI 13495, pp. 432–447, 2023.
https://doi.org/10.1007/978-3-031-28953-8_32

2 Review on the Existing Views of Classifying the Adverb *Dōu*

2.1 The Origins of the Existing Views of Classifying *Dōu*

In the existing literature, there are mainly *Quartation*, *Trichotomy*, *Dichotomy*, and *Univocal* on how to classify the semantic and pragmatic functions of the adverb *dōu*. In the existing literature, the first two works, which advocated the *Trichotomy* and comprehensively described their semantic and pragmatic functions, are *Xiàndài Hànyǔ Yǔfǎ Jiǎnghuà* (*Modern Chinese Grammar Speech*, after this *Speech*) edited by Ding et al. [3] and *Xiàndài Hànyǔ Xūcí Lìshì* (*Explanations of Functional Words in Modern Chinese*, from now on *Explanations*) [4], that the 1955 and 1977 language classes of the Chinese department of Peking university began to compile in the winter of 1959 and finalized it in July 1960, published in 1982.

The *Speech* [3] holds that the adverb *dōu* has three usages (this is the *Trichotomy* mentioned above): I. The totalized components, which express a scope or a totality, are always before *dōu*. II. *Lián...dōu...*means *shènzhì* (even). III. *Dōu...Le* means *yǐjīng* (already) *...Le*(Asp). After this, these three usages are called *dōu₁*, *dōu₂*, and *dōu₃*, respectively.

In the *Explanations* [4] the adverb *dōu* is also summarized into three usages: I. It totalizes the things mentioned before *dōu* that there is no exception to the following actions. II. *Dōu* indicates the tone of emphasis and can be used in different situations. A. *Dōu* is used in the subordinate clause of the compound sentences of inference to indicate the tone of emphasis while still totalizing the scope. *Dōu* means *shènzhì* (even) and is often matched with *lián* (including). B. It emphasizes a high degree and is often matched with *lián* (including). C. *Dōu...le* means *yǐjīng* (already) ... *le*(Asp) and emphasizes that the time is approaching or the situation already exists. III. *Dōu shì...* (All are...) is used to explain the reason, often with a complaining tone. From now on, these three usages are called *dōu*ₐ (*dōu₁*), *dōu*ᵦ(*dōu₂*, *dōu₃*), and *dōu*ᵧ, respectively.

Since then, the roots of the various classification views of the adverb *dōu* seem to be found in *Speech* and *Explanations*. For example, in *Modern Chinese Dictionary*, from the trial edition [5] to the 7th edition [6], the adverb *dōu* has been interpreted as four usages: I. It totalizes a component. Except for interrogative sentences, the totalized components are before *dōu*. II. *Dōu* collocating with *shì* explains the reason. III. It expresses *shènzhì* (even). IV. It expresses *yǐjīng* (already). This view of *Quartation* seems to be the addition of *dōu₁*, *dōu₂*, and *dōu₃* in *Speech* and *dōu*ᵧ in *Explanations*.

*Dōu*ᵧ is used to explain a reason and is attributed into *dōu₁* in *Eight Hundred Words of Mandarin Chinese* [7]. In addition to *Explanations* and *Modern Chinese Dictionary*, which takes *dōu*ᵧ as an independent sub-*dōu*, the academic circle usually classifies it as *dōu₁*. If there were no *dōu*ᵧ, the adverb *dōu* in *Explanations* could only be divided into *dōu*ₐ (*dōu₁*) and *dōu*ᵦ(*dōu₂*, *dōu₃*). Therefore, it is not difficult to understand that the academic circle later developed the viewpoint of *Dichotomy*. Such as Paris [8], Wang [9], Zhang [10], Xu [11], Zhong [12–14], and Zhou [15].

Later, under the influence of the minimal thought of formal linguistics, further developed the claim that *dōu*ᵦ in *Explanations* indicates the tone of emphasis while still playing the role of totalizing a scope, there is naturally the view of *Univocal* that *dōu* has only one meaning and usage of totalizing universal or a universal quantification. For example,

Nakagawa [16], Huang [17–19], Jiang [20], Dong [21], Pan [22], Yuan [23], Jiang & Pan [24], Shen [25], Wu & Mo [26], and so on.

To sum up, in the current views of classifying *dōu*, the three most influential ones are three kinds: *Trichotomy, Dichotomy,* and *Univocal,* which are reviewed and commented on respectively below.

2.2　To Review the Current Views on Classifying *Dōu*

The standard grammar works and documents, represented by *Eight Hundred Words of Mandarin Chinese* (Lü [7]), describe *dōu* as *dōu*₁, which means totalizing universal; *dōu*₂, which is equivalent to *shènzhì* (even); and *dōu*₃, which is equivalent to *yǐjīng* (already). They define the semantic and pragmatic functions of each sub-*dōu* with synonyms in Chinese analytical formulas. This description is simple, convenient, and intuitive but also relatively vague. Furthermore, it is impossible to carry out full-coverage verification operations which maintain consistency internally and are exclusive externally. Moreover, according to different collocations of words (such as *Lián...dōu...,* *Dōu...le*) and different contextual meanings of different sentence patterns, the original *dōu*ᵦ of the same sub-*dōu* is divided into *dōu*₂ and *dōu*₃, which stops at the surface of contextual usage and ignores the internal consistency of *dōu*₂ and *dōu*₃. Although widely used in teaching, these descriptions can only be an expedient measure before more rigorous and accurate definitions are produced, and a consensus is reached.

Therefore, the controversy over the classification of *dōu* is mainly between the *Dichotomy* and the *Univocal.*

In recent years, the *Univocal* theory tends to "unify the world", and its theoretical goal of pursuing the minimalist program (MP) is worth advocating. However, it is not possible to disregard chickens and ducks for the sake of simplicity. The diachronic connection between *dōu*ₐ and *dōu*ᵦ can be linked by totalizing universal or a universal/distributive quantification, which is no problem. Nevertheless, the *Univocal* takes it to define the synchronic relationship between *dōu*ₐ and *dōu*ᵦ, ignoring the opposition between them. This kind of scheme cannot avoid the distinctive oppositions between *dōu*ₐ and *dōu*ᵦ (see below for details).

Furthermore, the *Univocal* regards a universal or distributive quantification on a plural disordered set or ordered set as the consistency of *dōu*ₐ and *dōu*ᵦ, such as Jiang [20], Pan [22], and Jiang & Pan [24]. Nevertheless, they could not evade these problems: A. In a *dōu*ₐ sentence, the disordered set may be singular, such as *Nà ge pítigguǒ* (that apple) in *Tā bǎ nà ge píngguǒ dōu chī le.* B. In some sentences, even if there is a plural disordered set, such as **Tāmen liǎ dōu shāsǐ le nà tíao yú.* (*They both killed that fish), the *dōu*ₐ sentence may be untenable. C. The plural quantitative meaning of *dōu*ₐ is the objective truth of a proposition itself, rather than the pragmatic deduction meaning, which cannot be canceled. In contrast, the *dōu*ᵦ's universal or distribution quantification of an ordered set is not the objective truth of a proposition itself, which is entirely the result of a plausible inference and can be canceled (See Zhong [13, 14]). For example:

(1) Lián lǎoshī dōuᵦ dào le, nǐ hái méi dào.

Including teacher even arrived Le, you still not arrived.

Even the teacher has arrived. You haven't arrived yet.

In this sentence, the universal set implied in the clause *Lián...dōu...* is canceled by the latter clause.

When looking for the unified semantic core of the adverb *dōu*, many scholars of the *Univocal* theory find that the different sub-*dōu*s can not be covered by a universal quantification / totalizing universal, so they try various alternatives. For example, Xiang [27] regards the maximality operator as the semantic core of *dōu*. Li [28] argues that the semantics of *dōu₁* consists of two parallel components: The meaning of distribution and that of a relatively large quantity. And the semantics of *dōu₂* and *dōu₃* only consists of the meaning of a relatively large quantity. Xu [29] believes that the condition of using *dōu* in a sentence is whenever the speaker believes that a considerable degree of something has been attained. Shen [25] tried to use a universal quantification of the *Rightward Government Rule* to unify the sub-*dōu*s. Wu and Mo [26] attempted to use the universal quantification of semantics and a subjective polar quantity of pragmatics to make a consistent interpretation of the adverb *dōu*. Zhou & Wu [30] and Wu & Zhou [31] argue that the sememe shared by *dōu₁*, *dōu₂*, and *dōu₃* is an intensifier indicating 'degree.' Zhang [32] tried to uniformly account for the semantics of *dōu₁*, *dōu₂*, and *dōu₃* as a maximal quantity of events.

However, no matter what kind of *Univocal* theory is, it is impossible to ignore the opposite distinctive features between *dōu*ₐ and *dōu*ᵦ (see the following for details), so while they advocate the *Univocal*, the vast majority of them still advocate a classification view similar to the *Dichotomy*, such as Nakagawa [16], Jiang [20], Pan [22], Jiang & Pan [24], Li [28], Wu & Mo [26], Wu & Zhou [31]. Limited by space, we will not explore the ad hoc characters of the above alternatives here. The following table briefly illustrates several recent alternatives: The *Univocal* explicitly and the *Dichotomy* implicitly (Table 1).

Table 1. The semantic schemes of the adverb *dōu* in several recent *Univocal* theories

	dōu₁	*dōu₂*	*dōu₃*
Li [28]	The distribution and a relative large quantity	A relative large quantity	
Wu & Mo [26]	The universal quantification of semantics	A subjective polar quantity of pragmatics	
Wu & Zhou [31]	An explicit intensifier	An implicit intensifier	

Therefore, the *Univocal* is hard to unify the sub-*dōu*s.

Although correctly classified the adverb *dōu* as two, the existing *Dichotomy* describes *dōu*ₐ as a total/scope adverb or a universal quantifier, etc., and *dōu*ᵦ as a modal particle of subjectivity or emphasis that is also closer to the natives' intuition. The definitions of semantic and pragmatic functions of *dōu*ₐ and *dōu*ᵦ in most of the existing literature are still not rigorous and accurate enough and still unable to carry out full-coverage verifications that are internally consistent and externally exclusive. Furthermore, the worse problem is that the existing literature have not extracted the distinctive oppositions between $dōu_a$ and $dōu_b$.

Therefore, it is necessary to clarify the distinctive features between $dōu_a$ and $dōu_b$ to reach the *Dichotomy* consensus.

3   The Distinctive Features Between $Dōu_a$ and $Dōu_b$

3.1   What Semantic Features are the Distinctive Features of $Dōu_a$ and $Dōu_b$?

The descriptions of the $dōu$'s semantic features in the existing literature are very diverse. How do we extract the distinctive features of $dōu_a$ and $dōu_b$ from the various semantic features of the Adverb $dōu$? Or what kind of semantic features can become the distinctive features of $dōu_a$ and $dōu_b$?

Based on the principle of mutual verification of form and meaning, the author holds that the semantic feature associated with the common condition determining whether all $dōu_a$ or $dōu_b$ sentences are tenable is their respective semantic core. The opposite parts of their semantic cores are their distinctive features. If a condition applies only to part of $dōu_a$ or $dōu_b$ sentences, it is not the semantic core nor the distinctive feature. For example, there must be a plural NP before $dōu_a$ in some $dōu_a$ sentences, such as (2a). But it is also true that there are only singular before $dōu_a$ in others, such as (2b). And even some $dōu_a$ sentences in which there is a plural NP before $dōu_a$ are untenable, such as (2c):

(2) a. Tāmen dōu$_a$ huí jiā le | * Ta dōu$_a$ huí jiā le.

They all go home Asp |* He all go home Asp.

They all went home |* He all went home.

b. Tā bǎ nà ge píngguǒ dōu$_a$ chī le.

He BA that CL apple all eat Asp.

He ate all the apple.

c. *Xiǎo Fāng hé Xiǎo Juān, Tāmen dōu$_a$ shāsǐ le nà zhī jī.

Xiǎo Fāng and Xiǎo Juān, they both killed LE that CL chicken.

Xiǎo Fāng and Xiǎo Juān, they both killed the chicken.

Then, the condition that there must be a plural NP before $dōu_a$ only applies to some $dōu_a$ sentences. The plurality related to NP is not the semantic core, nor can it be selected as a distinctive feature. In addition, some interrogative pronouns/phrases before $dōu_a$ cannot express a question. When telling a question, they usually have to be moved after $dōu_a$, and some must be plural. For example:

(3) a.*Nǎ xiē diànyǐng nǐ dōu$_a$ kàn guo?

Which some movie you all watch Asp.

Which movies have you seen all?

→ b. Nǐ dōu$_a$ kàn guo nǎ xiē diànyǐng?

You all watch Asp which some movie.

What movies have you seen?

→ c.*Nǐ dōu$_a$ kàn guo nǎ bu diànyǐng?

You all watch Asp which CL movie.

Which movie have you seen all?

→ d. Nǐ dōu$_a$ kàn guo nǎ xiē diànyǐng?

You all watch Asp which some movie.

What movies have you seen?

The tenable condition of the interrogative *dōu*$_a$ sentence in example (3) only applies to some interrogative *dōu*$_a$ sentences (see Zhong [1]), and it cannot be selected as a distinctive feature. Similarly, those semantic features related to the non-common tenable conditions of some *dōu*$_b$ sentences cannot be selected as the distinctive features of *dōu*$_b$ (examples omitted). We should also note here that the relationship between the common tenable condition and the non-common tenable condition is the relationship between the commonality and individuality of the same things. The common tenable condition of sentences is the commonality, the semantic core, and conventionality, which will not change with the change of context. The non-common tenable conditions of sentences are individuality, different aspects of the same things, the semantic shell, temporary or partial, and variations caused by the change of context. The semantic core (commonality) lies in the semantic shell (individuality). No matter how the semantic shell changes, it will be restricted by the semantic core. And it is the presentation of the semantic core. If a non-common tenable condition of sentences (semantic shell) is misjudged as the common tenable condition (semantic core), then it is a partial generalization. For example, according to the mandatory requirement that there must be a plural NP before or after *dōu*$_a$ in some sentences, the existing literature judges *dōu*$_a$ as a scope adverb that totalizes a plural NP (see Zhong [2]).

Moreover, the author believes that after finding the semantic feature associated with the common tenable condition of all *dōu*$_a$ or *dōu*$_b$ sentences, we can finally clarify whether the adverb *dōu* should be divided into two parts or should be unified. That is to say, the common tenable conditions (semantic core) of *dōu*$_a$ and *dōu*$_b$ are different, so *dōu* is divided into two; if they are the same, the sub-*dōu*s are unified.

Then, what method can be used to find the respective semantic cores of *dōu*$_a$ and *dōu*$_b$? The author believes that Zhong's [2]) "seeking for differences comprehensively and seeking common ground in-depth" is adequate. Specifically, it is to comprehensively collect and investigate the tenable, untenable language facts and linguistic facts of *dōu*$_a$ and *dōu*$_b$ (see Shi [33], Zhong[1]) and find out the tenable and untenable minimal pairs in an all-round way. We will find their semantic core in these minimal pairs, excluding the non-common condition and finding the common condition. And what is opposite to each other is the distinctive feature.

3.2 The Semantic Core of $dōu_a$

Seeking differences in an all-around way, through a comprehensive investigation of the tenable, untenable language facts and linguistic facts of $dōu_a$, we have found the following minimal pairs of $dōu_a$ sentences.

(4) a. Tāmen dōu$_a$ huí jiā le.

They all go home Asp.

They all went home.

→ b.*Tā dōu$_a$ huí jiā le.

He all go home Asp.

He all went home.

(5) a. Nà xiē xuēshēng tā dōu$_a$ rènshí.

That some student he all know.

He knows all those students.

→ b.*Tā dōu$_a$ rènshí nà xiē xuēshēng.

He all know That some student.

He knows all those students.

(6) a. Shéi xué guo zhōngwén?

Who study Asp Chinese.

Who has studied Chinese?

→ b. Dōu$_a$ yǒu shéi xué guo zhōngwén?

All have who study Asp Chinese.

Who are all those who have studied Chinese?

→ c.*Shéi dōu$_a$ xué guo zhōngwén?

Who all study Asp Chinese.

Who are all those who have studied Chinese?

(7) a. Shéi měitiān dōu$_a$ xué zhōngwén?

Who everyday all learn Chinese.

Who learns Chinese every day?

→ b.*Shéi dōu$_a$ xué zhōngwén?

Who all learn Chinese.

Who are all those who learn Chinese?

→ c. Shéi dōu$_a$ xué zhōngwén.

Who all learn Chinese.

Everyone learns Chinese.

(8) a. Nǐ chàng nǎ shǒu gē?

You sing which CL song.

Which song do you sing?

→ b.*Nǐ dōu_a chàng nǎ shǒu gē?

You all sing which CL song.

Which song do you all sing?

→ c. Nǐ dōu_a chàng nǎ xiē gē?

You all sing which some song.

What are all those songs you sing?

(9) a.*Nǐ dōu_a chàng nǎ shǒu gē?

You all sing which CL song.

Which song do you all sing?

→ b. Nǐmen dōu_a chàng nǎ shǒu gē?

You all sing which CL song.

Which song do you all sing?

→ c. Nǐ měitiān dōu_a chàng nǎ shǒu gē?

You everyday all sing which CL song.

Which song do you sing every day?

(10) a. Tā bǎ nà jǐ ge júzi dōu_a chī le. A few oranges.

He BA that several CL orange all eat Asp.

He ate all those oranges.

→ b. Tā bǎ nà ge júzi dōu_a chī le.

He BA that CL orange all eat Asp.

He ate all the orange.

→ c. *Tā bǎ nà ge júzi dōu_a mǎi le.

He BA that CL orange all buy Asp.

He bought all the orange.

(11) a. Nà sì ge rén, tāmen dōu_a shì tóngxué.

That four CL people, they all are classmate.

Those four people, they are all classmates.

→ b. *Zhè liǎng rén, tāmen dōu_a shì tóngxué.

This two people, they all are classmate.

These two people, they are both classmates.

(12) a. Tāmen měitiān dōu_a bǎ gōngchǎng bāowéi zhe.

They everyday all BA factory surround Asp.

They surround the factory every day.

→ b. *Tāmen dōu_a bǎ gōngchǎng bāowéi zhe.

They all BA factory surround Asp.

They surround the factory.

(13) a. *Tā bǎ nà lì mǐfàn dōu$_a$ chī le.

He BA that CL rice all eat Asp.

He ate all that grain of rice.

→ b. Tā bǎ nà wǎn mǐfàn dōu$_a$ chī le.

He BA that CL rice all eat Asp.

He ate that bowl of rice.

→ c. Zhè zhī mǎyǐ bǎ nà lì mǐfàn dōu$_a$ chī le.

This CL ant BA that CL rice all eat Asp.

This ant ate all that grain of rice.

(14) a. Tāmen (*dōu$_a$) chī diào le nà ge júzi.

They (*all) eat finish Asp that CL orange.

They (*all) finished eating the orange.

→ b. Tāmen (dōu$_a$) chī diào le yí ge júzi.

They (all) eat finish Asp one CL orange.

They (all) finished eating an orange.

(15) a. Hěnduō / yídàbàn lǎoshī dōu$_a$ lái le.

Many / more-than-half teacher all come Asp.

Many / More than half of the teachers all came.

→ b. *Yíbàn lǎoshī dōu$_a$ lái le.

Half teacher all come Asp.

Half of the teachers all came.

→ c. Zhè yíbàn lǎoshī dōu$_a$ lái le.

This half teacher all come Asp.

This half of the teachers all came.

(16) a. *Yí xiē / shǎoshù / jǐ ge lǎoshī dōu$_a$ lái le.

One some / few /several CL teacher all come Asp.

Some / Few /Several teachers all came.

→ b. Zhè xiē / Zhè shǎoshù / Zhè jǐ ge lǎoshī dōu$_a$ lái le.

This some /the few / this several CL teacher all come Asp.

These / The few /These several teachers all came.

(17) a. *Hěn shǎo / Jí shǎoshù lǎoshī dōu$_a$ lái le.

Very few/ Tiny minority teachers all come Asp.

Very few/ Tiny minority teachers all came.

→ b. Zhè hěn shǎo / Zhè jí shǎoshù (de) lǎoshī dōu$_a$ lái le.

This very few/ This tiny minority (DE) teachers all come Asp.

The very few/ The tiny minority teachers all came.

Seeking common ground in-depth, among these minimal pairs, (4) (8) (9) (10) (11) indicate that the condition that there must be a plural NP before $dōu_a$ is a non-common tenable condition; (6)–(9) suggest that the requirement that interrogative pronouns/phrases (such as "who, what, which") can't be placed before $dōu_a$. The interrogative pronouns/phrases after $dōu_a$ are required to be plural is also a non-common tenable condition, etc. (There are other non-common tenable conditions, which are limited by space and not stated one by one.). These conditions, which only apply to some $dōu_a$ sentences, are excluded; finally, it is found that in (10)–(14), the tenable requirement which requires that the sentence must be plural eventualities applies to all $dōu_a$ sentences, which is the common tenable condition of all $dōu_a$ sentences. That is to say, the semantic core of $dōu_a$ expresses the plural semantics of eventualities. This condition restricts other non-common tenable conditions (limited to space and not expanded in detail. See Zhong [1, 2, 13, 14]).

3.3 The Semantic Core of $dōu_b$

Similarly, through a comprehensive investigation of the tenable, untenable language facts and linguistic facts of $dōu_b$, we have found the following minimal pairs of $dōu_b$ sentences.

(18) a. Tā (bù) xiǎng tǎohǎo xiàshǔ.

He (not) want please subordinate

He (does not) want to please his subordinates

b. Tā (bù) xiǎng tǎohǎo tóngshì.

He (not) want please colleague

He (does not) want to please his colleagues.

c. Tā (bù) xiǎng tǎohǎo lǐngdǎo.

He (not) want please leader

He (does not) want to please his leader.

d. Tā (bù) xiǎng tǎohǎo shàngdì.

He (not) want please God

He (does not) want to please God.

(19) a. Tā lián xiàshǔ dōu_b xiǎng tǎohǎo.

He including subordinate even want please

He even wants to please his subordinates.

b. Tā lián tóngshì dōu_b xiǎng tǎohǎo.

He including colleague even want please

He even wants to please his colleagues.

c. *?Tā lián lǐngdǎo dōu_b xiǎng tǎohǎo.

He including leader even want please

He even wants to please his leader.

d. *?Tā lián shàngdì dōu_b xiǎng tǎohǎo.

He including God even want please

He even wants to please God.

(20) a. *Tā lián xiàshǔ dōu_b bù xiǎng tǎohǎo.

He including subordinate even not want please

He even does not want to please his subordinates.

b. *Tā lián tóngshì dōu_b bù xiǎng tǎohǎo.

He including colleague even not want please

He even does not want to please his colleagues.

c. Tā lián lǐngdǎo dōu_b bù xiǎng tǎohǎo.

He including leader even not want please

He even does not want to please his leader.

d. Tā lián shàngdì dōu_b bù xiǎng tǎohǎo.

He including God even not want please

He even does not want to please God.

(21) a. *Tā lián māo dōu_b bù pà, hái pà lǎohǔ ma?

He including cat even not afraid, still afraid tiger Mod

He's not even afraid of cats. Is he still afraid of tigers?

b. Tā lián lǎohǔ dōu_b bù pà, hái pà māo ma?

He including tiger even not afraid, still afraid cat Mod

He's not even afraid of tigers. Is he still afraid of cats?

(22) a. Tā lián māo dōu_b pà, hái bù pà lǎohǔ ma?

He including cat even afraid, yet not afraid tiger Mod

He's even afraid of cats. Is he not afraid of tigers yet?

b. *Tā lián lǎohǔ dōu_b pà, hái bù pà māo ma?

He including tiger even afraid, yet not afraid cat Mod

He's even afraid of tigers. Is he not afraid of cats yet?

(23) a. *Dōu_b shísān suì le, Zěnme hái bù jiéhūn ne?

Already thirteen age Asp, why still not marry Mod

He is already thirteen years old, why doesn't he get married yet?

b. Dōu_b sānshí suì le, Zěnme hái bù jiéhūn ne?

Already thirty age Asp, why still not marry Mod

He is already thirty years old, why doesn't he get married yet?

(24) a. Dōu_b báitiān le, Zěnme hái yǒu yuèliang ne?

Already daytime Asp, why still have moon Mod.

It's already daytime. How can there be a moon?

b. *Dōu_b yèwǎn le, Zěnme hái yǒu yuèliang ne?

Already night Asp, why still have moon Mod

It's already night. How can there be a moon?

(25) a. [bādiǎn shàngbān]Xiànzài dōu_b jiǔdiǎn le, tā hái méi lái.

[Eight o'clock work] Now already nine-o'clock Asp, he still not come

[To work at eight o'clock] It's nine o'clock now, and he hasn't come yet.

b. *[bādiǎn shàngbān]Xiànzài dōu_b qīdiǎn le, tā hái méi lái.

[Eight o'clock work] Now already seven-o'clock Asp, he still not come

[To work at eight o'clock] It's seven o'clock now, and he hasn't come yet.

(26) a. *Yíngyíng bǐ tā māma dōu_b xiǎo

Yíngyíng than her mother even young

Yíngyíng is even younger than her mother.

b. *Yíngyíing bǐ tā māma dōu_b dà

Yíngyíng than her mother even older

Yíngyíng is even older than her mother.

c. Yíngyíing bǐ tā māma dōu_b piàoliang

Yíngyíng than her mother even pretty

Yíngyíng is even prettier than her mother.

(27) a. *Tā bǎ yīfu dōu_b lín shī le, kěshì zhè yǔ hěn dà.

He BA clothes even shower wet Asp, but this rain very heavy

He got his clothes wet, but it rained very heavily.

b. Tā bǎ yīfu dōu_b lín shī le, kěshì zhè yǔ hěn xiǎo.

He BA clothes even shower wet Asp, but this rain very light

He got his clothes wet, but it rained very lightly.

(28) a. Tā dōu_b sānshí suì le, kěyǐ xiǎngshòu rénshēng le.

He already thirty age Asp, can enjoy life Asp.

He is already thirty years old and can enjoy life.

b. Tā dōu_b sānshí suì le, yào nǔlì gōngzuò le.

He already thirty age Asp, has-to hard work Asp.

He is already thirty years old, so he has to work hard.

(29) Jiùjiu shì zhōngguó tōng, bǐ shàngdì dōu_b gèng liǎojiě zhōngguórén.

Uncle is Chinese expert, than God even more know Chinese

My uncle is a Chinese expert and knows Chinese better than God

(30) Shíyóu gōngrén yì shēng hǒu, dìqiú dōu_b děi dǒu sān dǒu.

Oil workers one CL roar, earth even must tremble three CL

When the oil workers roar once, the earth trembles three times.

Seeking common ground in-depth, among these minimal difference pairs, we can find that the common tenable condition of the dou_b sentences is that the possibility of the eventualities is inferior to the expectation/normal (see Zhong [2, 12]). Such as (19)–(30).

Therefore, the semantic core of dou_b can be regarded as a counter-expected discourse marker (see Zhong [12]). The conventional implicature of dou_b indicates that a speaker judges the eventuality described by a proposition, and he believes that the possibility of the eventuality is inferior to the expectation/normal. It is a non-truth procedural pragmatic meaning that carries interpersonal and textual functions in discourse.

3.4   The Opposition Between the Semantic Cores of dou_a and dou_b

The above investigation shows that the semantic cores of dou_a and dou_b are obviously different. By comparing the two, it is easy to find their distinctive oppositions. Dou_a has the semantics of plural eventualities, while dou_b has no; Dou_b has a pragmatic procedural meaning that a speaker judges on the eventuality described by a proposition, and he believes that the possibility of the eventuality is inferior to the expectation/normal, while dou_a does not. For example:

(31) a. Tāmen dōu$_a$ huí jiā le.

They all go home Asp

They all went home.

→ b.*Tā dōu$_a$ huí jiā le.

He all go home Asp.

He all went home.

(32) a. (Lián) Tāmen dōu$_b$ huí jiā le.

(Including) They even go home Asp

Even they went home.

→ b. (Lián) Tā dōu$_b$ huí jiā le.

(Including) He even go home Asp.

Even he went home.

(33) a. *Tāmen dōu$_a$ chī diào le nà ge júzi.

They all eat finish Asp that CL orange.

They all finished eating the orange.

→ b. Tāmen dōu$_a$ chī diào le yí ge júzi.

They all eat finish Asp one CL orange.

They all finished eating an orange.

(34) a. (Lián) Tāmen dōu$_b$ chī diào le nà ge júzi.

(Including) They even eat finish Asp that CL orange.

Even they finished eating the orange.

→ b. (Lián) Tāmen dōu$_b$ chī dī diào le yí ge júzi.

(Including) They even eat finish Asp one CL orange.

Even they finished eating an orange.

(35) a. Báitiān dōu$_a$ méiyǒu yuèliàng.

Daytime all have-not moon

There is no moon in all daytimes.

b. * (Lián) Báitiān dōu$_b$ méiyǒu yuèliàng.

(Including) Daytime even have-not moon

There is no moon even during the day.

c. (Lián) Yèwǎn dōu$_b$ méiyǒu yuèliàng.

(Including) Night even have-not moon

There is no moon even during the night.

(36) a. Tā wǎnshàng dōu$_a$ shuìjiào.

He night all sleep

He sleeps all nights.

b. Tā (lián) Báitiān dōu$_b$ shuìjiào.

He (including) Daytime even sleep

He even sleeps during the day.

c. * Tā (lián) wǎnshàng dōu$_b$ shuìjiào.

He (including) night even sleep

He even sleeps during the night.

The opposition between the semantic cores of $dōu_a$ and $dōu_b$ has been evident, and it is indisputable that the adverb $dōu$ has to be divided into two (See also Zhong [34]).

Acknowledgments. The study is supported by the Social Science Foundation of Fujian Province (FJ2020B130).

References

1. Zhong, H.: The distributive-index function of interrogative pronouns in $dōu$ sentences. Lang. Teach. Linguist. Stud. **4**, 79–90 (2021). in Chinese
2. Zhong, H.: Seeking differences, and seeking common ground deeply: methodological thinking of the case study of the adverb Dou. Linguist. Sci. **4**, 383–401 (2021). in Chinese
3. Ding, S., et al: Lectures on Modern Chinese Grammar. The Commercial Press, Beijing (1980[1961]). (In Chinese)
4. The 1955, 1977 L. CL. of Chin. D. of Pek. Un.: *Explanations of Functional Words in Mod-ern Chinese*. The commercial press, Beijing (1982). (in Chinese)
5. Dictionary Editing Room, Institute of Linguistics, Chinese Academy of Sciences. *Modern Chinese Dictionary* (Trial edn.). The commercial press, Beijing (1973). (in Chinese)
6. Dictionary Editing Room, Institute of Linguistics, Chinese Academy of Social Sciences. *Modern Chinese Dictionary* (7th edn.). The commercial press, Beijing (2016). (in Chinese)

7. Lü, S.X., et al.: Eight Hundred Words of Modern Chinese. The Commercial Press, Beijing (1980). in Chinese

8. Paris, M. C.: *Lián...Yě/Dōu* in Mandarin Chinese, *Ling. Abro.* 3, 50–55, 11.(1981[1979]). [In Chinese]

9. Wang, H.: Analysis of grammar meaning of adverb *Dōu*. Chin. Learn. **6**, 55–60 (1999). in Chinese

10. Zhang, Y.S.: Grammaticalization and subjectivization of adverbs *Dōu*. J. Xuzhou Norm. Univ. **3**, 56–62 (2005). in Chinese

11. Xu, L.J.: Similarities and differences of Shanghai Dialect Chai and Mandarin *Dōu*. Dial. **2**, 97–102 (2007). in Chinese

12. Zhong, H.: 都$_b$[*Dou*$_b$(*Dou*$_2$, *Dou*$_3$)] as a counter-expectation discourse-marker: On the pragmatic functions of *dou*$_b$ from the perspective of discourse analysis. Chin. Lex. Sem. **9332**, 392–407 (2015)

13. Zhong, H.: On the quantification of events in *dou*$_a$ construction. Chin. Lex. Sem. **10709**, 41–60 (2018)

14. Zhong, H.: The conventional implicature of *dōu*$_b$ (*dōu*$_2$, *dōu*$_3$): on semantics of *dōu*$_b$ from the perspective of discourse analysis. Chin. Lex. Sem. **11173**, 44–60 (2018)

15. Zhou, R.: The Syntactic, Semantic and Pragmatic Study ofDou. Academia Press, Shanghai (2019). (in Chinese)

16. Nakagawa, C.: Contextual analysis and analysis of tone of Chinese Adverbs *Dōu*. Chin.Transl. Jpn. Res. Pap. Anthol. Mod. Chin. (In Chinese) Translated by Xun Chunsheng, Yusunori Ohkochi, Shi Guangheng. Beijing, Beijing Languages College Press, pp. 309–322 (1993[1985])

17. Huang, S.Z.: Dou as an existential quantifier. In: Proceedings of the 6th North American Conference on Chinese Linguistics 11,114–125 (1994)

18. Huang, S.Z.: Quantification and predication in Mandarin Chinese: A case study of dou. University of Pennsylvania, Philadelphia, PhD. dissertation (1996)

19. Huang, S.Z.: Universal Quantification with Skolemization as Evidence in Chinese and English. The Edwin Mellen Press, New York (2005)

20. Jiang,Y.: Pragmatic reasoning and syntactic/semantic characterization of *Dōu*. Mod. Fore. Lang. **1**, 11–24 (1998). (in Chinese)

21. Dong, X.F.: Definite objects and relevant questions of *Dōu*. Stud. of the Chin. Lang. **6**, 495–507 (2002). in Chinese

22. Pan, H.H.: Focus Point and Trisection Structure and Semantic Interpretation of Chinese *Dōu*, *Grammar Study and Exploration* (XIII). The Commercial Press, Beijing (2006). in Chinese

23. Yuan, Y.: The information structure of the *Lian* construction in Mandarin. Linguist. Sci. **2**, 14–28 (2006). in Chinese

24. Jiang, J.Z., Haihua, P.: How many *Dōu*s do we really need? Stud. Chin. Lang. **1**, 38–50(2013). (in Chinese)

25. Shen, J.X.: Leftward or rightward? The quantifying of *Dōu*. Stud. Chin. Lang. **1**, (2015). (in Chinese)

26. Wu, P., Mo, C.: An interpretation of *Dōu* from perspective of semantics and pragmatics. Chin. Teach.**1**, 29–41 (2016). (in Chinese)

27. Xiang, M.: Plurality, maximality and scalar inferences: a case study of Mandarin *dou*. J. East Asian Ling. **17**, 227–245 (2008)

28. Li, W.S.: On the semantic complexity of *Dōu* in Mandarin: a partially unified account. Chin. Teach. **3**, 319–330 (2013). in Chinese

29. Xu, L.J.: Is *Dōu* a universal quantifier? Stud. Chin. Lang. **6**, 498–507 (2014). in Chinese

30. Zhou, Y., Wu, Y.C.: The intensification function of Dou in mandarin Chinese: an in teractive perspective. Fore. Lang. and Their Teach. **6**, 26–35 (2018). in Chinese

31. Wu, Y.C., Zhou, Y.: Towards a unified account of Dou in Mandarin Chinese: implicit and explicit domains. Cont. Lin. **2**, 159–180 (2019). in Chinese
32. Zhang, J.J.: A unified account on the semantics of Dou: maximal quantity of event. Lang. Teach. Linguist. Stud. **1**, 55–66 (2021). in Chinese
33. Shi, C.H.: Language fact and linguistic fact. Chin. Ling. **4**, 2–17 (2010). in Chinese
34. Zhong, H.: On the differences between *Dōua* and *Dōub*. In: Dong, M., Gu, Y., Hong, J.-F. (eds.) Chinese Lexical Semantics: 22nd Workshop, CLSW 2021, Nanjing, China, May 15–16, 2021, Revised Selected Papers, Part I, pp. 3–21. Springer International Publishing, Cham (2022). https://doi.org/10.1007/978-3-031-06703-7_1

The Syntactic Features of Chinese Verbs of Saluting

Shan Wang[1,2(✉)]

[1] Department of Chinese Language and Literature, Faculty of Arts and Humanities,
University of Macau, Macau SAR, China
shanwang@um.edu.mo
[2] Institute of Collaborative Innovation, University of Macau, Macau SAR, China

Abstract. Verbs involving the body can reflect the way of human cognition. A type of such body verbs which describes the whole body movements is less examined. This study has selected a typical category, namely, verbs of saluting, to examine their syntactic features. Single sentences have been extracted and filtered from several Chinese corpora and annotated based on dependency grammar. This study then analyzed their syntactic features from the aspects of syntactic dependencies and the intensity of syntactic collocations. It is found that this type of verbs often acts as heads of sentences, accounted for almost 60%. A case study of 行礼 xínglǐ 'salute' shows that its overall intensity of syntactic collocations is 1.90. This study provides a research paradigm for the research on Chinese verbs and lexicography.

Keywords: Syntactic features · Verbs · Verbs of saluting · Dependency grammar

1 Introduction

As the core of sentences, verbs carry the key syntactic and semantic information of sentences. *The Grammatical Knowledge-base of Contemporary Chinese—A Complete Specification* [1] established a part-of-speech system according to the principle of grammatical function distribution and more than 73,000 words were classified under this system. This knowledge-base displays the grammatical properties of verbs. [2] pointed out that tagging words can make the knowledge behind these words explicit in constructing various language knowledge bases such as dictionaries and grammatical bases. The corpus-based research on verbs shows that synonymous verbs differ in syntactic functions and collocations. For example, [3] found that the primary type of syntactic dependency of Chinese verbs of searching is the sentence-head relation (HED), followed by the verb-object relation (VOB) and the subject-verb relation (SBV). In contrast, the attribute-head relation (ATT) is rarely used. Some studies also analyzed the relationship between syntactic distribution and semantic information of different types of verbs [4, 5]. [6] divided the syntactic functions of verbs into principal functions, secondary functions, and local functions using the Chinese dependency tree bank based on the probabilistic

© The Author(s), under exclusive license to Springer Nature Switzerland AG 2023
Q. Su et al. (Eds.): CLSW 2022, LNAI 13495, pp. 448–463, 2023.
https://doi.org/10.1007/978-3-031-28953-8_33

valency pattern theory. [7] found that the syntactic environment of "V + P" is roughly the same as that of general verbs, but the proportions differ.

Dependency grammar focuses on the relations between words [8–10], whose advantages lie in its concise form, convenient annotation, and strong applicability. After years of development, dependency grammar has become one of the mainstream methods in natural language processing, and many relevant studies have emerged in recent years [11, 12]. Dependency grammar is suitable for Chinese information processing [13], and many achievements have been made in Chinese studies. For example, [14] proposed some statistical properties for Chinese syntactic dependency networks based on two types of Chinese treebanks. [15] investigated the syntactic functions in texts of different genres. The results showed that word classes used to fulfill certain syntactic functions in spoken Chinese and written Chinese are quite different. However, no study has used dependency grammar for the syntactic research of verbs involving the body. The human body is not only physical or psychological, but also a way of perceiving the world, which plays an essential perceptual function [16]. Various body movements form different verbs in a language [17, 18]. With the development of relevant research, the scope of verbs involving the body has also expanded from movements only performed by body parts to the actions performed by artificial tools [17–19] also discussed verbs involving the body in the book entitled *English Verb Classes and Alternations*. Current research in Chinese has examined several types of verbs. For example, according to the statistics on the diachronic evolution of Chinese frequently used verbs, existing studies have paid more attention to hand actions (such as 击 *jī* 'hit' and 打 *dǎ* 'hit'), feet actions (such as 行 *xíng* 'walk' and 走 *zǒu* 'walk'), mouth actions (such as 吃 *chī* 'eat' and 食 *shí* 'eat') [20], but less attention has been paid to saluting actions. The reason may be that verbs of saluting have strong social and communicative properties; that is, to show respect or gratitude to someone or something. [21] classified 鞠躬 *jūgōng* 'bow', 示威 *shìwēi* 'protest', and 辩护 *biànhù* 'defense' as verbs of targeting. These verbs with the semantic features of "movement", "active", and "targeting" are bivalent verbs, which take Agents and Datives. Agents act as subjects in sentences, while Datives act as adverbials with prepositions like 对 *duì* 'to' and 给 *gěi* 'to'. [21] also classified 致敬 *zhìjìng* 'pay tribute', 偏心 *piānxīn* 'show partiality', and 施暴 *shībào* 'abuse' as intransitive verbs whose Datives must be introduced by prepositions. The existing research on verbs of saluting lacks systematicness. The current study argues that verbs of saluting should generally have the meaning of saluting to someone, so this type of verbs may have similar syntactic structures. This study has selected some less discussed Chinese verbs of saluting and analyzed their syntactic features based on dependency grammar, which provides authentic examples and rich statistics for assisting Chinese lexicography and teaching Chinese as a second language.

2 Research Methodology

To find Chinese verbs of saluting, this study first referred to the classification of "verbs involving the body" in VerbNet [22]. It further referred to *A Thesaurus of Modern Chinese* (《现代汉语分类词典》) [23], *A Word Forest of Synonyms* (《同义词词林》) [24], and *Lexicon of Common Words in Contemporary Chinese* (《现代汉语常用词表》) [25]

to find out more synonyms. Finally, six verbs were selected. After determining the verbs, the next step was to use large-scale modern Chinese corpora to collect typical sentences containing these verbs and annotate their syntactic dependencies to summarize their syntactic characteristics. The corpora used in this study include Sogou Lab[1][26], BCC[2] (literature and newspapers) [27], CCL[3][28], People's Daily, Reference News, Tencent News[4], Chinese Gigaword (used via Chinese Word Sketch) [29, 30]. These corpora mainly consist of literature, newspapers, etc. Following [31] and [32], this study downloaded all the paragraphs containing verbs of saluting from these corpora and extracted single sentences that comply with standard Chinese according to the following steps. First, used the punctuation marks at the end to divide the downloaded paragraphs and deleted those without right windows. Secondly, deleted the sentences containing Chinese commas and Chinese semicolons. The purpose of this step is to exclude complex sentences to obtain a single-sentence set A. Thirdly, according to *General Rules for Punctuation*[5] (《标点符号用法》), single sentences that contain non-Chinese characters and non-Chinese punctuation marks are also deleted in the single sentence set A to obtain the single-sentence set B. Finally, conducted word segmentation and part-of-speech tagging for all single sentences in set B, leaving the single sentences (no more than 20 words) with the part-of-speech of the target words as verbs, which get a single sentence set C with 4098 sentences. 526 sentences were finally selected from the set C through equidistant sampling, as shown in Table 1.

A syntactic and semantic annotation tool [31, 32] was used for automatic tagging and manual annotation based on Language Technology Platform (LTP) [33, 34]. This study has then investigated the syntactic dependencies of verbs of saluting to summarize their syntactic features.

Table 1. The number of single sentences of Chinese verbs of saluting

Verbs	Set C	Sampling
鞠躬 *jūgōng* 'bow'	379	199
致敬 *zhìjìng* 'pay tribute'	3316	100
磕头 *kētóu* 'kowtow'	157	99
行礼 *xínglǐ* 'salute'	148	88
跪拜 *guìbài* 'kneel'	38	22
膜拜 *móbài* 'worship'	60	18

---

[1] Sogou lab: http://www.sogou.com/labs/resource/t.php.

[2] BCC: http://bcc.blcu.edu.cn.

[3] CCL: http://ccl.pku.edu.cn:8080/ccl_corpus/.

[4] People' s Daily, Reference News, Tencent News: https://github.com/liuhuanyong/ChineseDiachronicCorpus.

[5] https://people.ubuntu.com/~happyaron/l10n/GB(T) 15834–2011.html.

3 Syntactic Dependencies and the Intensity of Syntactic Collocations of Verbs of Saluting

Dependency grammar considers that a sentence is composed of relations between words. A governor and a dependent are connected: the dependent is subordinate to the governor, while the governor dominates the dependent. Sentence (1) is illustrated in Fig. 1. A dependency arc HED (the sentence-head relation) points to 知道 *zhīdào* 'know' from Root; that is, the verb 知道 *zhīdào* 'know' is syntactically subordinate to the entire sentence; another dependency arc VOB (the verb-object relation) points to 行礼 *xínglǐ* 'salute' from 知道 *zhīdào* 'know'; that is, 行礼 *xínglǐ* 'salute' is subordinate to 知道 *zhīdào* 'know', meaning that 知道 *zhīdào* 'know' is the governor and 行礼 *xínglǐ* 'salute' is the dependent. There are two dependency arcs ADV (the adverbial-head relation) from 行礼 *xínglǐ* 'salute' to 现在 *xiànzài* 'now' and to 该 *gāi* 'should', which means that 现在 *xiànzài* 'now' and 该 *gāi* 'should' are subordinates to 行礼 *xínglǐ* 'salute'; that is, 行礼 *xínglǐ* 'salute' is the governor, 现在 *xiànzài* 'now' and 该 *gāi* 'should' are dependents. It can be seen that 行礼 *xínglǐ* 'salute' can be used as both a governor and a dependent in this sentence.

(1) 他知道现在该<u>行礼</u>了'。

Tā zhīdào xiànzài gāi <u>*xínglǐ*</u> le.
he_know_now_should_salute_ASP
'He knew it was time to salute.'

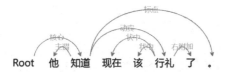

Fig. 1. An example of syntactic dependencies

This study first analyzes the syntactic dependency when verbs of saluting are dependents in the sentences. As shown in Table 2, the syntactic dependencies are, in descending order of proportion, sentence-head relations (HED), coordination relations (COO), verb-object relations (VOB), attribute-head relations (ATT), subject-verb relations (SBV), prepositional-object relations (POB), adverbial-head relations (ADV), and verb-complement relations (CMP). Among them, the proportion of sentence-head relations is the highest (58.37%), indicating that this is the most important syntactic dependency. The second one is the coordination relation. In contrast, other relations account for very small. From the perspective of specific verbs, the high-frequency dependencies of most verbs are sentence-head relations and coordination relations (including 鞠躬 *jūgōng* 'bow', 磕头 *kētóu* 'kowtow', 致敬 *zhìjìng* 'pay tribute', 行礼 *xínglǐ* 'salute', and 跪拜 *guìbài* 'kneel'). The highest frequency dependencies of 膜拜 *móbài* 'worship' are coordination relations and verb-object relations.

Table 2. Syntactic dependencies of verbs of saluting

Verbs	HED	ATT	SBV	VOB	COO	POB	ADV	CMP	Total
鞠躬	134	3	7	10	42	2	0	1	199
jūgōng 'bow'	67.34%	1.51%	3.52%	5.03%	21.11%	1.01%	0.00%	0.50%	100.00%
致敬	64	6	0	4	26	0	0	0	100
zhìjìng 'pay tribute'	64.00%	6.00%	0.00%	4.00%	26.00%	0.00%	0.00%	0.00%	100.00%
磕头	44	4	4	19	28	0	0	0	99
kētóu 'kowtow'	44.44%	4.04%	4.04%	19.19%	28.28%	0.00%	0.00%	0.00%	100.00%
行礼	53	4	2	3	25	1	0	0	88
xínglǐ 'salute'	60.23%	4.55%	2.27%	3.41%	28.41%	1.14%	0.00%	0.00%	100.00%
跪拜	8	5	0	0	8	0	1	0	22
guìbài 'kneel'	36.36%	22.73%	0.00%	0.00%	36.36%	0.00%	4.55%	0.00%	100.00%
膜拜	4	1	2	5	6	0	0	0	18
móbài 'worship'	22.22%	5.56%	11.11%	27.78%	33.33%	0.00%	0.00%	0.00%	100.00%
Total	307	23	15	41	135	3	1	1	526
	58.37%	4.37%	2.85%	7.79%	25.67%	0.57%	0.19%	0.19%	100.00%

The following part conducts a case study of 行礼 xínglǐ 'salute' due to space limit. 88 single sentences are automatically annotated, manually proofread, and statistically analyzed. As shown in Table 3, when 行礼 xínglǐ 'salute' is the dependent in the sentences, it appears in six types of syntactic dependencies with its governors: the sentence-head relations, the coordination relations, the attribute-head relations, the verb-object relations, the subject-object relations, and the preposition-object relations. There is no adverbial-head relations or verb-complement relations in the sampled sentences. There are 53 sentences of sentence-head relations formed by 行礼 xínglǐ 'salute' and its governors, accounting for 60.23%, which is much higher than the 25 sentences of coordination relations; there are 4 sentences of attribute-head relations formed by 行礼 xínglǐ 'salute' and its governors, accounting for 4.55%; there are 3 sentences of verb-object relations formed by 行礼 xínglǐ 'salute' and its governors, accounting for 3.41%; there are only 2 sentences of subject-object relations formed by 行礼 xínglǐ 'salute' and its governors, accounting for 2.27%, and only 1 sentence is the preposition-object relation, accounting for 1.14%. It shows that the most common type of syntactic dependency of 行礼 xínglǐ 'salute' as a dependent in these sentences is the sentence-head relation, while the rest are not common.

Table 3. Syntactic dependencies of 行礼 *xínglǐ* 'salute'[6]

Types	No	Percent	Examples
HED	53	60.23%	守卫向她行礼。 Shǒuwèi xiàng tā ***xínglǐ*** guard_to_she_salute 'The guard salutes her.'
COO	25	28.41%	他立即跪下去行礼。 Tā lìjí **guì** xiàqù *xínglǐ* he_immediately_kneel_down_salute 'He immediately kneeled and saluted.'
ATT	4	4.55%	法师行礼之后就下台休息。 Fǎshī *xínglǐ* **zhīhòu** jiù xiàtái xiūxi Master_salute_after_then_step down_rest 'After the Master saluted, he left the stage to rest.'
VOB	3	3.41%	他知道现在该行礼了。 Tā **zhīdào** xiànzài gāi *xínglǐ* le he_know_now_should_salute_ASP 'He knows it is time to salute.'
SBV	2	2.27%	行礼完毕。 *Xínglǐ* **wánbì** salute_over 'Saluting is over.'
POB	1	1.14%	梅克林格用郑重的一个行礼接受了皇帝拙劣的玩笑。 Méikèlíngé **yòng** zhèngzhòng de yī gè *xínglǐ* jiēshòu le huángdì zhuōliè de wánxiào Mecklinger_use_solemn_DE_one_Classifier_sal-ute_accept_ASP_Emperor_clumsy_DE_joke 'Mecklinger accepted the Emperor's clumsy joke with a solemn salute.'
Total	88	100.00%	/

Next, this study calculates the intensity of syntactic collocations when 行礼 *xínglǐ* 'salute' is a governor which dominates different dependents based on the formula (1) proposed by Wang and Zhou [35].

$$I_{\text{intensity of syntactic collocations}} = (A_{\text{number of syntactic dependencies directly governed by verbs}} - B_{\text{number of WP}})$$
$$\div S_{\text{number of single sentences}} \qquad (1)$$

The number of syntactic dependencies directly governed by 行礼 *xínglǐ* 'salute' is 221 (A = 221), and the number of WP is 54 (B = 54). The reason for subtracting the number of punctuation marks is that dependency grammar also regards them as a kind of syntactic dependency dominated by verbs in the sentences, but it contributes nothing to the syntactic features of verbs. The number of single sentences of 行礼 *xínglǐ* 'salute' is 88. After calculating, the intensity of syntactic collocations of 行礼 *xínglǐ* 'salute' is 1.90, showing that 行礼 *xínglǐ* 'salute' can govern nearly two syntactic dependencies in the sentences. For example, in (2), 行礼 *xínglǐ* 'salute' and 新郎 *xīnláng* 'groom' form a subject-verb relation; 行礼 *xínglǐ* 'salute' and 向 *xiàng* 'to' form an adverbial-head relation.

(2) 新郎新娘向主婚人行礼!

---

[6] Please refer to the appendix for the explanation of the terms.

Xīnláng xīnniáng **xiàng** zhǔhūnrén *xínglǐ*!
groom_bride_to_officiant_salute
The bride and groom salute the officiant!'

Referring to Wang and Zhou [35], this study calculates the intensity of syntactic collocations of 行礼 *xínglǐ* 'salute' under different syntactic governors. The calculation formula is:

$I_{\text{intensity of syntactic collocations under a syntactic governor}}$

$$= (A_{\text{number of syntactic dependencies directly governed by verbs under a syntactic governor}} \tag{2}$$

$$-B_{\text{number of WP under a syntactic governor}})$$

$$\div S_{\text{number of single sentences under a syntactic governor}}$$

As shown in Table 4, the intensity of syntactic collocations of 行礼 *xínglǐ* 'salute' under different syntactic governors are 2.81 (HED), 2.00 (VOB), 2.00 (POB), 0.50 (SBV), 0.50 (ATT) and 0.28 (COO). The result indicates that under the sentence-head relation, the intensity of syntactic collocations of 行礼 *xínglǐ* 'salute' is the strongest. In (3), 行礼 *xínglǐ* 'salute' is the head of this sentence. The governor 行礼 *xínglǐ* 'salute' and its dependents 员工 *yuángōng* 'employee', 向 *xiàng* 'to' and 致意 *zhìyì* 'greeting' form a subject-verb relation, an adverbial-head relation, and a coordination relation respectively.

(3) 华航员工向罹难者行礼致意。

Huáháng **yuángōng xiàng** línànzhě *xínglǐ* **zhìyì**.
China Airlines_employee_to_victim_salute_ give one's regards
'China Airlines employees saluted the victims and gave their regards.'

Table 4. The intensity of syntactic collocations of 行礼 *xínglǐ* 'salute' under different syntactic governors

The intensity of syntactic collocations of 行礼 *xínglǐ* 'salute'			
I_{HED}	2.81	I_{SBV}	0.50
I_{VOB}	2.00	I_{ATT}	0.50
I_{POB}	2.00	I_{COO}	0.28

4   The Entry Information of Verbs of Saluting

Chinese Verbs of saluting are often included in dictionaries. For example, *A Chinese Proficiency Test Vocabulary Guideline—A Dictionary of Usage: 8000 Words* (《HSK中国汉语水平考试词汇大纲: 汉语8000词词典》) [36], which is specially designed for learners of Chinese as a second language, contains 鞠躬 *jūgōng* 'bow' (a fourth-level word

Table 5. Verbs of saluting in *A Chinese Proficiency Test Vocabulary Guideline—A Dictionary of Usage: 8000 Words*

A Chinese Proficiency Test Vocabulary Guideline—A Dictionary of Usage: 8000 Words	Translation
鞠躬(丁级词) jūgōng (bow) 弯身行礼：～道谢|行了个～礼|深深地鞠了一个躬|他向老师鞠了个躬|他向父亲的遗像鞠了三个躬。	鞠躬 (fourth-level word) *jūgōng* (bow) Bent over to salute. ～道谢 *jūgōng* dàoxiè bow_express one's thanks
【近义词】行礼 【提示】 ①离合词，中间可插入其他成分，如：鞠了躬|鞠了三个躬。②鞠，姓。	'bow to express one's thanks' 行了个～礼 xíng le gè *jūgōng* lǐ make_ASP_Classifier_bow_ritual 'made a bow'
	深深地<u>鞠</u>了一个<u>躬</u> shēnshēn de *jū* le yī gè *gōng* deeply_DE_bow_ASP_one_Classifier_bow 'bow deeply'
	他向老师<u>鞠</u>了个<u>躬</u>。 Tā xiàng lǎoshī *jū* le gè *gōng*. he_to_teacher_bow_ASP_Classifier_bow 'He bows to the teacher.'
	他向父亲的遗像<u>鞠</u>了三个<u>躬</u>。 Tā xiàng fùqīn de yíxiàng *jū* le sān gè *gōng*. he_to_father_DE_portrait_bow_ASP_three_Classifier_bow 'He bows three times to the portrait of his father.'
	【Synonym】行礼 *xínglǐ* 'salute' 【Tips】 ① 离合词 A separable word, other components can be inserted in the middle: <u>鞠</u>了<u>躬</u> *jū* le *gōng* bow_ASP_bow 'bowed'
	<u>鞠</u>了三个<u>躬</u> *jū* le sān gè *gōng* bow_ASP_three_Classifier_bow

(continued)

Table 5. (*continued*)

	'bowed three times'
	②鞠 *jū* a surname
致敬(丁级词) zhìjìng (salute) ［动］向人敬礼或表示敬意：向解 放军～|向敬爱的首长～|向老师～	致敬 (fourth-level word) *zhìjìng* ('pay tribute') [Verb] Pay tribute to or show respect to someone. 向解放军～ xiàng jiěfàngjūn *zhìjìng* to_People's Liberation Army_pay tribute 'pay tribute to the People's Liberation Army' 向敬爱的首长～ xiàng jìng'ài de shǒuzhǎng *zhìjìng.* to_beloved_DE_chief_pay tribute 'pay tribute to the beloved chief' 向老师～ xiàng lǎoshī *zhìjìng.* to_teacher_pay tribute 'pay tribute to the teacher'

in this dictionary) and 致敬 *zhìjìng* 'pay tribute' (a fourth-level word in this dictionary). The information is shown in Table 5.

The following takes 行礼 *xínglǐ* 'salute' as an example to display its information that can be included in a dictionary, including *pinyin*, part of speech, meaning, syntactic functions, the intensity of syntactic collocations, examples, and frequency, as shown in Table 6. Dependency relations of 行礼 *xínglǐ* 'salute' show its syntactic functions to a certain extent. For instance, when 行礼 *xínglǐ* 'salute' is a dependent, the most frequent syntactic dependency with its governors is the sentence-head relation. This means that the syntactic function of 行礼 *xínglǐ* 'salute' or the clause in which 行礼 *xínglǐ* 'salute' is located is to act as a predicate. However, the syntactic dependency relation does not entirely correspond to syntactic functions. For example, in (4), according to dependency grammar, the dependent 行礼 *xínglǐ* 'salute' and its governor 知道 *zhīdào* 'know' form a verb-object relation. While in traditional linguistics, the clause (你给他们行礼 *nǐ gěi tāmen xínglǐ* 'you salute them') is an object and 行礼 *xínglǐ* 'salute' in this clause is a predicate.

(3) 他们未必知道你给他们行礼。

Tāmen wèibì zhīdào nǐ gěi tāmen *xínglǐ.*
they_may not_know_you_give_they_salute

'They may not know you saluted them.'

Table 6. The entry information of 行礼 *xínglǐ* 'salute'

Entry	行礼
pinyin	xínglǐ
Part of speech	verb
Meaning	Use a specific ritual or gesture to respect or welcome someone or something.
Syntactic Dependency	【Head】<60.23%>: [～]两人相对～。 Liǎng rén xiāngduì *xínglǐ*. two_people_face to face_salute 'The two saluted face to face.' 【Coordination】<28.41%>: [～]两岸嘉宾再度依次向始祖炎帝**敬香**、～。 Liǎng'àn jiābīn zàidù yīcì xiàng shǐzǔ Yándì **jìngxiāng**, *xínglǐ*. both sides of the Strait_guest_again_in turn_to_first ancestor_ Emperor Yan_offer incense_salute 'Guests from both sides of the Strait once again offered incense and saluted the first ancestor, Emperor Yan.' 【Attribute of its governor】<4.55%>: [～]两人～**后**站直身子。 Liǎng rén *xínglǐ* **hòu** zhànzhí shēnzi. two_people_salute_after_stand up_body 'The two people stood up after saluting.' (governor: 后 *hòu* 'after') [preposition + object +～]有向菩萨～的**法师**。 Yǒu xiàng púsà *xínglǐ* de **fǎshī**. be_to_Bodhisattva_salute_DE_Master 'There are masters who salute Bodhisattva.' (governor: 法师 *fǎshī* 'Master') 【Object of its governor】<3.41%>: [subject + preposition + object +～]他们未必知道你给他们 ～。

(*continued*)

Table 6. *(continued)*

Tāmen wèibì **zhīdào** nǐ gěi tāmen *xínglǐ*.
they_may not_know_you_give_they_salute
'They may not know you saluted them.'
(governor: 知道 *zhīdào* 'know')

【Subject】<2.27%>:
[～]～完毕。
Xínglǐ **wánbì**.
salute_be over
'Saluting is over.'

【Prepositional object】<1.14%>:
[～]梅克林格用郑重的一个～接受了皇帝拙劣的玩笑。
Méikèlíngé **yòng** zhèngzhòng de yī gè *xínglǐ* jiēshòu le
huángdì zhuōliè de wánxiào.
Meck-
lin-
ger_use_solemn_DE_one_Classifier_salute_accept_ASP_E
mperor_clumsy_DE_joke
'Mecklinger accepted the Emperor's clumsy joke with a
solemn salute.'

The intensity of syntactic collocations	this verb roughly has two dependents (not including punctuations): 两人<主语>相对<状语> ～ 。 **Liǎng rén** <subject> **xiāngduì** <adverbial> *xínglǐ*. two_people_face to face_salute The two saluted face to face.

5 Conclusion

Verbs involving the body are ubiquitous in human languages. They can reflect the way of human cognition based on embodied experience. A subtype of such verbs that describe the whole body movements are less examined. This study has selected a representative class of such verbs, namely, verbs of saluting. They are verbs that express respect to others through specific body movements. This study has then extracted and filtered 526 sentences from several Chinese corpora containing these verbs. Based on manual correction of the automatic tagging results, this study has further analyzed the syntactic features of these verbs from two aspects, including syntactic dependencies and the intensity of syntactic collocations. The results show that they as a whole often act as heads of sentences, taking up about 60%. A case study of 行礼 *xínglǐ* 'salute' indicates that the overall intensity of its syntactic collocations is 1.90 when 行礼 *xínglǐ* 'salute' is a governor. When 行礼 *xínglǐ* 'salute' acts as the head of the sentences, its intensity of syntactic collocations is the highest (2.81), showing that 行礼 *xínglǐ* 'salute' can govern nearly three dependents. This study further argues that syntactic dependencies can help us highlight verbs' core syntactic features when we compile dictionaries. Therefore, this study has enriched the entry of 行礼 *xínglǐ* 'salute' based on the statistical results and analysis. This study has quantitatively and qualitatively examined the syntactic features of verbs of saluting, which provides a research paradigm for the research on Chinese verbs and lexicography.

Acknowledgment. This study is funded by the University of Macau (Project No.: MYRG2022-00191-FAH and MYRG2019-00013-FAH). Ms. Shuchi Chen helped with making annotation in the very early stage. This study has re-annotated every sentence.

Appendix

Terms in LTP[7]	Terms in this study	Abbreviation of LTP	English translation in this study	Examples in this study
前置宾语-动词关系	前置宾语-动词关系	FOB	The fronting object-verb relation	/
兼语结构	兼语结构	DBL	The pivotal construction	/
主谓关系	主谓关系	SBV	The subject-object relation	行礼完毕。 Xínglǐ **wánbì** salute_ over 'Salute is over.' (完毕 wánbì 'over' → 行礼 xínglǐ 'salute')
动宾关系	动宾关系	VOB	The verb-object relation	他们未必知道你给他们行礼。 Tāmen wèibì **zhīdào** nǐ gěi tāmen xínglǐ they_ may not_know_you_give_they_salute 'They may not know you saluted them.' (知道 zhīdào 'know' → 行礼 xínglǐ 'salute')
定中关系	定中关系	ATT	The attribute-head relation	两人行礼后站直身子。 Liǎng rén xínglǐ **hòu** zhànzhí shēnzi two_people_salute_after stand up_body 'Two people stood up after saluting.' (后 hòu 'after' → 行礼 xínglǐ 'salute')
状中结构	状中关系	ADV	The adverbial-head relation	华航员工向罹难者行礼致意。 Huáháng yuángōng **xiàng** línànzhě xínglǐ zhìyì China Airlines employee_to_victim_salute_ give one's regards 'China Airlines employees saluted the victims and gave their regards.' (行礼 xínglǐ 'salute' → 向 xiàng 'to')

(continued)

---

7 https://ltp.ai/docs/appendix.html.

(continued)

Terms in LTP	Terms in this study	Abbreviation of LTP	English translation in this study	Examples in this study
动补结构	动补关系	CMP	The verb-complement relation	查干感动得向他们深深鞠躬致谢。 Chágàn gǎndòng de xiàng tāmen shēnshēn jūgōng zhìxiè Chagan moved_DE_to_they_deeply_bow_thanks 'Chagan was so moved that he bowed deeply to them.' (感动 gǎndòng 'moved' → 鞠躬 jūgōng 'bow')
并列关系	并列关系	COO	The coordination relation	他立即跪下去行礼。 Tā lìjí **guì** xiàqù **xínglǐ** he_immediately_kneel_down_salute 'He immediately kneeled and saluted.' (跪 guì 'kneel down' → 行礼 xínglǐ 'salute')
介宾关系	介宾关系	POB	The preposition-object relation	梅克林格用郑重的一个行礼接受了皇帝拙劣的玩笑。 Méikèlíngé **yòng** zhèngzhòng de yī gè **xínglǐ** jiēshòu le huángdì zhuōliè de wánxiào Mecklinger use solemn_DE_one_Classifier_salute_accept_ASP_Emperor_clumsy_DE_joke 'Mecklinger accepted the Emperor's clumsy joke with a solemn salute.' (用 yòng 'use' → 行礼 xínglǐ 'salute')
左附加关系	左附加关系	LAD	The left adjunct relation	/
右附加关系	右附加关系	RAD	The right adjunct relation	/
独立结构	独立结构	IS	The independent structure	/
核心	句子与核心的关系	HED	The sentence-head relation	守卫向她行礼。 Shǒuwèi xiàng tā **xínglǐ** guard_to_she_salute 'The guard salutes her.' (行礼 xínglǐ 'salute' is the head of this sentence.)

References

1. Yu, S., et al.: The Grammatical Knowledge-Base of Contemporary Chinese——A Complete Specification. Tsinghua University Press, Beijing (2003). (in Chinese)
2. Yu, S., Zhu, X.: Comprehensive language knowledge base and its preliminary application in international Chinese language education. Int. Chinese Lang. Educ,. 174–180+203 (2013). (in Chinese)
3. Wang, S., Chen, S.: The syntax and semantics of verbs of searching. In: Jia, W., et al. (eds.) International Symposium on Emerging Technologies for Education, vol. 01, pp. 174–180. Springer, Cham (2021)
4. White, A.S., Hacquard, V., Lidz, J.: Semantic information and the syntax of propositional attitude verbs. Cogn. Sci. **42**(2), 416–456 (2018)
5. Zhang, B.: The application of micro semantic roles in sentence pattern description: A case study of verbs meaning "making sth. by freehand". Chinese Lang. Learn. **6**, 57–68 (2021). (in Chinese)
6. Gao, S., Yan, W., Liu, H.: A quantitative study on syntactic functions of Chinese verbs based on dependency treebank. Chinese Lang. Learn. **5**, 105–112 (2010). (in Chinese)
7. Zhang, H.: A study on the syntactic function of "V+P" structure based on corpus. Chinese Lang. Learn.. **6**, 93–101 (2018). (in Chinese)
8. Tesnière, L.: Comment construire une syntaxe. Bullet de la Facultédes Lettres de Strasbourg **7**, 219–229 (1934)
9. Tesnière, L.: Eléments de syntaxe structurale. Klincksieck, Paris (1959)
10. Feng, Z.: Tesnière and dependency grammar: Commemorating the 60th anniversary of Tesnière's death. Mod. Chinese **11**, 4–9 (2014). (in Chinese)
11. Dashtipour, K., Gogate, M., Li, J., Jiang, F., Kong, B., Hussain, A.: A hybrid Persian sentiment analysis framework: Integrating dependency grammar based rules and deep neural networks. Neurocomputing **380**, 1–10 (2020)
12. Poiret, R., Liu, H.: Some quantitative aspects of written and spoken French based on syntactically annotated corpora. J. Fr. Lang. Stud. **30**(3), 355–380 (2020)
13. Niu, R., Osborne, T.: Chunks are components: a dependency grammar approach to the syntactic structure of Mandarin. Lingua **224**, 60–83 (2019)
14. Liu, H.: The complexity of Chinese syntactic dependency networks. Phys. A **387**(12), 3048–3058 (2008)
15. Liu, B., Niu, Y., Liu, H.: Word class, syntactic function and style: a comparative study based on annotated corpora. Appl. Linguis. **4**, 134–142 (2012). (in Chinese)
16. Merleau-Ponty, M.: Phénoménologie de la perception. The Commercial Press, Beijing (2001). (in Chinese)
17. Li, J.: The cognitive study of the modern chinese bodily verbs. Ph.D. East China Normal University, Shanghai (2006). (in Chinese)
18. Wang, J.: The Category of Animacy in Chinese. East China Normal University Press, Shanghai (2004). (in Chinese)
19. Levin, B.: English Verb Classes and Alternations. The University of Chicago Press, Chicago (1993)
20. Zhuang, H., Zhang, M.: Current situation and expectation of the research on the diachronic evolution of Chinese frequently used verbs. Overseas Chinese Educ. **3**, 28–40 (2019). (in Chinese)
21. Chen, C.: Syntactic and Semantic Properties of Modern Chinese Verbs. Academia Press, Shanghai (2002). (in Chinese)
22. Schuler, K.K.: VerbNet: A Broad-Coverage, Comprehensive Verb Lexicon. University of Pennsylvania, Pennsylvania (2005)

23. Su, X.: A Thesaurus of Modern Chinese. The Commercial Press, Beijing (2013). (in Chinese)
24. Mei, J., Zhu, Y., Gao, Y., Yin, H.: A Word Forest of Synonyms. Shanghai Lexicographical Publishing House, Shanghai (1983). (in Chinese)
25. Li, X., Su, X.: Lexicon of Common Words in Contemporary Chinese, 2nd edn. The Commercial Press, Beijing (2021). (in Chinese)
26. Liu, Y., et al.: Identifying web spam with the wisdom of the crowds. ACM Trans. Web 6(1), 1–30 (2012)
27. Xun, E., Gaoqi, R., Xiao, X., Zang, J.: The construction of the bcc corpus in the age of big data. Corpus Linguist. 3(1), 93–109+118 (2016). (in Chinese)
28. Zhan, W., Guo, R., Chang, B., Chen, Y., Chen, L.: The building of the CCL corpus: Its design and implementation. Corpus Linguisti. 6(1), 71–86+116 (2019). (in Chinese)
29. Huang, C.-R.: Tagged Chinese Gigaword Version 2.0 (https://catalog.ldc.upenn.edu/LDC200 9T14). Tagged from Chinese Gigaword version 2.0 (2009). (https://catalog.ldc.upenn.edu/LDC2005T14). https://catalog.ldc.upenn.edu/LDC2009T14
30. Kilgarriff, A., Huang, C.-R., Rychlý, P., Smith, S., Tugwell, D.: Chinese word sketches. ASIALEX 2005: Words in Asian Cultural Context, Singapore (2005)
31. Wang, S.: Investigating verbs of confession through a syntactic and semantic annotation tool. In: Dong, M., Gu, Y., Hong, J.-F. (eds.) Chinese Lexical Semantics, pp. 198–211. Springer, Cham (2022)
32. Wang, S., Liu, X., Zhou, J.: Developing a syntax and semantics annotation tool for research on Chinese vocabulary. In: Dong, M., Gu, Y., Hong, J.-F. (eds.) Chinese Lexical Semantics, pp. 272–294. Springer, Cham (2022)
33. Liu, T., Che, W., Li, Z.: Language technology platform. J. Chinese Inf. Process. 25(6), 53–62 (2011). (in Chinese)
34. Che, W., Li, Z., Liu, T.: LTP: A Chinese language technology platform. In: Liu, Y., Liu, T. (eds.) Proceedings of the Coling 2010: Demonstrations, pp. 13–16. Chinese Information Processing Society of China, Beijing (2010)
35. Wang, S., Zhou, J.: On the syntax and semantics of verbs of cheating. In: Li, S., et al. (eds.) Proceedings of the 20th Chinese national conference on computational linguistics, pp. 501–512. Chinese Information Processing Society of China, Huhhot (2021). (in Chinese)
36. Liu, L.: A Chinese Proficiency Test Vocabulary Guideline—A Dictionary of Usage: 8000 Words. Beijing Language and Culture University Press, Beijing (2000). (in Chinese)

The Semantic Roles of Chinese Verbs of Saluting

Shaoming Wang and Shan Wang$^{(\boxtimes)}$

Department of Chinese Language and Literature, Faculty of Arts and Humanities, University of Macau, Taipa, Macau SAR, China
shanwang@um.edu.mo

Abstract. The human body is the basis of a human's perception of the world. Verbs describing body actions are ubiquitous in human languages. Among different kinds of verbs involving the body, verbs of saluting express respect to others through saluting actions. This study has screened out single sentences from Chinese corpora and carried out semantic role annotation based on dependency grammar. The study found that more than half of the sentences are used with agent-like semantic roles; the most frequently used agent-like semantic role of these verbs is the Agent, which shows the originator of the action; the primary patient-like semantic role is the Dative, which shows the receiver of saluting actions in these sentences. The most frequently used situational role is the Manner, which indicates how the movement occurs. This study has investigated the semantic roles of verbs of saluting, which provides reference for the study of verbal semantics and the compilation of dictionaries.

Keywords: Verbs · Semantic roles · Verbs of saluting

1 Introduction

Current research on Chinese semantics is increasingly integrated with network technology, such as implementing lexical semantic classification of terms based on Wordnet to improve the accuracy of text analysis [1]. [2] pointed out that lexical semantic research for natural language processing should be based on quantitative research. Although many websites can provide some language knowledge and corpus queries, few provide knowledge about Chinese lexical, syntactic, and semantic knowledge [3]. Verbs are dominant in language expressions, so they have always been the focus of linguistic research. Verb-centered semantic role resources are significant for research on linguistics, language teaching, and natural language processing [4]. How to make language knowledge, especially for verbs, more prominent has always been the focus of studies. [5] mentioned that semantic role annotation can make syntactic and semantic knowledge explicit. Linguistic researchers at home and abroad have proposed some semantic role annotation systems [6–11].

Dependency grammar [12, 13] has become one of the most essential theoretical base for examining semantic roles in natural language processing. Dependency grammar does not need a fixed word order, which shows that it can be more suitable for modeling languages with flexible word order [14]. Much research on Chinese semantics has been

© The Author(s), under exclusive license to Springer Nature Switzerland AG 2023
Q. Su et al. (Eds.): CLSW 2022, LNAI 13495, pp. 464–473, 2023.
https://doi.org/10.1007/978-3-031-28953-8_34

produced. For example, [15] proposed an imperative sentence classification method based on keywords' semantics using dependency parsing.

The human body plays a vital role in perceiving the external world [16]. The verbs describing the movements and actions performed by body parts are sometimes named 身体动词 *shēntǐ dòngcí* 'body verbs' [17, 18]. The scope of these verbs has been extended to the actions with the help of artificial tools [17]. For example, 抱 *bào* 'hold' generally does not rely on any instrument, while 切 *qiē* 'cut' requires the help of knives. There is much research on hand actions (such as 擦 *cā* 'wipe', 拭 *shì* 'wipe'), foot actions (such as 跳 *tiào* 'jump', 跃 *yuè* 'jump'), and oral actions (such as 哭 *kū* 'cry', 泣 *qì* 'weep')[19]. [20] specifically discussed the classification of English "verbs involving the body" in the book entitled *English Verb Classes and Alternations*. Verbs that describe the whole body movements are often overlooked. Among them, verbs of saluting are not only a type of complex physical movement, but also a social behavior to show respect to others, so their semantics are more complicated. [21] noticed that collocating with Agents and Datives is the semantic feature of 鞠躬 *jūgōng* 'bow', but ignored whether other verbs of saluting (such as 跪拜 *guìbài* 'bow down' and 膜拜 *móbài* 'worship') has the same semantic feature.

This study selects verbs of saluting, a kind of less-mentioned verbs, as the research object and analyzes their semantic roles. The steps are as follows. We first referred to the curtsey verbs under verbs involving the body in VerbNet [22]. There are verbs such as *bob, salaam, salute, genuflect, knee,* and *bow*. This study also referred to *A Word Forest of Synonyms* [23], *A Thesaurus of Modern Chinese* [24], and *Lexicon of Common Words in Contemporary Chinese* [25] to select verbs of saluting in Chinese taking into account the Chinese etiquette culture. Next, we used large-scale Chinese corpora that are publicly available to collect sentences containing verbs of saluting. This study follows the steps of [26, 27] to filter out the single sentences containing verbs of saluting. Then, a syntactic and semantic annotation tool [26, 27] based on Language Technology Platform [28, 29] is used for automatic annotation and manual checking. Based on the above, this study has summarized the semantic roles of verbs of saluting by analyzing the agent-like semantic roles, patient-like semantic roles, and situational roles. This study provides reference for investigating Chinese verbs and compiling dictionaries.

2 Semantic Roles of Verbs of Saluting

Semantic peripheral arguments (semantic roles) include主体角色 *zhǔtǐ juésè* 'agent-like semantic roles', 客体角色 *kètǐ juésè* 'patient-like semantic roles', and 情境角色 *qíngjìng juésè* situational roles. The semantic roles in this study do not refer to the roles that these verbs themselves can be, but the role of the words that they collocate with. For example, the verb *wash* has two roles: an Agent (someone who does the washing) and a Theme (the thing being washed) [30]. Overall, over half of the sentences containing these verbs are used with agent-like semantic roles. For example, (1)a has an agent-like semantic role (i.e. 信徒们 *xìntúmen* 'believers'), while (2)b has no agent-like semantic role. 鞠躬 *jūgōng* 'bow' and 行礼 *xínglǐ* 'salute' tend to be used with agent-like semantic roles. 僧众 *sēngzhòng* 'monks' in (2)a is the performer of the saluting action. 膜拜 *móbài* 'worship' and 致敬 *zhìjìng* 'pay tribute' tend to be used without any agent-like semantic role. In (2)b, there is no specific performer. Only a few sentences of these verbs have patient-like semantic roles, such as (2)b, (3)a, (3)b.

(1) a. 信徒们一起跪拜。

Xìntúmen yīqǐ *guìbài.*

believers_together_bow down

'The believers bow down together.'

b. 还不快磕头谢恩!

Hái bù kuài *kētóu* xiè'ēn!

yet_not_quickly_kowtow_thanks

'Hurry up and kowtow!'

(2) a. 殿上僧众一齐躬身行礼。

Diànshàng **sēngzhòng** yīqí gōngshēn *xínglǐ.*

hall_monks_together_bow_salute

'The monks in the hall bow and salute together.'

b. 向英勇奋斗的伟大中国人民致敬!

Xiàng yīngyǒng fèndòu de wěidà Zhōngguó **rénmín** *zhìjìng*!

to_brave_fight_DE_great_China_people_pay tribute

'Pay tribute to the great Chinese people who fought bravely!'

(3) a. 向伟大的毛泽东致敬!

Xiàng wěidà de **Máozédōng** *zhìjìng!*

to_great_DE_Mao Zedong_ pay tribute

'Pay tribute to the great Mao Zedong!'

b. 向中国总理致敬!

Xiàng Zhōngguó **zǒnglǐ** *zhìjìng*!

to_Chinese_premier_ pay tribute.

'Pay tribute to the Chinese premier!'

Table 1 shows the agent-like semantic roles of verbs of saluting. The Agent (AGT) is the most common agent-like semantic role for these verbs, while the Experiencer (EXP) only appears in three sentences. Agents show that the saluting action always requires originators of the action, such as 我 *wǒ* 'I', 信徒 *xìntú* 'believer', 皇太子 *huángtàizǐ* 'the crown prince', 少年犯 *shàoniánfàn* 'juvenile delinquent', and 民众 *mínzhòng* 'people'. The Experiencer can't move on its initiative, such as 商约 *shāngyuē* 'commercial contract'.

Table 1. The agent-like semantic roles of verbs of saluting

Semantic role		Examples
Agent-like semantic roles	AGT	我给你们磕头了! **Wǒ gěi nǐmen** *kētóu* le! I_give_you_kowtow_ASP 'I kowtow to you!' 信徒们一起跪拜。 **Xìntúmen** yīqǐ *guìbài* believers_together_bow down 'The believers bow down together.' 皇后和皇太子随后也相继行礼。 Huánghòu hé **huángtàizǐ** suíhòu yě xiāngjì *xínglǐ* queen_and_crown prince_then_also_successively_salute 'The queen and the crown prince then also saluted successively.' 少年犯感激地鞠躬致谢。 **Shàoniánfàn** gǎnjī de *jūgōng* zhìxiè juvenile delinquent_gratefully_DE_bow_convey thanks 'The juvenile delinquent bows gratefully.' 当天就有数万民众前往膜拜。 Dàngtiān jiù yǒu shùwàn **mínzhòng** qiánwǎng *móbài* that day_ as many as_have_tens of thousands_people_come_worship 'Tens of thousands of people came to worship (sb./sth.) that day.'
	EXP	但他所经手签订的中美商约还不是在对美国人磕头? Dàn tā suǒ jīngshǒu qiāndìng de Zhōng-Měi **shāngyuē** hái bùshì zài duì Měiguórén *kētóu*? but_he_SUO_handle_sign_DE_Sino-US_business contract_still_not_at_to_American_kowtow 'But isn't the Sino-US business contract he signed still *kowtowing* to the Americans?'

Table 2 shows the patient-like semantic roles of verbs of saluting. The main patient-like semantic role is the Dative (DATV), which mainly shows the receiver of the action, such as 她 *tā* 'she', 解放军 *jiěfàngjūn* 'People's Liberation Army', 婆母 *pómǔ* 'mother-in-law', 你 *nǐ* 'you', and 大家 *dàjiā* 'everyone'.

Table 2. The patient-like semantic roles of verbs of saluting

Patient-like semantic roles	DATV	暗地里对她膜拜就好。 Àndìlǐ duì **tā** *móbài* jiù hǎo secretly_to_her_worship_just_fine 'Just worship her secretly.' 致敬伟大的中国人民解放军! *Zhìjìng* wěidà de Zhōngguó rénmín **jiěfàngjūn**! pay tribute_great_DE_China_people_Liberation Army 'Pay tribute to the great Chinese People's Liberation Army!' 新媳妇快向婆母行礼吧! Xīn xífù kuài xiàng **pómǔ** *xínglǐ* ba! new_daughter-in-law_immediately_to_mother-in-law_salute_an auxiliary word 'New daughter-in-law, please salute your mother-in-law immediately!' 你母亲的儿子向你跪拜。 Nǐ mǔqīn de érzi xiàng **nǐ** *guìbài* you_mother_DE_son_to_you_bow down 'Your mother's son bows down to you.' 我给大家鞠躬了。 Wǒ gěi **dàjiā** *jūgōng* le I_to_everyone_bow_ASP 'I bow to everyone.'

Table 3 shows the situational roles for verbs of saluting. The most frequent situational role is the Manner (MANN), followed by the Measure (MEAS) and the Location (LOC). The Material (MATL), the Tool (TOOL), and the State (STAT) do not appear in sampled sentences. The Manner describes how the movement takes place. For example, the way of 磕头 *kētóu* 'kowtow' is 拼命 *pīnmìng* 'desperately'.

Table 3. The situational roles of verbs of saluting

Most frequently used situational roles	MANN	还让我和您一起拼命地磕头。 Hái ràng wǒ hé nín yīqǐ **pīnmìng** de _kētóu_ also_let_I_and_you_together_desperately_DE_kowtow '(Someone) also let me kowtow with you desperately.'
Frequently used situational roles	MEAS	他深深地三鞠躬。 Tā shēnshēn de **sān** _jūgōng_ he_deeply_DE_three_bow 'He bows three times deeply.'
	LOC	我在这儿给你磕头了！ Wǒ zài zhè'er gěi nǐ _kētóu_ le! I_at_here_to_you_kowtow_ASP 'I kowtow to you here!'
Other situational roles	REAS	有些企业则为二三十万元资金四处磕头。 Yǒuxiē qǐyè zé wèi èr-sānshí wàn yuán **zījīn** sìchù _kētóu_ some_company_then_for_twenty to thirty_ten thousand_Yuan_fund_everywhere_kowtow 'Some companies kowtow for 200,000 to 300,000 Yuan of funds everywhere.'
	TIME	中山大学师生今天上午九时向校园内的国父铜像行礼、献花致敬。 Zhōngshān Dàxué shīshēng jīntiān shàngwǔ **jiǔshí** xiàng xiàoyuán nèi de guófù tóng xiàng _xínglǐ_, xiànhuā zhìjìng Sun Yat-sen_university_teacher and student_today_morning_nine o'clock_to_campus_inside_DE_the founding father_statue_salute_offer flowers_pay tribute 'The teachers and students of Sun Yat-sen University saluted and offered flowers to the bronze statue of the founding father on campus at 9:00 this morning.'
	FEAT	两个卡通形象同样引发了人人网友的膜拜。 Liǎng gè kǎtōng xíngxiàng tóngyàng yǐnfā le Rénrén **wǎngyǒu** de _móbài_ two_Classifier_cartoon_image_also_arouse_renren.com_netizen_DE_worship 'The two cartoon images also arouse the worship of netizens in RENN.'
	SCO	这一鞠躬里包含了他对祖国人民真诚的感谢。 Zhè yī _jūgōng_ lǐ bāohán le tā duì zǔguó rénmín zhēnchéng de gǎnxiè this_one_bow_in_contain_ASP_he_to_motherland_people_sincere_DE_gratitude 'This bow contains his sincere gratitude to the people of the motherland.'

3   The Entry Information of Verbs of Saluting

This section takes 行礼 _xínglǐ_ 'salute' as an example to show a semantic entry based on the above analysis, including the word, _pinyin_, part of speech, meaning, and semantic roles, as shown in Table 4.

The Knowledge-Base of Content Words (《现代汉语实词句法语义功能信息词典》) is composed of the knowledge of adjectives, verbs and nouns [31]. It has two semantic roles of 行礼 _xínglǐ_ 'salute', including the Agent and the Object in Table 5. Table 4 of this study has also listed the frequently used situational roles of 行礼 _xínglǐ_ 'salute', including the Manner, the Location, and the Time.

Table 4. The semantic entry information of 行礼 *xínglǐ* 'salute'

Entry	行礼
Chinese *pinyin*	xínglǐ
Part of speech	verb
Meaning	Use a specific ritual or gesture to show respect or welcome someone or something (e.g. statues, flags)
Semantic Roles	**Agent-like semantic roles:** Agent: 新郎新娘互相行礼! **Xīnláng xīnniáng** hùxiāng *xínglǐ*! groom_bride_to_each other_salute 'The groom and bride salute each other!'
	Patient-like semantic roles: Dative: 新媳妇快向婆母行礼吧! Xīn xífù kuài xiàng **pómǔ** *xínglǐ* ba! new_daughter-in-law_quickly_to_mother-in-law_salute_an auxiliary word 'The new daughter-in-law salutes to the mother-in-law!'
	Frequently used situational roles: Manner: 两人相对 ~ 。 Liǎng rén **xiāngduì** *xínglǐ*! two_people_each other_salute The two saluted each other
	Location: 在泥泞里默默地 ~ 。 Zài **nínìng** lǐ mòmò de *xínglǐ* At_mud_in_silently_DE_salute 'Salute silently in the mud.'
	Time: 有一天我故意慢 ~ 。 Yǒu yī **tiān** wǒ gùyì màn *xínglǐ* have_one_day_I_deliberately_slowly_salute 'One day I deliberately saluted slowly.'

4 Conclusion

Verbs involving the body can reflect how humans perceive the world. This study has examined a subtype of such verbs, namely, verbs of saluting. This study has screened out single sentences from several Chinese corpora and annotated their semantic roles. The results show that more than half of the sentences are used with agent-like semantic

Table 5. Semantic Information of 行礼 *xínglǐ* 'salute' in *The Knowledge-Base of Content Words*

Semantic roles	Our Translation
施事A: 向某人或某物致敬、施礼的人	Agent: a person who salutes someone or something
对象TA: 施事对他行礼的人或物	Target: a person or thing that an agent salutes
例句: 弟子们向师傅 ~ 。	Example sentences: 弟子们向师傅 ~ 。 **Dìzǐmen** xiàng **shīfù** *xínglǐ* disciple_to_master_salute 'The disciples salute the master.'
入学第一天, 学生们向孔子像磕头 ~ 。	入学第一天, 学生们向孔子像磕头 ~ 。 Rùxué dìyī tiān, **xuéshēngmen** xiàng **Kǒngzǐ** xiàng kētóu *xínglǐ* admission_the first_day, student_to_Confucius_statue_kowtow_salute 'On the first day of school, students kowtowed to the statue of Confucius.'
大家对国旗鞠躬 ~ 。	大家对国旗鞠躬 ~ 。 **Dàjiā** duì **guóqí** jūgōng *xínglǐ* everyone_to_flag_bow_salute 'Everyone bowed and saluted the flag.'

roles, while a few sentences are with patient-like semantic roles. In terms of agent-like semantic roles, the Agent is most common for verbs of saluting, indicating that live beings carrying out the actions often appear in these sentences. The important patient-like semantic role is the Dative, which mainly shows the receiver of saluting actions. The most frequently used situational role is the Manner, which describes how the action is performed. This study also takes 行礼 *xínglǐ* 'salute' as an example to show a semantic entry. This study can provide reference for the study of verbal semantics and dictionary compilation.

Acknowledgment. This study is funded by the University of Macau (Project No.: MYRG2022-00191-FAH and MYRG2019-00013-FAH). Ms. Shuchi Chen helped with the annotation at the initial stage. This study has done annotation again for each sentence.

References

1. Long, J., Wang, L., Li, Z., Zhang, Z.-P., Yang, L.: WordNetased lexical semantic classification for text corpus analysis. J. Central South Univ. **22**(5), 1833–1840 (2015). https://doi.org/10.1007/s11771-015-2702-8
2. Yu, S., Zhu, X.: Quantitative lexicon study and knowledge base construction for commonly used words. J. Chinese Inf. Process. **29**(3), 16–20 (2015). (in Chinese)
3. Yu, S., Zhu, X.: Comprehensive language knowledge base and its applications in language teaching. J. Beihua Univ. (Soc. Sci.). **15**(3), 4–9 (2014). (in Chinese)

4. Wang, C., Qian, Q., Xun, E., Xing, D., Li, M., Rao, G.: Construction of semantic role bank for Chinese verbs from the perspective of ternary collocation. J. Chinese Inf. Process. **34**(9), 19–27 (2020). (in Chinese)
5. Yu, S., Zhu, X.: Comprehensive language knowledge base and its preliminary application in international Chinese language education. Int. Chinese Lang. Educ. 174–180+203 (2013). (in Chinese)
6. Liu, Y., Yang, H., Li, Z., Zhang, M.: A lightweight annotation guideline of Chinese semantic role labeling. J. Chinese Inf. Process. **34**(4), 10–20 (2020). (in Chinese)
7. Bai, X., Xue, N.: Generalizing the semantic roles in the Chinese proposition bank. Lang. Resour. Eval. **50**(3), 643–666 (2016). https://doi.org/10.1007/s10579-016-9342-y
8. Lee, J.-Y., Song, Y.-I., Rim, H.-C., Han, K.-S.: Incorporating frame information to semantic role labeling. IEICE Trans. Inf. Syst. **93**(1), 201–204 (2010)
9. Munir, K., Zhao, H., Li, Z.: Neural unsupervised semantic role labeling. Trans. Asian Low-Resour. Lang. Inf. Process. **20**(6), 1–16 (2021)
10. Wang, X.: Semantic role labeling in Chinese using HowNet. Lang. Linguist. **9**(2), 449–461 (2008)
11. Xu, K., Wu, H., Song, L., Zhang, H., Song, L., Yu, D.: Conversational semantic role labeling. IEEE/ACM Trans. Audio, Speech Lang. Process. **29**, 2465–2475 (2021)
12. Tesnière, L.: Eléments de syntaxe structurale. Klincksieck, Paris (1959)
13. Tesnière, L.: Comment construire une syntaxe. Bullet de la Facultédes Lettres de Strasbourg. **7**, 219–229 (1934)
14. Nugues, P.: An Introduction to Language Processing with Perl and Prolog. Springer, Berlin (2006)
15. Tu, J., Zhu, M.: Imperative sentence classification based on dependency parsing. Comput. Appl. Softw. **36**(2), 279–283+322 (2019). (in Chinese)
16. Merleau-Ponty, M.: Phénoménologie de la perception. The Commercial Press, Beijing (2001). (in Chinese)
17. Li, J.: The Cognitive study of the modern Chinese bodily verbs. PhD. East China Normal University, Shanghai (2006). (in Chinese)
18. Wang, J.: The Category of Animacy in Chinese. East China Normal University Press, Shanghai (2004). (in Chinese)
19. Zhuang, H., Zhang, M.: Current situation and expectation of the research on the diachronic evolution of Chinese frequently used verbs. Overseas Chinese Educ. **3**, 28–40 (2019). (in Chinese)
20. Levin, B.: English Verb Classes and Alternations. The University of Chicago Press, Chicago (1993)
21. Chen, C.: Syntactic and Semantic Properties of Modern Chinese Verbs. Academia Press, Shanghai (2002). (in Chinese)
22. Schuler, K.K.: VerbNet: A Broad-Coverage, Comprehensive Verb Lexicon. University of Pennsylvania, Pennsylvania (2005)
23. Mei, J., Zhu, Y., Gao, Y., Yin, H.: A Word Forest of Synonyms. Shanghai Lexicographical Publishing House, Shanghai (1983). (in Chinese)
24. Su, X.: A Thesaurus of Modern Chinese. The Commercial Press, Beijing (2013). (in Chinese)
25. Li, X., Su, X.: Lexicon of Common Words in Contemporary Chinese, 2nd edn. The Commercial Press, Beijing (2021). (in Chinese)
26. Wang, S.: Investigating verbs of confession through a syntactic and semantic annotation tool. In: Dong, M., Gu, Y., Hong, J.-F. (eds.) Chinese lexical semantics, pp. 198–211. Springer, Cham (2022)
27. Wang, S., Liu, X., Zhou, J.: Developing a syntax and semantics annotation tool for research on Chinese vocabulary. In: Dong, M., Gu, Y., Hong, J.-F. (eds.) Chinese lexical semantics, pp. 272–294. Springer, Cham (2022)

28. Liu, T., Che, W., Li, Z.: Language technology platform. J. Chinese Inf. Process. **25**(6), 53–62 (2011). (in Chinese)
29. Che, W., Li, Z., Liu, T.: LTP: A Chinese language technology platform. In: Liu, Y., Liu, T. (eds.) Proceedings of the Coling 2010: Demonstrations, pp. 13–16. Chinese Information Processing Society of China, Beijing (2010)
30. Thompson, C.K., Lange, K.L., Schneider, S.L., Shapiro, L.P.: Agrammatic and non-brain-damaged subjects' verb and verb argument structure production. Aphasiology **11**(4–5), 473–490 (1997)
31. Yuan, Y., Cao, H.: An introduction to the syntactic-semantic knowledge-base of Chinese verbs. In: Sun, M., Li, S., Zhang, Y., Liu, Y. (eds.) Proceedings of the 19th Chinese National Conference on Computational Linguistics, pp. 518–527. Chinese Information Processing Society of China, Haikou (2020)

A Study on the Context Mode of the Linking Verb "Shì" Addressing a New Branch Naming

Zhihong Chen and Dawei Lu$^{(\boxtimes)}$

School of Literal Arts, Renmin University of China, Beijing, China
wedalu@163.com

Abstract. Complementing the missing elements in Chinese clauses contributes to computer understanding. Based on the naming-telling structure and Clause Complex Theory, the paper explores the effect of the context when the former clause is a "shì"-clause and the latter lacks naming. The object of "shì" in the former clause as the missing naming of the latter clause is called the new branch naming. The object as a new branch naming introduced by "shì" is determined by the intelligibility and the referential specificity of the object. The context mode contains literal features and semantic features for resolution.

Keywords: Linking verb · Shì · Naming-telling structure · New branch · Context mode

1 Introduction

In Chinese, the subject-predicate structure of clauses is often incomplete in discourse, such as in (1) and (2). It's easy for the human to understand and fill in the missing ingredients, but not for computers.

(1) 教育$_i$是培养人的一种社会活动，Ø$_i$是人类自身发展所必需的，Ø$_i$也是人类社会得以发展的必要条件。

Education is a social activity that nurtures human beings, and is necessary for their own development, and is also a necessary condition for the development of human society.

(2) 另一个得利最大的是沙俄$_i$，Ø$_i$以后延续到苏联。

The other country that benefited the most was Tsarist Russia, which later continued to the Soviet Union.

Both (1) and (2) have multiple clauses. In both (1) and (2), the first clause is complete while other clauses lack the subject. For the human, it is easy to understand that the clauses lacking subject are about "jiàoyù(教育)" in (1) and "Shāé(沙俄)" in (2). Wang et al. [1] argue that the sentences whose subjects are retrievable and restorable need

© The Author(s), under exclusive license to Springer Nature Switzerland AG 2023
Q. Su et al. (Eds.): CLSW 2022, LNAI 13495, pp. 474–489, 2023.
https://doi.org/10.1007/978-3-031-28953-8_35

two blueprints for natural language processing: identification and restoration. But it is difficult to restore the correct component for computer. The present natural language processing paradigm of "pre-trained language model + fine-tuning" has good results in many tasks. However, the models are changing with each passing day and the language rules do not change with the models, so it is still important to excavate the language rules.

Chen [2] defines the phenomenon that from the semantic perspective, there should be a referent object in the structure that refers to the same thing that appears above, but from the grammatical perspective, this object does not have a real visible form of word expression as zero anaphora. (1) and (2) show zero anaphora at the beginning of clauses. Chinese has a large number of zero anaphora phenomena and is therefore considered a topic-prominent language [3], a pro-drop language and a zero-topic language [4]. Wang [5] proposed that in a topic-prominent language such as Chinese, the salient entities can be inferred in a specific context and thus are often elliptic. This phenomenon also serves as a window into human cognition, whereby human linguistic cognitive processing can be explored in depth.

Song [6–9] referred to the zero anaphora at the beginning of clauses as component sharing and proposed the concept of naming and telling with Clause Complex Theory. Naming is the start of an utterance and is similar to topic, but the scope is not limited to noun phrase. Telling is the concept opposite of naming, defined as the component that explains the naming. Punctuation clauses as units, Clause Complex Theory summarizes four types of component sharing patterns, which include branch pattern, new branch pattern, postposition pattern, and influx pattern. As in (1), the case where the latter clause shares a component at the beginning of the former clause is called the branch pattern; as in (2), the case where the latter clause shares the component which is not at the beginning of the former clause and cannot share the component at the beginning of the former clause is called the new branch pattern. These two patterns are the main object of this paper.

In this paper, we choose the linking verb "shì(是)" as the entry point to distinguish the branch pattern and the new branch pattern. On the one hand, linking verbs are special among verbs. According to Zhang [10], linking verbs are different from ordinary verbs that represent events. Linking verbs represent the relationship between entities, and "shì(是)" is the core member of linking verbs in Chinese. Therefore, the subject and the object of "shì(是)" are usually equivalent in semantics, and from the point of view of anaphora, there is a theoretical competition of being the antecedent between the subject and the object, which increases the difficulty of natural language processing. Another reason is that "shì(是)" can be paired with almost all referential components, which can exclude the influence of the verb on the semantic type of the subject and object to the greatest extent possible. Also, "shì(是)" is the most frequent verb in Chinese, so the study of it has a greater practical value.

Therefore, this paper will take the linking verb "shì(是)" as the object of study and explore the conditions under which different component sharing patterns are formed between the former and the latter clauses when the former clause has "shì(是)" as the core verb, focusing on the influence of the core verb "shì(是)" on the introduction of new branch naming. In this paper, we refer to this condition of different component sharing patterns as contextual patterns.

2 Analysis of the Clause Group of the Object New Branch Pattern with "Shì(是)" -Clause

2.1 Clause Group, Subject Branch Pattern and Object New Branch Pattern

For the sake of convenience, we refer to the two successive punctuation clauses called the former clause and the latter clause as a clause group. To make the study workable, two requirements were met in the selection of our corpus: the former clause is a complete "subject + verb + object" structure with "shì(是)" as the core verb; the latter clause is missing the naming of the clause.

There are two main cases of complementing missing naming: the branch pattern in which the latter clause shares the subject of the former clause and the new branch pattern in which the latter clause shares the object of the former clause [8]. We call the first one the subject branch pattern, as in (1), and the second one the object new branch pattern, as in (2). There are three characteristics of the subject branch pattern: firstly, the latter clause shares the subject or the part of it; secondly, the latter clause does not share the core verb "shì(是)" and the object; thirdly, the shared component starts from the beginning of the clause. And there are two characteristics of the object new branch pattern: firstly, the latter clause shares the object or the part of it; secondly, the latter clause does not share the core verb "shì(是)" and its preceding component[1]. (1) and (2) are represented in the newline-intent schema as follows [6].

(1')　①教育是培养人的一种社会活动，

　　　②　　是人类自身发展所必需的，

　　　③　　也是人类社会得以发展的必要条件。[1]

①Education is a social activity that nurtures human beings,

②　　　　is necessary for their own development,

③　　　　and is also a necessary condition for the development of human society.

(2')　①另一个得利最大的是沙俄，

　　　②　　　　　　　｜　　以后延续到苏联。

①The other country that benefited the most was Tsarist Russia,

②　　　　　　　　　　　　　　　　　　｜　　　　　　later continued to the Soviet Union.

---

[1] Tokens like this have more than one overlapping clause groups. After sharing components in the first clause group consisting clause ① and clause ②, clause ② is complete, and clause ③ shares components of clause ②.

2.2 The Corpus of "Shì(是)" Addressing a New Branch Naming

Through the systematic sampling method, we first extracted 1000 tokens from the corpus[2], and "shì(是)" appeared 1631 times in total. After excluding the invalid token[3], there were 822 clause groups containing "shì(是)". Among them, 168 tokens are tokens of the subject branch pattern, accounting for 20.4%; 15 tokens are tokens of the object new branch pattern, accounting for 1.8%; the remaining 639 tokens include 416 tokens without component sharing and 223 tokens of other component sharing patterns.

The number of the tokens of the subject branch pattern is much larger than that of the object new branch pattern, which is consistent with the results of previous studies. Fang [11] mentions that zero anaphora ellipsis of the subject in complex sentences accounts for 83.5% and zero anaphora ellipsis of the object accounts for 2.6%. Pu [12] studies the zero anaphor in spoken Chinese, with 93.5% referring to the subject and 5.3% to the object. Lu [13] counted the frequency and capacity of verbs addressing a new branch naming, and among the 14 most frequent transitive verbs in Chinese, the highest percentage of addressing a new branch naming is 4.3%, with the percentage of "shì(是)" being 1.4%. The statistical results in this paper are consistent with this, and also suggest that the high number of "shì(是)" addressing a new branch naming in the results of Ji et al. [14] is more likely due to the high word frequency of "shì(是)" itself.

It can be seen that the object new branch pattern with a small proportion when there is component sharing is marked. Therefore, the syntactic, semantic, and pragmatic features of the tokens of the object new branch pattern deserve further study. There are 15 tokens of the object new branch patterns in our corpus in total. One of them is (2), and the remaining are as follows.

(3)　　①当时的经济生活主要是渔猎和采集，

　　　　②　　　　　　　　　|　　　　使用的工具以打制石器为主，

　　　　①The economic life at that time was mainly fishing, hunting and gathering,

　　　　②　　　　　　　　　　　　　|　　　　　　　and the

　　　　tools used were mainly made of stone tools.

(4)　　①他们的做法是"两动两不动"，

　　　　②　　　　　|　　　　即"分配形式变动，

　　　　①Their approach is "two moves and two stays",

　　　　②　　　　　　|　　　　　　which means "the form of

　　　　distribution changes, ...

---

[2] Unless otherwise noted, all the tokens in this paper are taken from the CCL corpus of Peking University, and because of the downloading limitation, the corpus we chose just contains the first 500,000 tokens.

[3] There are three types of invalid material: the material that "shì(是)" functions as a non-verb or morpheme; the material with repetition and slips of the tongue; the material that the clause with "shì(是)" as the core verb is the last punctuation clause.

(5) ①我不是块石头，

② | 拈来拎去，

①I am not a stone

② | to be carried around.

(6) ①一种是一次抽签定额偿还，

② | 即在规定的时间内，

①One type of repayment is a fixed amount in one lottery,

② | means in the time limit…

(7) ①二是分期抽签定额偿还，

② | 即在规定的偿还期内分几次抽签，

①The second is the installment draw for fixed repayment,

② | means several draws

within a specified reimbursement period…

(8) ①最令我难忘的是1990年的夏训，

② | 我曾创下过连滑4万米的个人训练纪录。

①The most memorable was the summer training in 1990,

② | when I had set a person-

al training record of 40,000 meters in a row.

(9) ①富有诱惑的是中国今后一段时间里可观的进口额：

② | 10年之内，

①What is tempting is the considerable amount of imports

② | that China will have for

some time to come: within 10 years, ...

(10) ①这套书需要的资金也是一个令人瞠目的数字：

② | 100万元人民币。

①The money needed for this set of books is also an eye-popping figure:

② | 1 million

RMB.

(11) ①{说"凡人皆有死"}⁴就是把已知的归予同类之未知的，

② | 即"以其所不取之同

于其所取者予之也"。

①{"All men die"} is, to categorize the known and the unknown as the same,

②   which

is "to categorize the proposition that the other side disagrees with and the proposi-

tion that the other side agrees with as the same, as a way to refute the other side's

argument".

(12) ①六是各种金融规章还不配套，

② | 相互之间缺少依托和保障，

①Sixth, various financial regulations are still mismatched,

② | lacking mutual support and protection, ...

(13) ①现在一是审批手续繁琐，

② | 贻误时机。

①Now one, the approval process is cumbersome

②   and delayed.

(14) ①列车车厢用的是铝合金整体压模，

② | 具有防腐蚀、隔热、减震等性能。

①The train carriage is made of aluminum alloy,

② | which has the properties of corro-

sion prevention, heat insulation and shock absorption.

(15) ①四是提职晋升方面实行双轨制，

② | 即对那些学术造诣较深、教学科研水平

高、贡献大{但受目前职数限制无法晋升的教师，可破格按要求晋升}，

①Fourth, a dual-track system is implemented for promotion,

② | meaning that teachers

who have deep academic attainments, high ability and great contribution in teach-

ing and research, {but cannot be promoted by the limit of the current number of

posts, can be promoted by exception on request, ...}

(16) ①五是全县开花。

② | (许多部、局、科、室，{均有来稿})}

①Fifth, the whole county blooms.

② | (Many ministries, bureaus, sections and offices, { have

contributed articles)}

2.3   The Literal Formal Feature of "Shì(是)" Addressing a New Branch Naming

An analysis of (2) – (16) shows that all tokens of the object new branch pattern, except for (3) and (5), have some literal formal features[4].

The first literal formal feature is "jí(即)" at the beginning of the latter clause. There are 5 tokens in total: (4), (6), (7), (11) and (15). "jí(即)" is a common marker in complex clauses, and the latter clause usually illustrates the object of the former clause. We expanded the corpus for examination and found that the objects in these tokens are often institutional words, understood only by a specific group, which also required interpretation, thus exhibiting a temporary topic shift. However, a small amount of naming is the entire former clause rather than the solitary object.

The second literal formal feature is the former clause ends with punctuation ":". There are 2 tokens in total: (9) and (10). ":" is also a common marker in complex clauses, and the latter clause often illustrates the object of the former clause. In (9) and (10), the object is a modifier-head structure, and the latter clause is interpreted with figures. However, the corpus without systematic sampling reveals that the usage of ":" is more diverse and complex than that of "jí(即)", and is not yet qualified as a formal marker for addressing a new branch naming.

The third literal formal feature is the former clause takes a solitary numeral or numeral-classifier structure as its subject. There are 6 tokens in total: (6), (7), (12), (13), (15) and (16). In this case, the subject of the former clause only plays the role of enumeration. The core meaning is expressed by the object, and the latter clause explains the specific content of the object of the former clause.

The last literal formal feature is the subject of the former clause is the "de(的)" structure. There are 4 tokens in total: (2), (8), (9) and (14). In this case, the subject of the former clause describes the property of the object, while the latter clause tends to give a more detailed description of the object as a noun phrase.

2.4   The Semantic Feature of "Shì(是)" Addressing a New Branch Naming

In terms of the semantic aspect, the subject and the object of the linking verb should be equational or classificational [15]. "Shì(是)" is a linking verb, and this paper focuses on its usages to express equation and classification. Other usages as a verb, such as expressing presence, is controversial and occurs infrequently, so we will not discuss them in this paper. Lyu [15] mentions that when "shì(是)" express equation, the subject and the object are generally interchangeable, and the meaning remains the same; when it is categorized, the subject and the object are not interchangeable. We take this as the criterion to distinguish the semantics of "shì(是)".

---

[4] The part in { } involves component sharing with the punctuation clause outside the clause group, and for ease of understanding, the post-complementary form is simply indicated.

In all the 15 tokens of the object new branch pattern in our corpus, there are 13 tokens with usage of expressing equation. Only (5) and (10) express classification.

Another point worth noting is that (3) and (5), which are not evidenced in the literal form, have one thing in common: "shì(是)" is modified. In (3), "shì(是)" is modified by "zhǔyào(主要)", if there is no "zhǔyào(主要)", the subject and the object of the former clause are equivalent, but after adding "zhǔyào(主要)", the object becomes included in the subject. In (5), "shì(是)" is modified by "bù(不)". If "bù(不)" is deleted, the subject and the object of the former clause are in a classification relationship, and after "bù(不)" is added, the relationship becomes antagonistic. This type of modifier changes the equation or classification of the two entities linked by "shì(是)" so that they express other relationships.

(17a) ①我和乔红是世界头两号选手，

②　　　　是全世界共同研究的对象。

①Qiao Hong and I are the top two players in the world

②　　　　and are the object of common study around the world.

(17b) ①我和乔红是世界头两号选手，

②　　　｜是全世界共同研究的对象。

①Qiao Hong and I are the top two players in the world

②　　　｜ as the object of common

study around the world.

(18a) ①这些形象工程项目是纯粹的挥霍消费，

②　　　　带来的是零回报。

①These image projects are purely profligate consumption,

②　　　　so brings zero return.

(18b) ①这些形象工程项目是纯粹的挥霍消费，

②　　　｜带来的是零回报。

①These image projects are purely profligate consumption,

②　　　｜ which brings zero

return.

Semantically, if the two entities in the former clause are equated, the subject and the object are ontologically equivalent, so it is difficult to determine the naming of the latter clause, as in (17), both the subject and the object can be used as the naming. If the two entities in the former clause are analogous and the subject is a hyponym of the object, they may both fit the description of the latter clause, such as in (18). The modifier of "shì(是)" in (5) also changes the relationship between the subject and the object. Therefore, we further examine "shì(是)" with a modifier.

3   Analysis of the Clause Group of the Object New Branch Pattern with "Bù Shì(不是) "-Clause

In the corpus of the object new branch pattern, there are tokens where "shì(是)" is modified, such as in (3) and (5), where the modifiers " zhǔyào(主要)" and "bù(不)" change the relationship between the two entities in the former clause to inclusion and opposition. As mentioned above, adding modifiers can change the relationship, better distinguish the subject and the object, clarify the component sharing pattern, and explore the context mode of "shì(是)" addressing a new branch naming.

The verb "shì(是)", which is modified by the adverb "bù(不)", was selected for further investigation in this paper. There are two reasons for this. First, "bù(不)" is the most frequent adverb, often used as an adverbial modifier, and is representative. And "bù(不)" has a significant effect on the relationship expressed by "shì(是)", changing the relationship of equation or classification to opposition. When the latter clause shares the naming of the former clause, there is no logical competition between the subject and the object of the former clause.

3.1   The Corpus of "Bù Shì(不是)" Addressing a New Branch Naming

In this study, 1008 tokens containing "bù shì(不是)" were extracted from the corpus of "shì(是)", and "bù shì(不是)" appeared 1140 times. After excluding the invalid corpus, there were 646 clause groups containing "bù shì(不是)". Among them, there are 268 tokens of the subject branch pattern and 3 tokens of the object new branch pattern. The remaining 375 tokens include 270 tokens without component sharing and 105 tokens of other component sharing patterns.

Compared to the overall proportion of "shì(是)" addressing a new branch naming (14/822), the proportion of "bù shì(不是)" addressing a new branch naming (3/646) was much lower. This shows that "bù shì(不是)" is more difficult to address a new branch naming than "shì(是)". Overall, the subject branch pattern is still much more frequent than the object new branch pattern in the corpus. In the tokens of the subject branch pattern, the core verb of the latter clause is also often "shì(是)", usually with the conjunction "ér(而), bìng(并)" appearing at the beginning of the latter clause, or the adverb "hái(还), yě(也), jiù(就)" modifying the core verb "shì(是)". In this paper, we believe that these words can be regarded as markers of the subject branch pattern.

3.2   The Literal Formal Feature of "Bù Shì(不是)" Addressing a New Branch Naming

The only 3 tokens of the object new branch pattern are as follows.

(19) ①西藏不是过去美国的西部，

② | 可以大批移民开发。

①Tibet is not the American West of the past,

② | which can be developed by mass
immigration.

(20) ①而不是相反，

② | 即t变k大。

①And not the other way around,

② | which means that t becomes k large.

(21) ①但是文艺的娱乐功能绝不是巴尔扎克所批评过的那种"街头戏子"式的娱
乐，

② |

即没有思想内容和社会意义｛的娱乐｝，

①But the entertainment function of literature is never the kind of entertainment
that Balzac criticized as "performance in the streets,"

② |

that is, entertainment without
intellectual content and social meaning, ...

(22) ①用人单位不是"菜园门"，

② | 想来就来，

①Employers are not "food markets",

② | they can come whenever they want, ...

(23) ①我也不是那种人：

② | 10岁离开中国，

①I am not that kind of person either:

② | left China at the age of 10, ...

In addition, a large number of tokens show that "shì(是)" could not address a new
branch naming when the conjunction "ér(而), bìng(并)" or the adverb "hái(还), yě(也),
jiù(就)" was used, so we further filtered the corpus to exclude the latter clause with these
words. After filtering the corpus with the above-mentioned conjunctions and adverbs,
343 relevant fragments were extracted by systematic sampling method, and there were
423 clause groups containing the word "bù shì(不是)", among which only 2 tokens of
the object new branch pattern. They are (22) and (23).

(5) and (19)–(22) are tokens of the object new branch pattern. (20), (21), and (23) have literal formal markers, while (5), (19), and (22) have no literal formal markers. The three tokens without literal formal markers are further discussed below in terms of semantic features.

3.3 The Semantic Feature of "Bù Shì(不是)" Addressing a New Branch Naming

From the semantic point of view, an important feature of the clause groups in which "bù shì(不是)" addresses a new branch naming is irrealis of the latter clause. Irrealis refers to the description of what might happen or what is assumed to happen in the possible world [16]. The latter clauses of (5), (19), and (22) without literal formal markers are all irrealis. The modal verb " kěyǐ(可以)" in the latter clause of (19) can be used as evidence of irrealis. Similarly, (5) and (22) can also add "kěyǐ(可以)" at the beginning of the latter clause, and the basic meaning remains unchanged, see below.

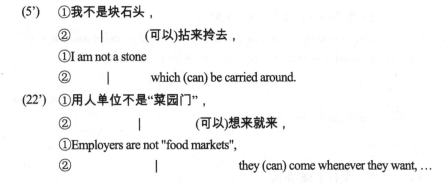

Accordingly, we examined another corpus[5], and retrieved 48 tokens with the structure of "noun phrase/pronoun phrase (+adverb) + bù shì(不是) (+noun phrase + de(的)) + noun phrase" in the former clause and " kěyǐ(可以)" as the beginning of the latter clause. After excluding 9 repetitive tokens, 11 of the 39 tokens are tokens of the subject branch pattern and 28 tokens are tokens of the object new branch pattern. The proportion of the object new branch pattern is 71.8%, which is much higher than the proportion of the object new branch pattern of "shì(是)". It can be seen that irrealis of the latter clause is an important feature in that the latter clause shares the new branch naming and becomes a new branch clause.

Another semantic feature is that there is no direct ontological hyponymy relationship between the subject and the object of the former clause. The clause is meant to express an attribute of the subject through the object. And the attribute is often not closely related to the object and needs to be explained.

---

[5] The tokens here are taken from the multi-domain, literary and newspaper databases of the BCC corpus of Beijing Language and Culture University.

(24) ①火车不是汽车，

②   ｜   可以叫得停的。

①Trains are not cars

②   ｜   that can be called to a halt.

(25) ①丫头都不是人，

②   可以由他当作礼物送来送去。

①The maid are not even human

②   and can be given around by him as gifts.

In (24), there is no direct subordination between "huǒchē(火车)" and "qìchē(汽车)", so the categorization is not based on common sense, and addressing "qìchē(汽车)" is actually to explain a certain property. However, "kěyǐ jiào dé tíng de(可以叫得停的)" is not a property of "qìchē(汽车)" with high psychological accessibility, so it needs to be explained. There are only 2 tokens of the object new branch pattern that do not meet this feature. In the tokens of the subject branch pattern, one case is that the subject is a hyponym the object[6], such as in (25), where the subject "yātou(丫头)" and the object "rén(人)" have an ontological hyponymy relationship, but the sentence denies the categorization; in the other case, the object is an abstract noun, which is also not a comparison but a description of some property, such as "bù shì wèntí(不是问题)", "bù shì bànfǎ(不是办法)", etc.

4 The Context Mode of the Linking Verb "Shì(是)" Addressing a New Branch Naming

4.1 The Feature of "Shì(是)" Addressing a New Branch Naming

In conclusion, we summarize the context mode of the linking verb "shì(是)" addressing a new branch naming.

Lu [17] considers that the new branch naming is a temporary topic shift. We argue that the underlying reason for the emergence of the object new branch pattern is the need for explanatory clarification of the object of the former clause. In some tokens of the object new branch pattern, the object of the former clause is presented as jargon or abbreviation, and its meaning needs a further explanation for the hearer to comprehend it. In some tokens, the object of the former clause is only a common noun, which seems to be easy to understand. This is evident in the tokens containing the phrase "bù shì(不是)". In fact, these nouns are not introduced to compare them ontologically with the subject, but to highlight a property. But when, in the perception of the hearer, or more precisely in the perception of the hearer as perceived by the speaker, this property is not so closely linked to the object and is difficult to psychologically access, an explanatory note is needed. The degree to which the object is easy to extract its connotation for the hearer is what we call intelligibility of the object.

---

[6] Here the pronoun is regarded as a specific range of people or corresponding things.

This paper also mentions two cases of a former clause with a solitary numeral or numeral-classifier structure as subject and "de(的)" structure that appear in the object new branch pattern, which we believe is related to the concreteness of the reference. Givón [18] argues that the somatic reference is the label of the mental document, which is used to store the input information. Thus, in cases where the subject and object referents are the same, the more concrete referential component is better able to fulfill this function, while the more abstract referential component tends to express with properties or evaluations, sometimes exhibiting a provisional nature. The degree to which this reference is more explicit and better reflects the referential function rather than the declarative function is what we call referential specificity.

Based on the corpus, we propose a sequence of the referential specificity: specific reference or definite reference > substantive reference > predicative reference > enumerative reference.

Specific reference is a proper name or term (e.g., "liǎng dòng liǎng bù dòng(两动两不动)" in (4)). Definite reference contains a personal pronoun or a demonstrative pronoun (e.g., "zhè(这), nà(那)"). The substantive reference is a noun or noun phrase without any proper name or term. Predicative reference contains at least one predicative component (e.g., "lǚhéjīn zhěngtǐ yāmó(铝合金整体压模)" in (14)). Enumerative reference is expressed as a solitary numeral or a numeral-classifier phrase (e.g., "èr(二)" in (7), "yī zhǒng(一种)" in (6)). In the case where the core verb of the former clause is "shì(是)", except when "shì(是)" is modified by "bù(不)", if the referential specificity of the subject is higher than or equal to the object, then the clause group is a clause group of the subject branch pattern; if it is lower than the object, then the clause group is a clause group of the object new branch pattern.

Therefore, we argue that in the case of the linking verb "shì(是)" as the core verb, the context mode to address a new branch naming depends to a large extent on the object. The first is the intelligibility of the object, both literally and intrinsically in relation to the subject; the second is the referential specificity of the object, which is based on the comprehensibility of the label chosen for storing information.

It is important to emphasize that intelligibility takes precedence over referential specificity. When the subject and the object do not belong to the same category, even if the subject is more specific, a new branch pattern may arise because of low intelligibility.

In addition, there are some sufficient conditions for the subject branch pattern, such as the latter clause still having "shì(是)" as the core verb. In tokens of the object new branch pattern, the meaning of "shì(是)" is expressed by the core verb "jí(即)". This may be related to parallelism. Another condition is a latter clause with the related conjunctions "ér(而), bìng(并), jì(既), yòu(又)" or the adverb "hái(还), yě(也), jiù(就)". This may indicate that the connectives cannot be used between the naming and telling of a clause in a temporary shift.

4.2   The Process of Interpreting the Linking Verb "Shì(是)" Addressing a New Branch Naming

Based on the above discussion, we have constructed a process to determine whether a clause group with "shì(是)" is a clause group of the subject branch pattern or the object new branch pattern, including both literal formal and semantic features, but we need to invoke the support of encyclopedic knowledge to determine the missing component completely and accurately.

There are literal formal features of the object new branch pattern itself. Besides, the sufficient condition of the subject branch pattern is also a necessary condition of the object new branch pattern. Although these rules cannot identify the object new branch pattern with absolute accuracy, they still help in the recognition of the object new branch pattern.

The above literal formal features are applicable in all cases where the core verb of the former clause is "shì(是)". If the core verb of the former clause is "shì(是)" modified by "bù(不)" to express negation, then the semantic features should be considered. If both are noun phrases or pronoun phrases, we need to determine whether the subject belongs to the object in the ontological category, and here it is necessary to bring in dictionaries to provide encyclopedic knowledge. If the subject is not a hyponym of the object and the object is not an exceptional abstract noun, then the clause group is a clause group of the object new branch pattern, otherwise, it is a clause group of the subject branch pattern.

Finally, in the absence of the above, the referential specificity of the subject and the object is compared, the component with high specificity is selected as the naming, and the clause group is grouped into the corresponding component sharing pattern (Fig. 1).

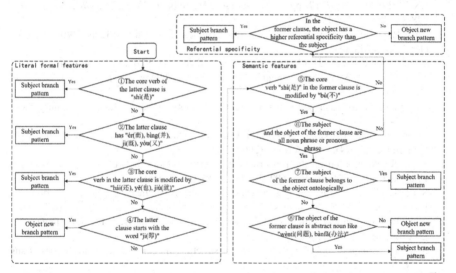

Fig. 1. The process of determining the component sharing pattern of the linking verb "shì(是)"

5 Conclusion

Complementing the missing elements in Chinese clauses contributes to computer understanding. This paper examines the linking verb "shì(是)" and "bù shì(不是)" based on the naming-telling structure and Clause Complex Theory, and explores the influence of verbs to address a new branch.

When "shì(是)" is used as a core verb, the component sharing of the next clause is mostly the subject branch pattern. The two main factors that determine whether "shì(

是)" addresses a new branch naming are the intelligibility and the referential specificity of the object. We propose a context mode for addressing new branch naming, including literal formal features and semantic features. The literal formal features include the core verb "shì(是)", the conjunction "ér(而), bìng(并), jì(既), yòu(又)", the adverb "hái(还), yě(也), jiù(就)" modifying the core verb in the latter clause, and the verb "jí(即)" at the beginning of the latter clause. The semantic features include the relationship between the subject and the object of the former clause in the ontological category and the effect of the adverb modifying the core verb in the latter clause on that relationship. Finally, we also propose a sequence of referential specificity and build a process for determining the component sharing pattern of the linking verb "shì(是)".

Acknowledgements. We thank the anonymous reviewers of this paper. We also thank the National Social Science Foundation of China for supporting the project (Grant No. 18CYY030).

References

1. Wang, G.-N., Qin, Y., Jiang, M., Zhao, Q.-R.: MT-oriented and computer-based subject restoration for Chinese empty-subject sentences. In: Ji, D., Xiao, G. (eds.) CLSW 2012. LNCS (LNAI), vol. 7717, pp. 1–10. Springer, Heidelberg (2013). https://doi.org/10.1007/978-3-642-36337-5_1
2. Chen, P.: Discourse analysis of zero Anphora in Chinese. Stud. Chinese Lang. **10**(05), 363–378 (1987). (in Chinese)
3. Li, C., Thompson, S.: Third-person pronouns and zero Anaphora in Chinese discourse. In: Givón, T. (eds.): Syntax and Semantics: Discourse and Syntax. Academic Press, New York (1979)
4. Huang, J.: On the distribution and reference of empty pronouns. Linguist. Inquiry **15**(4), 531–574 (1984)
5. Wang, D.: Zero Anaphora resolution in Chinese: a study based on centering theory. Mod. Foreign Lang. 27(4), 350–359+436 (2004). (in Chinese)
6. Song, R.: A research on the properties of syntactic relation between p-clause in modern Chinese. Chinese Teach. World **02**, 26–44 (2008). (in Chinese)
7. Song, R.: Chinese Clause Complex and Naming Structure. In: Jie C., Liu M. (eds.) Frontiers of Empirical and Corpus Linguistics. China Social Sciences Press, Beijing (2018). (in Chinese)
8. Song, R.: Grammatical Structure of Clause Complex. The Commercial Press, Beijing (2022). (in Chinese)
9. Song, R.: Stream model of generalized topic structure in Chinese text. Stud. Chinese Lang. **06**, 483–494 (2013). (in Chinese)
10. Zhang, B.: On the standards of copula identification in Chinese language. Lang. Teach. Linguist. Stud. **4**, 48–54 (2002). (in Chinese)
11. Fang, M.: Ellipsis of the subject of a clause in a complex sentence. J. Yanbian Univ. (Soc. Sci.) **01**, 44–54 (1985). (in Chinese)
12. Pu, M.: Zero Anaphora and grammatical relations in Mandarin. In: Givón T. (eds.) Grammatical Relations: A Functionalist Perspective. J. Benjamins, Amsterdam (1997)
13. Lu, D.: The Cognitive and Computational Research of Generalized Topic Structure in Chinese Discourse: A Corpus-driven Approach. Beijing Language and Culture University, Beijing (2015). (in Chinese)
14. Ji, C., Lu, D., Song, R.: Research on pragmatic function of verb addressing new branch topic. J. Chinese Inf. Process. **28**(03), 22–27 (2014). (in Chinese)

15. Lyu, S.: 800 Words of Modern Chinese, Updated The Commercial Press, Beijing (1999). (in Chinese)
16. Zhou, R.: A study of mandarin adverbs under realis-Irrealis distinction. Chinese Teach. World **29**(02), 167–183 (2015). (in Chinese)
17. Lu, D.: A study of syntactic constituent and semantic role of new branch topic. J. Chinese Inf. Process. **35**(10), 21–31 (2021). (in Chinese)
18. Givón, T.: The Story of Zero. J. Benjamins, Amsterdam (2017)

Taking Comparison Between the Degree Adverbs in Northeast Dialect and Taiwanese Mandarin from Three Perspectives——Taking *Lǎo* and *Chāo* as Examples

Jingying Rui[1] ⓘ, Jia-Fei Hong[2](✉) ⓘ, and Jie Song[3]

[1] School of Humanities, Minjiang University, Fuzhou, China
RaisingRui@mju.edu.cn
[2] Department of Chinese as a Second Language, Taiwan Normal University, Taipei, Taiwan
Jiafeihong@ntnu.edu.tw
[3] School of International Studies, Chengdu College of Arts and Sciences, Chengdu, China

Abstract. This paper uses the data from relevant corpora and multimedia resources to summarize the properties and features of the usages of *Lǎo* (老) and *Chāo* (超) from the semantic, grammatical and pragmatic perspectives as well as compare them at each level. It is found that *Lǎo* and *Chāo* are highly similar in terms of usages and they both belong to the sub-highest degree adverbs of the absolute degree adverbs with some exceptions. They can modify the same components, but they have different syntactic structures. From the pragmatic perspective, both *Lǎo* and *Chāo* can express subjective attitudes and strong sentiments, but there are differences in terms of writing, new and old information, accentuation, and inversion.

Keywords: Degree adverbs · Absolute degree adverbs · Corpora · *Lǎo* · *Chāo*

1 Introduction

It can be seen that degree adverbs are vast in numbers and usages among contemporary Chinese. Some of the degree adverbs are commonly found, such as *Hěn* (很)'very', *Fēicháng* (非常)'very', and *Tài* (太)'too', of which some scholars did a lot of research to define the specific degree [1–3]. While some other degree adverbs have local characteristics even the characters may not widely applicable which is worthy of further exploration [4–6]. As the prevalence of social media in Internet, Northeastern Mandarin and Taiwanese are compared in a lot of videos as they are considered as the most catchy and captivating accents in Chinese society. It is found that there are strong parallels between them even if they are far away regionally[1]. *Lǎo* and *Chāo* are very typical degree adverbs in Northeast China and Taiwan. Both of them have been used to indicate the degree of

---

[1] Website sources: https://www.sohu.com/a/69551589_391351.https://v.qq.com/x/page/d0750w mokou.html.

© The Author(s), under exclusive license to Springer Nature Switzerland AG 2023
Q. Su et al. (Eds.): CLSW 2022, LNAI 13495, pp. 490–505, 2023.
https://doi.org/10.1007/978-3-031-28953-8_36

the modifiers and can be interchangeable with other degree adverbs. The contexts that they can be used in are also highly overlapping. Whether there are differences between them in specific circumstances and how they differ from each other are the focuses of this paper. Through analyzing the relevant corpora of *Lǎo* and *Chāo* in a detailed way, this paper intends to clarify the following research questions:

1. Are there any differences between *Lǎo* and *Chāo* semantically? Which one conveys a stronger degree?
2. What are the grammatical features of *Lǎo* and *Chāo* respectively? Are the syntactic structures and the modifiers the same?
3. What are the pragmatic features of *Lǎo* and *Chāo*? Are there any differences in the contexts?

2 Corpus Resources

The existing corpora cannot take both Northeast Dialect and Taiwanese into account, and using a single corpus or data resource is not sufficient to carry out an overall investigation of specific features of *Lǎo* and *Chāo* from three perspectives. Therefore, this paper chooses multiple data resources combining the factors of regions, language styles, and expression patterns to conduct an objective and specific comparative analysis on the usage of *Lǎo* and *Chāo*. The sources of the data used in this paper mainly come from BLCU Chinese Corpus (BCC)[2], Academia Sinica Balanced Corpus (Sinca)[3], Corpus of Contemporary Taiwanese Mandarin (COCT)[4], the TV series *Mǎ Dàshuài* (马大帅) and *Xiāngcūn àiqíng* (乡村爱情), the short sketches *Zhōngdiǎngōng* (钟点工) and *Xiǎocuī shuōshì* (小崔说事), adding a small proportion of daily examples collected from forums, blogs, *Baidu Tieba* and so on.

3 The Usage of Lǎo

In this section, the usage of *Lǎo* is explained from semantic, syntactic, and pragmatic perspectives. The sources of the corpora mainly draw from the TV series *Mǎ Dàshuài*, *Xiāngcūn àiqíng*, the short sketches *Zhōngdiǎngōng* and *Xiǎocuī shuōshì*, etc., which rated as the most influential broadcasts in Northeast Dialect. Additionally, some data are from the BCC corpus, covering literary works, newspapers and *Weibo*.

3.1 The Semantic Features of Lǎo

Zhang [7] divides degree adverbs into two categories: comparative and absolute degree adverbs. The comparative degree adverb is divided into the superlative, minor superlative, comparative and the lower degree while the latter one is categorized into the extra, the highest, sub-highest, and slightly lower rank. In terms of [7]'s classification, *Lǎo* belongs

---

[2] BCC website: http://bcc.blcu.edu.cn/.
[3] Sinca website: http://asbc.iis.sinica.edu.tw/.
[4] COCT website: https://coct.naer.edu.tw/cqpweb/.

to the category of absolute degree adverbs and is explained as *Jí* (极) 'extremely' and *Hěn* (很) according to the online Xinhua dictionary[5]. They respectively belong to the highest and sub-highest rank of the absolute degree adverbs which are not of the same kind. Cao [8] regards *Lǎo* as the highest degree adverb, but some scholars [4, 9] classify *Lǎo* as the sub-highest degree adverb. Therefore, the categorization of *Lǎo* is controversial in the academia.

In this paper, a total of 50 sentences involving *Lǎo* acting as a degree adverb are randomly selected from the TV series *Mǎ Dàshuài* and *Xiāngcūn àiqíng*. These two TV series are the life portrayal of rural youth played by the local people in the Northeast of China, where the accents are regionally featured along with the expression habits of native speakers. To verify the semantic meaning, three native speakers were asked to judge the degree (which is *Lǎo* closer to, *Jí*, or *Hěn* and *Fēicháng*). If the three native speakers did not reach the same conclusion, another two will be asked to continue to make the judgment, and if the final result was 3:2, then another two native speakers would be asked to verify. After this round of verification, the semantic meaning of *Lǎo* in this sentence was finally divided based on the principle of majority rule. In the process of verification, 46 example sentences were passed in the first round, 3 example sentences were passed in the second round, and 1 example sentence was passed in the third round whose score was 5:2. The comprehensive statistics of the semantic judgment by the native speakers are as follows:

	Semantics is closer to *Jí*	Semantics is closer to *Hěn* and *Fēicháng*
Amount	5	45
Proportion	10%	90%

It was found that the word *Lǎo*, which is commonly used in the Northeast part of China, belongs to the sub-highest rank of the absolute degree adverb in most cases, and can be replaced with the same kind such as *Fēicháng*, *Tèbié* (特别) 'especially' in the context without changing the sentence meaning, for example:

(1) 我 姐夫 在 那里 老 好使 了。

Wǒ jiěfu zài nàlǐ lǎo hǎoshǐ le.

My brother-in-law is very powerful there. (《马大帅》7).

However, there are a few exceptions in the collected corpus, e.g.:

(2) 我 告诉 你 那 韵律 老毙 了, 老 有 感觉 了。

Wǒ gàosù nǐ nà yùnlǜ lǎobì le, lǎo yǒu gǎnjué le.

I tell you that the rhythm is extremely impressive. (《马大帅3》11).

(3) 小弟: 哎呀, 那 彪哥, 那你 现在 老 有 钱 了吧?

Xiǎodì: aiya, nà biāogē, nà nǐ xiànzài lǎo yǒuqián le ba?

Young fellow: Mr. Biao, you are very rich now, right?

彪哥: 钱啥呀, 钱是 身外之物。

---

[5] Xinhua dictionary online: http://xh.5156edu.com/.

Biāogē: qián sháya, qián shì shēnwàizhīwù.

Mr. Biao: What is money? Money is an external thing. (《马大帅》8)

The adjective *Bì* (毙) in example (2) is a unique adjective in Northeast Dialect, whose meaning is closer to *Hǎo* (好) 'good' and *Kù* (酷) 'cool'. Continuous uses of the word *Lǎo* emphasize the subject and convey richer emotional feelings. However, it cannot be replaced by *Hěn*, which is closer to *Jí* semantically; The context in example (3) that everyone sighs that Mr. Biao is now flourishing draws a sharp contrast and gap between the young fellow and Biao. The exclamation at the beginning of the sentence makes the phrase *Lǎo yǒuqián le* (老有钱了) closer to the expression of *Yǒuqián jí le* (有钱极了).

To sum up, *Lǎo*, as an absolute degree adverb, should be classified as the sub-highest degree adverb, except for individual cases and special contexts.

3.2   The Grammatical Features of *Lǎo*

This section will delve into the grammatical rules for the specific use of *Lǎo*.

3.2.1   Using with the Word *Le*

In a small number of the corpora, the grammatical structure of *Lǎo* as a degree adverb is *Lǎo + modified component* or *Lǎo + modified component + De*, such as:

(4) 爸妈 人 都 老 好, 待 我 也 好。

Bàmā rén dōu lǎo hǎo, dài wǒ yě hǎo.

My parents are very kind and treat me well. (《田园》陈忠实, BCC语料库).

The above example is found in the contemporary classical literature database, while in the Northeast part of China, the degree adverb *Lǎo* should follow the fixed syntactic structure *Lǎo + modified component + Le* in most cases. The function word *Le* has two usages: dynamic particle *Le*1 and modal particle *Le*2. The grammatical feature of *Le*2 is that it can be attached to the sentence or other words exclusively, which plays a certain grammatical role and often expresses mood together with intonation. Using *Le* with *Lǎo* usually emphasizes a positive tone or property change. For example:

(5) 这 小孩 穿 得 老 漂亮 了 (强调肯定语气) 。

Zhè xiǎohái chuān de lǎo piàoliang le.

The child dressed very beautifully. (emphasizing positive tone).

(6) 他 今天 老 不 舒服了 (强调性质变化) 。

Tā jīntiān lǎo bù shūfu le.

He is very uncomfortable today. (emphasizing property change).

The BCC corpus is rich in examples of *Lǎo + modified component + Le* which acts as a fixed syntactic structure. Taking the adjectives and verbs as examples of modified components, the specific statistical results are as follows:

The usage of *Lǎo*	*Lǎo* + *a* + *Le*	*Lǎo* + *v* + *Le*
Amount	1286	573

In addition, the pattern of *Lǎo* + *modified component* + *De* + *modified component* is also common when acting as attributive and adverbial, for example:

(7) 这 是 本 老 厚 的 书 了。

Zhè shì běn lǎo hòu de shū le.

This is a very thick book.

3.2.2 Diverse Modified Components

Lǎo can modify the following parts:

① Adjective.

(8) "你 觉得比 在家里 好 吗?".

Nǐ juéde bǐ zài jiā lǐ hǎo ma?

Do you think it's better than at home?

"老好了。".

Lǎo hǎo le.

"Very good. (《你在高原》张炜, BCC语料库).

② Verb

(9) 这 个 作者 我 老 喜欢 了!

Zhè gè zuòzhě wǒ lǎo xǐhuān le!

I like this author very much! (微博, BCC语料库)

③ Noun.

(10) 他 连 女朋友 都 保护 不 了, 老 孬种 了。

Tā lián nǚpéngyou dōu bǎohù bù liǎo, lǎo nāozhǒng le.

He can't even protect his girlfriend. He is really a coward.

④ Phrase.

(11) A. Verb phrase

这 笑话 老 招笑 了。

Zhè xiàohua lǎo zhāoxiào le.

This joke is very funny. (小品:《钟点工》).

(12) B. Adverbial phrase

最近 睡眠 老 不好 了!

Zuìjìn shuìmián lǎo bùhǎo le!

I slept very badly recently! (微博, BCC语料库)

C. Complement phrase

(13) 我 心 里老 过意 不去了。

Wǒ xīn lǐ lǎo guòyi búqù le.

I feel very sorry. (《马大帅3》32)

3.3 The Pragmatic Features of *Lǎo*

This section will delve into the pragmatic features of *Lǎo* and draw some conclusions.

3.3.1 Commonly Used in Colloquial Style

As an extremely common degree adverb in the Northeast part of China, *Lǎo* is mostly found in spoken language, but rarely in written expressions [10]. In BCC corpus, there are only four cases in which *Lǎo* is used in literature and newspaper as a degree adverbs, and most of them occur in conversational contexts. There are more data coming from *Weibo*, sketches, TV dramas, and other life languages.

3.3.2 Emotionally Rich in Expression

Ma [11] referred to *Lǎo* with a strong sentiment, which is usually an emotion that the speaker dislikes, for example:

(14) 被子 老 厚 的, 热死了。

Bèizi lǎo hòu de, rè sǐ le.

The quilt is very thick. It is so hot here.

(15) *这 姑娘 眼睫毛 老 长 的, 十分 好看。

Zhè gūniang yǎnjiémáo lǎo cháng de, shífēn hǎokàn.

The girl's eyelashes are very long and beautiful.

According to [11]'s analysis, example (15) is not valid since 'long eyelashes' belongs to positive emotion. However, *Lǎo* is not limited to this in Northeast China. Example (15) is quite common in Northeast Dialect which conveys adorable and positive feelings, for example:

(16) 这 辈子 还 能 住 上 小楼, 老 高兴 了。

Zhè bèizi hái néng zhù shang xiǎolóu, lǎo gāoxìng le.

It's very happy that I can live in a building in my life. (人民日报, BCC语料库)

The structure of *Lǎo* can also indicate negative and disgusting feelings, such as:

(17) 今天 古田路 店 送 餐! 全 焦! 老 伤心 了!

Jīntiān gǔtiánlù diàn sòng cān! Quán jiāo! Lǎo shāngxīn le!

The food delivered by the Gutian Road store today! All burnt out! I'm very sad! (微博, BCC语料库)

Sometimes, the structure of *Lǎo* is just a statement of facts without obvious emotions. For example:

(18) 我家门前有条老长的河。

Wǒ jiā mén qián yǒu tiáo lǎo cháng de hé.

There is a very long river in front of my house.

3.3.3   The Modified Components are Often New Information to Listeners

By analyzing the contexts in which *Lǎo* appears, it is easy to find that the phrases of *Lǎo* in non-interrogative sentences are usually new messages, which are unknown to the listeners, for example:

(19) 我爸对他印象老好了。

Wǒ bà duì tā yìnxiàng lǎo hǎo le.

My father is very impressed with him. (《马大帅》14).

The word *Hǎo* in example (19) is unknown to the listener, and the speaker allows the listener to understand the father's psychological state by using the structure of *Lǎo* + *modified component* + *Le*. Now let's assume a dialogue scene in which A buys a dress for 10,000 yuan:

(20) 甲: 这条裙子要一万块。

Jia: zhè tiáo qúnzi yào yíwàn kuài.

A: The dress costs 10,000 *yuan*.

乙: 哇!太贵了/ 好贵啊/贵极了 (*老贵了)。

Yi: Wa! Tài guì le/ hǎo guì a/ guì jí le (*lǎo guì le).

B: Wow! Too expensive/so expensive/extremely expensive (*very expensive).

(乙对丙).

(B to C).

乙: 甲买了一条裙子, 老贵了, 要一万块。

Yi: Jiǎ mǎi le yìtiáo qúnzi, lǎo guì le, yào yíwan kuài.

B: A bought a dress and it was very expensive costing 10,000 *yuan*.

丙: 哇, 真的好贵。

Bing: Wa, zhēn de hǎo guì.

C: Wow, really expensive.

During the conversation between A and B, we can infer that the high cost is not new to A, so it would be abrupt for B to say *Lǎo guì le* (老贵了), which is not suitable with native speakers' expression habits. It is necessary to use other adverbs of degree such as *Tài* instead. However, since C did not know the price of the dress in advance, it could be a new message to C. Therefore, B's conversation with C is valid and can be modified by the word *Lǎo*.

There are still a few exceptions. Objective facts mentioned to arouse a conversation or expressions with consensus can be modified with *Lǎo*. For example:

(21) 甲: 今天 天气 老 好 了!

Jia: Jīntiān tiānqì lǎo hǎo le!

A: The weather is so good today!

乙: 对啊, 天气 不 错。(客观事实).

Yi: duì a, tiānqì bú cuò.

B: Yes, the weather is not bad. (Objective facts).

The weather in this case is an objective fact that is clear to everyone, and it is not new to the listener.

3.3.4 Using Accentuation and Inversion to Emphasis

Lǎo is generally used by stressed and inversed which emphasizes the semantic meaning to highlight the degree of the expression:

(22) 崔: 大妈 这 衣服 挺 贵 吧?

Cui: dàmā zhè yīfu tǐng guì ba?

Cui: Aunt's dress is quite expensive, right?

赵: 老 贵 了, 40一天 租 的。

Zhao: lǎo guì le, 40 yìtiān zū de.

Zhao: Very expensive. It costs 40 yuan per day. (小品《小崔说事》).

Example (22) is a dialogue between the host and *Zhao Benshan*. The host asks *Song Dandan* about the price of the clothes she wears. *Zhao Benshan*, in order to highlight the degree of expensive clothes, advances the *Lǎo guì le* (老贵了) and then explains the price of clothes.

4 The Usage of *Chāo*

In this section, the usage of *Chāo* is explained from three perspectives: semantics, syntax, and pragmatics. The main sources of the corpora are from the Sinica Corpus, COCT Corpus, and a small number of discourses from daily life. The Sinica Corpus covers newspapers, general magazines, and books, etc.

4.1 The Semantic Features of *Chāo*

This section also defines the degree of *Chāo* according to [7]'s classification of degree adverbs. *Chāo* cannot be used in comparative sentences, so it is an absolute degree adverb. According to the semantic categorization of *Chāo* by Chinese Wordnet[6], there are seven meanings of *Chāo*. When it is used as a degree adverb, it always means more than the average degree, which is synonymous to the words *Fēicháng*, *Hěn*, and *Lǎo*. Similar to *Lǎo*, the categorization of *Chāo* is also controversial, and we can see many

---

[6] Chinese Wordnet website: http://lope.linguistics.ntu.edu.tw/cwn/.

viewpoints such as the highest degree adverb [12], between the highest degree and the sub-highest degree adverb [13], and the sub-highest degree adverb [14].

To find out the degree of *Chāo*, this paper analyzed 87 cases from the Sinica Corpus when it is used as a degree adverb and the verification method is the same as that of *Lǎo*. The native speakers were asked to judge the degree in the context. During the process, 82 sentences were verified in the first round and 5 in the second round. The results are as follows:

	Semantics is closer to *Jí*	Semantics is closer to *Hěn* and *Fēicháng*
Amount	5	82
Proportion	6%	94%

The results show that *Chāo* accounted for 94% as a sub-highest degree adverb while there are only 5 cases, accounting for 6% as a highest degree adverb. As the highest one, there are usually modifiers that emphasize the degree before *Chāo*. The use of exclamation marks will also play a role in strengthening tone and degree. For example:

(23) 黑糖 奶酪 真 是 超 赞 的!

Hēitáng nǎilào zhēn shì chāo zàn de!

Brown sugar cheese is really awesome! (平衡语料库)

More often, the use of *Chāo* as a degree adverb in the corpus is closer to the sub-highest degree adverb *Hěn* and *Fēicháng*, for example:

(24) 华原朋美 的 男友 是 超 多 金 的 企业家 第二 代。

Huáyuánpéngměi de nányǒu shì chāo duō jīn de qǐyèjiā dièr dài.

Hua's boyfriend is the second generation of super rich entrepreneurs. (平衡语料库)

The statement that *Chāo duō jīn* (超多金) can be replaced by *Yǒu hěnduō qián* (有很多钱). In summary, this paper suggests that the use of *Chāo* is closer to the sub-highest degree adverb, except for some contexts where the degrees are particularly emphasized.

4.2   The Grammatical Features of *Chāo*

In this section, we'll discuss the grammatical rules for the specific use of *Chāo*.

4.2.1   *Chāo* can be Used with *De.*

When *Chāo* is used as a degree adverb, the syntactic structure is *Chāo + modified component + De*. The word *De* could be omitted, for example:

(25) 小管 负责 回收 再 利用, 超 环保 的 唷!

Xiǎoguǎn fùzé huíshōu zài lìyòng, chāo huánbǎo de yo!

The small tube is used for recycling, which is super environmentally friendly! (平衡语料库)

In example (25), the character *De* could be used after *Huánbǎo* (环保) without affecting the semantics. *De* can also express an affirmative or intensified tone when acting as a sentence-final particle. Therefore, the adding of *De* after the modified component can convey a more emphatic feeling.

4.2.2 Diverse Modified Components

Chāo can modify the following parts:

① Adjective

(26) 平板 电脑 超 轻巧, 荧幕 可 旋转。

Píngbǎn diànnǎo chāo qīngqiǎo, yíngmù kě xuánzhuǎn.

The tablet is super light and the screen can rotate. (平衡语料库).

② Verb

(27) 她 的婆婆 是 一位 超 拜金 的老 女人。

Tā de pópo shì yíwèi chāo bàijīn de lǎo nǔrén.

Her mother-in-law is an old woman who worships money a lot. (平衡语料库)

③ Noun

(28) 他 吃 东西 都 挑三拣四, 超 机车 的。

Tā chī dōngxi dōu tiāosānjiǎnsì, chāo jīchē de.

He has lots of problems with what he eats. He is very picky.

④ Phrase

A. Verb phrase

(29) 我 超 注重 资源 回收 的。

Wǒ chāo zhùzhòng zīyuán huíshoū de.

I paid great attention to resource recovery. (《呼叫妙博士》99, COCT口语语料库)

B. Adverbial phrase

(30) 你 来借笔的 时候 都 超 没 礼貌。

Nǐ lái jiè bǐ de shíhou dōu chāo méi lǐmào.

Even when you came to borrow my pen, you were very rude. (《唐朝小栗子》138, COCT口语语料库)

C. Complement phrase

(31) 他 今天 没 来 帮忙, 超 靠 不 住 的。

Tā jīntiān méi lái bāngmáng, chāo kào bú zhù de.

It's very unreliable that he didn't come to help today.

4.3 The Pragmatic Features of *Chāo*

In this section, we will discuss the pragmatic features of *Chāo* and summarize its pragmatic characters.

4.3.1 Can be Used in Both Colloquial and Literary Languages

As a new degree adverb in recent years, the word *Chāo* firstly appeared as network or daily spoken language. However, with the popularization of its usage, the word *Chāo* has gradually appeared in newspapers, magazines, and other publications. Taking the Sinica Corpus as an example, there are totally 87 sentences and 78 of them are from newspapers, general magazines and general books. It can be seen that *Chāo* has spread from colloquial language and has been gradually absorbed and used in literary ones.

4.3.2 Emotionally Rich in Expression

Many scholars [12–14] mentioned that *Chāo* expresses strong emotions when it is used as a degree adverb, and the emotions are diverse. For example:

(32) 没错, 不 要 笑, 我 超 喜欢 她。

Méicuò, bú yào xiào, wǒ chāo xǐhuān tā.

That's right. Don't laugh! I like her very much. (COCT书面语语料库).

In the example above, the structure of *Chāo* shows a positive emotion. In addition, *Chāo* is often used to express a negative emotion too. For example:

(33) 现实 生活 里的 我, 其实 活 得 超 窝囊。

Xiànshí shēnghuó lǐ de wǒ, qíshí huó de chāo wōnang.

In real life, I'm actually living a very poor life. (平衡语料库).

Sometimes, the structure of *Chāo* does not express an obvious emotion, but simply states an objective fact. For example:

(34) 我 的 平板 电脑 超 轻巧。

Wǒ de píngbǎn diànnǎo chāo qīngqiǎo.

My tablet is super light.

4.4 The Modified Components can be New Information or Old Information

Unlike *Lǎo*, the components modified by *Chāo* are not limited by the old or new information. For example:

(35) "糟 了, 我们 少 买 一个 超 重要 的 东西。"

Zāo le, wǒmen shǎo mǎi yígè chāo zhòngyào de dōngxi.

That's too bad. We're missing one very important thing.

"什么 东西 啊?".

Shénme dōngxi a?

What is it? (《呼叫妙博士》183, COCT口语语料库2017).

(36) 甲: 我 在 语言 中心 已经 学 了3年 的 中文 了。

Jiǎ: wǒ zài yǔyán zhōngxīn yǐjīng xué le 3 nián de zhōngwén le.

A: I have learned Chinese in the language center for 3 years.

乙: 真 的?你的 中文 讲 得 超 棒 的!

Yi: zhēn de? Nǐ de zhōngwén jiǎng de chāo bàng de!

B: Really? Your Chinese is pretty good!

甲: 谢谢。

Jia: xièxie.

A: Thank you.

The *Chāo zhòngyào de dōngxi* (超重要的东西) in example (35) is unknown to the listener and belongs to new information. In example (36), B praises that A speaks Chinese well. A's Chinese level is not new to A, but it can still be modified by *Chāo*.

5 Comparative Analysis of *Lǎo* and *Chāo*

This section will comprehensively compare the similarities and differences between *Lǎo* and *Chāo* in the specific usage from the semantic, grammatical, and pragmatic perspectives.

5.1 From the Semantic Perspective

Lǎo and *Chāo* can not be used in comparative sentences and both of them belong to the absolute degree adverbs. Through the analysis of the corpora and video resources, *Lǎo* and *Chāo* belong to the sub-highest degree adverbs in most cases, and their semantics are similar to *Hen* and *Feichang*. In special contexts or with special modifiers, *Lǎo* and *Chāo* tend to be used as the highest degree adverbs due to semantic exaggeration. Therefore, the degree of *Lǎo* and *Chāo* needs to be judged in combination with specific contexts.

5.2 From the Grammatical Perspective

Based on the above analysis results, *Lǎo* and *Chāo* have both similarities and differences in grammatical rules.

5.2.1 The Syntactic Structures are Different Which Cannot be Interchanged When Modifying Nouns

There are three examples of *Lǎo* + *modified component* + *De* or *Lǎo* + *modified component* in the field of literature in the corpus. However, most of the time *Lǎo* should follow the fixed structure *Lǎo* + *modified component* + *Le*, in which *Le* cannot be omitted, for example:

(37) 他的衣服 老 漂亮 了。

Tā de yīfu lǎo piàoliang le.

His clothes are very beautiful.

(38) 他的衣服 超 漂亮 (的)。

Tā de yīfu chāo piàoliang (de).

His clothes are very beautiful.

In terms of modifying elements, there are no obvious differences between the modified components of *Lǎo* and *Chāo*, which can modify verbs, adjectives, and nouns. It can also modify verb-object, adverbial-verb, and verb-complement phrases. It is found that, except for nouns, other parts of speech and structures can be rewritten successfully, and both the meaning and the degree will not be changed. The collocation with nouns cannot be replaced optionally. On the one hand, it is related to the regional property of nouns. For example, the words *Jīchē* (机车) 'picky' and *Báimù* (白目) 'clueless' are unique in Taiwan; *Nāozhǒng* (孬种) 'coward' is a term commonly used in Northeast China but not used in Taiwan. On the other hand, from the syntactic perspective, degree adverbs cannot modify nouns directly. The reason why these nouns appear in the example sentences is that some usages have become fixed expressions in colloquial language due to the Noun-Verb Shift. For example, *Lǎo fèiwù le* (老废物了) is a common expression used to describe 'dead dog' in Northeast Dialect. Therefore, there are some differences between *Lǎo* and *Chāo* in modifying some noun components, and they cannot be replaced casually. However, in other modified components, they can basically be rewritten. In these examples, *Lǎo* + *modified component* + *Le* and *Chāo* + *modified component* + *(De)* can be regarded as synonymous structures.

5.2.2 When the Modified Component of *Lǎo* is a Phrase, It is Generally not Attributive

The structures of *Lǎo* and *Chāo* can be used as attributives (*Lǎo* / *Chāo* + *modified component* + *(De)* + *modified component*), but the usage of *Lǎo* is not as flexible as *Chāo*. Generally, when the modified component of *Lǎo* is a phrase, it can not be used as an attributive, for example:

(39) 超 爱 吃辣 的 舒淇 与 陈晓东、杨恭如 等 几位 同门 艺人, 在

Chāo ài chī là de Shūqí yǔ Chénxiǎodōng、Yánggōngrú děng jǐwèi tóngmén yìrén, zài

北京 合资 开 了 一家 宁记 麻辣 火锅店。

Běijīng hézī kāi le yìjiā níngjì málà huǒguōdiàn.

Shu Qi, who loves spicy food very much, has opened a Ningji spicy hotpot restaurant in Beijing with several artists from the same company, including Chen Xiaodong and Yang Gongru. (平衡语料库)

In this example, *Chāo* can be used as attributives when modifying phrases, and *Chāo* cannot be replaced by *Lǎo*. This point of view needs to be further studied and further supported by expanding the corpora research.

5.3   From the Pragmatic Perspective

Both *Lǎo* and *Chāo* have strong subjectivity and express abundant emotions. These emotions can be positive, negative, or neutral. However, there are still some differences between the two words in the process of specific language use.

5.3.1   Colloquial Language and Literary Language

Through a large number of corpora analysis, it can be shown that the degree adverb *Lǎo* appears mainly in oral expressions, while there are a large amount of data of *Chāo* in both oral language and written language, which is sufficient to prove that the degree adverb *Chāo* can be used in both colloquial language and literary language.

5.3.2   New Information and Old Information

The modified components of *Lǎo* are usually the unknown information of the listener in non-interrogative sentences, that is, the new information; *Chāo* can modify both new information and old information.

5.3.3   Inversion and Accentuation

Both *Lǎo* and *Chāo* can strengthen the degree and exaggeration through accentuation, but unlike *Lǎo*, *Chāo* does not often strengthen the semantics through inversion. For example:

(40) 老 热 了 屋里。

Lǎo rè le wūlǐ.

It's very hot in the room.

This is an example of *Lǎo* to emphasize the degree through inversion. We can rewrite it according to the vocabulary habits of people from Taiwan:

(41) *超 热 房间 里。

Chāo rè fángjiān lǐ .

It's very hot in the room.

This sentence is not correct and it must be expressed in normal word order:

(42) 房间 里 超 热。

Fángjiān lǐ chāo rè.

It's very hot in the room.

To sum up, the pragmatic features of *Lǎo* and *Chāo* are compared as follows:

Pragmatic Features	Colloquial Language	Literary Language	New Information	Old Information	Inversion	Accentuation
Lǎo	√			√	√	√
Chāo	√	√	√	√		√

6 Conclusion

With similar semantics, absolute degree adverbs *Lǎo* and *Chāo* are highly similar in their usages. Through the investigation of the corpora and oral materials, most of their usages belong to the sub-highest adverbs, with some exceptions in specific contexts, which are close to the extremely high degree adverbs. In the syntactic structure, *Lǎo* should strictly follow *Lǎo + modified component + Le* when it is not an attributive, while *De* inside *Chāo*'s structure *Chāo + modified component + De* can be omitted at any time. The modified components of them are highly similar except for modifying nouns. When modifying other components, they can be regarded as synonymous structures. *Lǎo* is not as flexible as *Chāo* when it is used as an attributive.

From the pragmatic perspective, both *Lǎo* and *Chāo* can express subjective attitudes and strong emotions. The structure of *Lǎo* can often be inverted and stressed to strengthen the exaggeration, while *Chāo* is usually not used for inversion. *Lǎo* is still mainly used in colloquial language, while *Chāo* can be used in both colloquial and literary language. Another pragmatic feature of *Lǎo* is that the modified contents are usually the new information to the listener, while *Chāo* has no such restriction.

There are many comparative studies on degree adverbs [10–12, 15] and this paper takes the lead in trying to compare the two local adverbs together. Through the comparative analysis, we can not only clarify the differences, and regulate the usages of the words, but also focus on teaching and helping students understand the language rules, which is a great benefit to the promotion of teaching Chinese as a second language.

Acknowledgements. This study is supported by the National Science and Technolo-gy Council, Taiwan, R.O.C., under Grant no. MOST 110-2511-H-003 -034 -MY3. It is also supported by National Taiwan Normal University's Chinese Language and Technology Center. The center is funded by Taiwan's Ministry of Education (MOE), as part of the Featured Areas Research Center Program, under the Higher Education Sprout Project.

References

1. Luo, Q., Liu, F.: The expressive content of the ad-adjectival *tai* 'too' in Mandarin Chinese: evidence from large online corpora. In: Hong, J.-F., Su, Q., Wu, J.-S. (eds.) Chinese Lexical Semantics. LNCS (LNAI), vol. 11173, pp. 311–320. Springer, Cham (2018). https://doi.org/10.1007/978-3-030-04015-4_26
2. Chu, Z.Y., Xiao, Y., et al.: A comparative structure of *Hen*. Chinese Teach. World. **1**, 37–44 (1999). (in Chinese)
3. Li, X.Z.: The Study of Adverb of Degree *Hen* in Mandarin Chinese. Master dissertation of Taiwan Normal University (2011). (in Chinese)

4. Teng, Y.B.: The study of Northeast Mandarin Degree Adverbs. Master dissertation of Jinan Unviersity (2014). (in Chinese)
5. Peng, X.C., Yan, L.M.: A Probe into the degree adverb *Chao* in the formation of Cantonese. Soc. Sci. Guangxi **2**, 158–162 (2006). (in Chinese)
6. Xiong, J., Hsieh, F.-F.: Degree intensification and sentential functions in chengdu chinese. In: Liu, M., Kit, C., Su, Q. (eds.) Chinese Lexical Semantics. LNCS (LNAI), vol. 12278, pp. 74–86. Springer, Cham (2021). https://doi.org/10.1007/978-3-030-81197-6_7
7. Zhang, Y.S.: The Study on Degree Adverbs in Modern Chinese. Academia Press, Shanghai (2000). (in Chinese)
8. Cao, M.L.: A Study on the Degree Word Lao in the Northeast Dialect. Master dissertation of Jiangxi Normal University (2009). (in Chinese)
9. Li, D.M., Yang, S.N.: Synchronic comparison of degree adverb Lao between the northeast dialect and Mandarin. J. Lang. Lit. Stud. **4**, 37–39 (2014). (in Chinese)
10. Li, X.Y.: A new probe into the differences of degree adverbs Hen, Tai and Lao. Bull. Chinese Lang. Teach. **9**, 49–50 (2015). (in Chinese)
11. Ma, Z.: Degree adverbs Hen, Ting, Guai, and Lao in Mandarin. Chinese Lang. Learn. **2**, 08–12 (1991). (in Chinese)
12. Zhao, F.: The modern new degree adverbs Ju, E, Kuang, Chao, and Bao. Overseas Chinese Educ. **4**, 64–70 (2006). (in Chinese)
13. Geng, Q.Q.: An analysis of new usages of the Chinese character *Chao*. J. Changshu Inst. Technol. **9**, 96–99 (2009). (in Chinese)
14. Jia, J.J.: Discussion on degree adverb Chao. Jiannan Lit. (Classic Inst.). **11**, 112–114 (2011). (in Chinese)
15. Luo, Q., Wang, Y.: A contrastive analysis of Hen and Ting in Chinese. In: Lu, Q., Gao, H., (eds.) LNCS (LNAI), vol. 9332, pp. 33-41. Springer, Cham (2015). https://doi.org/10.1007/978-3-319-27194-1_4

Exploration of the Semantic Differences of Motion Verbs from the Perspective of Image Schemas——Taking the Verbs "lā", " zhuài" and "tuō" as Examples

Changle Yin[✉]

Beijing Language and Culture University, Beijing 100083, China
yinchangle@126.com

Abstract. Taking the synonymous verbs *lā* (拉), *zhuài* (拽), and *tuō* (拖)as examples, this paper shows that image-schema analysis can help us better analyze the semantics of related verbs and find the semantic differences of synonymous motion verbs on this basis. Firstly, we review the analysis methods of motion meaning and illustrate the advantages of image-schema analysis in analyzing the semantics of motion verbs. Secondly, based on summarizing the image schema, we make a semantic analysis of the verb *tuō*. The verb *tuō* can be divided into three senses branches: (1) the agent forced the trajector to move in the direction of the agent; (2) the trajector is sagging (state meaning); (3) the trajector away from the landmark (generating meaning). Then, drawing on the research of Yin Changle (2018, 2021) on the verbs *lā* and *zhuài*, the article compares the differences between the synonymous verbs *lā*, *zhuài*,and *tuō* from the image schema and summarizes the differences in semantics. Finally, the paper illustrates the role of image schema in clarifying polysemy and semantic differences.

Keywords: *lā zhuài tuō* · image schemas · motion verbs · polysemy · semantic difference

1 Introduction

As for the semantics and polysemy of motion verbs, the previous scholars have paid more attention to them. They have used several methods to analyze the semantics of verbs, such as "seme analysis" "concept component analysis" "semantic component-pattern analysis", and "image-schema analysis". We find that the above methods have disadvantages in analyzing the semantics of verbs. In contrast, "image-schema analysis" is suitable for analyzing the semantics of motion verbs. This paper intends to analyze the semantics of motion verbs lā(拉), zhuài (拽), and tuō(拖)with the help of image schema to prove that "image-schema analysis" plays an essential role in analyzing the semantics of motion verbs and discovering the semantic differences of synonymous verbs.

Some scholars have studied verbs that have similar meanings to lā. Xu Meng and Zheng Hongyan [1] compared the differences in the collocation of verbs and objects

© The Author(s), under exclusive license to Springer Nature Switzerland AG 2023
Q. Su et al. (Eds.): CLSW 2022, LNAI 13495, pp. 506–520, 2023.
https://doi.org/10.1007/978-3-031-28953-8_37

between Chinese and English verbs with the meaning of "pull" and "drag" from the perspective of verb-object chunks. Zhang Yuhui [2] believes that the patient argument of monosyllabic verbs with the meaning of "pulling" can be divided into different semantic categories. Li Xiang [3] compared the similarities and differences of Chinese monosyllabic lāchě verbs from the perspective of semantic characteristics. The above research distinguishes Chinese lā verbs from different angles and provides some valuable findings. However, these studies ignore the following differences in lā verbs. Such as:[1]

(1) a. 谭功达 拽 了 拽 被子, 蒙住 了 自己 的 脸。

Tan Gongda drag LE drag quilt cover LE self DE face
Tan Gongda dragged the quilt and covered his face.
b. * 谭功达 拖 了 拖 被子, 蒙住 了 自己 的 脸。
Tan Gongda drag LE drag quilt cover LE self DE face
Tan Gongda dragged the quilt and covered his face.

(2) a. 她 拖 着 像 灌 了 铅 的 双腿, 吃 力

3sg drag ZHE look like filled with LE lead DE legs, laboriously
地 一步一步 挪 着。
DE step by step move ZHE
She dragged her legs, which looked they filled with lead, and moved laboriously step by step.
b. * 她 拉 着 像 灌 了 铅 的 双腿, 吃 力
3sg pull ZHE look like filled with LE lead DE legs, laboriously
地 一步一步 挪 着。
DE step by step move ZHE
She pulled her legs, which looked they filled with lead, and moved laboriously step by step.

In order to solve the above problems and better compare lā verbs, this paper first reviews the theory of analyzing the meaning of motion verbs. Then, the paper analyzes the semantic meaning of the verb tuō by inducing its image schemas. Finally, based on the research results of Yin Changle [4, 5] on the verbs lā and zhuài, this paper compares the differences of synonymous verbs lā, zhuài, and tuō from the perspective of image schema.

2 The Theory of Analyzing the Meaning of Motion Verbs

In this section, we first review the theory of analyzing the meaning of Chinese motion verbs, then explain the necessity of using image-schema theory to analyze motion verbs.

Su Xinchun [6] pointed out that "seme analysis" clarifies the way of meaning formation by analyzing the formation of sememes in a word. Many scholars have used "seme

---

[1] The examples listed in this paper are mainly from the modern Chinese corpus of the Chinese Linguistics Research Center (CCL) of Peking University, the modern Chinese corpus of Beijing Language and Culture University (BCC) and relevant literatures.

508   C. Yin

analysis" to analyze the meaning of motion verbs. For example, Li Xiang [3] expressed the semantic features of the motion verbs lā, zhuài, and tuō with the following sememes:

lā: [+hand] [+tool] [+long duration] [-fast] [-dispersed force directions] [+displace]

zhuài: [+hand] [-tool] [+long duration] [-fast] [+powerful] [-dispersed force directions] [+displace]

tuō: [+hand] [+tool] [+long duration] [-fast] [-dispersed force directions] [+displace]

"seme analysis" decomposes the meaning of a word into different sememes, which can well summarize the semantic characteristics of a word and provide an effective method for interpreting of word meaning.

However, there are also problems in the analysis of word meaning by "seme analysis". For example, Lyons [7] pointed out that several different analyses can be proposed for the same word. It can be seen that the results of "seme analysis" are often subjective. Secondly, Lyons believes that it is sometimes unreasonable to use the dichotomy of affirming or negating the existence of a constituent to explain the meaning of some words. The above disadvantages show that the "seme analysis" method has limitations in analyzing the meaning of verbs.

The second analysis method is "concept component analysis". Jiang Shaoyu [8] put forward this method against the background of the "concept field". The article points out that the "concept field" is a hierarchical structure which includes all concepts and can be subdivided into several levels. This paper analyzes "striking" verbs as an example, especially the semantics and differences of these verbs through the six dimensions in the conceptual field of "striking": motion, object, tool, mode, strength, and purpose. "Concept component analysis" sets a standard dimension for analyzing the meaning of words belonging to the same concept domain.

The third method is "component-pattern analysis". Fu Huaiqing [9, 10] proposed this method to analyze the words that express motion. The paper expresses the meaning formation pattern of those words as follows (Fig. 1):

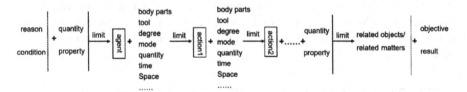

Fig. 1. Formation pattern of word meaning in Fu Huaiqing [9, 10].

The author thinks that we should determine the appropriate composition mode of word meaning based on the dictionary interpretation and the actual use of the word. This method has something in common with the "concept component analysis " mentioned above. The pattern of word meaning components are composed of different elements such as "actor" and "action", and the different dimensions in the "concept component analysis " actually refer to different elements of the components of word meaning.

However, this method could not show the subtle differences between synonymous verbs. For example, in sentences (1) and (2), the nuances of lā verbs cannot be summarized by such dimensions or elements as "action", "object", and other elements.

The fourth method is "image-schema analysis". Johnson [11] considers that image schema is the foundation of the conceptual system, directly related to people's feelings and experiences. Furthermore, image schema is an abstract generalization of a large number of experiences. image-schema analysis can express the different sense branches of words in schema form. The schema often includes "trajector", "landmark", and "path". For motion verbs that represent spatial movement, image schema can well represent different movement situations and summarize them into different sense branches. image-schema analysis can help us understand the meaning of words and summarize the use of words. In addition, this analytical method can also help us to conclude the subtle differences in the meaning of words. For example, Zhu Yan [12] summarized the meaning of the verb chuān(穿)into more than 20 kinds through image schema and analyzed the semantics of the verb chuān from a finer granularity. The researches which analyze modern Chinese verbs using image schema mainly includes Zhu Yan [12], Zhang Mengyun, Jiang Guiying [13], and Zong Qian [14]. Only Zhu Yan [12], Zhang Mengyun and Jiang Guiying [13] involve motion verbs. Based on the above, we should further extend this analytical method to the study of motion verbs. Next, we will start with the image schema and compare the differences between the three synonymous verbs lā, zhuài, and tuō.

3   Image Schemas of the Verb *tuō*

Yin Changle [4, 5] have studied the semantics of the verbs lā and zhuài from the perspective of image schema. In this section, we mainly analyze the semantics of the verb tuō.tuō is a spatial motion verb together with lā and zhuài. The description of its motion also involves the concepts of " trajector " "landmark", and "path". Trajector stands for the central part or the most prominent element in any relational structure. Landmark refers to the reference point for positioning. Path shows the trajectory of the main part moving from stage to stage.We introduce the above concepts into the analysis of the image schema of the verb tuō and conclude the polysemy system of tuō based on the corpus.

In this paper, the verb tuō is divided into three meanings: (1) the agent forces the trajector to move in the direction of the agent; (2) The trajector is drooping (state meaning); (3) The trajector is far away from the landmark (generation meaning).

3.1   The Agent Forces the Trajector to Move in the Direction of the Agent

This sense branch of tuō means that the agent exerts a force on the trajector in order to move the trajector in a specific direction. Trajectors are usually three-dimensional entities, and landmarks are the agent's location. Such as:

(3) 一群 纤夫 迈 着 沉重 而 疲惫 的 步伐 拖 着

a group of tracker make a step ZHE heavy and tired DE step drag ZHE
货 船, 艰难地 走 在 伏尔加河畔 的 沙滩上。

cargo ship with difficulty walk on Volga River DE beach
A group of trackers dragged cargo ships with heavy and tired steps on the beach along the Volga River.

(4) 战车 用 两匹马 拖 着, 士兵们 在 车内 驾驭 着 马......

chariot by two horses tow ZHE, soldiers in chariot rode ZHE horses
The chariot was towed by two horses, and the soldiers rode the horses in the chariot.
We take sentence (3) as an example. In sentence (3), tuō means that the agent 纤 夫(trackers)applies force to the three-dimensional trajector 货船(cargo ship)to move the trajector in the direction of the agent. It should be noted that when tuō expresses the above meaning, the trajector is close to the surface of the ground or other objects.
It can be shown in schema 1 (Fig. 2):[2]

TR

P   Ground

LM(A)

Fig. 2. Schema 1 3D A G/ S

In addition, this sense branch also includes the following special cases:

(5) 中华 优秀 儿 女 叶乔波, 拖 着 伤腿

Chinese outstanding son daughter YeQiaobo, drag ZHE broken leg
顽 强 拼 搏......
tenaciously struggle
Ye Qiaobo, an outstanding Chinese person, struggled tenaciously with a broken leg.
[Schema 2:3D A G/ S P(the trajector is part of the agent)].[3]

(6) 侯丹梅 丢下 病 儿, 自己 拖 着 病 体 准 时 赶来。

Hou Danmei leave sick child self drag ZHE sick body on time arrive
Hou Danmei left her sick child behind and arrived on time with her sick body.
[Schema 3:3D A G/ S C(the agent coincides with the trajector)].

---

[2] Due to the length limitation, this paper only shows this schema.3D indicates that the trajector is three-dimensional. A indicates that the landmark is the agent's location. G/ S indicates that the trajector is close to the ground or the surface of other objects.

[3] P indicates that the trajector is a part of the agent, and C indicates that the agent and the trajector coincide.

3.2   Trajector Dropping (State Meaning)

The verb tuō can also indicate a static state in which the trajector is drooping. Such as:

(7) 那时的女演员都穿着硬铁环支撑的

    At that time DE actresses all wear ZHE hard iron rings support DE
    拖地长裙, 戴着沉重的头饰和面具, 还穿着
    drag floor skirt wear ZHE heavy DE headdresses and masks, and wearZHE
    高跟鞋......
    high-heeled shoes.
    At that time, the actresses all wore floor-length skirts supported by hard iron rings,
heavy headdresses, masks, and high-heeled shoes.

(8) 我循声而望, 见松鼠拖着长长的尾巴

    1sg followed the sound and look see squirrel drag ZHE long DE tail
    窜入草丛深处。
    scurry grass deep
    I followed the sound and saw the squirrel scurrying into the grass with its long tail.
    [Schema 4:3D DR(trajector dropping)].[4]
    In sentence (7), the verb tuō means that the trajector 长裙(long skirt) hangs down
to the ground; In sentence (8), tuō means that the 尾巴(tail) of the trajector hangs down
behind the squirrel's body.

3.3   The Trajector is Away from the Landmark (Generation Meaning)

The third sense branch of the verb tuō is that the trajector is far away from the landmark,
and the result of the agent's movement is often to produce a particular substance. Such
as:

(9) 车在崎岖不平的公路上颠簸, 车后拖着长长的大雾般

    car on rough DE road bump car rear drag ZHE long DE fog like
    的黄尘。
    DE yellow dust
    The car bumped on the rough road, dragging long fog-like yellow dust behind the
car.

(10) 第一枚导弹拖着长长的尾焰, 像一道红色的

    first missile drag ZHE long DE tail flame like a bolt of red DE
    闪电, 将拖靶拦腰斩断。
    lightning take tow target in the middle cut off

---

[4] DR indicates that the trajector drops.

The first missile dragged a long tail flame which like a bolt of red lightning cut off the tow target.

[Schema 5: 3D A AF (射体远离界标the trajector is far from the landmark)].[5]

Take sentence (9) as an example. With time, 黄尘(yellow dust) continuously moves away from the 车(car). At this time, we can regard the agent as a landmark because the reference object for the relative movement of 黄尘(yellow dust) is the agent车(car). 车(car)is both an agent and a landmark. It can be seen that the process of the relative movement of the trajector away from the agent is precisely the process of generating the trajector. Therefore, we can conclude the meaning of the verb tuō as "generating".

4   The Difference Between the Verbs *lā, zhuài,*and *tuō*

Yin Chang [4, 5] has used image-schema analysis to analyze the semantics of the polysemous verbs lā and zhuài. In this section, based on Yin Changle [4, 5], combined with the analysis of the verb tuō in the third part of the article, we compare the semantic differences of the synonymous verbs lā、 zhuài and tuō from the perspective of image schema.

4.1   The Difference Between *lā* and *zhuài*

The verbs lā and zhuài are synonymous verbs. Dictionaries often use the more commonly used verb lā to explain zhuài. From the interpretation alone, we cannot understand the difference of the two verbs. In this section, we summarize the semantic differences between the two verbs by comparing the image schema and semantics of the verb lā and zhuài in Yin Changle [4, 5].

First, we replace the verb lā in different image schemas with the synonymous verb zhuài. Through replacement, we find that the verb zhuài cannot be used in the following situations. Such as:

(11)   a. 冬 日 的 阳光 投射 进来, 拉 出 他们 长长 的 影子。

winter DE sunshine cast in pull out 3pl long DE shadow
The winter sun casts in and pulls out their long shadows.
b. *冬 日 的 阳光 投射 进来, 拽 出 他们 长长 的 影子。
winter DE sunshine cast in drag out 3pl long DE shadow
The winter sun casts in and drags out their long shadows.

(12)   a. 阳 台 上 拉 了 一根 晾衣绳。[6]

balcony on pull LE a clothesline
A clothesline was pulled on the balcony.

---

[5] AF indicates that the trajector is away from the landmark.

[6] In this context, the English translation of the Chinese verb lā and zhuài is the same ("pull"). Sentence (13) and sentence (14) are the same as sentence(12).

b. *阳 台 上 拽 了 一根 晾衣绳。
balcony on pull LE a clothesline
A clothesline was pulled on the balcony.

In (11a), the verb lā means that the agent 阳光(sunshine) forces the trajector影子(shadow) away from the landmark. The movement of the agent 阳光(sunshine) makes the trajector影子(shadow) extend. When we replace lā with zhuài, the sentence does not hold, such as (11b). In sentence (12), the verb lā describes a trajector (usually a one-dimensional linear object) in a static state, and the trajector is stretched. When we replace lā with zhuài, the sentence does not hold, such as (12b). It can be seen that the verb zhuài cannot express the meaning of "generating" nor can it describe the state in which a one-dimensional trajector is being stretched.[7]

We replace the verb zhuài in different image schemas with the synonymy verb lā. We find that the verb lā cannot usually be used in the following situations. Such as:

(13) a. 口袋 揣 雨 蛙 的 女孩子 从 辫子上 拽下 一个 蝴蝶结……

pocket carry rain frog DE girl from braid pull a bow
The girl with a rain frog in her pocket pulled a bow from her braid.
b. *口袋 揣 雨 蛙 的 女孩子 从 辫子上 拉下 一个 蝴蝶结……
pocket carry rain frog DE girl from braid pull a bow
The girl with a rain frog in her pocket pulled a bow from her braid.

(14) a. 他的 左 手 还 紧紧 拽 着 歹徒 的 一 缕 头发。

his left hand still tightly drag ZHE gangster DE a strand of hair
His left hand was still holding a strand of the gangster's hair tightly.
b. *他的 左 手 还 紧紧 拉 着 歹徒 的 一 缕 头发。
his left hand still tightly tug ZHE gangster DE a strand of hair.
His left hand was still tugging at a strand of the gangster's hair."

In (13a), the verb zhuài means that the agent forces the trajector to disengage from the attachment. In (14a), the verb zhuài indicates that the agent holds/grasps the trajector or a part of the trajector (state meaning). (13b) and (14b) are not qualified which means that the verb lā cannot indicate " separate oneself from " or the state of "grasping ".

We find the difference of the synonymy verb lā and zhuài through the substitution test. As shown in the following Table 1:[8]

---

[7] The author has written two articles to analyze the image schemas of the verbs lā and zhuài. See Yin Chang [4, 5] for details. Due to space limitations, this paper only deals with the relevant schemata and their semantics and does not explain other situations.

[8] Another difference between the verbs *lā* and *zhuài* is that in the same context, *zhuài* tends to have higher strength than *lā* in. Such as:(1) a. 她 拉 着 平板车 往 前 走。3sg pull ZHE flatbed forward walk She pulled the flatbed forward.b. 她 毫不费力 地 拉 着 平板车 往 前 走。3sg without difficulty DE pull ZHE flatbed forward walk.She pulled the flatbed car forward without difficulty.(2) a. 她 拽 着 平板车 往 前 走。3sg drag ZHE flatbed forward walk She dragged the flatbed forward.b.* 她 毫不费力 地 拽 着 平板车 往前 走。3sg without difficulty DE pull ZHE flatbed forward walk.She dragged the flatbed car forward without difficulty.

Table 1. Semantic differences between the verbs *lā* and *zhuài*.

	lā	*zhuài*
Meaning of "generation" (the trajector is away from the landmark)	+	−
State meaning (trajector extension)	+	−
Meaning of "separation"	−	+
State meaning (the agent holds/grasps the trajector or part of the trajector)	−	+

4.2 The Difference Between *zhuài* and *tuō*

The verbs zhuài and tuō both mean "force the object to move in the direction of the agent or follow the agent". What are the differences between these two verbs?

Through the method of alternative test, we found that the verb zhuài can be used in the following cases, but the verb tuō cannot. Such as:

(15) a. 到 时 候 让 肖 科 平 穿 条 长 裙, 行 一 个
When the time comes let Xiao Keping wear a long skirt make a
欧 洲 宫 廷 的 那 种 拽 着 裙 边 的 屈 膝 礼。[9]
European court DE that drag ZHE skirt the edge of DE curtsey
When the time comes, let Xiao Keping wear a long skirt and make a curtsey like that of a European court by dragging the edge of the skirt.
b. *到 时 候 让 肖 科 平 穿 条 长 裙, 行 一 个
When the time comes let Xiao Keping wear a long skirt make a
欧 洲 宫 廷 的 那 种 拖 着 裙 边 的 屈 膝 礼。
European court DE that drag ZHE skirt the edge of DE curtsey
When the time comes, let Xiao Keping wear a long skirt and make a curtsey like that of a European court by dragging the edge of the skirt.

(16) a. 谭 功 达……拽 了 拽 被 头, 蒙 住 了 自 己 的 脸。
Tan Gongda pull LE pull quilt the edge of cover LE self DE face
Tan Gongda pulled the edge of the quilt head and covered his face.
b. *谭 功 达……拖 了 拖 被 头, 蒙 住 了 自 己 的 脸。
Tan Gongda drag LE drag quilt the edge of cover LE self DE face
Tan Gongda dragged the quilt head and covered his face.

(17) a. 口 袋 揣 雨 蛙 的 女 孩 子 从 辫 子 上 拽 下 一 个 蝴 蝶 结……
pocket carry rain frog DE girl from braid pull a bow
The girl with a rain frog in her pocket pulled a bow from her braid.
b. *口 袋 揣 雨 蛙 的 女 孩 子 从 辫 子 上 拖 下 一 个 蝴 蝶 结……
pocket carry rain frog DE girl from braid drag a bow
The girl with a rain frog in her pocket dragged a bow from her braid.

(18) a. 她 的 心 脏 已 停 止 跳 动, 僵 硬 的 手 里 却 还 紧 紧
3sg DE heart have stop beat stiff DE hand but still tightly
拽 着 医 药 箱。

---

[9] In this context, the English translation of the Chinese verb *zhuài* and *tuō* is the same ("drag").

pull ZHE medicine box

Her heart had stopped beating, but her stiff hand still clung tightly to the medicine box.

b. * 她 的 心脏 已 停止 跳动, 僵硬 的 手里 却 还 紧紧

3sg DE heart have stop beat stiff DE hand but still tightly

拖 着 医药箱。

drag ZHE medicine box

Her heart had stopped beating, but her stiff hand still clung tightly to the medicine box.

In (15a), zhuài means that the speaker intends to let the agent 肖科平(Xiao Keping) to exert force on the three-dimensional trajector 裙边 (the edge of the skirt) through the action of "zhuài" to move the trajector upward. The direction of motion is not the direction of the agent. However, tuō in (15b) cannot indicate that the moving direction is not the agent's direction. The verb tuō means that the agent forces the trajector裙边 (the edge of the skirt) to follow its movement, which does not meet the requirements of curtsey. Therefore, in this case, zhuài cannot be replaced by tuō. In (16a), the agent 谭功达(Tan Gongda) exerts a force on the two-dimensional trajector 被头(quilt head) through the action of zhuài, so that the trajector 被头(quilt head) moves in the direction where the agent他(he) is located. Finally, the trajector covers his face. (16b) is an unqualified sentence because the action "tuō" is generally not used to indicate the meaning of covering. In (17a), the agent女孩(girl) made the three-dimensional trajector 蝴蝶结(bow) separate from the landmark 辫子(braid) through the action of "tuō". The verb tuō does not mean deviating, so (17b) is unqualified. In (18a), zhuài means the state in which the agent (她she) holds/grasps the trajector (药箱medicine box). The verb tuō can not express the meaning of the state, so (18B) is unqualified.

We also found that some sentences can use tuō but cannot use zhuài. Such as:[10]

(19) a. 中华 优秀 儿 女 叶乔波, 拖着 伤 腿

Chinese outstanding son daughter YeQiaobo, drag ZHE broken leg

顽 强 拼 搏……

tenaciously struggle

Ye Qiaobo, an outstanding Chinese person, struggled tenaciously with a broken leg.

b. *中华 优秀 儿 女 叶乔波, 拽着 伤 腿

Chinese outstanding son daughter YeQiaobo, drag ZHE broken leg

顽 强 拼 搏……

tenaciously struggle

Ye Qiaobo, an outstanding Chinese person, struggled tenaciously with a broken leg.

(20) a. 我 循 声 而 望, 见 松鼠 拖着 长长 的 尾巴

1sg followed the sound and look see squirrel drag ZHE long DE tail

窜入 草丛 深处。

scurry grass deep

---

[10] In sentence (19)-(21), the English translation of the Chinese verb *tuō* and *zhuài* is the same ("drag").

I followed the sound and saw the squirrel scurrying into the grass with its long tail.

b. *我 循 声 而 望, 见 松鼠 拽 着 长长 的 尾巴

1sg followed the sound and look see squirrel drag ZHE long DE tail

窜入 草丛 深处。

scurry grass deep

I followed the sound and saw the squirrel scurrying into the grass with its long tail.

(21) a. 车 在 崎岖不平 的 公路上 颠簸, 车 后 拖 着 长长 的 大雾 般

Car on rough DE road bump car rear drag ZHE long DE fog like

的 黄 尘。

DE yellow dust

The car bumped on the rough road, dragging long fog-like yellow dust behind the car.

b. *车 在 崎岖不平 的 公路上 颠簸, 车 后 拽 着 长长 的 大雾 般

Car on rough DE road bump car rear drag ZHE long DE fog like

的 黄 尘。

DE yellow dust

The car bumped on the rough road, dragging long fog-like yellow dust behind the car.

The reason for the disqualification of sentence b is as follows: during the action indicated by zhuài, when the agent acts on the trajector to make the trajector move along with the agent in the direction of the agent, the trajector cannot be part of the agent or coincide with the agent; zhuài cannot indicate the state meaning of "trajector dropping"; zhuài cannot indicate that the trajector is away from the landmark.

We summarize the differences between the verbs zhuài and tuō as follows (Table 2):

Table 2. Semantic differences between the verbs *zhuài* and *tuō*.

	zhuài	*tuō*
The direction of movement (landmark) is not the direction of the agent	+	-
Trajector cover landmark	+	−
Meaning of "separate oneself from"	+	−
State meaning (the agent holds/grasps the trajector or part of the trajector)	+	−
(the agent forces the trajector to move with itself) the trajector is part of or coincides with the agent	−	+
State meaning (trajector dropping)	−	+
Meaning of "generation" (the trajector is away from the landmark)	−	+

4.3 The Difference Between *lā* and *tuō*

In this section, we continue the analysis methods of the above two sections to find the difference between lā and tuō through replacement. Such as:

(22) a. 海藻......上前拉住了肖梅的胳膊。
       Haizao come forward hold LE Xiao Mei DE arm
       Haizao comes forward and holds Xiao Mei's arm.
       b. *海藻......上前拖住了肖梅的胳膊。
       Haizao come forward drag LE Xiao Mei DE arm
       Haizao comes forward and drags Xiao Mei's arm.

(23) a. 徐义德拉了一下电线开关, 办公室被照得和白昼一般。
       Xu Yide pullLE once wire switch office by shine DE as bright as day time.
       Xu Yide pulled the wire switch, and the office was as bright as day time.
       b.*徐义德拖了一下电线开关, 办公室被照得和白昼一般。
       Xu Yide dragLE once wire switch office by shine DE as daytime as
       Xu Yide dragged the wire switch, and the office was as bright as day time.

(24) a. 墙上拉了五根麻绳, 各种干菜搭得
       wall on pull LE five hemp rope all kinds of dry vegetable hang DE
       满满的......
       full DE
       Five hemp ropes were pulled from the wall, and all kinds of dried vegetables
       were hung on.
       b. *墙上拖了五根麻绳, 各种干菜搭得
       wall on drag LE five hemp rope all kinds of dry vegetable hang DE
       满满的......
       full DE
       Five hemp ropes were dragged from the wall, and all kinds of dried vegetables
       were hung on.

(25) a. 我立刻缩回双脚, 拉了被子盖好。
       1sg immediately retract feet pull LE quilt cover
       I immediately retracted my feet and pulled the quilt to cover myself.
       b. *我立刻缩回双脚, 拖了被子盖好。
       1sg immediately retract feet drag LE quilt cover
       I immediately retracted my feet and dragged the quilt to cover myself.

(26) a. 这位年轻的大元帅......将剑锋拉出一半, 又推入鞘中。
       this young DE Marshal make blade pull half again push sheath
       The Young Marshal pulled half of the blade and pushed it into the sheath.
       b. *这位年轻的大元帅......将剑锋拖出一半, 又推入鞘中。
       this young DE Marshal make blade drag half again push sheath

The Young Marshal dragged half of the blade and pushed it into the sheath.
       As for (22b), the reason for the disqualification is that when the verb tuō indicates the meaning of "the agent forcefully moves the trajector in the direction of the agent", the trajector is usually close to the ground or the surface of another object. The motion mode of the trajector 胳膊(arm) in the sentence does not meet the semantic requirements of *tuō*. The reason for disqualification of (23b) is that during the movement of the object

described by *tuō*, the movement direction of the trajector must be the direction of the agent and the trajector cannot move in other directions. However, in (23a), the direction of movement of the trajector 开关(switch) is not the agent's direction. As for (24b), the reason for the disqualification is that *tuō* cannot indicate the state of the extension of the trajector. (25b) shows that *tuō* cannot indicate that the trajector covers the landmark. The detailed analysis is the same as the example (16). In sentence (26a), the landmark is a hollow three-dimensional entity, and the trajector is forcibly pulled out of the landmark by the agent through the action of *tuō*. Sentence (26b) is unqualified, which indicates that *tuō* does not have the meaning of "forcefully pulling out".

In addition, the difference between *lā* and *tuō* is also shown in the following aspects:

(27) a. 中华 优秀 儿 女 叶乔波, 拖 着 伤 腿,
      Chinese outstanding son daughter YeQiaobo, drag ZHE broken leg.
      顽 强 拼 搏……
      tenaciously struggle
      Ye Qiaobo, an outstanding Chinese person, struggled tenaciously with a broken leg.

      b. *中华 优秀 儿 女 叶乔波, 拉 着 伤 腿,
      Chinese outstanding son daughter YeQiaobo, drag ZHE broken leg
      顽 强 拼 搏……
      tenaciously struggle
      Ye Qiaobo, an outstanding Chinese person, struggled tenaciously with a broken leg.

(28) a. 我 循 声 而 望, 见 松鼠 拖 着 长长 的 尾巴
      1sg followed the sound and look see squirrel drag ZHE long DE tail
      窜入 草丛 深处。
      scurry grass deep
      I followed the sound and saw the squirrel scurrying into the grass with its long tail.

      b. *我 循 声 而 望, 见 松鼠 拉 着 长长 的 尾巴
      1sg followed the sound and look see squirrel pull ZHE long DE tail
      窜入 草丛 深处。
      scurry grass deep

I followed the sound and saw the squirrel scurrying into the grass with its long tail.

From the above examples, it can be seen that in the motion process indicated by the verb *lā*, when the agent forces the trajector to follow its movement, the trajector cannot be part of the agent or coincide with the agent, as shown in sentence (27b). Additionally, *zhuài* cannot indicate the state meaning of "trajector drooping", as shown in the sentence (28b).

Based on the above analysis, we summarize the differences between the verbs *lā* and *tuō* (Table 3):

Table 3. Semantic differences between the verbs *lā* and *tuō*.

	lā	*tuō*
Whether the trajector must be close to the ground or the surface of another object when Indicates the agent forces the trajector to move in the direction of the agent	−	+
The direction of movement (landmark) is not the direction of the agent	+	−
State meaning (trajector extension)	+	−
Trajector cover landmark	+	−
Draw out with strength	+	−
(the agent forces the trajector to move with itself) the trajector is part of or coincides with the agent	−	+
State meaning (trajector dropping)	−	+

4.4 Summary of Differences

Given the above analysis, we summarize the semantic differences between lā, zhuài, and tuō. The conclusions are as follows (Table 4):

Table 4. Semantic differences of verbs *lā*, *zhuài*, and *tuō*.

	lā	*zhuài*	*tuō*
(the agent forces the trajector to move with itself) the trajector is part of or coincides with the agent	−	−	+
Whether the trajector must be close to the ground or the surface of another object when Indicates the agent forces the trajector to move in the direction of the agent	−	+	+
The direction of movement (landmark) is not the direction of the agent	+	+	−
Trajector cover landmark	+	+	−
Draw out with strength	+	+	−
Meaning of "separate oneself from"	+	+	−
Meaning of "generation" (the trajector is away from the landmark)	+	−	+
State meaning (trajector extension)	+	−	−
State meaning (the agent holds/ rasps the trajector or part of the trajector)	−	+	−
State meaning (trajector sagging)	−	−	+

lā, zhuài, and tuō are frequently used motion verbs in Chinese. Previous studies on these verbs have not accurately revealed their semantic differences. This paper show that the image-schema analysis method can sufficiently express the differences between motion verbs. To sum up, image schema enables us to comprehensively and accurately summarize the semantics of motion verbs. More importantly, this analysis method can also help us to draw more convincing conclusions by comparing the semantic differences of synonymous verbs from the perspective of finer granularity. In addition, the conclusions obtained by this analysis are of great benefit to lexicography and second language teaching, and it is worth our further exploration.

Acknowledgments. This research project is supported by Science Foundation of Beijing Language and Culture University (supported by "the Fundamental Research Funds for the Central Universities") (No. 22YBB41), Beijing Philosophy and Social Sciences Youth Fund Project under the grant "A Study of Emphatic Markers Based on Beijing Natural Spoken Language Corpus" (No.19YYC019) and the Academic Research Projects of Beijing Union University (No. SK70202101). All errors remain my own.

References

1. Xu, M., Zheng, H,: A contrastive analysis of verb-object chunks of Chinese and English "La" Verbs -- a corpus based study. Mod. Chinese. **3**(1), 84–86 (2011). (in Chinese)
2. Zhang, Yuhui., Semantic Evolution of Pulling Type Monosyllable Verbs Based on the Corpus. Master's thesis of Xiangtan University (2017). (in Chinese)
3. Li, X.: A Study on the Monosyllable "Pulling" Verbs in Modern Chinese. Master's thesis of Yanbian University (2021). (in Chinese)
4. Yin, C.: Polysemy verb La: an image-schema- based approach. J. Chinese Lang. Lit. **112**, 37–56 (2018). in Chinese
5. Yin, C.:Polysemy Verb zhuai :An Image-schema- based Approach. CLSW2021, Hongkong (2021)
6. Su, X.: Chinese Word Meanings. Foreign Language Teaching and Research Press, Beijing (2008). in Chinese
7. Lyons, J.: Semantics:, vol. 1. Cambridge University Press, London (1977)
8. Jiang, S.: Semantic analyses of verbs of STRIKING. Stud. Chinese Lang. **15**(5), 387–401 (2007). in Chinese
9. Fu, H.: Componential analysis and word interpretation. Lexicogr. Stud. **8**(1), 48–55 (1988). in Chinese
10. Fu, H.: Analysis and Description of Word Meaning. Foreign Language Teaching and Research Press, Beijing (2006). in Chinese
11. Johnson, M.: The Body in the Mind: The Bodily Basis of Meaning, Imagination, and Reason. University of Chicago press, Chicago (2013)
12. Zhu, Y.: Polysemy of verb Chuan and the linking mechanisms among senses: an image-schema-based approach. Linguist. Sci. **9**(3), 67–80 (2010). in Chinese
13. Zhang, M., Jiang, G.: An image schema-based analysis on polysemy of "Rao." J. Longyan Univ. **8**(1), 63–69 (2014)
14. Zong, Q.: Semantic analysis and image schema construction of directional verbs "guolai" and "guoqu". J. Qingdao Agric. Univ. (Soc. Sci.) **27**(2), 89–92 (2015). (in Chinese)

A Corpus-Based Study of the Usage of Chinese Core Separable Words in the Use of Language

Changhao Li[(✉)] and Zezhi Zheng

Xiamen University, Xiamen 361000, Fujian, China
1131020549@qq.com

Abstract. The core separable words are typical words in modern Chinese. Based on previous studies, the article identifies nine core separable words, and uses the BCC corpus, CCL corpus and "HSK dynamic composition corpus" to investigate the usage and learning situation of the core separable words by native Chinese speakers and non-native Chinese speakers. We find that, for native speakers, the core separable words are still mainly not separated, which is the main usage pattern today; in terms of separated usage, the article summarizes the different types of core words insertion forms. From the perspective of Chinese as second language learners, it is necessary to examine the separable words as a special lexical phenomenon in Chinese to analyze, which is also an important element of contemporary International Chinese Language Education (ICLE). By dealing with and analyzing Chinese learner interlanguage corpus, our study indicates that the learners have a weak grasp of separable forms, as shown by the fact that they are mostly simple and short insertion components, learners' ability to use complex discrete forms is also low, and the types of errors are more concentrated, etc. By examining the use of Chinese core separable words by native speakers and Chinese as second language speakers, we can not only reveal the current usage of core separable words, but also help promote ontology research and the ICLE of separable words.

Keywords: Core Separable Words · Situation of Actual Usage · Separable Situation · Insertion Components Cases · ICLE

1 Introduction

Since Lu [1] proposed the concept of "separable words" (*li he ci*), there have been more than 60 years of research on separable words. The first phase (1950s to the late 1970s) focused on theoretical research, scholars explored the naming, nature, definition, types, attribution, separated causes and functions of separable words; the second phase (1980s to the present), in addition to theoretical research, also tends to applied research, including Teaching Chinese to Speaker of Other Language (TCSOL), Chinese information processing and dictionary compilation etc. The applied study of the separable word involves its usage characteristics, so it is necessary to further deepen the relevant research, with the goal of expanding its application in different domains. Further

© The Author(s), under exclusive license to Springer Nature Switzerland AG 2023
Q. Su et al. (Eds.): CLSW 2022, LNAI 13495, pp. 521–538, 2023.
https://doi.org/10.1007/978-3-031-28953-8_38

observation shows that previous studies on separable words have included introspective ontological analyses, corpus-based examinations, and the identification and translation of separable words in the context of Chinese information processing, but they have not gone far enough in the study of typical or core separable words, which are clearly representative of the entire separable words category and the role of such separable words in the study of second language teaching. This paper attempts to study the usage of the core separable words in Chinese corpus, mainly in terms of separated cases, insertion components, insertion types, etc., and usage among learners of TCSOL.

There are still some controversies about the nature of separable words, but in order to apply it to the content and scope of this study, it is important to clarify the nature of the object. As a unique language phenomenon in Chinese, separable words are special in that they are both combined and separated in usage; however, they are still words and not phrases, i.e. they are relatively special words that can be extended in structure, and they are integral in meaning [2], or conceptually intact [3]. Therefore, this study is dedicated to examining the usage of core separable words from the perspective of the nature of separable words as words, based on previous studies.

In modern Chinese, the separable words are an open category, and the number is always increasing [4]. It is difficult for researchers to include every separable word in study and it is a consensus in language research to select research objects that suit the actual needs [5]. Some researchers have pointed out that the majority of disyllabic words in Chinese are "separable words", which can be separated or combined, only the degree of separation varies; the combination of two syllable into a disyllabic words presupposes that they are divisible, because monosyllables are still quite active.[1] Although in term of the view, separable word is a broader concept, it also suggests that the production of separable words has its roots in linguistic development and is not a closed category. Therefore, we believe that, since Chinese presents a phenomenon in which most disyllabic words can be clasped together, and in the absence of highly applicable rules and methods of identification and the difficulty of exhausting all separable words, an attempt can be made to refine and deepen the study of separable words by selecting core words.

Core separable word is a representative and artificially specified category, which also have the characteristics of core words. Scholars have different understandings of the core words, and they also show a pluralistic tendency in definition and understanding [6]. Zhao [7] pointed out that core words should be determined according to specific situations and a combination of conditions, and believed that high usage degree, wide distribution, stability, wide circulation domain and strong combination power are important factors and conditions for screening various types of core words. Based on this view, we locate the selection of core separable words within the scope of expert language sense, and obtain core words in modern Chinese based on representative previous studies. Previous studies cover typical separable words dictionaries, syllabuses or standards in the TCSOL, and use a variety of exemplary corpora, so they are more representative in terms of the commonness, distribution and usage characteristics of separable words. The collection of separable words used and summarised therein also has reference value and significance.

---

[1] From the academic lecture "Keeping grammar theory up to date". (Shen, J. X., 23th March 2022) https://www.bilibili.com/video/BV1WL411A7Mp?spm_id_from=333.337.search-card. all.click.

Ren & Wang [8] compared the separable words in *Dictionary of Modern Chinese Separable Word Usage* (1995) and S*yllabus of Graded Words and Characters for Chinese Proficiency* (SGWCCP, 1992), selected common words and further identified a lexical list of 423 separable words; acquiring 12 core separable words with more than 100 examples and a discrete frequency of >50% based on a 13-million-word novel corpus. Wang [5] extracted 392 disyllabic separable structures from *Syllabus of Graded Words and Characters for Chinese Proficiency* (1992) contrasted with *The Modern Chinese Dictionary* (2005), and searched the CCL corpus to identify 60 separable words with a separable frequency of >10% as key separable words and regarded words with more than 100 example sentences as core separable words. Tong [9] examines 73 primary separable words in *The Graded Chinese Syllables, Characters and Words for the Application of Teaching Chinese to the Speakers of other Languages* (2010) based on two corpora, and the 26 words with a higher frequency of separated usage than the average value were selected. Liu [10] selected 388 separable words in S*yllabus of Graded Words and Characters for Chinese Proficiency* (1992), and compared them with *Dictionary of Modern Chinese Separable Word Usage* (1995) to obtain a total of 278 separable words, and listed the top 50 commonly used separable words according to the separable words frequency presented in the CNCORPUS.

In general, previous study have identified core or typical separable words from the perspective of separable frequencies, but have not done any in-depth analysis, and have basically only studied the overall category of separable words, so there is a lack of examination of core separable words, which provides a breakthrough point for us. In these studies, reference is made to existing dictionaries and lexical lists of separable words, such as the vocabulary of TCSOL and *The Modern Chinese Dictionary*, etc. Therefore, we will not repeat the examination of various dictionaries of separable words when studying. These dictionaries include Yang [11], Gao [12], Zhou [13] and Wang [14].

This paper provides further statistics based on the previous results. The separable words in the previous studies include, 12 typical separable words by Ren & Wang [8], 16 core separable words by Wang [5], 60 key separable words by Wang [5], 26 typical separable words by Tong [9], 50 common separable words by Liu [10], and 186 separable words by Gao [12], Zhou [13] 18 basic separable words, and Wang [14] 207 core separable words. We extracted these typical, common and frequent separable words from previous studies and further summarized them. Based on the scattering of different separable words in each study, we come up with nine words with a dispersion degree greater than or equal to 6 as the core separable words, including 睡觉(shuìjiào, 'sleep'), 洗澡(xǐzǎo, 'bathe'), 见面(jiànmiàn, 'meet'), 帮忙(bāngmáng, 'help'), 生气(shēngqì, 'take offence'), 吃惊(chījīng, 'be startled'), 听话(tīnghuà, 'heed what an elder or superior says'), 吃亏(chīkuī, 'suffer losses'), 干杯(gānbēi, 'drink a toast') (Fig. 1).

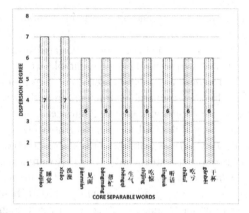

Fig. 1. Dispersion degree of the nine core separable words

2 Selection and Cleaning of the Language Materials

This paper takes use of the BCC "Dialogue" corpus of Beijing Language and Culture University (BLCU). At the same time, about 27 million words from three sub-corpora of the CCL modern Chinese corpus of Peking University," Oral, Crosstalk and sketch, Network Discourses", were used to examine the usage of core separable words accessorily. The separable usage of separable words is mostly found in spoken discourses, and the degree of solemnity of the discourses is a key condition for the emergence of the separable phenomenon [5]. The language selected above are mainly collected from oral corpora or oral conversations, while they also show obvious oral features, so the corpus selected in this paper is more oral and more representative. The paper's original corpus data of the BCC and CCL were obtained by searching the core separable words one by one. In view of the large number of confusing, redundant and misleading forms in the original corpus data, this paper was filtered by ourselves. In addition, considering the semantic wholeness of the separable words and the restricted freedom of the constituents or morphemes, we propose to follow a rule based on which the irrelevant corpus is further filtered out.

In this paper, the separable word is research object, which is a kind of disyllable structure in modern Chinese, in which other components can be inserted and can be separated or combined, but the meaning is solidified and has a whole. According to this rule, the original corpus data will be cleaned and collated, and some examples that did not meet the requirements of the research object will also be eliminated.

For example, *The Modern Chinese Dictionary* (7th edition, 2016) gives 3 word senses for 听话 *tīnghuà* [15]:

- Receiving the sounds of others' words with the ears.
- Listen to elders or leaders and be able to follow the willing of them.
- Waiting for someone to give a reply.

Therefore, according to the rules of this paper, in view of the separable use of 听话 *tīnghuà* in the original corpus data, separated forms such as 听远方的话 (*tīng yuǎnfāng de huà,* 'listen to the voice from afar'), which semantically consist of "听" and "话" as two free morphemes, so have been excluded; and separated forms such as 听长辈的话 (*tīng zhǎngbèi de huà,* 'heed what an elder or superior says'), which has a holistic meaning, have been retained. The corpus datas cleaned are suitable for the study and record the number of correct examples of 9 core separable words in the BCC and CCL (Table 1 and Fig. 2).

Table 1. The number of examples sentences of nine separable words in BCC and CCL

Core separable words	Number of examples sentences in CCL			Number of examples sentences in BCC		
	separated usage	combined usage	Total	separated usage	combined usage	Total
睡觉	162	685	847	22600	182020	204620
洗澡	52	260	312	8146	26424	34570
见面	102	1024	1126	2734	28526	31260
帮忙	106	324	430	2699	16168	18958
生气	34	464	498	1636	41072	42708
吃惊	138	258	396	40	1022	1062
听话	55	164	219	2218	8865	11083
吃亏	84	166	250	664	3102	3766
干杯	5	10	15	798	1638	2436

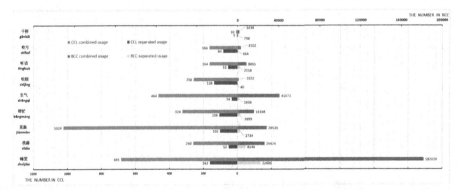

Fig. 2. Comparison of separated and combined cases for the core separable words in BCC and CCL

As shown in Table 1 and Fig. 2, the sentences number of core separable words in the different corpora clearly are different. The three sub-corpora of CCL are mainly spoken materials, but the actually contain some written materials, such as personal blogs in the "Network Discourses" and TV interviews" in the "Oral" corpus. Therefore, the CCL sub-corpus selected for this paper does not contain many valid sentences, and the total number of examples is less; however, in general, the three sub-corpora are predominantly spoken and rich in types, and can be used to support the research conducted using the BCC corpus.

The example sentences listed in the paper are mainly from the BCC, and the sources are not marked for these sentences; the remaining example sentences are marked with their sources. Through this study, we hope to help reveal some features of the core separable words in modern Chinese and provide some reference for TCSOL.

3 Characteristics of the Discrete Form of the Core Disjunctive

This section mainly uses materials to study the characteristics of the core separable words reflected in the separable frequency and the insertion components.

3.1 Features of Split Frequencies

The special feature of the separable word is that it can be both separated and combined, but how it is currently used, and which trends dominate, still requires further to examine. We focus on the state of the core separable words' separated situation. In this paper, we calculate the split frequencies of 9 words in two corpora (Table 2).

Table 2. Comparison of core separable words split frequencies in the BCC and CCL

Core separable words	BCC Corpus		CCL Corpus		Difference	
	split frequency	rank	split frequency	rank	rank difference	frequency difference
干杯	32.76%	1	33.33%	3	−2	−0.57%
洗澡	23.56%	2	16.67%	7	−5	6.90%
听话	20.01%	3	25.11%	4	−1	−5.10%
吃亏	17.63%	4	33.60%	2	2	−15.97%
帮忙	14.31%	5	24.65%	5	0	−10.35%
睡觉	11.04%	6	19.13%	6	0	−8.08%
见面	8.75%	7	9.06%	8	−1	−0.31%
生气	3.83%	8	6.83%	9	−1	−3.00%
吃惊	3.77%	9	34.85%	1	8	−31.08%

There is obvious difference in the number of examples in the core separable words. Table 1 shows that 睡觉 *shuìjiào* has the highest number in both combined and split use in BCC; 见面 *jiànmiàn* and 睡觉 *shuìjiào* has the top examples in CCL. The nine words show a greater difference in the number of split and combined usage in two corpora. However, it's difficult to find out the characteristics of each word only from the number of split examples, and since the content of the BCC and CCL is different and the number varies considerably, it is not accurate to rely on absolute numbers alone, and comparability is poor. Therefore, we also introduced split frequencies to find the ratio of the number of split sentences in the total number, and ranked them from split frequencies.

As shown in Table 2, only the split frequency of 干杯*gānbēi* in the BCC exceeds 30%; the split frequency of three words in the CCL, namely, 吃惊*chījīng*, 吃亏*chīkuī*, 干杯*gānbēi*, are greater than 30%; the split frequency of the remaining words is lower. In contrast, the split frequency of words in the BCC corpus is lower than that in the CCL, as can be seen in Table 1. This difference is related to both the amounts of examples in the corpus and the type of examples, with the BCC corpus being extremely large and therefore dominant in terms of the number of co-used examples, while the CCL corpus, despite having a small lot of written corpora, is mainly a very colloquial corpus, and therefore the latter represents a higher overall split frequency of the corpus.

It should be noted that, as shown in Table 2, the split frequencies of the nine words do not exceed the combined ratio. According to the statistical results, the core separable words are still mainly used with combined forms in the modern spoken Chinese. Is it a coincidence, or a feature of the development of separable words, or a natural phenomenon that the split frequency is higher?

Firstly, it can be explained from the perspective of the law of language development. Some studies have pointed out that in the dynamic usage of new words in modern Chinese, trisyllabic words dominate, but disyllabic words are actually still the mainstream, firmly in the first place of all words. [16] In the midst of the persistent trend of Chinese diphthongization, the internal components of most separable words are structurally tightly bound and steadily used, i.e. they still appear in a combined form as the main usage at present.

Secondly, previous studies can also support the point. Ren & Wang [8] examined 423 separable words and showed that the number of words with a split frequency of over 30% accounted for less than 17%; Wang [5] examined 392 separable words and found that the number of examples, more than 70% of the separable words, were was less than 100 examples, and only 22 words had a split frequency higher than 30%. Previous studies have basically shown that, whether in terms of the overall category or based on a few core words, separable words that can split and have a higher split frequency are in a minority position in modern Chinese.

We also examine the rank and frequency differences of two corpora (Table 2). Since the rank and frequency do not correspond exactly, we mainly examine their characteristics by the frequency difference. The four core separable words that are bold in Table 2 are significantly different from others. Results show that the split frequencies in BCC is lower than that in CCL.

As shown in Table 1, we can see that in terms of the total number of sentences and the number of split-usage sentences, the difference within the BCC corpus is significantly larger. For example, 睡觉*shuìjiào* has a difference of more than 100,000 sentences, while 吃惊*chījīng*, which has the least number, has a difference of more than 1000 sentences. Compared to CCL, 吃惊*chījī*, which has the largest frequency difference, has least number of sentences in BBC corpus. This phenomenon can be explained by two factors. Firstly, by examining the separated forms of BCC, we found that the main separated forms of 吃惊*chījīng* are very limited, and the types of insertable components are relatively few. These components include: numeral (吃一惊, *chī yī jīng*), auxiliary word (吃了惊, *chī le jīng*), auxiliary word + numeral (吃了一惊, *chī le yī jīng*), auxiliary word + numeral + adjective (吃了一大惊, *chī le yī dà jīng*), and interrogative pronouns (吃惊*chī shá jīng*). They are mainly concentrated in the auxiliary word + numeral form, so the split situation is limited and there is not much truly split examples. Secondly, the frequency difference between the four words is more obvious, but the frequency difference of 吃惊*chījīng* is the most prominent, which is related to the content of the two corpora. Although the BCC corpus is concerned with 'conversation' corpus, there are not many instances of 吃惊*chījīng* in real oral communication, and the separated forms of it are rarely used by people to describe their own or each other's emotion; whereas the CCL corpus is mostly descriptive and less conversation content, and the descriptive content contains more separated forms of 吃惊*chījīng*.

The split frequency is one of the characteristics of core separable words. At the same time, when examining the split frequency of core separable words, it is also important to be based on characteristic of separated forms and to analyze insertion components[2].

3.2 Features of Inserted Components

As dictionaries that collected separable words, Zhou [13] and Wang [14] have descriptions of the insertion components. Yang [11] published earlier, and the types and numbers of insertions are not comprehensive and need to be refined. For example, in the case of 睡觉*shuìjiào*, numeral, classifier and interrogative pronoun all could be inserted, which are not listed in the Yang [11]. Therefore, when examining the insertion components, we don't refer to the Usage Dictionary, but mainly make use of Zhou [13] and Wang [14].

Wang [17] examined the insertion components of separable words in *Dictionary of Commonly Used Chinese Separable Words*(2016) and showed that most of the separable words have only 1–3 insertion components and most of them are 了 (*le*), 过(guò), 个(*gè*), 什么(*shénme*) etc., but she did not study them in detail. We attempt to quantify and summarize the types of insertion components from a grammatical structure perspective, in order to reveal what insertion components are included in core separable words and what the main types are.

The division of the insertion components in the paper is word-centered, i.e. the insertion components are segmented in terms of words, in order to demonstrate the split features of the core separable words clearly and concretely, to facilitate the accurate identification of the separated forms of the words on the basis of word segmentation and thus to aid the interpretation, and also to make some sense of the reductive interpretation of split forms. With regard to insertion components, they are induced into 10 species on the basis of previous work. These species include the insertion words or structural forms, noun, predicate(verb/adjective), auxiliary word, numeral, classifier, pronoun (personal

---

[2] It also includes the inversion of a separable words' latter morpheme, in which no component is inserted in the middle of it, e.g. 澡洗了 (zǎo xǐ le, token a bath); or other component is inserted, e.g. 这个澡就别洗了(zhège zǎo jiù bié xǐ le, do not take the bath).

pronouns/finite pronouns), interrogative pronoun, complement, reduplication form, and morpheme inversion form.

With analysis of the insertion components of the BCC, we summarize 48 types of insertion components for the nine core separable words. These types are based on the combination of above 10 kinds of words. Despite of the limitation of corpus and the change of language usage, the types of insertion components are derived from a corpus of hundreds of millions of words, which shows high degree of usage in language, wide distribution and close relationship with the communicative reality.

Although the total number of insertion component types is larger, every core separable word corresponds to the different contexts, and the number of insertion type is also different (Table 3).

Table 3. The number of insertion types for the nine core separable words

Core separable word	睡觉	洗澡	帮忙	吃亏	生气	见面	听话	干杯	吃惊
The number of insertion type	23	19	18	16	14	13	13	8	5

Although the total number of insertion types is larger, it's actually a cross collection of the insertion components of each separable word. As shown in Table 3, the number of insertion types for each word does not cover all types, but we found that some core separable words still share some insertion components. We investigate the scattering cases of insertion components in the nine core separable words, and the data statistics showed six types of insertion components with a scattering number[3] greater than or equal to 5 (Table 4):

Table 4. Types of insertion components with a scattering number ≥ 5

Insertion type	Classifiers auxiliary	Interrogative	Pronouns	Numerals + quantifiers	Morpheme inversion	Complement
Scattering number	8	8	7	7	7	5

The dynamic auxiliaries are 了 *le*, 着 *zhē*, 过 *guò*, and the structural auxiliary is 的 *de*. Except 干杯 *gānbēi*, every core separable could be inserted with auxiliaries. For example:

(1) 昨晚忍着饥饿睡了觉，一夜没睡好.
    Zuówǎn rěn zhe jīè shuì le jiào, yī yè méi shuì hǎo.
    I slept with hunger last night and didn't sleep well all night.

---

[3] The scatter number is equal to some kind of insertion component, which appears in several words.

(2) 这算什么, 我一路洗着澡回家的!

   Zhè suàn shénme , wǒ yí lù xǐ zhe zǎo huíjiā de!

   That was nothing, because I showered all the way and went home!

(3) 你可能也见过很多他帮过忙的人, 谁他都帮的. (CCL)

   Nǐ kěnéng yě jiàn guò hěnduō tā bāng guò máng de rén, shuí tā dōu bāng de.

   You've probably met a lot of people he's helped, because he will help all those in need. (CCL)

(4) 吃的亏可多了去了.

   Chī de kuī kě duō le qù le.

   Someone has suffered losses too much.

The interrogative pronoun 什么(*shénme*, what) is inserted in the core separable words, mainly to express dissatisfaction, contempt or negation, and 啥*shá* is often used in spoken language, which is euqivalent to 什么*shénme*. According Ding [18], the separated form of "V + 什么 + O" only represents negation without the ambiguity, and the stress is on verb morpheme, which makes the intonation more subdued. However, when the stress is placed on 什么*shénme*, the whole structure changes to a questioning tone with the mark "?". Examples of negation are given below:

(5) 考试周还睡什么觉.

   Kǎoshì zhōu hái shuì shén me jiào.

   You should not sleep during exam week.

(6) 不过年不过节洗什么澡.

   Bù guònián bù guòjié xǐ shén me zǎo.

   You shouldn't take a bath until the new year or the festival.

(7) 你能在床上无聊地趟五个小时, 起来看电影吧, 睡啥觉.

   Nǐ néng zài chuángshàng wúliáo de tǎng wǔ gè xiǎoshí, qǐ lái kàn diànyǐng ba, shuì shà jiào.

   You can lie in bed for five hours bored, why not get up and watch a movie, please don't sleep.

Two types, the insertion form of "numeral + classifier" and the morpheme inversion, are concentrated in the seven words 睡觉*shuìjiào*, 洗澡*xǐzǎo*, 帮忙*bāngmáng*, 生气*shēngqì*, 听话*tīnghuà*, 见面*jiànmiàn*, 吃亏*chīkuī*. The "numeral + classifier" form is more common; the morpheme inversion often has a number of words inserted between the two morphemes. For example:

(8) 灯没关, 觉也没睡.

   Dēng méi guān, jiào yě méi shuì.

   No lights out, no sleep.

(9) 帮!这个忙一定帮!

   Bāng! zhè gè máng yí dìng bāng!

   Determined to help!

It should be noted that there are 8 core separable words that could be inserted with classifiers, 次*cì*, 回*huí*, 个*gè*, etc. These words include 睡觉*shuìjiào*, 洗澡*xǐzǎo*, 帮忙*bāngmáng*, 生气*shēngqì*, 听话*tī- nghuà*, 见面*jiànmiàn*, 吃亏*chīkuī*, 干杯*gānbēi*.

The complement inserted by the core separable word could be subdivided into possible complement and resultant complement, including the five words 睡觉*shuìjiào*, 洗澡*xǐzǎo*, 帮忙*bāngmáng*, 生气*shēngqì*, 见面*jiànmiàn*. For example:

(10) 正好等你洗完澡.
      Zhèng hǎo děng nǐ xǐ wán zǎo.
      Just waiting for you to take a shower.
(11) 看着好可怜虽然做错了,但是看着真的生不起气.
      Kàn zhe hǎo kělián suīrán zuò cuò le, dàn shì kàn zhe zhēn de shēng bù qǐ qì.
      Although the other made a mistake and looked pitiful, I really have no reason to be angry.

Statistics on the corpus show that the core separable words use some certain part of speech as the main separated forms, such as the auxiliaries "了 *le*, 着*zhē*, 过*guò*, 的*de*", the interrogative pronouns "什么*shénme*", the classifiers "个*gè*", etc. The seven words, 睡觉*shuìjiào*, 洗澡*xǐzǎo*, 帮忙*bāngmáng*, 生气*shēngqì*, 见面*jiànmiàn*, 吃亏*chīkuī*, 干杯*gānbēi*, could be inserted in 个*gè* individually; and it is also common to insert quantity phrases. The reason, why the insertion of classifiers is more common in the core separable words, is that the separated forms involving classifiers are very much more colloquial than other insertion types, and are simple and clear in structures, in line with the principle of economy of language communication. In the more complex separated forms, it is difficult to find an insertion type fitted to all core separable words, which is constrained by the limitations of the freedom of morphemes and the holistic meaning of the core separable words.

According to the insertion components types summarized in the paper, core separable words can not only insert words alone, such as, but can also combine different words to serve as insertion components. The latter case makes the nine core separable words not share common separated forms. Thus, it can be said that the main separated forms of the core separable words are not scattered and complex, but are concentrated in the six types of insertion forms counted in Table 3, among which classifier, auxiliary, interrogative pronoun, numeral + classifier, and morpheme inversion are the main types.

In addition to the insertion of alone auxiliaries, interrogative pronouns, numerals, classifiers, etc., the vast majority of the insertion components types have these words involved, e.g. 25 insertion types with auxiliaries and 25 insertion types with numerals or classifiers, in which there is inevitable crossover. In other words, the core separable words insertion component can hardly leave the participation of above a few major words, which constitute the bulk of separated forms.

The study of the core separable words can advance the study of modern Chinese ontology, while separable words are an important pedagogical component of TCSOL. Therefore, in addition to examining core separable words based on ontological perspective, we will introduce the perspective of TCSOL, and attempts to study learners' use of the core separable words in an examination of interlanguage corpus of Chinese.

4 Core Separable Words in International Chinese Language Education

Since the 1980s, separable words have been one of the more problematic aspects of TCSOL, but no good solution has yet been proposed. In ICLE, Yang [11] was the first tool for separable words which contains 4066 "separable words", including 1738 common separable words, and aims to provide learners with reference materials for learning separable words. Zhou [13] and Wang [14] individually compiled dictionary of separable words based on the SGWCCP, extracting commonly used separable words and explaining their syntactic functions, insertion forms and special usage. These scholars provided tools for non-native speakers of Chinese to learn separable words, but theses dictionaries lacked quantitative analysis and didn't obviously provide core separable words for learners to learn and imitate.

At present, the compilation and study of dictionaries of separable words for non-native learners of Chinese has been the academic study object. However, because of the wide range and large number of words included, the dictionaries didn't distinguish between the core separable words and the general separable words. The core separable words should be given special attention and examined independently, especially on the basis of the actual language usage state of Chinese learners.

4.1 Selection and Collation of the Corpus

Based on the "HSK Dynamic Composition Corpus" of Beijing Language and Culture University, we searched each of the nine core separable words to examine how non-native Chinese speakers learn to use these words, in the hope of providing a reference for TCSOL. The original language materials of core separable words were obtained by word-by-word search using the "specific condition search" mode in the corpus. In order to ensure the validity and accuracy of the corpus statistics, we clean and organize the original materials.

After cleaning, the paper obtained the separated and combined examples of the nine core separable words (Table 5).

To further compare the split situation of the different core separable words, their split frequencies are summarized in Fig. 3.

4.2 Characteristics of the Core Separable Words for Non-native Chinese Speakers

In this paper, we combine the correlation function to calculate the split frequencies correlation between of BCC, CCL corpus and HSK corpus respectively, and find that the correlation of both results is less than 0.3 (Fig. 4), i.e. there is no linear correlation between native and non-native speakers in the usage of the core separable words, and there are differences between them.

Firstly, Fig. 3 shows that the split rate of the word 听话tīnghuà is the most highest, 52.94%, which exceeds the combined rate, and the difference compared with native speakers is very obvious. In terms of learning errors, the original materials occasionally

Table 5. Non-native Chinese speaker's separated and combined usage of core separable words

Core separable words	Combined usage	Separated usage	Total number of examples	Split frequencies
听话	208	234	442	52.94%
帮忙	127	98	225	43.56%
吃惊	100	26	126	20.63%
洗澡	29	7	36	19.44%
吃亏	56	11	67	16.42%
见面	266	33	299	11.04%
生气	206	22	228	9.65%
睡觉	197	21	218	9.63%
干杯	0	0	0	0.00%

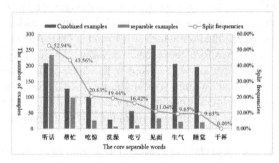

Fig. 3. Split frequency of core separable words for non-native Chinese speakers

treats the two components of 听话 *tī-nghuà* as free morphemes, i.e. learners do not really grasp the second sense of the word in *The Modern Chinese Dictionary* (7th edition). We deleted the type of incorrect material as well as other easily identified incorrect material (e.g., 其实当时我没注意听爸爸的话 *Qíshí dāngshí wǒ méi zhùyì tīng bàbà de huà,*), however, 听话 *tīnghuà* still has a higher split frequency than combined rate. The paper suggests that this may be due to the material limitations of the HSK corpus, such as the size of the corpus and the type of composition, etc.

Secondly, we did not find any examples of 干杯 *gānbēi*, which may involve thematic choice and cultural contextual considerations, but is beyond the scope of the paper.

In view of the special case of 听话 *tīnghuà* and 干杯 *gānbēi*, we considered temporarily excluding the two words, and called the materials containing nine separable words HSK-1, and the other materials excluding 听话 *tīnghuà* and 干杯 *gānbēi* HSK-2. By calculating the split frequencies correlation between the BCC, CCL materials and the HSK-2, we found that the results of calculation were around 0.3, which also can be regarded as uncorrelated, but, compared to the results of the HSK-1, this is a very significant improvement (Fig. 4).

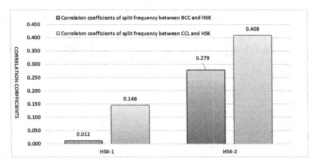

Fig. 4. Comparison between BCC and CCL corpus and HSK corpus about correlation coefficients of split frequency

As can be seen in Fig. 4, 听话*tīnghuà* and 干杯*gānbēi*, as special cases, interfere more with the split frequency correlations. Although the change in correlation is obvious, it cannot be said that there is a significant correlation between the native and interlanguage materials of the core separable words, which is thought to be related to the style of the corpus. According to the demonstration of the HSK Corpus, which collected learner's papers for composition examination which was from the HSK Advanced Chinese Language Proficiency Test. Therefore, these materials are well written style. The BCC and CCL corpus selected in paper are well spoken style, which means that there is a difference between the spoken and written style in the BCC, CCL corpus and HSK corpus, so the correlation between them is not high. In view of the difficulty and complexity of collecting spoken materials, the homogeneity of the native and non-native corpus is not intended to regulate.

In addition, the split usage of the core separable words by non-native speakers differs from native speakers, mainly in that the types of insertion components are fewer and more homogeneous, concentrating mainly on a few core types. After collating the insertion contents of the core separable words in interlanguage corpus, we first tried to examine the learners' usage from the perspective of the number of syllables in the insertion components (Fig. 5 and Fig. 6[4]).

As can be seen from Figs. 5 and 6, in the five syllable types, disyllables and trisyllables are the main insertions components of learners' usage about the core separable words; four syllables are the least. The pentasyllables and others contain a variety of cases; If these are subdivided further, there are fewer in the category. The monosyllables are moderately used. Therefore, the monosyllables will be examined together with disyllables and trisyllables. From the perspective of cognition and brain memory, the number of syllables inserted into the separable words basically conforms to the working memory and capabilities of information processing, that is, although the limit of human information processing is 7 components, 4 components are sensitive point of information processing. When the number is exceeded, the difficulty of understanding and processing the overall structure will increase. [19] Therefore, we can see that the number of inserted components equal to and exceeding four syllables is very small. However, in

---

[4] In Fig. 6, "pentasyllables and others", "others" includes the insertion components of more than five syllables, and the latter morpheme inversion.

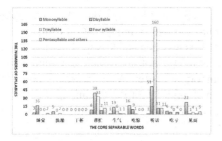

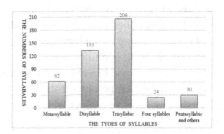

Fig. 5. The number of insertion components syllables about the core separable word about the insertion components

Fig. 6. The number of six types of insertion components syllables

addition to memory ability and information processing ability, second language learners themselves, as non-native Chinese speakers, are not familiar with the modern Chinese, which also has an impact on their learning and mastery of longer and more complex insertion components.

The number of syllables alone can reveal the usage of insertion components in core separable words as a whole, but it cannot reveal the specific types of insertion components and their internal composition. In the paper, we will study features of insertion components based on monosyllables, disyllables and trisyllables. We will analyze insertion components of eight core separable words other than 干杯*gānbēi* and their number according to the lexical classification of insertion components in the previous section (Table 6).

Table 6. Number of learner core disjunctive insertion component types

Core separable words	洗澡	听话	吃亏	帮忙	睡觉	见面	生气	吃惊
Number of separated forms	4	4	5	15	2	7	6	3

As can be seen, there are also significant quantitative differences in the types of insertion components of core separable words by learners. A further count of the eight separable word insertion types reveal that the five categories are the more common types of independent insertion, auxiliary, classifier, complement, pronoun + auxiliary, and noun + auxiliary. Among them, the auxiliaries include "了 *le*, 过*guò*, 的*de*"; the classifiers "个*gè*, 点*diǎn*"; pronouns focus on monosyllables (e.g., "你*nǐ*, you, 我*wǒ*, me, 他*tā*, he, 她*tā*, she") and disyllables (e.g., "我们*wǒmen*, we, 你们*nǐmen*, you, 他们*tāmen*, them"); nouns are special terms of address in the majority, mainly disyllables; complements are also predominantly monosyllables and disyllables. Thus, the split usage of the core separable words by non-native speakers of Chinese is concentrated in a few insertion types, with fewer syllables and simpler components, either as independent auxiliaries or classifiers, or in combinations between simple words. This is also evidenced by the small proportion of the four syllables and pentasyllables and other'. The number of four syllables is not only smaller and concentrated in the 帮忙*bāngmáng* and 听话*tīnghuà*;

the number of pentasyllables and above is only 23 examples, with only three examples of the latter morpheme inversion and only four examples of reduplication form.

Learners' usage of the core separable words is less rich and less well mastered than native speakers. In addition to the difference in the type of insertion, the learning error about the core separable words is also an important aspect. With the exception of 吃 亏 chīkuī, for which no any error example was found, six of the remaining seven core separable words have errors that they should be separable use while combined use. For example:

(12) 有时候, 爷爷到孩子家来住几天的话, 孩子不听话爷爷.*

   Yǒushíhou , yéye dào háizi jiā lái zhù jǐ tiān de huà, háizi bù tīng huà yéye.

   Sometimes, if the grandfather came to stay at the child's house for a few days, the child would not obey the grandfather.

(13) 我们艰难的时候, 她老是帮忙我们.

   Wǒmen jiānnán de shíhòu, tā lǎoshì bāngmáng wǒmen.

   She has been to help us when we were in trouble.

(14) 他是为了见面他的女朋友来到北京.

   Tā shì wèi le jiànmiàn tā de nǚpéngyǒu lái dào Běijīng.

   In order to meet his girlfriend, he came to Beijing.

Also, other types of errors exist, such as:

(15) 您们为了我常常担心而睡不觉的事. (missing component, 睡不着觉 *shuì bù zháo jiào*)

   Nín men wèi le wǒ chángcháng dānxīn ér shuì bù jiào de shì.

   You can't sleep because are worried about me.

(16) 可我不能在你身边照顾, 那时候, 我心疼得很, 连睡也好不觉了. (word order error, 连觉也睡不好 *lián jiào yě shuì bù hǎo*)

   Kě wǒ bùnéng zài nǐ shēnbiān zhàogù, nà shíhou , wǒ xīnténg de hěn , lián shuì yě hǎo bù jiào le.

   I couldn't take care of you by your side, so at that time, I was very distressed and couldn't sleep well.

(17) 父母的经验比我们年轻人多, 所以我们应该尊重他们, 听他们的说话. (semantic error, 听他们的话 *tīng tāmen de huà*)

   Fùmǔ de jīngyàn bǐ wǒmen niánqīngrén duō , suǒyǐ wǒmen yīnggāi zūnzhòng tāmen , tīng tāmen de shuōhuà.

   Parents have more experience than the young people, so we should respect them and follow their advice.

Among the seven core separable words, 34 errors were found, 16 of which were that should be separable use while combined use, while the rest of the errors were mainly due to missing components, word order error and semantic error. It can be seen that learners still have a certain psychology of escape learning separated forms or lack of mastery of the split usage of the core separable words. The usage of the separable words is characterized by the fact that they can be used in both separated and combined forms, and that separated forms are necessary for their grammatical, pragmatic and rhetorical effects, so it is important to guide and correct Chinese learners in the use of separated forms of the core separable words. However, as the number of examples of errors in corpus is smaller and unrepresentative, it is difficult to draw specific patterns of errors in the use of core separable words, and further research is needed.

In conclusion, in ICLE, a few major separated forms of the core separable words are relatively easy for non-native Chinese learners to master, and these forms can be used proficiently. However, compared to native speakers who use complex separated forms, learners still have greater difficulties in using core separable words flexibly. From the specific language example, we found that the separated forms that learners use are relatively few in type and simple in structure, and mainly consist of short insertion components such as monosyllabic, disyllabic, and trisyllabic. The learning errors focus on should be separable use while combined use. This is the type of error that needs to be focused on in TCSOL. It is important to note that the core separable words obtained from different perspectives should not be limited to these nine words, but as a refined category of core words, their representativeness in usage helps learners to master and expand the use of general separable words, and is a type of template that can be relied upon in the process of learning separable words. There is still a long way to go in teaching separable words today and in the future.

5   Conclusion

The paper uses nine core separable words as sample, and after statistical and comparative analysis of the corpus, we found that the split frequency of the core separable words does not exceed the rate of collocation for native Chinese speakers, and that the current usage of core separable words is predominantly combined, due to both corpus characteristics and Chinese development patterns. The split frequency of BCC and CLL is different clearly. It involves materials styles and also is related to the characteristics of the insertion component. In contrast, despite there are the large number of core separated forms, only a few simple types of insertion components, such as auxiliaries, classifiers and pronouns, could be widely used.

In International Chinese Language Education, learners' usage of core separable words differs significantly from that of native Chinese speakers. The study found that learners' usage of separated forms is relatively simple, suggesting that there is still much room for improvement in the teaching of the core separable words and general separable words, which is an important aspect that should not be taken lightly. The paper proposes to start with the core separable words, grasp their main separable laws and usage patterns, and gradually expand and deepen them so as to improve the ability to use separable words flexibly.

This paper is based on language sense of experts, and directly selects the core separable words from previous scholars' studies, and analyses them with the help of real language materials to present the usage patterns of the core separable words. In addition, such study can expand the selection range of the core separable words, so as to obtain a broader, more convincing and more typical research object, and conduct hierarchical research based on classification. At the same time, it increases the size and expands the scope of the mediated corpus, and enhance the homogenization of the corpora, thus revealing in more detail about the actual usage patterns and characteristics of non-native Chinese learners' core separable words and contributing to the ontology study of separable words and the International Chinese Language education.

References

1. Lu, Z.W.: The Construction of Words in Chinese. Science Press, Beijing (1957). (in Chinese)
2. Zhao, S.H., Zhang, B.L.: Determination and the nature of separable words. Lang. Teach. Linguist. Stud. **1**, 40–51 (1996). (in Chinese)
3. Packard, J.L.: The Morphology of Chinese: A Linguistic and Cognitive Approach. Cambridge University Press, Cambridge (2000)
4. Huang, X.Q.: A semantic research on separable character-group. Doctor's dissertation, Beijing Normal University (2003). (in Chinese)
5. Wang, H.F.: The study on the separable words' separated form function of mandarin Chinese. Doctor's dissertation, Beijing Language and Culture University (2008). (in Chinese)
6. Zhao, Y.H.: A review of core words research. Yangtze River Acad. **3**, 130–137 (2012). (in Chinese)
7. Zhao, S.J.: On core words and their types. Wuhan Univ. J. (Hum. Sci.) **67**(3), 63–70 (2014). (in Chinese)
8. Ren, H.B., Wang, G.: The analysis of split word in modern Chinese based on the large-scale corpus. Linguist. Sci. **4**(6), 75–87 (2005). (in Chinese)
9. Tong, L.: The investigation of the separable words in popularization level of vocabulary. Master's thesis, Shanghai Normal University (2013). (in Chinese)
10. Liu, X.: Modern Chinese acrostic verb-object constructions-Chunks theoretical analysis. Master's thesis, Sichuan Normal University (2013). (in Chinese)
11. Yang, Q.H.: Dictionary of Modern Chinese Separable Word Usage. Peking University Press, Beijing (1995). (in Chinese)
12. Gao, Y.A.: Dictionary of Listening and Remembering HSK Separable Word. Beijing Language and Culture University Press, Beijing (2009). (in Chinese)
13. Zhou, S.Z.: Dictionary of Commonly Used Chinese Separable Words. Beijing Language and Culture University Press, Beijing (2016). (in Chinese)
14. Wang, H.F.: Dictionary of Modern Chinese Separable Word Learning. Peking University Press, Beijing (2013). (in Chinese)
15. The Dictionary Department of the Institute of Linguistics of the Chinese Academy of Social Sciences: The Modern Chinese Dictionary Contemporary Chinese Dictionary (Revised edition). The Commercial Press, Beijing (2016). (in Chinese)
16. Zheng, Z.Z., Zhang, Y.Y.: A study on the dynamic evolution of three syllable neologisms in the new era. Appl. Linguist. (04), 81–91 (2020). (in Chinese)
17. Wang, C.X.: A Corpus-Based Study of Separable Words. Master's thesis, Beijing Language and Culture University (2001). (in Chinese)
18. Ding, Y.: A pragmatic analysis study of Chinese verb-object separable words. Stud. Lang. Linguist. (S1), 148–151. (in Chinese)
19. Han, X., Wang, H.: Human cognitive constraints on the separation frequency and limit of separable words. In: Dong, M., Gu, Y., Hong, J.-F. (eds.) CLSW 2021, pp. 18–41. Springer, Cham (2022). https://doi.org/10.1007/978-3-031-06547-7_2

Mandarin Analytic Causative Constructions with *Shǐ* and *Ràng*: A Usage-Based Collostructional Analysis

Na Liu[(✉)] ⓘ and Fuyin Li ⓘ

School of Foreign Languages, Beihang University, Beijing 100191, China
{selinaliu,thomasli}@buaa.edu.cn

Abstract. Analytic causative constructions with 使 *shǐ* 'make' and 让 *ràng* 'make, let', commonly used as [NP1 + SHI/RANG + NP2 + VP], are canonical constructions in Mandarin. Previous scholarship has rarely compared the interactions between the two constructions and the verbs in the VP slot. This study fills this gap by using a collostructional analysis. The prototypical verbs, prototypical constructional meanings and distinctive verbs are investigated. It is found that 1) The prototypical verbs used in SHI construction are change-of-state and change-of-possession verbs, whose constructional meaning refers to the change of NP2 in quantity or quality under the effect of NP1; for RANG construction, its prototypical verbs are psychological verbs and verbs of getting information, and its constructional meaning refers to NP2's perception of something under the influence of NP1; 2) The 17 distinctive verbs for SHI construction are change-of-possession verbs, existential verbs, motion verbs, verbs of phenomenon, change-of-state verbs, verbs of physical manipulation and creation; the 14 distinctive verbs for RANG construction are change-of-state verbs, psychological verbs, verbs of getting information, intellectual verbs and change-of-possession verbs. Although there is overlap in verb categories, the specific verbs which have different preferences for the two constructions are significantly different.

Keywords: Analytic Causative Construction · Collostructional Analysis · Mandarin · 使 *shǐ* · 让 *ràng*

1 Introduction

Causation is among the basic categories found in all languages. Linguists have classified causatives into three major types: lexical causatives, morphological causatives, and analytic causatives (cf. Comrie [1], Dixon [2]). Chinese has developed from a synthetic language to an analytic one (see Sapir [3]). Therefore, analytic causatives are prevalently used to express causation in Mandarin. Two most frequently used analytic causative verbs are 使 *shǐ* 'make' and 让 *ràng* 'make, let' (cf. Lyu [4] and Wang [5]), see examples (1–2):

© The Author(s), under exclusive license to Springer Nature Switzerland AG 2023
Q. Su et al. (Eds.): CLSW 2022, LNAI 13495, pp. 539–552, 2023.
https://doi.org/10.1007/978-3-031-28953-8_39

(1) 8月份以后美元汇率反弹使人民币对欧元、日元升值。
     8 yuèfèn yǐhòu měiyuán huìlǜ fǎntán shǐ rénmínbì duì ōuyuán
     August after dollar exchange rate rebound lead to RMB vs. Euro
     rì yuán shēngzhí
     Yen increase in value
     'The rebound of the dollar exchange rate after August made the RMB appreciate against the Euro and the Yen.'
(2) 精彩的演出仍让观众久久回味。
     Jīngcǎi de yǎnchū réng ràng guānzhòng jiǔjiǔ huíwèi
     Wonderful GEN show still get audience long-lasting appreciation
     'The wonderful performance is still lingering in the audience's mind.'

Syntactically, analytic causative constructions with *shǐ* and *ràng* have a three-slot structure in common: NP1 + SHI/RANG + NP2 + VP (SHI/RANG-cxn henceforth). In the matrix clause, NP1, the CAUSER, is the subject of *shǐ/ràng*, as illustrated in 'the rebound of the dollar' in (1) and 'the wonderful performance' in (2). NP2, the object of NP1 as well as the subject of the VP in the embedded clause, is the CAUSEE that undergoes change or influence, as 'RMB against Euro/Yen' and 'the audience' in (1–2). VP, the final result/state stems from the CAUSEE, can be realized by verbal phrase and adjective, e.g., 'to appreciate' and 'be unforgettable' in examples above. Semantically, a causative predicate can be defined as encoding two events: the causing and the caused event. In prototypical causative situations, the CAUSER succeeds in overriding the CAUSEE's natural tendency towards rest or action (see Talmy [6]). The force interaction between the two participants and its result can be profiled or gapped at the linguistic level, e.g., *The Queen killed Snow White* vs. *The apple killed Snow White* vs. *Snow White died* (see Langacker [7]). In many languages there is a division of labor between causatives, reflecting the integration and separability of components of the two events (see Shibatani [8]).

To account for the difference between *doen* 'do' and *laten* 'let', two analytic causative verbs in Dutch, Speelman and Geeraerts [9] built a usage-based multivariate model of causality, based on which it is shown that both lexical and semantic collocations with the causative lexemes play a significant role in distinguishing them. We are particularly interested in the applicability of the model in the use of Mandarin SHI-cxn and RANG-cxn. To this end, we test their model with Mandarin corpus data. Two questions will be addressed: 1) What are the prototypical meaning of SHI-cxn and RANG-cxn respectively? 2) How do SHI-cxn and RANG-cxn differ with respect to the verb collexemes occurring in the VP slot?

This article is structured as follows. In Sect. 2, we provide an overview of the existing accounts of Mandarin SHI-cxn and RANG-cxn. Next, we describe the data and method used for the corpus-based analysis (Sect. 3). In Sect. 4 we report and discuss the results. Section 5 rounds off with some conclusions.

2 Literature Review

In Mandarin, SHI and RANG represent a rather well-defined verbal category with similar morpho-syntactic properties, of which their common meaning -- 'send/demand sb. to do sth.' -- serves as the starting point (see Lyu [4]). In addition to *shǐ* and *ràng*, another two analytic causative verbs, 令 *lìng* 'demand' and 叫 *jiào* 'ask for', are sporadically used in Mandarin (cf. Lyu [4] and Wang [5]).

In more recent literatures, there has been a rising focus on *shǐ/ràng/lìng/jiào* in authentic use. For instance, Yang [10] conducted simple collexeme analyses of RANG, SHI and JIAO-cxn based on the Lancaster Corpus of Mandarin Chinese and a self-compiled corpus, and ended with a conclusion that SHI-cxn prefers change-of-state verbs, RANG-cxn favors motion verbs, and JIAO-cxn tends to co-occur with verbs of social interaction and communication. In CLSW 2020, Liesenfeld et al. [11] adopted a different statistical technique, i.e., behavioural profiling (BP), to examine the use of RANG, SHI and LING as near-synonyms. Liesenfeld et al. [11] investigated the semantic variation of the three constructions through analyzing 103 contextual features (ID tags) that characterize their collocational, lexical, semantic and frame semantic environment, summarizing that RANG, SHI and LING are each characterized by a combination of distinctive features. In a similar vein, Tian and Zhang [12] probed into the variation of SHI/RANG/LING-cxn in Mainland/Taiwan/Singapore Chinese, using multivariate analysis and concluding that language user's choice of the three verbs is jointly affected by multiple linguistic factors, in which the lectal variation is significantly influential. Meanwhile, Chen [13] modelled the semantic structure and lectal variation of Mandarin SHI and RANG-cxn, claiming that SHI-cxn normally denotes direct causation while RANG-cxn is specialized toward indirect causation. With various foci and methods, these studies indeed improve our understanding of the uses of Mandarin analytic causative verbs. What lacks from these previous corpus-based studies, however, is an integrative analysis of the lexical and semantic collocations with the causative verbs. Specifically, the interaction between the various types of verb lexemes in the VP slot and the constructions still needs to be determined. In an attempt to capture the whole spectrum of verbs and types of verbs occurring in the VP slot in Mandarin SHI and RANG-cxn, we adopt the usage-based collostructional analysis.

3 Data and Method

3.1 Corpora and Data Retrieval

In this study, we make use of the ToRCH[1] 2009 Corpus (see [14]) and ToRCH2014 Corpus (see [15]), which are both annotated and balanced corpora of about 1 million tokens containing texts from four subject domains: press, general prose, learned and fiction. 2009 and 2014 represent the year of publication of texts comprising the two corpora. All hits extracted with the string [SHI/RANG + N + V] from the two corpora are collected. We then manually check the data to exclude spurious and double hits. Instances of [RANG + N + V] used for permissive, demanding and passive meanings are removed. Table 1 presents the resulting dataset.

---

[1] ToRCH is the acronym of 'Texts Of Recent CHinese'.

Table 1. Overview of the dataset.

Construction	Type frequency	Token frequency	Type-Token ratio
NP1 + SHI + NP2 + VP	722	1476	0.47
NP1 + RANG + NP2 + VP	1074	2276	0.49

In the two corpora, we gather 1476 instances of SHI-cxn and 2276 instances of RANG-cxn. In a next phase, we collect 722 VPs from SHI-cxn and 1074 VPs from RANG-cxn. The type-token ratios of the two constructions, 0.49 and 0.47, are quite close.

The 3752 instances are annotated according for five variables: the lemma and the semantic domain of the VP, the (in)animacy of the CAUSER and the CAUSEE, and the genre of the text. While the lemma, genre, and (in)animacy of CAUSER/CAUSEE are straightforward in most cases, identifying the semantic domain of the lexical EP can be somewhat laborious. Based on previous research into verb classes in different languages (see Levin [16]), each occurrence is coded in line with the 15-class taxonomy of semantic domains developed by Levshina et al. [17], as listed and exemplified in Table 2:

Table 2. Taxonomy of semantic domains of VP.

Verb type	Meaning	Examples
V.Aspect	Aspectual verbs	保持-bǎo chí -keep, 停止-tíng zhǐ -stop
V.Body	Verbs related to body	哈哈大笑-hā hā dà xiào-laugh and loud, 昏睡-hūn shuì-lethargy
V.ChPoss	Verbs related to change of possession	获得-huò dé-get, 丧失-sàng shī-lose
V.ChState	Verbs related to change of state	提高-tí gāo-improve, 最大化-zuì dà huà-maximize
V.Create	Verbs related to creation, transformation and destruction of objects by an agent	产生-chǎn shēng-produce, 灭绝-miè jué-extinct
V.Exist	Verbs of existence, location, maintaining a position, etc.	存在-cún zài-exist, 植根于-zhí gēn yú-root in
V.Intel	Verbs related to intellectual processes and states, such as thinking, memory, beliefs, intentions	学以致用-xué yǐ zhì yòng-apply what you have learned, 怀疑-huái yí-suspect
V.PhysManip	Verbs related to exerting force to an object, without transforming it	把握-bǎ wò-grasp, 粘贴-zhān tiē-paste
V.Motion	Verbs of motion	陷入-xiàn rù-fall into, 走出-zǒu chū-go out

(continued)

Table 2. (*continued*)

Verb type	Meaning	Examples
V.GetInfo	Verbs related to obtaining information from the outside world	感受到-gǎn shòu dào-feel, 看到-kàn dào-see
V.Phenom	Verbs related to appearance, occurrence and other perceived phenomena	呈现-chéng xiàn-present, 显得-xiǎn dé-appear
V.Psych	Verbs related to emotions and desires experienced by the subject	惊恐-jīng kǒng-panic, 激动-jī dòng-excited
V.MentInfl	Verbs related to influencing someone's mind intentionally or unintentionally	影响-yǐng xiǎng-influence
V.SocInter	Verbs of social interaction and verbal communication, including performative verbs	服务-fú wù-serve, 原谅-yuán liàng-forgive
V.Oth	Other predicates, including light verbs and other abstract predicates	做-zuò-do, 工作-gōng zuò-work

3.2 Method: Collostructional Analysis

To account for the similarities and differences in the uses of SHI-cxn and RANG-cxn, this study investigates the interaction between the verb lexemes in the VP slot and the constructions, using the collostructional analysis developed by Stefanowitsch and Gries in a series of studies (cf. Stefanowitsch and Gries [18, 19] and Gries and Stefanowitsch [20–22]. As a family of methods, collostructional analysis aims at the associations between grammatical constructions and lexical items. In this study, we conducted simple collexeme analysis (SCA) and distinctive collexeme analysis (DCA). With SCA, we identify the degree to which the verb lexemes in the VP slot are attracted to SHI and RANG-cxn respectively. DCA measures the preference of a common VP collexeme for one particular construction over the other.

Table 3 exemplifies the data required for SCA. Taking the VP 具有-jù yǒu-*have*, apart from the frequency of *jù yǒu* in SHI-cxn (23), there are also the corpus frequency of SHI-cxn (1476), the corpus frequency of *jù yǒu* (1055) and the overall corpus size (2318758), from which the occurrence of *jù yǒu* in constructions other than SHI-cxn can be obtained.

DCA requires fewer input frequencies than SCA, as illustrated in Table 4.

In this paper, we use the G^2 statistic of the log-likelihood test, one of the commonly used association measures, to calculate the collostructional strength (cf. Stefanowitsch and Flach [23]). All subsequent calculations are performed using the R package {collostructions} (see Flach [24]) in the R environment (see R Development Core Team [25]). The cut-off p-value for attracted collexemes is 0.05.

Table 3. Input to a SCA for the verb *jù yǒu* in SHI-cxn.

	Frequency of *jù yǒu*	Frequency of ¬ *jù yǒu*	Total
Frequency of SHI-cxn	23	1453	1476
Frequency of ¬ SHI-cxn	1032	2316250	2317282
Total	1055	2317703	2318758

Table 4. Input to a DCA which compares verbs in the VP slot in SHI-cxn and RANG-cxn.

VP	Frequency in SHI-cxn	Frequency in RANG-cxn	Total
有-yǒu-have	61	77	138
感到-gǎn dào-feel	18	48	66
觉得-jiào dé-feel	4	44	48
…	…	…	…
Total	1476	2276	3752

4   Results and Discussion

4.1   SCA of SHI and RANG-Cxn

SCA computes the collostructional strength for each lexical item on the basis of the contingency table filled with the frequency information retrieved from the chosen corpora. We retrieve 556 VP collexemes for SHI-cxn, versus 802 for RANG-cxn. Table 5 and Table 6 present the 20 most attracted verb collexemes (COLLEX) of SHI and RANG-cxn respectively, including their total frequencies in the two corpora (CORP.FREQ), their observed (OBS) and expected (EXP) values in the construction, and the collostructional strength (G^2). All lexical items shown in Table 5 and Table 6 are significantly attracted at $p < .00001$.

As illustrated in Sect. 3, in order to investigate which semantic clusters are conceptualized by the most strongly attracted VPs of the two constructions, we group the VPs into 15 semantic classes. The ones that outperform in SHI-cxn and RANG-cxn will help us capture the semantic characteristics of the two constructions (cf. Dekalo and Hampe [26]).

At first glance, according to the semantic classes instantiated in Table 2, the most attracted VP collexemes in SHI-cxn can be classified into eight categories: V.Exist (成为-become, 处于-in); V.ChState (达到-achieve, 充满-full, 变-change); V.Create (产生-produce); V.GetInfo (感到-feel, 感受到-feel, 遭受-suffer); V.ChPoss (得到-get, 有-have, 获得-get, 具有-have); V.Phenom (显得-appear, 发生-occur, 形成-form); V.Motion (下降-decline, 陷入-fall into, 降低-reduce); and V.PhysManip (发挥-play). They mainly designate the change of state, be it physical or mental. In contrast, the most attracted VP collexemes in RANG-cxn can be summarized into seven categories: V.GetInfo (感到-feel, 感受到-feel, 看到-see, 体会-experience, 感觉-feel, 明白-clear);

Table 5. The 20 most attracted VP collexemes in [NP1 + SHI + NP2 + VP].

NO	COLLEX	CORP.FREQ	OBS	EXP	G^2	NO	COLLEX	CORP.FREQ	OBS	EXP	G^2
1	成为-chéng wéi-become	1481	79	0.9	551.97597	11	处于-chù yú-in	261	13	0.2	88.44325
2	得到-dé dào-get	759	33	0.5	215.88414	12	下降-xià jiàng-decline	211	11	0.1	75.83938
3	变-biàn-change	713	31	0.5	202.75883	13	陷入-xiàn rù-fall into	93	9	0.1	73.49516
4	有-yǒu-have	11845	61	7.5	150.35416	14	达到-dá dào-achieve	511	13	0.3	70.96582
5	获得-huò dé-get	592	23	0.4	145.10504	15	遭受-zāo shòu-suffer	60	8	0	70.73956
6	感到-gǎn dào -feel	366	18	0.2	122.05703	16	发生-fā shēng-occur	911	14	0.6	62.63214
7	具有-jù yǒu-have	1055	23	0.7	118.7071	17	发挥-fā huī-play	467	11	0.3	58.36212
8	产生-chǎn shēng-produce	701	20	0.4	113.81084	18	降低-jiàng dī-reduce	224	9	0.1	57.30419
9	感受到-gǎn shòu dào-feel	34	9	0	93.25804	19	充满-chōng mǎn-full	268	9	0.2	54.07088
10	显得-xiǎn dé -appear	241	13	0.2	90.54648	20	形成-xíng chéng-form	814	12	0.5	52.70631

Table 6. The 20 most attracted collexemes in [NP1 + RANG + NP2 + VP].

NO	COLLEX	CORP.FREQ	OBS	EXP	G^2	NO	COLLEX	CORP.FREQ	OBS	EXP	G^2
1	感到-gǎn dào -feel	366	48	0.4	382.13361	11	显得-xiǎn dé -appear	241	18	0.2	121.90624
2	感受到-gǎn shòu dào-feel	34	23	0	276.06119	12	了解-le jiě-understand	479	21	0.5	119.58589
3	觉得-jiào dé-feel	982	44	1	252.90899	13	体会-tǐ huì-experience	95	13	0.1	104.47404
4	变-biàn-change	713	35	0.7	207.45515	14	感觉-gǎn jiào-feel	606	20	0.6	102.59332
5	成为-chéng wéi -become	1481	42	1.5	203.29605	15	惊讶-jīng yà-surprise	76	11	0.1	89.71291
6	有-yǒu-have	11845	77	11.6	162.66143	16	明白-míng bái-clear	300	14	0.3	81.43424
7	看到-kàn dào -see	888	29	0.9	148.26636	17	变成-biàn chéng-become	311	14	0.3	80.42359
8	产生-chǎn shēng-produce	701	26	0.7	139.44687	18	失望-shī wàng-disappointed	61	9	0.1	73.76472
9	得到-dé dào-get	759	26	0.7	135.35035	19	想起-xiǎng qǐ-remember	179	11	0.2	70.08314
10	联想-lián xiǎng-associate	44	13	0	126.80762	20	充满-chōng mǎn-full	268	12	0.3	68.79591

V.ChState (变-change, 充满-full, 变成-become); V.Exist (成为-become); V.ChPoss (有-have, 得到-get,); V.Create (产生-produce); V.Intel (联想-associate, 想起-remember); and V.Psych (惊讶-surprise, 失望-disappointed). Additionally, we observe that in the list of the 30 most attracted VPs, SHI-cxn and RANG-cxn overlap greatly in VP categories, including V.GetInfo, V.ChState, V.ChPoss, V.Phenom, V.Motion, V.Exist, V.Create and V.Intel, reflecting their synonymous status regarding the interaction between VPs and SHI/RANG-cxn.

Figure 1 displays the distribution of the 15 types of VPs in the two constructions:

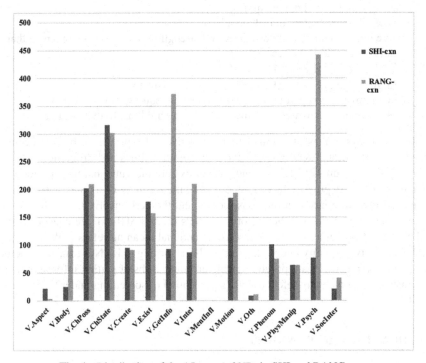

Fig. 1. Distribution of the 15 types of VPs in SHI and RANG-cxn.

In SHI-cxn, the sequence of 15 types of VPs based on their occurrences is V.ChState (21.41%) > V.ChPoss (13.75%) > V.Motion (12.53%) > V.Exist (12.06%) > V.Phenom (6.84%) > V.Create (6.44%) > V.GetInfo (6.30%) > V.Intel (5.89%) > V.Psych (5.22%) > V.PhysManip (4.34%) > V.Body (1.69%) > V.Aspect (1.49%) > V.SocInter (1.42%) > V.Oth (0.61%) > V.MentInfl (0%); in RANG-cxn, the sequence is V.Psych (19.42%) > V.GetInfo (16.34%) > V.ChState (13.27%) > V.ChPoss (9.23%) = V.Intel (9.23%) > V.Motion (8.52%) > V.Exist (6.94%) > V.Body (4.44%) > V.Create (4.00%) > V.Phenom (3.30%) > V.PhysManip (2.81%) > V.SocInter (1.80%) > V.Oth (0.48%) > V.Aspect (0.18%) > V.MentInfl (0.04%).

In previous studies, Furukawa [27] proposed that the VPs in SHI and JIAO-cxn habitually encode psychological or physiological feelings, while VPs in the SHI-cxn in particular rarely express actions or behaviors. Another scholar, Miyake [28] held that VP in the SHI-cxn is unable to represent an intentional action. In our analysis, however, it is found that both SHI and RANG-cxn can be used with verbs of physical manipulation, which refers to concrete or abstract actions and can be intentional, as indicated by the VP *kòngzhì* 'to control' and *wǔjǐn* 'to squeeze' in examples (3–4):

(3)   我们要锻炼小腹的弹性和力度，使其更好地控制气息。
       Wǒmen yào duànliàn xiǎofù de tánxìng hé lìdù,
       We need exercise low abdomen DE elasticity and strength,
       shǐ qí gènghǎode kòngzhì qìxí.
       make it more better control breath
       'We need to exercise the elasticity and strength of the lower abdomen so that it can better control the breath.'

(4)   经济不景气会使消费者捂紧钱包。
       Jīngjì bú jǐngqì huì shǐ xiāofèizhě wǔjǐn qiánbāo.
       Economy not prosperous will make consumer squeeze tightly wallet
       'An economic downturn can make consumers hold fast to their wallet

In our analysis, it is also found that the verbs and types of verbs that occur in Mandarin SHI-cxn and RANG-cxn have both commonalities and differences. Indeed, the syntactic structures of SHI-cxn and RANG-cxn are the same, but their prototypical meanings differ. As proposed by Goldberg [29], the meaning of a construction results from the interaction between the construction and the verb involved, and the two are closely related. Specifically, the prototypical VPs used in SHI-cxn are change-of-state and change-of-possession verbs, whose constructional meaning refers to the change of NP2 in quantity or quality under the effect of NP1; turning to RANG-cxn, we conclude that its prototypical VPs are psychological verbs and verbs of getting information, and its constructional meaning refers to NP2's perception of something under the influence of NP1.

4.2   DCA of SHI and RANG-Cxn

In the preceding section, we compare SHI-cxn and RANG-cxn based on two individual SCA, finding both semantic similarities and differences in their uses. In order to further distinguish the two constructions, we compare the two constructions with regard to the VP collexemes they have in common, using the method of DCA. Table 7 presents the result, in which the 17 distinctive collexemes for SHI-cxn and 14 distinctive collexemes for RANG-cxn are listed, along with their observed and expected frequencies and the G^2 value.

As shown in Table 7, the VPs listed have a higher observed frequency than the expected frequency with the construction they prefer to co-occur. For instance, the 17 VPs in the left column are strongly associated with SHI-cxn, while the 14 VPs in the right are strongly associated with RANG-cxn. The p-value ranges from $p < .00001 \sim p < .05$. To answer the second research question, we combine the results in Table 5, Table 6 and Table 7, and conclude that the 17 distinctive verbs of SHI-cxn are change-of-possession verbs, existential verbs, motion verbs, verbs of phenomenon, change-of-state

Table 7. The distinctive VP collexemes for [NP1 + SHI/RANG + NP2 + VP].

SHI-cxn					RANG-cxn				
COLLEX	SHI-cxn (O:E)	RANG-cxn (O:E)	G^2	ASSOC	COLLEX	SHI-cxn (O:E)	RANG-cxn (O:E)	G^2	ASSOC
具有 -jù yǒu- have	24:10.9	1:14.1	33.179 43	SHI-cxn	多 -duō- many	1:3.9	8:5.1	4.5186 5	RANG-cxn
成为 - chéng wéi- become	79:52.5	42:68.5	25.075 11	SHI-cxn	感 动 - gǎn dòng- touched	1:3.9	8:5.1	4.5186 5	RANG-cxn
下 降 - xià jiàng- decline	11:5.2	1:6.8	12.686 21	SHI-cxn	激 动 -jī dòng- excited	1:3.9	8:5.1	4.5186 5	RANG-cxn
获 得 - huò dé- get	23:13.5	8:17.5	12.293 86	SHI-cxn	明 白 - míng bái-clear	3:7.4	14:9.6	5.1478 1	RANG-cxn
陷 入 - xiàn rù- fall into	10:4.8	1:6.2	11.185 6	SHI-cxn	失望 -shī wàng- disap-pointed	1:4.3	9:5.7	5.4407 3	RANG-cxn
形 成 - xíng chéng- form	12:6.1	2:7.9	10.898 13	SHI-cxn	相 信 - xiàng xìn- believe	2:6.1	12:7.9	5.5564 2	RANG-cxn
出 现 - chū xiàn- appear	11:5.6	2:7.4	9.5359 6	SHI-cxn	享 受 - xiǎng shòu- enjoy	1:4.8	10:6.2	6.3860 1	RANG-cxn
发生 -fā shēng- occur	14:7.8	4:10.2	8.9344 4	SHI-cxn	惊 讶 - jīng yà- surprise	1:5.2	11:6.8	7.3503 8	RANG-cxn
达到 -dá dào- achieve	13:7.8	5:10.2	6.1782	SHI-cxn	感 到 - gǎn dào- feel	18:28.7	48:37.3	7.6125 3	RANG-cxn
增 加 - zēng jiā- increase	8:4.3	2:5.7	5.6498 3	SHI-cxn	知道 -zhī dào- know	2:9.1	19:11.9	11.878 07	RANG-cxn
发挥 -fā huī-play	11:6.5	4:8.5	5.5595 5	SHI-cxn	感 觉 - gǎn jiào- feel	2:9.6	20:12.4	12.835 73	RANG-cxn
满足 - mǎn zú- satisfy	6:3	1:4	5.4295 5	SHI-cxn	看 到 - kàn dào- see	4:14.3	29:18.7	15.561 96	RANG-cxn
生 - shēng - emerge	6:3	1:4	5.4295 5	SHI-cxn	得 到 -dé dào-get	1:11.7	26:15.3	22.978 69	RANG-cxn

(continued)

Table 7. (*continued*)

降 低 - jiàng dī- reduce	9:5.2	3:6.8	4.9716 5	SHI- cxn	觉 得 - jiào dé- feel	4:20. 8	44:27 .1	29.883 51	RAN G- cxn
呈 现 - chéng xiàn- present	7:3.9	2:5.1	4.4458 6	SHI- cxn					
发展-fā zhǎn- develop	7:3.9	2:5.1	4.4458 6	SHI- cxn					
实 现 - shí xiàn- accom- plish	5: 2.6	1: 3.4	4.0 8891	S HI- cxn					

verbs, verbs of physical manipulation and creation; the 14 distinctive verbs of RANG-cxn are change-of-state verbs, psychological verbs, verbs of getting information, intellectual verbs and change-of-possession verbs. Although there is overlap in verb categories, the specific verbs are significantly different.

5 Concluding Remarks

Within the usage-based framework, this study investigates the semantic similarities and differences in the uses of SHI-cxn and RANG-cxn in Mandarin, conducting a collostructional analysis. Major findings are:

1) The prototypical verbs used in SHI-cxn are change-of-state and change-of-possession verbs, whose constructional meaning refers to the change of NP2 in quantity or quality under the effect of NP1; turning to RANG-cxn, we classify its prototypical verbs as psychological verbs and verbs of getting information, and its constructional meaning refers to NP2's perception of something under the influence of NP1.
2) The 17 distinctive verbs for SHI-cxn are change-of-possession verbs, existential verbs, motion verbs, verbs of phenomenon, change-of-state verbs, verbs of physical manipulation and creation; the 14 distinctive verbs for RANG-cxn are change-of-state verbs, psychological verbs, verbs of getting information, intellectual verbs and change-of-possession verbs. The two constructions can be distinguished based on their distinctive VP collexemes.

Importantly, this study has shown that SHI-cxn and RANG-cxn can be compared and distinguished with respect to their interactions with the VP collexemes. Naturally, it would be interesting to investigate and compare more contextual features (e.g., syntactic, semantic, and pragmatic features) between the two constructions as well as among more synonymous constructions. This topic deserves to be investigated thoroughly in future research.

Acknowledgments. We would like to thank the anonymous reviewers of CLSW 2022 for helpful comments and suggestions. This study is supported by the Chinese Government Scholarship Project (Award number: 202006020199, PI: Na Liu) and the National Social Science Foundation Project titled *A Diachronic Typological Study on the Chinese Verb-complement of Macro-event* (Award number: 21BYY045, PI: Fuyin Li).

References

1. Comrie, B.: Language Universals and Linguistic Typology: Syntax and Morphology, 2nd edn. The University of Chicago Press, Chicago (1989)
2. Dixon, R.M.W.: A typology of causatives form, syntax and meaning. In: Dixon, R.M.W., Aikhenvald, A.Y. (eds.) Changing Valency: Case Studies in Transitivity, pp. 30–83. Cambridge University Press, Cambridge (2000)
3. Sapir, E.: Language: An Introduction to Study of Speech. Harhcount, Brance & Company, New York (1921)
4. Lyu, S.X.: The Essentials of Chinese Grammar. Commercial Press, Beijing (1942/1982). (in Chinese)
5. Wang, L.: Modern Chinese Grammar. Commercial Press, Beijing (1943/1985). (in Chinese)
6. Talmy, L.: Toward a Cognitive Semantics, Volume 1: Concept Structuring Systems. The MIT Press, Massachusetts (2000)
7. Langacker, R. W.: Settings, participants, and grammatical relations. In: Tsohatzidis, S.L. (ed.) Meanings and Prototypes. Studies in Linguistic Categorization, pp. 213–238. Routledge, London (1990)
8. Shibatani, M., Pardeshi, P.: The causative continuum. In: Shibatani, M. (ed.) The Grammar of Causation and Interpersonal Manipulation, pp. 85–126. John Benjamins Publishing Company, Amsterdam (2002). https://doi.org/10.1075/tsl.48.07shi
9. Speelman, D., Geeraerts, D.: Causes for causatives: the case of Dutch doen and laten. In: Sanders, T., Sweetser, E. (eds.) Linguistics of Causality, pp. 173–204. Mouton de Gruyter, Berlin (2009)
10. Yang, J.F.: A Multi-dimensional Study of Periphrastic Causative Constructions in Mandarin Chinese. Zhejiang University, Hangzhou, PhD dissertation (2016). (in Chinese)
11. Liesenfeld, A., Liu, M.C., Huang, C-R.: Profiling the Chinese causative constrution with rang (让), shi (使), and ling (令) using frame semantic features. CLSW (2020)
12. Tian, X.Y., Zhang, W.W.: Chinese analytic causative constructions and their lectal variation: a multinomial logistic regression. Foreign Lang. Teach. **3**, 22–33 (2020). (in Chinese)
13. Chen, Q.Y.: Creating a 3D semantic profile of causative shi and rang: a constructional approach. Australian J. Linguist. **40**(4), 405–427 (2020)
14. Xu, J.J.: ToRCH2009 Corpus (2014). (in Chinese)
15. Xu, J.J.: ToRCH2014 Corpus (2017). (in Chinese)
16. Levin, B.: English Verb Classes and Alternations: A Preliminary Investigation. The University of Chicago Press, Chicago (1993)
17. Levshina, N., Geeraerts, D., Speelman, D.: Mapping constructional spaces: a contrastive analysis of English and Dutch analytic causatives. Linguistics **51**(4), 825–854 (2013)

18. Stefanowitsch, A., Gries, S.: Collostructions: investigating the interaction of words and constructions. Int. J. Corpus Linguist. **8**(2), 209–243 (2003)
19. Stefanowitsch, A., Gries, S.: Covarying collexemes. Corpus Linguist. Linguist. Theory **1**(1), 1–43 (2005)
20. Gries, S., Stefanowitsch, A.: Co-varying collexemes in the into-causative. In: Achard, M., Kemmer, S. (eds.) Language, Culture and Mind, pp. 225–236. CSLI Publication, Stanford (2004)
21. Gries, S., Stefanowitsch, A.: Extending collostructional analysis: a corpus-based perspective on 'alternations.' Int. J. Corpus Linguist. **9**(1), 97–129 (2004)
22. Gries, S., Stefanowitsch, A.: Covarying collexemes. Corpus Linguist. Linguist. Theory **1**(1), 1–43 (2005)
23. Stefanowitsch, A., Flach, S.: Too big to fail but big enough to pay for their mistakes. A collostructional analysis of the patterns [too ADJ to V] and [ADJ enough to V]. In: Pastor, G. C., Colson, J-P. (eds.) Computational Phraseology, pp. 247–272. John Benjamins, Amsterdam/Philadelphia (2020)
24. Flach, S.: collostructions: An R implementation for the family of collostructional methods. R package version 0.1.0 (2017)
25. R Development Core Team. R: A language and environment for statistical computing (2021)
26. Dekalo, V., Hampe, B.: Networks of meanings: Complementing collostructional analysis by cluster and network analyses. GCLA **5**, 143–176 (2017)
27. Furukawa, Y.: Syntactic features of emotional predicates the voice-change relations between "Jiao/Rang/Shi/Ling" structure and "Wei" structure. Lang. Teach. Linguist. Stud. **2**, 28–37 (2003). (in Chinese)
28. Miyake, T.: A usage-based analysis of the causative verbs Shi in Mandarin Chinese. In: Takagaki, T., Zaima, S., Tsuruga, Y., Fernandez, F.M., Kawaguchi, Y. (eds.) Corpus-based Approaches to Sentence Structures, pp. 77–94. John Benjamins, Amsterdam/Philadelphia (2005)
29. Goldberg, A.E.: Constructions: A Construction Grammar Approach to Argument Structure. The University of Chicago Press, Chicago (1995)

Topic and Focus in the Left Periphery of Old Xiang: Syntactic Cartography and Semantic Constraints

Shunhua Fu[(✉)] [iD]

School of Foreign Languages, Xiangtan University, Xiangtan, Hunan, China
fshunhua@163.com

Abstract. In the syntactic cartography of the left periphery (LP), topic and focus are assumed to be hierarchically ordered with a typological divergence. In Indo-European languages like Italian, topics can be higher or lower than foci, whereas in Tibeto-Burman languages like Mandarin Chinese, topics must be higher than foci. This paper explores the LP in the Old Xiang dialect, a branch of Chinese dialects, and points out that topics and foci are distributed as "CP > 'lian' (*even*) Focus > AT > HT > DPLD > 'lian' (*even*) Focus > TP". The cartographic result shows that the hierarchical distribution of topics and foci is not typologically divergent between Italian and Chinese dialects (at least Old Xiang). The ordering is mainly restricted by semantic constraints, as well as constraints from other levels of language.

Keywords: Syntactic cartography · Semantic constraints · Focus · Topic · The Old Xiang dialect

1 Introduction

Information Structure (IS) describes the way information is formally packaged in a sentence [1]. Topic and focus are two primitives needed to account for all information structure phenomena [2]. Topic conveys old or given information, whereas focus conveys new information in the context [3, 4]. IS might be optionally divergent from basic word order formally, which is affected by factors from different levels of language, as well as prominence of information. Therefore, it serves as a bridge connecting syntax, semantics and discourse pragmatics, etc.

Extensive research has been done on IS (i.e. topic[1] and focus) within various theoretical frameworks, among which the syntactic cartography of IS has gained much attention. A hotly debated question is what is the exact cartographic mapping of IS in the left periphery (LP), and how it is constrained. The LP, which is on the left to the subject of a clause, is also called the CP (Complementiser Phrase) domain. It is assumed that the LP is where discourse concepts of IS are represented [6, 7]. In Italian, topics

---

[1] Topics in cartographic studies only refer to the structural topics, including non-subject topics [See Gao & Lyu [5]).

© The Author(s), under exclusive license to Springer Nature Switzerland AG 2023
Q. Su et al. (Eds.): CLSW 2022, LNAI 13495, pp. 553–566, 2023.
https://doi.org/10.1007/978-3-031-28953-8_40

and foci are distributed in a parallel way between the CP domain and the TP domain (the domain lower than TP but higher than vP); topics can be higher or lower than foci; topics can occur recursively on the LP [6, 8]. These assumptions have led to productive cross-linguistic studies, including the study of modern Mandarin Chinese. Nevertheless, in contrast to Italian, Mandarin has its own properties [9–12]: topics are always in the position higher than foci (typically the "lian" Focus); topics in the CP domain can appear recursively; there is a finer-grained map for IS.

This paper investigates the (Old) Xiang dialect, a branch of the Chinese language family, to provide further evidence to account for the divergences of syntactic distribution of IS cross-linguistically. The Xiang dialect, largely used by Hunan folks living in the Xiangjiang River basin, is divided into New Xiang and Old Xiang. The former is represented by Changsha dialect, whereas the latter Loudi-Shaodong dialect. Old Xiang is a comparatively less contaminated variety among Xiang dialects. The corpus of this paper mainly comes from native speakers of this dialect aged 50–70.

We concentrate our discussion on the Left Dislocation (LD, i.e. Left Dislocated Topic)[2], Hanging Topic (HT), Aboutness Topic (AT) and the "lian" (meaning even) Focus in the LP. The following questions will be addressed:

Q_1: What is the exact inventory of topics and foci in Old Xiang?

Q_2: What is the mapping of topics and the "lian" Focus in the LP in Old Xiang? How is the cartography semantically constrained at different levels of language?

Our goal in this paper is to examine whether Old Xiang exhibits the same ordering restrictions found in Mandarin and Italian with respect to topic and focus in the LP, and then discuss the typological significance of the cartographic divergences in IS. After the Introduction, Sect. 2 reviews the previous research on the cartography of IS in different languages, and inspects the debates on the inventory and mapping of topics and foci. Section 3 will testify and show that the typical topics including DPLD, HT, and AT in Mandarin can be found in Old Xiang, but as for PPLD, only the PP as the adjunct can be topicalized and is base-generated rather than generated by movement. Section 3 paves a way for Sect. 4, which offers a fine map of topics and the "lian" Focus and proposes that the ordering is mainly restricted by semantic constraints, as well as other factors like syntactic constraints and prominence of information. The last section draws a conclusion that topics are not necessarily higher than the "lian" Focus, and the hierarchy of topic and focus does not seem be a distinct typological divergence between Italian and Chinese dialects (at least Old Xiang).

2 Background

2.1 Cartography of Topic and Focus in Indo-European Languages

Most of the cartographic studies on IS have been carried out based on a comparative study of Italian, Italian dialects and other Indo-European languages. Rizzi [6] proposes that topics and foci in the left periphery of the CP in Italian are distributed as "CP >

---

[2] LD includes the Determiner Phrasal Left Dislocation (DPLD) and the Prepositional Phrasal Left dislocation (PPLD).

Topp* > FocP > Topp* > TP", which shows that topics are located on the position higher or lower than FocP, and topics can occur recursively. The distribution of IS in the CP domain is assumed be a property of typological universality. Benincà [13] points out that the topic and focus in Italian are distributed in clear-cut fields, and the topic field is higher than the focus field. The mapping of IS is shown as "ForceP > FrameP > TopP > FocP > FinP > TP". Benincà & Poletto [14] argue that the topic and focus in Italian and its varieties are distributed as "HT > SceS > LD > LI > CFoc > IFoc > TP"[3], which suggests that Rizzi's "topic recursion" is not an infinite set of identical TopPs or FocPs, but a finite set of different functional phrases. Frascarell & Hinterhölzl [15] find that the topic is above the focus by the comparison of German and Italian. However, Cruschina [10] finds that in Sicilian, the contrast focus (CFocus) is higher than the topic, which itself is higher than the information focus (IFocus). Therefore, the exact typological cartographic properties of IS are controversial.

2.2 Cartography of Topics and Foci in Mandarin

Studies on the mapping of topic and focus in the left periphery of Mandarin have also received attention. Through a comparative study of Mandarin and Italian, Paul [9] proposes that topics and foci of Mandarin in the CP and TP domains are distributed in a parallel way, which is "CP (force) > TopP* > 'even' FocP > TP > inner TopP > 'even' FocP > vP. The result indicates that similar to the conclusion drawn by Rizzi [6] and Belletti [8] in Italian, topics in the CP domain in Mandarin can occur recursively, however, the topics must be higher than the foci.

The fine-grained maps of information structure in Mandarin and its dialects have been investigated. Badan & Gobbo [11] propose that there are three typical topics in Mandarin—AT, HT, and LD, among which LD is classified into DPLD and PPLD. They reach a conclusion that IS in the CP domain is distributed as "CP > AT > HT > LD > lian-FocP > TP". Cheung [12] argues that syntactically, DPLD is distinct from PPLD, but similar to DPLD, and both DPLD and HT belong to "canonical topics". The cartography of Mandarin IS is "CP > AT > Canonical Topic > PPLD > Identificational Focus > 'lian' Focus > TP". Cheung [18] examines the wh-fronting structure in Cantonese, and advocates the analysis of such wh-phrases as identification focus (IdenF) with a syntactic distribution of "CP > AT > CT > PPT > IdentF > dak-F(ocus) > lin-F(ocus) > TP" (dar = only; lin = even; dar and lin are acted as a Cantonese focus markers). The conclusion is in favour of Beninca & Poletto's [14] claim that the IS consists of the topic field and the focus field, but differs from Rizzi's [6] view that topic can be lower than focus.

Previous studies show that there seems to be a typological distinction in the mapping of the topics and foci in the LP of CP among languages. Regarding the LP of Mandarin and its dialect Cantonese, the results support the assumption that topics must be higher than foci, though the detailed distributions are different. In the following sections, we shall provide evidence to testify to the typological property and then reach a new conclusion.

---

[3] HT = Hanging Topic; SceS = Scene Setting Topic; LD = Left Dislocation Topic; LI = List Interpretation Topic; CFocus = Contrastive Focus; IFocus = Information Focus.

3 Inventory of Topic and Focus in Old Xiang

To maintain consistency with the previous analysis, we shall adopt the definition and properties of the topics and foci discussed in Paul [9], Badan [10], Badan & Gobbo [11] and Cheung [12]. In this section, we shall point out that Old Xiang shares a similar inventory of Topics and Foci available in Mandarin, except that there are no real PPLDs.

3.1 Types of Topics and Foci

It is widely accepted that topics in Mandarin can be categorized into LD, HT, and AT [9, 12, 17–19], though there are different views on their sub-categorization. Each type of topic has its own properties.

 i. LD.

LD, which includes PPLD[4] and DPLD, has the following properties: it cannot be a pro; it is a topic structure with a gap; it is generated through movement; Weak Crossover (WCO) effects are observed; reconstruction is possible in a clause with LD. Also, both PPLD and DPLD topics can appear in the CP domain[5]. Such topics have their canonical thematic position after the verb, but are dislocated to the LP. Through reconstruction, a complete argument structure can be formed. The thematic assignment is strictly local, with the relevant local configurations provided by merge [20, p. 521]. Hence, both in (1) and (2), the topics in (b) are derived from the canonical positions below TP in (a) through internal merge.

(1)   a. lǎo zhāng [$_{PP}$ zài hé biān-hang]$_i$ zuò-gao dà bàn tiān.
        Lǎo Zhāng at river side- LOC sit-ASP good half day
        'Old Zhang spent a good part of the day sitting at the riverside.'
     b. [$_{PPLD}$ zài hé biān-hang]$_i$, lǎo zhāng e$_i$ zuò-gao dà bàn tiān. (PPLD[6])
        at river side-LOC Zhāng Sān e sit-ASP good half day
        'Old Zhāng spent a good part of the day sitting at the riverside.'
(2)   a. jǐ háng-gao [$_{DP}$ gē tiáo lù] liǎng huí.
        She walk-ASP this-CL road two times
        'She has walked this road twice.'

---

[4] Here PPLDs are named according to Badan & Gobbo [11] and Cheung [12]. In Sect. 3 we shall propose that adjunct PPs are based-generated through adjoining, so they are not left dislocated.

[5] Although (1) is available in Old Xiang, the PP is canonically generated on the position above the vP, as what is tested in the following examples.

a.   lǎo zhāng [$_{PP}$ zài hé biān-hang] zuò-gao dà bàn tiān. (PP in the TP domain)
     Old Zhāng at river side-LOC sit-ASP good half day
     'Old Zhāng spent a good part of the day sitting at the riverside.'
b.   * lǎo zhāng zuò-gao dà bàn tiān [$_{PP}$ zài hé biān hāng]. (PP in the vP domain)

     Old Zhāng sit-ASP good half day at river side-LOC.The ungrammaticality of (b) shows that the PP cannot be moved to the position above vP.

[6] Although (1) is available in Old Xiang, the PP is canonically generated on the position above vP.

b. [DP gē-tiáo lù]ᵢ jǐ háng-gao liǎng huí eⱼ. (DPLD)
This-CL road she walk-ASP twice times e
'She has walked this road twice.'

ii. HT.
HT (Hanging Topic) co-indexes with a resumptive pronoun in the sentence, and is base-generated. HT can only appear in the CP domain in the Old Xiang without manifesting reconstruction effects.

(3)   [HT nà-jiā dài ǎnjìng gè lǎozigǔ]ᵢ, [jǐ]ᵢ hái mǎo lái.
      That-CL with glasses De old man he yet not come
      'The old man with glasses has not come yet.'
      iii. AT
      AT is also base-generated. In a clause with AT, there is no real resumptive pronoun, pro, or trace co-indexing with AT.
(4)   [AT yú], háishìyào qiā [cǎo yú].
      fish had better eat grass carp
      'As for (the dish of) fish, you'd better choose grass carps.'
      As for focus, the "lian" Focus in Mandarin is also found in Old Xiang.
(5)   [lián yī-kǒu chá] nà jiā shīfù dōu máo qiā.
      even a-CL tea that-CL working man Dou not have
      'That working man didn't even take a sip of tea.'

(1)–(5) show that the above-mentioned three types of topics and the "lian" Focus in the LP in Mandarin also exist in Old Xiang.

3.2   DPLD, PPLD, and HT as Different Types of Topics

As mentioned in Sect. 2, Badan & Gobbo [11] hold that LD includes DPLD and PPLD. However, Cheung [12] argues that DPLD is different from PPLD, but similar to HT, so both DPLD and HT fall into one particular type called "canonical topics". The controversies regarding the classification of topics in Mandarin lead to the question: Should PPLD and DPLD, DPLD, and HT be distinguished in Old Xiang?

First of all, we find that in Old Xiang, PPLD can be higher or lower than DPLD through syntactic tests.

(6)   a. [zài shùxué kè gāo tóu], [zhāng sān]ᵢ (NA⁷), wǒ pèng-dao-gù [eᵢ] hǎojǐ huí
      In math class-TEMP Zhang San TOP I meet-ASP e several times
      'In the math class, I have met Zhang San several times.'
      PPLD > DPLD
      b. [zhāng sān] ᵢ(NA), [zài shùxué kè-gāo tóu], wǒ pèngdao-gù [eᵢ] hǎojǐ huí.
      Zhang San TOP, in math class-TEMP, I meet-ASP e several times
      'In the math class, I have met Zhang San several times.'
      DPLD > PPLD

---

⁷ "NA" is a topic maker, similar to the topic marker "a" in Mandarin.

(6) indicates that DPLD and PPLD have similar syntactic positions. It seems that a conclusion can be reached that DPLD and PPLD belong to the same type of topics in terms of their syntactic properties, which is in favour of Badan and Gobbo's [10] claim, but different from Cheung's [12].

However, it should be noted that there are two types of PPs: the complement PP (PP$_{-comp}$) as the argument of a transitive verb predicate, and the adjunct PP (PP$_{-adjunct}$) as the modifier of a TP or vP [21, 22]. Consider (7) below:

(7)   a. Mrs. Black baked a cake [PP-comp for her].

  b. Mrs. Black baked a cake [PP-adjunct for 5 dollars] / [PP-adjunct for an hour].

In (7a), the PP, as an object of the verb "bake", functions as the complement of the VP; in (7b), the PP, as a modifier of the verb "bake", acts as the adjunct of the VP.

Concerning the interpretation of PPs, a PP is an argument if its interpretation depends exclusively on the head with which it is associated, whereas it is an adjunct if its interpretation remains relatively constant when associated with different heads [23, p. 108]. Therefore, the distinction between PP-comp and PP-adjunct can be decided through tests. Consider the English examples.

(8)   a. * Mrs. Black baked a cake. ("bake" as a ditransitive verb)

  b. Mrs. Black baked a cake. ("bake" as a transitive verb)

In (8a), the omission "for her" results in ungrammaticality, indicating that the PP is an argument of the predicate. However, in (8b), the omission of "for 5 dollars/for an hour" does not affect the grammaticality of the sentence, hence, the PP is an adjunct.

In Mandarin, a PP also might function as a complement or as an adjunct. Consider the following examples.

(9)   a. wǒ gěi zhāng sān jì-le yī-fēng xìn.
    I to Zhang San post-ASP a-CL letter
    'I posted a letter to Zhang San.'
    b. wǒ zài jiǔdiàn chī-le zǎocān.
    I at hotel have-ASP breakfast
    'I had breakfast at the hotel.'

In (9), "gěi zhāng sān" is one of the arguments of the ditransitive verb predicate "jì", which cannot be omitted, as shown in (10a), whereas "zài jiǔdiàn" is used as a modifier of the whole TP "Mrs. Black baked a cake".

(10)   a. *wǒ jì-le yī fēng xìn. ("jì" as a ditransitive verb)
    I post-ASP a-CL letter
    b. wǒ chī le zǎocān. ("chī" as a transitive verb)
    I have-ASP breakfast
    'I had my breakfast.'

There is also PP as a complement of ditransitive verbs. However, in Old Xiang, the PP as a complement cannot be left-dislocated. Take "jì" as an example. "Jì" also is a ditransitive verb, which can choose a PP "bǎ..." as its argument, as in (11a). However, the dislocation of PP to the left of the subject results in the ungrammaticality of the sentence, as in (11b).

(11)   a. wǒ [PP-comp bǎ jǐ] jìgāo yī fēng xìn.
           I for him post-ASP a-CL letter
           'I posted a letter for him.'
        b. * [PP-comp bǎ jǐ] wǒ jìgāo yī fēng xìn.
           For him I post-ASP a-CL letter

The functions of PPs vary in terms of the canonical positions which they attach to in the sentence, despite that they can fulfill different functions in the sentence, as discussed in the above examples. In principle, the functions of a given PP in a particular sentence are semantically constrained. In practical, the linguistic and extralinguistic knowledge can help interpret arguments and adjuncts [24, p. 342]. As is shown in (11), in Old Xiang, a PP-comp, which serves as an internal argument of the predicate, is restricted by rigid semantic constraints, and cannot be dislocated to the LP.

Then consider PP-adjunct. Adjuncts (Adverbials) are adjoined to the sentence or the verb phrase to modify CP, TP, vP, or VP [25, p. 221]. The PP-adjunct, as one type of adjunct, can be topicalized and is generated through adjoining, rather than by movement (i.e. displacement). This is also the case in Old Xiang. Hence, we assume that there are no left dislocated PP-adjunct topics in Old Xiang, as in (12). Here we further test the syntactic distribution of PP-adjunct and HT and find that PP-adjunct can be put in a position either higher or lower than HT. Examples are shown as follows.

(12)   a. [PP-adjunct zài wǎngbā]j, [HT zhāng sān nàjiā guǐzǎizi]i, wǒ ej
           In cybercafe Zhang San that-CL guy I e
           pèngdàogù jǐi hǎojǐ huí.
           come-ASP across him several times
           'I came across the guy(called) Zhang San several times in the cybercafe.'
           CP > PP- adjunct > HT > TP
        b. [zhāng sān nàjiāguǐ zǎizi]i, [PP-adjunct zàiwǎngbā]j, wǒ ej pèngdào gù
           Zhang San that-CL guy in cybercafe I e come-ASP across
           jǐi hǎojǐ huí
           he several times
           'I came across the guy(called) Zhang San several times in the cybercafe.'
           CP > HT > PP-adjunct > TP
(13)   a. [CP [PP-adjunct (zài) xì shí jǐ], [AT wǒ], [TP gèzǐ ǎi]]
           (in) childhood, I height short
           'I was short in my childhood.'
           CP > PP-adjunct > AT > TP
        b. [CP [AT wǒ], [PP-adjunct (zài) xì shí jǐ], [TP gèzi ǎi]]
           I (in) childhood height short
           'I was short in my childhood.'
           CP > AT > PP-adjunct > TP

In (13), the PP is a temporal adverbial, so it functions as an adjunct. The grammaticality of both (13a) and (13b) indicates that AT can be lower or higher than the PP-adjunct in the left periphery of the CP. In terms of the definition of AT, the topic "wǒ" must have the semantic relationship of aboutness with the DP "gèzi" in the comment of the sentence. Then does the PP intervene in the aboutness relationship? When the PP is an adjunct modifying "gèzi ǎi", the PP is adjoined to the DP; when PP modifies "wǒ gèzi ǎi", it is adjoined to the TP. The semantic orientation of topics allows the PP to occur on the positions optionally. Hence the PP will not intervene in the aboutness relationship.

Here we have made a distinction of PP as an adjunct and PP as a complement. Through tests, we have reached the conclusion that there exists no PPLD$_{\text{-adjunct}}$ or PPLD$_{\text{-comp}}$ in Old Xiang. Despite that a PP can be topicalized and does occur in the left periphery of CP, it is not left-dislocated, and it can be positioned lower or higher than the DPLD, HT, or AT through adjoining to the constituents it modifies.

We continue to test the properties of HT and DPLD, and find that HT is higher than DPLD, as in (14).

(14) a. [$_{CP}$ [wáng lǎoshī]$_i$ (NA), [shū]$_j$, [$_{TP}$ wǒ zǎojiù bǎ jǐ$_i$ qìlī]]
        Teacher Wang TOP books I early-ASP give him FP
        'I have already given the book to Teacher Wang.'
        CP > HT > DPLD > TP
      b. * [CP [shū]$_j$, [wáng lǎoshī]$_i$ (NA), [$_{TP}$ wǒ zǎojiù bǎ jǐ$_i$ qì lī]]
        books Teacher Wang TOP, I early-ASP give him FP
        * CP > DPLD > HT > TP
        AT must be higher than HT, which is shown in (15)

(15) a. [$_{CP}$ [$_{AT}$ jǐ wūli gè ń], [$_{HT}$jǐi yálǎozi], [$_{TP}$ yòu bǎ jǐi
        his house-LOC De person his father again give him
        qǔ lī gè hòu niáng lī]]
        Marry-ASP CL stepmother FP
        '*His family member, his father, married him another stepmother'
        CP > AT > HT > TP
      b.*[CP [$_{HT}$jǐi yálǎozi], [$_{AT}$ jǐ wūli gè ń], [$_{TP}$ yòu bǎ jǐi
        his father his house-LOC De person again give him
        qǔ lī gè hòu niáng lī]]
        Marry-ASP CL stepmother FP
        * CP > HT > AT > TP

In terms of the definition of "aboutness", the topic has an inclusion relation with a constituent in the comment. In (15), DP2 should be semantically covered by DP1 when DP1 is topicalized.

The above tests indicate that Old Xiang does not contain real PPLDs. A PP can be topicalized, but it is base-generated through adjoining, not derived through left-dislocation. The position of PP topics can be higher or lower than that of DPLD, HT, and AT. PP topics have free syntactic distributions while DPLD does not, which shows that PPLD and DPLD are different types of topics. The observation leads to the following conclusion:

CP > PP-adjunct > AT > PP-adjunct > HT > PP-adjunct > DPLD > PP-adjunct > TP

Due to the fact that Pps-adjunct are not real LDs, PPLD will be excluded in the succeeding discussion. Then the hierarchy of DPLD, HT, and AT can be stated as follows:

CP > AT > HT > DPLD > TP

4 Mapping of Topics and Foci in the Left Periphery of Old Xiang

We have tested and found that PP-adjunct (which is called PPLD in the literature) and DPLD are two types of distinctive topics in accordance with their syntactic properties. We also find that DPLD, HT, and AT are three different types of topics. This section will discuss the mapping of DPLD, HT, and AT with the "lian" Focus in Old Xiang.

4.1 The "lian" (*Even*) Focus Lower Than the Topics Within the CP Domain

First, the "lian" Focus can appear in a position lower than DPLD.

(16)   [CP [DPLD nàjiā mèijǐ (NA)], [lián zìgāo gè yīshang] e$_i$ dōu ńdé xǐ]!
        That-CL girl TOP even self De clothes e even not wash
        'This girl even does not wash her own clothes!'
        CP > DPLD > "lian" Focus > IP
        Second, the "lian" Focus also appears in a position lower than HP

(17)   [CP [DPLDnàjiā mèi jǐ]$_i$ (NA), [lián zìgāo gè yīshang] jǐ$_i$ dōu wúdé xǐ]!
        That-CL girl TOP even self De clothes she Dou not wash
        'This girl even does not wash her own clothes'
        CP > HP > "lian" Focus > TP
        Third, the "lian" Focus can follow an AT in the LP

(18)   [CP [AT géjiā qí mò kǎoshì] (NA), [lián bān shàng chéngjī zuì chà
        this term final exam TOP even class-LOC grades most bad
        ge tóngxué], wǒ tīng dào gǎng yīngyǔ yě qǐgé lī!
        De classmate I hear-ASP speak English too pass-ASP
        'I heard that even the worst student in the class passed the English final exam this time'
        CP > AT > "lian" Focus > TP

Examples (16–18) show that DPLD, HT, and AT can co-occur with the "lian" Focus respectively. Then we shall test whether recursive topics can co-occur with the "lian" Focus. We find that these cases are impossible in Old Xiang.

First, HT, and DPLD do not appear on the position left to the "lian" Focus in the LP at the same time.

(19)   a.? *[HT wǒ yélǎozi]$_i$ (NA), [DPLD gé jiāshì]$_j$ (NE), [lián wǒ] jǐ$_i$ dōu
        My father TOP this-CL thing TOP even I he Dou
        yīzhí mán dào e$_j$ lī
        always hide-ASP e FP

'My father has even been hiding this from me for a long time'
*CP > HT > DPLD > "lian" Focus > TP

b. *[DPLD gé jiāshì]j (NE) , [HT wǒ yélǎozi]i (NA), lián wǒ jǐi dōu
this-CL thing TOP my father TOP even me he Dou
yīzhí mán dào ej lī
always hide-ASP e FP
* CP > DPLD > HT > "lian" Focus > TP

In (19), "jǐ" should be bound by its antecedent "wǒ yélǎozi" in terms of the definition of HT. The HT in (19a) is appropriately bound by its antecedent, while the one in (19b) is not. However, both clauses are not acceptable. It suggests that the ordering of topics and the "lian" Focus are not only subjected to semantic and syntactic constraints but also other factors. The ungrammaticality of (19) shows that the number of topic and focus is limited within two.

Second, AT and DPLD do not appear in the position left to the "lian" Focus in the LP, either.

(20)　*[ATshuǐguǒ](NA), [DPLD píngguǒ]i, lián kàn qí/pro dōu lǎndé kàn ei lī.
fruits (TOP) apple even look he/pro Dou not look e FP
*CP > AT > DPLD > "lian" Focus > TP

b. *[DPLD píngguǒ](NA)i, [AT shuǐguǒ], lián kàn jǐ/pro dōu lǎndé kàn ei lī
apples TOP fruits even look he/pro Dou not look e FP
'As for apples, he didn't even bother to look at fruits'
*CP > DPLD > AT > "lian" Focus > TP

Third, the "lian" Focus does not co-occur with AT and HT at the same time. Consider the following examples.

(21)　a. *[AT jǐ wū li gè én], [HT jǐ jiā lǎodì]i, lián xiǎo míng zì gāo
His family De member he De younger brother even Xiao Míng himself
dōu ń xiāngxìn jǐ i lī!
Dou not believe him FP
* CP > AT > HT > "lian" Focus > TP

b.* [HT jǐ jiā lǎo dì]i, [AT jǐ wū li gè én], lián xiǎo míng zì gāo
he De younger brother his family members even Xiao Ming himself
dōu ń xiāngxìn jǐi lī!
Dou not believe him FP
* CP > HT > AT > "lian" Focus > TP

In (21a), the HT can be the antecedent binding "jǐ", which suggests that the sentence is semantically and syntactically constrained appropriately. However, the sentence is unacceptable. It is found that the sentences in Old Xiang are comparatively simpler than in Mandarin. Basically, there is only one topic and one focus, or no more than two topics in a sentence. Therefore, it seems to be a requirement of information prominence that results in the ungrammaticality of (21a). As for (21b), the HT cannot bind the pronoun "jǐ" within the binding domain. Furthermore, the HT "lǎo dì" is semantically inclusive to the DP "jǐwū li gè én", which requires that DP must be lower than HT syntactically. Hence, (21b) is not acceptable.

From the above tests, we find that in Old Xiang, when topics are above the "lian" Focus, the distribution of IS is as follows:

CP > AT > HT > DPLD > "lian" Focus > TP

(No more than one topic co-occurs with the focus.)

4.2 The "lian" (Even) Focus Higher Than the Topics Within the CP Domain

Previous research shows that the "lian" focus cannot be lower than topics in Mandarin Chinese [9, 12, 18]. Here we shall check whether topics must be higher than the focus in Old Xiang through syntactic tests.

(22) a. [lián [yá lǎozi]$_j$], [$_{DPLD}$gé jiā shì]$_i$,[$_{TP}$ wǒ dōu mǎo gǎng sù e$_j$ e$_i$]
        Even father this-CL thing I Dou not tell e e
        'I even did not tell it to Father.'
        CP > "lian" Focus > DPLD > TP
      b. [lián [yá lǎozi]$_j$], [gé jiā shì]$_i$, [$_{TP}$ wǒ dōu mǎo gǎngsù jǐ$_i$ e$_j$]
        Even father this-CL thing I Dou not tell him e
        'I even did not tell it to Father.'
        CP > "lian" Focus > HT > TP
      c. [$_{CP}$ lián bān shàng chéngjī zuì chà ge tóngxué], [$_{AT}$ géjiā qí mò
        Even class-LOC grades most bad De classmate this term final
        kǎoshì (NA)], wǒ tīng dào gǎng yīngyǔ yě qǐgé lī!
        exam TOP I hear-ASP speak English too pass-ASP
        '*even the students with the worst grades in the class, this final exam I heard
        that he passed the English exam.'
        CP > "lian" Focus > AT > TP

(22) shows that the "lian" Focus can be higher than DPLD, HT or AT respectively in the LP. However, when topics co-occur with the "lian" Focus, there should be no more than one topic.

(23) a. *lián gé dà gè shì, wǒjiā rén (NA), wǒ yá lǎozi i (NA), [$_{TP}$ wǒ
        even so big De thing my family member TOP my father TOP I
        dōu mǎo gǎng sù e$_i$/qí$_i$]
        Dou not tell- ASP e$_i$/him
        * CP > "lian" Focus > AT > HT/DPLD > TP
      b. *lián wǒ yálǎozi i, wǒ jiārén (NA), gé jiā shì (NA), [$_{TP}$ wǒ
        even my father my family member TOP this-CL thing TOP I
        dōu mǎo gǎng sù qí$_i$]
        Dou not tell- ASP him
        * CP > "lian" Focus > HT > DPLD > TP
      c. *lián gé jiā shì, wǒ (NA), lǎoyázi (NA), e$_j$ dōu mǎo gǎng sù qí
        Even this-CL thing I TOP Father TOP e Dou didn't tell-ASP him
        * CP > "lian" Focus > DPLD > HT > TP

Compared to (22), there are two topics following the "lian" Focus in (23). The ungrammaticality of the clauses in (23) indicates that the prominence of the "lian" Focus refrains recursive topics co-occurring with it.

From the tests in this section, we find that the topics of DPLD and HP can appear recursively above the "lian" Focus, but cannot be lower than it, and no more than one topic can co-occur with the "lian" Focus in the LP. The distribution of Topics and the "lian"(even) Focus within the CP Domain can be summarized as follows:

CP > "lian" (*even*) Focus > AT > HT > DPLD > "lian" (*even*) Focus > TP

(No more than one topic co-occurs with the "lian" Focus; no more than two topics co-occur in the LP of a sentence without the "lian" Focus".)

5   Conclusion

This paper observes the syntactic cartography of toipcs and the "lian" Focus in Old Xiang and reaches the following conclusions:

Firstly, like Mandarin, Old Xiang also has DPLD, HT, AT, and "lian" Focus. In Old Xiang, PP can be classified into PP-comp and PP-adjunct. PP-comp cannot be left-dislocated to the LP of the CP domain. Although PP-adjunct can be topicalized in the LF, it displays great flexibility in syntactic representation and is base-generated. Thus, there are no PPLD topics in Old Xiang.

Secondly, the map of topics and the "lian" Focus in the LP in Old Xiang is represented as "CP > 'lian' Focus > AT > HT > DPLD > 'lian' Focus > TP", which is similar to the results in the previous studies, but displays its own characteristics.

Table 1. Comparison of the cartography of topics and focus in the CP domain

Language	Result
Italian	CP > TopP* > FocP > TopP* > TP [6]
Mandarin	CP (force) > TopP * > "lian" (*even*) FocP > TP [9]
Cantonese	CP > AT > CT > PPT > IdentF > dak-F(ocus) > lin-F(ocus) > TP [18]
Old Xiang	CP > "lian" (*even*) Focus > AT > HT > DPLD > "lian" (*even*) Focus > TP (this paper)

The Table 1 shows that cross-linguistically the IS can be split into two parts: the topic field and the focus field. There are also such specific fields in Old Xiang. However, whether topics are higher or lower than foci does not seem to be a distinct typological divergence between Italian and the Chinese dialects (at least Old Xiang). In Old Xiang, topics can appear recursively in the LP, but there should be no more than two topics in each clause. Only one topic can co-occur with the "lian" Focus in a clause. The ordering is mainly restricted by semantic constraints, as well as factors from other levels of language like syntax and prominence of information. The mapping clearly shows that the left periphery of the CP domain is the interface between syntax and pragmatics, the locus where informational characteristics of pragmatic relevance receive a syntactic encoding.

Acknowledgments. This paper is supported by the Key Scientific Research Project from Hunan Provincial Department of Education, China (Grant No.: 19A494; Project Title: A Comparative Study of Sentence Information Structure Between Modern Mandarin Chinese and Xiang Dialect based on the Theory of Syntactic Cartography). I thank Dr. Wu Ling, the anonymous reviewers and the participants of CLSW 2022 for helpful comments. All errors and misinterpretations remain entirely my responsibility.

References

1. Lambrecht, K.: Information Structure and Sentence Form: Topic, Focus, and the Mental Representations of Discourse Referents. Cambridge University Press, Cambridge (1994). https://doi.org/10.1017/CBO9780511620607
2. ErteschikShir, N.: Information Structure: The Syntax-Discourse Interface. Oxford University Press, Oxford/New York (2007)
3. Kou, X.: The restrictions on the genitive relative clauses triggered by relational nouns. In: Hong, J.-F., Zhang, Y., Liu, P. (eds.) CLSW 2019. LNCS (LNAI), vol. 11831, pp. 746–752. Springer, Cham (2020). https://doi.org/10.1007/978-3-030-38189-9_75
4. Fu, S.-H.: Relationship between discourse notions and the lexicon: from the perspective of Chinese information structure. In: Hong, J.-F., Zhang, Y., Liu, P. (eds.) CLSW 2019. LNCS (LNAI), vol. 11831, pp. 24–36. Springer, Cham (2020). https://doi.org/10.1007/978-3-030-38189-9_3
5. Gao, Y., Lyu, G.: Functions of non-subject topics in Mandarin conversations. In: Dong, M., Gu, Y., Hong, J.-F. (eds.) Chinese Lexical Semantics: 22nd Workshop, CLSW 2021, Nanjing, China, May 15–16, 2021, Revised Selected Papers, Part I, pp. 325–338. Springer International Publishing, Cham (2022). https://doi.org/10.1007/978-3-031-06703-7_25
6. Rizzi, L.: The Fine Structure of the Left Periphery. In: Haegeman, L. (ed.) Elements of Grammar, pp. 281–337. Springer, Dordrecht (1997). https://doi.org/10.1007/978-94-011-542 0-8_7
7. Zhong, H.: The Centennial controversy: how to classify the Chinese adverb Dōu? In: Hong, J.-F., Zhang, Y., Liu, P. (eds.) CLSW 2019. LNCS (LNAI), vol. 11831, pp. 63–73. Springer, Cham (2020). https://doi.org/10.1007/978-3-030-38189-9_6
8. Belletti, A.: Aspects of the low IP area. In: Rizzi, L. (ed.) The Structure of CP and IP: The Cartography of Syntactic Structures, vol. 2, pp. 16–51. Oxford University Press, New York (2004)
9. Paul, W.: Low IP and left periphery in Mandarin Chinese. Rech. Linguistiques de Vincennes **33**, 111–134 (2005). https://doi.org/10.4000/rlv.1303
10. Badan, L.: The even-construction in Mandarin Chinese. In: R. Djamouri, Sybesma, R. (eds.) Chinese Linguistics in Leipzig. EHESS-CRLAO, pp. 101–116, Paris (2008)
11. Badan, L., Gobbo, F.: On the syntax of topic and focus in Chinese. In: Beninca, P., Munaro, N.(eds.) Mapping the Left Periphery: The Cartography of Syntactic Structures, vol. 5, pp. 63–90. Oxford University Press, New York (2010). https://doi.org/10.1093/acprof:oso/978019 9740376.003.0003
12. Cheung, C.H.: cóng zhìtú lǐlùn tànsuǒ hànyǔ huàtí yǔ zhòngdiǎn de fēnbù. Xiàndài wàiyǔ. On the distribution of topics and foci in Mandarin: a cartographic solution. Mod. Foreign Lang. **36**(1), 10–17 (2013)

13. Benincà, P.: The position of topic and focus in the left periphery. In: Cinque, G., Salvi, G. (eds.) Current Studies in Italian Syntax: Essays Offered to Lorenzo Renzi, pp. 39–64. Elsevier-North Holland, Amsterdam (2001). https://doi.org/10.1163/9780585473949_005

14. Beninca, P., Poletto, C.: Topic, focus, and V2: defining the CP sublayers. In: Rizzi, L. (ed.) The Structure of CP and IP: The Cartography of Syntactic Structures, vol. 2, pp. 526–575. Oxford University Press, New York

15. Frascarelli, M., Hinterhölzl, R.: Types of topics in German and Italian. In: Schwabe, K., Winkler, S. (eds.) On Information Structure, Meaning and Form: Generalizations across languages, pp. 87–116. John Benjamins Publishing Company, Amsterdam (2007). https://doi.org/10.1075/la.100.07fra

16. Cruschina, S.: Informational focus in Sicilian and the left periphery. In: van Riemsdijk, H., van der Hulst, H., Koster, J. (eds.) Phases of Interpretation, pp. 363–385. Mouton de Gruyter, Berlin (2006). https://doi.org/10.1515/9783110197723.5.363

17. Badan, L., Gobbo, F.: The Even–construction and the low periphery in Mandarin Chinese. In: Tsai, W. D. (ed.) The Cartography of Chinese Syntax, pp. 33–74. Oxford University Press, New York (2015). https://doi.org/10.1093/acprof:oso/9780190210687.003.0002

18. Cheung, C. C.: On the fine structure of the left periphery: The positions of topic and focus in Cantonese. In: Tsai, W. D. (ed.) The Cartography of Chinese Syntax, pp. 75–130. Oxford University Press, New York (2015). https://doi.org/10.1093/acprof:oso/9780190210687.003.0003

19. Chen, P.: Pragmatic interpretations of structural topics and relativization in Chinese. J Pragmat. 26(3), 389–406 (1996). https://doi.org/10.1016/0378-2166(95)00042-9

20. Rizzi, L.: Syntactic cartography and the syntacticisation of scope-discourse semantics. In: Reboul, A. (ed.) Mind, Values, and Metaphysics, pp. 517–533. Springer, Cham (2014). https://doi.org/10.1007/978-3-319-05146-8_30

21. Hindle, D., Rooth, M.: Structural ambiguity and lexical relations. Comput. Linguist. 19(1), 103–120 (1993). https://doi.org/10.3115/981344.981374

22. Zhao, S., Lin, D.: A nearest-neighbor method for resolving PP-attachment ambiguity. In: Su, K.-Y., Tsujii, J., Lee, J.-H., Kwong, O.Y. (eds.) IJCNLP 2004. LNCS (LNAI), vol. 3248, pp. 545–554. Springer, Heidelberg (2005). https://doi.org/10.1007/978-3-540-30211-7_58

23. Grimshaw, J.: Argument Structure. MIT Press, Cambridge (1990)

24. Merlo, P., Ferrer, E.E.: The notion of argument in prepositional phrase attachment. Comput. Linguist 32(3), 341–378 (2006). https://doi.org/10.1162/coli.2006.32.3.341

25. Tang, S.-W.: xíngshì hànyǔ jù fǎxué. Shànghǎi jiàoyù chūbǎn shè, Shànghǎi. Formal Chinese Syntax. Shanghai Education Press, Shanghai (2010). (in Chinese)

Author Index

© The Editor(s) (if applicable) and The Author(s), under exclusive license
to Springer Nature Switzerland AG 2023
Q. Su et al. (Eds.): CLSW 2022, LNAI 13495, pp. 567–569, 2023.
https://doi.org/10.1007/978-3-031-28953-8

Printed in the United States
by Baker & Taylor Publisher Services